Human Behavior Understanding in Networked Sensing

Paolo Spagnolo · Pier Luigi Mazzeo
Cosimo Distante
Editors

Human Behavior Understanding in Networked Sensing

Theory and Applications of Networks of Sensors

Springer

Editors
Paolo Spagnolo
Pier Luigi Mazzeo
Cosimo Distante
National Research Council
Lecce
Italy

ISBN 978-3-319-10806-3 ISBN 978-3-319-10807-0 (eBook)
DOI 10.1007/978-3-319-10807-0

Library of Congress Control Number: 2014950650

Springer Cham Heidelberg New York Dordrecht London

Printed on acid-free paper

Springer is part of Springer Science+Business Media (www.springer.com)

Preface

In recent years, there has been increasing interest in human behavior understanding motivated by several societal needs that include security, natural interfaces, gaming, affective computing, and assisted living. Hundreds of papers have been published on the subject in the past, mostly focusing on single-device monitoring activities. Now, thanks to both the decreasing cost of sensors and the increasing performance of devices, the possibility of performing integration of forest of (homogeneous and heterogeneous) sensors is not only a theoretical issue but also a makeable solution in real contexts.

The exact aim of this book is to provide an overview of both the technical challenges in sensor network development (network discovery, control and routing, collaborative signal and information processing, tasking and querying), and real applications of them. Different aspects of distributed computing in large-scale networked sensor systems (including algorithms and applications, systems design techniques and tools, in-network signals and information processing) in the human behavior understanding context are analyzed. In addition, application scenarios ranging from surveillance to indexing and retrieval, from patient care to industrial safety, from social and ambient intelligence to sports analysis are introduced. The target audience is not only graduate students, but also scholars, researchers, and practitioners from different communities (such as Computer Vision, networked embedded sensing, artificial intelligence, and so on).

The book is a collection of chapters written specifically for this book by leading experts in the field. The chapters are organized into three parts.

Part I Distributed Sensing: Architectures (five chapters);
Part II Distributed Sensing: Applications (eight chapters);
Part III Multi-robot Systems (seven chapters).

All chapters are on topics related to the aim of the book, that is, applications of distributed systems. However, chapters belonging to the first part provide also a good analysis of some theoretic aspects: the design, implementation, and development of a distributed sensor network, as well as communication and computational remarks. The chapters in the second part are mostly focused on application of distributed sensing in the field of human behavior understanding, while in the third part specific distributed applications based on multi-robots (considered as a general term for autonomous intelligent vehicle) are presented. The first chapter in the first part can be considered as a high-level introduction to the argument of distributed sensing.

To support the reading of the book, in the final part a glossary with most used terms, and an analytic index are provided. In addition, the list of acronyms is present in the first part.

The editors would like to thank the authors of all contributions for the efforts they put on them. We would especially like to thank Simon Rees from Springer for his support and guidance during all the process of preparation of this book.

Italy, July 2014

Paolo Spagnolo
Pier Luigi Mazzeo
Cosimo Distante

Contents

Contributors

José J. Acevedo Grupo de Robótica, Visión y Control, Escuela Superior de Ingenieros, Universidad de Sevilla, Sevilla, Spain

Hamid Aghajan Department of Electrical Engineering, Stanford University, Stanford, CA, USA

Ryota Akai Graduate School of Engineering, Osaka University, Osaka, Japan

Toygar Akgun ASELSAN Elektronik Sanayi Ve Ticaret A.S., Yenimahalle Ankara, Turkey

David Alejo University of Seville, Seville, Spain

Begoña C. Arrue Grupo de Robótica, Visión y Control, Escuela Superior de Ingenieros, Universidad de Sevilla, Sevilla, Spain

Giovanni Attolico Institute of Intelligent Systems for Automation (ISSIA)—National Research Council (CNR), Bari, Italy

Charles Attwood THALES UK Limited, Research and Technology, Worton Drive, Reading, UK

Noboru Babaguchi Graduate School of Engineering, Osaka University, Osaka, Japan

Stanley Baek Department of Electrical and Computer Engineering, The University of Michigan, Dearborn, MI, USA

Bir Bhanu The Center for Research in Intelligent Systems, University of California, Riverside, CA, USA

Francisco A. Bonino Department of Computer Systems, Instituto Tecnologico de Mexicali, Mexicali, Mexico

Andrea Cavallaro Queen Mary University of London, London, UK

Müjdat Çetin Faculty of Engineering and Natural Sciences, Sabancı University, Istanbul, Turkey

Dang Viet Chau National Defense Academy, Yokosuka, Japan

Grazia Cicirelli Institute of Intelligent Systems for Automation (ISSIA)—National Research Council (CNR), Bari, Italy

José Antonio Cobano University of Seville, Seville, Spain

Serhan Coşar Faculty of Engineering and Natural Sciences, Sabancı University, Istanbul, Turkey

Arnoldo Díaz-Ramírez Department of Computer Systems, Instituto Tecnologico de Mexicali, Mexicali, Mexico

Christian Fabre CEA, LETI, MINATEC Campus, Grenoble, France; Université Grenoble Alpes, Grenoble, France

Antonios Gasteratos Department of Production and Management Engineering, Democritus University of Thrace, Xanthi, Greece

Ioakeim G. Georgoudas Department of Electrical and Computer Engineering, Democritus University of Thrace, Xanthi, Greece

Carsten Grenz Organic Computing, Universität Augsburg, Augsburg, Germany

Jörg Hähner Organic Computing, Universität Augsburg, Augsburg, Germany

Ali Hassan Department of Computer Science, LUMS School of Science and Engineering, Lahore, Pakistan

Guillermo Heredia University of Seville, Seville, Spain

Zhixing Jin The Center for Research in Intelligent Systems, University of California, Riverside, CA, USA

Abdul Rafay Khalid Department of Computer Science, LUMS School of Science and Engineering, Lahore, Pakistan

Masao Kubo National Defense Academy, Yokosuka, Japan

Huan Li School of Computer Science and Engineering, Beihang University, Beijing, China

Yuanyuan Li Biostatistics Branch, National Institute of Environmental Health Sciences, National Institutes of Health, Durham, USA

Pedro U. Lima Institute for Systems and Robotics—Instituto Superior Técnico, Universidade de Lisboa, Lisboa, Portugal

Chengnian Long Department of Automation, Shanghai Jiao Tong University, Shanghai, China

Kejie Lu Department of Electrical and Computer Engineering, University of Puerto Rico at Mayagüez, Mayagüez, PR, USA

Rafael Martín Universidad Autónoma de Madrid, Madrid, España

José M. Martínez Universidad Autónoma de Madrid, Madrid, España

Alcherio Martinoli Distributed Intelligent Systems and Algorithms Laboratory—EPFL, EPFL ENAC IIE DISAL, Lausanne, Switzerland

Iván Maza Grupo de Robótica, Visión y Control, Escuela Superior de Ingenieros, Universidad de Sevilla, Sevilla, Spain

Pier Luigi Mazzeo National Institute of Optics (INO)—National Research Council (CNR), Lecce, Italy

Pedro Mejía-Alvarez Department of Computer Sciences, CINVESTAV-IPN, Mexico City, Mexico

Annalisa Milella Institute of Intelligent Systems for Automation (ISSIA)—National Research Council (CNR), Bari, Italy

Akira Namatame National Defense Academy, Yokosuka, Japan

Naoko Nitta Graduate School of Engineering, Osaka University, Osaka, Japan

Aníbal Ollero Grupo de Robótica, Visión y Control, Escuela Superior de Ingenieros, Universidad de Sevilla, Sevilla, Spain

Daniel Pack Department of Electrical and Computer Engineering, The University of Texas at San Antonio, San Antonia, TX, USA

Donato Di Paola Institute of Intelligent Systems for Automation (ISSIA)—National Research Council (CNR), Bari, Italy

Lynne E. Parker Electrical Engineering and Computer Science, The University of Tennessee, Knoxville, USA

José N. Pereira Distributed Intelligent Systems and Algorithms Laboratory—EPFL, EPFL ENAC IIE DISAL, Lausanne, Switzerland

Antonio Petitti Institute of Intelligent Systems for Automation (ISSIA)—National Research Council (CNR), Bari, Italy

Fabio Poiesi Queen Mary University of London, London, UK

Dimitrios Portokalidis Department of Electrical and Computer Engineering, Democritus University of Thrace, Xanthi, Greece

David Portugal Institute of Systems and Robotics (ISR), University of Coimbra (UC), Coimbra, Portugal

Rui P. Rocha Institute of Systems and Robotics (ISR), University of Coimbra (UC), Coimbra, Portugal

Hiroshi Sato National Defense Academy, Yokosuka, Japan

Porfírio Silva Institute for Systems and Robotics—Instituto Superior Técnico, Universidade de Lisboa, Lisboa, Portugal

Georgios Ch. Sirakoulis Department of Electrical and Computer Engineering, Democritus University of Thrace, Xanthi, Greece

Paolo Spagnolo National Institute of Optics (INO)—National Research Council (CNR), Lecce, Italy

Salah Sukkarieh The University of Sydney, Sydney, NSW, Australia

Zhefeng Sun School of Computer Science and Engineering, Beihang University, Beijing, China

Liang Sun Department of Electrical and Computer Engineering, The University of Texas at San Antonio, San Antonia, TX, USA

Piotr Szczuko Gdansk University of Technology, Gdansk, Poland

Murtaza Taj Department of Computer Science, LUMS School of Science and Engineering, Lahore, Pakistan

Michael Thomason Electrical Engineering and Computer Science, The University of Tennessee, Knoxville, USA

Sven Tomforde Organic Computing, Universität Augsburg, Augsburg, Germany

Santiago Vera University of Seville, Seville, Spain

Kevin Bing-Yung Wong Department of Electrical Engineering, Stanford University, Stanford, CA, USA

Jing Wu Department of Automation, Shanghai Jiao Tong University, Shanghai, China

Tongda Zhang Department of Electrical Engineering, Stanford University, Stanford, CA, USA

Acronyms

AAL	Ambient Assisted Living
ADL	Activities of Daily Life
AI	Artificial Intelligence
AIA	Automated Imaging Association
ALMAS	Assisted Living Monitoring and Analysis System
AMCL	Adaptive Monte Carlo Localization
ANN	Artificial Neural Networks
ARMA	AutoRegressive Moving Average
AS	Articulated Skeleton
ASIC	Application-Specific Integrated Circuit
ASSP	Application Specific Standard Product
AUC	Area Under Curve
BBox	Bounding Box
BoW	Bag of Words
BP	Back Propagation
BPR	Bi-Perimeter Routing
BRHS	Bounded Recursive Heuristic Search method
BTF	Brightness Transfer Function
CA	Cellular Automata
CAN	Content-Addressable Network
CCA	Connected Component Analysis
CCTV	Closed-Circuit Television
CDR	Collision Detection and Resolution
CDTT	Consensus-Based Distributed Target Tracking
CENS	Center for Embedded Networked Sensing
CGA	Centralized Greedy Algorithm
CR	Catching Ratio
CRPF	Cost-Reference Particle Filter
DAAL	Distributed Ambient Assisted Living
DARPA	Defense Advanced Research Projects Agency
DCPBHA	Distributed Coverage-Probability-Based Heuristic Algorithm
DCS	Data-Centric Storage

DCT	Discrete Cosine Transformation
DFS	Depth-First Search
DGA	Distribute Greedy-Based Algorithm
DHT	Distributed Hash Table
DLT	Direct Linear Transformation
DMSA	Distributed Mean-Shift-Based heuristic Algorithm
DOT	Dynamical Object Tracking
DSN	Distributed Sensor Networks
DSP	Digital Signal Processing
DSR	Dynamic Source Routing
EKF	Extended Kalman Filters
EM	Expectation Maximization
EPN	Executable Petri Net
ETA	Estimated Time of Arrival
FD-SOI	Fully Depleted Silicon on Insulator
FLMM	Fixed Length Markov Model
FNR	False Negative Rate
FOV	Field of View
FP	False Positive
FPGA	Field Programmable Gate Array
FPR	False Positive Rate
FSA	Finite State Automata
GALS	Globally Asynchronous Locally Synchronous
GCM	Ground plane Color Map
GHT	Geographic Hash Table
GOM	Ground plane Occupancy Map
GPGPU	General-Purpose computing on Graphics Processing Units
GPS	Global Positioning System
GPSMP	General-Propose Symmetric Multi-Processors
GPSR	Greedy Perimeter Stateless Routing
GPU	Graphic Processing Unit
GUI	Graphical User Interface
HMM	Hidden Markov Model
HOG	Histogram of Oriented Gradient
HSV	Hue Saturation Value
IAC	Institutional Agent Controller
ILP	Integer Linear Programming
IMAC	Independent Markov Chain Occupancy Grid Map
IP	Internet Protocol
IR	Institutional Robotics
ISM	Implicit Shape Model
ISR	Intelligence Surveillance and Reconnaissance
KDE	Kernel Density Estimation
KTSSR	Kinematic and Temporal Search Space Reduction
LAN	Local Area Network

LBP	Local Binary Patterns
LDCA	Linear Deceleration and Constant Acceleration
LOF	Local Outlier Factor
LRF	Laser Range Finder
LUT	Look-Up Table
LZW	Lempel-Ziv-Welch
MAC	Multiply Accumulator
MAC	Medium Access Control
MAP	Maximum A Posteriori
MEMS	Micro-Electro-Mechanical Systems
ML	Machine Learning
MM	Mission Manager
MORRP	Mobile Orthogonal Rendezvous Routing Protocol
MOTA	Multi-Object Tracking Accuracy
MOTP	Multi-Object Tracking Precision
MRP	Multi-Robot Patrol
MRS	Multi-Robot Systems
MS	Mean-Shift
MSA	Mean-Shift-Based Heuristic Algorithm
MSE	Mean Square Error
NEST	Network Embedded Systems Technology
NOAA	National Oceanographic and Atmospheric Administration
NoC	Network on Chip
ONVIF	Open Network Video Interface Forum
ORCA	Optimal Reciprocal Collision Avoidance
ORRP	Orthogonal Rendezvous Routing Protocol
PC	Personal Computer
PCA	Principal Component Analysis
PCP	Percentage of Correctly estimated body Parts
PE	Processing Elements
PeMS	Performance Measurement System
PETS	Performance Evaluation of Tracking and Surveillance
PHD	Probability Hypothesis Density
PIR	Passive InfraRed
PLTS	Personal Localization and Tracking Sub-system
PN	Petri Net
PoI	Point-of-Interest
PP	Path Planner
PS	Pictorial Structures
PSA	Probabilistic Suffix Automata
PSIA	Physical Security Interoperability Alliance
PSO	Particle Swarm Optimization
PST	Probabilistic Suffix Tree
PTZ	Pan-Tilt-Zoom
QoS	Quality of Service

RaCM	Recording and Content Management
RF	Radio Frequency
ROC	Receiver Operating Characteristic
ROM	Read-Only Memory
ROS	Robot Operating System
RRT	Optimal Rapidly-Exploring Random Trees
RSI	Received Signal Indicator
RSS	Received Signal Strength
RVO	Reciprocal Velocity Obstacles
SDP	SemiDefinite Programming
SEBS	State-Exchange Bayesian Strategy
SensIT	Sensor Information Technology
SM	State Machine
SMP	Symmetric Multi-Processors
SoC	Systems on a Chip
SOPC	System-on-a-Programmable-Chip
SOSUS	Sound Surveillance System
SPSA	Simultaneous Perturbation Stochastic Approximation
SSR	Search Space Reduction
SVDD	Support Vector Data Descriptors
SVM	Support Vector Machine
TD	Thermal Detector
TLD	Tracking-Learning Detection
TM	Thermal Manager
TOA	Time of Arrival
TP	Thermal Point
TP	True Positive
TPR	True Positive Rate
TSP	Traveling Salesman Problem
UAV	Unmanned Aerial Vehicle
UBM	Universal Background Model
UCSD	University of California San Diego
UGV	Unmanned Ground Vehicle
VD	Voronoi Diagrams
VDS	Vehicle Detector Station
VHDL	VHSIC Hardware Description Language
VHSIC	Very High Speed Integrated Circuits
VLMM	Variable Length Markov Models
VRPTW	Vehicle Routing Problem with Time Windows
VSN	Visual Sensor Networks
WEBS	Wireless Embedded Systems
WHO	World Health Organization
WINS	Wireless Integrated Network Sensors
ZGHT	Zonal Geographic Hash Table

Part I
Distributed Sensing: Architectures

Sensing technologies have received a huge amount of advancement in the last decades, with the opportunity to miniaturize and communicate wirelessly in low power fashion modalities. To this aim, applications where deploying interconnected heterogeneous sensing technologies are needed as user and scenarios demand continuous changing operations. This poses several research issues ranging from data storage, wireless communication coverage that allows self-organization of the topology of the networked sensors, to their coordination in terms of optimizing computation and where to focalize sensing and what to sense.

The first chapter can be considered as a general introduction to the argument, providing an exhaustive overview of the problems that affect the distributed systems (communications, processing constraints), but also analyzing other aspects that only a quick view can consider as marginal (privacy issues, market expectations).

Chapter 1
Towards Cognitive and Perceptive Video Systems

Toygar Akgun, Charles Attwood, Andrea Cavallaro, Christian Fabre, Fabio Poiesi and Piotr Szczuko

Abstract In this chapter we cover research and development issues related to smart cameras. We discuss challenges, new technologies and algorithms, applications and the evaluation of today's technologies. We will cover problems related to software, hardware, communication, embedded and distributed systems, multi-modal sensors, privacy and security. We also discuss future trends and market expectations from the customer's point of view.

T. Akgun
ASELSAN Elektronik Sanayi Ve Ticaret A.S., Mehmet Akif Ersoy Mahallesi 296
Cadde 16, 06172 Yenimahalle Ankara, Turkey
e-mail: takgun@aselsan.com.tr

C. Attwood
THALES UK Limited, Research and Technology, Worton Drive, Worton Grange
Business Park, Reading RG2 0SB, UK
e-mail: charles.attwood@uk.thalesgroup.com

A. Cavallaro · F. Poiesi (✉)
Queen Mary University of London, Mile End Road, London E1 4NS, UK
e-mail: fabio.poiesi@qmul.ac.uk

A. Cavallaro
e-mail: a.cavallaro@qmul.ac.uk

C. Fabre
CEA, LETI, MINATEC Campus, 38054 Grenoble, France
e-mail: christian.fabre1@cea.fr

C. Fabre
Université Grenoble Alpes, 38000 Grenoble, France

P. Szczuko
Faculty of Electronics, Telecommunications and Informatics, Gdansk University of Technology,
Ul. Gabriela Narutowicza 11/12, 80-233 Gdansk, Poland
e-mail: szczuko@ssound.eti.pg.gda.pl

P. Spagnolo et al. (eds.), *Human Behavior Understanding in Networked Sensing*,
DOI 10.1007/978-3-319-10807-0_1

1.1 Introduction

A smart camera is an image capturing optical device with additional embedded hardware. The device is capable of extracting, processing and communicating information. The data processing and communication capabilities of these embedded devices enable a variety of video-based applications, which include surveillance [1], quality assessment in industrial production [2] and object tracking for security applications [3]. Smart cameras are employed to lower the amount of visual information shared in a network and analysed by an operator, and also to increase situational awareness.

A smart camera system must react to events that a human operator would find of interest with the implicit assumption that some of the events reported by the system might not be of interest to the operator. The goal is therefore to have no missed detections with the minimum false alarm rate. Events of interest are defined within the context of the application. In perimeter-control applications where the activity within the coverage area is expected to be very limited, a typical event of interest is meaningful or intentional motion within the coverage area [4, 5]. Not all changes in pixel values are considered meaningful or intentional. Moving shadows due to changing illumination conditions or terrain specific motion due to wind or water are considered to be part of the background and should not normally be reported to the operator. In the case of airport terminal security, where structured or intentional activities are expected within the coverage area, a typical event of interest is detecting unattended luggage [6–8]. For monitoring in industrial production, smart cameras must be flexible enough to adapt to various kinds of tasks, such as health and safety or quality control. Video analytics algorithms for quality control vary with the object being manufactured [9].

Market expectations for smart cameras (e.g. in the CCTV market) have traditionally been over-optimistic, compared to the current performance levels of video analytics algorithms and systems. By employing new low cost, low size, low weight and low power processing developments, significant performance improvements are possible. A combination of improved robustness in algorithms with clearly understood user needs coupled with new business models that fulfil both security requirements and offer a return on investment should generate increased user confidence and a cycle of good market growth.

The chapter is organised as follows. Section 1.2 describes recent advances of processing units and algorithms for smart cameras. Section 1.3 defines standards for interoperability of smart camera networks and cooperation of different sensor types. Section 1.4 discusses the communication among cameras while considering privacy. Section 1.5 covers market expectations and Sect. 1.6 draws the conclusions.

1.2 Processing Units and Algorithms for Smart Cameras

Cognitive and perceptive video systems involve largely distributed smart cameras that have limited power/thermal budgets and can communicate with each other to achieve

Table 1.1 Power/performance figures for selected mobile/embedded GPUs

	Release date	GFLOPs	Architecture	Thermal designing power (max/min watts)	Process node (nm)
NVIDIA-GT640	Q2 2012	691	GK104	65/15	28
AMD-E6760	Q2 2011	576	VLIW5	35/5	40
Intel-HD5200	Q3 2013	640	GT3e	47/2.4	22

Giga FLoating-point Operations Per Second (GFLOPs) represent the theoretical peak, single precision, combination of fused multiply-add operations (floating-point multiply-add operations performed in one step)

shared goals. Smart cameras can, for example, be mounted on mobile platforms that introduce constraints on the supportable algorithmic complexity and the need for increased power efficiency.

Video data can be processed on smart cameras using Graphics Processing Unit (GPU) platforms [10]. GPUs can achieve high performance in terms of Floating-point Operations Per Second (~8 TeraFLOPs or TFLOPs) but have several drawbacks. The power consumption of such devices is high (~250 W) and great effort is required to maintain low working temperatures. In turn, devices get physically heavier and are not employable for mobile platforms (e.g. unmanned aerial vehicles). However, embedded GPUs can offer an interesting trade-off among processing power, power consumption and operating temperatures. Examples of embedded GPUs are from NVIDIA (Tegra K1), AMD (E6760, E8860) and Intel (HD5200) (Table 1.1). These embedded GPUs offer substantial floating point compute power for inherently massively data parallel processing tasks, which are quite common in image and video processing.

As embedded platforms are being used for computing tasks with ever increasing computational complexity, the level of performance expected from embedded processors is also increasing. The main trend in both embedded and desktop computing is shifting from highest performance to highest performance per watt [11].

Engineers are moving towards many-core platforms with much lower power consumption (~2 W) at the cost of lower performance (~80 GigaFLOPs or GFLOPs). By implementing many-core template architectures [12] on advanced silicon technologies like FD-SOI (Fully Depleted Silicon on Insulator), the GFLOPs/W ratio can be improved [13]. For example, a ratio of 20 GFLOPs for 105 mW, or 380 GFLOPs for 2 W, could be achieved in the next few years.

In order to have flexible platforms that simultaneously meet performance and power efficiency targets, fixed function hardware blocks can be combined with specialised accelerators (e.g. DSP, FPGA, GPU) and/or general purpose processors (e.g. ARM, x86). This approach is already in use in modern Systems on a Chip (SoC) with successful results. Specialised accelerators and general-purpose processors have fixed function hardware blocks that implement frequently used mathematical operations (e.g. transcendental functions) or application-specific tasks (e.g. block sum of absolute values computation for motion estimation). Even larger fixed function hardware blocks with limited control parameter programming functionality are used for tasks such as video encoding and image/video filtering.

Heterogeneous platform architectures for smart cameras are available and we can identify two broad processing architectures, namely General-Propose Symmetric Multi-Processors (GPSMP), and General-Purpose computing on Graphics Processing Units (GPGPU) or programmable graphics units. GPSMPs have strong memory consistency models that limit them to (about) a dozen cores, while GPGPUs exhibit much more parallelism with thousands of cores and the same program/instruction executed on several datasets simultaneously.

For example, many-core architectures are based on a Globally Asynchronous Locally Synchronous (GALS) architecture [14] where a number of synchronous tiles are connected through an asynchronous NoC (Network on Chip). Each tile can have its own clock and power domain and is made of up to 16 Processing Elements (PE), each with their own flow of instructions, connected in an SMP fashion around local memory [12]. Because each cluster is controllable in frequency and voltage, the overall available computing power can be adjusted to the computing demand, therefore also controlling electrical power (Fig. 1.1). This kind of architecture can be further tuned for video analytics by means of hardware accelerating blocks in clusters (i.e. a mixed hardware-software many-core) or by dedicated instructions (e.g. 16 bit floating point arithmetic or specific instructions to compute the sum of absolute difference on arrays).

Solutions from low-power embedded systems, such as GALS many-cores on FD-SOI, can bring significant benefits faster than the downscaling of desktop tech-

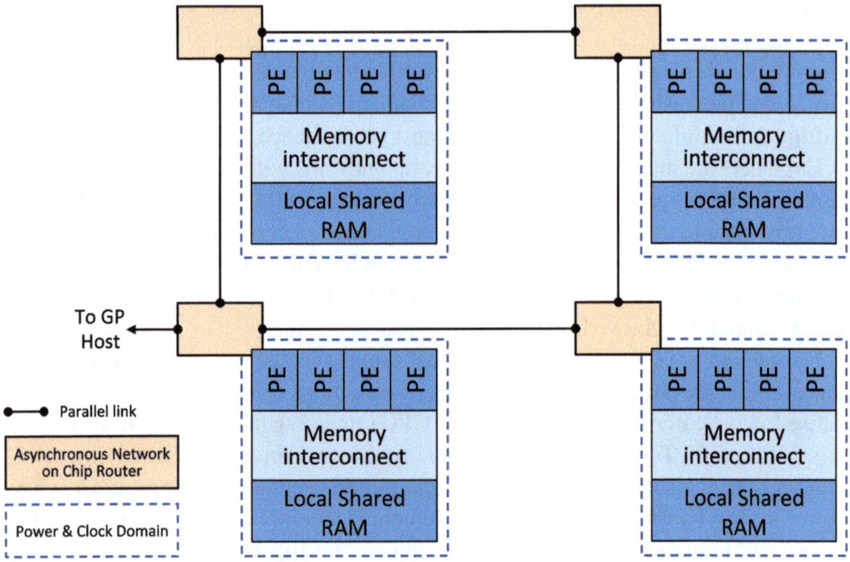

Fig. 1.1 NoC-based GALS architecture with four many-core clusters (power + clock) with four Processing Elements (*PE*) per cluster. Key: *GP* general purpose

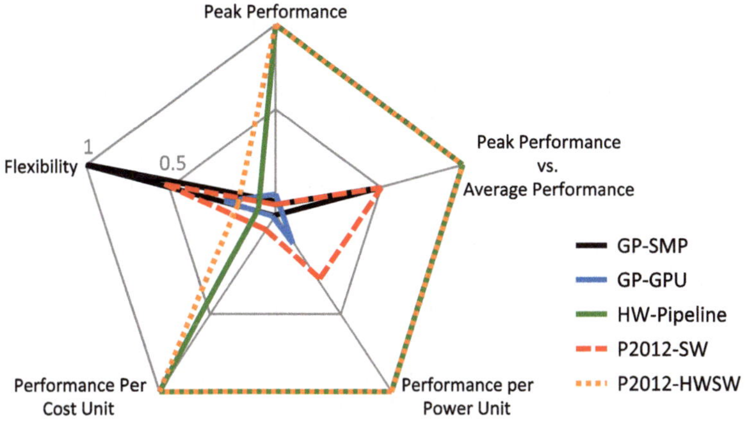

	GP	GPGPU	16 Processing Element Cluster	Hardware blocks
GFLOPs/mm^2	1	3	6	>100
GFLOPs/mm^2/W	1	2.3	25	>100

Fig. 1.2 Positioning of many-core with respect to General-Propose Symmetric Multi-Processors (GPSMP) and General-Purpose Computing on Graphics Processing Units (GPGPU) [12]

nologies. For instance, many-core template architectures can be specialised by class of applications. This can be done either through dedicated hardware blocks or by means of additional instructions, and can also provide fine-grain power control, e.g. at the cluster level. These architectures are more programmable, especially when data-dependent algorithms are being used, such as in video analytics and data fusion.

Such a variety of platforms leaves room for more flexible, fully programmable, and possibly heterogeneous many-core platforms that can serve data-dependent classes of algorithms. Figure 1.2 summarises the positioning of many-core with respect to traditional architectures.

Real-time algorithms currently running on smart cameras include motion detection, block-based motion estimation, adaptive histogram equalisation, bounding-box drawing, denoising, sharpening along with basic raw sensor data processing such as demosaicing, normalisation and colour processing [15, 16]. Most of these algorithms achieve real-time performance for standard definition frame resolution (PAL, NTSC or VGA) and typically with the help of platform (ARM + ASIC or ARM + ASIC + DSP/FPGA) optimised code. However, increasing frame rates, bit depths and frame resolutions are affecting current implementations. The need for hardware improvements providing higher memory bandwidth and processing is thus increasing.

The adoption of compute-capable GPUs in embedded systems can enable multi-threaded data parallelism [17]. OpenCL [18] can be used for programming heterogeneous multi/many-core platforms to achieve data and task-level parallelism. It is possible to off-load compute and memory bandwidth intensive frame processing to GPUs, or similar multi-core co-processors, leaving the remaining embedded processors available for additional functionality that best fits their architecture [19–21]. However, it is possible that the porting of some algorithms on smart cameras, which integrate parallel devices such as GPUs or multi-core accelerators, may not be able to achieve user-expected performance levels. This concern is mainly due to algorithm specifics, limited memory and core clock speeds, limited power consumption requirements or strict thermal budgets. Importantly, the nature of some algorithms may also not allow parallelisation [22–24].

Engineers are hence coping with the portability of algorithms from non-integrated to embedded processors. The major issue is achieving the same performance on both device types. This target motivates the integration of programmable accelerators inside the board to speed-up basic operations such as pixel-wise frame difference. Another key aspect is the programmability of the various kinds of architectures and portability of the application code [25]. This will be achieved by using industrial frameworks that bring together extensions to existing languages with their runtime systems [18, 26, 27], or by using emerging frameworks that address the specific needs of image processing algorithms and video analytics [28, 29].

1.3 Networks of Smart Cameras

Modern large area surveillance networks support multiple high-resolution cameras with high frame-rate video streams. Centralised data processing requirements can be addressed by increasing the memory and compute bandwidth, for example via processing units that employ high memory bandwidth and hardware accelerators such as GPUs. Such hardware accelerators can provide substantial performance gains and subsequently achieve much larger camera-feed per processor ratios [30]. Alternatively, a mixed centralised and distributed processing model can reduce both the transmission bandwidth between edge nodes (e.g. smart cameras) and a central control station and, possibly, the amount of processing that needs to be done at the central station.

Manual configuration of cameras in large area surveillance networks is costly, thus making autonomous and self-adaptive smart cameras desirable. Self-adaptive smart cameras must be capable of self-calibration, cooperation with heterogeneous hardware to identify neighbouring cameras and satisfy task requirements [31]. The advances in low-power computing discussed in the previous section bring computing power near to the sensors, which is key to reducing communication overheads.

Several solutions exist that attempt to interface heterogeneous cameras in a network, although none claim outright universality. An example is the Camera Link standard, version 2.0 managed by the Automated Imaging Association (AIA) [32]. Camera Link specifies camera connectors and a real-time communications protocol, provides standardised connections to programmable circuit hardware (e.g. Frame grabbers, FPGAs), and has enjoyed some market adoption. Hybrid analog and digital cameras are currently necessary to allow heterogeneous network devices to inter-connect. Analog to IP converters help integrate legacy analog systems into

IP-networks, though with very limited sensor control. Since components within smart cameras, or smart cameras themselves, are produced by multiple vendors, the collaboration among cameras has to be achieved among bespoke systems.

Two standards for IP cameras are emerging as dominant players in the market, the Physical Security Interoperability Alliance (PSIA) standard [33] and the Open Network Video Interface Forum (ONVIF) specification [34].

PSIA covers a range of products, not limited to IP cameras. The group behind PSIA formed from smaller companies and has seen reasonable adoption of its standard for IP video. The PSIA Recording and Content Management (RaCM) specification, combined with the PSIA IP Media Device specification, enables Digital Video Recorders, Network Video Recorders and Video Management Systems from different manufacturers to interoperate and to control different devices (e.g. cameras and encoders) in a video surveillance network.

ONVIF (started in 2008 by Axis communications) defines a common protocol for the exchange of information between network video devices, including automatic device discovery, video streaming and metadata. The standard is aimed at the surveillance market for intelligent cameras and analytics. In September 2013 more than 3,700 products were ONVIF conformant and more than 460 manufacturers, distributors and others were ONVIF members.

Software interoperability solutions have also been emerging. Genetec, for example, provides a software solution by the name of Omnicast [35], which claims to integrate a large number of IP cameras in such a way that an existing infrastructure should be interoperable with any new hardware selected by a customer.

A smart platform may incorporate multiple sensors, and blend them to boost event detection and classification performance. Night vision modules [36] and stereo pairs [37] can be embedded in smart cameras to boost perceptive capabilities. 3D object measurements can be used to improve type classifications [38] and to increase robustness in the case of occlusions [39, 40]. Smart cameras can perceive the surroundings also by integrating other sensors, such as microphones for gunshot detection and localisation, infrared motion sensors and radio-frequency identification for staff authorisation [41]. A video stream associated to an audio stream to enhance detection, identification and classification of events, and can broaden the type of applications that can be addressed, such as automatic camera re-orientation when an audio source location of interest is detected [42], or multi-modal object tracking [40, 43]. Some classes of sound events have been accurately detected and classified in research [44, 45] and in market products [46, 47]. Further enhancements involve robustness against difficult noise conditions and source localisation [48]. For the latter, dedicated acoustic sensors can be based on direction of air particles flow [49, 50] or beam-forming with time difference of arrival [51]. In order to increase the detection rate, one can employ an integrated solution of an acoustic-enabled Pan-Tilt-Zoom camera with sound source classification and localisation [42] (Fig. 1.3).

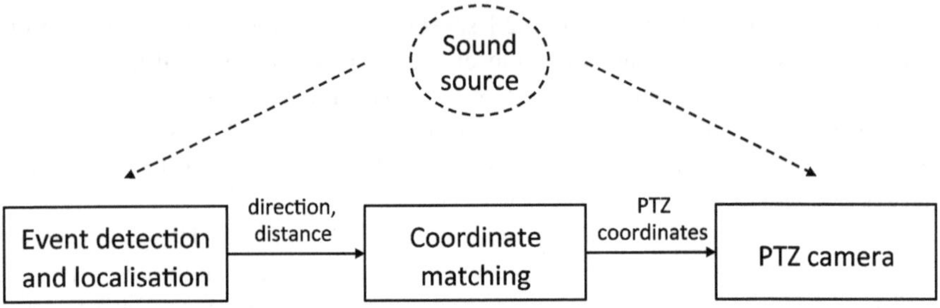

Fig. 1.3 General scheme of sound source detection, localisation and tracking, with automatic camera positioning. Key. *PTZ* pan-tilt-zoom

1.4 Privacy

Cooperation between smart cameras may lead to potential security problems as data communications may be accessible to unauthorised third-parties [52]. Moreover, because of the use of images of individuals, privacy has to be considered in the design of cognitive and perceptive video systems. Since embedded image processing supports detection of objects of interest using raw sensor data, object masking, as the simplest mean of privacy protection, can be performed before stream encoding for transmission [53]. The original images could be encrypted and stored in the camera itself for a short period of time. Privacy in surveillance can be addressed in numerous ways [54]. Generally, people's faces and license plates are the most prominent personal information readily extracted. A range of privacy-protection algorithms can be directly implemented in smart cameras in order to achieve a sufficient level of privacy in secure data communications. One simple approach is streaming-on-demand, in which the camera notifies an operator of detected events, and the operator engages the video stream if required. In such an approach the processing and archiving could be done within the camera itself [53].

Real-time anonymisation can also be a solution to the privacy problem [52]. People in a scene can be made anonymous by blurring the portion of the images representing their face and by storing the original non-blurred face for future use, e.g. inside an encrypted watermark. To reduce privacy-loss due to low face detection accuracy the whole top part of the detected object's silhouette can be masked. This reduces false-negatives as moving object detection can be considered reliable in most cases. Face blurring ensures that identities of people are safely managed, but at the same time the process of anonymisation can make other tasks difficult to perform, such as person re-identification. This can be dealt with by parameterisation of the original face images. Instead of distributing an image, the re-identification among numerous cameras could be based on numerical description—image features are not directly associated with the person identity, but are useful in confirming a visual similarity of objects seen by various cameras [55, 56].

Selective data erasure for privacy protection assumes that all footage, except identifiably important videos, should be deleted after predefined short periods of time. Important videos could be defined by event detection and re-identification of individuals [57] or with abandoned luggage, counter-flow and barrier crossing detection [58].

Smart camera networks could generate a fully symbolic representation of the monitored scene state (e.g. number of people entering through a particular door or in a highly sensitive zone or events of barrier crossing per hour). These could be the only data transmitted to an end-user application by re-creating a virtual reality representation of the real scene—anonymous avatars walking in a 3D environment, mimicking a person's behaviour, providing an operator with a comparable situational awareness to that of a traditional video feed [59].

1.5 Market Expectations

Typical CCTV (smart cameras for surveillance) end-user budgets allow them to spend only a small amount per camera as CCTV procurement is often part of a small physical security budget which tends to be seen as a drain on an organisation's resources. CCTV installation is traditionally a highly competitive, price-sensitive market with slow-growth. The addition of smart cameras has allowed a small increase in prices to be introduced, but in general CCTV users commonly expect the same or only marginal increases in price per camera. This effective cap on unit cost may have tended to force manufacturers, and their algorithm developers, to constrain their approaches to low computational cost processes that will run on standard Personal Computer (PC) architectures, thus tending to force smart camera system developers to limit themselves to low-computational complexity approaches to basic visual processing steps such as object detection, classification and tracking. Besides the constant search for better algorithmic approaches, huge increases in processing power are needed to ultimately allow high frame-rates, image resolutions and motion, texture and colour modelling to be utilised. For example, global minimisation techniques such as Simulated Annealing or Gibbs Markov Random Fields [60] can require millions of operations per pixel, and these might be a small part of a much larger set of complex processing stages. Whilst optimisations and cuts often help, they do not allow the developer free reign in combining the ideal combination of processing steps. In a recent thorough review of pedestrian classifiers [1], the best performing classifier was running at roughly five minutes per frame on standard NTSC images (although the authors note that many speed-ups are possible).

The introduction of cameras, with at-the-edge processing capabilities, is beginning to improve the situation, but cannot currently offer the level of processing that the most robust visual processing would consume.

CCTV end users tend to either have little or no conception of the potential offered by the current breed of commercial systems. Or have wildly over-optimistic expectations, perhaps fuelled by film and television (and also over-selling by some systems salespersons), of what is possible using smart cameras. Worse still, developers seldom get to understand the true needs or requirements of CCTV end-users. This lack of dialogue leads to a technology driven set of applications that seldom meet a genuine end-user need. A case in point might be the smart camera systems offering 'loitering' detection, often marketed into the public transport sector. 'Loitering' detection is a natural spin-off of people tracking technologies. However, in the transport domain, the incident of 'loitering' passengers is so high (i.e. waiting for connections is a natural part of travel) as to have little or no value to the end user. At the time of marketing, the purchaser would be presented with the scenario that loitering individuals up to no good would be detected, which sounds attractive, due to the semantic overloading of the term 'loitering'. Unfortunately, after a system is in operational use they then discover it cannot distinguish between 'good' and 'bad' loitering. This poor experience then feeds into the end user's negative perceptions of the benefits of smart cameras, and reduces their confidence in the concept, and reinforces the resistance to pay a significant mark-up on top of the CCTV cost for smart camera capabilities. High false alarm rates and the mismatching of capability to user needs therefore holds up both commercial progress and application performance, in a negative feedback loop (Fig. 1.4).

The smart camera market has seen a plethora of relatively low-cost systems appear in the last few years. Typical systems use a standard PC-based architecture and most

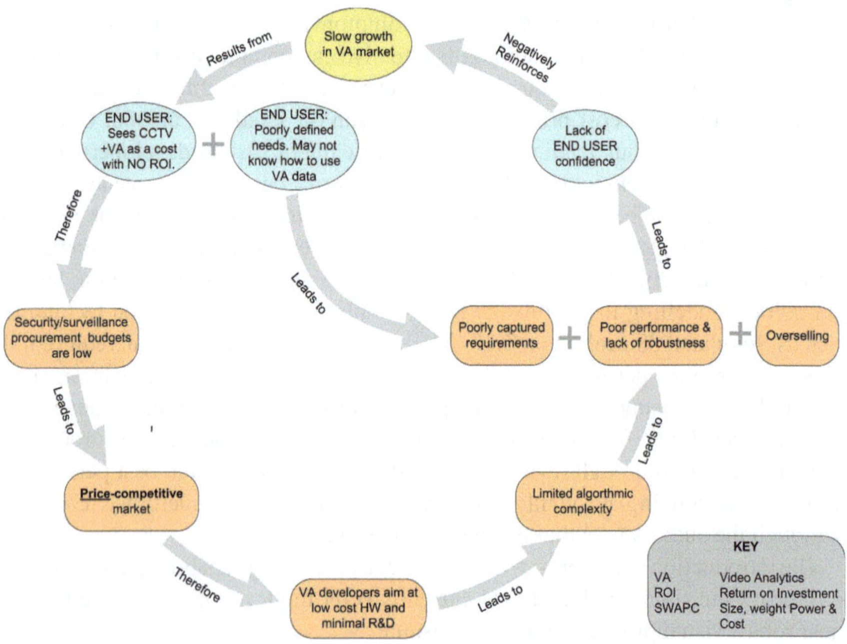

Fig. 1.4 Perceived market failure due to poor requirements definition and low smart CCTV user confidence

use standard CPU processing, although smart cameras with embedded systems have improved the computational power available per camera.

The preceding comments (summarised in Fig. 1.4) might seem to paint a rather bleak future for smart cameras; however, there are ways forward. The push for business innovation over the last decade has shown that by merging previously disparate information sources new and valuable knowledge can be gained. Such gains can be the basis of developing new business cases that change the smart camera system from being seen as a drain on resources to being a business opportunity and a revenue generator in itself. In essence, we should try and offer a surveillance capability that pays for itself. For example (i) reduce human work load or increase productivity (e.g. monitor more cameras with same number of staff) by using analytics to pre-filter large video archives for relevant information; (ii) preventative security (e.g. reduce vandalism repair costs in the Rail industry via detection of intruders at Rail stock yards and preventing graffiti tagging; (iii) create metadata that can be sold or aid the business and show a customer how to do it (e.g. counting the number of people passing specific locations in transport hubs to set advertising rates, and subsequently verify to advertisers that "hit rate" targets were met).

Another key aspect to managing user expectations and the acceptance of smart cameras is that the installation and maintenance of such systems should be as easy, robust and self-adaptive as possible. Additionally, honest collaboration with the end

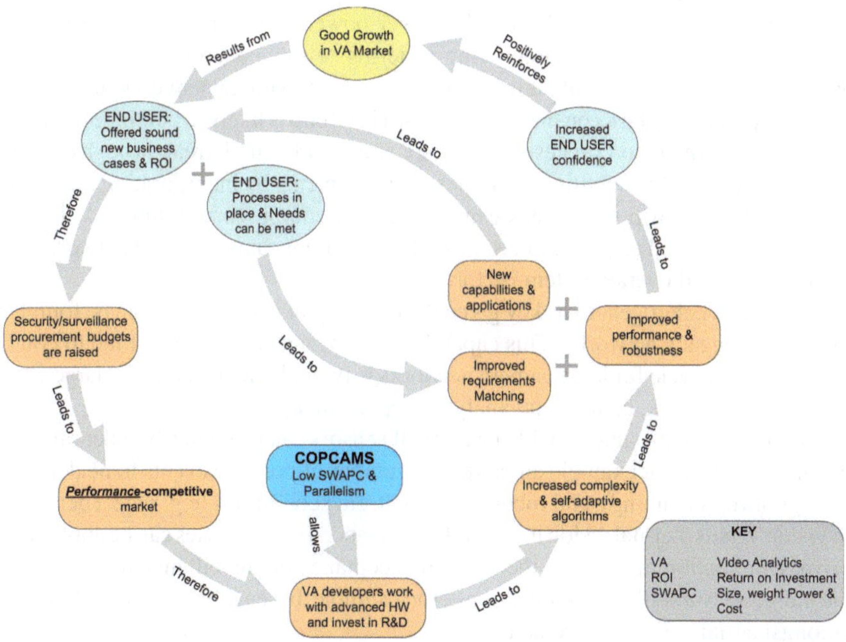

Fig. 1.5 Market success model that would allow end users to see smart CCTV systems as a benefit. COPCAMS cognitive and perceptive cameras (http://copcams.eu)

users is important to meet their expectations as opposed to proposing products that are a poor fit or unsuitable for their purposes. A recent trend in this area has been for sellers to appoint a "Customer's friend" (an extension of the Account Manager role). This individual works with the user organisation and challenges their own company where they see any sign of a mismatch or over-selling.

The goal is to create a beneficial circle (Fig. 1.5) so that as end users start to see a smart CCTV system as a net benefit, there is a potential for procurement budgets to be raised because they can now pay for themselves. That could (or should) lead to a more performance-based competitive market as opposed to a cost-competitive one, and it would enable the advancement of video analytics work using superior hardware and heavier investment in research and development costs.

New capabilities can therefore be generated, new products can be offered to customers and new applications can be better matched to real customer requirements. Finally, we should achieve the removal of existing negative feedback loops and the closure of a positive beneficial circle with a new level of end user confidence and approval.

1.6 Conclusions

Today's mobile and embedded processors are capable of what desktop computers could do ten years ago at substantially lower power consumption levels [61, 62]. As embedded platforms are improving in terms of raw computational power and available memory bandwidth, it is becoming possible to implement computationally complex processing tasks on these platforms. This trend is likely to continue thanks to developments in silicon process technology and architectural breakthroughs. Smart cameras are already benefiting from these developments by incorporating the newly available processing power to tackle more and more complex processing tasks locally leading to improved response times, more capable algorithms, lowered network traffic and enhanced overall system performance.

Nowadays heterogeneity is key given the diversity of cameras that can be found in many large legacy networks. This capability will be needed for some time to come, as the renewal cycle for large camera networks is typically long due to the large costs involved in network, camera and analytics replacement.

Equipping smart cameras with a variety of sensors can result in a broader range of business models, for example an increased number of possible events to be detected (e.g. gunfire, screaming), and robustness in extreme conditions (e.g. object detection in vision versus thermal vision in low light). Advanced technologies can be applied for privacy protection, increasing the societal acceptance of surveillance or to broaden the range of surveillance applications, for example by enabling the collaboration amongst aerial and terrain vehicles.

Acknowledgments This work has been partially funded by the Artemis JU and partially by TÜBİTAK—The Scientific and Technological Research Council of Turkey (Toygar Akgun), the UK

Technology Strategy Board (Charles Attwood, Andrea Cavallaro, Fabio Poiesi), French *Ministère de l'économie, du redressement productif et du numérique* (Christian Fabre) and Polish National Centre for Research and Development (Piotr Szczuko) as part of the COPCAMS project (http://copcams.eu) under Grant Agreement number 332913.

References

1. Dollar P, Wojek C, Schiele B, Perona P (2012) Pedestrian detection: an evaluation of the state of the art. IEEE Trans Pattern Anal Mach Intell 34(4):743–761
2. Koblar V, Filipic B (2013) Designing a quality-control procedure for commutator manufacturing. In: Proceedings of multiconference information society, Ljubljana, Slovenia, Oct 2013, pp 55–58
3. Stalder S, Grabner H, Van Gool L (2010) Cascaded confidence filtering for improved tracking-by-detection. In: Proceedings of European conference on computer vision, Crete, Greece, Sept 2010, pp 369–382
4. Abdelkader MF, Chellappa R, Zheng Q, Chan AL (2006) Integrated motion detection and tracking for visual surveillance. In: Proceedings of the computer visionsystems, New York, pp 28–34
5. Kiryati N, Raviv TR, Ivanchenko Y, Rochel S (2008) Real-time abnormal motion detection in surveillance video. In: Proceedings of international conference on patternrecognition, Tampa, Dec 2008, pp 1–4
6. Bhargava M, Chen CC, Ryoo MS, Aggarwal JK (2009) Detection of object abandonment using temporal logic. Mach Vis Appl 20(5):271–281
7. Smith K, Quelhas P, Gatica-Perez D (2006) Detecting abandoned luggage items in a public space. In: Proceedings of computer vision and pattern recognition, workshop on performance evaluation of tracking and surveillance, New York, June 2006, pp 75–82
8. Szwoch G, Dalka P, Czyzewski A (2010) A framework for automatic detection of abandoned luggage in airport terminal. In: Tsihrintzis GA, Damiani E, Virvou M, Howlett RJ, Jain LC (eds) Smart innovation, systems and technologies, intelligent interactive multimedia systems and services. Springer, Heidelberg, pp 13–22
9. Chen X, Yang SX (2013) A practical solution for ripe tomato recognition and localization. J Real-Time Image Proc 8(1):35–51
10. What is GPU accelerated computing? (2014) http://www.nvidia.com/object/what-is-gpu-computing.html. Last accessed June 2014
11. DARPA PERFECT (2014) http://www.darpa.mil/Our_Work/MTO/Programs/Power_Efficiency_Revolution_for_Embedded_Computing_Technologies_(PERFECT).aspx. Last accessed June 2014
12. Melpignano D et al (2012) Platform 2012, a many-core computing accelerator for embedded SoCs: performance evaluation of visual analytics applications. In: Proceedings of design automation conference, San Francisco, June 2012, pp 1137–1142
13. Wilson R et al (2014) A 460mhz at 397mv, 2.6ghz at 1.3v, 32b vliw dsp, embedding fmax tracking. In: Proceedings of solid-state circuits conference digest of technical papers, San Francisco, Feb 2014, pp 452–453
14. Meincke T et al (1999) Globally asynchronous locally synchronous architecture for large high-performance ASICs. In: Proceedings of circuits and systems, Orlando, July 1999, pp 512–515
15. Smart camera NI (2014) http://sine.ni.com/nips/cds/view/p/lang/en/nid/210036. Last accessed June 2014
16. Belbachir AN, Nabil A (eds) (2010) Smart cameras. Springer, New York
17. MALI OpenCL SDK (2014) http://malideveloper.arm.com/develop-for-mali/sdks/mali-opencl-sdk/. Last accessed June 2014
18. Open Computing Language (2014) https://www.khronos.org/opencl. Last accessed June 2014

19. Gaster B, Howes L, Kaeli DR, Mistry P, Schaa D (eds) (2011) Heterogeneous computing with OpenCL. Elsevier, Amsterdam
20. Munshi A, Gaster B, Mattson TG, Fung J, Ginsburg D (eds) (2011) OpenCL programming guide. Addison-Wesley Professional, New Delhi
21. Scarpino M (ed) (2011) OpenCL in action: how to accelerate graphics and computations. Manning Publications, Waltham
22. Jaja J (ed) (1992) Introduction to parallel algorithms. Addison-Wesley Professional, Reading
23. Kirk DB, Hwu WW (eds) (2012) Programming massively parallel processors: a hands-on approach. Morgan Kaufmann, San Francisco
24. Roosta SH (ed) (2000) Parallel processing and parallel algorithms: theory and computation. Springer, New York
25. Fabre C et al (2013) PRO3D, programming for future 3D manycore architectures: project interim status. Formal Methods Compon Objects Lect Notes Comput Sci 7542:277–293
26. A parallel computing platform and programming model (2014) http://www.nvidia.com/object/cuda_home_new.html. Last accessed June 2014
27. A specification for parallel programming (2014) http://openmp.org/wp/. Last accessed June 2014
28. Lepley T, Paulin P, Flamand E (2013) A novel compilation approach for image processing graphs on a many-core platform with explicitly managed memory. In: Proceedings of compilers, architecture and synthesis for embedded systems, Montreal, pp 1–10
29. Llopard I, Cohen A, Fabre C, Hili N (2014) A parallel action language for embedded applications and its compilation flow. In: Proceedings of software and compilers for embedded systems, St. Goar, June 2014, pp 118–127
30. Guler P, Emeksiz D, Temizel A, Teke M, Temizel T (2013) Real-time multi-camera video analytics system on GPU. J Real-Time Image Process 8(4):389–401
31. SanMiguel JC, Micheloni C, Shoop K, Foresti GL, Cavallaro A (2014) Self-reconfigurable smart camera networks. IEEE Comput 47(5):67–73
32. Camera Link Standard (2014) http://www.visiononline.org/vision-standards-details.cfm?type=6. Last accessed June 2014
33. Open Network Video Interface Forum (2014) http://www.onvif.org/. Last accessed June 2014
34. The Physical Security Interoperability Alliance (2014) http://www.psialliance.org/. Last accessed June 2014
35. OmniCast (2014) http://www.genetec.com/solutions/all-products/omnicast. Last accessed June 2014
36. Corsi C (2014) Infrared: a key technology for security systems. In: Baldini F et al (eds) Sensors, lecture notes in electrical engineering, vol 162. Springer, Heidelberg, pp 37–42
37. Houben Q, Czyz J, Tocino D, Debeir O, Warzee N (2009) Feature-based stereo vision using smart cameras for traffic surveillance. In: Fritz M, Schiele B, Piater JH (eds) Computer vision systems. Springer, Heidelberg, pp 144–153
38. Wang Y, Kato J (2012) Integrated pedestrian detection and localization using stereo cameras. In: Hansen J, Boyraz P, Takeda K, Abut H (eds) Signal processing for in-vehicle systems and safety. Springer, Heidelberg, pp 229–238
39. Mittal A, Davis LS (2002) M2Tracker: a multi-view approach to segmenting and tracking people in a cluttered scene using region-based stereo. In: Proceedings of European conference on computer vision, Copenhagen, May 2002, pp 18–22
40. Szwoch G, Dalka P, Czyzewski A (2013) Spatial calibration of a dual PTZ-fixed camera system for tracking moving objects in video. J Imaging Sci Technol 57(2):1–10
41. Haering N, Venetianer PL, Lipton A (2008) The evolution of video surveillance: an overview. Mach Vis Appl 19(5–6):279–290
42. Lopatka K, Kotus J, Czyzewski A (2011) Application of vector sensors to acoustic surveillance of a public interior space. Arch Acoust 36(4):851–860
43. Arguedas VF, Zhang Q, Izquierdo E (2014) Multimodal fusion in surveillance applications. In: Ionescu B, Benois-Pineau J, Piatrik T, Qunot G (eds) Fusion in computer vision. Springer, Heidelberg, pp 161–184

44. Kotus J (2010) Application of passive acoustic radar to automatic localization, tracking and classification of sound sources. In: Proceedings of information technology, Gdansk, June 2010, pp 67–70
45. Kotus J, Lopatka K, Czyzewski A (2014) Detection and localization of selected acoustic events in acoustic field for smart surveillance applications. Multimed Tools Appl 68(1):5–21
46. Cisco Gunshot Location Surveillance (2014) http://www.cisco.com/web/strategy/government/solution_GunshotLocationSurveillance.html. Last accessed June 2014
47. SST, Shotspotter Flex (2014) http://www.shotspotter.com/solutions. Last accessed June 2014
48. Lopatka K, Kotus J, Czyzewski A (2014) Evaluation of sound event detection, classification and localization in the presence of background noise for acoustic surveillance of hazardous situations. In: Andrzej D, Andrzej C (eds) Multimedia communications, services and security communications in computer and information science, vol 429. Springer, pp 96–110
49. Microflown (2014) http://www.microflown.com/. Last accessed June 2014
50. Wind J, de Bree H-E, Buye X (2010) 3D sound source localization and sound mapping using a PU sensor array. In: Proceedings of AIAA/CEAS aeroacoustics, Stockholm, June 2010
51. Kellermann W (2008) Beamforming for speech and audio signals. In: Havelock D, Kuwano S, Vorlander M (eds) Handbook of signal processing in acoustics, vol 691–702. Springer, Heidelberg
52. Cichowski J, Czyzewski A (2011) Reversible video stream anonymization for video surveillance systems based on pixels relocation and watermarking. In: Proceedings of international conference on computer vision workshops, Barcelona, Nov 2011, pp 1971–1977
53. Helten F, Fischer B (2004) Reactive attention: video surveillance in Berlin shopping malls. Surveill Soc 2(2/3):323–345
54. Cavallaro A (2007) Privacy in video surveillance. IEEE Signal Process Mag 24(2):166–168
55. Dalka P (2012) Multi-camera vehicle tracking using local image features and neural networks. In: Andrzej D, Andrzej C (eds) Multimedia communications, services and security. Communications in computer and information science, vol 287. Springer, Heidelberg, pp 58–67
56. Hamdoun O, Moutarde F, Stanciulescu B, Steux B (2008) Person re-identification in multi-camera system by signature based on interest point descriptors collected on short video sequences. In: Proceedings of distributed smart cameras, Stanford, Sept 2008, pp 1–6
57. D'Arminio P et al (2012) Technologies for granting balance between security and privacy in video-surveillance. In: Proceedings of intelligence and security informatics, Arlington, VA, Aug. 2012, pp 278–283
58. Dalka P, Bratoszewski P (2013) Visual detection of people movement rules violation in crowded indoor scenes. In: Andrzej D, Andrzej C (eds) Multimedia communications, services and security. Communications in computer and information science, vol 368. Springer, Berlin, pp 48–58
59. Szczuko P (2014) Augmented reality for privacy-sensitive visual monitoring. In: Dziech A, Czyzewski A (eds) Multimedia communications, services and security. Communications in computer and information science, vol 429. Springer, Switzerland, pp 229–241
60. Kato Z, Zerubia J (2012) Markov random fields in image segmentation. Found Trends Sig Process 5(1–2):1–155
61. NVIDIA Whitepaper (2014) http://www.nvidia.com/content/PDF/tegra_white_papers/tegra-K1-whitepaper.pdf. Last accessed June 2014
62. SAMSUNG Whitepaper (2014) http://www.samsung.com/global/business/semiconductor/minisite/Exynos/data/Enjoy_the_Ultimate_WQXGA_Solution_with_Exynos_5_Dual_WP.pdf. Last accessed June 2014

[illegible]

Chapter 2
Access-Centric In-Network Storage Optimization in Distributed Sensing Networks

Carsten Grenz, Sven Tomforde and Jörg Hähner

Abstract Distributed sensing networks are getting increasingly complex these days. The main reason are the changing demands of the users and application scenarios, which require multipurpose systems. Enabled by continuously improving computational and storage capacities of sensors, this development leads to an increasing number of different algorithms which run concurrently in a sensing network. Thereby, they enable sensor-actuator platforms to perform various kinds of analysis and actions in parallel. Within such a sensor network a variety of algorithms is performed simultaneously. When developing distributed vision and control algorithms, developers focus mainly on the consecutive processing stages. Such a process typically begins with perceiving raw sensor data and terminates with delivering high-level event data to responsible entities. Thereby, different stages may be performed at varying locations within the underlying network. Although the researchers may apply custom optimizations to their data flows, these are highly specific. During design time, it is impossible to anticipate each system environment or predict their algorithms' possible interactions and synergies with other data flows. We propose a generic storage architecture which separates algorithms from data storage and retrieval. By making use of the fact that most data in sensing networks refers to geographic areas, our architecture takes care of the data flow and its online optimization throughout the network at runtime. By decoupling the processing stages from the data flow, we allow for self-organizing meta-level optimizations of data placement in the network. Moreover, this approach even makes inter-algorithmic optimizations possible,

C. Grenz (✉) · S. Tomforde · J. Hähner
Organic Computing, Universität Augsburg, Augsburg, Germany
e-mail: carsten.grenz@informatik.uni-augsburg.de

S. Tomforde
e-mail: sven.tomforde@informatik.uni-augsburg.de

J. Hähner
e-mail: joerg.haehner@informatik.uni-augsburg.de

P. Spagnolo et al. (eds.), *Human Behavior Understanding in Networked Sensing*,
DOI 10.1007/978-3-319-10807-0_2

if different algorithms process similar data within their step-wise processing logic. With the introduction of the access-centric storage paradigm, we prove to reduce network load and query latency at the same time at runtime.

2.1 Introduction

The ongoing advances in the field of smart sensing applications lead to new challenges concerning requirements of communication middlewares and protocols for such systems. Especially, the trend toward integration of different kinds of sensors, on the same hardware platform as well as on different hardware platforms, can be observed. This diversification process leads to new data-aggregation and -fusion algorithms and, therefore, to many kinds of generated data and metadata.

Classical sensing networks mostly focused on specific tasks they were designed for. These networks are called *mono-tasked* systems. One representative of this class are wireless sensor networks assembled of low-powered Mica2 motes which take temperature and humidity measurements, and transport them to a base station. Typically, these systems were optimized by domain specialists to efficiently and effectively solve their specific task.

The advances in the field of computational power and network capacities led to much more elaborated kinds of sensing networks and applications, e.g., the integration of visual sensors into sensing nodes led to the development of smart camera networks. The main goal of such a *smart* camera is the extraction of high-level information from pictures taken by the camera. While the development started with vision algorithms applied to single cameras, nowadays, researchers apply various data-fusion algorithms to combine data of different cameras using networking capabilities [22]. This way, they generate contextual metadata to gain person-specific information or create situational descriptions like movement patterns. One step in the further research of smart cameras was the application of movement capabilities, e.g., pan-tilt-zoom actuators or moving robots, which enable the cameras to change their field of views (see [11, 26]). Using communication protocols from the peer-to-peer computing domain, researchers built distributed and self-organizing vision and control algorithms, which increased the efficiency and effectiveness of those systems.

Nowadays, the trend goes toward multipurpose systems integrating various sensor platforms and their specific algorithms [2]. This rise of heterogeneous systems leads to sensor data being fed into the systems from different kinds of sensors. Simultaneously, an increasing number of algorithms works concurrently to fuse and aggregate many kinds of descriptive metadata. Originally, the algorithms working in these heterogeneous systems were not developed with such an integration in mind. Moreover, they may even come from very different domains and it is not feasible for any developer to anticipate every application scenario of their algorithms during design-time, since an engineer naturally focuses on the main application scenario.

Due to this different focus, today's sensing networks are occupied with uncountable flows of data and control packets of various applications which leads to new challenges on different layers of the networks' protocol stacks. This challenge is arising in all complex smart sensing networks [6, 19].

A main concern of developers of distributed sensing algorithms is the emitted network load and, from an application's point of view, the latency of queries as well as the responsiveness of their applications during runtime. Latency is especially an issue, if the system serves some security-related function or if human operators are part of the interaction loop. Although developers of distributed algorithms put in huge efforts to optimize their own algorithms' data flows, the effects of interaction resulting from various distributed algorithms working on different subsets of the available data is not predictable. Moreover, the algorithms have their own, and often different, ways of coping with situations like node churn and other disturbances. However, there mostly exists no notion of how the algorithms may share their data. Therefore, each algorithm's optimizations take only its own expected data flows into account. Since the set of running algorithms accessing specific data items cannot be determined, this may lead to unnecessary high network traffic and contention. In the end, it is not possible for a developer to anticipate any future application scenario.

As a conclusion, it is unfeasible and often impossible for any developer to anticipate their algorithms' application context, which consists of the system's hardware-parameters, the concurrently running other algorithms, and the behavior of people interacting with the system and triggering events.

In this chapter, we meet these challenges presenting algorithms for a distributed online storage optimization build into a storage framework. On the one hand, our approach is general enough to be easily applied to various application scenarios of smart sensor systems. On the other hand, it is specialized enough to allow dynamic optimizations during runtime. Therefore, our framework offers a generalized interface for georeferenced data items.

After characterizing our system model, we present the storage-latency search problem. Afterwards, we introduce a generic storage layer for smart sensor nodes. We investigate the architecture's design space by discussing relevant parameters and their dependencies, and analyze the interactions with the underlying routing model. In the evaluation, we present appropriate metrics and show how our framework optimizes the storage allocation during runtime proving the benefits of our approach.

2.1.1 Case Study: CamInSens

One example for a smart sensing system which uses multistage processing is the CamInSens system [6, 10], which runs different high-level algorithms at the same time relying on each others data. It integrates PC-based smart cameras with pan-tilt-zoom functionality with Mica2 motes [3]. The system's main goal is the online extraction of persons' trajectories and their annotation with adjacent event data. The trajectories are acquired by single-camera multi-person trackers processing images

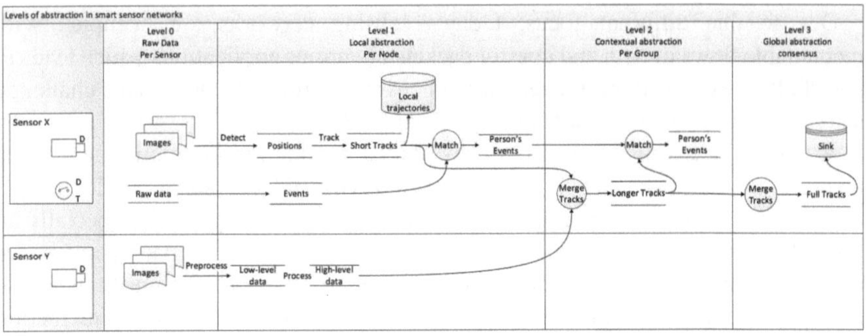

Fig. 2.1 Example data flow of a multistaged algorithm

next to the source—meaning as closely to the visual sensor as possible [18]. Distributed multi-camera trackers, which use the output of trackers on different cameras, build overall trajectories [19]. The smart cameras base their viewshed-planning on current and predicted trajectories [12, 13]. In addition, another set of algorithms annotates these trajectories with other events based on data from nearby sensors, i.e., recognized events in the surroundings of the Mica2 motes.

To illustrate this statement, Fig. 2.1 depicts an exemplary data flow for two sensors. The figure shows the data flows of two smart cameras with the upper one being accompanied by an additional mote sensor. From left to right, one can see the different levels of abstractions that match different communication primitives used. Level 0 represents the local recording of raw sensor data. At level 1, this data is processed locally in order to extract first metadata, i.e., people's positions and events like glass breakage. This information is merged into short annotated tracks of people. On the next level, geographically adjacent sensors merge their findings into contextual abstractions. This behavior is applied gradually until a global abstraction is reached. Depending on the user's needs, he may access the merged global data at the control room, or the contextual data stores of the different sensors. The latter case is especially useful, if the user moves through the region under observation and accesses the system with an ad hoc connected device.

This example shows how people from different domains cooperate to develop high-level algorithms for such systems. A modern sensor middleware should offer a universal interface to integrate such heterogeneous entities. Moreover, it shows a dimension of the incalculability of access patterns on data during design time of system components, since the number of nodes, their distribution in the environment and their interconnection is not set at design-time.

We are going to research this new area of interacting algorithms and present a generalized self-organizing storage framework for smart sensing networks. Our work enables developers and maintainers of self-organizing networks to concentrate on their algorithmic developments while our distributed storage framework manages and optimizes storage locations adaptively based on the current demand.

2.2 Related Work

Our work originates from the idea of using a virtual coordinate overlay for fast and transparent access to distributed resources which offers the interface of a distributed hash table (DHT). Well-known examples of distributed hash tables for peer-to-peer systems like the internet are Chord [24] and content-addressable network (CAN) [20]. These approaches form an overlay network whose topology is independent from the underlying network. Although they offer a general approach for the distributed implementation of hash tables, they may impose significant detours in the underlying network. This leads to unwanted network load and is unfeasible for sensor networks with their limited capabilities (e.g., bandwidth, energy consumption).

Considering in-network storage algorithms for sensor networks, the authors of [23] proposed a widely adopted data-centric storage (DCS) paradigm. It makes use of the position of the nodes and the data to store. Therefore, it uses a geographic routing protocol, i.e., *Greedy Perimeter Stateless Routing* (GPSR) [14], to determine actual storage positions. Depending on the position that is assigned to data, different storage patterns can be reached. One example is location-centric storage, which ensures that data is stored near its origin [7].

The authors of the *Geographic Hash Table* (GHT) combined the idea of determining storage positions using hash functions and the routing on the underlay network using GPSR [21]. Their application of a hash function leads to an equal distribution of data on the network nodes (given an uniform distribution of the nodes in space), but they do not consider the imposed load on the network or individual nodes caused by their distribution. Moreover, the authors of GHT consider a fixed number of queries per second independently of the number of participating nodes. Consequently, they argue that the overall usage of nodes decreases with an increasing number of nodes. This differs from application scenarios such as smart camera networks, where many nodes are considered to produce and consume data. We also make use of a virtual coordinate space in our Lookup table while routing on real geocoordinates using geographic routing protocols. But our approach uses a mutable virtual coordinate space to optimize the storage allocation w.r.t. latencies.

Since GHT does not take the actual network topology into account, different efforts have been made to distribute the workload equally upon suited nodes: The authors of ZGHT [16] try to improve the storage behavior by introducing zones, which are responsible for similar amounts of replicated data. The goal when choosing the size of a zone is to achieve a load balancing in terms of contained number of nodes. In contrast to our approach, the ZGHT algorithm computes all zones centrally with the knowledge of all nodes' positions. A similiar approach is Q-NiGHT [4] which uses nonuniform hash functions to meet the challenge of unequally distributed sensor nodes. Another load-balancing approach is presented in [17] proposing a temporally rotating hash function which changes the storage location in a predefined way during runtime. Our approach, in contrast, focuses on the actual access patterns to data as primary optimization objective and adapts the storage locations to a dynamically changing system in a self-organizing way during runtime.

The authors of [1] also consider the hop count as a criterion for data placement. As part of their approach, a multicast-tree is generated. Nodes have to proactively join and leave this tree. As opposed to our approach, there may only be one producer of a data item and they solve the problem to optimally place successive replications of the measured data items. Furthermore, they assume a fixed update rate of each data item by its producer. Our approach, in contrast, is significantly more flexible as it supports any number of producers and consumers with changing access frequencies. Moreover, our algorithm has a smaller message overhead since no tree management is necessary.

The authors of [5] argue for a layered architecture representing standardized interfaces and semantics. Within our concept, we utilize their notion and representation, while presenting an approach with a varying focus.

2.3 System Model

Our system model extends a previously developed system model of smart camera networks, see [9, 11]. The smart cameras and security personnel's devices are distributed in a convex area of surveillance. All participating entities in the network, i.e., smart cameras and the security personells' hardware, are connected using IEEE 802.11b/g wireless LAN. The smart cameras are equipped with processing and networking capabilities. Therefore, all cameras are able to communicate with each other using appropriate routing protocols.

As outlined above, all participating devices may acquire, aggregate, and store data at the same time. Therefore, we introduced the notion of *producers* and *consumers* in smart sensing networks [8]. The common case of these roles is the following: The sensors, i.e., cameras in the system, are the producers of data. The security personnel consumes this data using their workstations. These workstations may be central control rooms as well as moving mobile entities, such as tablets or smartphones, which are part of the wireless network. Furthermore, different algorithms on the sensors may be *consumers* of each other's data (see Fig. 2.2a, b).

Since all data in a smart camera network refers to geolocations, the data model consists of two parts: the *geolocation of an event* and the *event* itself. The *event* represents any event and may originate from an extraction from a visual algorithm, e.g., a person's position in space, or even an aggregated vector of data, e.g., a person's trajectory. Since the actual data is not of interest to our algorithm, we adapt the notion of a distributed key-value store or distributed hash table (DHT). All anticipated data items are relatively small compared to the storage of images, so they can easily reside and migrate throughout the network.

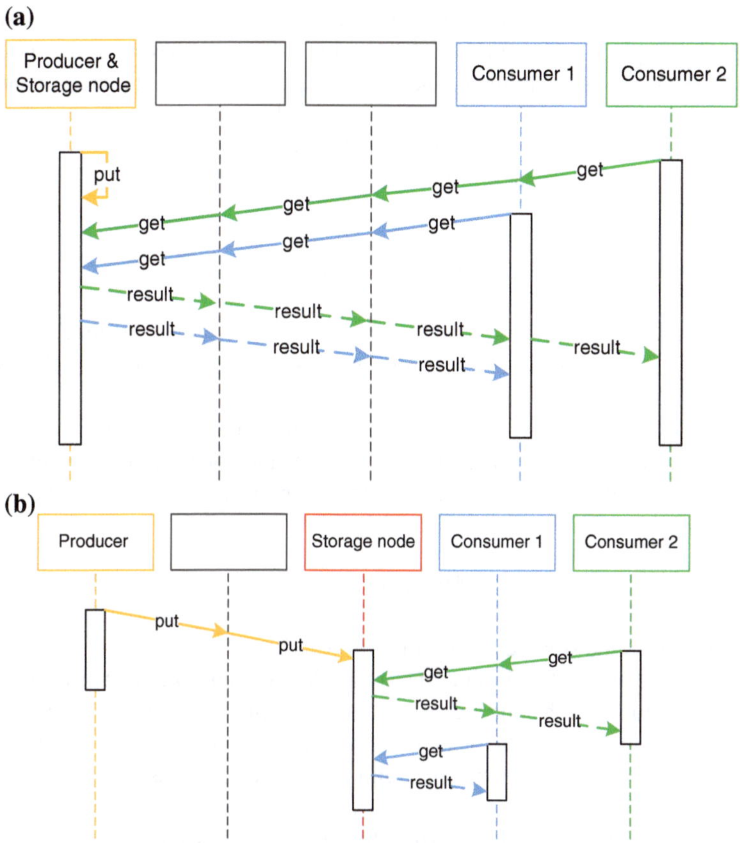

Fig. 2.2 **a** Initial query latency. The figure depicts a producer (*left*, *yellow*) and two consumers (*blue* and *green*, *right*). Access is realized using *put*, *get*, and *result* messages. The latency expressed in terms of hops in the network, i.e., the number of messages sent, sums up to 14 in this example. **b** Optimized query latency. After data migration took place, the data is now allocated to the storage node in the middle (*red*). Considering the current access pattern this leads to an optimized hop count of 8. Thus, the overall network load is reduced significantly

2.4 Problem Definition

In order to demonstrate the applicability of our framework to different classes of sensor networks, we present a formal representation of the storage allocation problem. By examining the key parameters of this problem, we give an overview of possible application scenarios. Afterwards, we formulate the optimization problem resulting from the storage allocation problem. Thereafter, we present our storage framework for peer-to-peer systems and show how the problem becomes feasible if it is solved in a distributed manner.

The formal problem definition models the problem of assigning suitable storage positions as a graph-based optimization problem [9]. It is based on an undirected graph $G = (V, E)$, namely the *connectivity graph*. Therefore, the graph contains a set of vertices v_i for every node i in the network. Furthermore, edges $e_j = \{v_k, v_l\}$ exist iff node k and node l can bidirectionally communicate.

The nodes have the capability to store (atomic) data items σ_i consisting of a *key* and a *value*, i.e.,

$$\sigma_i = \langle key, value \rangle$$

The `key` represents the geographical reference-position of the data item, the `value` may be any kind of data. The overall data stored in the network is denoted by $\Sigma = \cup \sigma_i$.

The goal of an in-network data storage algorithm is to assign each data item $\sigma \in \Sigma$ to a node $v \in V$, which will be responsible for its storage, delivery, and update management. Therefore, the data-item-to-node assignment can be expressed as a function

$$Allocate : \Sigma \to V$$

which represents the storage location for all data items.

Furthermore, the nodes' limitations are modeled as constraints. For example, the storage limitation of each node is expressed by a function $Mem: V \to \mathbb{N}$ representing the number of objects σ_i, which can be stored at a node at the same time. Using this function, the problem's memory constraint can be expressed as:

$$\forall v_i \in V : |\{ \sigma \mid Allocate(\sigma) = v_i \}| \leq Mem(v_i) \tag{2.1}$$

Each data item σ_i can be accessed by various nodes with varying frequencies and different operations, i.e., *put*, *get*, or *delete* operations. Therefore, the number of accesses n of a specific access-*type* to σ_i from a node $v \in V$ may be modeled as a tuple:

$$acc_{\sigma_i} = \langle v, type, num \rangle$$

$$\text{with } v \in V, type \in \mathbb{N}_+, num \in \mathbb{N}_+$$

A set of n different accesses to σ_i is denoted as

$$ACC_{\sigma_i} = \{\langle v_1, type_1, num_1 \rangle, \ldots, \langle v_n, type_n, num_n \rangle\}$$

To calculate the costs of an access, the following definitions from graph theory are used:

A path between two nodes from u to w is defined as a tuple:

$$p(u, w) = (\{u, v_1\}, \{v_1, v_2\}, \ldots, \{v_{n-1}, v_n\}, \{v_n, w\})$$

The length of a path $p(v_1, v_2)$ is equal to the number of edges in the path and is denoted by $|p(v_1, v_2)|$. The set of all paths connecting nodes u and w is $P(u, w)$.

Let the shortest path between two nodes v_1 and v_2 in G be denoted as $d_G(v_1, v_2)$ and be defined as:

$$d_G(v_1, v_2) = \begin{cases} 0 & v_1 = v_2 \\ \min_{p \in P(v_1, v_2)} |p(v_1, v_2)| & P(v_1, v_2) \neq \emptyset \\ \infty & \text{otherwise} \end{cases}$$

The costs of an access represent the impact it has on the network's resources.

Since we are going to minimize the latency of accesses, the cost of an access is defined as the minimal number of hops needed to access a data item given an instance of a graph G. Moreover, the *access type* determines the messaging pattern used, i.e., the number of messages exchanged for a successful transaction. Therefore, the costs for one access pattern $acc_{\sigma_i} = \langle v, type, num \rangle$ given a graph G and an allocation $Allocate$ is defined as

$$costs(G, Allocate, acc_{\sigma_i}) = type \cdot num \cdot d_G(v, Allocate(\sigma_i))$$

2.4.1 Storage Latency Search Problem

The goal of the access-centric storage paradigm is to find an optimal solution for the placement of data items in a distributed peer-to-peer system with the primary goal to minimize the latency of issued queries measured by their hop counts. Given the problem description and constraints above, the *storage latency search problem* is defined as follows: Given a graph G and an access pattern ACC, find a complete data allocation function $Allocate$ which minimizes the following access costs:

$$\min \sum_{\sigma_i \in \Sigma} \sum_{acc \in Acc_{\sigma_i}} costs(G, Allocate, acc)$$
$$= \min \sum_{\sigma_i \in \Sigma} \sum_{acc \in Acc_{\sigma_i}} acc.type \cdot acc.num \cdot d_G(acc.v, Allocate(\sigma_i))$$

and meets all constraints in the form of formula (2.1).

2.5 Storage Framework

In the following section, we present our storage framework as a middleware which can be integrated into any sensor node model by implementing its interfaces. Figure 2.3 depicts an exemplary three-layered sensor node model with the storage middleware

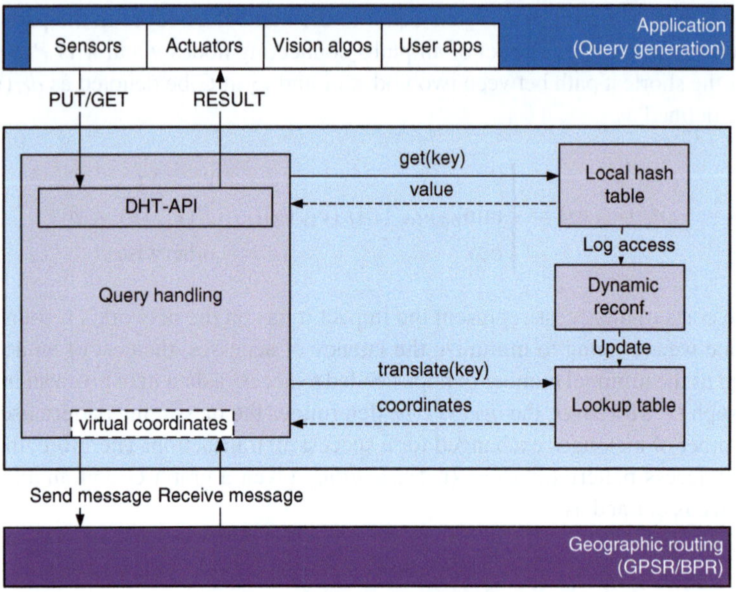

Fig. 2.3 Node architecture. The figure shows a three-layered sensor node with the storage middleware located between the *application* and the *routing* layer. The *arrows* represent the collaboration between the modules

placed between the application and the routing layer. In Sect. 2.5.2 we explain our distributed online optimization algorithm for self-organizing data storage.

2.5.1 Architecture

Our *storage middleware* is located between the *application layer* and the *routing layer* (see Fig. 2.3). As will be explained, our algorithm makes as few assumptions about these other layers as possible.

The *application layer* encapsulates any sensing or control algorithm that stores and retrieves georeference-based data. These algorithms may interact with any kind of sensor or abstract data. To make use of the storage framework, an application has to use the sleek interface of a distributed hash table as described in Sect. 2.5.1.1. Therefore, the placement and distribution of data in the network is fully transparent to the application. We abstract certain kinds of applications' behavior in *producer* and *consumer* modules.

The *routing layer* contains a geographic routing protocol, which operates on the nodes' positions during packet forwarding. In particular, our algorithms make use of the capability of these protocols to determine so called *home nodes*. A node is considered a *home node* for a specific coordinate, if it is the nearest node available w.r.t. the euclidean distance. However, it is important to note that the home node might change due to node churn or movement.

The *storage middleware* is located in the layer between. It translates coordinates, which are the keys of the queries, to virtual coordinates, which represent the actual storage location of data items. This is done using a Lookup table that is available at each node (see Sect. 2.5.1.2). Due to this translation, the whole optimization and migration process is transparent to both, the routing and the application layer. Therefore, standard geographic routing algorithms may be used on the lower layer. However, cross-layer optimizations may improve the performance as will be discussed in Sect. 2.5.1.3.

To offer a general and extensible framework, we follow a clean tier-based approach as suggested in [5]. We chose a three-tiered approach which well be presented in the following sections: *Tier 2* contains the interface to the application layer. *Tier 1* contains the key-space transformation which translates real geocoordinates to their respective virtual coordinates, which represent the storage location of the associated data items. And *Tier 0* implements the interface to a geographic routing protocol.

2.5.1.1 Tier 2—API

In order to achieve a generic applicability for all kinds of application-level algorithms, the storage layer offers a concise and general-purpose frontend API of a distributed hash table (DHT-API). This way, the applications can make use of a highly standardized interface. The available operations are:

- `put(key,value)`
- `value = get(key)`
- `delete(key)`

In the context of network performance and workload, the main difference between these operations is whether they are one-way messages with no return value, in this case *put* operations, or if they require a returning message, e.g., *get*. Therefore, delete messages are considered as to resemble one of the two kinds. In fact, this behavior is represented by an *access type* parameter (see Sect. 2.4) which contains the number of messages necessary for a complete interaction. This way, even more complex query-response-acknowledgment-patterns can be represented.

2.5.1.2 Tier 1—Key-Space Transformation

The key-space transformation tier represents the main part of the algorithm. Its main purpose is to translate keys, i.e., their geopositions, to their virtual pendants in order to determine the current storage positions. Therefore, it implements the following function:

```
geoposition = translate(key)
```

While the `translate` operation is the main external function, this layer needs some internal helper modules to offer its adaptive service. These three modules are (see Fig. 2.3):

- The layer's **Lookup table** provides valid, up-to-date storage nodes for queries at any point in time.
- The **dynamic reconfiguration module** contains a statistics module. It takes care of creating access models and determines the time and amount of migrations (see Sect. 2.5.2).
- The **local hash table** stores data for which the node is responsible and logs accesses.

2.5.1.3 Tier 0—Key-Based Routing

Although the storage position is determined based on virtual coordinates, the routing happens on the actual network using geographic routing mechanisms, e.g., GPSR [14] or Bi-Perimeter Routing (BPR) [7]. The implementation of the virtual address translation allows for using standardized and thoroughly researched geo-routing protocols on the routing layer.

Since all changes of storage locations are transparent to the routing layer, a mechanism is necessary to enable the storage layer to update packets so that they reach their correct destinations. Depending on the implementation of the storage layer and the possibilities to extend the geo-routing protocol in use, different options are available (see 1 and 2 in the following):

1. *No changes to the routing protocol*: If it is unfeasible to modify the routing protocol's behavior, this means that every packet handed over to the routing layer will be routed all the way to its destination, i.e., the home node for the destination's coordinates. If the destination is no longer responsible for a data item, it has to reroute the arriving packets. As long as the key-space transformation information is kept synchronized on all nodes, this standard behavior of a routing protocol is sufficient for the algorithm to work efficiently.
2. *Cross-layer design*: There are several reasons why every intermediate node on a route of a network packet should be able to update its destination. The most important reason is that a fully synchronized state of the Lookup table during runtime is unfeasible for most application scenarios. While there is only a small probability for them to happen while a packet transmission is in the progress, many events may lead to an invalid destination coordinate in a packet, e.g., data migration, node churn, node's memory exceeded. Moreover, as will be pointed out below, due to performance and scalability reasons, most implementations of the proposed storage framework will include a distributed solution of the key-space transformation. For instance, the usage of an information distribution strategy, which only ensures *eventual consistency*, may lead to inconsistent states of the Lookup table.

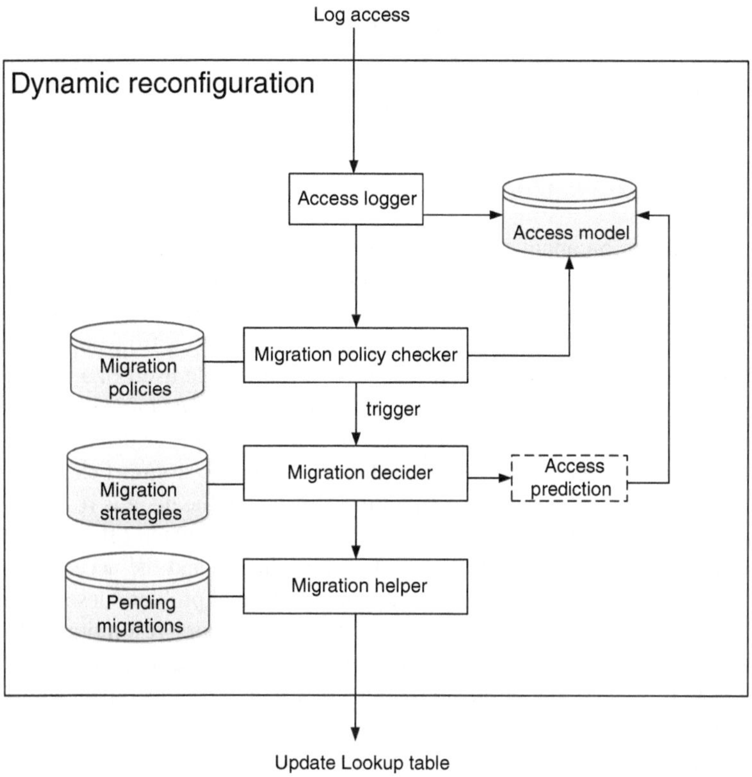

Fig. 2.4 Dynamic reconfiguration module. This module is a submodule of Fig. 2.3 and contains the distributed online optimization algorithm

2.5.2 Dynamic Online Storage Reconfiguration

The main goal of access-centric storage is to reach an optimal storage allocation that minimizes the network load according to Sect. 2.4.1. Our algorithm solves this problem in a distributed way as each node is responsible for the initialization, handling, and announcement of migrations of data items which it currently stores.

The main functionality of our algorithm is encapsulated in the *dynamic reconfiguration module* of our architecture (see Fig. 2.4). The data migration algorithm is separated into two phases:

1. At first, the *migration policy checker* identifies potential migration pressure in the access-log and decides *when* to perform a migration.
2. Afterwards, the *migration decision* module is triggered to decide on the actual migrations, i.e., *where* to migrate data.

Such a separation is reasonable especially to offer different sets of configurations for both submodules. While the migration policy checker and the migration decision modules implement the main functionality of the access-centric storage allocation, additional helper modules take care of the access-logging and the migration execution.

2.5.2.1 Data Migration Algorithm

Since no assumption about the behavior of possible consumers of data is made at start-up time, a location-centric storage approach is chosen at first. This means each node is responsible for its surrounding key space, i.e., they store data associated with close-by events. Considering the locality of the sensing ranges from applied sensors, this means that most data will be stored at the sensing node itself or a nearby node. From the algorithm's point of view, this means that the *Lookup table* is empty during startup. For as long as no migration has taken place, it simply returns the real-world location of an event leading to the desired location-centric storage behavior.

During runtime, the accesses to data items for which the node is responsible are recorded. This is done by the *access logging* submodule which offers an interface to log the source coordinate, the destination coordinate, and the access type. This information resembles the access format from the formal problem description from above. Its main configuration parameters are its spatiotemporal resolution and the size of its backlog. Depending on the application domain and its requirements, this module can be used for converting or quantizing the coordinates to a specific resolution.

The migration policy checker regularly applies data mining techniques to recognize potential optimizations through data migration. When a data item σ_i is accessed, it tests the accesses against the given migration policies. If the number of accesses surpasses a given threshold τ, the *migration decider* module is triggered. Based on the current access model, the optimal position for a data item is determined using the following formula:

$$\text{Optimal Position}(\sigma_i) = \frac{\sum_{acc \in Acc_{\sigma_i}} acc.pos \cdot acc.n}{\sum_{acc \in Acc_{\sigma_i}} acc.n}$$

Typically, the calculated coordinate of the optimal position is located somewhere between nodes. Therefore, the actual target position for the migration is determined by sending a soliciting message toward the optimal position. The geographic-routing protocol delivers it to the nearest node next to this position which is nominated the new home node of the data. After the migration took place, the Lookup table is updated accordingly.

The migration policy checker may not only evaluate accesses to single data items but also to chunks of them. The size of the data mined key-space around an accessed data item is given by the *migration chunk size* m. If a group of data items gets migrated, the optimal position is computed over the whole set of σ_i in the chunk. As the evaluation will show, m is an important design parameter (see Sect. 2.6.6).

considers the number of updates since the last migration of σ_i. More elaborate statistic modules can easily be applied to the presented architecture.

2.6 Evaluation

In this section, we explore the main characteristics of our proposed solution. We created a reference implementation of the storage framework presented in Sect. 2.5.

As has been discussed in Sect. 2.5.2.3, some components of the framework need a thorough examination of whether they are implemented in a centralized, synchronized, or distributed way. To get a grasp of the framework's main attributes and to maintain as application scenario independent as possible, the Lookup table is implemented in a fully synchronized data structure. In a real-world application, this could either be a centralized server component or a data store which is synchronized between all nodes. Depending on the actual implementation, this leads to different types and amounts of message exchanges. Since these decisions are more application specific, they are not explicitly modeled here. More specific evaluations can be performed for specific application scenarios.

The metric used to quantify the results is the hop count of messages issued for the different access types, i.e., *put* and *get* operations. After explaining the experimental setup, we present the results of different scenarios.

2.6.1 Experimental Setup

Our experiments are carried out using the discrete-event simulator *OMNeT++* [25] extended by the *MiXiM* [15] simulation package, which offers simulation models for IEEE 802.11b/g wireless LAN. All network nodes are placed randomly for each run and were connected through their wireless LAN interface with a radio range of 160 m. On the routing layer, we use an implementation of GPSR [14]. During a start-up period of 60 s the *producer* and *consumer* applications are paused so that the graph planarization of the routing protocol can take place. Although graph planarization runs all the time to handle nodes joining and leaving, this period ensures a reasonable starting point.

To model the characteristics of smart sensing systems, all *producers* output sensing data with keys originating in a surrounding 100 m^2 square. Each *consumer* queries equally distributed geolocations in up to five regions. These regions are chosen randomly by each consumer during initialization. Both types of applications generate queries at regular time intervals according to Table 2.1. The number of *producers* and *consumers* are varied to demonstrate the adaptability of the system to different and dynamically changing scenarios. The migration threshold τ is set to 10 accesses. The scenario-specific parameters of the experimental setup are listed in Table 2.1.

Table 2.1 Simulation setup

Parameter	Scenario 1 + 2 dynamic appl.	Scenario 3 network size	Scenario 4 query rates	Scenario 5 migration
Field size	$1{,}000 \times 600\,m^2$	$1{,}500 \times 1{,}500\,m^2$	$1{,}000 \times 600\,m^2$	$1{,}000 \times 600\,m^2$
Number of nodes	20	50, 100, 150	30	20
Simulation time	2.75 h	4 h	4 h	4 h, 80 h
Number of producers	**5→10→15→20**	**50, 100, 150**	**30**	**20**
PUT generation rate	12/min	12/min	12/min	**20/min**
Size of PUT fields	100×100	100×100	100×100	100×100
Number of consumers	**5→10→15→20**	**10**	**10, 20, 30**	**10**
GET generation rate	6/min	6/min	6/min	12/min
Size of GET fields	20×20	40×40	40×40	20×20
GET areas per consumer	5	5	5	**1**
Migration field size *m*	20×20	20×20	20×20	$1 \times 1, 4 \times 4, 10 \times 10, 16 \times 16, 20 \times 20, 60 \times 60$

The following graphs show the average number of hops across the network for *get* and *put* operations, respectively. The hop counts for *get* operations accumulate both, the queries and the resulting replies. Furthermore, we show the moving average of the accumulated hop counts for *puts* and *gets* to research the overall hop count optimization.

2.6.2 Scenario 1: Fixed Behavior of Applications

At first, we present results from an experiment in which the characteristic behavior of the *producers* and *consumers* are chosen at the start of the simulation and remain unchanged during the simulation's run. This way, the general behavior of our framework can be observed.

This scenario contains 20 sensing nodes, which acquire data from their surroundings and store it using the storage framework. Five of the nodes are equipped with *consumers*, which represent algorithms consuming data from the storage layer. Therefore, each consumer chooses five regions of interest with a size of $20 \times 20\,m^2$ during start-up. They frequently query their regions of interest by accessing randomly chosen keys from them using *get* operations issued to the storage framework.

Figure 2.6 shows the results from this experiment. At the beginning, one can observe the hop counts that arise from the initial distribution of the data. Since the Lookup table is empty at start-up, all data is stored on the node that is next to the event's position. This resembles the behavior of a location-centric storage paradigm. The average hop count for the put operations is greater than zero, since the sensing node is not necessarily the nearest node to the event. The mean number of hops for

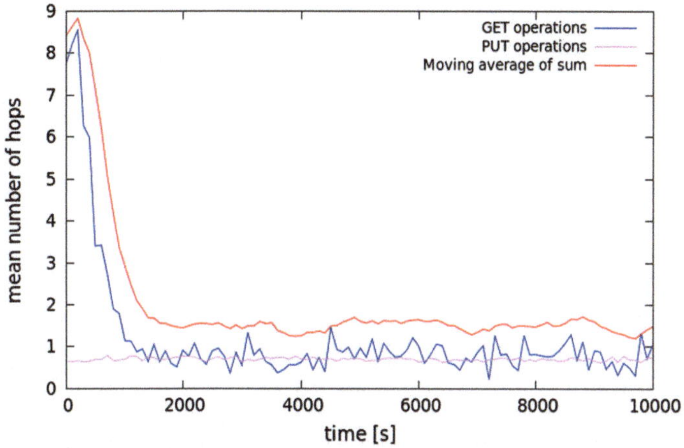

Fig. 2.6 Fixed behavior of applications. The figure depicts the development of the mean hop count over time for fixed application behavior. The *red line* shows the accumulated and smoothed sum of the hop counts for PUT and GET operations. It can be seen that the system adapts to the given access behavior by migrating accessed data to optimal positions between producers and consumers leading to a huge reduction in network load

get operations of consumers querying the data is high. It can be seen that the network load is mainly caused by the get operations. Due to the huge migration pressure issued by the accesses, the system optimized the storage locations quickly and the mean hop count decreases by about 75 % until 2,000 s.

Since the nodes generate queries that are equally but randomly distributed in their regions of interest, small amounts of migration pressure arise and vanish throughout the remainder of the experiment. The algorithm's continuous optimization leads to localized short-way migrations. This behavior causes the jitter of the hop counts. It could be avoided by more elaborated migration policies which adapt to this situation and avoid short-way migrations.

2.6.3 Scenario 2: Dynamic Behavior of Applications

In order to demonstrate the adaptability of our algorithm, we applied dynamically changing application behavior during runtime. While the *put* operations mainly depend on the sensors' characteristics and settings, the *consuming* applications may appear and vanish unpredictably during runtime. We modeled this behavior by spawning five new *consumers* periodically every 2,500 s. While we only change the behavior of the consumers in this experiment, the results would be similar if we changed the producers accordingly. As stated above, from the framework's point of view, the access type only determines the number of message exchanges necessary. This way, the actual operation is in fact reduced to this relative value.

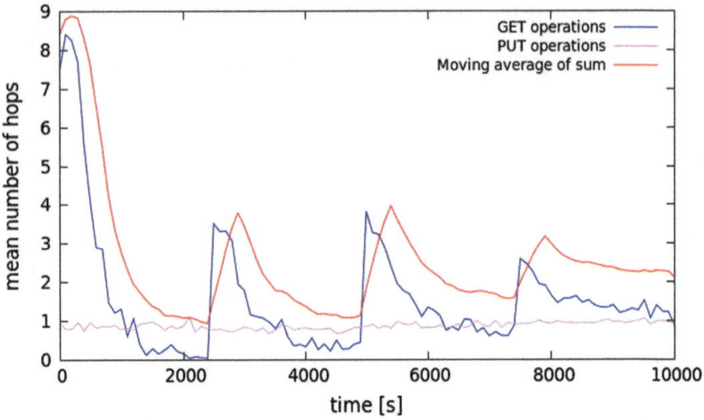

Fig. 2.7 Dynamic behavior of applications. This scenario extends the scenario of Fig. 2.6 by adding five consumers at $t = 2{,}500$ s, $t = 5{,}000$ s, and $t = 7{,}500$ s, respectively. The changing access patterns lead to a rising mean number of hops. The algorithm reacts to the changing behavior with new migrations which quickly lowers the mean hop count again

The results of these runs are depicted in Fig. 2.7 and show the fast adaptations taking place. After start-up, the first 2,500 s yield results that qualitatively resemble the results in Fig. 2.6. The periodic introduction of new consumers (first time at $t = 2{,}500$ s) leads to new access patterns and, thus, the hop count increases. The dynamic reconfiguration of our algorithm reacts to the migration pressure with storage reallocations. As a consequence, it drastically reduces the hop counts for subsequent access operations. The same qualitative performance increases are achieved after the subsequent introductions of new consumer nodes at $t = 5{,}000$ s and $t = 7{,}500$ s.

One can observe that the lower limit of hops required after the optimizations increased slightly, e.g., by comparing the mean hop counts at $t = 2{,}000$ s and at $t = 7{,}000$ s. This is due to the increased number of consumers which lead to an absolute increase in access operations. Moreover, it can be observed that the mean hop counts of put operations increase only slightly. The reason for this is that still much data is stored locally, since only accessed data items (and their surrounding key space) are migrated. This shows the main advantage of our framework which only migrates data which is actually accessed or in the vicinity of accessed data.

2.6.4 Scenario 3: Different Network Sizes

This scenario shows how the framework scales in networks of different size. A larger field size of $1{,}500 \times 1{,}500$ m^2 is chosen for these experiments to investigate networks containing up to 150 nodes. This way, the node density of the network with 100 nodes has a similar node density compared to the other scenarios. The experiments with

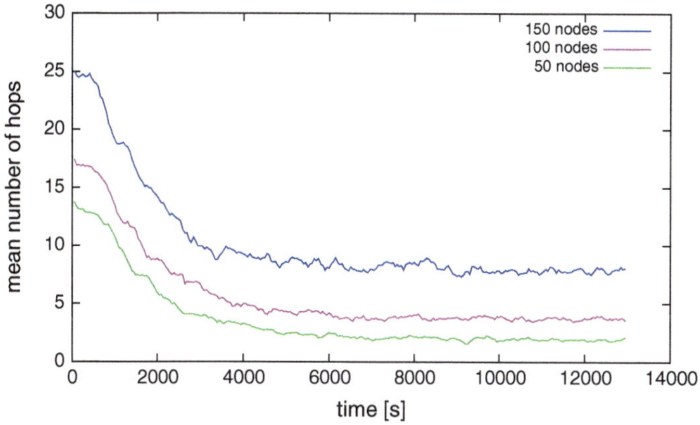

Fig. 2.8 Different network sizes. The figure depicts the development of the sum of the mean hop counts over time. It shows the results for three scenarios containing 50 (*bottom line*), 100 (*middle line*), and 150 nodes (*top line*). It can be seen that the algorithm's performance scales with the size of the network and always leads to huge latency reductions

50 and 150 nodes show the behavior in relation to this value. While increasing the number of nodes (each one acting as a producer), we keep the number of consumers constant. This models a given set of accessing algorithms with different numbers of sensors available.

We present the results for networks of 50, 100, and 150 nodes in Fig. 2.8. The graphs show the sum of mean hop counts for put and get operations in each scenario. It is obvious that the qualitative reduction of the hop counts is similar in all optimizations and leads to reductions from 60 to 80 % of the initial values. The absolute hop counts increase proportionally to the number of nodes in the network. This is caused by the higher density of nodes which directly leads to longer shortest paths between two nodes in the connectivity graph.

2.6.5 Scenario 4: Different Query Rates

After examining the consequences of different networks sizes given a fixed number of consuming algorithms, this experiment researches the optimization results for different numbers of consumers in a network with 30 nodes. Therefore, the number of consumers is increased from 10 up to 30 consuming nodes. This drastic increase in consumers in comparison to the number of sensing nodes enforces more overlaps in the areas of interest of the consumers. This leads to migration decisions that take more access nodes into account.

As can be seen in Fig. 2.9, the optimization leads to a reduced mean number of hops between 40 and 60 %. This shows that the algorithm even copes with a large number of algorithms consuming data and reduces the network load significantly.

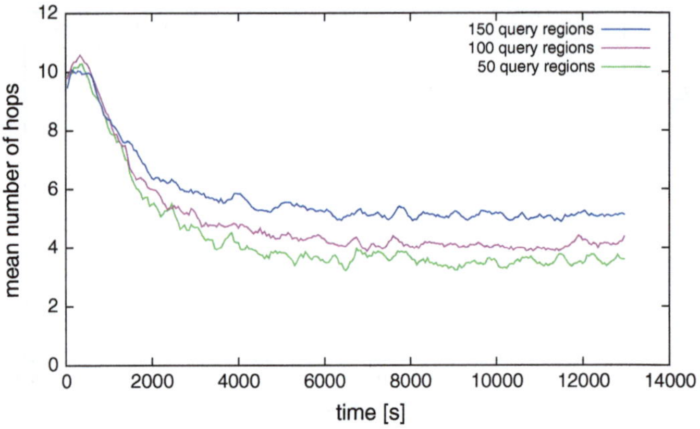

Fig. 2.9 Different query rates. This figure shows the evaluation of a scenario with 30 nodes and with 10 (*bottom line*), 20 (*middle line*), and 30 consumer applications (*top line*). It shows that the algorithm performs very well with a large number of consumers

2.6.6 Scenario 5: Migration Field Size

As stated in Sect. 2.5.2.3, an important parameter of the optimization algorithm is the chunk size of migrations performed. The migration chunk size m is a parameter for the migration policy checker as well as the migration decider. If a data item is accessed, itself and its neighborhood of size m is considered as one chunk and checked by the migration policy checker. If the number of accesses in this area reaches the access threshold τ, a migration is triggered and the migration decider calculates the new storage location. Therefore, it takes into account all accesses to data items in the chunk and initiates a migration of the whole chunk. While the theoretical optimum of the search problem can only be reached if the storage position of every single key is optimized, such a behavior is unfeasible for most applications and scenarios.

Figure 2.10 shows the results for a given network configuration with migration chunk sizes m from $4 \times 4\,\mathrm{m}^2$ up to $60 \times 60\,\mathrm{m}^2$. The results for $m = 1 \times 1\,\mathrm{m}^2$, which represents the exact solution that considers every data key on its own, are depicted in Fig. 2.11. Since the applications scatter their accesses using an equal distribution in each area of interest, the exact solution has the drawback that it runs a long time until the access threshold τ is reached. To show its long-term development, the exact scenario has been run over 80 h of simulation time.

As can be seen, the migration chunk size directly influences how fast a migration is triggered. This is because all keys in the chunk are considered by the migration policy checker. While the exact migration is the slowest, it should reach the best result in the long run. However, this setup already shows its drawback. Especially in a real-world setup, the measured location of an event will be subject to different kinds of noise, e.g., a tracking event which gets converted into world coordinates. To handle this kind of noisy data, the framework should quantize the key space.

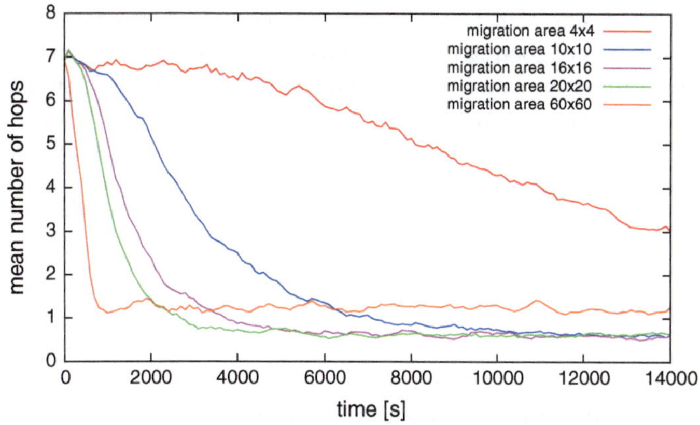

Fig. 2.10 Different migration chunk sizes. The figure shows the algorithm's behavior for the same scenario using different migration chunk sizes from 4 × 4 (*red line*) up to 60 × 60 (*orange line*). An increasing chunk size leads to a much faster decrease in the mean number of hops. A drawback of too large chunks are suboptimal migration decisions by taking to many different accesses into account, as can be seen from the *orange line*, which does not reach the minimum

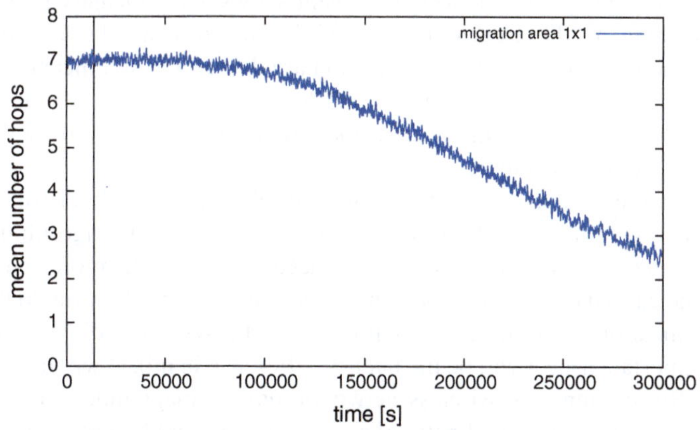

Fig. 2.11 Different migration chunk sizes—the exact solution. This scenario shows the algorithm's behavior if accesses to single data items are considered. The vertical line marks the runtime of the other scenarios. It shows the same qualitative behavior of the runs in Fig. 2.10 but requires a long time for the optimizations to take place. It could be speeded up by lowering τ

On the other hand, if the chosen chunk size gets to large, the resulting optimizations may be worse than for smaller chunk sizes. This can be observed for chunks of $60 \times 60\,\text{m}^2$ which lead to a suboptimal storage allocation. This happens since too many unrelated accesses are considered at once. This leads to suboptimal migration decisions.

The evaluation shows that a reasonable chunk size, between $10 \times 10\,\mathrm{m}^2$ and $20 \times 20\,\mathrm{m}^2$, offers very good storage location optimizations incorporating the advantages of being responsive as well as robust towards noisy data. Migration chunks are especially useful if the consuming algorithms issue queries concerning certain ranges or to quantify the key-space to a scale applicable for the application scenario, e.g., appropriate for the magnitude of noise induced by other system components.

2.7 Conclusion

This chapter presented a novel approach to usage-centric storage and access of sensor data. Based on the insight that current geolocated sensor networks perceive large amounts of data while simultaneously accessing this data within the network, we discussed different approach of the state of the art to optimise this data access. We presented a distributed storage algorithm whose design goal is the online optimization of in-network storage allocation of georeferenced data.

The evaluation demonstrates the potential benefit of this novel approach. We investigated the effects of varying consumers (i.e., applications accessing data items in the network) and varying network size. The result shows a significantly improved hop count—meaning that the latencies in terms of visited nodes until the desired information is available to the requesting application are decreasing significantly. Thereby, the algorithm is robust against joining and leaving nodes. It also scales with the number of nodes contained in the network and is not characterized by drawbacks such as single-points-of-failure.

Our current and future work investigates possibilities to apply distributed algorithms which rely on eventual consistency. We aim for a robust algorithm which is able to offer the presented benefits with a reduced overhead. Therefore, we are going to model the caused costs by overhead messages and their relationship to the degree of synchronization. Moreover, we want to apply the system to different technologies. An important aspect will be the latency difference in mixed wired and wireless networks. Since latency in wireless networks may be magnitudes worse and less predictable compared to wired networks, wired nodes could be used as a dynamic backbone for queries issued from mobile units. Therefore, such queries may be handled by a query proxy which is chosen w.r.t. node characteristics. Another direction of research will cover the extension to accompanying replication algorithms to handle unexpected node failure.

References

1. Abdelzaher T, Bhattacharya S, Kim H, Prabh S (2003) Energy-conserving data placement and asynchronous multicast in wireless sensor networks. In: Proceedings of mobisys 2003: the first international conference on mobile systems, applications, and services

2. Aghajan H, Cavallaro A (eds) (2009) Multi-camera networks-principles and applications. Elsevier
3. Akyildiz IF, Vuran MC (2010) Wireless sensor networks. Wiley, New York
4. Albano M, Chessa S, Nidito F, Pelagatti S (2007) Q-NiGHT: adding QoS to data centric storage in non-uniform sensor networks. Sensors (Peterborough, NH), pp 166–173
5. Dabek F, Zhao B, Druschel P, Kubiatowicz J, Stoica I (2003) Towards a common API for structured P2P overlays. In: Proceedings of the 2nd international workshop on peer-to-peer systems (IPTPS03), vol 2735, pp 33–44
6. D'Angelo D, Grenz C, Kuntzsch C, Bogen M (2012) CamInSens-an intelligent in-situ security system for public spaces. In: International conference on security and management (SAM), Las Vegas, Nevada
7. Dudkowski D (2009) Fundamental storage mechanisms for location-based services in mobile ad-hoc networks. Ph.D. thesis, Universität Stuttgart
8. Grenz C, Hähner J (2011) PhD forum: adaptive storage management in highly heterogeneous smart sensor systems. In: 5th ACM/IEEE international conference on distributed smart cameras, ICDSC 2011
9. Grenz C, Hähner J, Asam F (2013) Application-independent in-network storage optimization for distributed smart camera systems. In: Seventh international conference on distributed smart cameras (ICDSC)
10. Grenz C, Jänen U, Hähner J, Kuntzsch C, Menze M, D'Angelo D, Bogen M, Monari E (2012) CamInSens-demonstration of a distributed smart camera system for in-situ threat detection. In Proceedings of international conference on distributed smart cameras (ICDSC)
11. Hoffmann M, Wittke M, Hähner J, Müller-Schloer C (2008) Spatial partitioning in self-organizing smart camera systems. IEEE J Sel Top Signal Process 2(4):480–492
12. Jaenen U, Feuerhake U, Klinger T, Muhle D, Hähner J, Sester M, Heipke C (2012) Qtrajectories: improving the quality of object tracking using self-organizing camera networks. In: ISPRS annals of the photogrammetry, remote sensing and spatial information sciences, vol I-4, pp 269–274
13. Jaenen U, Spiegelberg H, Sommer L, von Mammen S, Brehm J, Haehner J (2013) Object tracking as job-scheduling problem. In: Seventh international conference on distributed smart cameras (ICDSC) IEEE, pp 1–7
14. Karp B, Kung HT (2000) Greedy perimeter stateless routing for wireless networks. In: Proceedings of the sixth annual ACM/IEEE international conference on mobile computing and networking (MobiCom), Boston, pp 243–254
15. Köpke A, Swigulski M, Wessel K, Willkomm D, Klein Haneveld PT, Parker TEV, Visser OW, Lichte HS, Valentin S (2008) Simulating wireless and mobile networks in OMNeT++ the MiXiM vision. In: Proceedings of the first international conference on simulation tools and techniques for communications networks and systems (ICST)
16. Kumar B (2008) ZGHT- a zonal hash-table for data-centric storage. TAMU Comp Sci, College station, TX 77840
17. Nam Le T, Yu W, Bai X, Xuan D (2006) A dynamic geographic hash table for data-centric storage in sensor networks. In: IEEE wireless communications and networking conference (WCNC), pp 2168–2174
18. Monari E, Pollok T (2011) A real-time image-to-panorama registration approach for background subtraction using pan-tilt-cameras. In: International conference on advanced video and signal based surveillance (AVSS), IEEE computer Society, pp 237–242
19. Monari E, Voth S, Kroschel K (2008) An object-and task-oriented architecture for automated video surveillance in distributed sensor networks. In: IEEE fifth international conference on advanced video and signal based surveillance (AVSS), pp 339–346
20. Ratnasamy S, Francis P, Handley M, Karp R,Shenker S (2001) A scalable content addressable network. In: Proceedings of the 2001 conference on applications., technologies, architectures, and protocols for computer communications (ACM SIGCOMM), vol TR-00-010, University of Berkeley,CA, pp 161–172

21. Ratnasamy S, Karp B, Yin L, Yu F, Estrin D, Govindan R (2002) GHT: a geographic hash table for data-centric storage. In: Proceedings of the first ACM international workshop on wireless sensor networks and applications (WSNA)
22. Rinner B, Wolf W (2008) Proc IEEE 96(10):1565–1575
23. Shenker S, Ratnasamy S, Karp B, Govindan R, Estrin D (2003) Data-centric storage in sensornets. ACM SIGCOMM Comput Commun Rev 33(1):137–142
24. Stoica I, Morris R, Karger D, Frans Kaashoek M, Balakrishnan H (2001) Chord: a scalable peer-to-peer lookup service for internet applications. In: Proceedings of the 2001 conference on applications, technologies, architectures, and protocols for computer communications, New York, pp 149–160
25. Varga A, Hornig R (2008) An overview of the OMNeT++ simulation environment. In: Proceedings of the 1st international conference on Simulation tools and techniques for communications, networks and systems & workshops (Simutools)
26. Wittke M, Grenz C, Hähner J (2011) Towards organic active vision systems for visual surveillance. In: Berekovic M, Fornaciari W, Brinkschulte U, Silvano C (eds) Architecture of computing systems-ARCS 2011. Springer, Berlin, pp 195–206

Chapter 3
Decentralized Human Tracking in Visual Sensor Networks: Using Sparse Representation for Efficient Communication

Serhan Coşar and Müjdat Çetin

Abstract The recent advances in camera sensors and development of new distributed processing algorithms have enabled a new kind of wireless sensor networks namely the visual sensor networks (VSNs). VSNs consist of a network of image sensors, embedded processors, and wireless transceivers which are powered by batteries. The constraints on energy and bandwidth resources challenge setting up a tracking system in VSNs. In this chapter, we present a sparsity-driven decentralized framework for multi-camera human tracking in VSNs. The traditional centralized approaches involve sending compressed images to a central processing unit, which, in the case of severe bandwidth constraints, can hurt the performance of further processing (i.e., tracking) because of low-quality images. Instead, we propose a decentralized tracking framework in which each camera node performs feature extraction and obtains likelihood functions. We propose a sparsity-driven method that can obtain bandwidth-efficient representation of likelihoods. Our approach involves the design of special overscomplete dictionaries that match the structure of the likelihoods and the transmission of likelihood information in the network through sparse representation in such dictionaries. By exploiting information from the sparse representation obtained in the previous frame, we spatially constrain the set of allowed dictionary coefficients in the current frame to reduce the size of the optimization problem and hence, the computation time. Experimental results show that our sparse representation framework is an effective approach that can be used together with any probabilistic tracker and that can provide major savings in communication bandwidth without significant degradation in tracking performance.

S. Coşar (✉) · M. Çetin
Faculty of Engineering and Natural Sciences, Sabancı University, Istanbul, Turkey
e-mail: serhancosar@sabanciuniv.edu

M. Çetin
e-mail: mcetin@sabanciuniv.edu

P. Spagnolo et al. (eds.), *Human Behavior Understanding in Networked Sensing*,
DOI 10.1007/978-3-319-10807-0_3

3.1 Introduction

Over the past decade, large-scale camera networks have been a topic of increasing interest in security and surveillance. Following, the developments in wireless sensor networks and the availability of inexpensive imaging sensors, a new field called visual sensor networks (VSNs) has emerged [27]. VSNs primarily consist of a network of devices with local processing capabilities that can capture video data and use wireless links.

The potentially high-volume visual information captured in these wireless networks creates unique and challenging problems that are more complex than the traditional multi-camera video analysis systems and wireless sensor networks might have. Conventional wireless sensor networks usually collect scalar or low-dimensional data at each time instant, whereas in VSNs sensors provide image data, i.e., N-dimensional vectors where N is the number of pixels in the images. In most of the multi-camera analysis systems, the image or video analysis task of interest is performed in a centralized fashion by collecting the raw data acquired by cameras in a central unit and doing processing in this unit. However, performing complex tasks, such as tracking, recognition, etc., in a communication-constrained VSN environment is extremely challenging, as it is not feasible to send all the measured data over the bandwidth-constrained network [27]. For such constraints, the common approach is to follow a data compression perspective and compress images in the process of transmission to the central unit [8]. This strategy essentially focuses on low-level data compression without regard to the final inference goal. Such a strategy may not be appropriate for use under scenarios with severe bandwidth limitations and might cause significant degradation in tracking performance in the case of large compression ratios. We provide a more in-depth review of existing work in Sect. 3.2.

In this chapter, we follow a different strategy that is better matched to the final inference goal, which, in the context of this chapter, is tracking. We propose a sparsity-driven tracking method that is suitable for energy and bandwidth constraints in VSNs. Our method is a decentralized tracking approach in which each camera node in the network performs feature extraction by itself and obtains image features (likelihood functions). Instead of directly sending likelihood functions to the fusion node, we compute and transmit sparse representations of the likelihoods. By sending such sparse representations to the fusion node, multiview tracking can be performed without overloading the network. We design special overcomplete dictionaries for the sparse representation of likelihood functions. The main contribution of this work is building a sparse representation framework and designing overcomplete dictionaries that are matched to the structure of likelihoods. In particular, our dictionaries are designed in an adaptive manner by exploiting the specific known geometry of the measurement scenario and by focusing on the problem of human tracking. Each element in the dictionary for each camera corresponds to the likelihood that would result from a single human at a particular location in the scene. Hence, actual likelihoods extracted from real observations from scenes containing multiple individuals can be very sparsely represented in our approach. By using these dictionaries, we can represent likelihoods with a very small number of coefficients, and thereby, decrease the communication between camera and fusion nodes. In addition, we exploit the sparse representation obtained in the previous frame and reduce the computation time of the optimization problem to be solved in the current frame. We use the sparse coefficient vectors computed in the previous frame in order to spatially constrain the set of allowed dictionary elements in the current frame, thereby, reducing the size of the problem.

Furthermore, we have used our method within the context of two multi-camera human tracking algorithms [10, 14]. We have modified these methods in order to obtain decentralized tracking algorithms. Both by qualitative and quantitative results, we have shown that our method is better than using the block-based compression scheme in [4], the decentralized tracking method in [17], and the distributed tracking method in [26]. The sparse likelihood representation framework we present can be used within any probabilistic tracking method under VSN constraints without significantly degrading the tracking performance.

In Sect. 3.2, existing pieces of work on tracking in VSNs are reviewed. Section 3.3 presents our decentralized approach for multi-camera tracking in detail. In Sect. 3.4, our sparse representation framework and the details of our specially designed over-complete dictionaries are described. Experimental results are presented in Sect. 3.5. Finally in Sect. 3.6, we provide a summary and conclusions.

3.2 Related Work

The main differences between wireless sensor networks and visual sensor networks are in acquiring, processing, and transferring data. Therefore, methods proposed for wireless sensor networks cannot directly be applied in VSNs and new approaches for VSNs have been proposed. In several pieces of work, basic features, or techniques are used to adapt centralized tracking methods to VSNs. For instance, visual hulls are used in [34, 35] to detect the presence and number of people. However, since a visual hull presents the largest volume in which an individual can reside, the exact number of people cannot be determined when humans are positioned close to one another. To minimize the amount of data to be communicated, in some methods simple features are used for communication. For instance, 2D trajectories are used in [21]. In [9], 3D trajectories together with color histograms are used. Hue histograms along with 2D position are used in [20].

Moreover, there are decentralized approaches in which cameras are grouped into clusters and tracking is performed by local cluster fusion nodes. This kind of approach has been applied to the multi-camera target tracking problem in various ways [17, 25, 38]. For a nonoverlapping camera setup, tracking is performed by maximizing the similarity between the observed features from each camera and minimizing the long-term variation in appearance using graph matching at the fusion node [25]. For an overlapping camera setup, a cluster-based Kalman filter in a network of wireless cameras has been proposed in [17, 38]. In this work, local measurements of the target acquired by members of the cluster are sent to the fusion node. Then, the fusion node estimates the target position via an extended Kalman filter, relating the measurements acquired by the cameras to the actual position of the target by nonlinear transformations.

To further increase scalability and to reduce communication costs, distributed estimation operates without local fusion centers. The estimates generated in a camera are transmitted to its immediate neighbors only. The received estimates are used to refine the estimates at these immediate neighbors, and these refined estimates are then transmitted to the next group of neighbors [26, 30]. This process concludes within a predefined number of steps after all cameras viewing the target are visited or when the uncertainty has decreased below a desired value. In [26], the Kalman-Consensus algorithm [19] is adapted to take into account the directional nature of video sensors and the network topology. Each camera estimates the locations of the people in the scene based on its own sensed data which is then shared locally with the neighboring cameras in an iterative fashion, and a final estimate is arrived at in the network using the Kalman-Consensus algorithm. A wireless embedded smart camera system for cooperative human tracking has been proposed in [30]. At each camera lightweight foreground detection and color histogram-based tracking algorithms are implemented and run. Important portions of video and trajectories are determined by detecting events of interest that are predefined by users. Communication in the network is minimized by sending messages only when an event of interest occurs.

There are certain limitations of previous work which motivate further research. The methods in [9, 20, 21, 34, 35] that use simple features may be capable of decreasing the communication, but they are not capable of maintaining robustness of tracking performance in the case of reduced communication. For the sake of bandwidth efficiency, these methods choose to change the features from complex and robust to simpler, but not so effective ones. Distributed tracking methods [26, 30] fit well to the needs of VSNs, but suffer from several disadvantages. In the literature of multi-camera tracking, there are many algorithms that can perform robust tracking. In order to use such algorithms in VSN environments, we need to implement existing centralized trackers in a distributed way. In order to do that, usually, one needs to modify pretty much each step from feature extraction to final inference, which is not a straightforward task and which can affect the performance of the tracker. Performing local processing and collecting features to the fusion node, as in [17, 25, 38], may not satisfy the bandwidth requirements in a communication-constrained VSN environment. In particular, depending on the size of image features and the number of cameras in the network, even collecting features to the fusion node may become expensive for the network. In such cases, further approximations on features are necessary.

Over the last decade, an alternative sampling/sensing theory, known as "compressed sensing" has emerged. Compressed sensing enables the recovery of signals, images, and other data from what appear to be undersampled observations. Compressed sensing is a technique for acquiring and reconstructing a signal from small amount of measurements utilizing the prior knowledge that the signal has a sparse representation in a proper space. As a consequence, compressed sensing and sparse representation (SR) have become important signal recovery techniques because of their success for acquiring, representing, and compressing high-dimensional signals in various application areas [7, 15, 23]. In the past few years, variations and extensions of l_1 minimization have been applied to many vision tasks, including face recognition [32], denoising and inpainting [15], background modeling [2], and image classification [16]. In almost all of these applications, using sparsity as a prior leads to state-of-the-art results [33].

3.3 Decentralized Human Tracking in Visual Sensor Networks

3.3.1 Overview

In a traditional setup of camera networks, which we call centralized tracking, each camera acquires an image and sends this raw data to a central unit. In the central unit, multiview data are collected, relevant features are extracted and combined, finally, using these features, the positions of the humans are estimated. Hence, integration of multiview information is done at the raw-data level by pooling all images into a central unit. The presence of a single global fusion center leads to the need for high data-transfer rates and the need for a computationally powerful machine. Such an approach cannot satisfy the scalability, bandwidth efficiency, and energy-efficiency requirements of a VSN. Compressing raw image data may decrease the communication in the network, however high- compression ratios imposed by severe bandwidth limitations could lead to degraded tracking performance. For this reason, centralized trackers are not very appropriate for use in VSN environments. In decentralized tracking, there is no central unit that collects all raw data from the cameras. Cameras are grouped into clusters and nodes communicate with their local cluster fusion nodes only [28]. Multi-camera tracking is performed in the local cluster fusion nodes and fusion nodes communicate with each other to handoff the tracking over the network. Communication overhead is reduced by limiting the cooperation within each cluster and among fusion nodes. In this chapter we are concerned with the tracking task within one cluster.

After acquiring the images, each camera extracts useful features from the images it has observed and sends these features to the local fusion node. The processing capability of camera nodes in emerging VSNs enable feature extraction at the camera nodes without the need to send the images to the central unit [1, 12, 29, 31]. Using the multiview image features, tracking is performed in the fusion node. Hence, in decentralized tracking, multiview information is integrated in feature-level by combining the features in small clusters. This both reduces the communication in the network and removes the need of powerful processors in the local fusion node. Decentralized approaches are appropriate for VSNs in many aspects. The processing capability of each camera is utilized by performing feature extraction at the camera-level. Since cameras are grouped into clusters, feature extraction, and communication are distributed among cameras in clusters, therefore, efficient estimation can be performed.

Modeling the dynamics of humans in a probabilistic framework is a common perspective of many multi-camera human tracking methods [10, 11, 13, 37]. In tracking methods based on a probabilistic framework, data, and/or extracted features are represented by likelihood functions, $p(y|x)$ where $y \in \mathbb{R}^d$ and $x \in \mathbb{R}^m$ are the observation and state vectors, respectively. In other words, for each camera, a likelihood function is defined in terms of the observations obtained from its field of view ($p(y|x) = \prod_{c=1,\ldots,N} p(y^c|x)$). In centralized tracking, of course, the likelihood functions are computed after collecting the image data of each camera at the central unit. For a decentralized approach, since each camera node extracts local features from its field of view, these likelihood functions can be evaluated at the camera nodes and they can be sent to the fusion node. Then, in the fusion node the likelihoods can be combined and tracking can be performed in the probabilistic framework ($p(x|y) = \prod_{c=1,\ldots,N} p(y^c|x) \cdot p(x)$). A flow diagram of a generic decentralized approach is illustrated in Fig. 3.1. Following this line of thought, we have converted the tracking approaches in [10, 14] to decentralized trackers as explained in the next section.

Fusion node selection and sensor resource management (sensor tasking) is out of scope of this chapter. We have assumed that one of the camera nodes, a relatively more powerful one, has been selected as the fusion node. In a practical implementation, resource management can be performed using existing work in [6, 39].

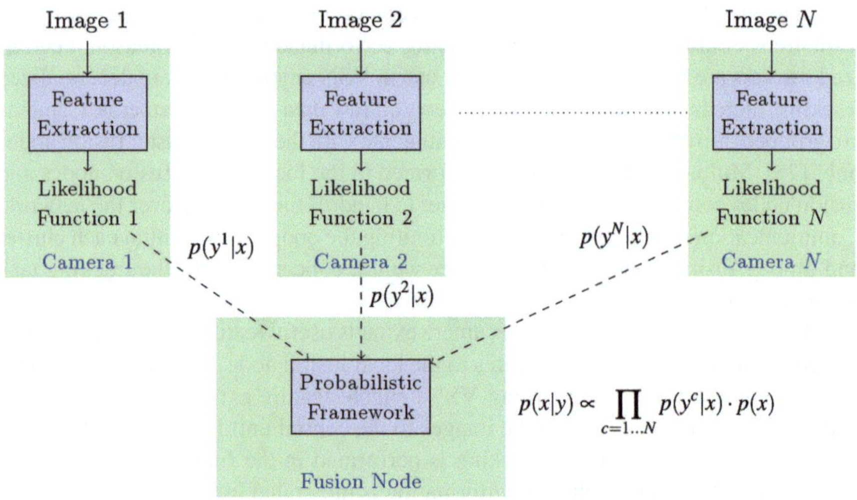

Fig. 3.1 The flow diagram of a decentralized tracker that is based on a probabilistic framework

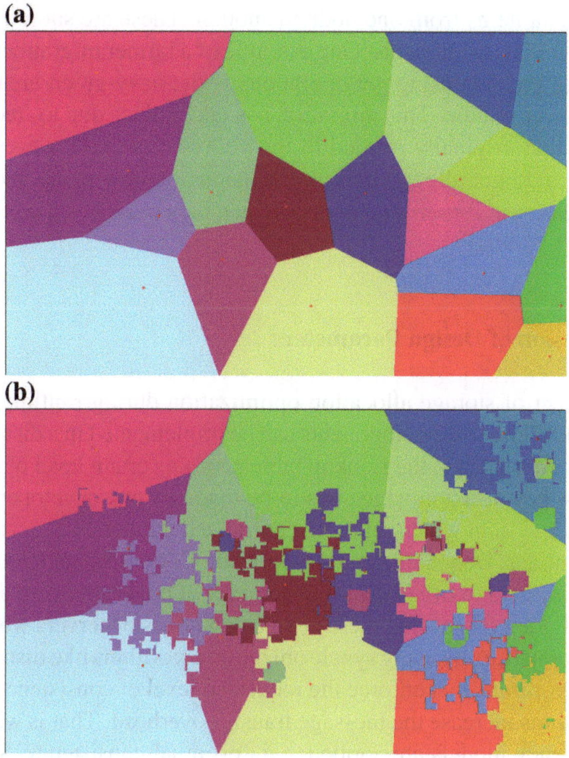

Fig. 2.5 **a** Initial storage allocation. The nodes are represented by *red dots*. Their surrounding areas represent their current area of responsibility for which they store data. Since the Lookup table is empty at start-up, the storage allocation resembles a Voronoi distribution. **b** Exemplary storage allocation after a certain simulation period of Fig. 2.5a scenario. Again, the positions of the nodes are indicated by *small red dots*. Still, the different responsibilities are illustrated by different colors, where each specific color defines one of the nodes. Each migration resembles an entry in the Lookup table

2.5.2.2 Example

An initial storage allocation of the algorithm, which results from an empty Lookup table, is shown in Fig. 2.5. The map represents the distribution area of the sensors. Each sensor is represented by a red dot surrounded by its region of responsibility, i.e., it stores all events whose geolocation lies inside this area. This location-centric behavior resembles a Voronoi partition.

Figure 2.5b depicts the virtual coordinate space after a certain simulation period. With the colors still representing the nodes' responsibilities, one can see that a number of migrations took place. The frayed borders where the colors mix may originate from neighboring nodes surveying events in the other nodes' vicinities. In the given example, access-optimization with respect to *put* operations is responsible for migrating the data items from one node to another. These are short-way migrations optimizing the initial assignments. One example of a farther migration due to various nodes accessing the data using *get* operations is the navy-green area in the yellow region in the lower middle. This migration has taken place due to frequent accesses to a data item that originally resided in the yellow region. However, these virtual coordinate maps do not allow reliable conclusions on how many and which nodes have actually accessed certain data items. Rather, they provide a qualitative overview of the migration results.

2.5.2.3 Discussion of Design Parameters

One major aspect of storage allocation optimization during runtime is the kind of algorithm used. While some components can be implemented in a distributed fashion without loss of consistency, the Lookup table needs a certain level of internode synchronization. A key decision which has to be made by any developer is whether he wants to create a system which relies on centralized entities like servers or synchronized network nodes. Depending on the application's constraints it will be necessary for the storage system to offer certain guarantees of consistency. In distributed systems, this most often means that there are elected nodes or servers which act as synchronization points, i.e., by using synchronization algorithms like distributed barriers and election algorithms that enforce the requested level of consistency. However, all of these algorithms increase the message transfer overhead. That is why, most often, weaker consistency models are applied, e.g., eventual consistency. So the decision for a consistency model may have great impact on the network load, which is caused by the exchange of synchronization messages.

Another important design parameter of our algorithm is the choice of statistics which the nodes use during runtime. This choice has a direct impact on the algorithms performance. A main design parameter is the *quantization* or *accumulation* of key space which is the size of distinct regions for which access models are build. With an increase of detail, the local access models will grow and, proportionally, the algorithm's memory footprint. At the same time, the increase in detail enables for much more fine-grained migration decisions. Therefore, the key-space quantization is one important tradeoff criteria between the nodes' local resources, i.e., memory usage and computation time, and lowered network utilization as benefit from more fine-grained migration decisions. Since memory is getting cheap, the benefits of the proposed algorithm will overhaul its costs.

To show the applicability of the algorithm, the access-log uses a *per data item* statistical approach. This resembles the notion in the problem description (see Sect. 2.4). We analyze the design space of the parameter key-space quantizations for the access models in Sect. 2.6.6, showing that this parameter has a great impact on the performance. Therefore, not only single data items but also chunks of adjacent data items are considered.

Another design parameter of the statistics module is the model-building characteristic of accesses, i.e., the *sample size* of Acc_{σ_i} (see Sect. 2.4). The current approach

3.3.2 Multi-camera Human Tracking Algorithms

We have applied our proposed framework within the context of two different tracking methods. In this section, we describe these tracking methods and explain how we have converted these trackers to decentralized trackers.

3.3.2.1 Algorithm 1

In this section, we describe the tracking method of [10], as we apply our proposed approach within this method. In [10], the ground plane is discretized into a finite number G of regularly spaced 2D locations. Let $\mathbf{L}_t = (L_t^1, \ldots, L_t^{N^*})$ be the locations of individuals at time t, where N^* is the maximum number of individuals. Given T temporal frames from C cameras, $\mathbf{I}_t = (I_t^1, \ldots, I_t^C),\ t = \{1, \ldots, T\}$, the goal is to estimate the trajectory of person n, $\mathbf{L}^n = (L_1^n, \ldots, L_T^n)$, by seeking the maximum of the probability of both the observations and the trajectory ending up at location k at time t:

$$\Phi_t^n(k) = \max_{l_1^n, \ldots, l_{t-1}^n} P(\mathbf{I}_1, L_1^n = l_1^n, \ldots, \mathbf{I}_t, L_t^n = k) \tag{3.1}$$

Under a hidden Markov model, the above expression turns into the classical recursive expression:

$$\Phi_t^n(k) = \underbrace{P(\mathbf{I}_t | L_t^n = k)}_{\text{Appearance model}} \max_{\tau} \{ \underbrace{P(L_t^n = k | L_{t-1}^n = \tau)}_{\text{Motion model}} \Phi_{t-1}^n(\tau) \} \tag{3.2}$$

The motion model is a circular uniform distribution with limited radius and center τ, which corresponds to a loose bound on the maximum speed of a walking human.

From the input images $\mathbf{I}_t$, by using background subtraction, foreground binary masks, $\mathbf{B}_t$, are obtained. Let the colors of the pixels inside a blob in foreground mask be denoted by $\mathbf{T}_t$ and let X_k^t be a Boolean random variable denoting the presence of an individual at location k of the grid at time t. It is shown in [10] that the appearance model in Eq. 3.2 can be decomposed as:

$$P(\mathbf{I}_t | L_t^n = k) \propto \underbrace{P(L_t^n = k | X_k^t = 1, \mathbf{T}_t)}_{\text{Color model}} \quad \underbrace{P(X_k^t = 1 | \mathbf{B}_t)}_{\text{Ground plane occup.}} \tag{3.3}$$

In [10], humans are represented simply by rectangles used to create synthetic ideal images that would be observed if people were at given locations. Within this model, the ground plane occupancy is approximated by measuring the similarity between ideal images and foreground binary masks.

Let $T_t^c(k)$ denote the color of the pixels taken at the intersection of the foreground binary mask, B_t^c, from camera c at time t and the rectangle A_k^c corresponding to location k in that same field of view. Say we have the color distributions of the N^* individuals present in the scene, $\mu_1^c, \ldots, \mu_{N^*}^c$. The color model of person n in Eq. 3.3 can be expressed as:

$$P(L_t^n = k | X_k^t = 1, \mathbf{T}_t) \propto P(\mathbf{T}_t | L_t^n = k) = P(T_t^1(k), \ldots, T_t^C(k) | L_t^n = k)$$
$$= \prod_{c=1}^{C} P(T_t^c(k) | L_t^n = k) \qquad (3.4)$$

As in [4], we represent $P(T_t^c(k)|L_t^n = k)$ by comparing the estimated color distribution (histogram) of the pixels in $T_t^c(k)$ and the color distribution μ_n^c with the Bhattacharya coefficient between two distributions. By performing a global search with dynamic programming using Eq. 3.2, the trajectory of each person can be estimated.

From the above formulation, we can see that there are two different likelihood functions defined in the method. One is the ground plane occupancy map (GOM), $P(X_k^t = 1|\mathbf{B}_t)$, approximated using the foreground binary masks. The other is the ground plane color map (GCM), $P(L_t^n = k|X_k^t = 1, \mathbf{T}_t)$, which is a multiview color likelihood function defined for each person individually. This map is obtained by combining the individual color maps, $P(T_t^c(k)|L_t^n = k)$, evaluated using the images acquired by each camera. Since foreground binary masks are binary images that can be easily compressed by a lossless compression method, they can be directly sent to the fusion node without overloading the network. Therefore, as in the original method, GOM is evaluated at the fusion node. In our framework, we evaluate GCM in a decentralized way (as presented in Fig. 3.1): At each camera node ($c = 1, \ldots, C$), the local color likelihood function for the person of interest ($P(T_t^c(k)|L_t^n = k)$) is evaluated by using the image acquired from that camera. Then, these likelihood functions are sent to the fusion node. At the fusion node, these likelihood functions are integrated to obtain the multiview color likelihood function (GCM) (Eq. 3.4). By combining GCM and GOM with the motion model, the trajectory of the person of interest is estimated at the fusion node using dynamic programming (Eq. 3.2). The whole process is run for each person in the scene.

Since each camera keeps a reference color histogram individually for each person in the scene, data association between different people is performed at the camera-level. Then, at the fusion node, assuming there is only one person in the scene in the beginning of the tracking process, we assign an ID number for each likelihood function coming from cameras to the fusion node. Likelihoods with the same ID number from different cameras are associated with one another at the fusion node.

3.3.2.2 Algorithm 2

This section describes the second tracking algorithm [14] upon which we implement our proposed approach. In [14], a planar homographic occupancy constraint that fuses foreground likelihood information from multiple views to resolve occlusions and localize people on a reference scene plane has been developed. For better performance, this process has been extended to multiple planes parallel to the reference plane in the framework of plane to plane homologies. The formulation of likelihood function in this approach ($p(y|x)$ where y and x are the image observation and position of the person, respectively) is compactly described by:

$$p(y|x) = \prod_{h=1}^{H} p(y_h|x) = \prod_{h=1}^{H} \prod_{c=1}^{C} p(y_{c,h}|x) \tag{3.5}$$

Here, $p(y_{c,h}|x)$ represents the foreground likelihood information extracted from camera c and projected onto plane h, $p(y_h|x)$ represents the fused foreground likelihood information from multiple views on plane h, and finally H and C represent the number of parallel planes and cameras, respectively.

Unlike the method in [14], we have used the human detection algorithm in [36] for extracting foreground likelihood information ($p(y_{c,h}|x)$). The human detector outputs a probability map that represents the probable locations of people in the image plane. We project this probability map onto the ground plane (Z = 0) and onto planes at different heights (Z = 200, 400, ..., 1,600) that are parallel to the ground. Then, we combine these multilayered projected probability maps and obtain a likelihood function for a camera view. Similar to the first tracker described in Sect. 3.3.2.1, after the fusion of likelihoods from multiple views for multiple planes, a posterior probability is obtained by combining the likelihood with a motion model and the position of people are estimated by running dynamic programming on the posterior probability. The association of observations to people is achieved in two levels: at the camera level based upon appearance (color) and at the fusion node based on motion information.

In our framework, we evaluate the multilayer projected probability maps ($p(y_h|x)$) in a decentralized way (Fig. 3.1). In [14], fusion is first performed on camera views and then on parallel homography planes. Here, we switch this order by first fusing the likelihood information on parallel planes. At each camera node, the likelihood functions obtained by the human detection algorithm [36] ($p(y_{c,h}|x)$) are projected on multiple parallel planes and combined to obtain the singleview likelihood function:

$$p(y_c|x) = \prod_{h=1}^{H} p(y_{c,h}|x) \tag{3.6}$$

Then, this likelihood is sent to the fusion node. In the fusion node, the likelihoods are fused on camera views to obtain the multiview likelihood function:

$$p(y|x) = \prod_{c=1}^{C} p(y_c|x) \tag{3.7}$$

Using the multiview likelihood function and the motion model, the position of people in the scene are estimated at the fusion node using dynamic programming.

3.4 Sparse Representation of Likelihoods

3.4.1 Overview

The bandwidth required for sending local likelihood functions depends on the size of likelihoods (i.e., the number of "pixels" in a 2D likelihood function) and the number of cameras in the network. To make the communication in the network feasible, in [4] a block-based transform domain compression scheme is followed. In this block-based compression scheme, after each camera node performs feature extraction and obtains likelihood functions, likelihood functions are split into blocks and each block is transformed to an appropriate wavelet domain. Then, by taking only the significant coefficients, the likelihood functions are compressed and this new representation is sent to the fusion node. Here, following the great success of compressed sensing in different application areas, we propose a sparse representation framework. At each camera node we propose to represent the likelihood functions sparsely in a proper dictionary and then send this representation instead of sending the function itself. If one can find a dictionary through which the likelihood functions can be represented accurately by a small number of coefficients, then this approach would have the potential to contribute to accurate tracking with minimal use of communication resources. Thanks to the developments in processor technology and fast solver algorithms for l_1-minimization problems, we believe sparse representation-based methods, such as our approach, also have a high potential for real-world scenarios.

Mathematically, we have the following linear system:

$$y_c = A_c \cdot b_c \tag{3.8}$$

where y_c and b_c represents the likelihood function of the camera c (e.g., $P(T_t^c(k)|L_t^n = k)$ in Eq. 3.4 or $p(y_c|x)$ in Eq. 3.6) and its sparse coefficients, respectively, and A_c is the overcomplete[1] dictionary matrix for camera c that represents the domain in which y_c has a sparse representation. To obtain the sparse representation of the likelihood function, at each camera we solve the optimization problem[2] in Eq. 3.9.

$$\min_{b_c}\{||y_c - A_c \cdot b_c||_2 + \lambda ||b_c||_1\} \tag{3.9}$$

Notice that in our sparse representation framework, we do not require the use of specific image features or likelihood functions. The only requirement is that the

[1] The number of columns is bigger than the number of rows.

[2] The algorithm selected for solving the optimization problem is specified in Sect. 3.5.

tracking method should be based on a probabilistic framework, which is a common approach for modeling the dynamics of humans. Hence, our framework is a generic framework that can be used with many probabilistic tracking algorithms in a VSN environment. In fact, we have applied our framework using two different tracking algorithms (Sect. 3.3.2) and shown the tracking results in Sect. 3.5.

At the fusion node, likelihood functions of each camera can be reconstructed simply by multiplying the new representation with the matrix A_c. In general, this may require an initialization step to decide the sparsifying space (A_c) at each camera that is matched with the task of interest and to send all dictionary matrices to the fusion node. In the next subsection, we go through the question of which space should be selected in Eq. 3.8.

3.4.2 *Designing Overcomplete Dictionaries*

One of the well-known approaches in data compression involves using wavelet transforms to obtain a compact representation of signal of interest. As in [4], we can perform likelihood compression through orthogonal transforms of blocks of the likelihood functions and achieve some level of sparsity. However, by using such orthogonal transforms, we cannot fully exploit the structure of the likelihood functions, instead we may distort the structure. For computational reasons, these orthogonal transforms should be applied to blocks of the likelihood functions, leading to blocking artifacts in the reconstructed likelihoods. Focusing on scenarios involving extreme bandwidth constraints, in this chapter we propose designing overcomplete dictionaries that are matched to the structures of the full likelihood functions and that will enable a representation with higher level of sparsity.

For instance, the likelihood functions we obtain from the color model in [10] have a special structure. As it has been explained in Sect. 3.3.2.1, the color model likelihood functions for a person of interest are obtained by comparing the color histogram of rectangular patches in the foreground image and the color distribution of the person of interest. In Fig. 3.2, two sample foreground images and the likelihood function obtained from these foreground images are shown. Figure 3.2a, c show foreground

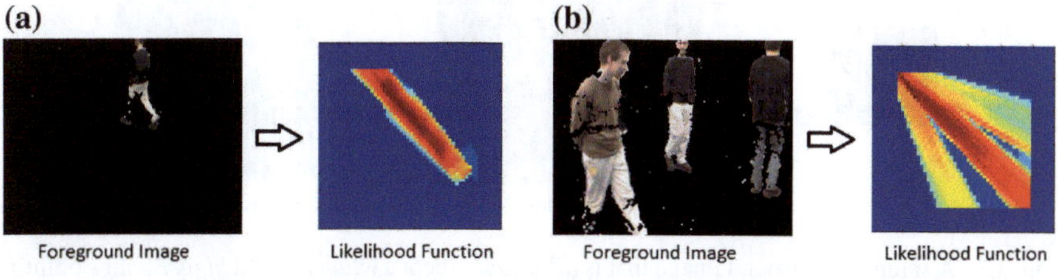

Fig. 3.2 Foreground images captured from two different camera views and corresponding color model likelihood functions extracted from these images based on the approach in [10]. **a** when there is only one person in the scene, **b** when the scene is crowded

images captured from two different camera views when there is only one person in the scene and when the scene is crowded, respectively. The likelihood functions obtained from these image are shown in Fig. 3.2b, d. We can clearly see that likelihood functions consist of quadrilateral-shaped components. A person in the scene creates a quadrilateral-shaped component in the likelihood function. One of the important properties of these components is that their shape do not depend on the value of the foreground pixels. The values inside the quadrilateral change according to the color pixel intensities in the foreground image. But the shape of the quadrilateral only depends on the camera view and the position of the foreground pixels. For this reason, we can say that these quadrilateral-shaped components are building blocks of likelihood functions. By creating a dictionary from these building blocks, we can naturally and properly exploit the structure of the likelihood functions.

As we have mentioned above, the scale and orientation of the quadrilaterals depend on the camera view and the position of the foreground pixels. In order to find all the building blocks of likelihood functions, we need to create likelihood functions from all the possible foreground images. Similar to a 2D Dirac delta function, we create a foreground image that is all-black except a single white pixel and obtain a likelihood function from this image. By changing the position of the white pixel and obtaining the likelihood function from that foreground image, we can create a pool composed of building blocks. Note that dictionaries constructed in this manner depend on the geometry of the observation scenario. Hence, our dictionaries naturally adapt to and exploit the geometry of the sensing scenario (Fig. 3.3).

In the tracking method [14], the likelihood functions of each camera view are obtained by fusing the projection of foreground maps obtained by the human detection step on parallel planes. A sample foreground image and a foreground map obtained from this foreground image are shown in Fig. 3.4a. Again we can observe that a person in the scene creates a quadrilateral-shaped component in the projected likelihood function. In order to find the building blocks of these likelihood functions, we imitate a person in the scene by setting a 100×30 rectangular patch in an all-zero likelihood function and projecting this likelihood onto the ground plane (Fig. 3.4b). Similar to the procedure above, as we shift this rectangular patch, we can create a pool of building blocks and consequently build the dictionary.

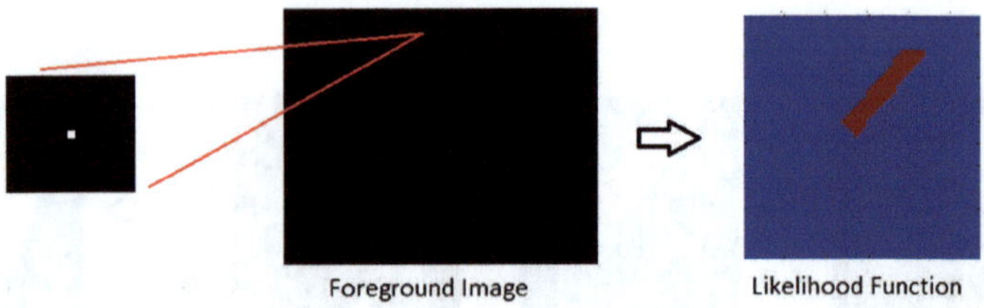

Fig. 3.3 A sample foreground image that is *all-black* except a *white* pixel (a *bigger image* pointing the pixel is given on *left*) and the likelihood function obtained from this foreground

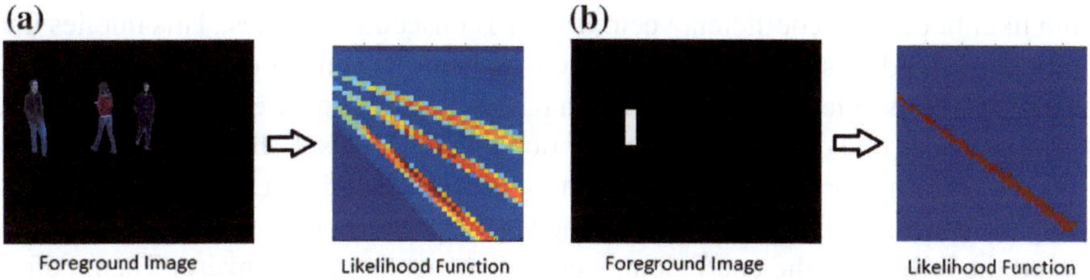

Fig. 3.4 **a** A foreground image and likelihood function obtained from the image based on the approach in [14], **b** A sample foreground map that is *all-black* except a *white* 100×30 rectangular patch and the likelihood function obtained from this foreground

3.4.3 Exploiting Previous Tracking Results

In tracking human dynamics, we expect small differences in movements in two consecutive instances of time. Although this depends on the image resolution and frame rate, it is a well-known assumption and it is used nearly in all motion estimation methods. In this chapter, we exploit this fact in order to reduce the computation time of the optimization problem in Eq. 3.9.

Figure 3.5a, b show two likelihood functions obtained from the tracker in Sect. 3.3.2.1 at two consecutive frames and the corresponding sparse coefficient vectors (x_c in Eq. 3.8). We can clearly see that there are very small differences between

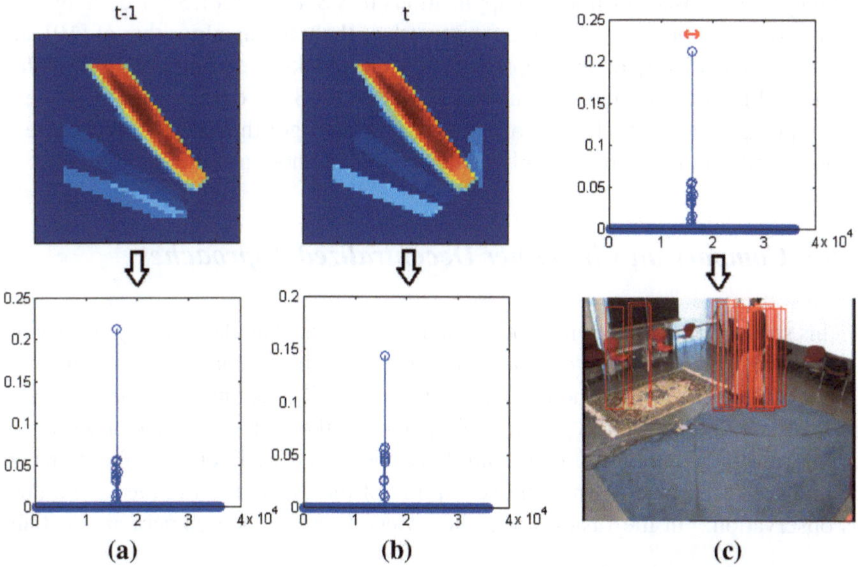

Fig. 3.5 **a** Likelihoods obtained at two consecutive frames and **b** corresponding sparse coefficient vectors, **c** an example of a set around a nonzero element (*red line*) in the sparse coefficient vector together with the corresponding positions in the image

both likelihoods and coefficient vectors of two consecutive frames. This implies that there is no need to solve the optimization problem that includes all the dictionary elements (full problem). By using only a part of the dictionary elements, it could be still possible to find the sparse representation of likelihoods. Following this observation, we perform a procedure to reduce the size of dictionaries at the current frame by using the sparse coefficient vector obtained at the previous frame. At each frame, we record the indices of the coefficient vector elements that are nonzero. Then, before solving the optimization problem, we reduce the dictionaries by taking the elements that are in the neighborhood of the nonzero elements of the coefficient vector, corresponding to spatial neighboring positions of the person (Fig. 3.5c). By changing the neighborhood set, we can achieve different levels of reduction. After we constrain the dictionary elements with neighborhood set, we solve the optimization problem with the new dictionary in Eq. 3.10.

$$\min_{b_c}\{||y_c - A_c^k \cdot b_c||_2 + \lambda||b_c||_1\} \tag{3.10}$$

Here, k denotes number of elements taken in the neighborhood of nonzero elements.

3.5 Experimental Results

This section contains results of a set of experiments testing the performance of our approach in various tracking scenarios and comparing it with several existing techniques proposed for tracking applications in VSNs. Section 3.5.1 demonstrates the use of our approach within the framework of the tracking algorithm of [10], and presents comparisons of our approach with the block-based compression method in [4] and the decentralized method in [17]. Section 3.5.2 demonstrates the use of our approach within the framework of the tracking algorithm of [14], and presents comparisons of our approach with the distributed method in [26].

3.5.1 Comparison with Other Decentralized Approaches

In this subsection, we present experimental results based on the tracking framework in [10]. We have compared our method with a block-based compression framework [4] and a decentralized method in which, similar to [17], a Kalman filter is used in the fusion node to estimate the position of a person in the scene using the observations coming from cameras. In this decentralized method, after likelihood functions are computed, each camera sends the peak point of the distribution to the fusion node as observation.[3] In the fusion node, the observations of each camera are spatially

[3] Previously, the word "observation" was used to refer to the data acquired by cameras. Here, we use it as the information that is obtained by feature extraction at the camera nodes, shared by cameras to be used as "data" by the tracker.

averaged and using the average position as its observation, a Kalman filter is applied to estimate the position of the person on the ground plane. The positions of all people in the scene are estimated by running an individual Kalman filter for each person.

3.5.1.1 Setup

In the experiments, we have simulated the VSN environment by using the indoor and outdoor multi-camera dataset used in [10]. The indoor dataset consists of a video sequence of four people sequentially entering a room and walking around. The sequence was shot by four synchronized cameras that were located at each corner of the room. In this sequence, the area of interest was discretized into $G = 56 \times 56 = 3{,}136$ locations, which determines the size of the likelihood vectors. The outdoor dataset was shot in a university campus and it includes up to four individuals appearing simultaneously. This sequence was shot by three synchronized cameras. The area of interest for this sequence was discretized into $G = 40 \times 40 = 1{,}600$ locations. For the correspondence between camera views and the top view, the homography matrices provided with the dataset are used. The size of the images are 360×288 pixels and the frame rate for all of the cameras is 25 fps.

Using the procedure described in Sect. 3.4.2, we have created the dictionaries for each view. For the indoor dataset, we end up with dictionaries with 36,073, 46,986, 28,155, and 30,195 atoms for the first, second, third, and fourth view, respectively. Note that these numbers are equal to the number of columns of the matrix A_c, $c \in \{1, 2, 3, 4\}$. The number of rows in each dictionary A_c is equal to G. Some elements of these dictionaries are presented in Fig. 3.6. For the outdoor dataset, we end up with dictionaries with 12,777, 11,984, and 19,846 atoms for the first, second, and third view, respectively.Following the comparison between l_1 minimization solvers in [5], we have solved the optimization problem using the Homotopy algorithm [24] with λ set to 0.1 for all dictionaries.

3.5.1.2 Indoor Tracking Results

In this subsection, we present the performance of our method used for indoor multi-person tracking and compare it with the block-based compression approach of [4], as well as with our implementation of the decentralized approach in [17]. For the block-based compression framework, we consider the version that uses DCT for feature compression with a block size of 8×8 and with several levels of compression, taking 1, 2, 3, 4, 5, 10, and 25 most significant coefficient(s) per block. Consequently, with 56×56 likelihoods, at each camera we end up with at most 49, 98, 147, 196, 245, 490, and 1,225 total number of coefficients per person. Since there are four individuals in the scene at most, each camera sends at most 196, 392, 588, 784, 980, 1,960, and 4,900 coefficients per frame. In our method, after the sparse representation of the color model likelihood of a person of interest is found, we consider transmission of 10, 15, 20, 25, 50, and 100 most significant coefficients. Since there are four individuals

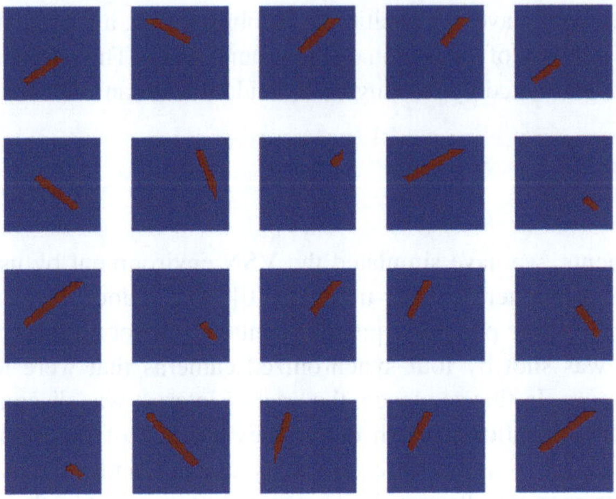

Fig. 3.6 Some elements of the dictionary created for the indoor dataset by the procedure described in Sect. 3.4.2

in the scene at most, each camera ends up sending at most 40, 60, 80, 100, 200, and 400 coefficients per frame to the fusion node. In the decentralized method that uses a Kalman filter, for each person, each camera sends only two points, namely the 2D position of the peak point, to the fusion node. In total, we end up with eight points in maximum for four individuals.

A ground truth for this sequence is obtained by manually marking the people in the ground plane, in intervals of 25 frames. Tracking errors are evaluated via Euclidean distance between the tracking and manual marking results (in intervals of 25 frames). Figure 3.7 presents the average of tracking errors of the methods considered over all people versus the total number of significant coefficients used in communication by each method. Note that the actual number of significant coefficients sent by a camera at each time point depends on the number of people in the scene at that moment. The number of significant coefficients shown in Fig. 3.7 is computed based on the worst case assumption of the presence of four people in the scene all the time. So this is actually an upper bound on the number of coefficients that will be sent by each camera at each time point. Note this is handled in exactly the same way for all methods, so our comparison is fair. Note that the block-based approach is labeled as "fc" in the figure legend, which corresponds to "feature compression".

It can be clearly seen that by using custom-designed dictionaries, our sparse representation framework achieves much more bandwidth reduction than the block-based compression framework. To achieve an error of 1 pixel in the grid on average, our sparse representation framework using custom-designed dictionaries needs at least 20 coefficients per person, whereas the block-based compression framework needs at least 147 coefficients per person. By using the decentralized Kalman approach, we can obtain a huge reduction in communication, but we cannot perform robust tracking. Our framework is also advantageous over an ordinary decentralized approach

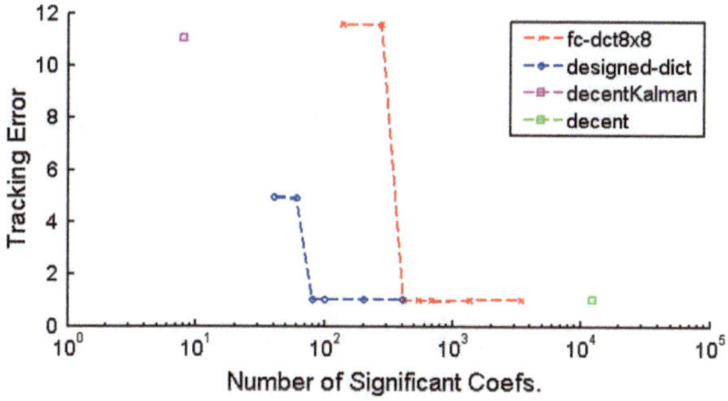

Fig. 3.7 Indoor sequence: average tracking errors versus the number of coefficients for the block-based compression framework (*red*), our sparse representation framework (*blue*), the decentralized Kalman approach (*purple*) and a decentralized method (*green*) that directly sends the likelihoods

that directly sends likelihood functions to the fusion node. In such an approach, we send each data point in the likelihood function, resulting in the transmission of 3,136 values per person. It can be seen that our approach can significantly reduce the amount of communication in the network as compared to this approach while achieving the same level of tracking accuracy.

The tracking results of the block-based compression framework using 49 coefficients per person, the decentralized Kalman approach, and our sparse representation framework using 20 coefficients per person are given in Figs. 3.8, 3.9, and 3.10, respectively. It can be seen that, although the block-based compression approach can track the first and the second individuals very well, there is an identity association problem for the third and fourth individuals. The decentralized Kalman approach fails to track the people in the scene. Nearly for all people, there occurs identity association problems. In some frames, it loses the track of the person and starts tracking a virtual person in the scene (frame no. 1,175 in Fig. 3.9b). These failures

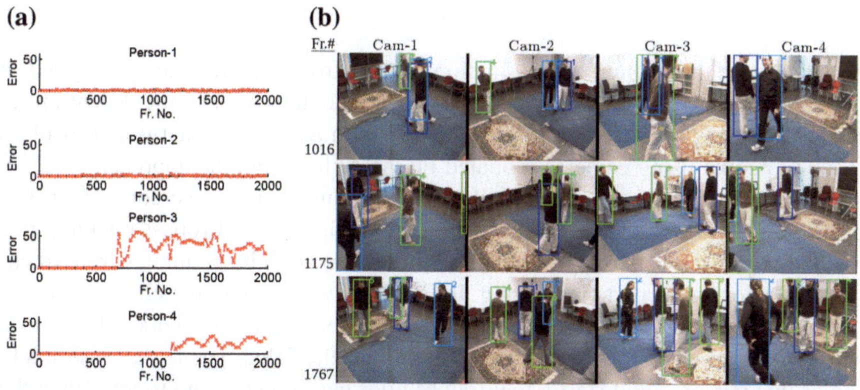

Fig. 3.8 **a** Tracking errors for each person and **b** tracking results for the indoor dataset obtained by the block-based compression framework in [4] using 49 coefficients per person used in communication

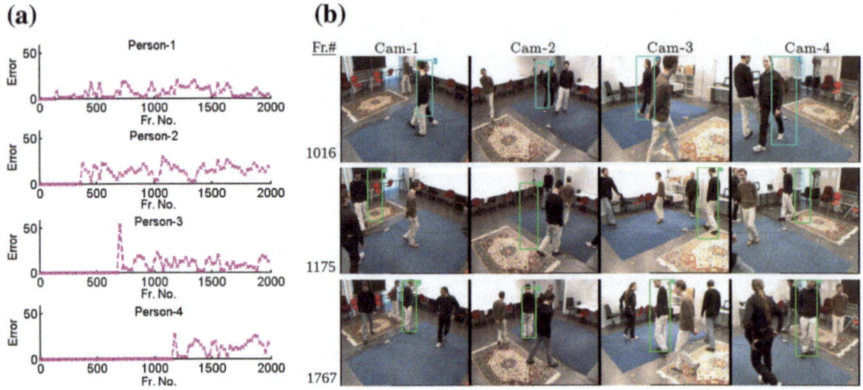

Fig. 3.9 **a** Tracking errors for each person and **b** tracking results for the indoor dataset obtained by the decentralized Kalman approach

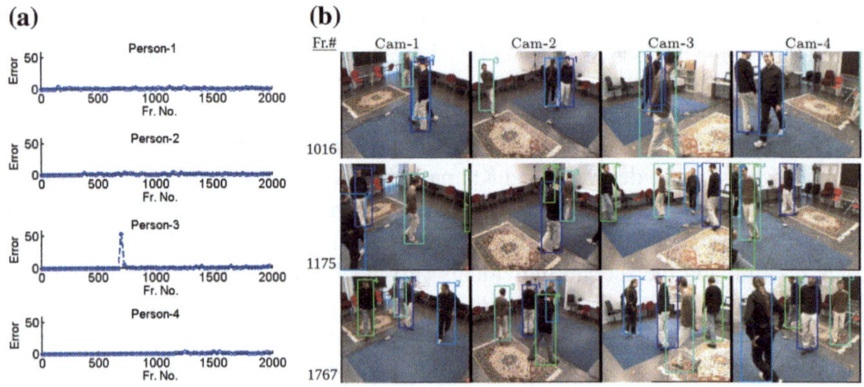

Fig. 3.10 **a** Tracking errors for each person and **b** tracking results for the indoor dataset obtained by our sparse representation framework using 20 coefficients per person used in communication

occur because the amount of information coming from cameras (i.e., peak point of the likelihood) is not enough to perform robust tracking. In [17], the decentralized Kalman filtering approach has only been tested on a simple scenario that involves tracking people using cameras mounted on the ceiling, and the approach does not perform very well on the more challenging tracking scenario we consider in this chapter. In order to achieve reduction in communication and robust tracking, this method requires a better approximation of likelihoods such as samples from likelihood functions as in particle filtering. In Fig. 3.10, we observe that all people in the scene can be tracked very well by our sparse representation framework. All methods suffer from an error for the third person around the 700th frame, because tracking of this person could start a few frames after he/she enters the room. When the number of coefficients taken per person is fewer then 20, we also observe identity problems. However, by selecting the number of coefficients per person greater than

or equal to 20, we can track all the people in the scene accurately. The block-based compression framework requires at least five times more coefficients to achieve this level of accuracy.

In the light of the results we obtained, for the same tracking performance, our sparse representation based method saves 86.39 % of the bandwidth used by the block-based compression approach. As compared to the ordinary decentralized approach transmitting full likelihood functions, our approach saves 99.37 % of the bandwidth, while achieving the same level of tracking accuracy.

3.5.1.3 Outdoor Tracking Results

The performance of our sparse representation-based method for outdoor multi-person tracking is presented in this subsection. Again, we have compared our sparse representation framework with the block-based compression framework in [4] using DCT domain with a block size of 8×8 and the decentralized Kalman approach in [17]. For the block-based compression approach, we take only the 5, 10, 15, 20, 30, and 50 most significant coefficient(s) per block. Consequently, with 40×40 likelihoods, at each camera in total we end up with at most 125, 250, 375, 500, 750, and 1,250 total number of coefficients per person. Since there are four individuals in the scene at most, each camera sends at most 500, 1,000, 1,500, 2,000, 3,000, and 5,000 coefficients per frame. In our method, after the sparse representation of the color model likelihood of a person of interest is found, we only took 5, 10, 15, 20, 25, 50, and 100 the most significant coefficients. Since there are four individuals in the scene at most, each camera ends up sending at most 20, 40, 60, 80, 100, 200, and 400 coefficients per frame to the fusion node. As mentioned in the previous section, in the decentralized Kalman approach, we end up sending at most 8 points for four individuals.

As in the indoor sequence, tracking errors are evaluated via the Euclidean distance between the tracking and manual marking results. Figure 3.11 presents the average of tracking errors of the methods considered over all people versus the total number of significant coefficients used in communication by each method. It can be clearly seen that our sparse representation framework works better in decreasing the communication than the block-based compression framework. The block-based compression framework requires at least 375 coefficients per person to achieve an error of 2 pixel in the grid on average. Using fewer coefficients with this approach causes identity association problems. On the other hand, by using our sparse representation framework, we achieve the same tracking performance with 10 coefficients per person. The decentralized Kalman approach enables a huge reduction in communication, but we cannot perform robust tracking. Our framework is also advantageous over an ordinary decentralized approach that directly sends each data point in the likelihood functions to the fusion node. Such an approach requires sending 1,600 values per person. It can be seen that we can achieve the same level of tracking accuracy with the ordinary decentralized method while significantly decreasing the communication in the network.

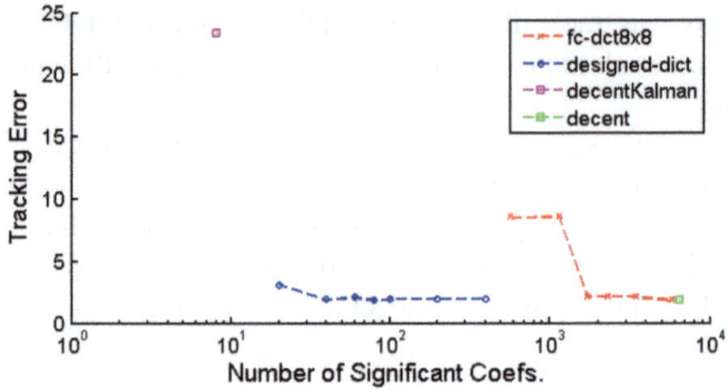

Fig. 3.11 Outdoor sequence: average tracking errors versus the number of coefficients for the block-based compression framework (*red*), our sparse representation framework (*blue*), the decentralized Kalman approach (*purple*), and a decentralized method (*green*) that directly sends likelihoods

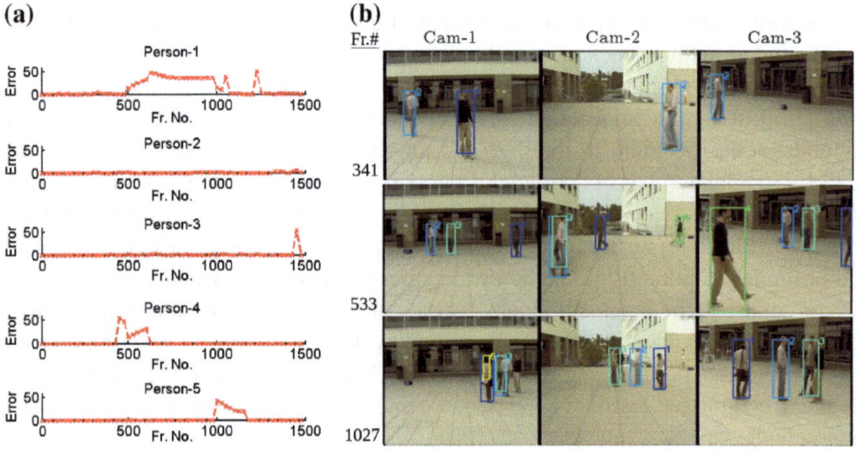

Fig. 3.12 **a** Tracking errors for each person and **b** tracking results for the outdoor dataset obtained by the block-based compression framework in [4] using 250 coefficients per person in communication

The tracking results of the block-based compression framework using 250 coefficients per person, the decentralized Kalman approach, and our sparse representation-based approach with custom-designed dictionaries using 10 coefficients per person are presented in Figs. 3.12, 3.13, and 3.14, respectively. It can be seen that, block-based compression fails to preserve identities with this level of compression. In particular, when a person leaves the scene and comes back, the person cannot be recognized and he or she is considered as a new person in the scene. For the decentralized Kalman approach, nearly for all people, there occurs identity association problems. Usually, it loses the track of the person and starts tracking a virtual person in the scene (Fig. 3.13b). As in the indoor tracking results presented in the previous section, these failures occur because the amount of information coming from cameras is not enough to perform robust tracking. In Fig. 3.14, we observe that all

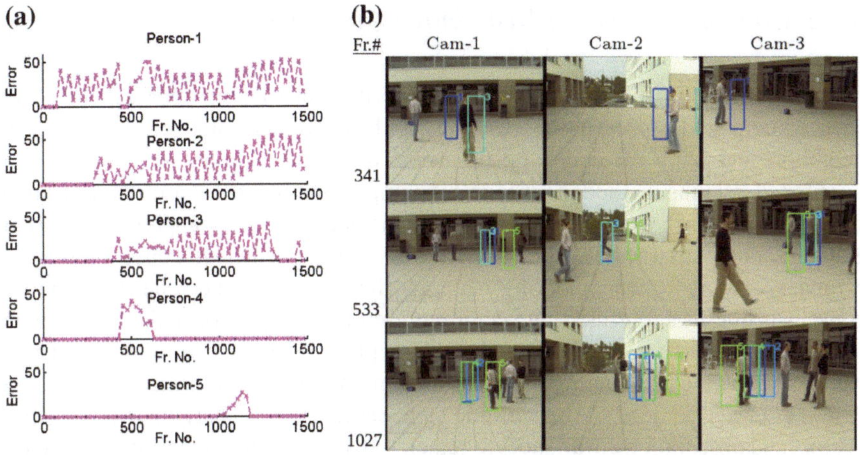

Fig. 3.13 **a** Tracking errors for each person and **b** tracking results for the outdoor dataset obtained by the decentralized Kalman approach

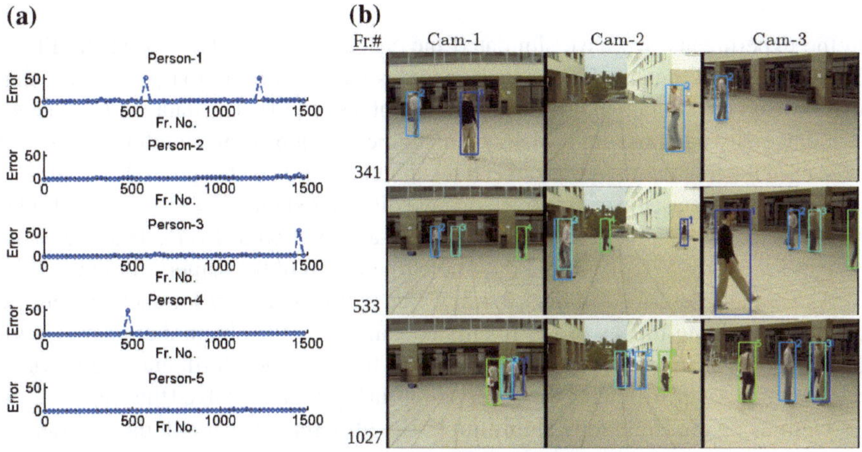

Fig. 3.14 **a** Tracking errors for each person and **b** tracking results for the outdoor dataset obtained by our sparse representation framework using 10 coefficients per person in communication

people in the scene can be tracked very well by our approach with custom-designed dictionaries using 25 times fewer coefficients.

Based on these results, we can say that, by using the custom-designed dictionaries, our sparse representation framework successfully decreases communication load in the network without significantly degrading tracking performance. Hence, what we propose is a bandwidth-efficient approach. Our sparse representation based method is also advantageous over an ordinary decentralized approach that sends 6,400 values for tracking four people (Fig. 3.11). Our approach uses only 0.63 % of the bandwidth needed by the decentralized approach.

3.5.2 Comparison with a Distributed Approach

In this subsection, we compare our method with a distributed approach in which each camera node fuses its observations with tracking results received from its neighbors and sends the updated estimates to the next neighbor. We have used the distributed tracking method in [26] for this comparison. In [26], at each camera node, the position of each person on the ground plane is estimated by applying individual Kalman-consensus filters [19] on its own observations together with observations and estimates coming from neighboring cameras. The state of each person in the Kalman-consensus filter is a four-element vector representing the position and velocity in the horizontal and vertical directions on the ground plane. The observation vector of each camera is obtained by finding the local maximum points of its likelihood function ($p(y_c|x)$ in Sect. 3.3.2.2). At each time step, camera nodes share their observation vectors and observation covariances together with the predicted states of each person.

3.5.2.1 Setup

In the experiments, we have simulated the VSN environment by using the PETS 2009 benchmark dataset [22], which includes camera calibration parameters that will be used to estimate multi-plane homographies in [14]. The data were collected in a university campus and it includes many people appearing simultaneously. We have used the four cameras that cover a rectangular region on the ground. The area of interest in this dataset is of size $6 \times 6\,\mathrm{m}^2$ and discretized into $G = 40 \times 40 = 1,600$ locations, corresponding to a regular grid with a resolution of 15 cm. The size of the images are 720×576 pixels and the frame rate for all of the cameras is 7 fps.

As we have described in Sect. 3.4.2, we design a dictionary for each camera by using the building blocks of the likelihood functions. We obtain dictionaries with 6,932, 7,870, 7,768, and 6,844 atoms for the first, second, third, and fourth view, respectively. Again following the observations in [5], we have solved the optimization problem using the Homotopy algorithm [24] with λ set to 0.1 for all dictionaries.

3.5.2.2 Tracking Results

The results of the comparison between our method and the distributed method in [26] is presented in this subsection. In the distributed approach, at each iteration of the Kalman-consensus filter, each camera shares the observation[4] vector (2 element vector) and observation covariance (2×2 matrix) together with the predicted states (4 element vector) with neighboring cameras. In our implementation, we have selected a common observation covariance at each camera, hence, we save on communications by not sending. In the experiments, we have observed that the Kalman-consensus filter converges to an estimate in all cameras in three iterations.

[4] We refer to the information shared by cameras.

Consequently, to estimate the position of a person, in total 18 elements are shared among cameras. Since there are four individuals in the scene at most, each camera sends at most 72 elements. In our method, after the sparse representation of the likelihood of a person of interest is found, we consider the transmission of 15, 30, 40, 50, 75, 100, and 250 most significant coefficients. Since there are four individuals in the scene at most, each camera sends at most 120, 160, 200, 300, 400, and 1,000 coefficients per frame to the fusion node.

A ground truth for this sequence is obtained by manually marking the people in the ground plane. Tracking errors are evaluated via Euclidean distance between the tracking and manual marking results. Figure 3.15 presents the average of tracking errors over all people versus the total number of significant coefficients used in communication by each method. Since the actual number of significant coefficients sent by a camera depends on the number of people at that moment, an upper bound on the number of coefficients is shown in Fig. 3.15. It can be clearly seen that the distributed approach can provide a huge reduction in communication in the network, but it cannot perform robust tracking. The distributed approach we consider here appears to depend on each camera to provide good tracking performance on its own, and may not perform well in a challenging tracking scenario when that is not satisfied as we observe in our experiments. Our sparse representation framework achieves a smaller bandwidth reduction than the distributed approach, but, by using the custom-designed dictionaries, our framework has the ability to decrease the communication without affecting the tracking performance significantly. By using at least 50 coefficients per person, our sparse representation framework achieves an error of 2.5 pixels in the grid on average. On the other hand, the distributed approach has a tracking error of 24 pixels in the grid on average while using 18 coefficients per person. Our method is also advantageous over an ordinary decentralized approach that directly sends likelihood functions to the fusion node. In such an approach, we send each data point in the likelihood function, resulting in the transmission of 1,600 values per person. The performance of this approach is also given in Fig. 3.15. By using all the information in likelihoods, the ordinary decentralized approach achieves marginally

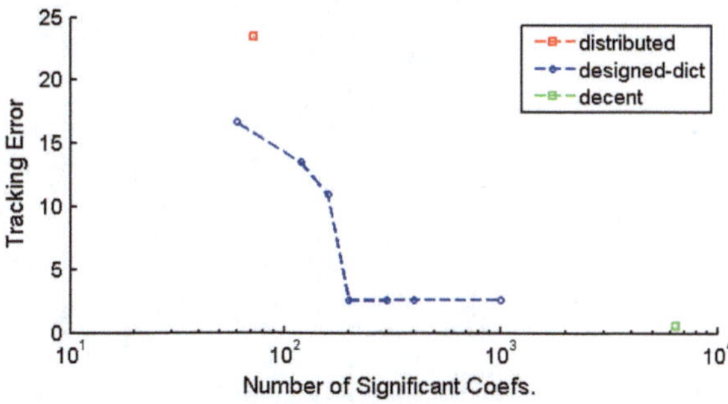

Fig. 3.15 PETS 2009 sequence: The average tracking errors versus the number of coefficients for the distributed approach in [26] (*red*), our sparse representation framework (*blue*) and a decentralized method (*green*) that directly sends likelihoods

better tracking performance than our method. However, our framework provides a significant reduction in bandwidth use while achieving a tracking performance very close to the performance of the ordinary decentralized method.

The tracking results of the distributed approach in [26] per person and our sparse representation framework using 50 coefficients per person are shown in Figs. 3.16 and 3.17, respectively. It can be seen that, the distributed approach fails to preserve identities. For all people in the scene, there occurs identity switches. One of the main reasons of this problem is that the observations extracted from singleview likelihood functions are not sufficient for representing the whole likelihood function. The distributed approach appears to equally incorporate all observations coming from cameras. Since the observations are not extracted after fusing the multiview likelihoods, noisy singleview likelihoods cause inaccurate observations for tracking. An example for such a case is given in Fig. 3.18. We can see that, since the observations

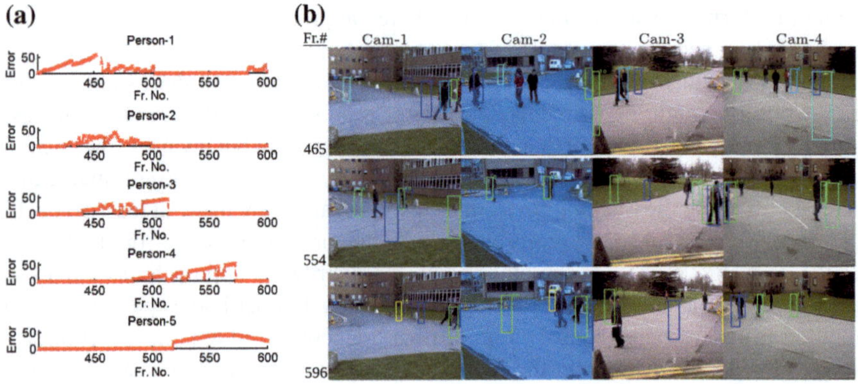

Fig. 3.16 **a** Tracking errors for each person and **b** tracking results for the PETS 2009 dataset obtained by the distributed approach in [26]

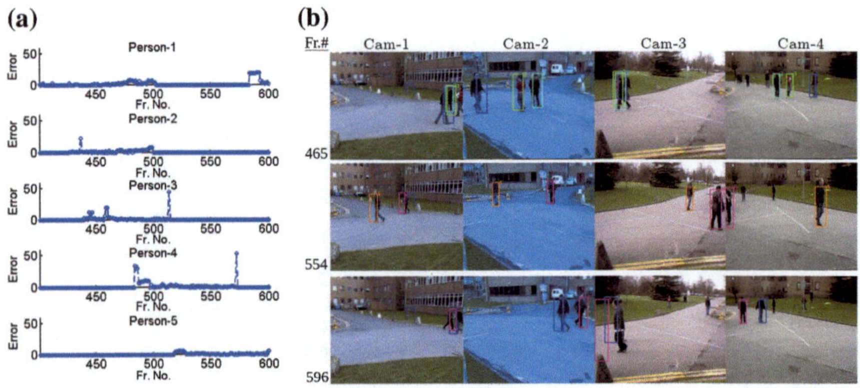

Fig. 3.17 **a** Tracking errors for each person and **b** tracking results for the PETS 2009 dataset obtained by our sparse representation framework using 50 coefficients per person used in communication

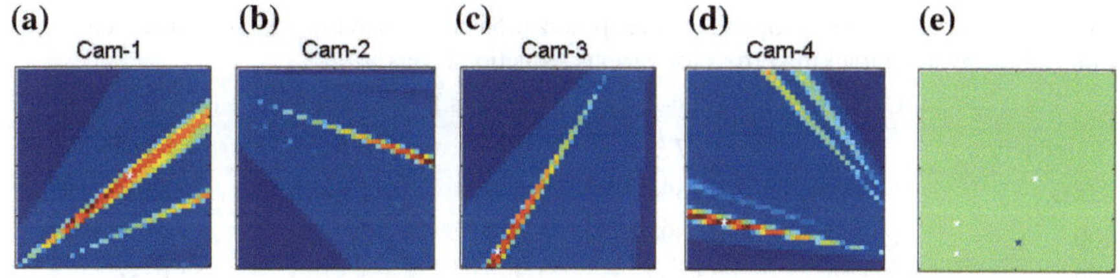

Fig. 3.18 a–d Inaccurate observations extracted from the likelihoods of camera 1, 3, and 4 (*white stars*) lead to **e** inaccurate estimation (*blue star*) in the distributed approach in [26]. Since the person of interest is not visible in camera 2, we do not have an observation coming from this view

extracted from likelihoods of each view are inaccurate, the estimated position of the person is not accurate. Hence, the distributed approach fails to track the people. On the other hand, in our sparse representation framework, we first fuse the singleview likelihoods and then use the multiview likelihood function in tracking. By using the custom-designed dictionaries, we represent the likelihood functions with small number of coefficients without significantly reducing the amount of information they contain. Thus, the multiview likelihoods, obtained by fusing the reconstructed single view likelihoods, are accurate enough to perform robust tracking under severe bandwidth limitations. In Fig. 3.17, it can be seen that our framework can successfully preserve identities and track all people in the scene robustly. Even if a person leaves the scene and comes back (the first person in Fig. 3.17b), he or she is recognized and a true label is assigned to the person. Occasionally in this sequence, a person enters the scene while another person leaves. For this reason, sometimes our method starts tracking a few frames after the person enters the scene or ends tracking before the person leaves the scene. Thereby, it suffers from some errors. When the number of coefficients taken per person is fewer then 50, we also observe identity problems. But by selecting the number of coefficients per person greater than or equal to 50, we can track all the people in the scene accurately.

In the light of the results we obtained, we can say that our sparse representation based method outperforms the distributed approach in [26]. By using the custom-designed dictionaries, we can both decrease the communication in the network and perform robust tracking. Our method requires only 3.12 % of the bandwidth needed by the ordinary decentralized method in order to achieve a tracking performance very close to that method. In the distributed approach in [26], since the observations are modeled with single Gaussian distributions, we only share mean and covariance information with the fusion center. However, such a simple model is often insufficient for robust tracking [18]. In addition, there are particle filtering-based distributed algorithms in which the particles sampled from likelihood functions are approximated using models (e.g., mixture of Gaussians) or quantized in order to reduce communications [3, 18]. Since our approach involves representing likelihood functions using custom-designed dictionaries, we expect to obtain more parsimonious representations, and hence, more efficient communication than such methods.

Table 3.1 Average computation time of the optimization problem in Eq. 3.10 solved at each camera node and the average tracking errors for various reduction levels

k	Cam-1(s.)	Cam-2(s.)	Cam-3(s.)	Cam-4(s.)	Tracking error
No reduction	1.5881	1.7775	3.1716	3.2509	1.9156
2,000	1.1450	0.9386	2.6199	2.8685	1.9156
400	1.1291	0.9394	3.0321	3.2320	1.9175
200	0.6672	0.5507	1.4621	1.5179	1.9156
150	0.2670	0.2132	0.3565	0.3675	1.9175

3.5.3 Decreasing the Computation Time

In this section, we present an analysis of the performance of our procedure to decrease computation time using the indoor dataset described in Sect. 3.5.1.1. Based on the procedure explained in Sect. 3.4.3, we have reduced the size of the optimization problems solved at each camera node (Eq. 3.10). In particular, rather than using the full-size dictionary at each frame, we spatially constrain the dictionary elements in the current frame, by considering only 2,000, 400, 200 and 150 elements in the neighborhood of each nonzero element of the sparse coefficient vector obtained in the previous frame. Table 3.1 presents the average computation time recorded at each camera node and average tracking errors computed as in Sect. 3.5.1.2 for various reduction levels. The average computation times obtained by the non-reduced dictionaries are also presented in Table 3.1. The computation times are recorded on a Intel Xeon E5645 dual 2.35 GHz CPU using Matlab implementation.

It can be observed that by spatially constraining the dictionary elements, we can decrease the computation time without affecting the tracking performance significantly. The results show that using our reduction procedure, it is possible to decrease the computation time to satisfy the constrain on processor capability of camera nodes in VSNs.

3.6 Conclusion

Using a camera in a wireless network poses unique and challenging problems that do not exist in the traditional multi-camera video analysis systems and wireless sensor networks. This chapter presents a novel method that can be used in VSNs for multi-camera person tracking applications. In our method, tracking is performed in a decentralized way: each camera extracts useful features from the images and sends them to a fusion node which performs tracking. Most probabilistic tracking systems involve computation of a likelihood function. Instead of sending the likelihood functions themselves to the fusion node, we compress the likelihoods via sparse representation. Special overcomplete dictionaries that are matched to the structure of the likelihood functions are designed in an adaptive fashion exploiting information about the geometry of the sensing scenario and used for sparse representation of likelihoods. This enables us to decrease the communication between cameras and fusion nodes. Thereby, for the same tracking performance, we achieve more bandwidth savings compared to existing methods. Additionally, we have presented a procedure to decrease the computation time of the optimization problems by exploiting the sparse representation obtained in the previous frame. By using the sparse coefficient vectors computed in the previous frame, we can spatially constrain the set of allowed dictionary elements in the current frame and reduce the size of the problem, thereby, decreasing the computation time.

This framework fits well within the needs of the VSN environment. By extracting image features at the camera-level, the processing capabilities of cameras are utilized. Transmitting only the most significant coefficients, obtained from the sparse representation of likelihoods, saves energy, and bandwidth resources. In this manner, we have achieved a goal-directed compression scheme for the tracking problem in VSNs by performing local processing at the nodes and compressing the resulting likelihood functions which are related to the tracking goal, rather than compressing raw images. Another advantage of this framework is that it does not require the use of a specific tracking method. In our experiments, we have used two different tracking algorithms and achieved bandwidth reduction in the network without degrading the tracking performance significantly. We believe our sparse representation framework is an effective approach that can be used together with any probabilistic tracker in VSNs. Thereby, existing centralized methods can be used within our framework in VSN environments without making significant changes (e.g., using simpler features, etc.) which may degrade their performance.

References

1. Akyildiz IF, Melodia T, Chowdury KR (2007) Wireless multimedia sensor networks: a survey. IEEE Wirel Commun 14(6):32–39
2. Cevher V, Sankaranarayanan AC, Duarte MF, Reddy D, Baraniuk RG, Chellappa R (2008) Compressive sensing for background subtraction. In: ECCV, Marseille, France. Springer, pp 155–168
3. Coates M (2004) Distributed particle filters for sensor networks. In: Proceedings of the 3rd international symposium on information processing in sensor networks, IPSN'04. ACM, New York, pp 99–107
4. Coşar S (2014) Feature compression: a framework for multi-view multi-person tracking in visual sensor networks. J Vis Commun Image Represent 25(5):864–873
5. Coşar S, Çetin M, Sparsity-driven bandwidth-efficient decentralized tracking in visual sensor networks. submitted to Comput Vis Image Underst
6. Dieber B, Micheloni C, Rinner B (2011) Resource-aware coverage and task assignment in visual sensor networks. IEEE Trans Circ Syst Video Technol 21(10):1424–1437
7. Duarte MF, Davenport MA, Takhar D, Laska JN, Sun T, Kelly KF, Baraniuk RG (2008) Single-pixel imaging via compressive sampling. IEEE Signal Process Mag 25(2):83–91
8. Ferrigno L, Marano S, Paciello V, Pietrosanto A (2005) Balancing computational and transmission power consumption in wireless image sensor networks. In: Proceedings of the IEEE

international conference on virtual environments, human-computer interfaces and measurement systems, VECIMS 2005, p 6
9. Fleck S, Busch F, Straßer W (2007) Adaptive probabilistic tracking embedded in smart cameras for distributed surveillance in a 3d model. EURASIP J Embed Syst 2007(1):24–24
10. Fleuret F, Berclaz J, Lengagne R, Fua P (2008) Multicamera people tracking with a probabilistic occupancy map. IEEE Trans Pattern Anal Mach Intell 30(2):267–282
11. Gupta A, Mittal A, Davis LS (2008) Constraint integration for efficient multiview pose estimation with self-occlusions. IEEE Trans Pattern Anal Mach Intell 30(3):493–506
12. Hengstler S, Prashanth D, Fong S, Aghajan H (2007) Mesheye: a hybrid-resolution smart camera mote for applications in distributed intelligent surveillance. In: Proceedings of the 6th international conference on information processing in sensor networks, IPSN'07. ACM, New York, pp 360–369
13. Hofmann M, Gavrila DM (2009) Multi-view 3d human pose estimation combining single-frame recovery, temporal integration and model adaptation. In: Proceedings of the IEEE conference on computer vision and pattern recognition (CVPR), pp 2214–2221
14. Khan SM, Shah M (2009) Tracking multiple occluding people by localizing on multiple scene planes. IEEE Trans Pattern Anal Mach Intell 31(3):19–505
15. Mairal J, Elad M, Sapiro G (2008) Sparse representation for color image restoration. IEEE Trans Image Process 17(1):53–69
16. Mairal J, Bach F, Ponce J, Sapiro G, Zisserman A (2008) Discriminative learned dictionaries for local image analysis. In: Proceedings of the IEEE conference on computer vision and pattern recognition, CVPR, pp 1–8
17. Medeiros H, Park J, Kak A (2008) Distributed object tracking using a cluster-based Kalman filter in wireless camera networks. IEEE J Sel Top Signal Process 2(4):448–463
18. Ni Z, Sunderrajan S, Rahimi A, Manjunath BS (2010) Distributed particle filter tracking with online multiple instance learning in a camera sensor network. In: Proceedings of the 17th IEEE international conference on image processing (ICIP), pp 37–40
19. Olfati-Saber R (2007) Distributed kalman filtering for sensor networks. In: Proceedings of the 46th IEEE conference on decision and control, pp 5492–5498
20. Oto E, Lau F, Aghajan H (2006) Color-based multiple agent tracking for wireless image sensor networks. In: Proceedings of ACIVS06, pp 299–310
21. Pahalawatta PV, Katsaggelos AK (2004) Optimal sensor selection for video-based target tracking in a wireless sensor network. In: Proceedings of the international conference on image processing (ICIP'04), pp 3073–3076
22. PETS (2009) 11th IEEE International workshop on performance evaluation of tracking and surveillance
23. Potter LC, Ertin E, Parker JT, Cetin M (2010) Sparsity and compressed sensing in radar imaging. Proc IEEE 98(6):1006–1020
24. Salman Asif M, Romberg J (2012) Fast and accurate algorithms for re-weighted l_1 norm minimization. Submitted to IEEE Trans Signal Process
25. Song B, Roy-Chowdhury AK (2008) Robust tracking in a camera network: a multi-objective optimization framework. IEEE J Sel Top Signal Process 2(4):582–596
26. Song B, Kamal AT, Soto C, Ding C, Farrell JA, Roy-Chowdhury AK (2010) Tracking and activity recognition through consensus in distributed camera networks. IEEE Trans Image Process 19(10):2564–2579
27. Soro S, Heinzelman W (2009) A survey of visual sensor networks. Adv Multimed 1–22:2009
28. Taj M, Cavallaro A (2011) Distributed and decentralized multicamera tracking. IEEE Signal Process Mag 28(3):46–58
29. Tavli B, Bicakci K, Zilan R, Barcelo-Ordinas JM (2012) A survey of visual sensor network platforms. Multimed Tool Appl 60(3):689–726
30. Wang Y, Velipasalar S, Casares M (2010) Cooperative object tracking and composite event detection with wireless embedded smart cameras. IEEE Trans Image Process 19(10):2614–2633

31. Wolf W, Ozer B, Tiehan Lv (2002) Smart cameras as embedded systems. Computer 35(9): 48–53
32. Wright J, Yang AY, Ganesh A (2009) Robust face recognition via sparse representation. IEEE Trans Pattern Anal Mach Intell 31(2):210–227
33. Wright J, Ma Y, Mairal J, Sapiro G, Huang TS, Yan S (2010) Sparse representation for computer vision and pattern recognition. Proc IEEE 98(6):1031–1044
34. Yang DB, Gonzalez-Banos HH, Guibas LJ (2003) Counting people in crowds with a real-time network of simple image sensors. In: Proceedings of ninth IEEE international conference on computer vision, vol 1, pp 122–129
35. Yang D, Shin J, Ercan AO, Guibas L (2004) Sensor tasking for occupancy reasoning in a camera network. In: Proceedings of IEEE/ICST 1st workshop on broadband advanced sensor networks (BASENETS 2004)
36. Yao J, Odobez JM (2008) Fast human detection from videos using covariance features. In: Proceedings of European conference on computer vision, workshop on visual surveillance (ECCV-VS), p 10
37. Yao J, Odobez JM (2008) Multi-camera multi-person 3d space tracking with mcmc in surveillance scenarios. In: Proceedings of ECCV workshop on multi camera and multi-modal sensor fusion algorithms and applications
38. Yoder J, Medeiros H, Park J, Kak AC (2010) Cluster-based distributed face tracking in camera networks. IEEE Trans Image Process 19(10):2551–2563
39. Yu C, Sharma G (2010) Camera scheduling and energy allocation for lifetime maximization in user-centric visual sensor networks. IEEE Trans Image Process 19(8):2042–2055

[illegible]

Chapter 4
Real-Time Tracking for Moving Target in WSN with Uncovered Holes

Huan Li, Zhefeng Sun and Kejie Lu

Abstract In many practical scenarios, tracking moving targets in the field is very important but also challenging. To effectively track targets, a promising solution is to deploy a target-tracking wireless sensor network (WSN), which has attracted significant attention in the literature. In the past few years, most existing studies in this area have been focused on improving the accuracy and energy efficiency based on the assumption that the field is fully covered. However, this assumption may be invalid because sensors may fail due to various reasons. In this chapter, we tackle this important but largely overlooked problem. Specifically, we consider a WSN in which there exist uncovered areas, a.k.a. *holes*, in the field, due to the failures of sensors. We propose a novel signaling protocol where the main idea is to identify the hole and boundary nodes at the same time during the tracking course when the target moves into the hole. To quickly discover the boundary, we also propose to adopt directional antenna to achieve wireless communication. Simulation results show that the proposed approach can realize the real-time detection of a moving target when it runs into and out of the hole, and at the same time, consume much less energy than the omnidirectional antenna-based methods.

4.1 Introduction

Wireless sensor network (WSN) is a promising technology that can efficiently collect information from the unattended field and thus can facilitate the interactions between the physical world and human beings. One of the most important applications of

H. Li (✉) · Z. Sun
School of Computer Science and Engineering, Beihang University, Beijing, China
e-mail: lihuan@buaa.edu.cn

Z. Sun
e-mail: sunzhefengsandy@gmail.com

K. Lu
Department of Electrical and Computer Engineering, University of Puerto Rico at Mayagüez, Mayagüez, PR, USA
e-mail: kejie.lu@upr.edu

P. Spagnolo et al. (eds.), *Human Behavior Understanding in Networked Sensing*,
DOI 10.1007/978-3-319-10807-0_4

WSNs is to check moving target continuously, in scenarios such as monitoring wild animal and human detection and tracking. Unlike the centralized surveillance system, the advantages of target-tracking WSN include higher accuracy and shorter detection delay.

Typically, a target-tracking WSN consists of a set of sensor motes, each of which can sense moving targets nearby and communicate with other motes using wireless communication. In general, sensor motes are deployed with a certain density so as to provide full coverage of the field. On the other hand, since motes are usually powered by battery, to prolong the lifetime of WSN, a sensor shall be on the sleeping mode until it is notified by neighbors that a moving target is about to enter its sensing field.

Despite the importance of these studies, in practical scenarios, sensors can fail due to various reasons such as low battery, software bugs, natural disaster, etc. Consequently, uncovered areas, a.k.a. *holes*, can occur dynamically over time. In the literature, most existing studies on target-tracking WSN concentrate on improving the accuracy and energy efficiency in a fully covered area [18, 40]. In this chapter, we investigate how to keep tracking moving target in WSN with holes that are not known in advance.

This problem is challenging because of a few reasons. First of all, the hole can appear dynamically until a particular sensor identifies that one or more of its neighbors cannot be waked up. Secondly, once a hole is detected the particular sensor must initiate a procedure to quickly determine the border of the hole and activate sensors around the hole so as not to miss the moving target, which is difficult. Here we note that, although there are some studies on boundary detection [10, 12, 25], none of them were designed to deal with our problem, in which we have the requirement to detect moving target in real-time.

In this chapter, we address this challenging problem. In particular, our major contributions are listed below.

- We apply directional antenna for target-tracking WSNs, which is different from most studies in the literature. To the best of the authors' knowledge, this is the first study that uses directional antenna for continuous tracking moving target for WSN with holes.
- We propose a novel prediction algorithm that can not only achieve continuous tracking, but also minimize the energy consumption by automatically setting the mode of boundary sensors. To realize real-time and accurate path prediction, we also design a signaling protocol.
- We conducted extensive simulation experiments. The results show that the proposed protocol can achieve the real-time detection of a moving target when it runs into and out of the hole. Moreover, the energy consumption of the proposed scheme is lower than that of schemes using omnidirectional antenna.

The rest of the chapter is organized as follows. Section 4.2 surveys the related work. Section 4.3 presents the system models and problem statement. Section 4.4 introduces the real-time tracking protocol. Section 4.5 discusses the performance evaluation. Finally, Sect. 4.6 concludes the chapter and points out the future work.

4.2 Related Work

4.2.1 Target Tracking in WSN

Technical advances in micro-sensing, wireless communications, and microelectro-mechanical systems have enabled the development of wireless sensor network (WSN) to bridge the interaction gap between the physical world and human beings. A sensor network is composed of a large number of sensor nodes (also called motes) that are deployed inside the phenomenon to realize a wide range of applications, including remote environmental monitoring, real-time tracking, precision agriculture, etc. [13]. In WSN, the main components of a mote include microcontroller, transceiver, external memory, power source, and some sensors. Each individual mote is capable of performing some processing, gathering sensory information and communicating with other nodes via wireless transmission in the network.

Tracking moving target is one of the most important applications in WSNs. Different from the centralized monitoring system, the advantages of applying WSN in these applications are distinguished, since it catches with the physical world in real-time and thus can satisfy the quality of service, e.g., the demand of high accuracy of path detection [5, 18]. In [42], the position and the velocity are both considered in the state of the target in Cartesian coordinates, and a new approach, which is based on the combination of Kalman filter and maximum likelihood estimator, is investigated to avoid the instability problem and thus can offer superior tracking performances. In [46], the authors proposed to extract an ordered list from unreliable sensor readings to estimate the movement trace and developed a multidimensional smoothing scheme to enhance tracking accuracy.

In addition to accuracy objective, some other issues such as real-time and energy are also studied. With regard to real-time tracking, Finding HuMo [9] proposes a real-time user tracking system for smart environments, in which individual targets can be fast identified by investigating binary motion data stream. Earlier work has also investigated how to guarantee real-time communications in wireless sensor network [20, 21] or robot sensing systems [22]. Some special scenarios, such as how to track a single target in WSN that includes sensor motes with controlled mobility, have been studied in [27].

While in traditional WSN, static sensor motes are the *de facto* nodes used in the infrastructure for investigated areas of interest, some researchers considered the tracking problem in a distributed heterogeneous WSN that includes cameras [37] and multi-sensor mobile robots [32]. For instance, multi-agent surveillance systems have been proposed for tracking and monitoring in [26, 32, 33]. Different from other discussions that focused on a specific algorithm or protocol design, the multi-agent system was proposed to provide robot-assisted system that can exploit a distributed control architecture to enable the network to autonomously accomplish general-purpose and complex monitoring tasks. Moreover, some other artificial intelligence (AI) techniques, such as machine learning algorithms (e.g., a support vector machine (SVM) classifier in [38, 39]) have been introduced to realize the high-accuracy tracking. These works provided a new way of thinking for tracking task using WSN, however, the proposed methods are normally too complicated for real-time scenarios in practice.

4.2.2 Hole Detection and Boundary Discovery

As defined in [35], a boundary separates two regions of interest in a phenomenon, which can be visualized as an edge if there is a sharp change in the field value between the two regions, or alternatively, as a contour with a field value $f = \tau$ separating two regions with field values $f > \tau$ and $f < \tau$. Under this condition, holes can be defined as the area not covered by the sensing area of any nodes as $\tau = 0$. This is different from the definition in [5], where a hole refers to a target that is covered by less than three sensors. In this chapter, we adopt the first definition.

With regard to boundary discovery in WSN, several problems have been discussed in the literature, including field estimation, localized estimation, and adaptive estimation. Field estimation is to sample the entire field and query for the points on boundary. For instance, in [24], contour maps are generated at the sink by gathering information from the whole network. Localized estimation is to identify which sensors lie on the boundary. In [11, 12], the authors examined the problem of tracking dynamic boundaries occurring in natural phenomena using a network of range sensors. In this work, a low energy algorithm, which combines the spatial estimation and temporal estimation techniques, has shown good performance in the estimation accuracy, compared to similar periodic update techniques to track boundaries without requiring a priori knowledge about the dynamics. In [36], mobile agents were proposed to optimally approximate the boundary with a polygon, in order to monitor an environmental boundary. The mobile sensors rely only on sensed local information to position some interpolation points that lead to an approximating polygon.

According to our survey, no existing studies have investigated the mobile target tracking under the hole detection scenario. Moreover, most previous algorithms focus on the improvement of the boundary detection's accuracy and the reduction of calculation time. Besides, how to utilize directional antenna to save energy is not considered in existing studies.

4.2.3 Directional Antenna in WSN

Compared to omnidirectional antenna, directional antenna has several advantages, especially in the energy consumption and reduction of collisions among multiple sensor nodes. In WSN, topics on using directional antenna include capacity improvement, medium access control (MAC) design, routing protocol, coverage study, location discovery, etc.

Here we note that, for directional antenna, the amplifier energy consumption is proportional to the angle [7].

$$\varepsilon_{\text{amp}} \propto \text{Angle} \tag{4.4}$$

Combining Eqs. (4.3) and (4.4), we have the following expression for energy consumption, as illustrated in Eq. (4.5):

$$\sum_{i=1}^{N} E_{\text{comm}}(i) = \sum_{i=1}^{N} E_{\text{comm}}(i) \propto (\sum_{i=1}^{N} k_{\text{s}}(i) + \sum_{i=1}^{N} k_{\text{r}}(i) + \sum_{i=1}^{N} (\text{Angle}(i) * k_{\text{s}}(i) * M')) \tag{4.5}$$

4.3.4 Problem Statement

In a randomly deployed WSN, when a sensor node is active in packet transmission, reception, and sensing, the energy consumption for those activities is much higher than the consumption when the node is on the sleeping mode. Therefore, after the nodes are deployed and self-organize the network, on-demand cooperation and notification are useful to reduce the energy consumption and thus can significantly prolong the lifetime of WSN.

In the domain of long-term real-time target tracking, the term of on-demand means that, if a mobile target is located in the sensing area of some sensor nodes, these sensor nodes shall be notified in time to start sensing and shall keep sensing whenever necessary with the help of neighboring nodes' cooperation. For such applications, any attempt to save energy in the target tracking process shall be based on the guarantee of sensing accuracy. Specifically, accuracy means that the related nodes must keep sensing and record the results whenever the target is in its sensing range.

In this study, we consider a scenario that some fields are not covered by any sensing nodes, as shown in Fig. 4.3. These specific uncovered fields are called *holes*

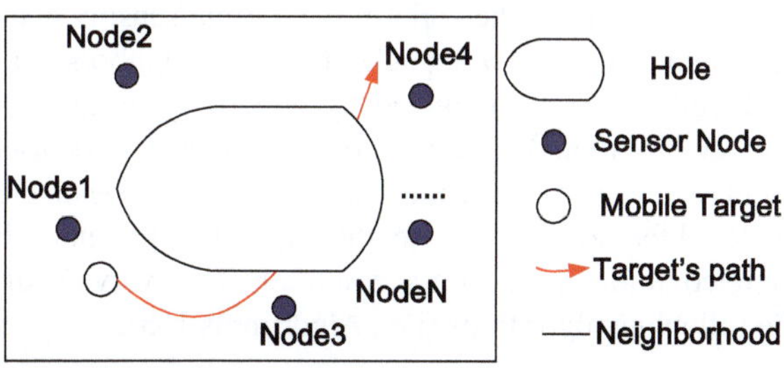

Fig. 4.3 Mobile target's tracking in the area where hole exists

in this work. In such scenarios, suppose a moving target is walking/running across a big hole (The diameter of the hole is much larger than the sensing range.) in a field with a predictable average speed, our first problem is how to detect that the target has entered the hole in real-time and initiate a signaling protocol to notify the nodes along the border of the hole to keep tracking.

When the target is in the hole, the reduction of energy consumption is of great importance in order to prolong the network lifetime. However, in order to catch up the target, it is required to keep some sensor nodes awake to achieve necessary tracking accuracy. Hence, the trade-off between accuracy and energy efficiency is another important problem to be solved.

To facilitate further discussion, we suppose that each sensor node knows its position and its one-hop neighbors' information. In summary, the problem is: how the nodes can cooperate with one another to discover the hole accurately and detect the mobile target in time before it enters the hole and after it runs out of the hole. For this problem, there are two possible objectives: (1) to minimize the energy consumption in the communication and sensing processes; and (2) to guarantee the accuracy in real-time detection.

4.4 Real-Time Mobile Target Detection Protocol

In this section, we elaborate on the aforementioned problem and discuss how to design a protocol to guarantee a real-time and low-energy consumption detection of the mobile target when it runs into and out of the hole. Specifically, we investigate three subproblems: (1) detection of the hole, (2) boundary node discovery, and (3) convergence of the protocol. To simplify the discussions, we assume that the design is based on a lossless channel.

4.4.1 Overview

Suppose the nodes keep sensing with the interval of Δt until the target moves out of their sensing coverage area. At the moment when the node cannot catch the moving target, we can prove that the target must be in the neighbors' sensing area. So once the target moves out of the sight of the current sensing nodes, these nodes will immediately send a *start-sensing* packet to all its neighbors at a pre-calculated direction (The direction can be predicted by previously received sensing signals sent from its former neighbors.), and wait for the replies. If no sensed-ACK (ACK: acknowledgement) is received, the senders are considered to be on the boundary and the target has entered the hole; otherwise, the target does not enter the hole and the sensing procedure continues as in normal condition. The overview of the protocol is presented in the following algorithms (i.e., Algorithms 1–3).

Algorithm 1: Sensing-process

```
repeat
    Sensing the targets;
until cannot sense the target anymore;
send out start-sensing signal at one direction to its one-hop neighbors;
wait for replies for a given interval;
if received ACK(sensed) then
    Stop sensors; return // The neighbors have sensed the target
else                                  /* start Hole-detection process */
    broadcasts hole-detection signal to its one-hop neighbors;
```

Algorithm 2: Hole-detection (*hole-detection*)

```
if it is the first time receiving hole-detection then      /* upon receipt of
hole-detection */
    if (boundary-discovery( hole-detection) == TRUE) then
        broadcasts hole-detection signal to its one-hop neighbors;
        start Sensors till the target caught or received target-catch-up signal;
    else
        Stop sensors; Return Sleep
else                              /* have received the signal before */
    Return
```

Algorithm 3: Boundary-discovery (*hole-detection*)

```
calculate the direction;
broadcast boundary-discovery signal to neighbors on that direction;
wait for the ACKs;
calculate the number of the received ACKs (#ACK);
if #ACK / #neighbors ⩽ Threshold then
    return (TRUE);
else
    return(FALSE);
```

4.4.2 Detection of the Hole

At the initial stage, the nodes that first detect the existence of the hole will broadcast a *hole-detection* query signal to the nodes in all directions, and then initiate the boundary detection process (see the next section). Once the node can tell that it is on the boundary, it will then continue to send out *hole-detection* signal to the next nodes on some directions using direction antenna and start sensing process till the target-catch-up signal feedbacked/propagated to it, which indicates that the target

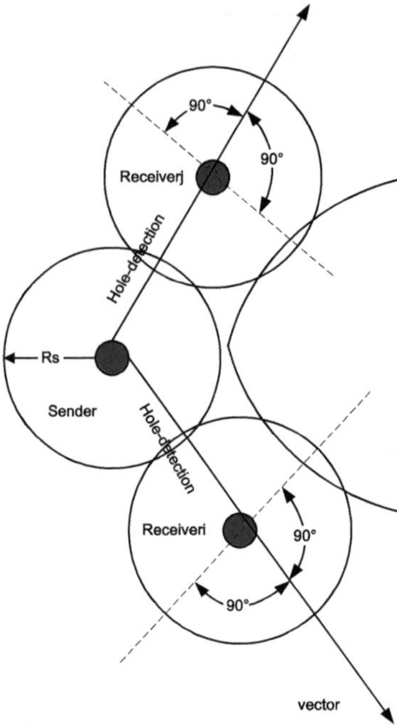

Fig. 4.4 Hole detection signaling process

has moved out of the hole and has been successfully detected by some sensing nodes on the boundary, the whole hole-detection process can thus stop.

Except for the initial stage, to save energy, we design an efficient scheme to utilize direction antenna to transmit the signal to the neighboring nodes on the boundary. The problem is how to calculate the angle so that all nodes on the boundary can be covered. In this study, we apply a simple scheme, as illustrated in Fig. 4.4. Particularly, the receiver will choose a direction that is the same as the direction from the sender to the receiver. With this direction, the receiver will select 180° in total from the sum of the angle of clockwise and counterclockwise directions (each covering 90°). Note here, we use a relative large angle to make sure that all boundary nodes can be covered for the signaling propagation. In fact, to save the energy, the angle can be smaller and more adaptive to the scenario if the algorithm can predict the speed and the shape of the hole in more precise manners, which will be investigated in our future work.

4.4.3 Boundary Node Discovery

Although one node may receive several *hole-detection* signals from different nodes from one direction, for simplicity, upon receipt of the first signal, this node will send

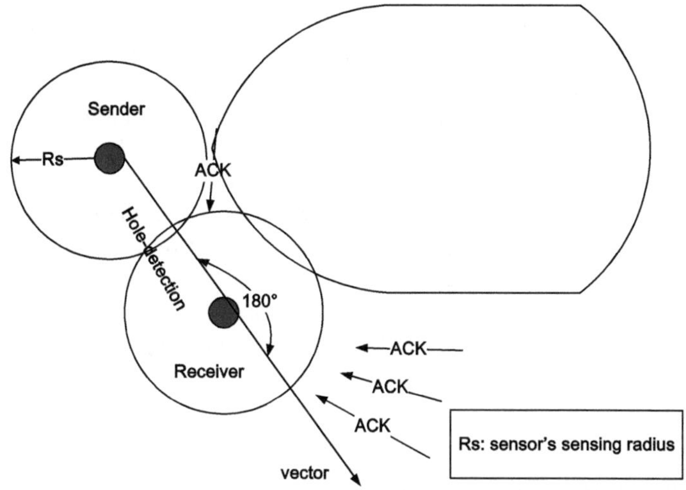

Fig. 4.5 Boundary discovery process

out *boundary-discovery* query packet right away to the nodes in all directions at initial stage or some directions for the following steps, and then wait for the ACKs from those that received this packet. Other detection signals will be ignored because the first one already contains the proximity of the curve.

Suppose the underlying protocol is CSMA-based MAC layer protocol [19], it will not guarantee that all ACKs can reach the sender without collision. To solve this problem, we introduce a threshold to help proceed with the boundary discovery process. That is: if $\frac{\#\text{ACK}}{\#\text{neighbors}} \leq$ Threshold, this node will be identified as a boundary node. For any identified boundary node, it (1) starts *hole-detection* signal to some direction as discussed before; and (2) starts sensing target procedure. Otherwise, this node is not on the boundary, and it will stop involving in the hole detection process. Note here, #neighbors refers to the number of active neighbors on the direction that can be obtained using regular neighboring discovering process, and Threshold is an empirical value that may be affected by the property of physical/MAC layer protocols.

Still, nodes that need to determine if they are boundary nodes will also use directional antenna to send out the *boundary-discovery* packet instead of flooding to all directions, as illustrated in Fig. 4.5. Here, we use the *hole-detection* signal to calculate the 180° angle along the vector, to cover the area that faces toward the hole.

4.4.4 Convergence of the Protocol

The hole-detection signal may transit along the two directions of the hole. So if a sensor node receives a hole-detection signal later again, it should check if it is from a different direction than the previous ones. Since the time for one-hop neighboring transition is relatively much shorter than the signal transition from another direction, we can easily design the timer to handle the neighboring case. Thus, we can draw a conclusion if the signal is received from another direction the first time, that the signaling protocol actually converges and no more signals need to be sent out.

In practice, the target may keep moving or stay for a while inside the hole and will eventually move out. To handle the move-out event, in the protocol we use a *Stop* signal to indicate the target-catch-up event on the reversed path of the hole detection message. All sensing nodes that received this signal will stop sensing process immediately. Although the state of the neighboring boundary nodes should be maintained, the cost is very small because the number of these nodes is very limited.

4.5 Performance Evaluation

In this section, we conduct extensive simulation to demonstrate the effectiveness of the proposed real-time tracking protocol. We evaluate the performance in terms of accuracy and energy efficiency using simulation testbed developed in NS3. We compare the proposed directional transmission method to a flooding approach that makes use of omnidirectional antenna to achieve the communication. The results in each figure in this section is the average value of 25 trials, each having a new node deployment in the network for a given path.

4.5.1 Experimental Settings

In the experiments, 450 sensor motes are randomly deployed and connected in a field with length and width of 1,000 m. According to the relationship between R_S and R_T (i.e., $R_S = 1/3R_T$), the transmission range R_T and sensing range R_S are set to be 150 and 50 m respectively, to ensure that the whole field is covered by the WSN. The sensing interval Δt is set to 0.1 s, and the total simulation time is 80 s for each trial.

In our experiments, we consider four different moving paths, as shown in Figs. 4.6, 4.7, 4.8 and 4.9, each of them corresponds to one of the four distinct holes in Table 4.2.

Table 4.2 Coordinate area of failure nodes

Holes	Coordinate representation of failure nodes
area1	$\{(x, y) \mid x \in [575, 800], y \in [135, 285]\}$
area2	$\{(x, y) \mid x \in [575, 800], y \in [135, 285]\}$
area3	$\{(x, y) \mid x \in [650, 750], y \in [500, 700]\}$
area4	$\{(x, y) \mid x \in [0, 200], y \in [800, 1,000]\}$

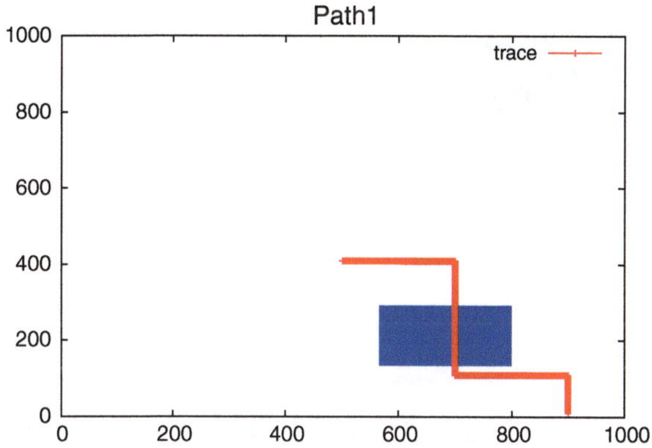

Fig. 4.6 Target starts at (900, 10), moving speed is 10 m/s, turns around 4 times when it moves at 0, 100, 300 and 600 m at the direction: *up*, *left*, *up* and *left*

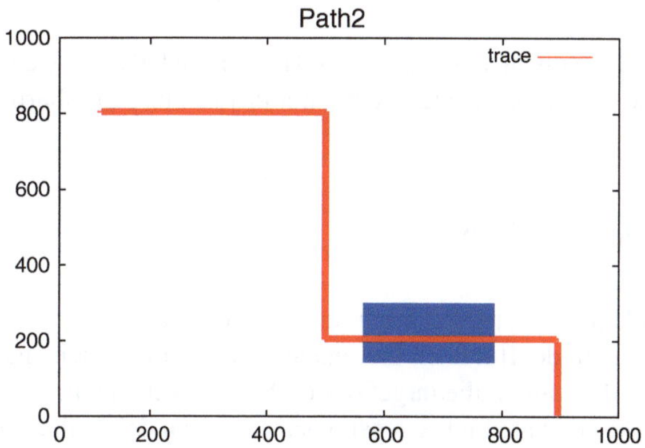

Fig. 4.7 Target starts at (900, 10), moving speed is 20 m/s, turns around 4 times when it moves at 0, 200, 600 and 1,200 m at the direction: *up*, *left*, *up* and *left*

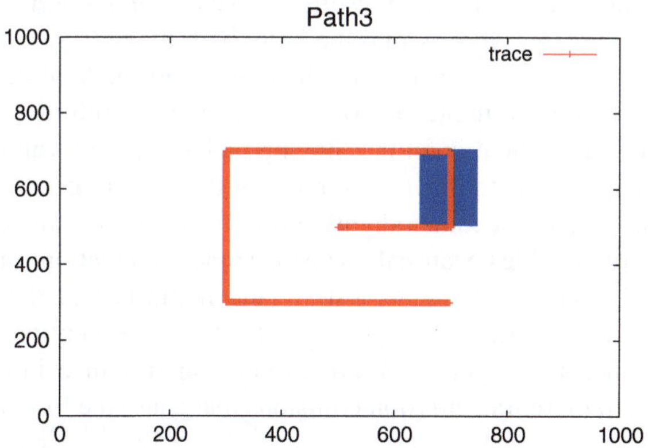

Fig. 4.8 Target starts at (500, 500), moving speed is 20 m/s, turns around 5 times when it moves at 0, 200, 400, 800 and 1,200 m at the direction: *right*, *up*, *left*, *down* and *right*

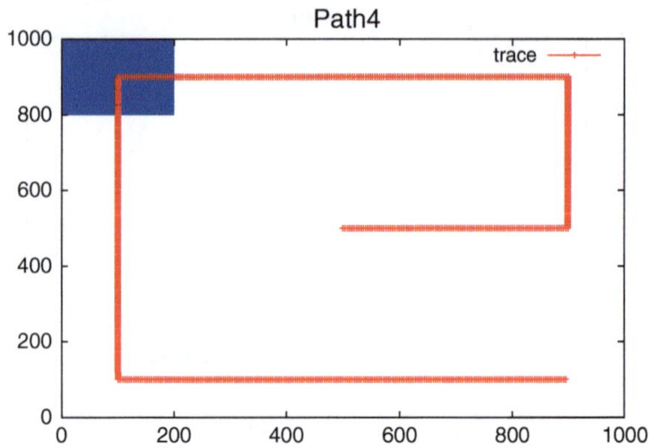

Fig. 4.9 Target starts at (500, 500), moving speed is 20 m/s, turns around 5 times when it moves at 0, 400, 800, 1,600 and 2,400 m at the direction: *right*, *up*, *left*, *down* and *right*

The nodes within the given hole are assumed to be failed. Paths are chosen to evaluate the impact of moving area, turning angle, smoothly running and sharp turn, and speed.

4.5.2 Accuracy Analysis

During the whole tracking period, each sensor mote can be either on the sensing state or on the sleeping mode. If it is on the sensing state, for each sensing event there are two possible results: caught the target or not. So at any moment, if we only consider those sensor motes that are on the sensing state, we can define the catching ratio CR as the ratio of motes that are actually catching the target during the state, which is CR = #Caught/#Sensing_nodes.

Based on the definition of CR, we plot CR over time in Figs. 4.10, 4.11, 4.12 and 4.13, for different paths. From these results, we have several observations. First, for each path when the target moves into the hole, both the proposed scheme and the existing one can tell the existence of the hole and start the hole detection process in real-time. Second, from the results of all paths, the algorithms can always catch the target whenever the hole is on the moving path or at the turning-around point. Finally, as the target starts to move into or out of the hole, in general, the CR when using directional antenna becomes slightly lower than the one using omnidirectional antenna. This is reasonable because the sensing angle for directional antenna is much smaller than 360°. On the other hand, it shows that in most cases, the results of using directional antenna converged very quickly to 1. The only exception happens for the third path, in which the target turns around more sharply than in other scenarios, which may lead to more transmission collisions that cause the loss of catches.

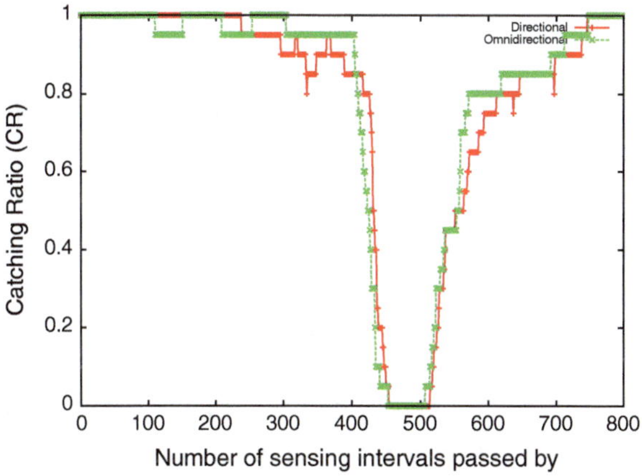

Fig. 4.10 Catching ratio for Path1

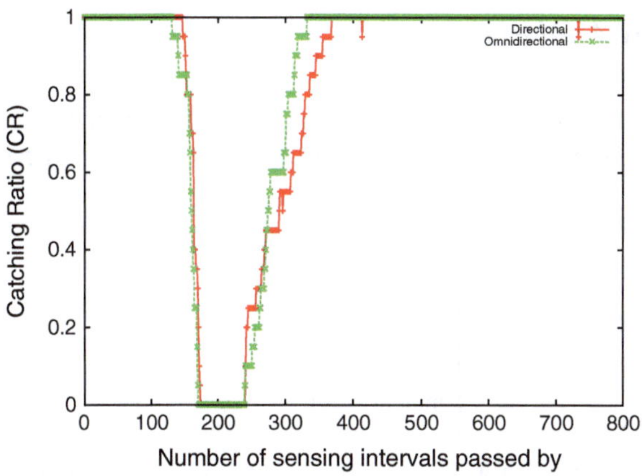

Fig. 4.11 Catching ratio for Path2

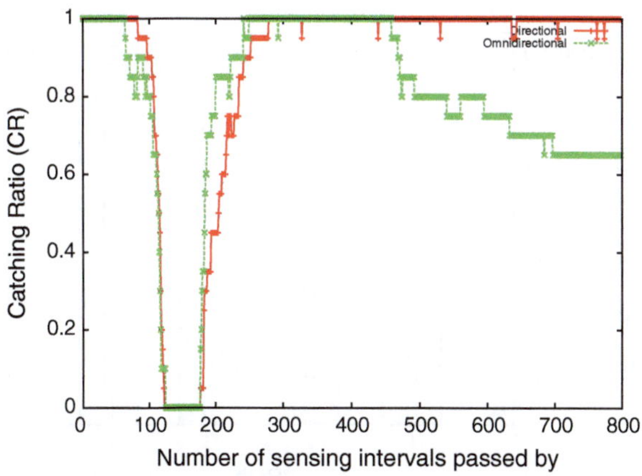

Fig. 4.12 Catching ratio for Path3

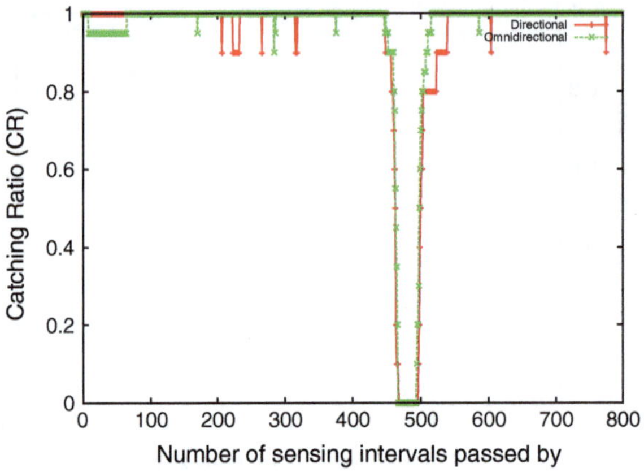

Fig. 4.13 Catching ratio for Path4

4.5.3 Energy Analysis

According to the energy consumption models depicted in Eqs. (4.1) and (4.3), the minimization of energy consumption can be obtained by the following three objectives:

$$\begin{cases} \min(\sum_{i=1}^{N} k_s(i) + \sum_{i=1}^{N} k_r(i)) \\ \min(\sum_{i=1}^{N} (\text{angle}(i) * k_s(i))) \\ \min(\sum_{i=1}^{N} t_s(i)) \end{cases} \tag{4.6}$$

In Figs. 4.14, 4.15 and 4.16, we compare the proposed scheme and the omni-directional antenna-based scheme according to these three objectives, respectively.

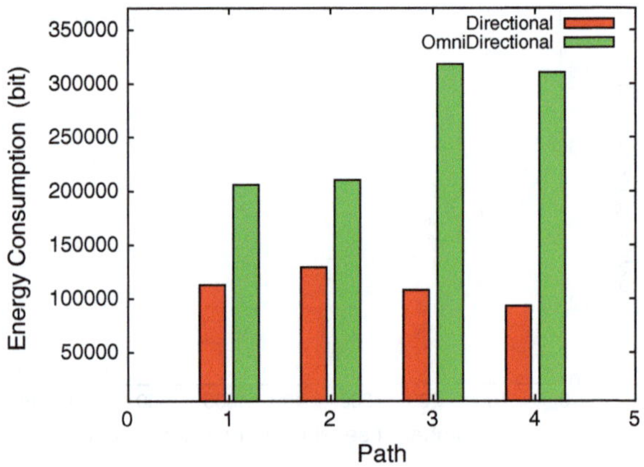

Fig. 4.14 Objective one

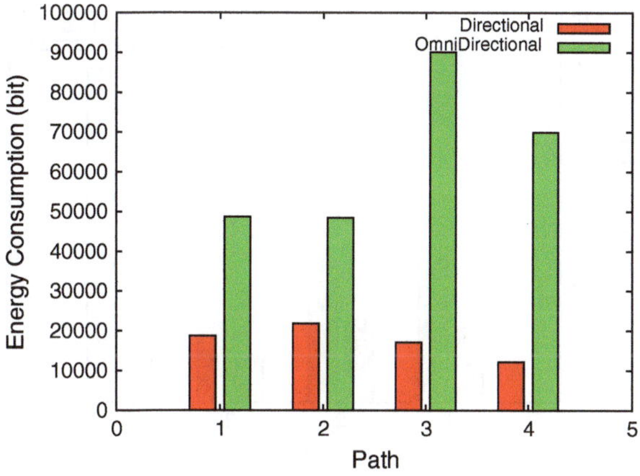

Fig. 4.15 Objective two

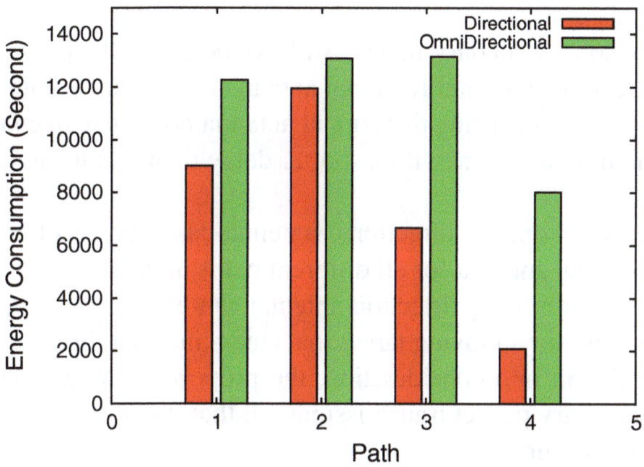

Fig. 4.16 Objective three

As shown in Fig. 4.14, the total number of bits sent and received in the approach using omnidirectional antenna is 1.6–3.3 times as much as that of using directional antenna. And the ratio is even larger (as much as 6) in Fig. 4.15 when the transmission angle is taken into consideration. Furthermore, the total sensing time (Fig. 4.16) of the proposed scheme is less than that of using omnidirectional antenna, for all paths.

4.5.4 Real-Time Analysis

The performance evaluation for real-time target tracking can be measured by the delay between the moment when the target is moving out of the hole and the moment

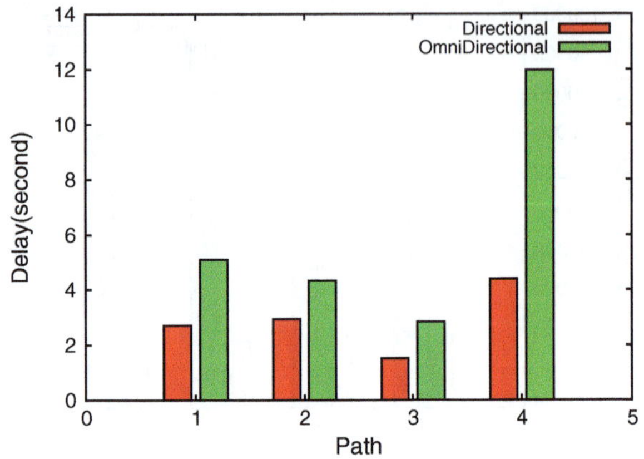

Fig. 4.17 Real-time detection

it is detected by some boundary nodes. Still, we compare the proposed directional antenna-based scheme to omnidirectional antenna based one. Figure 4.17 illustrates the results. As we can see, using directional antenna not only can converge, but also can catch up the moving target with a shorter delay than that using omnidirectional antenna.

In summary, the proposed directional antenna-based protocol outperforms that using omnidirectional antenna for all different paths under different uncovered scenarios. This is because using direction antenna can efficiently achieve on-demand sensing and tracking for a moving target that enters into/out the hole. Taking packet transmission collision into consideration, the proposed scheme can avoid a large number of unnecessary packet transmissions, so that it can track target in real-time without scarifying accuracy.

4.6 Conclusions and Future Work

In this chapter, we have investigated continuous moving-target tracking in WSN with uncovered holes. On the one hand, we have introduced the idea of using directional antenna, which breaks the omnidirectional antenna's presumption in this field. On the other hand, we have proposed a collaborative prediction algorithm and a signal protocol to realize real-time and low-energy-consumption target tracking. To evaluate the proposed scheme, we have conducted extensive simulation experiments to compare the proposed scheme with the existing approach that utilizes omnidirectional antenna. Simulation results demonstrate that our scheme can outperform the existing one and guarantee both real-time detection and energy consumption reduction.

Although we have tackled the fundamental problem of using directional antenna to make continuous tracking possible in WSN under holes, several issues remain to be considered. For example, how to handle the unreliable and lossy channel are among the future work.

Acknowledgments This work has been supported by National Natural Science Foundation of China, NSFC 61170293.

References

1. Abdullah AA, Cai L, Gebali F (2012) Dsdmac: dual sensing directional mac protocol for ad hoc networks with directional antennas. IEEE Trans Veh Technol 61(3):1266–1275
2. Anastasi G, Conti M, Di Francesco M, Passarella A (2009) Energy conservation in wireless sensor networks: a survey. Ad Hoc Netw 7(3):537–568
3. Bow-Nan C, Murat Y, Shivkumar K (2010) Using directionality in mobile routing. Wireless Netw 16(7):2065–2086
4. Carr JJ (1993) Directional or omnidirectional antenna? In: Receiving antenna handbook. High-Text, 189p. http://www.dxing.com/tnotes/tnote01.pdf
5. Chen P, Zhong Z, He T (2011) Bubble trace: mobile target tracking under insufficient anchor coverage. In: Proceedings of the 31st international conference on distributed computing systems (ICDCS2011), pp 770–779, Minnesota, USA, June 2011
6. Cheng B-N, Yuksel M, Kalyanaraman S (2009) Orthogonal rendezvous routing protocol for wireless mesh networks. IEEE/ACM Trans Netw 17(2):542–555
7. Cho J, Lee J, Kwon T, Choi Y (2006) Directional antenna at sink (daas) to prolong network lifetime in wireless sensor networks. In: Proceedings of the 12th European wireless conference 2006—enabling technologies for wireless multimedia communications (European wireless), pp 1–5, Athens, Greece, April 2006
8. Choudhury RR, Vaidya NH (2005) Performance of ad hoc routing using directional antennas. Ad Hoc Netw 3(2):157–173
9. De D, Song W, Xu M, Wang C, Cook D, Huo X (2012) Findinghumo: real-time tracking of motion trajectories from anonymous binary sensing in smart environments. In: Proceedings IEEE of 32nd international conference on distributed computing systems (ICDCS2012), pp 163–172, Macau, China, June 2012
10. Ding M, Chen D, Xing K, Cheng X (2005) Localized fault-tolerant event boundary detection in sensor networks. In: Proceedings of INFOCOM 2005, 24th annual joint conference of the IEEE computer and communications societies, Florida, USA, pp 902–913
11. Duttagupta S, Ramamritham K, Kulkarni P (2011) Tracking dynamic boundaries using sensor network. IEEE Trans Parallel Distrib Syst 22(10):1766–1774
12. Duttagupta S, Ramamritham K, Kulkarni P, Moudgalya K (2008) Tracking dynamic boundary fronts using range sensors. In: Proceedings of the 5th European conference on wireless sensor networks (EWSN2008), pp 125–140, Bologna, Italy, Jan 2008
13. Estrin D, Girod L, Pottie G, Srivastava M (2001) Instrumenting the world with wireless sensor networks. In: Proceedings of IEEE international conference on acoustics, speech, and signal processing (ICASSP '01), pp 2033–2036, Salt Lake City, UT, USA, 7–11 May 2001
14. Felemban E, Vural S, Murawski R, Ekici E, Lee K, Moon Y, Samac SP (2010) A cross-layer communication protocol for sensor networks with sectored antennas. IEEE Trans Mob Comput 9(8):1072–1088
15. Heinzelman WB, Chandrakasan AP, Balakrishnan H (2002) An application-specific protocol architecture for wireless microsensor networks. IEEE Trans Wireless Commun 1(4):660–670
16. Heinzelman WB (2000) Application-specific protocol architectures for wireless networks. PhD Dissertation, Massachusetts Institute of Technology
17. Jain RK, Katiyar S, Agrawal NK (2011) Smart antenna for cellular mobile communication. IEEE Antennas Propag Mag 1(9):530–541

18. Jing T, Snoussi H, Richard C (2010) Decentralized variational filtering for target tracking in binary sensor networks. IEEE Trans Mob Comput 9(10):1465–1477
19. Kurose J, Ross K (2012) Computer networking: a top down approach, 6th edn. chapter 6, pp 513–578. Addison-Wesley, Boston
20. Li H, Shenoy P, Ramamritham K (2004) Scheduling communication in real-time sensor applications. In: Proceedings of the 10th IEEE real-time embedded technology and applications symposium (RTAS04), Toronto, Canada, May 2004, pp 10–18
21. Li H, Shenoy P, Ramamritham K (2004) Scheduling messages with deadlines in multi-hop real-time sensor networks. In: Proceedings of the 11th IEEE real-time embedded technology and applications symposium (RTAS05), San Francisco, California, USA, March 2004, pp 415–425
22. Li H, Sweeney J, Ramamritham K, Grupen R, Shenoy P (2003) Real-time support for mobile robotics. In: Proceedings of the 9th IEEE real-time embedded technology and applications symposium (RTAS03), Washington DC, USA, May 2003, pp 10–18
23. Maloratsky LG (2009) Switched directional/omnidirectional antenna module for amplitude monopulse systems. IEEE Antennas Propag Mag 51(5):90–102
24. Meng X, Nandagopal T, Li L, Lu S (2006) Contour maps: monitoring and diagnosis in sensor networks. Comput Netw 50(15):2820–2838
25. Miao H, Ooi C, Wu X, Schindelhauer C (2010) Coverage-hole trap model in target tracking using distributed relay-robot network. In: Proceedings of 2010 ACM symposium on applied computing (SAC2010), Sierre, Switzerland, March 2010, pp 1299–1304
26. Milella A, Paola DD, Mazzeo PL, Spagnolo P, Leo M, Cicirelli G, DOrazio T (2010) Active surveillance of dynamic environments using a multi-agent system. In: 7th IFAC symposium on intelligent autonomous vehicles, IAV 2010, vol 7, pp 13–18
27. Mourad F, Chehade H, Snoussi H, Yalaoui F, Amodeo L, Richard C (2012) Controlled mobility sensor networks for target tracking using ant colony optimization. IEEE Trans Mob Comput 11(8):1261–1273
28. Murawski R, Felemban E, Ekici E, Park S, Yoo S, Lee K, Park J, Mir ZH (2012) Neighbor discovery in wireless networks with sectored antennas. Ad Hoc Netw 10(1):1–18
29. Nasipuri A, Li K (2002) A directionality based location discovery scheme for wireless sensor networks. In: Proceedings of WSNA '02, Proceedings of the 1st ACM international workshop on wireless sensor networks and applications, Atlanta, Georgia, USA, 28 September 2002, pp 105–111
30. Navda V, Subramanian AP, Dhanasekaran K, Timm-Giel A, Mobisteer SRD (2007) Using steerable beam directional antenna for vehicular network access. In: Proceedings of the 5th international conference on mobile systems, applications and services (MobiSys), San Juan, Puerto Rico, USA, pp 192–205
31. Orda A, Yassour B-A (2005) Maximum-lifetime routing algorithms for networks with omnidirectional and directional antennas. In: Proceedings of the 6th ACM international symposium on mobile ad hoc networking and computing (MobiHoc2005), IL, USA, May 2005, pp 426–437
32. Petitti A, Paola DD, Milella A, Mazzeo PL, Spagnolo P, Cicirelli G, Attolico G (2013) A distributed heterogeneous sensor network for tracking and monitoring. In: 10th IEEE international conference on advanced video and signal based surveillance (AVSS) 2013, pp 426–431
33. Petitti A, Paola DD, Rizzo A, Cicirelli G (2011) Consensus-based distributed estimation for target tracking in heterogeneous sensor networks. In: 50th IEEE conference on decision and control and European control conference (CDC-ECC) 2011, pp 6648–6653
34. Rappaport Theodore (2001) Wireless communications: principles and practice. Prentice Hall, Upper Saddle River
35. Srinivasan S, Duttagupta S, Kulkarni P, Ramamritham K (2012) A survey of sensory data boundary estimation, covering and tracking techniques using collaborating sensors. Pervasive Mob Comput 8(3):358–375
36. Susca S, Bullo F, Martinez S (2008) Monitoring environmental boundaries with a robotic sensor network. IEEE Trans Control Syst Technol 16(2):288–296
37. Taj M, Cavallaro A (2011) Distributed and decentralized multicamera tracking. IEEE Signal Process Mag 28(3):46–58

38. Viani F, Rocca P, Oliveri G, Massa A (2011) Electromagnetic tracking of transceiver-free targets in wireless networked environments. In: Proceedings of the 5th European conference on antennas and propagation (EUCAP), pp 3650–3653
39. Viani F, Rocca P, Oliveri G, Trinchero D, Massa A (2011) Localization, tracking, and imaging of targets in wireless sensor networks: an invited review. Radio Sci 46(5), RS5002. doi: 10.1029/2010RS004561
40. Vicaire P, He T, Cao Q, Yan T, Zhou G, Gu L, Luo L, Stoleru R, Stankovic JA, Abdelzaher TF (2009) Achieving long-term surveillance in vigilnet. ACM trans Sens Netw 5(1):1–39
41. Wang X, Xing G, Zhang Y, Lu C, Pless R, Gill C (2003) Integrated coverage and connectivity configuration in wireless sensor networks. In: Proceedings of the 1st international conference on embedded networked sensor systems (SenSys2003), California, USA, pp 28–39
42. Wang X, Minyue F, Zhang H (2012) Target tracking in wireless sensor networks based on the combination of KF and MLE using distance measurements. IEEE Trans Mob Comput 11(4):567–576
43. Yi S, Pei Y, Kalyanaraman S (2003) On the capacity improvement of ad hoc wireless networks using directional antennas. In: Proceedings of the 4th ACM international symposium on mobile ad hoc networking & computing (MobiHoc '03), Annapolis, Maryland, USA, June 2003, pp 108–116
44. Yu Z, Teng J, Bai X, Xuan D, Jia W (2011) Connected coverage in wireless networks with directional antennas. In: Proceedings IEEE of INFOCOM 2011, pp 2264–2272, Shanghai, China, April 2011
45. Zhang S, Datta A (2005) A directional-antenna based mac protocol for wireless sensor networks. In: Proceedings of the 2005 international conference on computational science and its applications (ICCSA2005), Singapore, May 2005, pp 686–695
46. Zhong Z, Zhu T, Wang D, He T (2009) Tracking with unreliable node sequences. In: Proceedings IEEE of INFOCOM2009, Rio de Janeiro, Brazil, April 2009, pp 1215–1223
47. Zhou H, Luo D, Gao Y, Zuo D (2011) Modeling of node energy consumption for wireless sensor networks. Wireless Sens Netw 3(1):18–23

58. Mani F, Rocca P, Oliveri G, Massa A (2011) Electromagnetic [illegible] of arrays [illegible] wireless [illegible] environments. In: Proceedings of the 5th European conference on antennas and propagation (EuCAP), pp 1650–1653
59. [illegible]

Chapter 5
Sequential Anomaly Detection Using Wireless Sensor Networks in Unknown Environment

Yuanyuan Li, Michael Thomason and Lynne E. Parker

Abstract Anomaly detection is an important problem for environment, fault diagnosis and intruder detection in Wireless Sensor Networks (WSNs). A key challenge is to minimize the communication overhead and energy consumption in the network when identifying these abnormal events. We present a machine learning (ML) framework that is suitable for WSNs to sequentially detect sensory level anomalies and time-related anomalies in an unknown environment. Our system consists of a set of modular, unsupervised, machine learning algorithms that are adaptive. The modularity of the ML algorithms to maximize the use of resource constrains sensor nodes in different environmental monitoring tasks without reprogramming. The developed ML framework consists of the following modular components. First, an unsupervised neural network is used to map multi-dimensional sensor data into discrete environmental states/classes and detect sensor level anomalies. Over time, the labeled classes form a sequence of environmental states. Next, we use a variable length Markov model in the form of a Probabilistic Suffix Tree (PST) to model the relationship between temporal events. Depending on the types of applications, high order Markov models can be expensive. We use a symbol compression technique to bring down the cost of PST models by extracting the semantic meaning out of temporal sequences. Lastly, we use a likelihood-ratio test to verify whether there are anomalous events. We demonstrate the efficiency our approach by applying it in two real-world applications: volcano monitoring and traffic monitoring applications. Our experimental results show that the developed approach yields high performances based on different benchmarks compared to traditional fixed length Markov models.

Y. Li (✉)
Biostatistics Branch, National Institute of Environmental Health Sciences,
National Institutes of Health,
Research Triangle Park, Durham, NC 27709, USA
e-mail: yuanyuan.li@nih.gov

M. Thomason · L.E. Parker
Electrical Engineering and Computer Science, The University of Tennessee,
1520 Middle Drive, Knoxville, TN 37996, USA
e-mail: leparker@utk.edu

M. Thomason
e-mail: thomason@eecs.utk.edu

P. Spagnolo et al. (eds.), *Human Behavior Understanding in Networked Sensing*,
DOI 10.1007/978-3-319-10807-0_5

5.1 Introduction

Wireless Sensor Networks (WSNs) of spatially distributed autonomous sensor nodes collect information and make inferences about the environments that they are sensing. Size and cost constraints on these sensor nodes result in corresponding constraints on resources such as energy, memory, computational speed, and communications bandwidth. As a result, WSNs have inspired resurgence in research on machine learning (ML) methodologies with the objective of overcoming the physical constraints of sensors. Research in WSNs area has focused on networking issues, such as connectivity, deployment, scheduling, allocations, etc; and application issues such as environment monitoring [1–9]. Identifying events or observations that do not conform to an expected pattern (anomaly detection) is one of the most important challenges for environment monitoring, fault diagnosis, surveillance, and intrusion detection in WSNs. A key problem is to minimize communication overhead and energy consumptions in the WSN while identifying these anomalous events.

This paper focuses on the ML issues from the application perspective. Our goal is to develop a distributed ML framework for WSNs to detect sensory level anomalies and time-related anomalous events in previously unknown environments. The term "unknown environment" means that it is infeasible to pre-program the state of the environment and the types of anomalies before system deployment. Both the state of the environment and the types of anomalies must be learned by the system autonomously over an initial period of time.

The development of the ML procedure is inspired by the following design criteria. WSNs typically consist of a large number of sensor nodes; flooding a large amount of collected data through the network for central decision-making can be a huge burden on resource-constrained sensors. It has been shown that hierarchical learning structures in WSNs can significantly reduce data transmitted [3, 10]. Because of a large number of sensors, tuning the parameters of ML algorithms can be a long and tedious process. Therefore, it is important to have the ML algorithms be unsupervised, adaptive, and have as few parameters to adjust as possible. In addition, we believe that the ML framework should be modular, so that the system can serve as many applications as possible without reprogramming. Each ML component can be removed (turned off) if its capability is not required. Due to the nature of WSNs, it is important to have detection decisions in real-time in order to be meaningful to end-users. Besides accurately detecting anomalous events, we also desire the ML algorithms to be computationally efficient. Our online approach is different from conventional approaches because ML techniques like Expectation Maximization (EM)-based and gradient-based algorithms are offline and computationally expensive.

In this work, we propose a hierarchical, distributed, and modular anomaly detection system that can make decisions continuously in real-time. The system uses an online unsupervised classifier to perform sensor fusion from multiple sensors and classify the sensor signals online. We further extend the classifier to detect time-related anomalies through the use of a more robust, high performance and memory efficient anomaly detection method. This method consists of symbol compression approach that extracts the semantic meaning from the raw data, along with a Probabilistic Suffix Tree (PST) that is a data-driven and memory efficient method for anomaly detection. In addition, we use an unsupervised likelihood-ratio detector to make sequential anomaly detection decisions over time.

The contribution of this chapter is the development of a sequential anomaly detection system—a novel general approach that autonomously detects anomalies using sensor data that is collected by a WSN in a distributed fashion. This system exhibits all of the desired characteristics outlined earlier in this section. Our research makes use of a number of existing techniques, combining them in such a way that the system is able to achieve general capabilities that have not been previously achieved for anomaly detection in WSNs. Thus, our contributions are primarily at the systems level. Specifically, this research makes several important contributions to WSN research, including:

- Makes PST practical for time modeling in WSNs by extracting semantics out of temporal sequences.
- Enables the system to save communications costs by compressing temporal sequences in WSNs.
- Enables the system to making sequential decisions without prior knowledge of the types of anomalies in the environment.
- Uses an anomaly detection system that is modular and flexible in design.

The rest of this chapter is organized as follows. We first review the related work in Sect. 5.2. We then present our proposed approach in Sect. 5.3, which includes our network architecture, the time analysis module, and likelihood ratio detector. In Sect. 5.4, we test the approach in two application domains: volcano monitoring and highway traffic monitoring. Finally, we summarize our findings in Sect. 5.5.

5.2 Related Work

Following an iterative design process, we first designed a heuristic finite state machine approach to time series analysis in WSNs in [11]. This prior approach was demonstrated to be successful in detecting time-related anomalies for a robot working with a WSN in an intruder detection problem. However, we subsequently developed a more sophisticated approach to time series analysis, which includes a more powerful variable length Markov model representation, and the ability to compress time sequence data, reported partially in [12], with significant new details and new experiments reported in this current chapter.

Various regression models have been proposed for time-related analysis in WSNs (e.g., [6]). Wang et al. have used AutoRegressive Moving Average (ARMA) models to predict future target positions in a WSN [7]. Most of these systems are linear regression models, which have been widely used outside the wireless sensor network domain as a way to approximate and summarize time series, with applications in finance, communication, weather prediction, and a variety of other areas. However, regression models involve a complex parameter estimation process and may suffer from model mismatch and bias-variance trade-off problems. There has been some work on the use of probabilistic time-series models in WSNs, such as the Kalman Filters (e.g., [13]). These systems rely on a combination of local and global probabilistic models, which are kept in sync to reduce communication between sensor nodes and the sink (e.g., [13]). In general, Kalman Filter-based models are sophisticated and require significant computation, thus making them unsuitable for resource-constrained WSNs.

The fixed length Markov model is another commonly used technique for time series analysis [14]. Examples of fixed order Markov models include the Markov chain and Hidden Markov Model. Due to the limited resources in WSNs, building fixed, high order Markov models is not feasible. Instead, variable length Markov models (VLMMs) are more appropriate [15]. Mazeroff et al [16] implemented VLMM in the forms of PST models and Probabilistic Suffix Automata (PSAs) to build models of benign application behavior with the goal of detecting malicious applications in Windows XP, which can be easily applied to WSNs. The VLMM is a data-driven Markov model that supports online learning and online detection. Note that in practice, the VLMM is usually implemented in the form of a PST or a PSA model. The two models are proven to be equivalent [17]. A PSA model can be inferred directly from a PST model by using the algorithm described in [16]. The PST models depend on a fixed number of random variables; in PST models this number of conditioning random variables may vary based on the specific observed realization. PST model is a data-driven technique, which can be easily applied to WSNs. Our research makes use of the PST to model time sequence data and to detect time-related anomalies. PST models can be expensive in both space and time if not implemented carefully. Many researchers have proposed algorithms to build PST models in linear time and space (e.g., [18]). Lin et al. have proposed an online PST-based time-series visualization tool to aid aerospace analysts [19]. In addition, the method is automatic, and can be applied without assuming any preliminary information. PST models have been applied in WSNs for object tracking (e.g., [5]). To the best of our knowledge, our work is the first work that makes use of a PST model to detect time-related anomalies in WSNs. Our results show that a PST has the same performance as the same order Markov model with less memory cost. The PST model has been shown in applications involving prediction (in non-WSN applications) in [20] as well.

5.3 Approach

In this section, we first introduce the overall system architecture. Then, we discuss temporal models in detail. Lastly, we describe our sequential anomaly detection process via likelihood-ratio test.

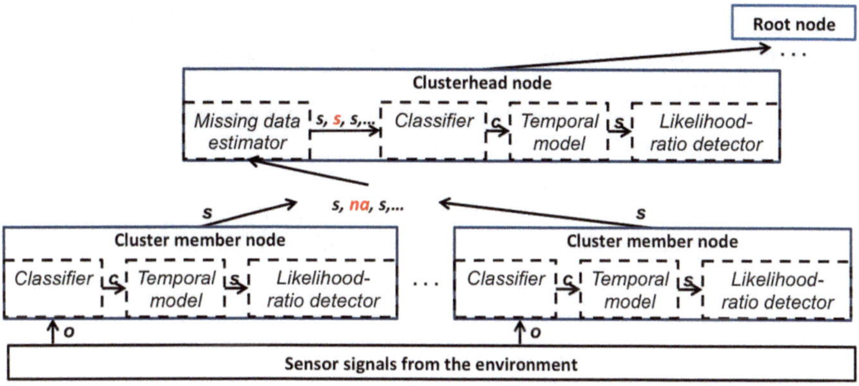

Fig. 5.1 The overall learning architecture for WSN. All sensor nodes run the same programming image. Depending on the role of the sensor node (clusterhead/cluster member), the assigned modules are activated. The cluster members use raw sensor signals as input and detect anomalies at a local level. The (compressed) sequences of class labels are then sent to the clusterhead to detect anomalies at a higher level. The root clusterhead has an overall representation of the environment

5.3.1 Architecture for the WSNs

We use a hierarchical learning/communication structure for our WSN. The sensor nodes in the WSN are divided into clusters, as shown in Fig. 5.1. Each cluster has a clusterhead and multiple cluster members. Each cluster covers a geographic region and is responsible for detecting the environmental changes in that region. Both cluster members and clusterheads run an identical detection system—a classifier, a time analysis model, a likelihood-ratio test detector, and a missing data estimator. Cluster members read in vectors of raw sensor signals (e.g., light and sound) from the environment as input, and then perform sensor fusion and classify sensor signals into corresponding classes. If the signals do not match those of the existing classes, an abnormal alert is raised. The details of our unsupervised classifier can be found in [11]. Over time, our system accumulates a sequence of environmental states/class that describe the temporal events in the environment. Cluster members build temporal models that describe the temporal events in their monitoring regions. Then, likelihood-ratio tests are performed to verify if there are anomalous temporal events at local levels. After the classification process, class labels are transmitted to their higher level clusterheads. Clusterheads often cannot receive complete labels from all of their cluster members, due to unstable wireless communications. Ignoring missing data would result in too many false positives (as justified in our previous work [21, 22]). Thus, the clusterheads first preprocess the collected class labels by identifying and estimating the missing values (using our technique described in [21]). Since the learning system has a hierarchical structure, clusterheads may have higher level clusterheads, which classify their class labels. Finally, the root node obtains the final model of the environment. With this learning architecture, the system is able to detect both abnormal environmental changes and time-related changes. Note that we assume cluster assignment is given. Therefore, optimal cluster design is not in the scope of this research.

We keep our design in a modular form because it gives human operators the flexibility of turning off the modules that are not needed. For example, the operator can turn off the time analysis module if analyzing time is not of interest. In addition, the WSN can be easily scaled to a large number of sensors. At the same time, this hierarchical approach reduces communication, which in turn saves energy in the WSN.

5.3.2 Temporal Models

After the sensor fusion and classification process is finished, the system further checks whether there are time-related changes. Figure 5.2 demonstrates the flow of the sensor signals of an individual sensor node in our system, which is a significant extension over our prior design in [11]. The temporal sequence model is a two-step process. First, the sequence of classes is compressed with a symbol compressor (described in Sect. 5.3.2.1). It operates efficiently by sampling the string statistics in a manner that allows a compressed representation and exact reconstruction of the original string. Depending on the implementation, learning and generating can be offline or online, real-time or non-real-time. Then, the compressed events are built into a PST model (described in Sect. 5.3.2.1). In order to detect time-related changes, the system measures the likelihood of the current compressed sequence, compared to the PST model(s) learned during the training phase (described in Sect. 5.3.2.2).

Note that we propose this two-step structure to make our system more flexible when capturing the temporal sequence information. For example, system designers may substitute another symbol compression method or Markov-based model as desired. When modeling the temporal sequence, if time duration within a state (class) is not of interest, the designers can simply remove all consecutive repeated class labels in the symbol compression stage and let the PST model only the state sequences.

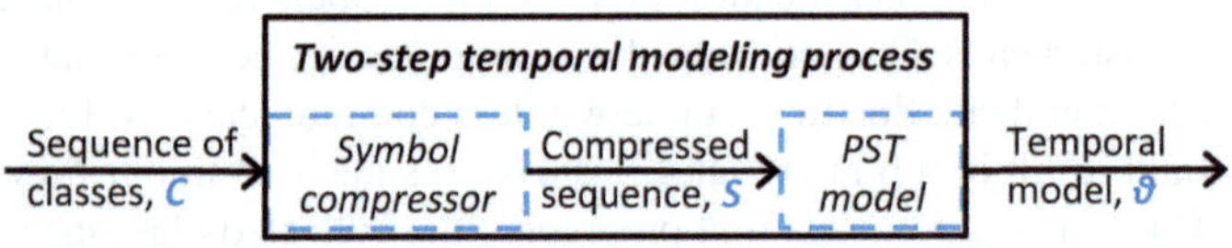

Fig. 5.2 The proposed architecture for an individual sensor node. Each sensor node consists of three components: a classifier to detect anomalies in the sensor signals, a symbol compressor to compress the temporal sequence, and a time model to detect time-related anomalies

5.3.2.1 Identifying Semantic Symbols from Temporal Classes

Identifying semantic symbols is of particular interest since it allows reasoning to be extended from individual temporal classes to a higher semantic level. These semantic symbols can be constructed using compression algorithms. Compression algorithms can roughly be categorized into lossless or lossy compression. Lempel-Ziv 77/78 and Lempel-Ziv-Welch (LZW) are the most widely used dictionary-based compression techniques [23]. The main mechanism in both schemes is pattern matching: find sequence patterns that have occurred in the past and compress them by encoding a reference to the previous occurrence. Our temporal sequence compression process is defined as follows. The encoder/compression algorithm takes a sequence of class labels $C = \{c_1, \ldots, c_T\}$ and compresses it into another sequence denoted by S, which encodes higher-level semantic meaning.

The LZW algorithm performs limited analysis to the sequence. Thus, it is designed to be fast but may not be optimal. With the limited resources of a WSN, it is important to reduce the amount of processing. In a typical compression run, the algorithm takes a string as input, and processes the string using a dictionary of distinct substrings. The algorithm encodes the string (and builds the dictionary) by making a single left to right traversal of a sequence. Initially, the dictionary contains the alphabet with its corresponding encoding. Then it sequentially adds every new substring that differs by a single last character from the longest match that already exists in the dictionary. This repeats until the string is consumed. The idea is that, as the string is being processed, the dictionary is populated with longer strings, and allows encoding of longer substrings of the string at each replacement. For example, suppose we have a source temporal sequence with a three-letter alphabet $\Sigma = \{1, 2, 3\}$, and we wish to compress the temporal sequence $C = \{1, 2, 2, 2, 2, 3, 3, 1, 2, 3, 2, 2, 2, 2, 1, 3\}$. Based on knowledge about the source sequence C, LZW builds the dictionary shown in Table 5.1. The output encoded string of S in this example is $\{0, 1, 4, 1, 2, 2, 3, 2, 5, 1, 0, 2\}$.

The interpretation of the temporal sequence compression process is as follows. Each entry in the dictionary denotes a subsequence in the initial temporal sequence to be compressed, while the corresponding index is the "new" compressed temporal symbol with higher semantic meaning. The compressed sequence carries the higher

Table 5.1 Example dictionary built by LZW algorithm

Dictionary			
Index (code)	Entry (class labels)	Index (code)	Entry (class labels)
0	1	7	33
1	2	8	31
2	3	9	123
3	12	10	32
4	22	11	2222
5	222	12	21
6	23	13	13

level semantic meaning of the initial temporal sequence. The length of each dictionary entry corresponds to a real-world event in discrete time. Specifically, the length of a single-alphabet entry in the dictionary denotes the time duration of the event's occurrence and the corresponding index carries that semantic meaning. For example, the entry "2222" in Table 5.1 indicates the environment is in state "2" for 4 time units. The corresponding index "11" indicates 4 time units of state "2" in the compressed temporal sequence. Dictionary entries with multiple alphabets may have a real-world meaning as well. For example, the entry "12" could correspond in the real world to a person taking 1 min to add coffee powder and water into a coffee machine, and then it takes the machine 1 min to make a pot of coffee. The whole process is now associated with an index "3" that has the real semantic meaning "making-coffee". Therefore, the compressed temporal sequence is able to maintain the higher level semantics of the initial temporal sequence while using a shorter length.

In WSNs, transmitting a compressed sequence saves communication costs compared to transmitting uncompressed raw data. Note that with the proposed two-step temporal modeling process, it is not necessary to keep all entries in the dictionary. Especially with limited memory in the wireless sensor nodes, we wish to build a small dictionary. If a system can afford to build a PST with order up to M, dictionary entries with length shorter than M can be pruned, since they can be modeled by an Mth order PST. System designers may choose to further prune the dictionary entries based on their knowledge of the application. To further prune the dictionary, system designers may select relevant features based on the application. The relevant features are the dictionary entries with real-world meanings that are relevant to the specified application.

5.3.2.2 Modeling Semantic Interactions Using PSTs

A practical application may have days or months of normal activity followed by an anomaly lasting only minutes. A WSN that is designed to model time sequences should be able to model this process and be able to detect such anomalies. However, it is infeasible to model the activity using a traditional high order Markov chain, since an Lth order Markov model requires $|\Sigma|^L$ states, where $|\Sigma|$ denotes the number of alphabet symbols and L is the length of past history/memory being modeled. For a large variety of time-related sequential data, statistical correlations decrease rapidly with the distance between symbols in the sequence. If the statistical correlations are indeed decreasing, then there exists a *memory* length M such that the empirical probability changes very little if conditioned on subsequences longer than M. Ron et al. [17] proposed a solution to this problem. The underlying observation in that work is that in many natural sequences, the memory length depends on the context and therefore is not fixed. Therefore, as in [17], we propose to use a Variable Length Markov Model (VLMM) to preserve the minimal subsequences (of variable lengths) that are necessary for precise modeling of the given statistical source. This results in a more flexible and efficient sequence representation. It is particularly attractive in cases where we need to capture higher order temporal dependencies in some parts of the behavior and lower order dependencies elsewhere. The VLMM model can be implemented in the form of Probabilistic Suffix Tree (PST). A PST is a tree whose nodes are organized such that the root node gives the probability of each symbol of the alphabet while nodes at subsequent levels give next-symbol probabilities conditioned on a combination of one or more symbols having been seen first.

The constructed PST model is a symbolic predictive model: the underlying continuous time signals are first abstracted to a discrete space, analogous to a set of finite classes. In some cases, this has the advantage of being more immune to the problems of noise while still preserving the essential underlying patterns or dependencies that govern behavior in the observed domain. Arguably, it also produces a more understandable model since its components are higher level abstractions. All these advantages of the PST model make it suitable to model temporal sequences in WSNs.

One of the challenges of using a PST model on resource constrained sensor nodes is that the model complexity may grow exponentially with the memory depending on the data, which makes it impractical for resource constrained sensor nodes. Using PST models directly to model the sensor data is computationally prohibitive. Thus, we use a data-driven approach to automatically infer discrete and abstract representations (symbols) of primitive object interactions. These symbols are then used as an alphabet to infer the high level structures of typical interactive behaviors using PST models. This Markov model represents high-level semantic notions. These environment features are invariant of the sensor classes and time dependencies. They constitute the input to a statistical learning framework where discrete representations of interactive behaviors can be learned by modeling the probability distribution of the feature vectors within the interaction feature space.

Symbolic modeling and processing have several advantages over continuous measurements and models, including: (1) sensor data is often discrete (e.g., certain radar systems [14]); (2) environments that are modeled with discrete states that have clear physical interpretations are natural and easy for humans to interpret (e.g., volcanic eruption or no eruption vs. vibration measurements); and (3) data compression techniques, which we use to reduce the size of the observations, typically require discrete state representations.

The PST model [17], which was originally designed for classification purposes, has the advantage of improved extraction of statistical information from sequences. The trade-off is that it deliberately throws away some of the original subsequences during the analysis process to maintain a compact representation. In resource constrained WSNs, compact data models save energy in nodes by reducing the amount of data being transferred among the nodes. We are interested in building models of the environment that are able to support both interpretation and anomaly detection. We achieve this by using PSTs to efficiently encode the sequences of the classes corresponding to observed interactive behavior in the feature space. In the following, we provide more details of the PST. Then, we explain how the PST is used to detect time-related anomalies in the WSN.

The PST is a stochastic model that uses a suffix tree as the index structure. This approach is based on the "memory" of natural sequences. That is, the root node of the PST gives the empirical probability of each symbol in the alphabet while each node at subsequent levels is associated with a vector that gives the next symbol given the label of the node as the preceding segment. For example, $P(s_{i+1}|s_0 \ldots s_i) = P(s_{i+1}|s_{i-M} \ldots s_i)$, where $i > M$, gives the empirical probability distribution P of the next symbol s_{i+1} given the last M symbols in the preceding segment. Furthermore, a tree of order M has M levels beyond the root. To illustrate, consider a (compressed) sequence $S = \{1, 2, 3, 1, 2, 3, 2, 1, 3\}$ with a three-letter alphabet $\Sigma = \{1, 2, 3\}$. Figure 5.3 shows the order-2 PST inferred from the observation. Beginning with the root node, which represents the empty string, each node is a suffix of all its children. The probability vector below the nodes gives the conditional next-symbol probabilities. Moreover, all symbols are shown on the same level of the tree. Next symbol "transitions" jump from one branch to another, not from a parent node to its children. This transition pattern is due to the suffix format of the node labels. Some branches typically die out early while other branches propagate to the maximum depth of the tree. Additionally, if a child node carries an identical next-symbol probability distribution as its parent node, the child node is pruned. Detailed PST inference and pruning procedures can be found in [16].

Let $S = \{s_u : u \in U\}$ denote a compressed temporal sequence of size U, where u denotes the discrete time unit after compression. To model the normal behavior using the Maximum Likelihood criterion, we find a model that maximizes the probability of a given sequence of observations. Given a PST θ, the total likelihood of the observations can be expressed mathematically as $L = P(S|\theta)$. If the probability of

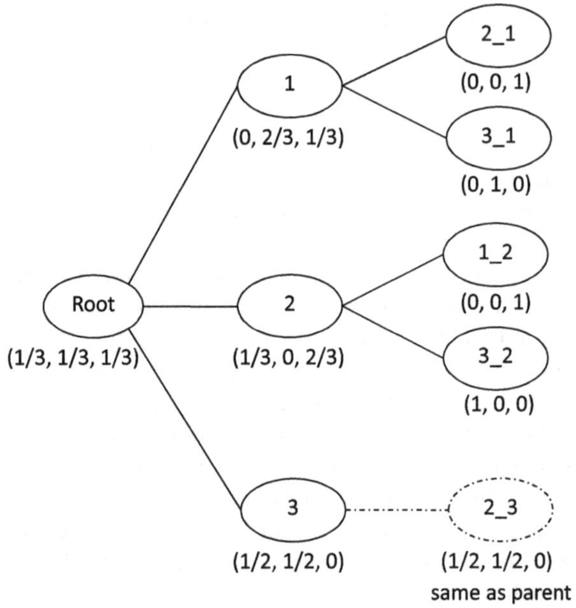

Fig. 5.3 An example order-2 PST based on a compressed sequence $S = \{1, 2, 3, 1, 2, 3, 2, 1, 3\}$

the observation sequence given the model is below a threshold c, then an anomaly is detected. A likelihood-ratio detection scheme is addressed in detail in the following subsection.

The computation for this procedure is fast and inexpensive. The PST model has been shown to be implementable in linear time and space [18]. Let the length of the training sequence be n, the memory length of PST be M, the alphabet be Σ, and the length of a testing sequence be k. Apostolico and Bejerano's PST building algorithm takes $O(n|\Sigma|)$ time [18]. This procedure is a one-time overhead cost to the system during the initial period (unless the PST needs to be updated). To detect anomalies after the PST is constructed, the system has to calculate the likelihood that the testing sequence matches the built PST. The sequence matching procedure is a simple tree traversal, and the detection procedure takes $O(mk)$ time. Thus, it is practical for sensor nodes that have limited resources.

5.3.3 Likelihood-Ratio Test for Anomaly Detection

In statistics, a likelihood ratio test is used to compare the fit of two models, one of which (the null model) is a special case of the other (the alternative model). The test is based on the likelihood ratio, which expresses how many times more likely the data are under one model than the other. Like statistical hypothesis testing in general, it has been widely used in many different areas of applications such as speaker verification [24].

Let X denote a hypothesized sequence of events, f_0 denote the distribution of a normal sequence of events, and f_1 denote the distribution of abnormal sequence of events. Suppose that the testing sequence X has one of two possible distributions f_0 or f_1. The task of anomaly detection is to determine if X is has probability density function f_0. The anomaly detection task can be restated as a hypothesis test between:

H_0: X has probability density function f_0

and

H_1: X has probability density function f_1

The test that we construct is based on the following idea: if we observe $X = x$, then the condition $f_1(x) > f_0(x)$ is evidence in favor of the alternative; the opposite inequality if evidence against the alternative.

We are interested in detecting anomalies in an unknown environment. We assume that during the initial training time, we can observe typical normal events; in addition to the normal events, there could be abnormal events and/or unknown events. Ideally, we could build a typical normal model of the environment and use χ^2 statistics to determine the abnormal events that deviate from the normal model. However, the maximum probability of observed sequence given an alternative model is not easy to calculate. Therefore, we use a simple-versus-simple hypotheses test that has completely specified models under both the null and alternative hypotheses.

The parameter space is $\Theta = \{\theta_0, \theta_1\}$, and f_0 denotes the probability density function of X when $\theta = \theta_0$ and f_1 denotes the probability density function of X when $\theta = \theta_1$. The hypotheses are equivalent to:

$$H_0 : \theta = \theta_0 \text{ versus } H_1 : \theta = \theta_1 \tag{5.1}$$

The likelihood ratio test statistics can be written as

$$\Lambda(x) = \frac{L(\theta_0|x)}{L(\theta_1|x)} = \frac{f(x|\theta_0)}{f(x|\theta_1)} \tag{5.2}$$

In the form stated above, the likelihood ratio is small if the alternative model is better than the null model; the likelihood ratio test provides the decision rule as

$$\begin{cases} \text{if } \Lambda \geq c & \text{accept } H_0 \\ \text{if } \Lambda < c & \text{reject } H_0 \end{cases} \tag{5.3}$$

where the decision threshold for accepting or rejecting H_0 is a constant c. For our temporal anomaly detection, the null and alternative hypotheses use PST models θ. Hence, we denote the PST model for the null hypothesis as $p(x|H_0; \theta_0)$ and for the alternative hypothesis as $p(x|H_1; \theta_1)$. The likelihood-ratio sequential decision process is given by $p(x|H_0; \theta_0)/p(x|H_1; \theta_1)$. Usually, the logarithm of this statistic is used giving the log-likelihood ratio,

$$\Lambda(x) = \log(x|H_0; \theta_0) - \log(x|H_1; \theta_1) \tag{5.4}$$

Ideally, we would use normal events to train the PST model θ_0, and abnormal events to train the PST model θ_1; the likelihood-ratio $\Lambda(x)$ is the ratio of normal model versus abnormal model. However, in practice, it is often difficult to obtain typical abnormal models. A solution to this problem is to use all available events as the abnormal model. This is known as the Universal Background Model (UBM) [24]. Therefore, we train the PST model θ_0 using normal events and θ_1 using all possible events including normal, abnormal, and unknown events. The reason is that during the training period, we may encounter various event sequences that are normal, abnormal, and/or undetermined. The model for H_0 can be estimated using a normal event sequence. However, the model for H_1 is less well-defined since it potentially must represent every abnormal situation possible. Since the environments that WSNs operate in are typically unknown, it is not possible to train H_1 with every abnormal situation. Therefore, we believe the UWB, which uses all sequences of events, is a more suitable way to define H_1.

5.4 Experiments

The primary objective of this research is to design a robust sequential anomaly detection system for resource constrained WSNs that is applicable to a wide range of applications. Thus, to validate our approach, we illustrate it in two domains—volcano monitoring and highway traffic monitoring. Each experiment illustrates different aspects of our approach. In the volcano monitoring application we show the system making sequential detections using a single seismic sensor, while in the highway traffic monitoring application, we show a network of sensors detecting unusual events in traffic patterns.

5.4.1 Performance Metrics

The following performance metrics are used to evaluate our system: compression ratio, and the receiver operating characteristic (ROC) curve. The compression ratio refers to the ratio of the size of data before compression and the size of data after compression, i.e., *uncompressed data/compressed data*. The detection outcome can be described in the contengency table shown in Table 5.2. The ROC curve is created by plotting the fraction of true positives out of the true positive rate (TPR) versus the false positive rate (FPR), at various likelihood-ratio threshold settings. Finally, the FPR or false alarm rate is the fraction of negative examples predicted as positive class, i.e., $\text{FPR} = \text{FP}/(\text{TN} + \text{FP})$, while the FNR or miss rate is the fraction of positive examples predicated as a negative class, i.e., $\text{FNR} = \text{FN}/(\text{TP} + \text{FN})$. Ideally, the values of sensitivity and specificity are at 100 %; and the values of false alarm rate and miss rate are at 0 %.

5.4.2 Volcano Monitoring Application

We use a volcano monitoring dataset to test the proposed anomaly detection system. Specifically, this test serves as a proof-of-concept to illustrate how our enhanced time modeling module works on a real-world dataset. The dataset was collected by

Table 5.2 2 × 2 Contingency

Ground truth (gold standard)			
Detection	True positive (TP)	False positive (FP)	Precision PPV $= \frac{\text{TP}}{\text{TP+FN}}$
Outcome	False negative (FN)	True negative (TN)	Negative predictive value NPV $= \frac{\text{TN}}{\text{TN+FN}}$
	Sensitivity TPR $= \frac{\text{TP}}{\text{TP+FN}}$	Specificity SPC $= \frac{\text{TN}}{(\text{FP+TN})}$	Accuracy ACC $= \frac{\text{TP+TN}}{(\text{TP+FP+TN+FN})}$

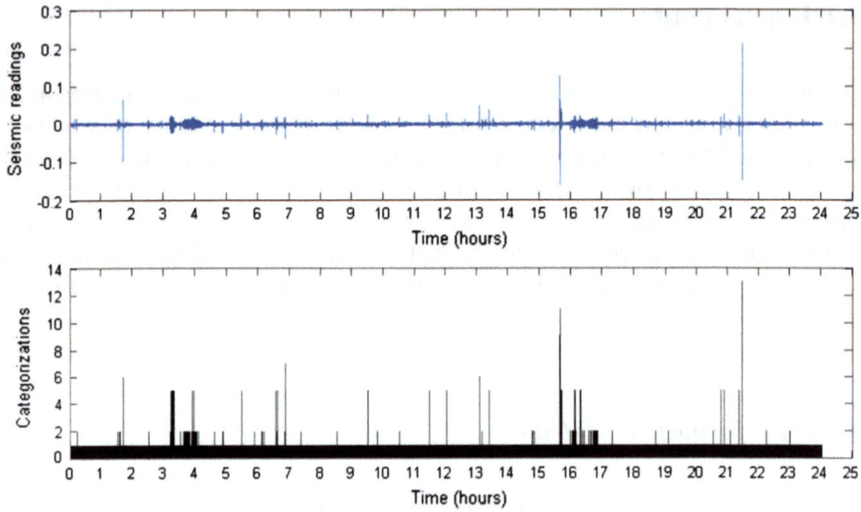

Fig. 5.4 *Top* Raw seismic readings over a time period of 24 h [9]. *Bottom* The classifications based on the raw seismic readings

Werner-Allen et al. over a 24 h time period at the Volcano Reventador [9]. The data used in our experiments was obtained from one of the seismic stations, which samples the environment at 120 Hz. Since the data are voluminous, we have analyzed one day's worth of data, which is approximately 200 Mb. These data are from a single station (a single sensor node). The classes are assumed to carry the higher semantic meaning of the data, such as different levels of volcanic activities. Then, we can analyze the sequence of activities to understand their temporal semantic meanings. Observe that in the data of Fig. 5.4 there are more than 15 h of no activities followed by an eruption of less than a minute. The top part of Fig. 5.4 shows the raw seismic sensor readings recorded over a 24 h time period. We applied the unsupervised classifier (described in [11]) to classify the sensor signals into 13 distinct classes (see the bottom part of Fig. 5.4).

Our experiments with volcano data do not involve clusters or clusterheads. However, the detection process for the entire WSN work is described in Sect. 5.3. We have also demonstrated in our prior work [11, 21] that our developed detection system works with multiple layers of clusters of sensor nodes that use multiple sensors in our lab environments. Our approach in [11, 21] uses heuristic discrete states to model time; however since the 2-step temporal modeling approach proposed in this chapter also uses discrete state representations, we believe this should work with the existing system architecture when implemented on the physical nodes. We also illustrate the hierarchical approach in the traffic monitoring application, which follows this subsection. The current approach is more robust when detecting multiple anomalies in the environment and takes less communication by transmitting compressed temporal sequences.

5.4.2.1 Preprocessing

The top part of Fig. 5.4 depicts the raw seismic readings recorded over a 24 h time period. The raw seismic data O is normalized and classed by our classifier described in [11]. as shown in the bottom part of Fig. 5.4. The raw sensor data O is classified into $|\Sigma| = 13$ classes by setting the vigilance parameter ρ of the classifier to 0.93. Hence, the output temporal classification sequence C has an alphabet size $|\Sigma|$ of 13. Note that the physical meaning of these 13 classes is unknown, since we do not have a seismic geologists's analysis of this data. In the future work, if we have the groundtruth of the seismic data, the classifier can assign more meaningful classes (e.g., magnitudes of eruptions) by adjusting its vigilance parameter ρ. The data are grouped into hour-long subsets. Based on visual inspection, there are no volcanic activities during the period between the 1st hour and the 15th hour; we regard this period as the normal period. There is an anomaly/eruption between the 15th hour and the 16th hour. Thus, we regard this hour as an abnormal period. We are unable to determine whether the periods following the eruption are "normal after eruption" or "abnormal". As a result, we currently discard the data after the 16th hour. In summary, we treat hours 1–15 as a normal period and hour 16 as an abnormal period.

5.4.2.2 PST Versus Fixed Length Markov Model

We first compare the performances between the PST model and the traditional fixed length Markov model on the volcano monitoring dataset. In this experiment, we use the abnormal period's class sequence (hour 16) as training data and the normal periods' (hours 1–15) class sequences as testing data. The performance is measured by the negative log-likelihood of the normal class sequence given the observation of the abnormal class sequence. Specifically, we construct both PST and fixed length Markov models from the training data with Markov orders 1, 2, 3, 4, 5, and 10. For each PST/fixed length Markov model, we calculate the negative log-likelihood $P(C|\lambda)$ of the testing sequence C given the PST/fixed length Markov model λ. The larger the negative log-likelihood value is, the more dissimilar are the compared sequences. We expect the dissimilarity between the abnormal period and the normal period to grow as the memory order grows.

Our results are summarized in Table 5.3. The empirical results indicate that the sizes of PST models are much smaller than the traditional fixed length Markov models as the order increases. For example, observe that the 10th order fixed length Markov model uses 981 states, while the order-10 PST model only uses 205 states. The negative log-likelihood is the same between a sequence given a PST model and a fixed length Markov model with the same order, since we eliminate nodes that have the same probabilities as their parent nodes when constructing the PST models. The model is lossless in terms of capturing the information of the training data. Therefore, we prefer a PST model over a fixed-length Markov model because it is purely data-driven, flexible, and most importantly, takes less space. Note that the PST models can be pruned to remove some low probability nodes (see [17]); however, this will

Table 5.3 Comparison of fixed length Markov models versus PST models

	Order	Number of nodes	Negative log-likelihood
Fixed length Markov	1	12	−0.0141
	2	45	−0.0112
	3	104	−0.0092
	4	190	−0.0078
	5	296	−0.0069
	10	**981**	−0.0046
PST	1	12	−0.0141
	2	41	−0.0112
	3	76	−0.0092
	4	116	−0.0078
	5	146	−0.0069
	10	**205**	−0.0046

lead to information loss. In the future work, we will evaluate the proposed detection system based on PST models with thresholds to remove low probability nodes. In addition, we explore a systematic procedure for deciding the threshold values for PST models in the proposed detection system.

5.4.2.3 PST Model with Compressed Temporal Sequence

As shown in the previous section, using the PST model directly on the volcano monitoring dataset is still not practical for the resource limited sensor nodes, i.e., it takes 208 states to build a PST model with a memory of 10 observations. An observation with 10 samples can hardly capture any meaningful sequences in the environment monitoring type of applications. In reality, daily-life activities usually take more than 10 observations to capture. If modeling such a long sequence of actions is important to an application, the PST model will not be a practical solution if used directly on the raw samples. Our proposed compression technique, in which the PST is built from the higher level symbol representation rather than the original data, addresses this issue.

We applied the standard LZW symbol compression algorithm on the class sequences of the dataset. The average dictionary size for 16 h (excluding the pre-built characters in the dictionary) is approximately 61 entries per hour. Table 5.4 shows some sample entries. Based on the given data, we observe that there are long periods of inactivity, which are denoted by sequences of class "1". Then, we apply the compression algorithm to all 16 h of data independently. The average compression ratio for the 16 h is approximately 33:1. The compressed representation of data saves on both processing power and reduces the amount of storage on the sensor nodes. Most importantly, when the local sensor nodes transmit the temporal models to the clusterheads, they are able to save the transmission power as well.

Table 5.4 Partial dictionary of the volcano data

Entry (class labels)
...
1111111122
211111115
51511
111112111111
11111111111111111111111111111...11111111115
51111111
...

For sequential detection decisions, we employ a universal likelihood-ratio detection scheme as given in Eq. (5.3). The detection procedure works as follows: during the training period, we use semantics (compressed symbols) from hours 1 to 16 to obtain the alternative hypothesis $p(S|H_1)$, and hour 16 to obtain the null hypothesis $p(S|H_0)$. In order to determine the detection threshold c, we use the Receiver Operating Characteristic (ROC). ROC is a graphical plot of the *TPR*/sensitivity versus the FPR/false alarm rate for a binary classifier system as its discrimination threshold is varied. We have built two PST models for the dataset of orders 5 and 10. Figure 5.5 shows the ROC curve for the order-5 PST model (left), as well as the ROC curve for the order-10 PST (right). Note that each prediction result (or one instance of a confusion matrix) represents one point in the ROC space. The best possible prediction method would yield a point in the upper left corner representing no false negatives and no false positives. From Fig. 5.5 (left), we observe that the optimal operating point for the order-5 PST model is with a TPR of 84 % and a FPR of 19 %. From Fig. 5.5 (right), we observe that the optimal operating point for the order-10 PST model is with a TPR of 98 % and a FPR of 5 %. We use the optimal operating points as references to choose likelihood ratio threshold c values in Eq. (5.3). Table 5.5 shows the results of different values of the threshold θ. Based on the detection performances,

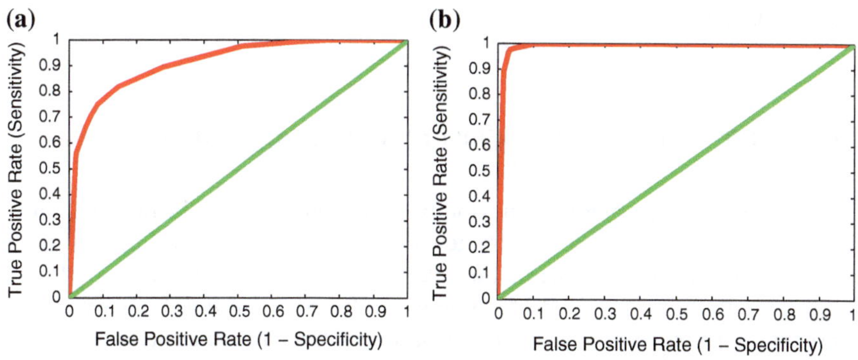

Fig. 5.5 ROC curves built from order-5 PST model and order-10 PST model. **a** ROC curve for order-5 PST model. **b** ROC curve for order-10 PST model

Table 5.5 Performances for PST orders 5 and 10 w compression

PST order	Threshold (c)	Sensitivity (TPR) %	Specificity (TNR) %
5	0.4803	89.47	71.59
	0.493	**83.63**	**81.44**
	0.5057	81.87	84.79
	0.5184	80.70	86.24
10	0.4911	100.00	89.84
	0.5039	98.25	93.69
	0.5167	**98.25**	**95.20**
	0.5295	96.49	97.10

the sensitivity (TPR) for the order-5 PST model is 83.63 % when $c = 0.493$, which has the best trade-off between sensitivity and specificity. The sensitivity (TPR) for the order-10 PST model is 98.25 % when $c = 0.5167$, which has the best trade-off between sensitivity and specificity. It is the closest value to the order-10 PST ROC optimal point. Therefore, we choose c values of 0.493 and 0.5167 for PSTs of orders 5 and 10, respectively. In addition, the specificity for PST orders 5 and 10 PST models are 81.44 and 95.2 %, respectively. The sensitivity and specificity are relatively high for both PST models. This indicates the ROC curves provide good reference when choosing the values for threshold θ. The tree sizes for the orders 5 and 10 PST models are 186 and 241 nodes, respectively. Note that the nodes of PST models that are built from compressed sequences represent higher semantic temporal meanings. Therefore, the nodes represent much longer observations compared to the nodes of the PSTs that are built from the uncompressed sequences, (i.e., the order 10 PST is modeling a sequence with approximately 330 observations compared to 10 observations). The detection results show that our proposed PST model with symbol compression method is able to detect anomalies with high performance. Additionally, the UWB-based likelihood ratio detector is robust and able to detect multiple anomalies in a time sequence with high performance. The robustness and the ability of detecting multiple anomalies are significant enhancements to our previous heuristic state machine [11].

5.4.3 Caltrans Highway Traffic Monitoring Application

To evaluate the effectiveness and flexibility of our approach for a hierarchical sensor network, we have evaluated our framework in the application of highway traffic monitoring using data from the Caltrans Performance Measurement System (PeMS) project. The traffic data of the PeMS system is collected in real-time from over 25,000 sensors that span the freeway system across all major metropolitan areas of the State of California [25]. Existing research studies using the PeMS database include sensor fault detection [26], detection of spatial configuration errors in traffic surveillance

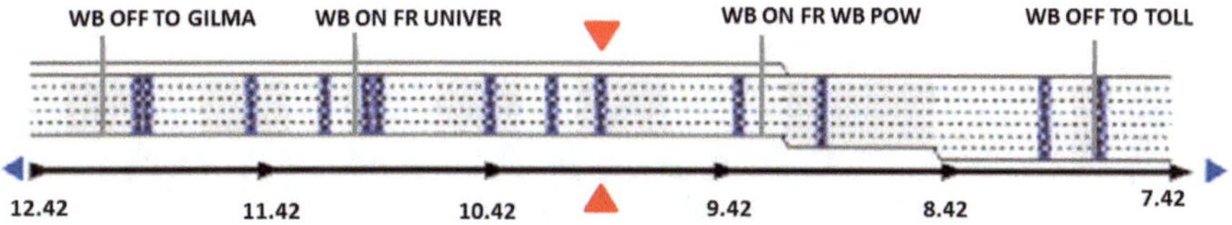

Fig. 5.6 Sensor network deployment on highway I-80 west. The chosen location is marked in *red*

sensors [4], and analysis of highway congestion [27]. Our goal in this study is to determine whether our proposed anomaly detection system is flexible enough to be applied in very different domains; in this case, for detecting highway incidents, which is a significantly different domain from seismic analysis.

In a typical highway sensor deployment under PeMS, a single sensor is positioned in each highway lane, as illustrated in Fig. 5.6. For our study, we chose four highway segments on highway I-80 with various traffic patterns. Highway I-80 has been studied in many research projects such as [28–30]. One of the highway segments is very congested—specifically, the highway I-80 westbound lanes near the 9.92 mile marker in the San Francisco Bay Area. The Vehicle Detector Station (VDS) located at the chosen location is 400803. The rest of the highway segments are VDS 314491 in District 3, Sacramento Country, at the 95.85 mile marker; VDS 400929 in District 4 Contra Costa County, at the 42.45 mile marker; and VDS 401790 in District 4, Solano County, at the 20.62 mile marker. All chosen highway segments have five (5) lanes, each lane has one detector. For example, VDS 400803 has lane detection IDs 405018 to 405022 for lanes 1–5, respectively. We treat sensor data collected from each lane as an individual cluster member sensor node. We obtain data from PeMS over a period of three (3) weeks, from August 2 to 22, 2010. This dataset gives us 6,048 data samples per detector, totaling 30,240 samples across the five (5) sensors and 120,960 samples for all four (4) VDS. This particular subset of the data had 65 incidents associated with VDS 400803, 14 incidents associated with VDS 401790, 49 incidents associated with VDS 400929, and 62 incidents associated with VDS 314491. These incidents served as the ground truth for our studies. Each sensor is sampled once every five (5) minutes (i.e., 12 samples per hour), and returns four (4) features: flow, speed, delay(35), and delay(45). The flow feature measures the number of vehicles that pass by the sensor in a given period of time. The 5 min speed is computed from the flow and occupancy using the usual formula speed $=$ flow$/$occupancy $*\ G$, where G is the average effective vehicle length, and is set to 6 m (20 ft). The delay(x) feature, where x is either 35 or 45, is the additional travel time required for a vehicle to travel a given distance, compared to a standard speed of 35 or 45 miles per hour. In addition to the raw sensor measurements, the PeMS dataset also includes manual notations of traffic events that are reported at given time periods. Sensors that are within one (1) mile of these events are tagged with the associated event data. Example traffic events that are noted in PeMS include traffic collision, hit and run, vehicle driving on center divider, traffic hazard, pedestrian on road, etc (Fig. 5.7).

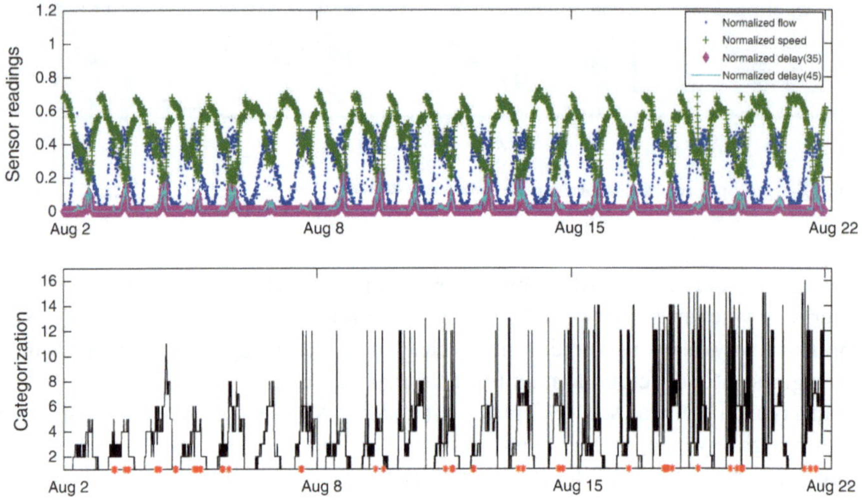

Fig. 5.7 *Top* Normalized sensor readings for lane 5 at VDS 400803, including: flow, speed, delay(35) and delay(45). *Bottom* Unsupervised classifer for lane 5. The *red stars* indicate incidents

To illustrate our hierarchical sensor network approach, we simulated an additional clusterhead sensor for these five (5) traffic lane sensors. Thus, each of the five cluster member nodes would use the real traffic data as input to our anomaly detection system to detect incidents based on local observations. Each cluster member would then send its learned class labels to the clusterhead, which would detect anomalies based on the combination of the local sensors' class labels. To train our sensor network, we divided the samples by week, due to the natural temporal patterns of the traffic data. That is, the traffic data tends to follow daily and weekly cycles. Since the data is relatively sparse (e.g., 5 min per sample), we decided to train the system using weekly cycles. Therefore, we use the first week's data as training samples and the rest of the two weeks' data as testing samples. We further divide the training samples by each hour. We marked the hour as normal if the hour has no accident (as classified by the PeMS dataset), and we marked the data samples that fell into the incident periods as abnormal traffic patterns. We build a normal PST model using all the normal temporal sequences and a universal PST model using all the training samples (i.e., normal + abnormal samples). Since the sample rate is sparse, we turned off the temporal symbol compressor module. This demonstrates the modularity of our approach.

Using our approach, the raw sensor data are first processed by the unsupervised classifier. We set the vigilance levels as 0.9 and 0.8 for cluster members and the clusterhead, respectively. The parameters roughly represent natural traffic patterns over a week. For example, using the threshold 0.9 for lane 5 at the VDS 400803, the traffic data was classified into 16 classes by the classifier, as illustrated in Fig. 5.8. The top figure shows the normalized sensor readings, and the bottom figure shows

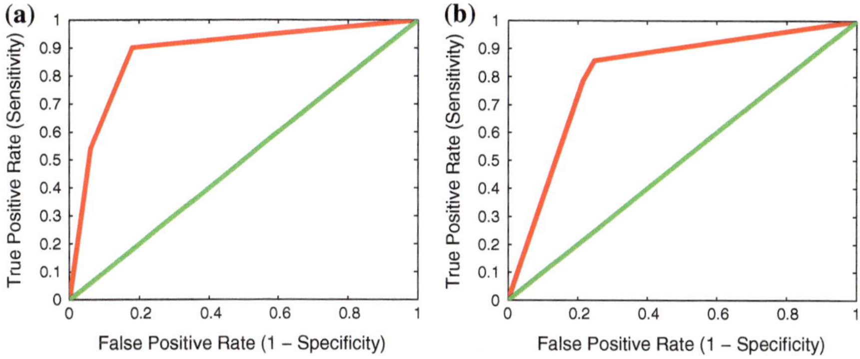

Fig. 5.8 ROC curves built from order-1 PST model (**a**) and 1-state HMM model (**b**) for the clusterhead's detection system of the VDS 400803

the classifications. The incidents are marked in red. We can clearly see the daily patterns over a week with the chosen vigilance levels.

For comparison purposes, we also train a Hidden Markov Model (HMM). In the HMM approach, we replace the PST model with a HMM model, keeping the classifier module and the UBM likelihood-ratio detection module the same as our proposed system. To train the HMM, we first randomly initialize the prior, transition matrix and the observation matrix. Then, we apply the Expectation-Maximization (EM) [31] algorithm to learn the parameters of the HMM model offline. The EM algorithm runs until convergence or for a maximum of 15 iterations. We have run both HMM and PST versions with model sizes from 1 to 15 states/orders. We found order-1 PST and 1-state HMM performances to be the best. We believe this is because the traffic data is quite sparse. It is much sparser than the volcano dataset, i.e., the 5 min data volume for the traffic monitoring application consists of 1 sample, while the volcano monitoring application has 36,000 samples. Hence, the traffic dataset does not contain a sufficient number of samples to train a large PST/HMM model. The average model size for 1-order PSTs are 6, 6.7, and 6.8 nodes for VDS314491, VDS400803 and VDS400929, respectively. The HMM model consists of one start probability matrix, one transition probability matrix and one emission matrix. The model size for the 1-state HMM model is 18 nodes, which is always fixed for all sensor nodes. Thus, the PST model has a smaller size in this application.

Figure 5.9 shows the ROC curves for the order-1 PST (left) and 1-state HMM (right) of the VDS 400803. Figure 5.8 (left) shows the ROC curve for the clusterhead node with a PST of order-1 of the VDS 400803, whereas Fig. 5.8 (right) shows the ROC curve for the clusterhead built with a 1-state HMM of the VDS 400803. The PST models have better performances than HMM models as indicated by the large Area Under Curve (AUC)s in the ROC graphs (see Table 5.6). We believe this is caused by the random initialization of the model parameters. Based on the initial parameter values, the EM algorithm may not find global optimal results. In addition, the data size not may not be large enough to train both the emission matrix and the

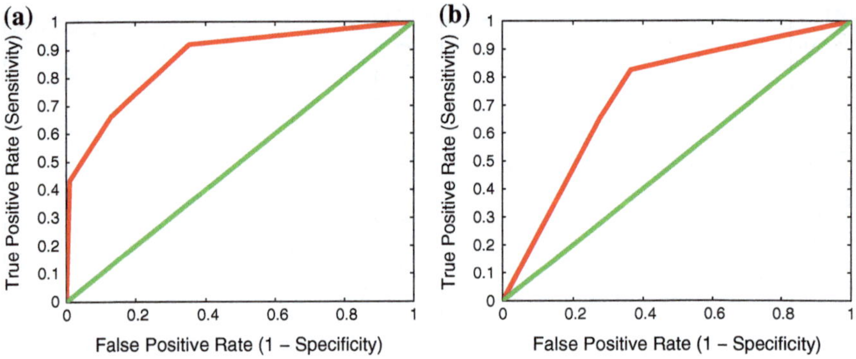

Fig. 5.9 ROC curves built from order-1 PST model (**a**) and 1-state HMM model (**b**) for the lane 5 sensor node of the VDS 400803.

Table 5.6 Area under curve comparisons of 1-order PST and 1-state HMM model for all VDS

	Lane1	Lane2	Lane3	Lane4	Lane5	Clusterhead
PST (std. dev)	72 % (13 %)	70 % (8 %)	69 % (6 %)	74 % (6 %)	74 % (8 %)	89 % (1 %)
HMM (std. dev)	66 % (5 %)	63 % (15 %)	61 % (7 %)	64 % (7 %)	68 % (10 %)	80 % (3 %)

transition matrix. We can also observe that the clusterhead is more capable than the cluster members in terms of the percentage of anomalies detected. This illustrates that the clusterhead's more global perspective is able to detect anomalies that individual nodes cannot. For example, if an incident occurred in an outer traffic lane, it is more likely to affect the adjacent lane than it is to affect the inner traffic lane. The clusterhead may catch this anomaly if it is sensitive enough to the change.

Table 5.6 shows the AUC of ROC for all four VDS. The AUC of ROC can be treated as one form of model comparison. To determine the significance of the differences in the results, the Student's T-test is applied. The assumption of the test is that the underlying distributions of accuracies/errors are Gaussian, because of the Central Limit Theorem—as the number of testing sets approaches infinity the distribution of the mean of accuracy/error approaches a Normal distribution. The Student's T-test was applied to the accuracy (AUC) results for the clusterhead performance compared against other lanes' performances. This test confirms that the differences in these results are statistically significant, with a confidence level of 95 %. In addition, the PST models have better performance compared to HMM algorithm. The student's T-test confirms that the differences in these results are statistically significant, with a confidence level of 99 %.

In summary, we believe that these results, combined with the seismic application, illustrate that our proposed sequential anomaly detection system is flexible enough to be applied in very different applications domains, and can achieve a satisfactorily high performance.

5.5 Conclusions

Using resource constrained WSNs for environment monitoring of applications such as volcanic eruptions and traffic flows are challenging, because the events of interest are usually preceded by a long periods of inactivity and the event itself may last only for a short period of time. The main objective of this chapter is to propose a distributed sequential anomaly detection system in an unknown environment using a WSN. In this chapter, we have proposed a sequential detection procedure to analyze and extract semantic symbols from a sequence of observations. The system first detects sensory level anomalies using an unsupervised neural network and then detects time-related changes online using a likelihood-ratio detection scheme. Our proposed temporal modeling technique is able to capture high-order temporal dependencies in some parts of the behavior and lower order dependencies elsewhere. We have verified the proposed approach using a volcano monitoring dataset and a traffic monitoring application. Results show that our system yields high performance. Our iterative temporal learning approach captures the temporal dependencies in data and removes redundancies, which translates into energy savings in the WSN. The algorithm is distributed, and supports a hierarchical learning structure, which we believe will scale to a large number of sensors and will be practical for resource constrained sensor nodes.

Acknowledgments We sincerely thank Dr. Matt Welsh, of Harvard University, who made the Reventador data from Volcano Tingurahua available to us. We also thank Dr. Nicholas Compin and Jane Berner, of California Department of Transportation, who made the PeMS data available to us.

References

1. Dongbing G (2011) A game theory approach to target tracking in sensor networks. IEEE Trans Syst Man Cybern Part B Cybern 41(1):2–13
2. Janakiram D, Reddy VA, Kumar AVUP (2006) Outlier detection in wireless sensor networks using Bayesian belief networks. In: First international conference on communication system software and middleware, pp 1–6
3. Kulakov A, Davcev D (2005) Tracking of unusual events in wireless sensor networks based on artificial neural-network algorithms. Inf Technol Coding Comput (ITCC) 2:534–539
4. Kwon J, Chen C, Varaiya P (2004) Statistical methods for detecting spatial configuration errors in traffic surveillance sensors. Transp Res Record J Transp Res Board 1870(-1):124–132
5. Tsai H, Yang D, Peng W, Chen M (2007) Exploring group moving pattern for an energy-constrained object tracking sensor network. In: Pacific-Asia conference on knowledge discovery and data mining, Nanjing, May 2007. Springer, pp 825–832
6. Tulone D, Madden S (2006) PAQ: Time series forecasting for approximate query answering in sensor networks. In: The 3rd European workshop on wireless sensor networks (EWSN), ETH Zurich, vol 3868, Feb 2006. Springer, pp 21–37
7. Wang X, Ma J-J, Wang S, Bi D-W (2007) Time series forecasting energy-efficient organization of wireless sensor networks. Sensors 7:1766–1792
8. Wang X, Wang S, Bi D (2009) Distributed visual-target-surveillance system in wireless sensor networks. IEEE Trans Syst Man Cybern B Cybern 39(5):1134–1146

9. Werner-Allen G, Lorincz K, Johnson J, Lees J, Welsh M (2006) Fidelity and yield in a volcano monitoring sensor network. In: Proceedings of the 7th symposium on operating systems design and implementation (OSDI), Berkeley, Nov 2006. USENIX Association, pp 381–396
10. Heinzelman W, Chandrakasan A, Balakrishnan H (2000) Energy-efficient communication protocols for wireless microsensor networks. In: International conference on system sciences, Maui
11. Li Y, Parker LE (2008) Detecting and monitoring time-related abnormal events using a wireless sensor network and mobile robot. In: IEEE/RSJ 2008 international conference on intelligent robots and systems (IROS), Nice, Sept 2008
12. Li YY, Thomason M, Parker LE (2010) Detecting time-related changes in wireless sensor networks using symbol compression and probabilistic suffix trees. In: IEEE/RSJ 2008 international conference on intelligent robots and systems (IROS), Taipei, Oct 2010
13. Jain A, Chang EY, Wang Y-F (2004) Adaptive stream management using Kalman filters. In: Proceedings of the 2004 ACM SIGMOD international conference on management of data, Paris. ACM, pp 11–22
14. Wang A, Krishnamurthy Vikram (2008) Signal interpretation of multifunction radars: modeling and statistical signal processing with stochastic context free grammar. IEEE Trans Signal Process 56(3):1106–1119
15. Liang Y-M, Shih S-W, Shih AC-C, Liao H-YM, Lin C-C (2009) Learning atomic human actions using variable-length markov models. IEEE Trans Syst Man Cybern B Cybern 39(1):268–280
16. Mazeroff G, Gregor J, Thomason M, Ford R (2008) Probabilistic suffix models for api sequence analysis of windows xp applications. Pattern Recognit 41(1):90–101
17. Dana R, Yoram S, Naftali T (1996) The power of amnesia: learning probabilistic automata with variable memory length. Mach Learn 25(2–3):117–149
18. Apostolico A, Bejerano G (2000) Optimal amnesic probabilistic automata or how to learn and classify proteins in linear time and space. In: Proceedings of the fourth annual international conference on computational molecular biology, Tokyo. ACM, pp 25–32
19. Lin J, Keogh E, Lonardi S, Lankford JP, Nystrom DM (2004) Visually mining and monitoring massive time series. In: Proceedings of the 10th ACM international conference on Knowledge discovery and data mining. ACM, pp 460–469
20. Begleiter R, Yona G (2004) On prediction using variable order markov models. J Artif Intell Res 22:385–421
21. Li Y, Parker LE (2008) A spatial-temporal imputation technique for classification with missing data in a wireless sensor network. In: IEEE/RSJ 2008 international conference on intelligent robots and systems (IROS), Nice, Sept 2008
22. Li Y, Parker LE (2014) Nearest neighbor imputation using spatialtemporal correlations in wireless sensor networks. Inf Fusion 15:64–79
23. Sayood K (2000) Introduction to data compression. Morgan Kaufmann, San Mateo
24. Reynolds DA, Quatieri TF, Dunn RB (2000) Speaker verification using adapted gaussian mixture models. Dig Signal Process 10:19–41
25. Caltrans performance measurement system (pems) (2010) http://pems.dot.ca.gov/
26. Claudel CG, Nahoum M, Bayen AM (2009) Minimal error certificates for detection of faulty sensors using convex optimization. In: Proceedings of the 47th annual Allerton conference on communication, control, and computing, Piscataway. IEEE Press, pp 1177–1186
27. Varaiya P (2005) What we've learned about highway congestion. Access 27:2–10
28. Hoh B, Gruteser M, Herring R, Ban J, Work D, Herrera J-C, Bayen AM, Annavaram M, Jacobson Q (2008) Virtual trip lines for distributed privacy-preserving traffic monitoring. In: Proceeding of the 6th international conference on mobile systems, applications, and services, MobiSys'08, New York, ACM, pp 15–28
29. Jia Z, Chen C, Coifman B, Varaiya P (2001) The pems algorithms for accurate, real-time estimates of g-factors and speeds from single-loop detectors. In: Proceedings of the IEEE ITS council annual meeting, Oakland, Aug 2001, pp 536–541

30. Kwon J, Varaiya P, Skabardonis A (1856) Estimation of truck traffic volume from single loop detectors with lane-to-lane speed correlation. Transp Res Record J Transp Res Board 106–117:2003
31. Murphy K (2012) machine learning: a probabilistic perspective, in preparation, to be published by MIT Press

Part II
Distributed Sensing: Applications

Sensor network research was initially driven by expensive military applications such as battlefield surveillance and enemy tracking. Nowadays, the sudden diffusion of cheaper fixed and mobile sensors that has greatly changed everyday human life lets us think about the wide diffusion of smartphones. Many applications based on distributed sensing systems for civil applications have been developed. These applications can be classified into habitat monitoring, environment observation and forecast systems, human activity monitoring for health, security, and surveillance.

As previously remarked in the preface, these chapters are mainly focused on the applications, providing also a good theoretical contribution, but reserving the majority of the efforts to the implementation of real applications based on distributed systems.

Chapter 6
A Full-Scale Hardware Solution for Crowd Evacuation via Multiple Cameras

Dimitrios Portokalidis, Ioakeim G. Georgoudas, Antonios Gasteratos and Georgios Ch. Sirakoulis

Abstract Crowd evacuation is thoroughly investigated in recent years. All efforts focus on improving safety standards of such a process. Past and latest life-threatening incidents related to evacuation procedures justify both the growing scientific interest as well as the interdisciplinary character of most research approaches. In this chapter, we describe the hardware implementation of a management system that aims at acting anticipatively against crowd congestion during evacuation. The system consists of two structural components. The first one relies on an elaborated form of the Viola et al. [55] detection and tracking algorithm, which incorporates both appearance and motion in real-time. Being supported by cameras, this algorithm realises the initialisation process. In principal, it consists of simple sum-of-pixel filters that are boosted into a strong classifier. A linear combination of these filters properly set thresholds, thus succeeding detection. The second part consists of a Cellular Automata (CA) based route estimation model. Presumable congestion in front of exits during crowd egress, leads to the prompt activation of sound and optical signals that guide pedestrians towards alternative escaping points. The CA model, as well as the tracking algorithm are implemented by means of Field Programmable Gate Array (FPGA) logic. Hardware accelerates the response of the model by exploiting the distinct feature of parallelism that CA structures inherently possess. Furthermore, implementing the model on an FPGA device takes advantage of their natural parallelism, thus reaching significant speed-ups with respect to software simulation.The incorporation of the

D. Portokalidis · I.G. Georgoudas · G.C. Sirakoulis (✉)
Department of Electrical and Computer Engineering,
Democritus University of Thrace, 67100 Xanthi, Greece
e-mail: gsirak@ee.duth.gr

D. Portokalidis
e-mail: dportoc@gmail.com

I.G. Georgoudas
e-mail: igeorg@ee.duth.gr

A. Gasteratos
Department of Production and Management Engineering,
Democritus University of Thrace, 67100 Xanthi, Greece
e-mail: agaster@pme.duth.gr

P. Spagnolo et al. (eds.), *Human Behavior Understanding in Networked Sensing*,
DOI 10.1007/978-3-319-10807-0_6

design as a fast processing module of an embedded system dedicated to surveillance is also advantageous in terms of compactness, portability and low cost.

6.1 Introduction

The approach that has been recently adopted in crowd modelling addresses crowd as composed of discrete individuals, rather than a homogeneous mass that behaves like a flowing fluid [19]. As a result, certain attributes of crowd behavior, such as collective effects, collisions and delaying factors have been successfully encountered during simulation process [49]. On the other hand, such complexities in crowd activities as emergent behaviors or self-organizing, hinder the visual understanding of crowd scene. Human activity recognition and crowd behavior analysis from videos remains a challenging problem due to the inherent complexity and vast diversity found in crowded scenes [35]. Simultaneously, the progress in human detection and tracking processes, which both comprise a complicated field of scientific research, can be combined with crowd evacuation simulation approaches aiming at the development of more efficient crowd management systems. Recently, an integrated system has been proposed that operates as an anticipative management tool in cases of crowd evacuation [14]. The scope of such a system is to establish a near real-time processing mechanism that could prevent clogging in exits, especially in cases of emergent evacuations. The system estimates plausible congestion zones within the area that the crowd moves based on the actual (computed almost in real-time) position of individuals composing the crowd. Two interconnected structural parts comprise the system; the detecting and tracking mechanism and the CA-based model that estimates the route of members of the crowd. The initialisation process is established by the detecting and tracking algorithm, which is supported by cameras. The automatic response of the algorithm provides the current location of pedestrians around exits, thus enabling dynamic initialisation of the CA model, followed by the estimation of their possible route for the very near future. Among all possible exit points, the most suitable is proposed as an alternative and the crowd is proactively re-directed towards the chosen one by means of of appropriate audial and visual guiding signals.

Many different approaches of crowd dynamics' simulation have been reported in the literature, as for example based on CAs [3, 7], lattice-gas and social force models [19], fluid-dynamics [15], agent-based modelling [5], game theory [28], and biomimetics [2]. In some models, pedestrians are considered as homogeneous individuals [60], whereas in others, they are treated as heterogeneous [30]. Some methods that describe pedestrian dynamics in a microscopic scale and collective phenomena emerge from the complex interactions among individuals [44]. Besides, there are macroscopic scale models of crowd dynamics [23]. Moreover, these models can also be distinguished into discrete or continuous in space and time [13, 17, 40]. Literature also reports a variety of CA-based models investigating crowd behavior. CA based methods model human behaviors, such as inertial effects, unadventurous effect and group effect [8] or treat pedestrians as particles subject to long-range forces [58].

Furthermore, the impact of environmental conditions [52] and bi-directional pedestrian behavior [27] has been studied with the use of CA as well as interactions among pedestrians, friction effects [25] and herding behavior [11].

Literature review also indicates several different detection techniques. The most common ones include recognition of parts of the human-body [42] or extraction of information from the foreground of the frames [47]. The main drawback of such processes is that they require large amounts of computational resources. Hence implementation of real-time computer vision systems is difficult due to the huge amount of data that is processed. Yet, efficient tracking models based on video technology and sensor networks have been developed [8]. Motion detection focuses on the segmentation of moving objects in a scene. A common method is the application of background subtraction algorithms [18], which however is sensitive to changes in dynamic scenes. Furthermore, optical-flow, a method based on flow vectors of moving objects, is computationally complex and sensitive to noise [36]. Finally, Viola et al. [55], have proposed a system able to detect and track people in almost real time. This is succeeded with the use of simple filters, i.e. sum-of-pixels filters, which form a strong classifier.

Traditional closed-circuit television (CCTV) systems tend to be ineffective as the number of cameras exceeds the capability of human operators to monitor them. Visual surveillance in dynamic scenes attempts to detect, recognise and track certain objects from image sequences, or even to understand and describe object behaviors. In general, the processing framework of visual surveillance in dynamic scenes includes a set of successive stages that incorporate modelling of environments, detection of motion, classification of moving objects, tracking and human identification from multiple cameras [21]. A common method is the application of background subtraction algorithms in order foreground information to be isolated from background images, continuing with the segmentation of the foreground pixels [18, 34]. The method is simple but extremely sensitive to changes in dynamic scenes. Optical-flow based methods use characteristics of flow vectors of moving objects over time to detect moving regions in an image section [37]. The major drawback of the methods are that they are computationally heavy and very sensitive to noise. Hence, they can hardly be applied to video streams in real-time. Another conventional approach, temporal differencing, makes use of the pixel differences between two successive frames in a sequence of images to extract moving regions. The method is very adaptive to dynamic environments [55]. Correct classification of moving objects is an essential step before tracking. It is a standard issue of pattern recognition, commonly based either on shape attributes (e.g. human body patterns [26]) or on motion characteristics of the classified objects (e.g. periodic properties of moving objects [10]). Tracking of the moving objects is finally succeeded by comparing consecutive frames under various criteria. Tracking over time typically involves matching objects in consecutive frames using features such as points, lines or blobs. Tracking methods make use of mathematical tools such as the Kalman filter [29], Bayesian networks [46], etc. There are algorithms that apply tracking of moving objects based on shadow processing running in real-time in low-cost hardware [24]. Another approach that reduces computational complexity performs tracking by dynamically updating bounding contours that correspond to the outlines of the moving elements [39]. Furthermore, matching based tracking is established either by extracting elements with certain features and matching features between images [9] or by matching image elements to models of a data basis [45].

Regarding occlusion, the problem can hardly be addressed since motion segmentation may become unreliable. When multiple moving objects occlude each other, especially when their speeds, directions and shapes are very close, their motion regions coalesce, which makes the location and tracking of objects particularly difficult. Manipulating the problem by using statistical methods into available image information severely downgrades the response of the system. Nevertheless, a solution based on the use of multiple cameras may constitute a reliable solution.

In this chapter, a Field Programmable Gate Array (FPGA) implementation of the overall assisting management system is described. To the best of our knowledge, hardware implementation of evacuation systems has not been extensively investigated and it is rarely reported in literature [12]. The system comprises of two structural components, which are presented sequentially. On the one hand, detection and tracking is based on an elaborated form of the method of Viola et al. [55]. The design of the human detection system relies on an Artificial Neural Networks (ANNs) model [59].

On the other hand, the automatic response of the processor that realises the CA-based evacuation model provides the location of pedestrians near exits. The evacuation model operates as a 'short term' simulator of the plausible evolution of the crowd-system focusing on a very specific situation (evacuation). The implementation of the model is motivated by parallelism, an inherent feature of CA that contributes to further acceleration of the models operation. The main motivation for using FPGAs is that their regular, two-dimensional structure provides an ideal architecture for mapping the structure of a CA model. Consequently, the realisation of the model on an FPGA device takes advantage of the natural parallelism of FPGAs, thus reaching to significant speed-ups with respect to software simulation [56].

Moreover, in terms of circuit design and layout, ease of mask generation, silicon-area utilisation and maximisation of achievable clock speed CA are perhaps the computational structures best suited for a fully parallel hardware realisation [12]. Using FPGAs, it is possible to parallelise the algorithm processing. The dedicated processor is utilised as a real-time processing module of the embedded system dedicated to surveillance that responds fast. The implementation of the overall system is advantageous in terms of low-cost, high-speed, compactness and portability features.

Essentially, the proposed hardware embedded system acts as a unifying mechanism that coherently combines data/information from different sources in order to achieve a specific goal, by deriving decisions and reducing uncertainty. In other words, it realises the main principles of information fusion.

The following sections describe thoroughly the structural parts of the system. Particularly, Sect. 6.2 presents the major implementation directions of the detection and tracking algorithm. In Sect. 6.3 the multi-camera approach is further analysed, while in Sect. 6.4, the design principles of the CA-based evacuation model are described. Finally, conclusions are drawn in Sect. 6.5, along with future work prospects.

6.2 Main Implementation Principles of the Detection and Tracking Algorithms

The algorithm deciding whether an individual appears in a frame or not, follows a discrete sequence of steps (Figs. 6.1 and 6.2): (a) a continuous flow of images (video) is separated into discrete frames (images), (b) each of these images is converted into greyscale, (c) each image is divided into separate windows of size 610×930 pixels, (d) each window is examined whether it contains an individual or not with the use of a strong classifier, (e) a window and, therefore, the corresponding image is supposed to contain an individual, in the case that it undergoes all the stages of the strong classifier. If at any stage, a classifier rejects the window being examined, no further processing is performed and searching continues to the next sub-part of the window.

The circuit implements the corresponding algorithm, which enables processing in near real time and that can be realised on a low-cost execution platform. Though efficient detection and tracking implementations have been reported in literature, the incorporation of such a circuit in an overall crowd management system is the motivational primary objective.

The strong classifier is modelled according to the principles of Neural Networks. Each individual weak classifier of the overall strong classifier acts like a simple neuron (perceptron), to which a threshold function is applied. Each weak classifier has its own threshold value. Provided that the response of the function corresponding to each neuron-classifier is higher than the threshold value, the classifier becomes active; otherwise, it remains inactive. Moreover, each classifier consists of a properly selected feature (filter) or a group of them. These features are arranged in a cascade formation, in order this mechanism to reject quickly windows that are not likely to contain an individual. The main aim is the real-time implementation of the system. Thus, it enables fast decisions without consuming useful computational resources and easy communication with the video cameras that supply the system with the image sequences.

As soon as the appropriate filters that generate the neurons of the neural network (strong classifier) have been delineated, the hardware (FPGA) implementation is activated in order to train the neural network and apply the filters as well. In practice, the circuit sets and changes the weight values that correspond to each feature in order to optimise the process.

Additionally, an appropriate model has been developed in Matlab, which completes automatically the above procedure. This software tool also functions as a testing tool of the overall behavior of the system by checking the results accrued. The reason for creating such a tool is to prevent hardware level from errors and to improve the hardware implementation. Software enables easy identification of errors (debugging) in the source code. Hence, the implementation at hardware level mainly pertains to the calculation of the responses of the filters, which are applied to each window, as well as to the construction of the neural network (specifically of the strong classifier), which comprises the decision-making mechanism.

(a)

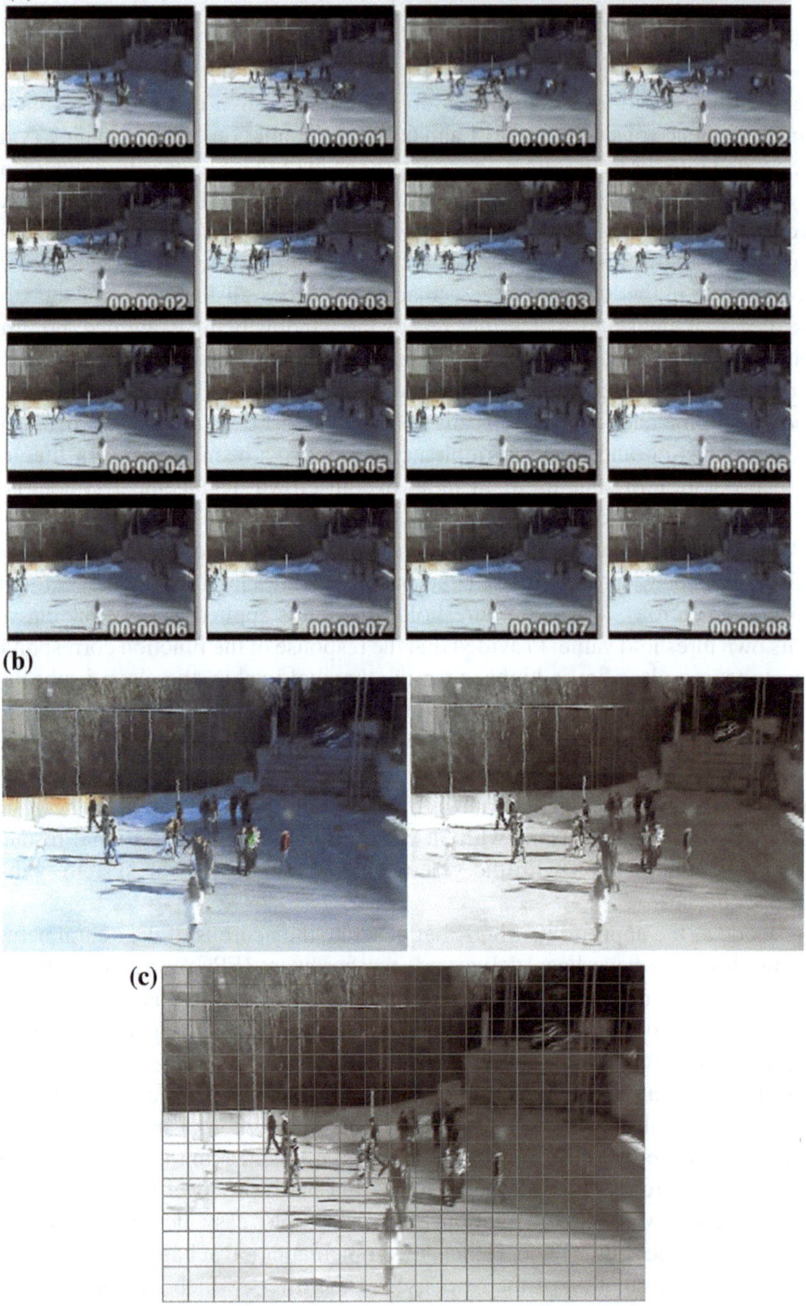

(b)

(c)

Fig. 6.1 The first three main steps of the detection and tracking algorithm, **a** a continuous flow of images (video) is separated into discrete frames (images), **b** each of the images is converted into greyscale mode, **c** each image is divided into separate windows

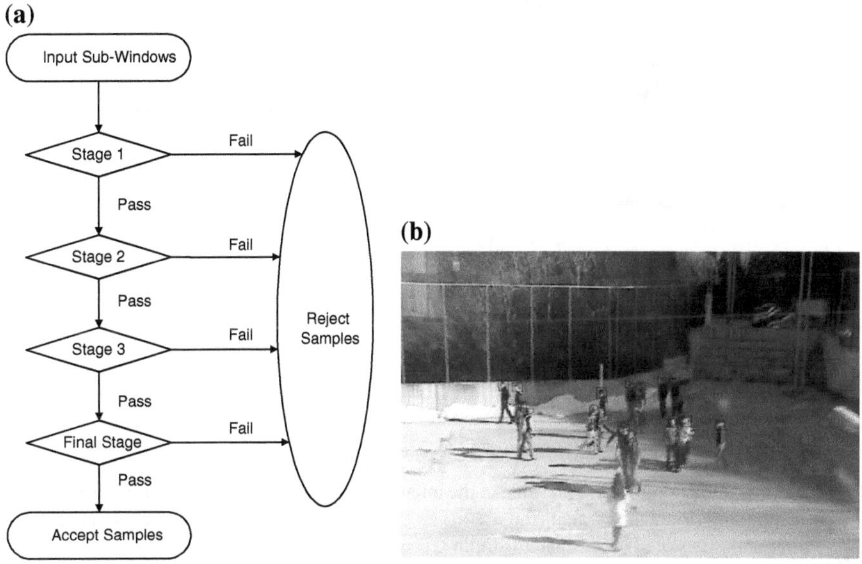

Fig. 6.2 The rest of the main steps of the detection and tracking algorithm follow: **a** the topology of the strong classifier, **b** a window and therefore the corresponding image is supposed to contain an individual

6.2.1 Filter Response

Filters applied to each sub-window of the whole image (frame) are all of the same type, i.e. Haar-type (sum of pixel filters) [38]. Their response is the sum of the intensities in the image area, which the filters are applied to. The images are converted to greyscale mode, thus the values are integer. The intensity of each pixel is represented by an integer ranging between 0 and 255. This is a total of 256 values, which represent different shades of grey color. Hence, 8 bits (unsigned type) are required for the representation of each pixel. Provided that the range includes also negative values then an extra bit is used, thus leading to a total of 9 bits representation. Thus, negative from positive values can be separated.

The most common method to calculate the response of a sum of pixel filters would be a simple addition of the corresponding intensities. However, this kind of implementation, especially at hardware level, would not be particularly efficient as far as processing time concerns. Consequently, it is more efficient to apply a multiplication between the value of the intensity of a given pixel times the corresponding orientation value. The latter defines the orientation of each of the orthogonal regions of the image that a filter consists of. Then the corresponding result is driven into a register. This process takes advantage of the Multiply Accumulator (MAC) component that is available in FPGA logic. Furthermore, the operations are controlled more effectively and the majority of the required calculations are taking place faster (Fig. 6.3).

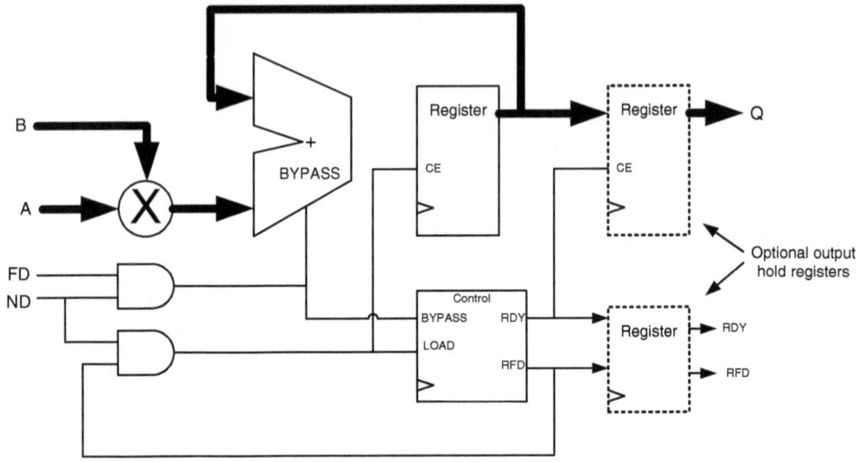

Fig. 6.3 Multiply accumulator. The value of the intensity of a given pixel (input A) is multiplied with the corresponding orientation value (input B). The corresponding product represents the response of the filter and it is stored to a register (output Q)

In Fig. 6.3, parameters A and B represent respectively the value of each pixel (ranging from 0 to 255 in the case of greyscale form) and the value 1 or -1 (depending on the orientation) that corresponds to each of these pixels depending on the form of the filter that is applied each time. Parameter Q represents the resulting value of the multiplication that takes place and the addition of that result to the already existed value that is stored in the register. As shown in Fig. 6.3, Q holds, each time, the value that exists inside the accumulator. The boldface lines indicate data conduits, whereas plain lines represent control signals.

Depending on its size, i.e. the number of pixels that it covers, each type of filter performs a multiplication between the value of each pixel times the corresponding orientation, i.e. $+1$ represents a positive orientation, whereas -1 a negative one. Hence, there is a maximum value that can be assigned to each filter. Then, an accumulator is required to sum up the multiplication results, thus generating the final response. Therefore, two multiply-accumulating units are required for each filter depending only on its dimensions and not on its orientation. For example, for each of the 8×12 filters two such units will be used, for each of the 16×24 filters two more units will be used and so on. Obviously, multiply accumulators are also used during the multiplication of the values of the weights with the values of the filters inside each neuron. It should be noted that following the original proposal for the calculation of the response of the filter, i.e. following continuing additions of the values of the filters, the results would also be correct, but in the cost of extra time and resources.

In order to enable the detection system to identify the orientation values of the pixels (Fig. 6.4) for each of the filters applied to windows, it is necessary to use a component that can store and easily match values, i.e. a Look Up Table (LUT) (Fig. 6.5). For each filter, according to its size, there is a corresponding LUT. In fact,

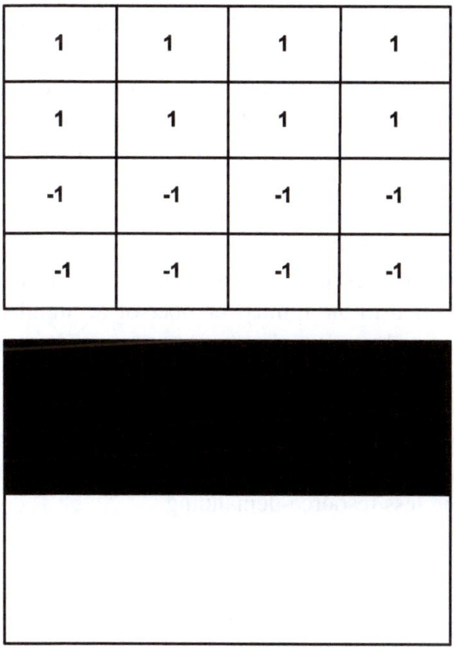

Fig. 6.4 An example of a filter and the corresponding operations required for the calculation of its response. Each pixel value is multiplied by the corresponding value

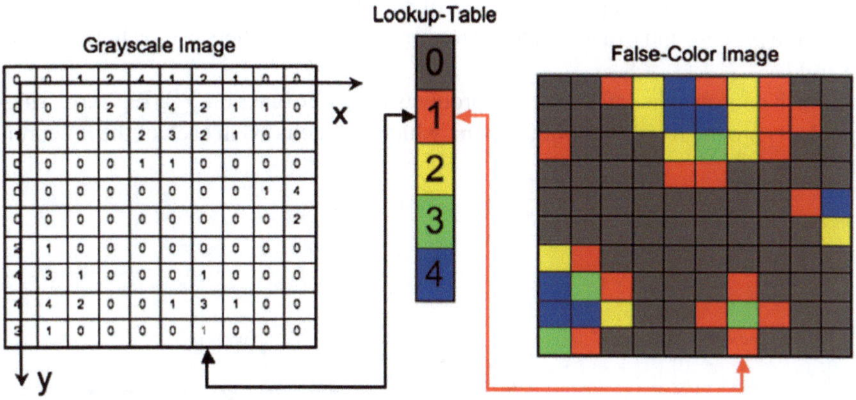

Fig. 6.5 An example of LUTs function. A false-colored (or pseudo-colored) image is a single channel *gray* image (8, 16 or 32-bit) that has color assigned to it via a LUT. Thus, differences in color in the pseudo-colored image reflect differences in intensity of the object

this is a two-dimensional array $2 \times K$, where parameter K represents the number of columns of each filter. For filters of 8×12 pixels, the size of the corresponding LUT is 2×12. The first row contains the value 1, whereas the second row contains the value -1 or 1, depending on the orientation of the filter. According to the area that a filter covers, the values of the pixels are multiplied with the elements of the corresponding row. Thus, easy indexing is succeeded. Clearly, the speed optimisation is one of the main advantages of using such a component, as the memory access operation is much faster than a simple operation (addition or abstraction) at hardware level.

As far as the memory, thus, the time concerns, the major overhead of the implementation can be spotted to the limited number of accumulators. Following such an approach, an increased number of memory accesses is required. As a result, the corresponding time is augmented, compared to an implementation that would use different accumulators for each of the filters.

The prominent benefit of the implementation as far as the speed concerns is that the training of the neural network takes place offline, keeping the performing burden of the system low and less resource-demanding.

6.2.2 Neurons

Having calculated the responses of the filters, the next step is to create a strong classifier using hardware components. As already mentioned, the strong classifier consists of individual weak classifiers, which are modelled by using neurons. An activation function is applied to each of these neurons. In order to simplify the decision process and to accelerate the response of the classifiers, a threshold function is used.

Each neuron calculates a sum of products (transfer function $\sum$) (Fig. 6.6). These products are the responses of the filters, which are included in each of the n neurons

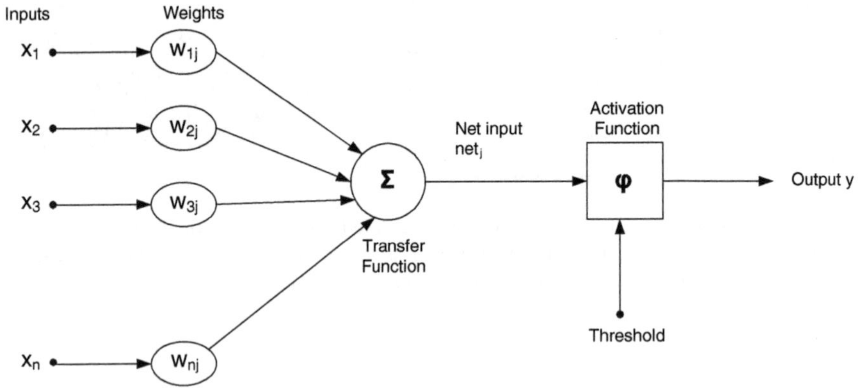

Fig. 6.6 A block functional diagram of a neuron

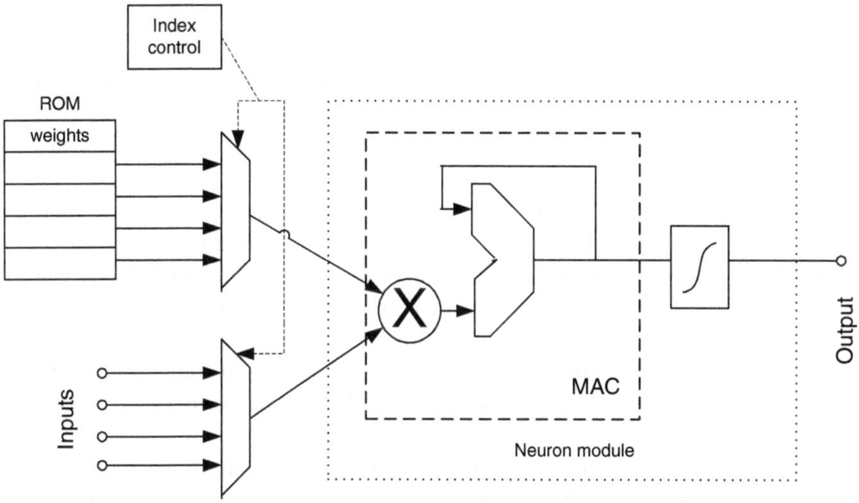

Fig. 6.7 Schematic design of an artificial neuron

$(x_1, x_2, \ldots, x_n)$, multiplied with the corresponding weight value $(w_1, w_2, \ldots, w_n)$. Then, a function called activation function (ϕ) is applied. The goal of this function is to match the previous calculated value to another one, depending on the type of the function. The aim of the proposed implementation is to check whether the result of the sum of products of each neuron exceeds (or not) the corresponding threshold value. Equation 6.1, which describes this operation, forms the output of the strong classifier, while F_i represents the output of each of the filters that corresponds to a neuron.

$$o(\text{classifier}) = \begin{cases} 1, & \text{if } \sum w_i o(F_i) \geq \text{th}_{\text{classifier}} \\ 0, & \text{otherwise} \end{cases} \quad (6.1)$$

Each of the neurons (Fig. 6.7), which form the strong classifier, can be represented at hardware level by using a MAC component (Fig. 6.3). Also a ROM memory is required, so as to store the weight values of the filter permanently. These values have already been calculated during the training process of the strong classifier. Each neuron has its own ROM for storing the corresponding weights. The transactions made in each neuron take place simultaneously (in parallel) and for that reason a synchronization signal is necessary (clock). Each accumulator unit uses a load signal, which either allows or forbids the loading of the values.

The next step of the construction of the proposed detection system requires the definition of the appropriate filters in the neurons (classifiers). As stated before, this procedure is performed by the corresponding simulation tool that has been developed. This process is based on Adaboost algorithm [54]. A thorough description of its operation is out of the purpose of this chapter. Nevertheless, it should be noted that the strong classifier is built by selecting the most powerful features (filters), which separate training examples with the greatest possible certainty. These are the features with the lowest error rate. Along with other randomly selected filters, they form the neurons classifiers, thus leading to the creation of the strong classifier. The weight values of the more powerful features are greater than the respective values of other filters. Both these values and the way that the filters are placed into the neurons, are random.

Regarding the implementation of the particular system, only 7 neurons are used. The choice was based on the corresponding measures that took place with the use of the auxiliary software program in Matlab. More particularly, the main target regarded savings of resources (spatial and temporal) during the implementation of a flexible system. The latter could be applied in real time and could provide satisfactory results as well. After a number of tests, the minimum number of neurons that accomplished the desired requirements was defined equal to seven. More information can be found in [54].

As far as the operation of the software tool concerns, its main purpose is to examine each window whether it contains an individual or not (1 or 0 are the results respectively at the final classifier). In this implementation, such a window is supposed to have a size of 16 × 24 pixels. Consequently, 16 vectors have been used, each one with 24 elements. Hence, 16 signals are required in order the places of the vectors to be filled. Furthermore, 24 clock cycles are required so as these 16 vectors to be filled and thus the window under test to be successfully introduced. Right after, during the next clock cycle, the computation of the responses of all the filters that have been chosen commences. Particularly, all necessary operations to all accumulators take place and the upcoming values are compared with the corresponding thresholds. In the case that the value calculated is greater than the corresponding threshold then the filter is supposed to have a response equal to 1, otherwise equal to 0. Provided that all these responses are available, they are guided to the appropriate neurons, where they are multiplied with the value of the corresponding weight. As a result, for each neuron a sum of products comes up (multiply-accumulate operation). In case that this specific sum is greater than the value of the threshold of each particular neuron then the output of this neuron—weak classifier is equal to 1, otherwise to 0. A window and therefore the frame that this window comes from is accepted only in the case that it passes successfully all the stages of the strong classifier. The latter process is implemented through the performance of the logic operation AND between subsequent classifiers.

6.2.3 Validating the Implementation of the Tracking Algorithm

The final step in creating the strong classifier is to find the appropriate values of the weights of the features that the neurons consist of. For this purpose the Error Back Propagation algorithm is applied [4]. The Back Propagation (BP) method is a supervised training method of ANNs, where it is necessary for the teacher (trainer) to know or to be able to calculate the desired output for any input.

The training method is implemented as follows: a window that is part of a frame that contains an individual is selected. Consequently, the outputs of all neurons are set to 1. This window is a training example that helps the corresponding process of the ANN leading to the correct estimation of the weights. This procedure is applied to all neurons.

The overall system consists of seven (7) neurons, which are responsible for making decisions. Each neuron consists of a number of filters, which have been chosen properly [55]. These filters are assigned values that reflect the importance of each of them in the decision process. The activation function is principally the same for all neurons, i.e. a binary-like function. The input values of each neuron, i.e. the responses of the filters, are multiplied with the respective weight values, which are calculated during the training process of the ANN. The goal of this part is to apply the BP method to each of the seven neurons and observe whether the appropriate weight adjustment is achieved.

The implementation process of the BP algorithm follows the steps below:

1. The weights and the threshold values of each classifier are defined randomly.
2. Certain examples are applied and the sum of products between the weights and the corresponding values of inputs in each neuron are calculated. These are actually the responses of the filters.
3. The responses of the filters should exceed the threshold value that corresponds to each neuron-classifier in order the output of the neuron to be the desired one, i.e. 1. Hence, if this value does not exceed the threshold, then the weight values are redefined.
4. The formula for calculating the new weights is:

$$w_{\text{new}} = w_{\text{old}} + \alpha\delta x \tag{6.2}$$

   where α is the learning rate factor of the neural network, varying from 0 to 1 and δ is the error.
5. Step 4 is repeated until the desired convergence is succeeded.

The term $\alpha\delta x$ appearing in Eq. (6.2) is essentially the application of the delta rule, which is given by:

$$w_{\text{new}} = w_{\text{old}} + \Delta w, \quad \Delta w_{ji} = \alpha(t_j - y_j)g'(h_j)x_i \tag{6.3}$$

where t is the desired output, y is the real output, x is the input of each neuron, $g'(h)$ is the derivative of the neurons activation function and parameter h represents the sum of products between the weights and the respective inputs of the neuron.

The activation function of each neuron is a binary like function, which by definition is not a continuous function, thus its derivative cannot be defined. In order to overcome this irregularity, the following approach is adopted:

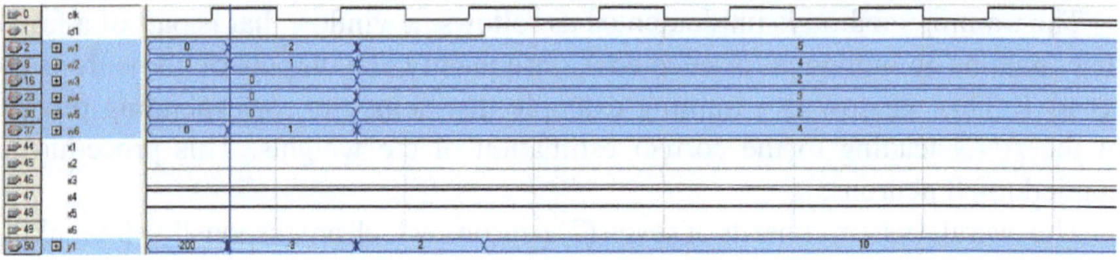

Fig. 6.8 The implementation of BP for neuron no. 3 in Quartus

$$w_{\text{new}} = w_{dd} + a \times (\text{threshold}_{\text{neuron}} - |\text{threshold}_{\text{current}}|)/2 + (w_{\text{desired}} - |w_{\text{current}}|)/2 \tag{6.4}$$

In essence, each new weight value is a function of (a) its previous value, (b) the value of the learning rate multiplied by the normalized difference of the neurons threshold minus the current value of the threshold and (c) the outcome of the normalized difference of the desired weight value minus the current weight value. This method achieves the appropriate weight correction which is actually the goal. Yet, it does not extremely differ from the original version of the BP algorithm, which cannot be fully applied as the proposed method also contains feedback and there is propagation of the error as well. The second column of Table 6.1 presents the values of the weights of one of the neurons, namely no. 3, as they were calculated during the training process. Next column shows the values obtained through the implementation of the BP algorithm at hardware level. Additionally, it is provided the standard deviation value of the weights, as it was obtained before and after the implementation of the BP algorithm. As expected, right after the implementation of the algorithm the values of the standard deviation in each neuron are smaller than the values obtained before. Along with, the results of the implementation of BP in the FPGA design platform of Altera [1] are provided (Fig. 6.8).

Table 6.1 Application results of BP algorithm in neuron no. 3

Input values of neuron no. 3		
1, 0, 0, 1, 1, 0		
No. of weight	Value (before)	Value (after)
1	5	5
2	3	4
3	1	2
4	2	3
5	1	2
6	3	4
Standard deviation	Before	After
	1.38	1.1

In order to verify the validity of the results, (both in Matlab and Quartus platforms) the new weight values were tested after the implementation of the BP algorithm. The response of the circuit remained the same. Additionally, there is a reduction of the standard deviation of the weights, which proves that the implementation responds more accurately and reliably. These results indicate that several weight values obtained after the implementation of the algorithm are not identical to those originally specified. This occurs because it was not used a floating point representation of the numbers. Such a decision was motivated by the fact that an FPGA of smaller size would be utilized in order to decrease the cost of the implementation as well as to accelerate its real-time performance. As a result, there was a loss of decimal parts, which should have been added during the algorithm processing. In several cases, this caused weights to increase similarly. Naturally, the correction of the weight values would be more accurate, but then the number of required iterations to achieve adequate convergence would be higher. In general, the new values of the weights were not far from their original values, a fact that proves the validity of this implementation. Moreover, the reduction of the standard deviation values enforces the effectiveness of the implementation. Once the best possible values of the weights of each neuron were calculated, the circuit was able to detect whether a person was appearing in a sub-window or not. Figure 6.9 depicts the response of the proposed implementation, for a window that contains a person (Fig. 6.10). It should be pointed out that frames of different types were successfully tested, e.g. for indoor/outdoor activities. The resolution of the frames was 320 × 480 pixels and the recording size was 24 frames/s. Video recording took place from a significant distance, thus further downgrading the detection conditions. Nevertheless, the hardware implementation proved effective in detection process.

The system was designed with the use of a hardware description language, i.e. VHDL and the simulation was performed in Altera FPGA design platform [1]. The representation of the values of the pixels required 16 signals, denoted as $x_1, x_2, \ldots, x_{16}$ in Fig. 6.9. Each of these signals was responsible for representing the pixels contained in the 16 rows of the window. The windows' dimensions were 16×24

Fig. 6.9 The response of the system right after introducing the selected sub-window

Fig. 6.10 The response of the system right after introducing the selected sub-window. The frame and the selected sub-window (in *red box*)

pixels. Hence, each of the x_i, $i = 1, \ldots, 16$ signals was actually a vector consisting of 24 values, i.e. $x_1(p_1, \ldots, p_{24}), x_2(p_1, \ldots, p_{24}), \ldots, x_{16}(p_1, \ldots, p_{24})$. The time required for providing an entire window as an input to the system was 24 clock cycles following a semi-parallel loading technique. Nevertheless, the exact duration of this period depends on the value of the clock signal. For the results presented here, a clock with a period of 15 ns was applied. Thus, the processing time of each of the sub-windows was $15 \times 24 = 360$ ns. Moreover, an extra clock period was required for the neural network to respond, i.e. to make a decision. This is a total time of 375 ns. Taking into consideration that a 320×480 frame was divided into 400 such sub-windows, then the total time required for each frame to be processed was $400 \times 375 = 150{,}000$ ns. The number of cycles does not change, since it depends on the width of the window, which is equal to 24 pixels. The area enclosed in red in Fig. 6.9 represents the window in greyscale mode. As soon as all values of pixels' intensities are provided to the system, the responses of the filters in the seven neurons are calculated. Then the neurons' responses are evaluated. The signals used to represent the output of each neuron in Fig. 6.9 are: classifier$_i$, where $i = 1, \ldots, 7$ respectively. In order a window to be considered as containing a person, the outputs of all neurons should be 1, as shown in the first case. If even a single neurons' output is 0, then this particular window is rejected. Under the testing conditions described above, the response of the system presented almost 80 % success rate. The exact model of the FPGA used for the implementation of the system is Altera Stratix II. This FPGA uses 90 nm technology and it allows the use of up to 180,000 logic elements. It also includes 96 Digital Signal Processing (DSP) blocks with 385 multipliers

Table 6.2 The resources of the FPGA circuit

Stratix II compilation report	
Combinational ALUTs	23,148/48,352 (48 %)
Dedicated logic registers	3,268/48,352 (7 %)
Total registers	3268
Total pins	138/335 (41 %)
Logic utilization	48 %

for efficient implementation of filters and other functions that require digital signal processing. Table 6.2 shows the use of the resources provided, for the implementation described.

6.3 Multi-camera Approach

Following the principles that are thoroughly described in Altera's white paper [43], video surveillance based on analog Closed Circuit Television (CCTV) cameras and interfaces is not easily expandable, and has low video resolution with little or no signal processing. However, more recent video surveillance systems replace these components with newer digital Local Area Network (LAN) cameras, complex image processing, and video-over-IP routing. They are no longer simply surveillance camera systems, but also video communication systems.

The Internet protocol (IP)-based structure of the new surveillance systems allows for scalability, flexibility, and cyber security. Various encoding and decoding standards transport the video stream (MPEG4 CODEC is the standard used today). Besides the CODEC function, image pre- and post- processing enhances the picture quality in real time with low latency. Programmable logic with embedded digital signal processing (DSP) blocks, memories, interfaces, and off-the-shelf IP solutions allows a designer to meet the new system requirements.

There are many different standards for video data compression, with the most popular including JPEG, H.263, Motion JPEG, MPEG, Wavelet and newer H.264. The type of compression used has an impact on hardware system requirements, including memory, data rate, and storage space. Compression efficiency is a key factor in the transmission of high-quality video over a bandwidth-limited network. For example, a color transmission at 30 fps at 640×480 pixels requires a data rate of 26 Mbytes/s. This data rate must be reduced (compressed) to a more manageable data rate that can be routed over a twisted pair of copper wires.

Pre- and post-processing techniques, such as de-interlacing, scaling, noise reduction using 2D filtering, and color space conversion, are also critical parts of a video surveillance system. Figure 6.11 illustrates a typical video surveillance system setup using field programmable gate arrays (FPGAs) and application specific standard product (ASSPs).

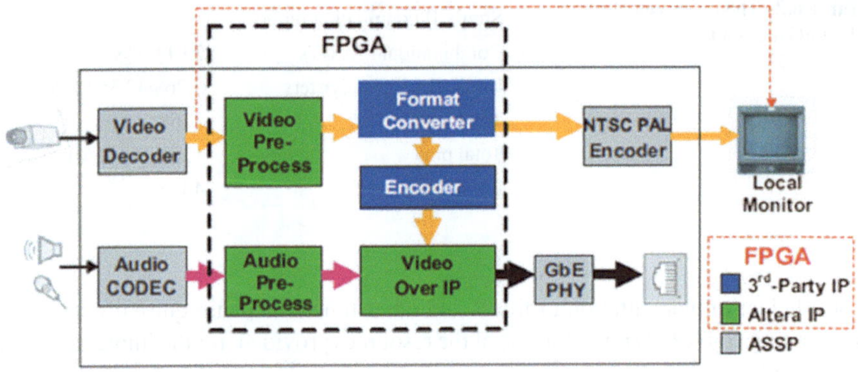

Fig. 6.11 Surveillance camera system with FPGA [43]

With expanding resolutions and evolving compression, there is a need for high performance while keeping architectures flexible to allow for quick upgradeability. As technology matures and volumes increase, the focus will move to cost reduction. System architecture choices include standard cell application-specific integrated circuit (ASICs), ASSPs, and programmable solutions such as digital signal processing (DSP) or media processors and FPGAs. Each of the approaches has advantages and disadvantages, with the ultimate choice depending on end-equipment requirements and solution availability. The ideal surveillance architecture would have the following characteristics: high performance, flexibility, easy upgradability, low development cost, and a migration path to lower cost as the application matures and volume ramps.

Performance not only applies to compression, but also pre- and post-processing functions. In fact, in many cases these functions are more computationally demanding, than the compression algorithm itself. Examples of these functions include scaling, de-interlacing, filtering, and color space conversion. For video surveillance, the need for high performance rules out processor-only architectures. They simply cannot meet the performance requirements with a single device. This FPGA co-processing approach can deliver significantly higher performance, since the designer can partition the system to take advantage of the benefits of each device. Figure 6.12 shows the block diagram.

Mackay et al. [33] propose another interesting solution. According to their approach, early research on the tracking and recognition of human form and actions have used single-camera computer-vision systems, while assuming ideal conditions, with un-occluded views of the subject readily available [50]. Recent works, however, have proposed the use of multiple (static) cameras to improve upon the sensing objective [48, 57]. An alternative approach to improving recognition has been the use of reconfigurable multi-camera active vision systems, which can select performance-optimal viewpoints [31, 32, 50]. An agent-based sensing-system applies reconfiguration strategy for the recognition of a human form moving under real-world conditions. The strategy is designed to be adaptable to a wide variety

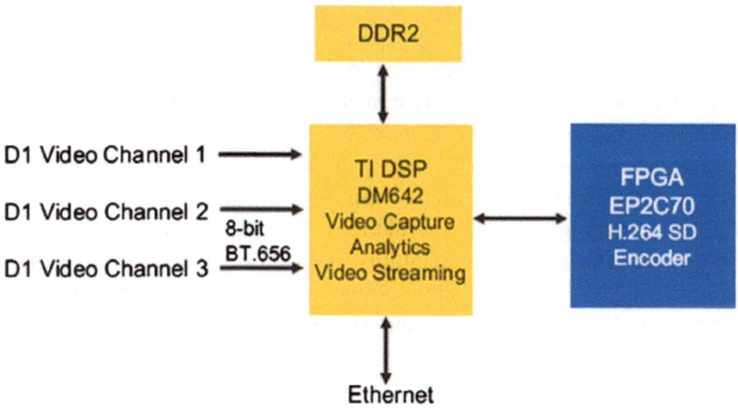

Fig. 6.12 Architecture with FPGA and Texas Instruments (TI) DSP [43]

of real-world time-varying-geometry object action-sensing tasks, while addressing real-time operation, presence of multiple static or dynamic (maneuvering) obstacles, differentiated importance of viewpoints, and object self-occlusion.

More recent, a multi-camera surveillance system based on the use of self-organizing neural networks to represent events on video has been developed, proposed by Orts-Escolano et al. [41]. According to them, the development of the visual surveillance process in dynamic scenes often includes steps for modeling the environment, motion detection, classification of moving objects, tracking and the recognition of actions. Most of the work is focused on applications related to tracking people or vehicles that have a large number of potential applications, such as: controlling access to special areas, the identification of people, traffic analysis, anomaly detection, security management or interactive monitoring using multiple cameras [22, 53]. The majority of visual surveillance systems for scene analysis and surveillance depend on the use of knowledge about the scenes where the objects move in a predefined manner [6, 20]. In recent years, work in the analysis of behaviors has been successful, because of the use of effective and robust techniques for detecting and tracking objects and people. Moreover, thanks to the proliferation of low-cost vision sensors, embedded processors and the efficiency of wireless networks, a large amount of research has focused on the use of multiple sources of information for the analysis of behavior. In particular, multi-camera networks are used for interpreting the dynamics of objects moving in wide areas or for observing objects from different viewpoints to achieve a 3D interpretation. Multiple viewpoints help in dealing with ambiguities and occlusions and can lead to a more reliable analysis of the scene. Third generation surveillance systems usually refer to system conceived of to deal with a large number of cameras, a geographical spread of resources and many monitoring points and to mirror the hierarchical and distributed nature of the human process of surveillance [53]. The system proposed by Orts-Escolano et al. [41], that constitutes an efficient multi-camera approach for the proposed implementation, processes several tasks in parallel using graphic processor units (GPUs). It addresses multiple vision tasks at various levels, such as segmentation, representation or characterization, analysis and monitoring of the movement. These features allow the construction of a robust representation of the environment and interpret the behavior of mobile agents in the scene. Furthermore, the vision module is integrated into a global system that operates in a complex environment by receiving images from multiple acquisition devices at video frequency. Offering relevant information to higher level systems, monitoring and making decisions in real time, it accomplishes a set of requirements, such as: time constraints, high availability, robustness, high processing speed and re-configurability. The system is able to represent and analyze the motion in video acquired by a multi-camera network and to process multi-source data in parallel on a multi-GPU architecture.

6.4 Main Implementation Principles of the CA-Based Crowd Evacuation Model

The response of the management system is structurally based on two operationally connected components. Supported by cameras, the first one elaborates detection and tracking, thus providing updated initial conditions to the CA-based, route estimation model that constitutes the second operational part. The CA model is two-dimensional and it is based on virtual potential field. Certain attributes of crowd behavior, have been successfully incorporated in the model. According to the motion mechanism individuals are attracted to exit points or they are repelled from obstacles and walls. The virtual potential field is established by the superposition of two independent fields [16]. The first one is attractive and triggers the direction towards exits, following the relationships below:

$$d = \sqrt{(x_E - x)^2 + (y_E - y)^2} \tag{6.5}$$

$$\theta = \tan^{-1}\left(\frac{y_E - y}{x_E - x}\right) \tag{6.6}$$

$$\mathrm{d}_E x = \alpha\cos(\theta) \quad \text{and} \quad \mathrm{d}_E y = \alpha\sin(\theta) \quad \text{if; } d > 0 \tag{6.7}$$

$$\mathrm{d}_E x = 0 \quad \text{and} \quad \mathrm{d}_E y = 0 \quad \text{if; } d = 0 \tag{6.8}$$

where d denotes the Euclidean distance between the pedestrian located at (x, y) and the exit (x_E, y_E), θ the angle between the pedestrian and the exit, α a constant that allows the adjustment of the strength of the field and $\mathrm{d}x$, $\mathrm{d}y$ the components of the gradient vector $\overrightarrow{\Delta_E v} = [\mathrm{d}_E x, \mathrm{d}_E y]^T$ of the vector $\overrightarrow{v} = [x, y]^T$.

The repulsive module of the overall field is generated by the following relationships:

$$d = \sqrt{(x_o - x)^2 + (y_o - y)^2} \tag{6.9}$$

$$\theta = \tan^{-1}(\frac{y_o - y}{x_o - x}) \tag{6.10}$$

$$\mathrm{d}_o x = -\beta \cos(\theta) \quad \text{and} \quad \mathrm{d}_o y = -\beta \sin(\theta) \quad \text{if; } d < r \tag{6.11}$$

$$\mathrm{d}_o x = 0 \quad \text{and} \quad \mathrm{d}_o y = 0 \quad \text{if; } d > r \tag{6.12}$$

where d denotes the Euclidean distance between a pedestrian located at (x, y) and an obstacle (x_o, y_o), θ the angle between the pedestrian and the obstacle, β a constant that allows the adjustment of the strength of the field, r the radius of the area that the repulsive field is effective and $\mathrm{d}x, \mathrm{d}y$ the components of the gradient vector $\overrightarrow{\Delta_o v} = [\mathrm{d}_o x, \mathrm{d}_o y]^T$ of the vector $\overrightarrow{v} = [x, y]^T$.

Then the total field originates in accordance to the relationship:

$$\mathrm{d}_x = \mathrm{d}_E x + \mathrm{d}_o x, \mathrm{d}_y = \mathrm{d}_E y + \mathrm{d}_o y \tag{6.13}$$

The motion mechanism is generated according to the attracting direction from the exit and the repelling directions from obstacles and walls, leading to the calculation of the coordinates of the next target-cell. In case that this is free, which also means that it has not been targeted by any another individual, the given individual moves on. Otherwise, the individual is looking for another choice, i.e. for a neighbouring cell with equal potential value. In case that the target-cell is an exit, it is checked whether this is free or not. The individual moves if the exit is free.

Algorithmically, for each individual the following parameters are calculated: (i) the distance from the exit, as well as parameters $\mathrm{d}_E x, \mathrm{d}_E y$, (ii) the distance from each cell that represents a wall or an obstacle. In case that this distance is less than two cells, parameters $\mathrm{d}_o x, \mathrm{d}_o y$ are calculated and (iii) the total vector, as described by the equations above.

In the view of the foregoing, the fundamental structural principles of the hardware implementation of the CA based model are presented as follows. The dedicated processor has been designed with the use of the Altera Quartus II software multi-platform, a comprehensive environment available for system-on-a-programmable-chip (SOPC) design. The design of the CA model follows updated implementation principles of the corresponding realisation presented in [12].

Prominent disadvantages of a general-purpose computer, such as high power consumption and significant size may sometimes hinder their utilisation. Furthermore, taking into consideration that a CA circuit design is reduced to the design of a single one, with a relatively simple cell and a uniform layout, the prospect of a dedicated

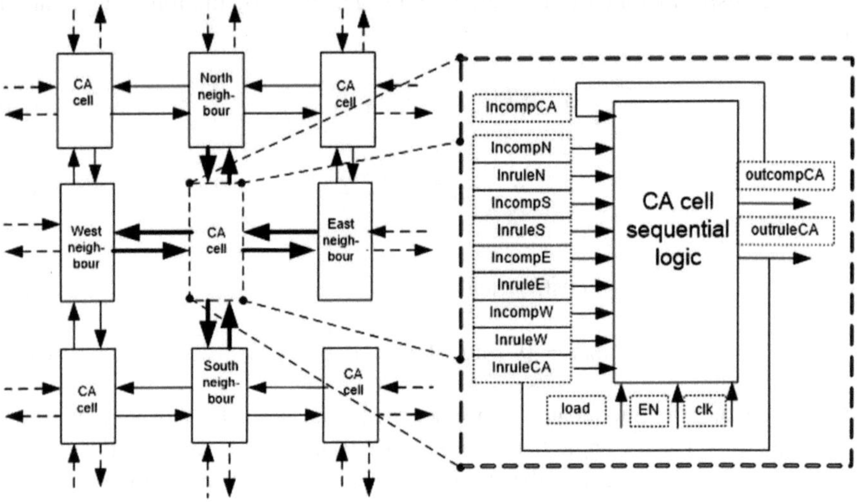

Fig. 6.13 Description of the constructional part of the CA grid

processor becomes attractive. The whole mask implementation regarding a large CA array (the cells with their internal connections as well as the interconnection between cells) constitutes a repetitive procedure, with no silicon area overhead on long interconnection lines. Moreover, the locality of the processing allows minimisation of the length of critical paths no matter what the number of cells is [51].

The device used for this realisation is the Stratix EP1S80B956C6 that belongs to the ALTERA family. The fundamental structural part of the design is the cell of the CA grid (Fig. 6.13). Each cell is supplied with nine input signals; the given cell itself `outcompCA` and each eight closest neighbours; `inruleN`, `inruleS`, `inruleE`, `inruleW`, `incompN`, `incompS`, `incompE` and `incompW`. `Clock` input is used for synchronisation reasons, whereas `clear` input is included for efficient initialisation purposes of the memory parts of the system. Evacuation mechanism is triggered, as soon as the load signal is provided with the values '11', '10', '01', '00', followed by all necessary operational processes that enable evacuation estimation. All these inputs are one-bit inputs which are serially provided to the processor. One-to-eight (1/8) bit converters intermediate so as data further to proceed in parallel, as eight-bit strings.

According to the operation process, there is an array that holds the current values of all parameters. Given the value '11' to input `load`, input `inruleS` loads its current value to the array of the present state. Hence, the value of the cell changes during the current clock pulse. The general exit of the area under study is represented by value '10'. As soon as the value of input `inruleS`, holds that value, signals `xe`, `ye` are supplied with the values of the coordinates of the cell that is `i` and `j`, respectively. Provided that (a) the value of input load is '10', (b) the value of input `inruleS` is different than '11' and (c) at the same time there is at least one of the signals that describe the state of neighbouring cells with value '11', then the value of signals sumx and sumy increase or decrease to one. sumx and sumy are intermediate signals of a cell. The exact location of the neighbouring cell defines the state of signals sumx and sumy.

The determination of the vectors due to the attractive force of the general exit corresponds to the following step of the design process. It is realised by increasing (or decreasing) the state of signals sumx and sumy by a value of 2. In fact that depends on the direction of the vector. Increasing (or decreasing) these values by two units, indicates that the magnitude of the attractive force of general exit is two times greater than the magnitude of the repulsive force of walls or obstacles. The array of Euclidean distances stores the current distances between cells and the general exit. The computation of the array is triggered in the case that the value of input load is defined to '01'. In order the evacuation process to begin, this value is defined to '00'. The states of occupied cells during next time step are stored in the array of next state, d.

The main advantage of this approach is that the internal update of the states of the cells is reassured, avoiding feeding back inputs with output values. The only variable that is user-dependant is the size of the area. The efficiency of the design is enhanced by the fact that all other parameters are modified automatically and computed according to the current conditions.

Figure 6.14 displays a typical pipelined interconnection between cells. Pipelined circuits contain registers in-between the logic blocks that break up the circuit into smaller pipeline stages. Applying this technique, the inclusion of eight-bit registers in-between structural devices is also essential for reasons of synchronisation, further increasing latency. The essence of pipelining is to break up a long process into smaller parts, and then to have each part to accomplish its mission and pass the result to the next part. Nevertheless, the appearance of a result at a constant period is reassured, hence increasing the throughput and/or the frequency of the entire circuit [16]. Memory components are used in order to balance delays during signal propagation.

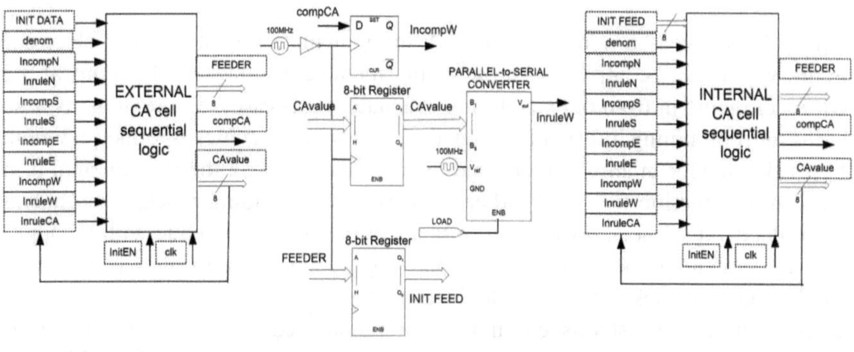

Fig. 6.14 Interconnection between cells

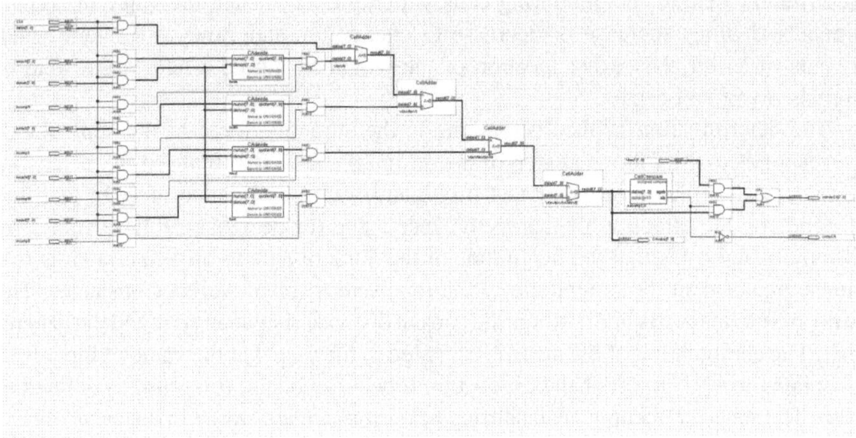

Fig. 6.15 The structural elements of the combinational part of the CA cell

Following sequential logic, each cell is separated into two parts; the combinational and the memory one. The former realises all computations that take place into cells. The latter part forwards the combinational results to the cells of the vicinity during each time step. Focusing on the design of the combinational part, Fig. 6.15 indicates the main structural elements of that module of the cell that realises all necessary arithmetic and logic operations. Finally, regarding the initialization process of the CA model implementation part, this is characterized as semi-parallel. Specifically, data starts to be loaded simultaneously, that is in parallel, whereas the process continues serially with initial bit strings moving from one cell to its adjacent at the same row of the grid until all cells are properly initiated. A parallel load register realises the parallel part of the semi-parallel method.

6.5 Conclusions and Future Work

In this chapter, it is proposed the FPGA implementation of an overall electronic circuit, which can be applied as an assisting management system that aims at preventing clogging in front of exits during evacuation processes. The system, by associating and combining information from different sources, achieves refined estimates of crowd behavior in an observed field of view, thus serving the fundamental principles of information fusion. It rather realizes a human-aiding process for analysis and/or decision support, providing the security manager of a venue with all appropriate information to perform some actions (e.g. opening additional exits, activating visual or audible cues to try to guide the crowd, etc.).

The structure is established in two interconnected parts that consist of the detection-tracking implementation and the corresponding realisation of the CA-based crowd movement model. The implementation is advantageous in terms of compactness, portability, high-speed, low-power consumption and low cost. Initialisation is processed with the detecting and tracking algorithm supported by cameras and the automatic response of the processor provides an estimation of the position of individuals near exits.

The main advantage of the structural part that realises detection and tracking initialisation mechanism is its ability to manipulate an enhanced number of frames compared to an embedded processor that requires increased amounts of processing time for such operations. Though it constitutes a simplified version of the Viola, Jones and Snow system [55], it has been proven quite accurate as far as its detection precision concerns. Among its main characteristics is the fact that the number of filters and the number of positive and negative examples during the training part is significantly smaller. The implementation of the CA model structural part facilitates the incorporation of the design as a near real-time processing module of the embedded system dedicated to anticipative crowd management. CA are efficient, as far as hardware realisation concerns, in terms of circuit design and layout, silicon-area utilisation and maximisation of clock speed. Thus, the corresponding realisation accelerates the response of the model by developing the distinct feature of parallelism that CA structures nest.

The overall implementation could be further improved by optimizing certain attributes of both constructional components. As far as the detection and tracking circuit concerns, the threshold values have been selected following the normalization method. The available features have been derived from all examples and the threshold value for each of the filters has been evaluated as the mean value of their responses. In essence, the training of the ANN (strong classifier) has not taken place automatically, as proposed by the Adaboost algorithm. Furthermore, all examples have been considered of equal importance and they were not assigned with different weight values. Consequently, the circuit can further improve its efficiency by enhancing its qualitative features as well as its training procedure. The application of more filters would obviously improve its response, since more characteristics of the frames would be incorporated. Furthermore, more examples would lead to more accurate threshold and weight values. Finally, detection rate could be increased by using more neurons.

References

1. Altera: Quartus II handbook version 13.1. Altera Corporation (2013). http://www.altera.com/literature/hb/qts/quartusii_handbook.pdf
2. Altshuler E, Ramos O, Nunez Y, Fernandez J, Batista-Leyva AJ, Noda C (2005) Symmetry breaking in escaping ants. Am Nat 166(6):643–649
3. Bandini S, Federici ML, Vizzari G (2007) Situated cellular agents approach to crowd modeling and simulation. Cybern Syst 38:729–753
4. Girau B, Tisserand A (1996) On-line arithmetic based reprogrammable hardware implementation of multilayer perceptron back-propagation. Technical report, Ecole Normale Superieure de Lyon

5. Bonabeau E (2002) Agent-based modeling: methods and techniques for simulating human systems. Proc Natl Acad Sci USA (PNAS) 99(3):7280–7287
6. Brand M, Kettnaker V (2000) Discovery and segmentation of activities in video. IEEE Trans Pattern Anal Mach Intell 22:844–851
7. Burstedde C, Klauck K, Schadschneider A, Zittartz J (2001) Simulation of pedestrian dynamics using a two-dimensional cellular automaton. Physica A 295:507–525
8. Vihas C, Georgoudas IG, Sirakoulis GC (2013) Cellular automata incorporating follow-the-leader principles to model crowd dynamics. J Cell Autom 8(5–6):333–346
9. Coifman B, Beymer D, McLauchlan P, Malik J (1998) A real-time computer vision system for vehicle tracking and traffic surveillance. Transp Res: Part C 6(4):271–288
10. Cutler R, Davis LS (2000) Robust real-time periodic motion detection, analysis, and applications. IEEE Trans Pattern Anal Machine Intell 22:781–796
11. Georgoudas IG, Sirakoulis GC, Andreadis I (2007) An intelligent cellular automaton model for crowd evacuation in fire spreading conditions. In: Proceedings of the 19th IEEE international conference on tools with artificial intelligence (ICTAI 2007), vol 1, pp 36–43
12. Georgoudas IG, Kyriakos P, Sirakoulis GC, Andreadis I (2010) An fpga implemented cellular automaton crowd evacuation model inspired by the electrostatic-induced potential fields. Microprocess Microsyst 34(7–8):285–300
13. Georgoudas IG, Sirakoulis GC, Andreadis I (2007) Modelling earthquake activity features using cellular automata. Math Comput Model 46(1–2):124–137
14. Georgoudas IG, Sirakoulis GC, Andreadis I (2011) An anticipative crowd management system preventing clogging in exits during pedestrian evacuation processes. IEEE Syst 5(1):129–141
15. Goldstone RL, Janssen MA (2005) Computational models of collective behavior. Trends Cognitive Sci 9(9):424–430
16. Goodrich MA Potential fields tutorial. http://www.ee.byu.edu/ugrad/srprojects/robotsoccer/papers/goodrich_potential_fields.pdf
17. Haldera C, Madeja L, Pietrzyka M (2014) Discrete micro-scale cellular automata model for modelling phase transformation during heating of dual phase steels. Arch Civil Mech Eng 14:96–103
18. Haritaoglu I, Harwood D, Davis LS (2000) W4: Real-time surveillance of people and their activities. IEEE Trans Pattern Anal Machine Intell 22(8):809–822
19. Helbing D, Farkas I, Vicsek T (2000) Simulating dynamical features of escape panic. Nature 407:487–490
20. Howarth RJ, Buxton H (1992) Analogical representation of space and time. Image Vis Comput 10:467–478
21. Hu W, Tan T, Wang L, Maybank S (2004) A survey on visual surveillance of object motion and behaviors. IEEE Trans Syst Man Cybern - C: Appl Rev 34(3):334–352
22. Hu WHW, Tan TTT, Wang LWL, Maybank SMS (2004) A survey on visual surveillance of object motion and behaviors. IEEE Trans Syst Man Cybern C 34:334–352
23. Hughes R (2002) A continuum theory for the flow of pedestrians. Transp Res B 36:507–535
24. Kilger M (1992) A shadow handler in a video-based real-time traffic monitoring system. In: Proceedings of the IEEE workshop applications of computer vision. IEEE, Palm Springs, pp 11–18
25. Kirchner A, Klupfel H, Nishinari K, Schadschneider A, Schreckenberg M (2003) Simulation of competitive egress behavior: comparison with aircraft evacuation data. Physica A 324:689–697
26. Kuno Y, Watanabe T, Shimosakoda Y, Nakagawa S (1996) Automated detection of human for visual surveillance system. In: Proceedings of the international conference on pattern recognition, pp 865–869
27. Li J, Yang L, Zhao D (2005) Simulation of bi-direction pedestrian movement in corridor. Physica A 354:619–628
28. Lo SM, Huang HC, Wang P, Yuen KK (2006) A game theory based exit selection model for evacuation. Fire Saf J 41:364–369
29. Lou JG, Yang H, Hu WM, Tan TN (2002) Visual vehicle tracking using an improved ekf. In: Proceedings of the Asian conference on computer vision, pp 296–301

30. Schultz M, Lehmann S, Fricke H (2007) A discrete microscopic model for pedestrian dynamics to manage emergency situations in airport terminals. In: Waldau N, Gattermann P, Knoflacher H, Schreckenberg M (eds) Pedestrian andevacuation dynamics 2005. Springer, Berlin, pp 369–375
31. Mackay M, Benhabib B (2007) A multi-camera active-vision system for dynamic form recognition. In: Proceedings of international conference on computer, information, and systems sciences, and engineering (CISSE2007)
32. Mackay M, Fenton RG, Benhabib B (2008) Time-varying-geometry object surveillance using a multi-camera active-vision system. Int J Smart Sens Intell Syst 1(3):679–704
33. Mackay M, Fenton RG, Benhabib B (2011) Multi-camera active surveillance of an articulated human form - an implementation strategy. Comput Vis Image Underst 115:1395–1413
34. McKenna S, Jabri S, Duric Z, Rosenfeld A, Wechsler H (2000) Tracking groups of people. Comput Vis Image Underst 80(1):42–56
35. Mehran R (2011) Analysis of behaviors in crowd videos. Ph.D. thesis, University of Central Florida. http://crcv.ucf.edu/papers/theses/thesis-mehra005_300.pdf
36. Meyer D, Denzler J, Niemann H (1998) Model based extraction of articulated objects in image sequences for gait analysis. In: Proceedings of the IEEE international conference on image processing, pp 78–81
37. Meyer D, Denzler J, Niemann H (1998) Model based extraction of articulated objects in image sequences for gait analysis. In: Proceedings of the IEEE international conference on image processing, pp 78–81
38. Mita T, Kaneko T, Hori O (2005) Joint haar-like features for face detection. Multimed Lab Corp Res Dev Cent Toshiba Corp 2:1619–1626
39. Mohan A, Papageorgiou C, Poggio T (2001) Example-based object detection in images by components. IEEE Trans Pattern Recognit Machine Intell 23:349–361
40. Nalpantidis L, Sirakoulis GC, Gasteratos A (2011) Non-probabilistic cellular automata-enhanced stereo vision simultaneous localisation and mapping (slam). Meas Sci Technol 22(11):114027
41. Orts-Escolano S, Garcia-Rodriguez J, Morell V, Cazorla M, Azorin J, Garcia-Chamizo JM (2014) Parallel computational intelligence-based multi-camera surveillance system. J Sens Actuator Netw 3:95–112
42. Panagiotakis C, Tziritas G (2004) Recognition and tracking of the members of a moving human body. In: Perales FJ, Draper BA (eds) AMDO 2004, LNCS 3179, Springer, pp 86–98
43. Papers AW (2007) Video surveillance implementation using FPGAs. Altera Corporation. http://www.altera.com/literature/wp/wp-videosrvl.pdf
44. Parisi D, Dorso C (2005) Microscopic dynamics of pedestrian evacuation. Physica A 354: 606–618
45. Recatala G, Carloni R, Melchiorri C, Sanz PJ, Cervera E, del Pobil AP (2008) Vision-based grasp tracking for planar objects. IEEE Trans Syst Man Cybern - C: Appl Rev 38(6):844–849
46. Remagnino P, Tan T, Baker K (1998) Agent orientated annotation in model based visual surveillance. In: Proceedings of the IEEE international conference on computer vision, pp 857–862
47. Rother C, Kolmogorov V, Blake A (2004) Grabcut: interactive foreground extraction using iterated graph cuts. In: Proceeding ACM SIGGRAPH '04. ACM, pp 309–314
48. Roy A, Sural S (2009) A fuzzy interfacing system for gait recognition. In: Proceedings of the 28th north american fuzzy information processing society annual conference, pp 1–6
49. Shiwakoti N, Sarvi M, Rose G, Burd M (2011) Animal dynamics based approach for modeling pedestrian crowd egress under panic conditions. Transp Res B: Methodol 45(9):1433–1449
50. Tarabanis KA, Allen PK, Tsai RY (1995) A survey of sensor planning in computer vision. IEEE Trans Robot Autom 11(1):86–104
51. Toffoli T (1984) Cam: a high-performance cellular automaton machine. Physica D 10(1–2):195–204
52. Varas A, Cornejo M, Mainemer D, Toledo B, Rogan J, Munoz V, Valdivia JA (2007) Cellular automaton model for evacuation process with obstacles. Physica A 382:631–642

53. Velastin S, Remagnino P, (2006) Intelligent distributed video surveillance systems., IEE Computing Series, Institution of Engineering and Technology, Stevenage
54. Viola P, Jones M (2001) Fast and robust classification using asymmetric adaboost and a detector cascade. In: Advances in Neural Information Processing System, vol 14. MIT Press, Cambridge, pp 1311–1318
55. Viola P, Jones MJ, Snow D (2003) Detecting pedestrians using patterns of motion and appearance. In: Proceedings of the IEEE international conference on computer vision, pp 734–741
56. Vlassopoulos N, Fates NA, Berry H, Girau B (2010) An fpga design for the stochastic greenberg-hastings cellular automata. In: International conference on high performance computing & simulation - HPCS, IEEE Computer Society, pp 565–574
57. Wang X, Wang S, Bi D (2009) Distributed visual-target-surveillance system in wireless sensor networks. IEEE Trans Syst Man Cybern - B: Cybern 39(5):1134–1146
58. Yuan WF, Tan KH (2007) An evacuation model using cellular automata. Phys A 384:549–66
59. Zhang W, Tong R, Dong J (2009) Boosting 2-thresholded weak classifiers over scattered rectangle features for object detection. Institute of Artificial Intelligence Zhejiang University Hangzhou, pp 397–404
60. Zhao D, Yang L, Li J (2006) Exit dynamics of occupant evacuation in an emergency. Physica A 363:501–511

Chapter 7
Visual Sensor Networks—Adaptive Online Configuration of Surveillance Networks with Distributed Smart Cameras

Chengnian Long and Jing Wu

Abstract Distributed smart cameras have been increasingly employed to capture dynamic events for tasks such as surveillance and training. When events distribute throughout a large area, many issues may occur, two of which are inevitable and critical, that is, limited computational capabilities and battery energy constraints. These two issues bring both challenge and opportunity to researchers all over the world. Different approaches for camera configurations are presented. In this chapter, we propose an adaptive online configuration for large-scale camera networks. By exploiting tracking-inspired local search and cluster-based cooperating coverage, a distributed coverage-probability-based heuristic algorithm (DCPBHA) is designed with the consideration of limited camera computational capacities and energy constraints. Furthermore, a point corresponding method is built to implement the dynamic configuration, which can minimize the overall energy consumption and balance energy distribution among camera nodes. Simulations show the camera networks can response to dynamic events quickly and last for a longer lifetime, which demonstrate the effectiveness of our proposed methods.

7.1 Introduction

Since last decade, a significant amount of surveillance applications have been seen in wireless sensor networks by deploying multiple smart cameras, such as business buildings [1], high-speed railways and train stations [2], and airports and public parks [3]. Compared to the traditional camera network, embedded smart camera incorporates image sensor, on-board processor, and wireless communication interface, which make it low-cost, self-organized and easy-deployed [4]. Thus, it can facilitate a large-scale surveillance by eliminating wired connection constraints, releasing communication bandwidths by on-board process, and reducing system's overall cost.

C. Long · J. Wu (✉)
Department of Automation, Shanghai Jiao Tong University, Shanghai, China
e-mail: jingwu@sjtu.edu.cn

C. Long
e-mail: longcn@sjtu.edu.cn

P. Spagnolo et al. (eds.), *Human Behavior Understanding in Networked Sensing*,
DOI 10.1007/978-3-319-10807-0_7

However, there is a fundamental problem in the surveillance application when the targets and coverage demand are mobile and dynamic [5]. That is, how can we configure a camera network to cover the regions of interest continuously and efficiently? We call this problem as online configuration.

The first consideration for online configuration is how to consistently achieve a satisfactory coverage quality with least amount of cameras. It deserves more concerns in a large-scale situation. One general idea that optimize the placement of cameras is reducing the redundance of cameras' Field of View (FoV) [6, 7]. Besides that, another choice will be extending camera's FoV [6]. Since a large viewing angle is impossible due to the cost and energy constraints of smart cameras embedded in wireless sensors [8], a feasible way is to use camera's patrolling behavior to create the so-called potential FoV. Here, the potential FoV means a p-coverage framework that has been firstly presented in [9]. On the other hand, using static cameras to monitor dynamic scene needs to pre-deploy a lot of cameras, whose sensor regions are usually heavy overlapped with each other to adapt network's topology to the changes of scene. This adaption procedure is called sensor selection [10]. Consequently, pre-deploy redundant cameras would result in unacceptable system cost especially for large scale situation.

As a result, if we adopt mobile platforms in [11] to eliminate the shortcoming of sensor selection, use camera's patrol behavior to enlarge camera's FoV, and continually optimize the configuration of network, our coverage goal could be fulfilled. However, it will bring some new problems: (a) p-coverage framework, mobile behavior and large-scale situation have imposed extra computation overhead on network configuration, whereas smart camera's process ability is highly restricted for its low-cost design [12]. (b) Mobile platform is usually powered by battery, which means energy efficiency should be carefully considered when implementing the configuration. Consequently, the following two critical issues need to be considered:

- How to find an efficient algorithm which could calculate the online configuration of a large-scale camera network in real time?
- How to consider the energy efficiency to prolong the network lifetime when implementing the configuration of the mobile camera networks?

In this chapter, we propose a distributed coverage-probability-based heuristic algorithm (DCPBHA) to tackle the first issue. The basic idea of DCPBHA is: online configuration could use former optimal solutions to search the current one efficiently, which is different from the network initial deployment. We also notice that with the increase of problem's complexity, collect, and process information in a centralized manner would introduce extra communication and computation overhead. Therefore, we have decentralized our algorithm to meet the network's scalable requirement. Furthermore, DCPBHA is cluster-based so that it could take the advantage of cooperative coverage in p-coverage framework, which results in a better coverage performance comparing with other distributed algorithms.

To deal with the second issue, the major energy consumption of camera node is considered by its position configuration, which means the node changes its current position to a give place. A point corresponding method is proposed to minimize the overall traveled distance when configuring the network. Moreover, some nodes may continuously changing their position in a series of configurations, which result in the prematurely run-out of their energy. Thus, the balance distribution of node energy, which can prolong the network lifetime, is also considered and evaluated by our proposed method.

The remainder of this chapter is structured as follows. Section 7.2 describes the system model and two problems in mathematical form. Section 7.3 describes the DCPBHA and the point corresponding method. The performance evaluations is shown in Sect. 7.4. We finally conclude our chapter in Sect. 7.5.

7.2 System Modeling and Problem Formulation

In this section, we will provide a probability-based optimal coverage framework for distributed camera network. Then an energy cost function is formulated for configuration. Finally, two optimization problems are presented to derive maximum camera coverage and minimum energy cost, respectively. Before we start, some notations used in this chapter are listed in Table 7.1.

7.2.1 p-Coverage and Coverage Metric

Assume one surveillance camera patrols an target periodically, its FoV could be extended to a potential FoV, see Fig. 7.1, from which the coverage definition is transformed from *cover* or *uncovered* to *p-covered*. Here *p-coverage* means the percentage of a target j is covered by a camera i in its patrol period and is denoted by λ_{ij}, which is defined as follows:

Table 7.1 Constant and variable notations

θ_i	The max pan angle of camera i
ϕ, R	The view angle and depth of patrol camera
x_i, y_i	The position of camera i
$\overrightarrow{e_i}$	The vector which defining the orientation of FoV
φ_i, ϕ_i	Orientation angle and patrol angle of patrolling
x_j, y_j	The positions of target j
$\overrightarrow{v_{ij}}$	The camera-object vector from camera i to object j
β_{ij}	The angle between v_{ij} and e_i
λ_j	The *coverage probability* of target j

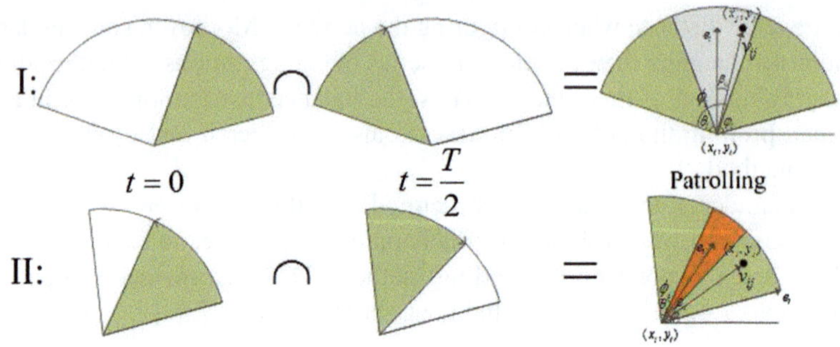

Fig. 7.1 A target is covered by patrol camera's dynamic FoV: situation I happens when $\phi_i > \theta_i$, otherwise is situation II

$$\text{If } \phi_i > \theta_i, \lambda_{ij} = \begin{cases} \frac{\theta_i}{\phi_i}, & \beta_{ij} < \frac{\phi_i - \theta_i}{2} \\ \frac{\phi_i + \theta_i - 2\beta_{ij}}{2\phi_i}, & \frac{\phi_i - \theta_i}{2} \le \beta_{ij} < \frac{\phi_i + \theta_i}{2} \\ 0, & \text{else} \end{cases} \tag{7.1}$$

$$\text{Else} \qquad \lambda_{ij} = \begin{cases} 1, & \beta_{ij} < \frac{\theta_i - \phi_i}{2} \\ \frac{\phi_i + \theta_i - 2\beta_{ij}}{2\phi_i}, & \frac{\theta_i - \phi_i}{2} \le \beta_{ij} < \frac{\phi_i + \theta_i}{2} \\ 0, & \text{else} \end{cases} \tag{7.2}$$

Moreover, when multiple cameras are used to cooperatively cover a target j, the corresponding coverage probability for the target j can be obtained as follows:

$$\lambda_j = 1 - \prod\nolimits_{i=1}^{n} (1 - \lambda_{ij}) \tag{7.3}$$

We use U to represent the set of camera's all possible configurations, including both positions (x_i, y_i) and patrol parameters (φ_i, ϕ_i). We use C_n to represent the configuration set which contains n cameras in a network. Then the camera model is:

$$C_n = \{c_1, \ldots, c_n\}, \quad \text{where} \quad c_i = (x_i, y_i, \varphi_i, \phi_i) \subset U \tag{7.4}$$

Assume each target j has a *coverage demand* p_j which varies from 0 to 1 to represent the target's important level. For a set of m targets, we ca use the following model to represent their positions and coverage demands.

$$T_m = \{t_1, \ldots, t_m\}, \quad \text{where} \quad t_j = (x_j, y_j, p_j) \tag{7.5}$$

As a result, the satisfactory rate r_j for coverage demand of target t_j is given as follows:

$$r_j = \begin{cases} \lambda_j / p_j & \text{if} \quad \lambda_j < p_j \\ 1 & \text{if} \quad \lambda_j \ge p_j \end{cases} \tag{7.6}$$

Given T_m and C_n, the average coverage rate can be obtained as follows:

$$P(C_n, T_m) = \left(\sum\nolimits_{j=1}^{m} r_j\right) / m \tag{7.7}$$

7.2.2 Energy Cost

To derive the energy cost of camera network configuration, we represent C_n as the current configuration set of cameras while C_n^* is the expected configuration set. Then a match matrix A can be defined when C_n is configured to a new status C_n^*, where the element a_{ij} indicates the ith camera in C_n is configured to a new status c_j^* in C_n^*.

$$A = \begin{pmatrix} a_{11} & \cdots & a_{1n} \\ \vdots & \ddots & \vdots \\ a_{n1} & \cdots & a_{nn} \end{pmatrix} \tag{7.8}$$

$$a_{ij} = \begin{cases} 0, & \text{others} \\ 1, & c_i \rightarrow c_j^* \end{cases}, \quad \sum_i a_{ij} = \sum_j a_{ij} = 1 \tag{7.9}$$

Assume energy cost is proportional to camera's traveled distance, it can be calculated as following:

$$E(C_n, C_n^*, A) = \sum\nolimits_{i,j}^{n} a_{ij} \operatorname{dist}(c_i, c_j^*) \tag{7.10}$$

7.2.3 Problem Formulation

Two optimal problems, *MAX-COVERAGE* and *MIN-ENERGY*, are formulated based on patrol camera's configurable FoV and mobile characteristic. By solving these two optimal problems, an optimal online configuration can be derived with less energy and larger coverage for a set of cameras.

MAX-COVERAGE: Given a set of camera's possible configuration U, camera's number n and a set of m targets T_m. One of our objectives is to find a possible configuration set C_n such that the average coverage rate $P(C_n, T_m)$ is maximum. This can be stated as:

$$\text{Given } T_m, U, n \quad \text{Max } P(C_n, T_m) \quad s.t.\ C_n \subset U \tag{7.11}$$

MIN-ENERGY: Given camera network's current configuration set C_n and expected configuration set C_n^*, another objective is to find the match matrix A such that the power consumption for implementing network configuration $E(C_n, C_n^*, A)$ is minimum. That is:

$$\begin{aligned} &\text{Given } C_n, C_n^* \quad \text{Min } E(C_n, C_n^*, A) \\ &s.t. \; \textstyle\sum_i a_{ij} = \sum_j a_{ij} = 1, a_{ij} \in \{0, 1\} \end{aligned} \tag{7.12}$$

The MAX-COVERAGE and MIN-ENERGY are combinatorial optimization problems and they are NP-hard [9]. The brute-force searching method such as ILP [13] is unfeasible to solve the problem especially for the first one. In the next section, we will introduce our distributed coverage-probability-based heuristic algorithm (DCPBHA) to solve the first problem, and a point corresponding method to solve the second one to prolong the network lifetime.

7.3 Approaches for Online Configuration

In this section, we first introduce a two-step event-based framework to solve the *MAX-COVERAGE* problem. Then we detail the framework: a distributed coverage-probability-based heuristic Algorithm (DCPBHA) is presented, which calculates optimal configuration of network under dynamic scene. Moreover, a point corresponding method is also proposed to solve the *MIN-ENERGY* problem for configuration implementation, in which both of the overall energy cost and the energy's balance distribution are considered. Finally, complexity analysis of our proposed methods is given.

7.3.1 Event-Based Online Configuration

As Eq. (7.4) states, we have 4 parameters for every camera, which can be classified as patrol parameters (φ_i, ϕ_i) and position/topology parameters (x_i, y_i). Notice that the patrol parameters are easy and cheap to configure, but lots of energy are required when moving nodes to configure its topology. Furthermore, topology change is usually slow. Therefore, our strategy is to configure the patrol behavior in real time while keeping network's topology unchanged for a given period, and we will change the topology only if it is over a given period or the network's performance is severely deteriorated, whatever comes first.

Consequently, we introduce a two-step event-based strategy for network's online configuration. We assume that with the help of additional sensors (e.g., acoustic sensors), every event could be detected and reported to corresponding camera. Therefore, every camera detects events happened in its potential FoV, and immediately configure itself (patrol behavior) as well as broadcasting its new status to neighbors. Every node which receives the message from its neighbors would also determine whether to configure itself (patrol behavior) and then update status. On the other hand, we implement the topology configuration periodically to save energy. Actually, the configuration of network's topology could also be triggered by other application-based events which are not covered in our chapter, such as severely deteriorated performance of the network. Details of this strategy could be seen in the following Algorithm 1.

Algorithm 1 Event-based DCPBHA

1: **init:** use [9] to set up the camera network
2: *//for ith camera's patrol configuration*
3: **on** *observe target t_j changed* **do**
4: $N_{hop} \leftarrow 0$, execute line 9-15
5: **end on**
6: **on** *incoming message from neighbors* **do**
7: update $N(c_i)$
8: **if** $N(c_i)$ changed **then**
9: $N_{hop} \leftarrow N_{hop+1}$ *// trigger iteration.*
10: **while** $\|M_i^k\| > \zeta$ **do**
11: shift to new status c_i^k through Eq. (7.14)
12: calculating shift vector M_i^k through Eq. (7.13)
13: **end while**
14: **Configure** (φ_i, ϕ_i) **using Eq. (7.17)**
15: broadcast c_i to its neighbors $N(c_i)$
16: **end if**
17: **end on**
18: *//for network's topology configuration*
19: **on** *Times up or application-based trigger* **do**
20: use line 2-17 to calculate config. set $C^* = \{c_i^*\}$
21: **Configure** $\{(x_i, y_i)\}$ **(Alg. 2)**
22: **end on**

7.3.2 Distributed Coverage-Probability-Based Heuristic Algorithm (DCPBHA)

Mean shift is an iterative algorithm for locating the maxima point of a density function when giving the discrete data sampled from that function. It could be used to detect the modes of the density function [14]. Thus, if we regard $P(C_n, T_m)$ as a density function, we could borrow the idea from Mean shift to find the optimal configuration set C_n^* to maximize $P(C_n, T_m)$.

The general form of mean-shift iteration for optimization is defined as follows:

$$M^k = \frac{\sum_{s \in S} K(s - x^k) F(s)(s - x^k)}{\sum_{s \in S} K(s - x^k) F(s)} \tag{7.13}$$

$$x^{k+1} = x^k + M^k, \lim_{k \to \infty} x^k = x^*, \tag{7.14}$$

where S denotes the sample set which contains possible solutions of x. It can be used to calculate the shift vector M^k. k denotes the iteration times. $K(\bullet)$ is the kernel function, which indicates the samples' contribution to the shift vector and can be used to control the sampling strategy. $F(\bullet)$ is the fitness function which equals to the function we want to maximize. After the shift vector M^k is obtained, we repeatedly move x^k to next position x^{k+1}, then it would finally converge to the optimal solution x^* that maximize $F(x)$.

In our online configuration, it should notice that a centralized algorithm would introduce extra communication and computation overhead, especially for the large-scale situation. Thus we decentralize the general Mean-Shift algorithm to meet the scalable requirement and communication and computation constraints. A cluster-based strategy which would improve the coverage rate through the cooperativity among cameras is proposed.

7.3.2.1 Cluster-Based Cooperative Coverage

We have stated in Eq. (7.3) that p-coverage framework is a cooperative coverage, which means a target could be cooperatively covered by multiple cameras. Comparing to coverage definition such as k-coverage or binary coverage, cooperative coverage could achieve better coverage performance with the same amount of cameras [9]. Thus, we should take this advantage in DCPBHA. Specifically, for every single camera i, its fitness function $F(\bullet)$ in Eq. (7.13) should not only reflect a single camera's coverage performance but also the cluster's, in which cameras could cooperate with each other to achieve a better coverage performance. The cluster for camera i is defined as $\mathcal{N}(i)$. Generally, $\mathcal{N}(i) = \{k\}$, $\text{dist}(i, k) < 2R$, where the threshold $2R$ indicates that node i and k could cooperatively cover target only if they have possible intersection of sensing region. Then we could get $F(s_i) = P(\mathcal{N}(i), T_m)$ in Eq. (7.13), where $P(\mathcal{N}(i), T_m)$ means the coverage rate of camera cluster $\mathcal{N}(i)$ monitor m targets. Thus, node i should gather neighbors' information and maximize cluster's coverage performance instead of itself. The shift vector for camera i is rewritten as:

$$M_i^k = \frac{\sum\limits_{s_i \in S_i} K(s_i - c_i^k) P(\mathcal{N}(i), T_m)(s_i^j - c_i^k)}{\sum\limits_{s_i \in S_i} K(s_i - c_i^k) P(\mathcal{N}(i), T_m)}, \tag{7.15}$$

Moreover, as we should sample S_i over whole solution space for Mean-Shift iteration, above-mentioned strategy seems not much efficient, especially, when the solution space is high dimension. Nevertheless, We argue that online configuration, dislike the initial deployment, could use the former optimal solution to find the current one locally. Inspire from the tracking idea, we incorporate local search strategy in DCPBHA to improve its efficiency.

7.3.2.2 Tracking-Inspired Local Search

We should notice that dynamic target or scene usually result in a continuous changing instead of a mutation, which means the optimal solution in the feasible solution space is also a continuous motion. Therefore, we can treat online configuration as a tracking procedure of the motion, in which just local information should be considered. For example, if a target moves, the camera which observes this target should adjust its configuration to optimally cover the target. As target's velocity is constrained, its moving distance is short with respect to the small time slot. Thus the camera only need to change a little to adjust this movement. In other word, we could sample a reduced solution space, to calculate the shift vector in Mean-Shift iteration. In our DCPBHA, we achieve this kind of local sampling through using the following truncated gaussian function as kernel function $K(\bullet)$ in Eq. (7.15).

$$K(s_i - c_i) = \begin{cases} e^{-\beta \|s_i - c_i\|_2^2}, & \|s_i - c_i\|_2 < \lambda \\ 0, & \text{others} \end{cases}, \tag{7.16}$$

where the condition $\left\| s_i^j - c_i \right\|_2 < \lambda$ means a truncation, namely, only the local configurations (marked by λ) can be sampled and then used to calculate shift vector M_i^k.

7.3.2.3 Convergence of DCPBHA

At last, in order to make the DCPBHA convergence in a finite time, we define a factor which gradually hampers the changes of the node's configuration after a given event. That is:

$$c_i^{*'} = \frac{1}{N_{\text{hop}}(c_i^* - c_i) + c_i}, \tag{7.17}$$

where N_{hop} means hops from the node which capture the event to current node. c_i^* means the expect configuration while $c_i^{*'}$ is the actual adopted configuration for camera node i. Obviously, after a given event, N_{hop} would consistently increase with the time, thus $\lim_{N_{\text{hop}} \to \infty} c_i^{*'} = c_i$. It guarantees every node would stop changing their configuration in a finite time.

In a word, the tracking-inspired local sampling and distribute feature can make DCPBHA highly efficient compared to the related heuristic algorithm, which will be discussed in Sect. 7.3.4. Moreover, cluster-based cooperating coverage also guarantees DCPBHA's better coverage performance comparing to other distributed methods, see Sect. 7.4. In Algorithm 1, we have listed the entire procedure of DCPBHA and its event-based mechanism.

7.3.3 MIN-ENERGY in Implementing Configuration

After obtaining the expected configuration parameters, the second problem MIN-ENERGY should be handled when implementing the new configurations to the camera network. As we have discussed before, node energy is mainly costed by its mobile behavior. Therefore, the goal of our point corresponding method is to build an effective match matrix to minimize the overall traveled distance. Figure 7.2 demonstrates the point corresponding method: it firstly builds the entire possible matches, then iteratively remove bad matches until the final one-one mapping is found. Details can be seen in Algorithm 2.

Algorithm 2 Point corresponding in implementation

1: Defines object set $O = \{o_1, \cdots, o_n\}$ from $C_n(t)$. Define Label set $L = \{l_1, \cdots, l_n\}$ from $C_n(t+1)$.
2: *//init*
3: Establish an initial match set $A(0)$, each object node aligned to all labels.
4: *//calculating*
5: Using Eq. (7.18) to compute the similarity of each node with respect to matched pair. e.g. $\omega_{i,l}$:similarity between object o_i with label l_j
6: Probability of match between o_i and l_l: $p_i(l|i) = \frac{\omega_{i,l}}{\sum_k \omega_{i,k}}$
7: *//Iteratively update match set $A(k)$*
8: **while** exist nodes have more tha one label in $A(k)$ **do**
9:   **for** every match pair (o_i, l_l) **do**
10:     *//o_j, l_h means the neighbors of o_i, l_l, respectively*
11:     $q_{il}^{(k)} = \sum_{o_j} \sum_{l_h} p_j^{(k)}(h|j)$
12:     $p_i^{(k+1)}(l|i) = p_i^{(k)}(l|i)(\alpha + \beta q_{il}^{(k)})$
13:   **end for**
14:   **for** each match probability $p_i^{(k+1)}(l|i)$ **do**
15:     $p_i^{(k+1)}(l|i) = \frac{p_i^{(k+1)}(l|i)}{\sum_j p_j^{(k+1)}(l|j)}$
16:     **if** $p_i^{(k+1)}(l|i) < \varepsilon$ **then**
17:       Remove the match pair (o_i, l_l) from $A(k)$
18:       $p_i^{(k+1)}(l|i) = 0$
19:     **end if**
20:   **end for**
21: **end while**

In initialization part (line 2–3) of Algorithm 2, we set the all elements of match matrix equal to 1. In calculating part (line 4–6), we use the following equation to calculate every match pair's similarity, after that the match probability is conducted.

$$\omega_{i,l} = \frac{1}{1 + d_{i.l}} + \alpha \frac{E_i^{\text{reserved}} - E_{\min}^{\text{reserved}}}{E_{\text{initial}}} \times \frac{d_{ij}}{d_{\max}} \tag{7.18}$$

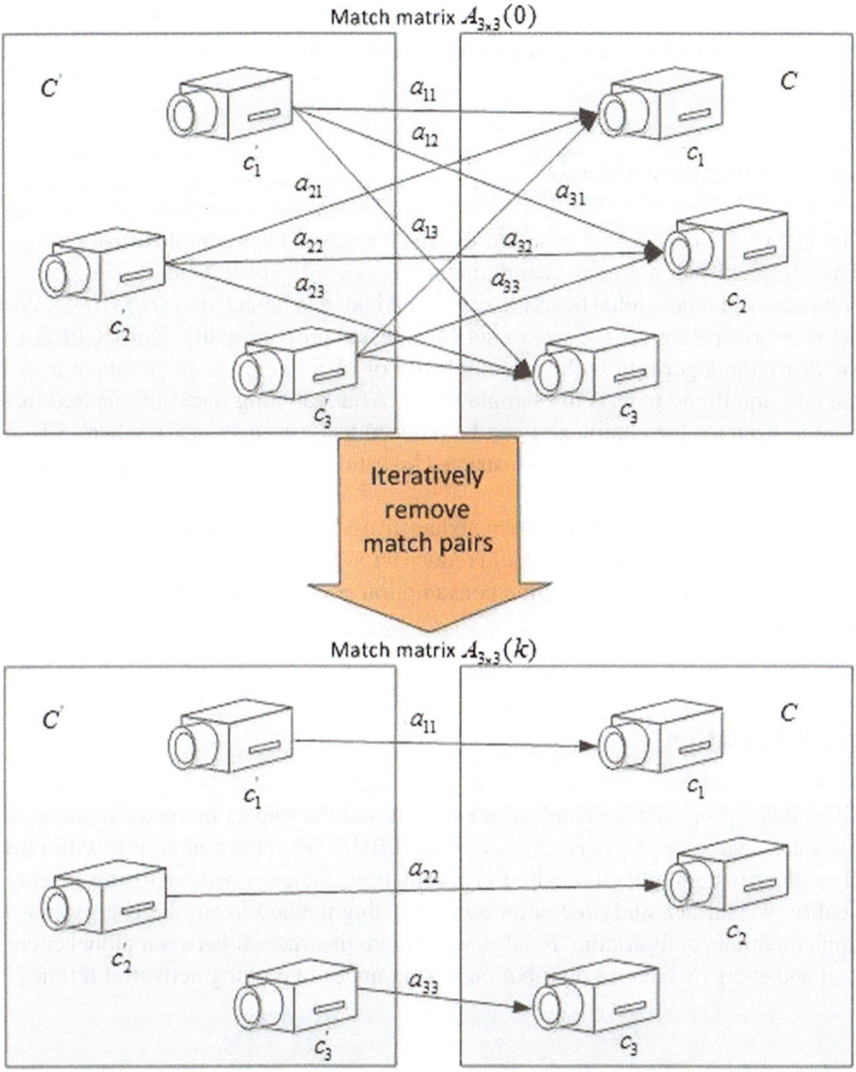

Fig. 7.2 Point corresponding for implementing topology configuration

where $d_{i,l}$ means the distance between $c_i(t)$ with $c_l(t+1)$, E_i^{reserved} means the energy reserved in the ith mote, $E_{\text{min}}^{\text{reserved}}$ means the least value of E_i^{reserved}, and E_{initial} is a constant which means the initial energy of nodes. Note that the first part is used to minimize the global energy cost while the second part can balance the node's energy distribution to prolong the network lifetime. α is a weight to adjust two parts' influence. Line 7–21 is the iterative part. We first discourage the weak match pairs and encourage the strong pairs, which is based on the status of its neighbor pairs (line 11–14), then normalize the match probability, and remove the lower ones (line 15–21). The iteration keeps going until a one-one map is found.

7.3.4 Complexity Analysis

For the MAX-COVERAGE problem, exhaustive-search has a complexity of $O(C^n_{|U|})$. The complexity of a greedy-search method is $O(n \cdot |U|)$ [9]. Due to $|U| \gg n$, the complexity of other global heuristic search methods can be stated as $O(f(|U|))$. With the network scaling up, the size of set U increases proportionally. Our DCPBHA is the distribute algorithm with the complexity of $O(n \cdot iters \cdot \iota \cdot |U|)$, where *iters* is the iteration times and ι is the sample factor. After adopting tracking-inspired local sample strategy, the complexity can be reduced to $O(n \cdot iters \cdot |S|)$, where S is the local sample set. The size of S is restricted by ι and λ in Eq. (7.16). It is usually much less than $\iota \cdot |U|$.

For the MIN-ENERGY problem, exhaustive-search has a complexity of $O(n!)$. Our points-correspond method could reduce it to $O(n^2)$. Given that $n \ll |U|$ as well as $n \ll m$, second problem's time consumption could be omitted comparing to the first problem.

7.4 Simulation

To evaluate proposed approaches, we have tested the impact of surveillance area's dynamic degree on the performance of DCPBHA. We also compare it with other algorithms to highlight our method's computation efficiency without losing coverage quality. We further study the point corresponding method to cut the energy cost in implementing configuration. Finally, we explore the tradeoff between global energy cost and energy's balance distribution among nodes to prolong network lifetime.

7.4.1 Scenario

The scenario consists of 250 target points which are randomly distributed on a 300×300 m area initially. Every target has a random probability-based coverage demand, which is uniformly ranging from 0 to 1. We have used a greedy-search method [9] to do the initial deployment of cameras. Totally 40 cameras are needed to achieve a 85 % coverage rate. After the network is set up, we assume that every single target would have a random speed to move, both on x and y directions. The speed is uniformly distributed on range $[-v_{\max}, v_{\max}]$. Suppose that a target moves, a event will be produced and then captured by camera. Thus, a series online configuration is conducted to adapt to the change. See Algorithm 1.

7.4.2 Evaluation of DCPBHA

We have discussed in Sect. 7.3.4 that DCPBHA has a very low-computation complexity for its local search and distribute feature. Notice that DCPBHA's local search is influenced by parameters λ. Thus we simulate its time consumption with different λ, and compare it with other distributed algorithms, for example, Distribute Greedy-based Algorithm (DGA) [15]. The simulation is under the condition of different number of events happened in the network, which is used to reflect the dynamic degree. Furthermore, we also compare the average coverage rate of DCPBHA with DGA and three other centralized algorithm: CGA—Centralized Greedy Algorithm—[15], PSO—Particle Swarm Optimization—[16] and MSA (Mean-Shift-based heuristic Algorithm, centralized version of DMSA—Distributed Mean-Shift-based heuristic Algorithm). The comparison is under the condition of different $v_{\max}$. In Fig. 7.3a, we can see DCPBHA ($\lambda = 1.13$) could achieve faster speed than DGA. Especially for the small amount of events, DCPBHA with different λ outperform DGA in terms of speed. In Fig. 7.3b, we can see DCPBHA's coverage rate has slightly deteriorated compared to its centralized version MSA, whereas DGA has dropped a lot from CGA. Actually, DCPBHA has the similar performance of PSO and better than DGA. By Fig. 7.3a, b, we can see that larger λ could slow DCPBHA but improve its coverage rate.

7.4.3 Evaluation of Point Corresponding Method

In Fig. 7.4, we see the energy cost of implementing 2,000 times sequential online configuration, in which the energy is measured by the distance that a camera could

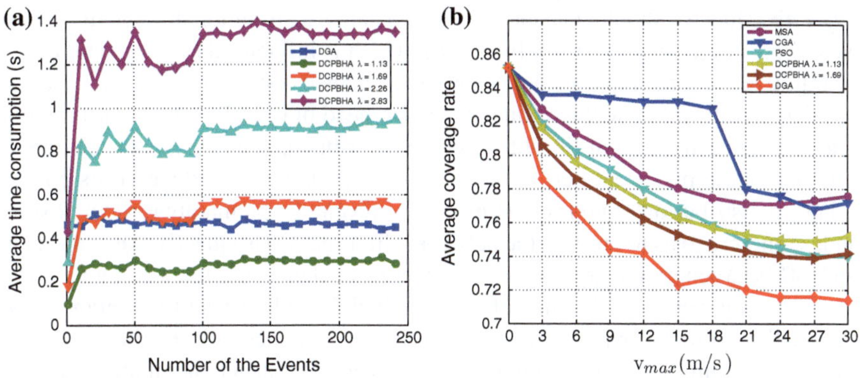

time cost of event-response

network's average coverage rate

Fig. 7.3 DCPBHA's efficiency and coverage quality under dynamic scene: **a** is under different number of events; **b** is under different target speed $v_{\max}$

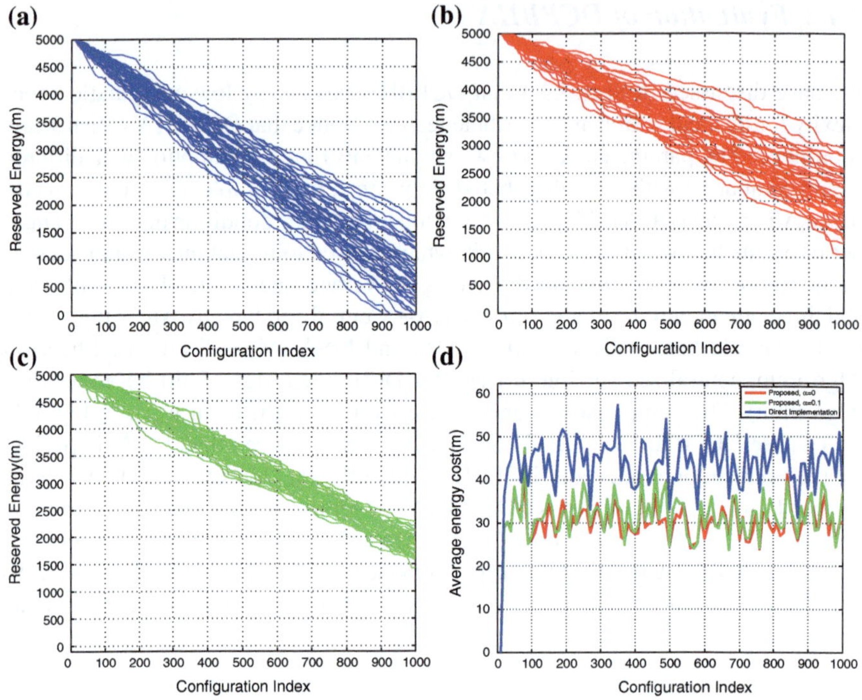

Fig. 7.4 Energy cost of different implementation of configuration. **a** Direct implementation, **b** point corresponding $a = 0$, **c** point corresponding $a = 0.1$, **d** average energy cost

totally move. The comparison between Fig. 7.4a, b shows that the point corresponding method could dramatically reduce the energy cost. However, unbalanced distribution of nodes' energy could prematurely exhaust some nodes, which is depicted in Fig. 7.4b. Thus we should consider energy's balance distribution through discussing the effects of the second part of Eq. (7.18), which is influenced by parameter α.

Intuitively, more emphasis on the energy's balance distribution, which is marked by a larger value of α, will introduce extra overhead of overall energy consumption. This can be easily seen in Fig. 7.5a. On the other hand, if we define the lifetime of network as the persistent period before any single node has exhausted its energy, balanced distribution of nodes' energy could prevent the premature run-out of some nodes' energy, so as to prolong the network's lifetime. Consequently, we explore the tradeoff between global energy cost and energies balance distribution among nodes to prolong the network lifetime in Fig. 7.5, which is with respect to different α. We can see the optimal α approximately equals to 0.08, and network could live for more than 1,500 configurations. The ignorance of energy's balance distribution ($\alpha = 0$) will shorten lifetime to 1,300, while overemphasis will make the lifetime even shorter than direct implementation.

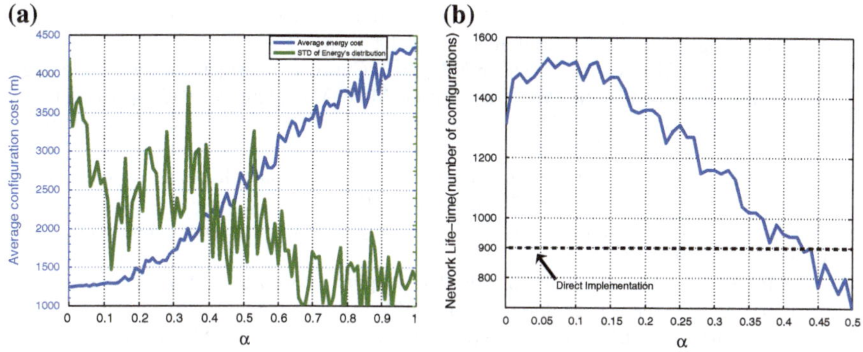

Fig. 7.5 The impacts of α on the network lifetime. **a** Impacts on energy cost and balance distribution, **b** impacts on network lifetime

7.5 Conclusion

In this chapter, we explored the problems of online configuration for a large-scale surveillance network using mobile smart cameras. A distributed coverage-probability-based heuristic algorithm (DCPBHA) is proposed to tackle the efficiency as well as the accuracy problem of online configuration. We also propose a point corresponding method to implement these configuration, in which both of network's overall energy consumption and energy's balance distribution among camera nodes are considered. Simulations show that DCPBHA is highly efficient without losing too much accuracy, which can overcome the bottlenecks of smart camera's computation ability for somehow. Network lifetime could also be prolonged by adopting our point corresponding method.

Acknowledgments The research was supported in part by the grants from NSFC (No. 61172064, 61104091), China Ministry of Railway (No. 2010X020), Shanghai PUJIANG Talents (No. 09PJ1406300), China Ministry of Education (No. 20100073120061), SJTU Science and Technology Innovation Funding (No. AE0300006).

References

1. Hengstler S, Prashanth D, Fong S, Aghajan H (2011) MeshEye: a hybrid-resolution smart camera mote for applications in distributed intelligent surveillance. In: Proceedings of the IPSN conference, July 2011, pp 360–369
2. Bramberger M, Brunner J, Rinner B, Schwabach H (2004) Real-time video analysis on an embedded smart camera for traffic surveillance. In: Proceedings of the ITAS conference, Toronto, May 2004, pp 174–178
3. Fleck S, Strasser W (2005) Adaptive probabilistic tracking embedded in a smart camera. In: Proceedings of the CVPR conference, San Diego, June 2005, pp 134–134

4. Rinner B, Winkler T, Schriebl W (2008) The evolution from single to pervasive smart cameras. In: Proceedings of the ICDSC conference, Sept 2008, pp 1–10
5. Munishwar VP, Tilak S, Abu-Ghazaleh NB (2012) Coverage management for mobile targets in visual sensor networks. In: Proceedings of the MSWiM conference 2012, pp 107–116
6. Costa DG, Guedes LA (2010) The coverage problem in video-based wireless sensor networks: a survey. Sensors 10(9):8215–8247
7. Horster E, Lienhart R (2006) On the optimal placement of multiple visual sensors. In: Proceedings of the VSSN conference 2006, pp 111–120
8. Akyildiz I, Melodia T, Chowdhury K (2007) A survey on wireless multimedia sensor networks. Comp Netw 51:921–960
9. Zhou P, Wu J, Long C (2012) Probability-based optimal coverage of PTZ camera networks. In: Proceedings of the ICC conference, June 2012
10. Park J, Micheloni C, Bhat PC, Kak AC (2006) A look-up table based approach for solving the camera selection problem in large camera networks. In: Proceedings of the international workshop on distributed smart cameras (DCS 06), 2006
11. cDrones: http://uav.lakeside-labs.com/
12. Chen P, Ahammad P, Boyer C (2008) CITRIC: a low-bandwidth wireless camera network platform. In: Proceedings of the ICDSC conference, Aug 2008, pp 1–10
13. Munishwar VP, Abu-Ghazaleh NB (2010) Scalable target coverage in smart camera networks. In: Proceedings of the ICDSC conference, Sept 2010, pp 206–213
14. Cheng Y (1995) Mean shift, mode seeking, and clustering. IEEE Trans Pattern Anal Mach Intell 17(8):790–799
15. Ai J, Abouzeid A (2006) Coverage by directional sensors in randomly deployed wireless sensor networks. J Comb Optim 11:22–41
16. Zhou P, Long C (2011) Optimal coverage of camera networks using PSO algorithm. In: Proceedings of the CISP conference, Shanghai

Chapter 8
Human Detection and Tracking in Healthcare Applications Through the Use of a Network of Sensors

Arnoldo Díaz-Ramírez, Francisco A. Bonino and Pedro Mejía-Alvarez

Abstract One of the most appealing applications of wireless sensor networks (WSNs) is in human detection and tracking. The aim of these applications is to detect if a person is in an area of interest, and to keep track of his location at every instant of time. In recent years, we have seen a growing interest in the development of proposals for the use of WSNs in detection and tracking applications for healthcare. In the particular case of a patient suffering from dementia, it is very important to detect him and keep track of his location at every time, to avoid that the patient may enter to a zone of risk without supervision. When an event of interest is detected, such as wandering, an action may be taken by sending out a notification to the caregiver personnel. In this chapter, we review the most important proposals regarding the use of WSNs for human detection and tracking in healthcare applications. Moreover, we introduce a model for detection of patients suffering from dementia, based on a WSN that uses binary sensors. The proposed model is able to detect if a patient leaves a secure zone without supervision, and to emit alerts directed to caregivers.

8.1 Introduction

Human detection and tracking is one of the most attractive fields of application of Wireless Sensor Networks (WSNs). The nodes of a WSN, known as *motes*, work together to monitor the presence of people in the sensed area, and to keep track of their location as they move. Since the motes have limited resources, an important

A. Díaz-Ramírez (✉) · F.A. Bonino
Department of Computer Systems, Instituto Tecnologico de Mexicali, Mexicali, Mexico
e-mail: adiaz@itmexicali.edu.mx

F.A. Bonino
e-mail: abonino@itmexicali.edu.mx

P. Mejía-Alvarez
Department of Computer Sciences, CINVESTAV-IPN, Mexico City, Mexico
e-mail: pmalvarez@cs.cinvestav.mx

P. Spagnolo et al. (eds.), *Human Behavior Understanding in Networked Sensing*,
DOI 10.1007/978-3-319-10807-0_8

design goal for these applications is to achieve a reliable detection of targets with minimal resources consumption. Examples of areas where they can be used are habitat monitoring, surveillance, intruder tracking, and healthcare.

New problems have emerged as a consequence of the fast growth of the urban population experienced during the past few years. Even though people now live longer, the number of deaths caused by neurodegenerative diseases has grown considerably [38]. Among them we have Psychiatric Illness, Dementia (of which Alzheimer's is the major cause), Parkinson's disease, and Autism Spectrum disorders [34]. Unfortunately, these diseases are starting earlier and affecting people under 55 years.

Most of the brain disorders are chronic and incurable, and may last for years or decades. Their economic costs are huge. In Europe, the 2010s total estimated cost was 798 billion euros, of which the 60 % was attributable to direct costs and 40 % to lost productivity [15]. For the family members that take care of patients with brain diseases, it can represent an enormous source of emotional, practical, and financial burden. As world's population ages, the healthcare systems may collapse.

Among brain disorders, one of the major health problems is dementia. Dementia describes a set of symptoms that includes loss of memory, mood issues, and problems with communication and reasoning. The causes of this disease may include a number of progressive illness that affect behavior and the ability to perform daily activities. Two of the most common types of dementia are the Alzheimer's disease and vascular dementia.

Accordingly to the Alzheimer's Disease International, 36 million people suffered from dementia worldwide in 2010, and it is estimated that this number will grow to 66 million by 2030, and to 115 million by 2050. Also, nearly two-thirds of these people live in middle and low-income countries. In addition, the global cost of dementia was estimated at $604 billion USD in 2010, and this cost is expected to grow in proportion to the number of people affected by this disorder [2]. Dementia is the main cause of dependency in the elderly, since they need constant monitoring, imposing a severe burden to caregivers.

To address these issues, the use of WSNs to implement ubiquitous systems to support healthcare activities has been the subject of intense research [1]. To ease the burden on caregivers, in-home and in-hospital WSN-based applications may provide continuous patient tracking, medical monitoring, medical data access, and emergency notifications [43]. In the case of people with cognitive and physical disabilities, the capability of continuous monitoring will increase the chance of early detection of emergency and risk conditions [24]. In addition to the elderly and patients with cognitive disorders, the care services for children may also benefit from these applications.

In this chapter, we review the most important proposals regarding the use of WSNs for human detection and tracking in healthcare applications. Moreover, we introduce a model for detection of patients suffering from dementia, based on a WSN that uses binary sensors. The proposed model is able to detect if a patient leaves without supervision a secure zone, and to emit alerts directed to caregivers.

The rest of the chapter is organized as follows. In Sect. 8.2 we briefly discuss the state of the art of the detection and tracking proposals that use networks of sensors.

Section 8.3 introduces the related work regarding human detection and tracking for healthcare applications. In Sect. 8.4, the proposed model for detection of patients suffering from dementia is presented, and in Sect. 8.5 this model is evaluated and the results are discussed. Finally, Sect. 8.6 is for conclusions.

8.2 Target Tracking Based on the Use of a WSN

Target tracking using wireless sensor networks has been the subject of intensive research in the last decade [9]. A WSN tracking application must periodically collect sensed data and use it to reconstruct the overall status of the monitored area using data fusion techniques. The centralized approach is the most commonly used in target tracking algorithms. In it, when the motes detect an event, they record it, and rely on a routing protocol to send the relevant and preprocessed information toward a base station or *sink*. The sink, which is a device with more resources than the motes, collects the data received from the sensor nodes, processes it, and takes the appropriate actions.

The algorithms designed to be used in WSN tracking applications are targeted for the network and application layers, and may assume a static or a mobile sink [8]. Regarding the application layer, two approaches have been used: coarse-grained and fine-grained [25]. Coarse-grained localization uses minimal information, which can include binary proximity [22] or near-far information [16]. In contrast, fine-grained approaches use more detailed information and are based on different types of measurements, such as the received signal strength (RSS) [37], angle of arrival (AOA) [14, 37], time of arrival (TOA) [35], time difference of arrival (TDOA) [36], extended Kalman filters (EKF) [30], and hybrid approaches [23, 47].

Concerning coarse-grained localization proposals, in [22] Kim et al. proposed a target tracking model that relies on the use of binary sensors. Such sensors provide only 1-bit information regarding the presence or absence of a target in the sensed area. Past and current sensor outputs are used to determine the trajectory of the target during small intervals. This trajectory is approximated by a straight line segment. In [41], Shrivastava et al. analyzed fundamental performance limits of target tracking using binary proximity sensors, and determined the accuracy with which a target's trajectory can be tracked. They introduced a geometric algorithm to derive linear paths that approximate the trajectory of the target, and they extended their proposal for multiple target tracking in [42]. The *Dynamical Object Tracking* (DOT) algorithm was introduced by Tsaia et al. [44]. It assumes a mobile sink since it was devised to guide a mobile user to chase a moving target. The motes that detect an intruder record the event. When the mobile user requires the target location, it sends queries that are replied by those motes that have tracking information, guiding the mobile user until he catches the target. The algorithm uses the knowledge of spatial neighborhood defined on a planar graph, where the face neighbors are identified by a Gabriel Graph. Bugallo et al. [7] addressed the problem of multiple target tracking using particle filtering. Under this approach, the algorithms need a very large number of particles when the sensed area is moderately large. To face this problem, they partition the state space of the system into different subspaces, and run a separate particle filter for each subspace.

In [12], Djuric et al. proposed the use of the auxiliary particle filtering (AFP) and the cost-reference particle filter (CRPF) algorithms for tracking a single target using data from binary sensors. The adopted model for sensor measurements was the signal strength. Vu and Zheng addressed the problem of target detection and tracking using binary proximity sensors with location uncertainty in [45]. The uncertainty was modeled as disks of possibly different radius around the nominal positions. They introduced the concept of order-k max Voronoi Diagrams (VD) that tessellates the area of interest into regions that are closer to k sensors in the worst case, to determine the minimum sensing radius needed to ensure worst-case k-coverage. Their work was extended in [46]. Le and Kaplan [27], proposed a probability hypothesis density (PHD) filter for multi-target tracking using proximity sensors. This method was able to estimate the number of targets and localize them regardless the target separation for sufficient sensor density.

Concerning the fine-grained detection approach, Arora et al. [4] introduced a surveillance system using inexpensive sensor nodes. In their model, intrusion data are processed locally at each node, and if an anomaly situation is detected, data are shared with neighboring nodes, and communicated to a gateway with wide area networking capability. The model considers three user requirements: target detection, classification, and tracking. The user may specify the QoS parameters that affect how well the system detects, classifies, and tracks targets. Sheng and Hu proposed a target location method using microphones in [40]. This method is based on a maximum likelihood estimation of both the source locations and corresponding acoustic energy readings. Since this method uses nonlinear optimization, two complementary methods were proposed to solve this nonlinear optimization problem.

He et al. proposed in [17] a monitoring system for use in military applications, such as a surveillance system, that is able to operate for long periods of time. Using magnetic sensors, the system allows a group of cooperating motes to detect and track the positions of moving vehicles. It is able to tradeoff between energy-awareness and surveillance performance by adaptively adjusting the sensitivity of the system. Based on this work, He et al. later developed *VigilNet* [18], a large-scale real-time WSN system that allows detecting, tracking, and classifying targets within a reasonable period of time, while making efficient use of energy. *VigilNet* is a system designed for spontaneous military operations in remote areas, where events of interest happen infrequently and with a short duration, such as intruder-related events. The system is organized into a layered architecture comprised of higher-level services and lower-level components. The latter includes time synchronization, localization, and routing, and forms the basis for implementing the higher-level services, such as aggregation and power management.

In [30], Lin et al. introduced an EKF-based distributed adaptive multisensor scheduling scheme for energy efficiency, to improve tracking accuracy. Since more sensors can achieve better tracking accuracy, the proposed scheduling scheme calculates the optimal sampling interval, selects the nodes that will conform the cluster, and designates one of them as the cluster coordinator. The sensor scheduling problem is formulated as an optimization problem and solved by a sequential three-step heuristic algorithm. Wang et al. proposed in [47] an approach for target tracking for WSN by combining maximum likelihood estimation and Kalman filtering using the distance measurement. The maximum likelihood estimator is used for pre-localization of the target and measurement conversion. The converted measurement and its associated noise statistics are then used in a standard Kalman filter for recursive update of the target state.

A method for RF tomographic tracking of a single target using a wireless sensor network was introduced by Li et al. [29]. RF tomographic imaging involves an image reconstruction step to estimate target locations. To avoid imaging processing, the proposed method uses a particle filtering (Sequential Monte Carlo) approach. In order to reduce the computational complexity of the algorithm, they introduced a new measurement model that does not *pixelize* the region of interest. In [49], Xu et al. addressed the problem of mobile target tracking based on a TOA measurement model. The signals emitted by the mobile target are collected by the sensor nodes, which records the signal's time of arrival (TOA). A mobile sensor also emits signals to allow the motes to collect the needed information to determine its location. This mobile sensor can also measure signal from the target. In the data fusion center, a mobile sensor controller directs the mobile sensor toward the target location. To track a moving target with a mobile sensor, the data fusion center must estimate the locations of both the target and the mobile sensor. The proposed model accounts for the measurement noise due to multipath propagation and sensing error. It uses a min-max approximation approach to estimate the targets location that can be efficiently solved by means of semidefinite programming (SDP) relaxation.

8.3 Human Detection and Tracking for Healthcare Applications

As the world's population ages, there has been a great interest in the development of ambient intelligence solutions to assist the elderly, particularly, those suffering from the Alzheimer's disease and related problems [24]. We can categorize the proposals regarding human detection and tracking for healthcare as invasive and non-invasive. In the former, the detection and tracking model considers the use of devices attached to the target's body. In contrast, in non-invasive models, the use of these devices is not required.

Regarding invasive proposals, the *Assisted Living Monitoring and Analysis System (ALMAS)*, introduced in [33] by Marques et al., extended the concepts and ideas of the *CodeBlue* project [31] by incorporating RFID technology, and employing sophisticated video analysis algorithms for patient location, tracking, and monitoring. Wireless transceivers are located throughout the facility (e.g., a geriatric residence), which communicate with the RFID tags and wearable units worn by the patients to track and locate them. The video analysis software examines the information that is continuously recorded by the video cameras, in order to detect if there is any anomalous situation, such as when a patient leaves his room toward an unauthorized area, or if a patient has fallen down.

In [19], the location tracking *Ultra Badge* system was proposed to be used in a hospital setting, with the aim of detecting falls and wandering. The system was composed of two subsystems: an ultrasonic radar subsystem, and a wheelchair locator subsystem. The first one monitors the human head's position on and around the bed, in order to detect falls. The second one is used to detect wandering, assuming that the patient uses a wheelchair. The system consists of embedded ultrasonic receivers, embedded/wireless ultrasonic emitters (named *Ultra Badges*), and a WSN that connects receivers and emitters. In [21], Intille et al. introduced *PlaceLab*, which is part of the *House_n* project, and share some of their experiences in regard to constructing and operating the living laboratory. It included the use of hundreds of sensors deployed in a live in laboratory, in order to research the use of ubiquitous computer technologies in home settings. The laboratory was designed to support the collection of rich, multimodal sensor datasets of domestic activity, which are intended to be shared among researchers working on context-aware ubiquitous computing technology, preventive healthcare, energy conservation, and education.

Bardram et al. proposed in [6] a set of context-awareness applications and technologies to be used in hospitals. The proposed system consisted, among other components, of an indoor location tracking system that uses the Bluetooth technology, and a context-aware mobile phone application. The location and tracking system was designed to locate staff, patients, and equipment, using smartphones and Bluetooth tags.

AlarmNet, introduced in [48] by Wood et al., is a system for assisted living and residential monitoring which uses a WSN. *AlamNet* consists of wearable body networks, emplaced wireless sensors, user interfaces, and back-end processing elements. The body network includes sensors for heart rate, oxygen saturation, and ECG. Emplaced sensors are deployed in living spaces to sense environmental quality, such as temperature, dust, and light, or resident activities. Motion and tripwire sensors enable location tracking. However, it is not explained how the location and tracking processes are conducted. In [10], Corchado et al. proposed *GerAmi*, an intelligent environment that integrates multiagent systems, mobile devices, RFID bracelets, and Wi-Fi technologies, to facilitate the management and control of geriatric residences. To track the location of a patient, the signal emitted from the bracelets is used by the ID readers installed on the doors. The readers forward the data to a controller, which sends a notification to a system agent that manages and forwards the information to a mobile device, where the medical staff can identify the patient's location.

An indoor system for patient tracking and monitoring system was proposed in [13]. The system is capable of determining the location of a patient, and monitoring motion activity. In this proposal, patients must carry a mobile node comprised of a RF transceiver and a 3-axis accelerometer. A localization WSN is used, consisting of static nodes, placed at known positions throughout a house or geriatric residence. The mobile nodes transmit a beacon message every 50 ms. The static nodes that receive the message will forward it to the sink, where a localization module runs.

It uses the number of the received beacon messages per static node that has the same sequence number to determine which static nodes are in proximity to the mobile node. Delaunay triangles are used to create a grid of possible regions where the target could be located. If three static nodes are found to be in proximity, the corresponding Delaunay triangle is used to determine the position of the patient. A tracking system for the elderly is proposed by Yan et al. [50]. It is based on a mixed localization algorithm that relies on sensors attached to the wrist of the patients, and the received signal indicator (RSI). The system is able to track the location of a patient regardless of whether or not he is wearing the sensor node.

Armaini et al. proposed in [3] a tracking system based on the combination of wearable sensors and a video analysis module. The wearable sensor is a mobile node that is fixed on the belt of the patient. It embeds an Inertial Navigation System (INS) consisting of gyroscopes, accelerometers, and a compass. Data is fused using an Extended Kalman Filtering (EKF). Once the wearable node detects the patient's location, the corresponding video camera is activated to confirm the presence of the patient in the predicted area.

Concerning non-invasive proposals, Marco et al. introduced *ZUPS* in [32], a ZigBee and ultrasound-based positioning system. *ZUPS* was intended to emit an alarm when a risky situation is detected, such as wandering. The system uses ZigBee (radio-frequency) and ultra-sound to measure distances between tags carried by the patients, and beacons with known locations. Additionally, an accelerometer and a button are integrated into the devices worn by the patients, to detect falls. A similar approach was used in [20], where Huang et al. proposed a patient alert system for fall management. It is a ZigBee-based location awareness and fall detection system that provides immediate position information to the caregivers as soon as it detects that a patient fell. Redondi et al. proposed *LAURA*, the *Localization and Ubiquitous Monitoring of Patients for Healthcare Support* in [39], which is an integrated system based on wireless sensor networks for patient monitoring, localization, and tracking. In their paper, the authors discuss the two proposed approaches of the localization and tracking engine. The first one is a centralized implementation, where localization is executed centrally using the information collected locally. The second approach is a distributed solution, where the localization is performed at the mobile nodes and the outcome is delivered to the central controller. The personal localization and tracking subsystem (PLTS) uses a localization algorithm based on the received signal strength and the fixed distance between nodes.

In [26], Laoudias et al. discuss the proposal of an architecture which combines the sensor health state estimation together with fault tolerant localization algorithms, to be used in a binary WSN. The proposed architecture has three main components. The Sensor State Estimation component determines the health state of each sensor. The Localization component uses the information generated by the previous module, and ignores any information coming from what are thought as faulty sensors. Finally, the target location estimate is sent to the Smoothing component, which filters the current location estimate using a particle filter.

As it can be observed, most of the proposals described here require the use of physical devices attached to the person that is being monitored or tracked, such as

RFID bracelets. However, patients with dementia tend to reject noticeable gadgets. For this kind of patients, we need a device-free passive localization [51], which is able to detect and track persons that do not carry any device.

8.4 Architecture of the Proposed System

Healthcare applications may benefit greatly by the use of networks of sensors. For instance, since it is not necessary the existence of a previous infrastructure (e.g., cables) to deploy it, the system may have a high degree of flexibility. Additionally, they provide the possibility of implementing homogeneous systems by integrating almost any sensor to the nodes constituting the WSN. This means that using only the WSN it is possible to detect a large number of events. Also, they allow the development of ambient intelligence healthcare solutions through the integration of wireless sensor networks with pervasive computing, fusion information, and artificial intelligence techniques.

The aim of the proposed model is to support the care process of patients with dementia. It is an extension of the model introduced in [11]. In particular, the objective of the extended model is to add robustness to the former one, when detecting a patient leaving a safe location without supervision. The specific objective is to identify if a patient leaves a room, having arrived there by himself or by someone else, such as a nurse.

As discussed previously, some proposals that have been published to date also consider the use of ubiquitous computing to implement healthcare monitoring and tracking applications. However, most of them include the use of devices attached to the person that is being monitored, and that are hardly accepted by dementia patients. Our purpose has been to investigate how to monitor dementia patients using non-invasive techniques, as the one used in the system discussed in [51] for patient location, or the one discussed in [5] for falls detection. However, unlike these proposals that use the strength of the signal detected by the sensors, we wanted to develop a simpler solution using inexpensive binary sensors. In addition, the use of binary sensors reduces the processing overhead, allowing a faster system response. In our model, the sensors produce binary outputs without the need of filter them to achieve binary signals.

Non-invasive techniques are helpful when it is not possible or convenient use invasive methods. Additionally, the proposed model can be used together with an invasive model to improve the system's performance. It can be used also as a redundant system to detect events of interest, in case that the main systems fails. For instance, if the patient removed the RFID bracelet attached to him.

In order to select the most suitable sensors to successfully detect if a patient leaves a room, and taking into consideration the results published in the literature, we conducted several tests using different types of sensors. The choice was made based on the accuracy in detecting the changes in the environment, and their relationship with the amount of processing to be given to the output received from the sensor.

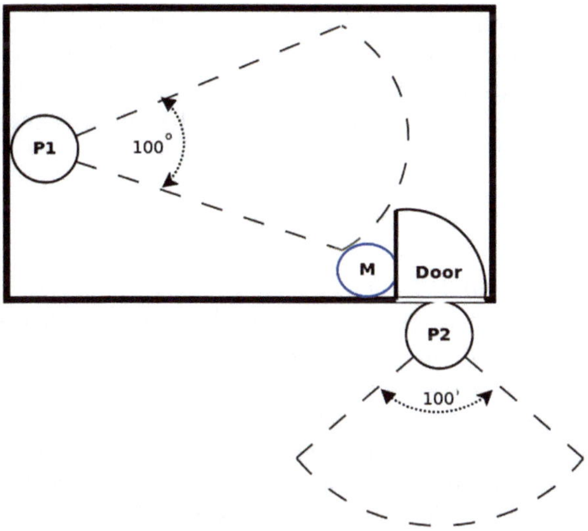

Fig. 8.1 System deployment

Two of the sensors tested showed a very good performance: passive infrared sensors, and magnetometers.

Passive InfraRed (PIR) sensors measure the infrared light emanating from objects. They are cheap sensors that detect the presence of heat from an object or body nearby. They are also capable of detecting the movement of people when a temperature change occurs. Motion detectors usually use PIR sensors. On the other hand, magnetometers are sensors that detect the change of direction of a magnetic field. When placed on the doors of the rooms, it is possible to know if they were opened or closed. However, we require that the system would be able to decide if the door was opened because someone entered the room, or opened for a person to leave the room. For this, we propose an algorithm that uses information fusion techniques to combine the values measured by PIRs and magnetometers, to determine whether a person enters a room (I), or leaves a room (O).

Because there are many scenarios to consider for the detection of wander, we propose another algorithm that combines the measured values of the sensors, and the events I and O, to determine if a patient leaves a room without authorization. The system deployment is shown in Fig. 8.1.

8.4.1 Non-invasive Tracking Algorithms

In order to be able to design a WSN-based algorithm to detect when a patient enters or leaves a room, it was important to understand the relationship between the data collected by the sensors. To achieve this, we conducted a set of experiments using the deployment shown in Fig. 8.1. As it can be observed, a node equipped with a magnetometer (M) was placed on the door of the room, whereas two nodes using a PIR sensor were placed on a wall inside the room (P_1), and on top of door (P_2), outside the room, respectively. It is important to note that the deployment of the sensors is important in our model. The PIR sensor placed on the wall (P_1) must detect any event around the room's door. The second PIR (P_2) must sense any movement close to the door, outside the room. The magnetometer must be able to detect any movement of the door.

The sensors were activated when an event of interest took place (e.g., motion is detected in the room). Afterward, they periodically sensed the environment until no activity was detected. The data collected by the sensors was sent to the sink.

An important observation from the analysis of the data obtained from the experiments, is that it is possible to differentiate the event of a *person entering the room* (I), from the event of a *person leaving the room* (O), using the values recorded from the sensors. To illustrate this, Fig. 8.2 shows the data collected from the sensors when a person enters the room, and later when a person leaves the room. We can observe that in the former case, we first got data from the magnetometer, followed by data received from both M and P_1 sensors, and finally data from the P_1 sensor. In contrast, in the later case we first received data from the P_1 sensor, followed by data received from both M and P_1 sensors, and finally we received data from the magnetometer, and also from the P_1 sensor if a person stays in the room. Using the above relationships between the values measured by the sensors as a function of the time, it was possible to design an algorithm based on information fusion techniques, to determine the type of event occurred (i.e., I or O).

In our model, S_t represents a sample recorded by a sensor node, where t is the time when the event was detected. $S \in (M, P)$, where M is a sample recorder by the

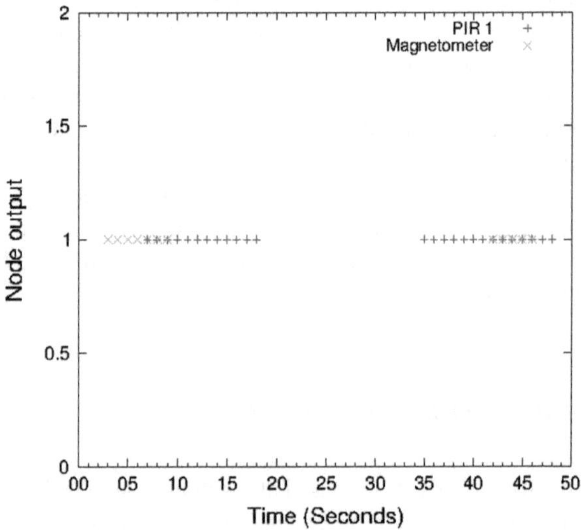

Fig. 8.2 Values measured by the sensor when a person enters and leaves a room

magnetometer, and P by the PIR sensor on the wall of the room, which are the only sensors needed to detect either I and O events. The events of interest are: I, a person entering the room, and O, a person leaving the room. For instance, considering the behavior of an I event, and assuming, without loss of generality, that the event starts at $t = 1$, and that the sampling period T is 1 second, the event can be represented as:

$$I = (M_1, M_2, \ldots, M_i, P_j, M_{i+1}, P_{j+1}, \ldots, M_k, P_{k+1}, \ldots, P_{n-1}, P_n).$$

As it can be observed, the event takes place in the interval $(1, n)$. The magnetometer detects activity in the interval $(1, k)$, whereas the PIR sensor detects it in the interval (j, n). During the interval (i, k), we have that the time elapsed between two consecutive samples, named t, satisfies the relationship $0 \leq t \leq T$. We call *intersection* the interval (i, k). The samples S_t are stored in a sliding window W of size ws.

The characteristics of the patients can vary depending on the age, type of disease, among other things. Also, the conditions of the rooms vary considerably in size, distribution, weight, and orientation of the doors, just to name a few. Because of this reason, the proposed model requires a training stage, to determine the values of parameters of interest of the events that are used by the algorithm. The parameters of interest are: the mean and standard deviation of the number of samples of the I and O events, named $\bar{S_I}$, σ_{S_I}, $\bar{S_O}$, and σ_{S_O}, respectively. Also, the mean and standard deviation of the number of samples collected by the magnetometer before the intersection in an I event, $\bar{M_I}$ and σ_{M_I}, respectively; the mean and standard deviation of the number of samples collected by the PIR sensor after the intersection in an I event, $\bar{P_I}$ and σ_{P_I}, respectively; the mean and standard deviation of the number of samples collected by the PIR sensor before the intersection in a O event, $\bar{P_O}$ and σ_{P_O}, respectively; and the mean and standard deviation of the number of samples collected by the magnetometer sensor after the intersection in a O event, $\bar{M_O}$ and σ_{M_O}, respectively. Finally, the threshold values TM_I, TM_O, TP_I, and TP_o, which are of the maximum number of samples recorded by the magnetometer and PIR sensors, and their respective standard deviations, before and after an intersection, for both events. To obtain these parameters, data is collected in the training stage, from the I and O events, for each patient and a room.

When the nodes discover activity, they send the collected data to the sink, where each sample is stored in the sliding window. The algorithm detects the beginning of an event when the time elapsed between two consecutive samples is equal or less than T. The event finishes when the previous condition is not satisfied, or when the number of samples is large enough to conclude that an event of interest has taken place. To determine if an event I or O has taken place, the following expression is used,

$$E = 1 - \frac{|NS - \bar{S}_E|}{\lambda \cdot \sigma_{S_E}}, \tag{8.1}$$

where NS is the number of samples of the event, and λ is a constant. If $E \geq 0$, the algorithm concludes that an event has occurred.

The NS parameter is the sum of the number of samples before, during and after the intersection. In the former and latter cases, if the number of samples are greater than a threshold, then the threshold value is used. The mean and the standard deviation of the number of samples can be used as a threshold value. The algorithm is described in Fig. 8.3. It can be observed that the function `event()` is used to determine the type of event, which can be I, or O.

For instance, consider the case of the I event discussed previously. The algorithm first receives the data sent by the magnetometer collected in the interval $(1, i)$, followed by an intersection (data sent by both nodes) collected in the interval (j, k), and finally the data sent by the PIR sensor, collected in the interval $(k + 1, n)$. Then, it calculates the following, as shown in the algorithm of Fig. 8.3:

- $b = \sum_{t=1}^{i} M_t$ if $b \leq \bar{M}_I + \sigma_{M_I}$; $b = \bar{M}_I + \sigma_{M_I}$ otherwise;
- $m = \sum_{t=j}^{k} S_t$;
- $l = \sum_{t=k+1}^{n} P_t$ if $l \leq \bar{P}_I + \sigma_{P_I}$; $l = \bar{P}_I + \sigma_{P_I}$ otherwise; and
- $NS = b + m + l$.

To determine if an I event has occurred, the algorithm evaluates the following expression:

$$E_I = 1 - \frac{|NS - \bar{S}_I|}{\lambda \cdot \sigma_{S_I}}. \tag{8.2}$$

Finally, if $E_I \geq 0$, the algorithm concludes that an I event occurred.

The second algorithm uses the temporal relationship maintained by the order in which the sensors are activated, when someone leaves a room without supervision. Through various experiments, it was observed that this is the occurrence of events, or a change of states in the environment in a particular order. For instance, when a patient leaves a room, he first performs an activity within it (such as walking), later the door is opened, and finally, there is no activity in the room. We assume that only authorized individuals can enter the room through a security mechanism. The state machine (SM) shown in Fig. 8.4 depicts the proposed algorithm.

The SM has five states representing changes in the patient's environment. State 0 represents that the room is empty, while State 4 represents a patient left the room without supervision. States 1, 2, and 3 are transitional states, and represent: one or two people entered the room, another person entered the room with the patient inside, and that a person has left the room leaving inside the patient, respectively. State changes may occur as a consequence of the events produced by the sensor measurements, evaluated as a function of time. The events that cause state changes are: I, representing an input is detected; O, representing that an output was detected; P_1, which means that the PIR sensor placed on the wall detects activity in the room; N_1, which represents a period of inactivity inside the room, P_2, which means that the PIR sensor placed on the door detects activity outside the room; and finally N_2, which represents no activity is detected outside the room. In our former model [11],

```
/* Input: S_t, samples collected by sensors,
   conformed of a timestamp (ts) and node id. */
/* Output: e, type of event (I, O, P, or N) */
while (true) do
   i=b=m=l=0;
   b_node_id = l_node_id = NULL;
   w[i]=S_t;
   i++;
   w[i]=S_t;
   while ( w[i].ts - w[i-1].ts ≤T ) do
      b_node_id = w[i].id;
      b = 2;
      i++;
      w[i]=S_t;
      while [ ( w[i].ts - w[i-1].ts ≤T ) and
               (w[i].id == w[i-1].id) ] do
         b++;
         i++;
         w[i]=S_t;
      m = 1;
      i++;
      w[i]=S_t;
      while [ ( w[i].ts - w[i-1].ts ≤T ) and
         !( w[i].id == w[i-1].id == w[i-2].id ) ] do
         if(w[i].lastElement.id == P2)
               m++;
         i++;
         w[i]=S_t;
      l = 1;
      i++;
      w[i]=S_t;
      if(b_node_id == INPUT)
         b_threshold = b_thresholdInput;
         l_threshold = l_thresholdInput;
      else
         b_threshold = b_thresholdOutput;
         l_threshold = l_thresholdOutput;

      while [ ( w[i].ts - w[i-1].ts ≤T ) and
               (l ≤l_threshold) ] do
         l_node_id = w[i].id;
         l++;
         i++;
         w[i]=S_t;
      if (b ¿ b_threshold)
         b = l_threshold;
      e = event(b, m, l, b_node_id, l_node_id); // using Eqn. 1
      send_event(e);
   i++;
   w[i]=S_t;
```

Fig. 8.3 Algorithm 1

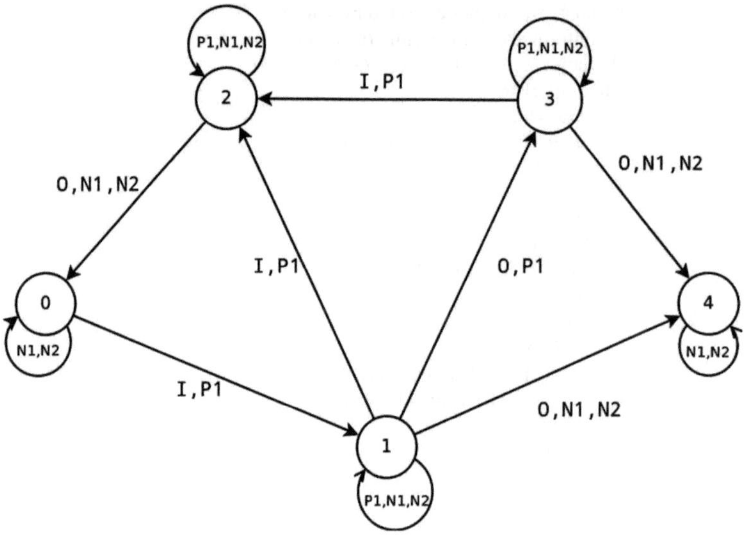

Fig. 8.4 State machine

it was difficult to detect the transition from State1 to State2, and from State2 to State0. The inclusion of the PIR outside the room's door enables a more accurate detection of these cases. Additionally, the model is able to detect a patient leaving the room even when there are people standing or moving outside the patient's room.

We restricted our model to the scenarios described above since they represent common situations in geriatric residences, or at home, where family members take care of a person affected by the Alzheimer's disease. In these cases, the patient is under constant supervision, with the exception of special situations. For instance, when the patient goes to sleep, or when the caregiver is busy preparing meal. Our model is aimed to be used in these and similar cases. Otherwise, the system can be deactivated. It is important to note that our model is able to distinguish whether the patient or caregivers are leaving the room.

On the other hand, if the proposed system is deployed to be used in different scenarios, some minor modifications to the proposed algorithm are required, and perhaps it would be necessary the addition of more sensors. It is important to note that our purpose has been to show that is possible to define a non-invasive method to detect events of interest, using inexpensive binary sensors.

8.5 Evaluation

The proposed algorithms were evaluated using a room with only one access, and simulating various activity scenarios. We implemented a prototype of the proposed model and conducted a series of experiments to evaluate it.

To implement the prototype, the nodes used were equipped with two types of sensors. One was the PIR sensor, which can detect people's movement through the energy they emit. The PIR sensor used has a maximum radial detection distance (straight ahead) of 7 m, and a detection angle of 100°. The second PIR sensor was placed on the outside wall of the room, above the door. The other sensor used was the magnetometer, which detects the change in the magnetic field direction. This sensor is used in conjunction with a magnet integrated in the door, to detect when it is opened.

The WSN was composed of four nodes. Three of them used an IRIS hardware platform, which was programmed using the *nesC* language and the *TinyOS* operating system [28]. These nodes have a MTS300CA board, one of them containing a magnetometer and two of them containing PIR sensors. The third node was used as a sink, and was connected to a personal computer via an interface board MIB520.

We used a DYP-ME003 model PIR sensor. It is a digital sensor that has a *true* output when someone enters to its detection area. The PIR sensor output depends on the electric current in its power source. This implies that, when the magnitude of the current decreases, so it does the magnitude of the high level output of the PIR sensor.

To increase the lifetime of the PIR sensor node, and for a more certainty in its measurements, the PIR sensor was connected to an LM741C model operational amplifier (Opamp), which is connected using a magnitude comparator configuration. The amplifier output was connected to a MDA300CA board. This connection is illustrated in Fig. 8.5. Note that the values of resistors connected have 10 KΩ, and $V_{cc} = 5$ VDC.

We conducted a set of controlled experiments to evaluate our first algorithm. The goal of this set of experiments was to corroborate whether the algorithm was able to detect a person entering and leaving the room. From the training stage, we obtained the following parameters values: $\bar{S}_I = 18.45$, $\sigma_{S_I} = 1.67$, $\bar{S}_O = 21.9$, and

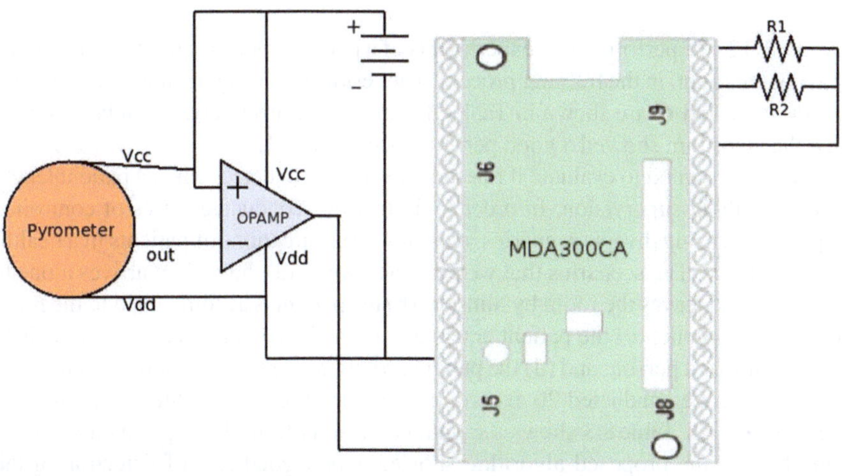

Fig. 8.5 PIR sensor connected to aMDA300CA board

Table 8.1 Results obtained from the evaluation of event I

λ	Detected	False negatives
1	13	7
1.1	13	7
1.2	14	6
1.3	14	6
1.4	14	6
1.5	15	5
1.6	15	5
1.7	17	3
1.8	17	3
1.9	18	2
2	18	2

Table 8.2 Results obtained from the evaluation of event O

λ	Detected	False negatives
1	13	7
1.1	13	7
1.2	13	7
1.3	16	4
1.4	16	4
1.5	16	4
1.6	18	2
1.7	18	2
1.8	18	2
1.9	19	1
2	19	1

$\sigma_{S_O} = 1.12$. We performed 20 experiments of a person entering a room, and 20 more leaving the room, in the training process. The results of the algorithms evaluation for the events I and O are shown in Tables 8.1 and 8.2, respectively. It can be observed that the algorithm showed a good performance for $\lambda \geq 1.8$.

Next, we wanted to evaluate if our model was able to detect when a patient leaves a room without supervision. In order to do that, we conducted series of controlled experiments using diverse scenarios, recreating real situations of patients in a health-care residence. The scenarios that we evaluated were: (a) the patient arrives alone to the room, and leaves the room by himself; (b) the patient is accompanied to the room and leaves it alone; (c) the patient enters the room alone, and leaves it with the help of an authorized person; and (d) the patient arrives and leaves the room accompanied by a person. We conducted 20 experiments of each scenario. In these experiments, we used $\lambda = 2$. Table 8.3 shows the obtained results from the experiments. As we can observe, the proposed algorithm showed a very good rate of detection of the events of interest. As we can observe from Table 8.3, scenario d showed the worst

Table 8.3 Evaluation of the second algorithm

Scenario	Rate of detection (%)
a	90
b	80
c	80
d	70

detection rate. This is because the parameters of the system were obtained from the training stage considering only one person, and in this scenario two people are involved: the patient and the caregiver. A change in the parameters (e.g., a larger λ) may provide a better detection rate.

8.6 Conclusions

The fast urban population growth and the aging of the world population are imposing a heavy burden in the government's healthcare and financial systems. One of the major health problems of the elderly is dementia. Dementia is the main cause of dependency in older people, since they need constant supervision. Alzheimer's disease and vascular dementia are the most common types of dementia. The use of sensors of networks to assist the elderly has been a subject of intensive research in recent years. In this chapter, we reviewed some of the most important proposals regarding the use of wireless sensor networks for target tracking. Also, we discussed some of the proposals published to date about human detection and tracking for healthcare applications.

We introduced a pervasive computing model, based on the use of a WSN, to support the activities of assistance and monitoring of patients with dementia. Using high-availability and low-cost binary sensors, the proposed model has been designed to detect in real-time when the patient enters a secure zone, and to emit alerts if he leaves it. Particularly, we proposed two algorithms to determine if a patient leaves a room without supervision, assuming the use of a WSN equipped with passive infrared sensors and magnetometers. The evaluation of the proposed algorithms showed that they are able to detect efficiently when a patient leaves a room without supervision. In addition, the proposed model can detect events in more complex scenarios with minor modifications and the addition of more sensors.

References

1. Alemdar H, Ersoy C (2010) Wireless sensor networks for healthcare: a survey. Comp Netw 54(15):2688–2710
2. Alzheimer's Disease International. www.alz.co.uk

3. Armanini A, Colombo A, Conci N, Daldoss M, Fontanelli D, Palopoli L (2012) Wireless sensor networks and video analysis for scalable people tracking. In: Proceedings of the 5th international symposium on communications control and signal processing, Rome, Italy, May 2012, pp 1–4
4. Arora A, Dutta P, Bapat S, Kulathumani V, Zhang H, Naik V, Mittal V, Cao H, Gouda M, Choi Y, Herman T, Kulkarni S, Arumugam U, Nesterenko M, Vora A, Miyashita M (2004) A line in the sand: a wireless sensor network for target detection, classification, and tracking. Comp Netw 46(5):605–634
5. Avvenuti M, Baker C, Light J, Tulpan D, Vecchio A (2009) Non-intrusive patient monitoring of alzheimers disease subjects using wireless sensor networks. In: Proceedings of the 2009 world congress on privacy, security, trust and the management of e-Business, Saint John, New Brunswick, pp 161–165
6. Bardram JE, Hansen TR, Mogensen M, Soegaard M (2006) Experiences from real-world deployment of context-aware technologies in a hospital environment. In: Proceedings of the 8th international conference on ubiquitous computing, Orange County, September 2006, pp 369–386
7. Bugallo MF, Lu T, Djuric PM (2007) Target tracking by multiple particle filtering. In: Proceedings of the IEEE aerospace conference, Big Sky, March 2007, pp 1–7
8. Calafate CT, Lino C, Diaz-Ramirez A, Cano J-C, Manzoni P (2013) An integral model for target tracking based on the use of a wsn. Sensors 13(6):7250–7278
9. Cao Q, Yan T, Stankovic J, Abdelzaher T (2005) Analysis of target detection performance for wireless sensor networks. In: Distributed computing in sensor systems proceedings, vol 3560. Springer, pp 276–292
10. Corchado JM, Bajo J, Abraham A (2008) Gerami: improving healthcare delivery in geriatric residences. IEEE Intell Syst 23(2):19–25
11. Diaz-Ramirez A, Murrieta FN, Atempa JA, Bonino FA (2013) Non-intrusive tracking of patients with dementia using a wireless sensor network. In: Proceedings of the IEEE international conference on distributed computing in sensor systems, Cambridge, May 2013, pp 460–465
12. Djuric MP, Mahesh V (2008) Target tracking by particle filtering in binary sensor networks. IEEE Trans Signal Process 56(6):2229–2238
13. D'Souza M, Wark T, Ros M (2008) Wireless localisation network for patient tracking. In: Proceedings of the IEEE international conference on intelligent sensors, sensor networks and information processing, Sydney, pp 79–84
14. Girod L, Lukac M, Trifa V, Estrin D (2006) The design and implementation of a self-calibrating distributed acoustic sensing platform. In: Proceedings of the 4th international conference on embedded networked sensor systems, Boulder, Colorado, Oct 2006, pp 71–84
15. Gustavsson A, Svensson M, Jacobi F, Allgulander C, Alonso J, Beghi E, Dodel R, Ekman M, Faravelli C, Fratiglioni L (2011) Cost of disorders of the brain in europe 2010. Eur Neuropsychopharmacol 21(10):718–779
16. He T, Huang C, Blum BM, Stankovic JA, Abdelzaher T (2003) Range-free localization schemes for large scale sensor networks. In: Proceedings of the 9th annual international conference on mobile computing and networking, San Diego, Sept 2003, pp 81–95
17. He T, Krishnamurthy S, Stankovic JA, Abdelzaher T, Luo L, Stoleru R, Yan T, Gu L, Hui J, Krogh B (2004) Energy-efficient surveillance system using wireless sensor networks. In: MobiSys'04: proceedings of the 2nd international conference on mobile systems, applications, and services, New York, 2004, ACM, pp 270–283
18. He T, Vicaire P, Yan T, Luo L, Gu L, Zhou G, Stoleru R, Cao Q, Stankovic JA, Abdelzaher T (2006) Achieving real-time target tracking usingwireless sensor networks. In: 12th IEEE real-time and embedded technology and applications symposium (RTAS'06). IEEE, pp 37–48
19. Hori T, Nishida Y (2005) Ultrasonic sensors for the elderly and caregivers in a nursing home. In: Proceedings of the 7th international conference on enterprise information systems, Miami, May 2005, pp 110–115
20. Huang CN, Chiang CY, Chang JS, Chou YC, Hong YX, Hsu SJ, Chu WC, Chan CT (2009) Location-aware fall detection system for medical care quality improvement. In: Proceedings

of the 3rd international conference on multimedia and ubiquitous engineering, Qingdao, June 2009, pp 477–480
21. Intille SS, Larson K, Tapia EM, Beaudin JS, Kaushik P, Nawyn J, Rockinson R (2006) Using a live-in laboratory for ubiquitous computing research. In: Proceedings of the 4th international conference on pervasive computing, Dublin, May 2006, pp 349–365
22. Kim W, Mechitov K, Choi J-Y, Ham SK (2005) On target tracking with binary proximity sensors. In: Proceedings of the 4th international symposium on information processing in sensor networks, Los Angeles, April 2005, pp 301–308
23. Kleine-Ostmann T, Bell AE (2001) A data fusion architecture for enhanced position estimation in wireless networks. IEEE Comm Lett 5(8):343–345
24. JeongGil K, Chenyang L (2010) Wireless sensor networks for healthcare. Proc IEEE 98(11):1947–1960
25. Krishnamachari B (2005) Networking wireless sensors. Cambridge University Press, Cambridge
26. Laoudias C, Michaelides MP, Panayiotou C (2013) Fault tolerant target localization and tracking in binary wsns using sensor health state estimation. In: Proceedings of the IEEE international conference on communications, Budapest, June 2013, pp 1469–1473
27. Le Q, Kaplan Lance M (2013) Probability hypothesis density-based multitarget tracking for proximity sensor networks. IEEE Trans Aerosp Electron Syst 49(3):1476–1496
28. Levis P, Gay D (2009) TinyOS programming. Cambridge University Press, Cambridge
29. Li Y, Chen X, Coates M, Yang B (2011) Sequential monte carlo radio-frequency tomographic tracking. In: Proceedings of the IEEE international conference on acoustics, speech and signal processing, Czech Republic, pp 3976–3979
30. Lin J, Xiao W, Lewis FL, Xie L (2009) Energy-efficient distributed adaptive multisensor scheduling for target tracking in wireless sensor networks. IEEE Trans Image Process Instr Meas 58(6):1886–1896
31. Malan D, Fulford-Jones T, Welsh M, Moulton S (2004) Codeblue: an ad hoc sensor network infrastructure for emergency medical care. In: Procedings of international workshop on wearable and implantable body sensor networks, London, April 2004
32. Marco A, Casas R, Falco J, Gracia H, Artigas J, Roy A (2008) Location-based services for elderly and disabled people. Comput Comm 31(6):1055–1066
33. Marques O, Chilamakuri P, Bowser S, Woodworth J (2004) Wireless multimedia technologies for assisted living. In: Proceedings of the 2nd international Latin American and Caribbean conference for engineering and technology, Miami, June 2004
34. National Institute of Mental Health. http://www.nimh.nih.gov/ Last visted: May 2014
35. Niculescu D, Nath B (2003) Ad hoc positioning system (aps) using aoa. In: Proceedings of the INFOCOM 2003, vol 3CA, San Francisco, pp 1734–1743
36. Patwari N, Ash JN, Kyperountas S, Hero III AO, Moses RL, Correal NS (2005) Locating the nodes: cooperative localization in wireless sensor networks. IEEE Signal Process Mag 22(4):54–69
37. Patwari N, Hero III AO, Perkins M, Correal NS, O'Dea RJ (2003)Relative location estimation in wireless sensor networks. IEEE Trans Signal Process 51(8):2137–2148
38. Pritchard C, Mayers A, Baldwin D (2013) Changing patterns of neurological mortality in the 10 major developed countries 1979–2010. Public Health 127(4):357–368
39. Redondi A, Chirico M, Borsani L, Cesana M, Tagliasacchi M (2013) An integrated system based on wireless sensor networks for patient monitoring, localization and tracking. Ad Hoc Netw 11(1):39–53
40. Sheng X, Hu Y (2005) Maximum likelihood multiple-source localization using acoustic energy measurements with wireless sensor networks. IEEE Trans Signal Process 53(1):44–53
41. Shrivastava N, Mudumbai R, Madhow U, Suri S (2006) Target tracking with binary proximity sensors: fundamental limits, minimal descriptions, and algorithms. In: Proceedings of the 4th international conference on embedded networked sensor systems, Nov 2006, pp 251–264
42. Singh J, Kumar R, Madhow U, Suri S, Cagley R (2011) Multiple-target tracking with binary proximity sensor. ACM Trans Sensor Netw 8(1):5:1–5:26

43. Stanford V (2002) Using pervasive computing to deliver elder care. IEEE Pervasive Comput 1(1):10–13
44. Tsaia H-W, Chua C-P, Chenb T-S (2007) Mobile object tracking in wireless sensor networks. Comput Comm 30(8):1811–1825
45. Vu K, Zheng R (2011) Robust coverage under uncertainty in wireless sensor networks. In: Proceedings IEEE INFOCOM, Shanghai, April 2011, pp 2015–2023
46. Vu K, Zheng R (2012) Geometric algorithms for target localization and tracking under location uncertainties in wireless sensor networks. In: Proceedings of the IEEE INFOCOM, Orlando, March 2012, pp 1835–1843
47. Wang X, Fu M (2012) Target tracking in wireless sensor networks based on the combination of kf and mle using distance measurements. IEEE Trans Mobile Comput 11(4):567–576
48. Wood A, Stankovic J, Virone G, Selavo L, He Z, Cao Q, Doan T, Wu Y, Fang L, Stoleru R (2008) Context-aware wireless sensor networks for assisted-living and residential monitoring. IEEE Netw 22(4):26–33
49. Xu E, Ding Z, Dasgupta S (2013) Target tracking and mobile sensor navigation in wireless sensor networks. IEEE Trans Mobile Comput 12(1):177–186
50. Yan H, Huo H, Gidlund M (2010) Wireless sensor network based e-health system—implementation and experimental results. IEEE Trans Consumer Electron 56(4):2288–2295
51. Youssef M, Mah M, Agrawala A (2007) Challenges: device-free passive localization for wireless environments. In: Proceedings of the 13th annual ACM international conference on mobile computing and networking, Montreal, Sept 2007, pp 222–229

Chapter 9
Automatic Players Detection and Tracking in Multi-camera Tennis Videos

Rafael Martín and José M. Martínez

Abstract This chapter presents a multi-camera system designed to detect and track players in individual sports. This system requires an initial configuration comprised of scene background, field distances, and the correspondence between some points from each camera and those points in the field. With the resulting positions of each player generated by the system, individual players statistics are extracted allowing performance analytics for each player. This system can be used in any sport in which each player has a unique own space, not shared with the other players. Some examples of these sports are tennis, badminton or paddle tennis.

9.1 Introduction

The analysis of sports videos has been one of the research fields that has grown further due to the high demand of the public. Specifically, tennis is one of the most popular sports in most countries. It is played by millions of players and is also a worldwide broadcasted sport. Analysis systems of sports videos are interesting not only for the public but also for the players and coaches as these systems allow them to improve their training, skills, and performance during training and matches. Basic algorithmic techniques and their applications are described in [19] where an overview of the research focused on sports video is given. In that overview, sports video research is classified in two categories: indexing and retrieval systems (based on high-level semantic queries) and augmented reality presentation (to present additional information and to provide new viewing experiences to the users).

Moreover, depending on the type of sports videos, another classification can be considered differentiating edited for broadcast [6, 13, 20, 22] and non edited mono- [2, 8, 21] or multi-camera [9]. The broadcast sequences include game scenes,

R. Martín (✉) · J.M. Martínez
Universidad Autónoma de Madrid, Madrid, España
e-mail: rafael.martinn@uam.es

J.M. Martínez
e-mail: josem.martinez@uam.es

P. Spagnolo et al. (eds.), *Human Behavior Understanding in Networked Sensing*,
DOI 10.1007/978-3-319-10807-0_9

repetition, and viewpoint changes. The non-edited sequences can be recorded by mobile cameras.

Some examples of works centered on individual sports are [8] (player detection and tracking), [2] (tennis strokes detection) and [21, 22] (ball detection and tracking).

For team sports the problem is harder as there are multiple players with half of them wearing the same clothes. Some application examples of processing these kinds of sports are those presented in [7] (virtual view synthesis), [10] (ball-player interactions) or [17] (players performance and skills).

The system presented in this chapter is centered on individual sports. With individual sports we refer to sports in which each player has his own area of the field and no other player can enter in the area of the tracked player.

The remainder of the chapter is structured as follows: after the introduction in Sect. 9.1, Sect. 9.2 describes the designed system; Sect. 9.3 presents the adjustments, testing, and results of the implementation of the system, including the description of the used dataset; Sect. 9.4 shows the developed GUI of the system; finally, Sect. 9.5 includes the conclusions and some lines of future work.

9.2 Video Analysis System

9.2.1 Canonical System

The canonical system for detecting and tracking players in a field can be decomposed into several main blocks, as depicted in Fig. 9.1. The different techniques and associated algorithms that are key for any sports video analysis system are described below.

Background Extraction is a very common method used for moving players segmentation which consists of differentiating between the moving objects (generally players and ball) and the background model. The background model is generally obtained from an empty image of the field (if it is available) or from a video sequence without static players. Some of the main problems in background extraction in sports

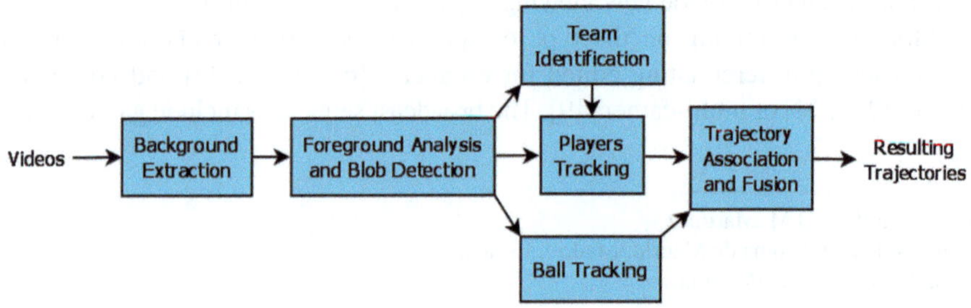

Fig. 9.1 Block diagram of a general sport system

are the same than for generic computer vision approaches: illumination changes, shadow removal, and dynamic background components.

Foreground Analysis and Blob Detection is based on associating the pixels of the foreground. The goal is to adjust the contour of the player's blob, separating (if possible) overlapping players. The correct determination of the blob's pixels is important for making correct decisions during the tracking.

The teams' uniform information is used for the *Team Identification* of the blobs and allows differentiating between different teams' players, goalkeepers, and referees. Generally, a player can be modeled as a group of regions, each region having some predominant colors. This block is optional and not all systems use it. This is, especially, useful in team sports to help to discriminate between different players.

When the position of each player is detected, the next objective is to track the player to know where the player is at each moment. The objective of the *Players Tracking* block is to associate target objects in consecutive video frames.

The method for *ball tracking* is similar to the methods used for player tracking, but ball tracking is more difficult than player tracking as automatic detection of the ball is harder due to its reduced dimensions in the image. If a player has the ball, its tracking is difficult because the ball is frequently occluded.

Finally, the *Trajectory Association and Fusion* block fuses the information obtained from different sources of information (usually cameras). The reconstruction of global trajectories fusing multiple points of view requires the combination of multiple information sources of the same object as well as the fusion of trajectory fragments captured by individual sensors. The trajectory data from individual sensors may contain errors and inaccuracies such as bounding box distortion caused by noise, object exits and entrances from the visual field, or occlusions.

9.2.2 System Overview

As the system has been designed for tracking one player, two individual instances of the system are necessary for a game. That is, there will be two parallel instances of the system for a game, with three cameras for each instance. The videos used from the content set are those covering only the areas of each player, without using global views.

The system block diagram is shown in Fig. 9.2. Each one of the blocks is described below.

The Initialization block is executed first. It generates the field representation (using the field measurements), the backgrounds (obtained from an initial empty image, or generated from the first frames of the game or players warming up) and the homography reference points (selected manually from each one of the cameras and indicating its correspondence in the top view resulting perspective).

The Detection and Tracking block receives the videos and the backgrounds from the different recording cameras. The tracking block generates the tracking trajectories

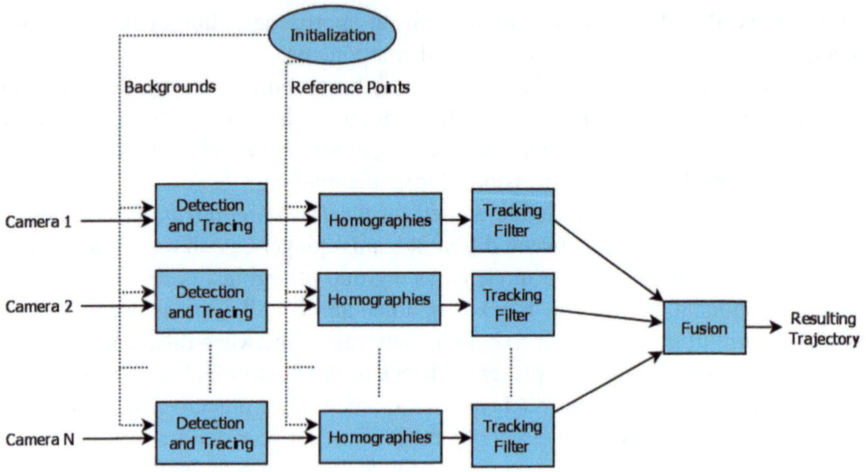

Fig. 9.2 Block diagram of the system

from its own perspective processing the frames of the sequences of each camera. Each instance of this module only process one of the cameras.

The Homographies block receives the coordinates of the player from each camera (in pixels) and the reference points. The results of this block are the top view player coordinates from each camera.

The Tracking filter block receives and filters the tracking coordinates from the topview tracking from each camera. There are plenty of restrictions that can be defined for this block. Some examples of these constraints are: maximum distance to the previous resulting coordinates, restricted regions in the field (own side of the field), blob continuity for a minimum number of frames (in order to remove spurious and noisy blobs), etc.

Finally, *the Fusion block* combines the processed trajectories from each one of the cameras and generates the overall trajectory using the information from the different cameras.

9.2.3 Initialization

The initialization of the system can be obtained from a previous capture of the field without players, or from the first frames of the match video (if the first option is not available).

The initialization step defines the field representation, the backgrounds and the homography reference points. The field distances are needed for the field representation to generate accurate sports analytics. Each one of the components of the initialization block are described below.

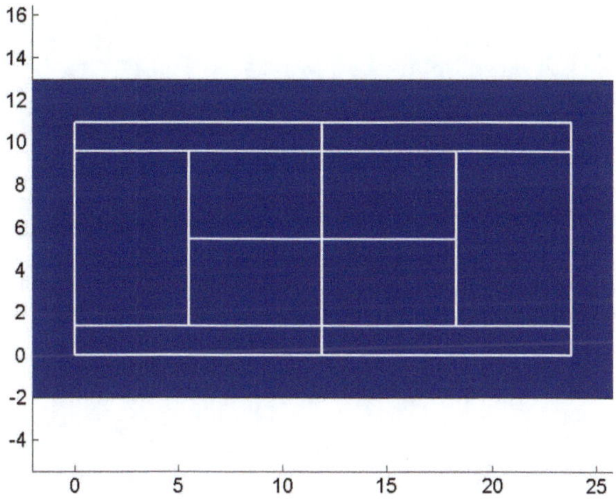

Fig. 9.3 Field representation

9.2.3.1 Field Representation

For the representation of the field the standard dimensions have been used, but they can be easily changed in the initialization module if the filmed field has specific dimensions (generally there are some distances in standard dimensions which can take a range of values instead of a constant dimension). The resulting field representation is shown in Fig. 9.3.

9.2.3.2 Background Generation

The tracking system used needs an initial background image of the scene for each video analyzed. These methods are necessary when an image of the background without players is not available. In Computer Vision more complex methods are used for hot start up (to start without initialization) or with updating background, but this method covers quickly and easily the objective. In live applications, players usually warm up some minutes before the game. These sequences can be used for system initialization, including, among others, background generation. In the system designed both methods have been used: first, the mean method (automatic) is used. If the generated background is not correct, the junction of portion from different frames method (supervised) is used. The two methods used are described below.

- Mode of pixels from a set of frames: this automatic method is based on choosing (watching the video using a video player as in the case above) a set of frames and generating each pixel of the background with the mode of all the pixels in the position of the pixel generated. Other operations like mean or median have been tested with worse results. The advantage of this method is that it needs less supervision

Fig. 9.4 Background generation process for the median-based background generator. From *left* to *right*, background obtained using 10, 30, and 90 frames for the median, respectively

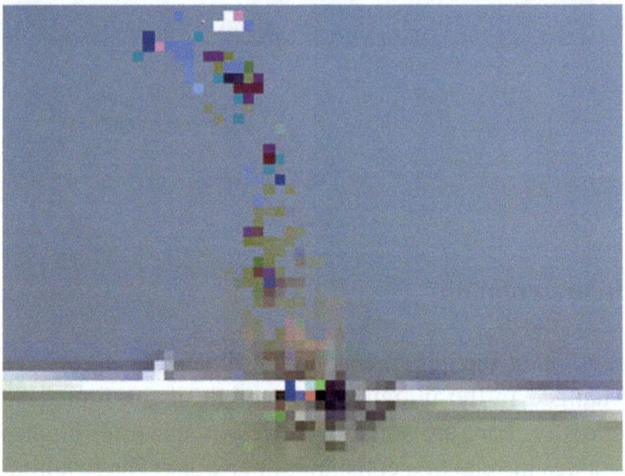

Fig. 9.5 Example (detail) of malfunction in junction-based background generator

than the other method. The script requests an initial frame and a number of frames to analyze. The original frame is chosen after watching video display frames with few players and without static players, which may cause problems when generating the background. By increasing the number of frames processed improves the results, increasing the computational cost. The results obtained using a different number of frames for the median are shown in Fig. 9.4. The disadvantage of this method is the high-computational cost due to mode operation. Using this method sometimes small areas with strange colors appear caused by any person or object moving slowly in the set of chosen frames to generate the background. One example of this area is shown in Fig. 9.5. This colored area is caused by a person moving behind the advertising. These areas generally do not cause malfunction because the erosion and reconstruction operations make them disappear from tracking. An example of incorrect and correct background using this method is shown in Fig. 9.6.

- Junction of portion from different frames: this supervised method is based on finding some portion in frames without players in the field. Once enough frames to compose a full background are found, the final image is created. The portions used in this project are halves, but smaller portions can be taken, such as quarter-frame

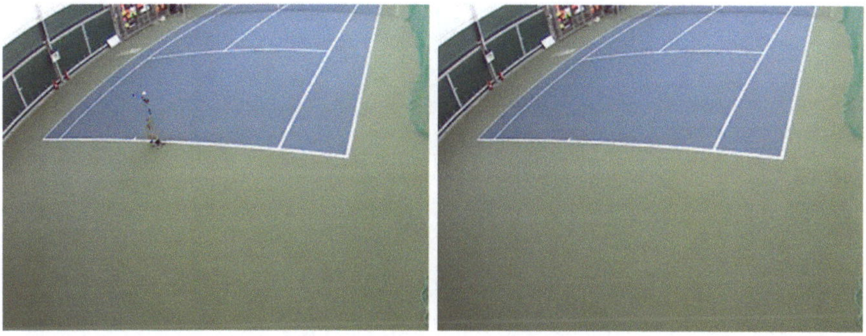

Fig. 9.6 Example of incorrect (*left*) and correct (*right*) background using the mode-based background generation method

or vertical strips less than half frame. The (non assisted) procedure used is as follows: first, the video frames are watched using a video player trying to locate regions where there are no players. Then a first approximation of the background is generated with the frames located in the previous step. If a region contains background generated players (or part), the frame number chosen for that region can be increased or decreased to get an empty region, and the background is generated again. If players appear completely, another frame should be chosen by visualizing the video again. The advantage of this method is the reduced computational cost. The disadvantages of this method are that sometimes finding frames without players is not easy and that it is a supervised method. An example of the process followed for the generation of one of the backgrounds is shown in Fig. 9.7. An example of incorrect and correct background using this method with part of a player is shown in Fig. 9.8. This correct example is very similar to the one obtained with the previous method.

9.2.4 Mono-camera Detection and Tracking

The mono-camera detection and tracking module is based on a video-surveillance analysis system for event detection [15]. It was designed to work in real time. This feature imposes time complexity limitations on the used algorithms in each of the analysis modules.

Figure 9.9 presents the block diagram of this module. A foreground mask is generated for each frame at the *background substraction* module [1]. This foreground mask consists on a binary image that identifies the pixels that belong to moving or stationary blobs, and it is obtained by subtracting the background image from each of the frames, thresholding the result to obtain a binary mask. The *background model*

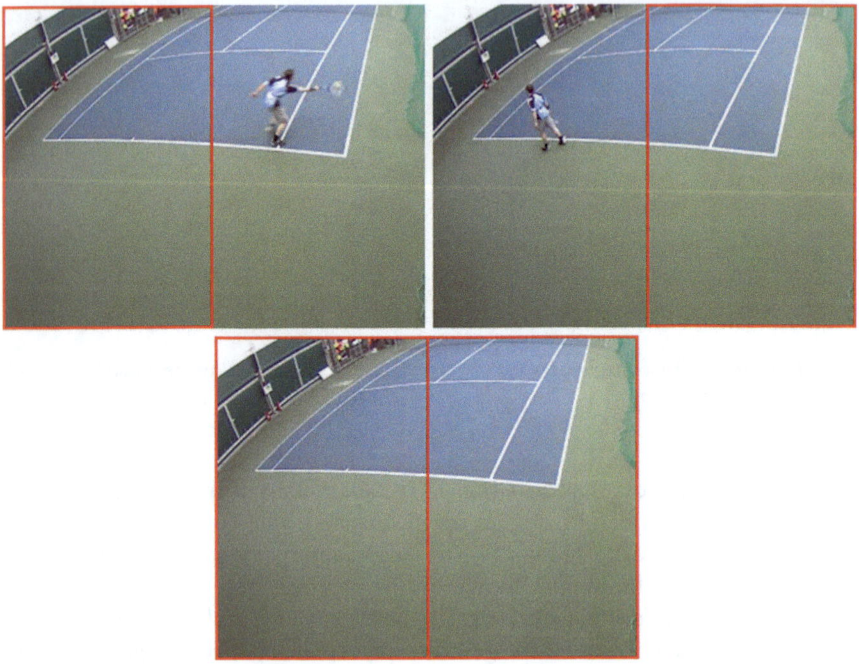

Fig. 9.7 Background generation process for the junction-based background generator. The *two red rectangles* in the *two top frames* show the selected region in the original frames and the *bottom frame* represents the generated background

Fig. 9.8 Example of incorrect (*left*) and correct (*right*) background using the junction of portion from different frames background generation method

is initialized with the initial background image and updated then with the frames received by the system using a running average method [12].

The *shadow removal* block is used for removing the pixels belonging to the shadows of the players. For this stage of the system, the image is converted to the HSV (Hue Saturation Value) color space [16], allowing to locate those shadow

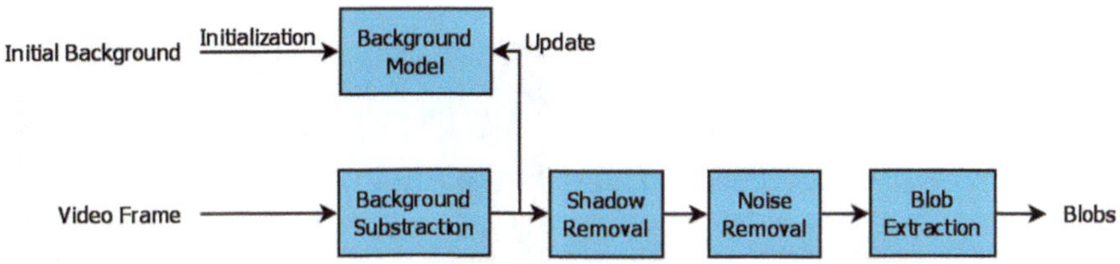

Fig. 9.9 Block diagram of the mono-camera detection and tracking module

pixels [3]. In the *noise removal* block, morphological operations are applied on the previous step resulting mask for removing noise artifacts. A combination of erosion and reconstruction operations is applied [14]. Its purpose is to remove small objects (small blobs due to noise) without distorting the shape and size of the player's blob.

Finally, the *blob extraction* block labels the groups of pixels in the mask using CCA (Connected Component Analysis) using 8-connectivity as the connectivity criteria.

9.2.5 Extraction of the Base Mid-Point

The base system obtains two points (p1 and p2) for the player in each frame, defining the bounding box of the player. Each point has its coordinates x and y: p1 corresponds to the upper left point of the bounding box and p2 corresponds with the lower right point of the bounding box. In Fig. 9.10 some examples of bounding box and base mid-points are shown to clarify. Base mid-point (b) coordinates (x_b and y_b) are defined as follows:

The base mid-point is taken because when the homography is applied, the correspondence is calculated for points on the floor of the field. The base point is closer to the floor and presents a minor error than selecting, for example, the center point on the bounding box (which is typically used in other tracking applications).

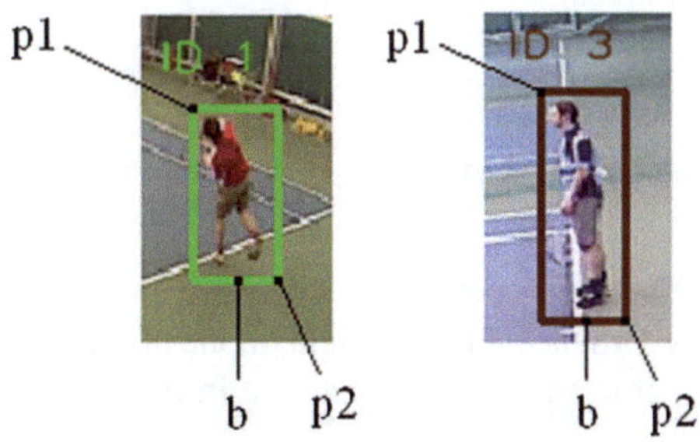

Fig. 9.10 Examples of bounding box (*yellow* and *red*) indicating the base mid-point (*b*) and points *p1* and *p2*

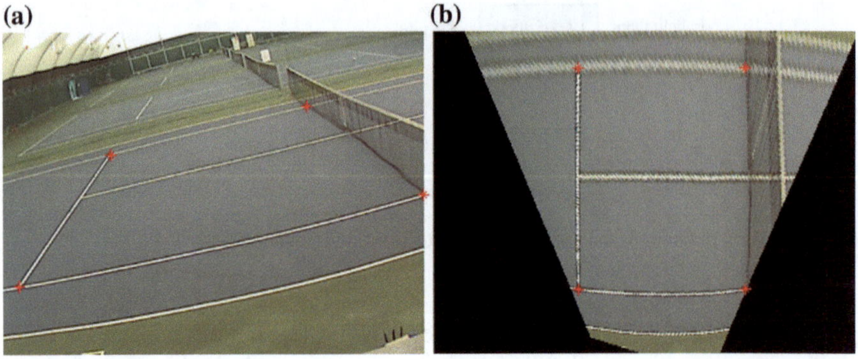

Fig. 9.11 Example of homography: **a** image plane, **b** top view

9.2.6 Homographies

Homographic transformations are used to change camera perspectives. The homographic techniques used in this work follow the normalized direct linear transformation algorithm (DLT) [5]. Four points (more than the minimum number of points needed, but this helps to improve the accuracy) are selected in the original image plane (generally characteristic points of the field) and its correspondence is indicated in the top view. The code used for this block is public.[1] In Fig. 9.11, an example of the process is presented. Note that in the system the homography is applied to a single point (the base mid-point) of the tracked player (blob) as the conversion of the whole image is a slow and unnecessary process. The red crosses in the figure indicate the selected points, in both the original image and the corrected perspective.

Resulting projected coordinates from two cameras may have different positions, due to different error sources: players' volumes, camera distances, lens, etc. Note that the higher the distance from the camera to the points, the lower precision in the projection. In the case of Fig. 9.11, the field lines closer to the camera are sharper than the lines located at greater distance. In the case of people detection and tracking, these differences use to be moderate and the fusion block can also reduce these error sources.

9.2.7 Fusion

The fusion process is relatively simple for this system as all the cameras can only record the half of the field of one of the players. The main advantage is that every blob extracted from each camera in frame t belongs to the tracked player. The resulting

[1] http://www.csse.uwa.edu.au/~pk/research/matlabfns/.

fusion coordinates are obtained with a coordinate mean between each camera individual coordinates:

$$x_{\mathrm{t}} = \frac{1}{N}\sum_{i=1}^{N_{\mathrm{t}}} x_{i,\mathrm{t}} \qquad y_{\mathrm{t}} = \frac{1}{N}\sum_{i=1}^{N_{\mathrm{t}}} y_{i,\mathrm{t}} \tag{9.1}$$

where $(x_{\mathrm{t}}, y_{\mathrm{t}})$ are the combined coordinates in frame t, $(x_{i,\mathrm{t}}, y_{i,\mathrm{t}})$ are the individual camera coordinates in frame t from the i-camera, and $i = 1 \ldots N_{\mathrm{t}}$ are the N_{t} cameras which have a blob corresponding to the player in frame t.

9.3 Adjustments, Testings and Results

A web page has been made available online to show some videos and results, where examples with the obtained results of the systems have been uploaded [11].

9.3.1 Content Set: 3DLife ACM Multimedia Grand Challenge 2010 Dataset

The dataset [4] features video from nine CCTV-like cameras placed at different points around the entire court [18]. Videos are ASF files and encoded using an MPEG-4 codec. Seven of the videos are recorded with a resolution of 640×480 pixels from Axis 212PTZ network cameras. The two other cameras have a resolution of 704×576 pixels and are captured using Axis 215PTZ network cameras. The start time of each video is synchronized via software at the start of each sequence. There are two games sequences availables in the datas (about 2 min per game). Note that each game sequence is composed of nine videos, one for each of the cameras.

9.3.2 System Configuration

For the system configuration, the 3DLife ACM Multimedia Grand Challenge 2010 Dataset used videos are from the cameras 1, 3, and 4 for the first player, and from the cameras 5, 6, and 8 for the second player. The homography reference points are selected manually. In the Tracking filter module, the criteria (heuristically set) for filtering are:

- The detected blobs must be visible during a minimum of 10 consecutive frames.
- The detection area is limited to the player own side of the field.
- A maximum distance of one meter between two consecutive frames is allowed for each camera blob.

If the defined restrictions are not enough to filter some of the sequence frames and errors occur, the player's position can be corrected manually using the graphical user interface (GUI, see Sect. 9.4)

9.3.3 Results

9.3.3.1 Players' Detection and Tracking

This subsection shows the results obtained with the system. Figures 9.12 and 9.13 present the players trajectories obtained from the two game sequences.

Some examples of the different possible number of cameras tracking simultaneously the player are shown in Fig. 9.14. In this figure, the resulting point of the fusion is shown as a yellow square, and the resulting point of each camera tracking is shown as a cross (whose color depends on the corresponding camera).

Due to the location of each camera and depending on the point at which the player is on the field and on the number of cameras with the player located, the error will be larger or smaller. In Fig. 9.15 two different points are shown with two simultaneously camera projected points. In the right of the figure, the points tracked from each camera are closer between them, different from the case in the left of the image, where the points are more distant. Some possibilities to compensate this distortion are proposed in the future work section. In the presented case this problem is solved by the fusion method, as shown in the results.

A study of the projected distance error has been performed to estimate the distance between the estimated point by the system and the (subjective) ideal point. To achieve

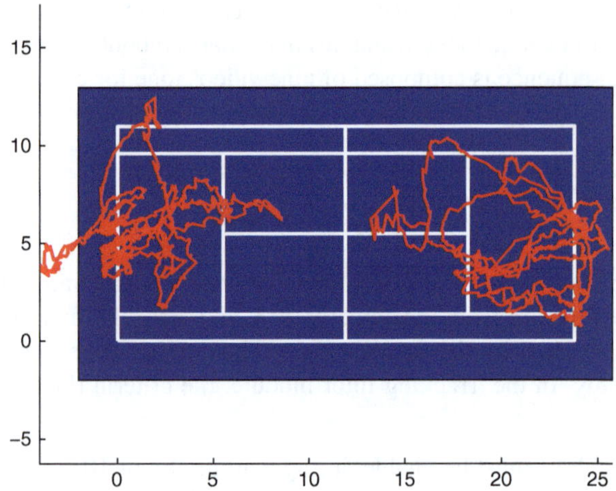

Fig. 9.12 Resulting trajectories extracted from the first game sequence

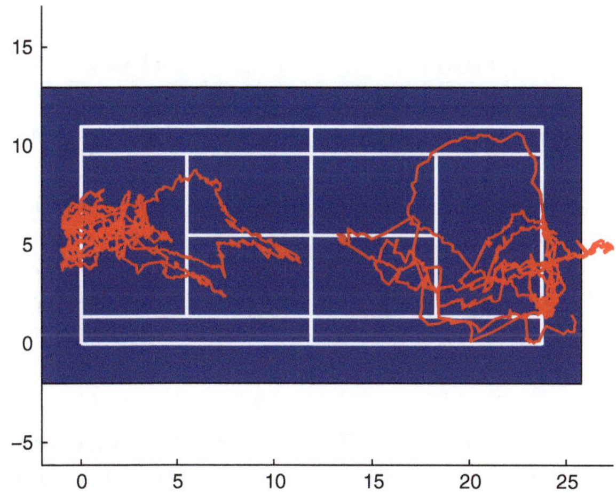

Fig. 9.13 Resulting trajectories extracted from the second game sequence

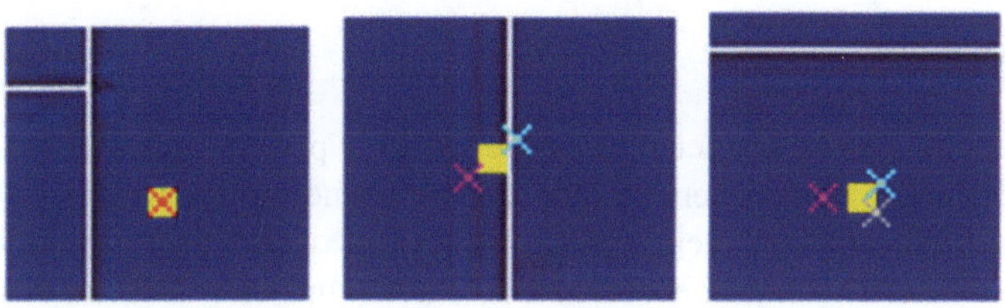

Fig. 9.14 Examples of the possible number of cameras tracking simultaneously the player, from *left* to *right*: one camera, two cameras and three cameras

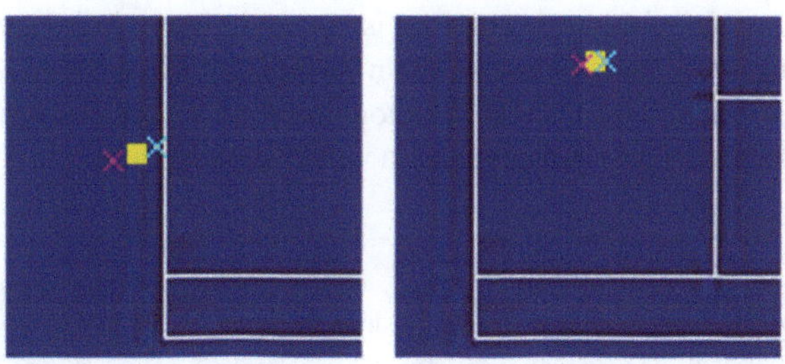

Fig. 9.15 Examples of the major or minor error depending on the position of the player

this, the ground plane position of the player has been manually annotated in each camera of the two game sequences. The annotations [11] have been made every 25 frames, the same frames of which the analytics are later extracted (Table 9.1).

The average time of the system processing is about 21.0 fps. The computer characteristics are: Intel(R) Core(TM) 2 Duo, E7500 @2.93 GHz, 4GB RAM, Windows 7 Professional 32 Bits. Therefore, even the current implementation could work in

Table 9.1 Distance error (in pixels) between the manually and the automatic extracted points

		Player 1			Player 2		
		C1	C3	C4	C5	C6	C8
Game1	d_x	6,0	8,5	5,9	18,9	7,4	5,5
	d_y	5,8	8,7	5,7	6,2	6,8	6,6
	d_{total}	8,7	12,7	8,7	20,6	10,7	9,1
Game 2	d_x	6,8	10,3	5,0	26,4	11,1	5,2
	d_y	5,6	8,2	6,6	9,0	7,6	6,0
	d_{total}	9,2	13,8	9,6	29,3	14,7	8,3

real time using a typical current-day PC. This time analysis has been obtained with a sequential processing of the frames from each camera. If it is parallelized then the execution time would decrease considerably.

9.3.3.2 Analytics

Player analytics can be extracted using the resulting players' trajectories.

A zigzag effect appears between consecutive frames, as shown in Fig. 9.16 (left). As commented previously, there are multiple sources of error that cause this problem: different camera lenses, user accuracy errors in the manually selected homography points, background-foreground segmentation, etc. This effect causes an error in the obtained analytics if they are calculated for each frame. To reduce this error, the statistics are calculated after postprocessing the trajectory (subsampling every 25 frames). An example of this subsampling is shown in the right image of Fig. 9.16.

The resulting sport analytics are shown in Figs. 9.17 and 9.18, which show the following player information: field position, covered distance, average speed, and instant speed. In addition to these figures, a video showing the evolution of analytical

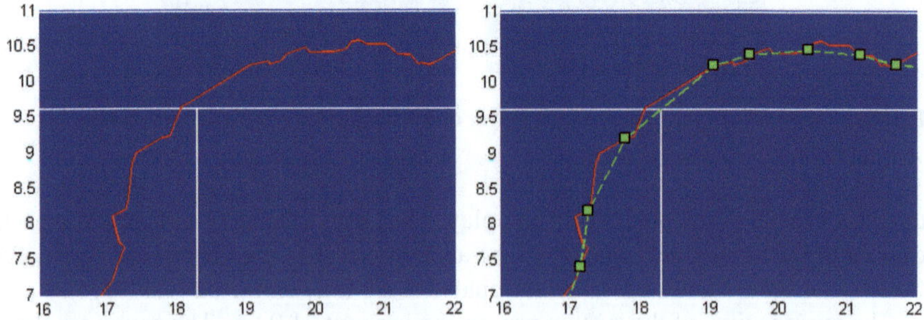

Fig. 9.16 Example of the zigzag effect in the trajectories (*left, red line*) and the subsampling result (*right, green line*)

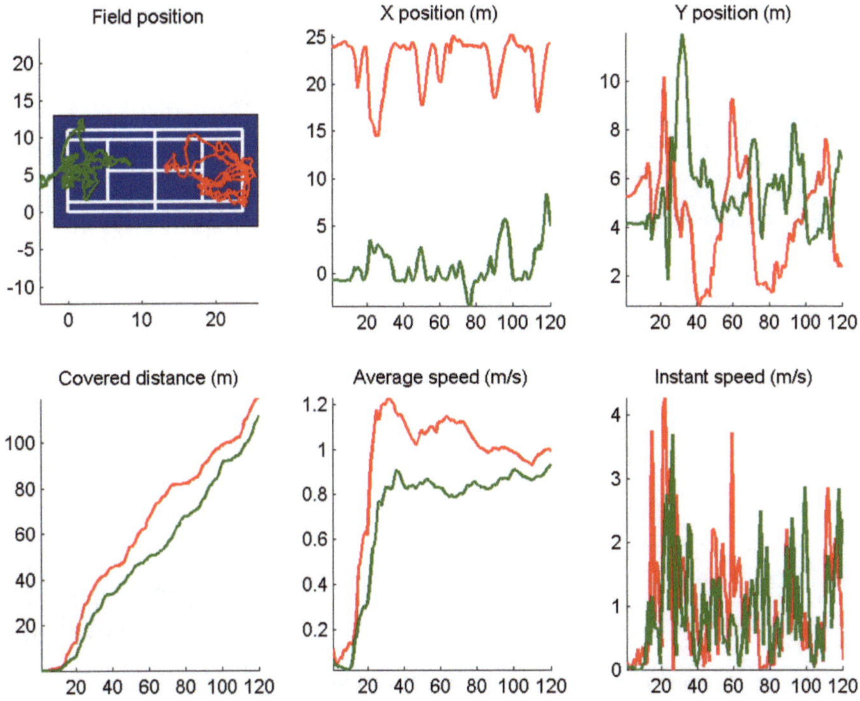

Fig. 9.17 Sport analytics for the first game sequence

belonging to one of the players can be watched visiting the publication website [11]. A sample frame of this video is shown in Fig. 9.19.

9.4 Graphic User Interface

A real-time interactive Graphical User Interface (GUI) has been developed for the system operators or supervisors. This Qt-based[2] GUI allows to manually correct errors in certain frames to get precise trajectories for the tracked Players. Some of the most common errors that can be corrected by improving the accuracy of the bounding box are: situations in which the player extends the racket horizontally, jumps, player inclinations (especially when he/she starts running), etc.

Some examples of the GUI windows are presented. Figure 9.20 shows the main window of the system during an execution and the position edit window.

[2] http://qt-project.org/.

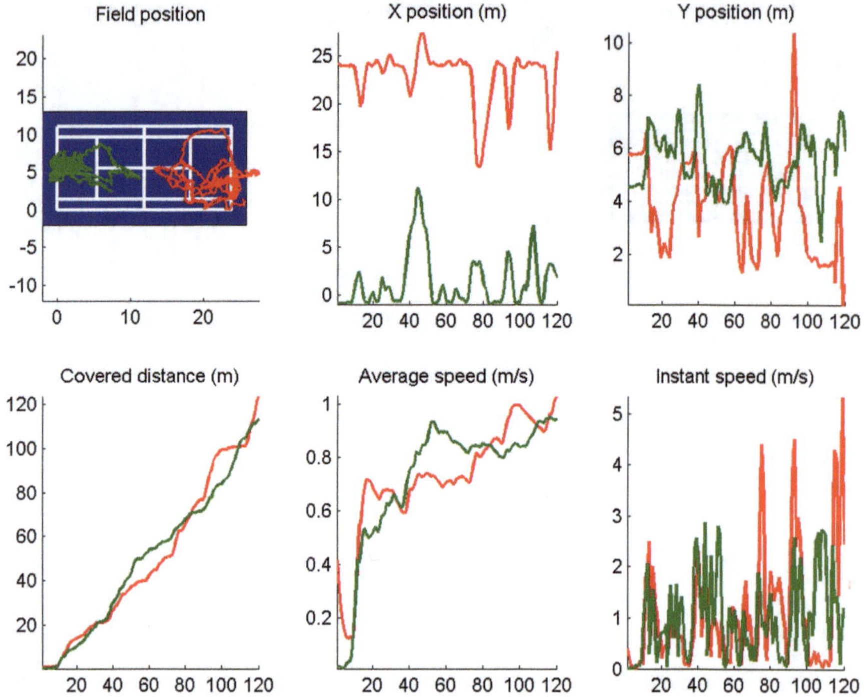

Fig. 9.18 Sport analytics for the second game sequence

9.5 Conclusions

This chapter presents a multi-camera system designed to detect and track players in individual sports. Thanks to the initial configuration, the resulting positions of each player is generated by the system. The players statistics are extracted using the trajectory of the player, allowing performance analytics for each player. Moreover, the system has been designed interconnecting separate modules, which allows system improvements modifying independently each one of the modules.

The sports video analysis with static cameras has advantages over the general video processing as background can be easily modeled. Some problems that may appear in this background are the audience or the advertisements, which can be removed using masks or constraints in the tracking filter block.

The deployment of the cameras is one of the key aspects. The objective is to place symmetrically the cameras trying to cancel the position errors produced by each camera. Placing the cameras at higher elevations also reduces the tracking errors but this option may not be available.

There are many lines of future work for this system. The precision of each trajectory projection depends on the players' location in the field. An evaluation of the precision which depends on the position in the field can reduce these precision

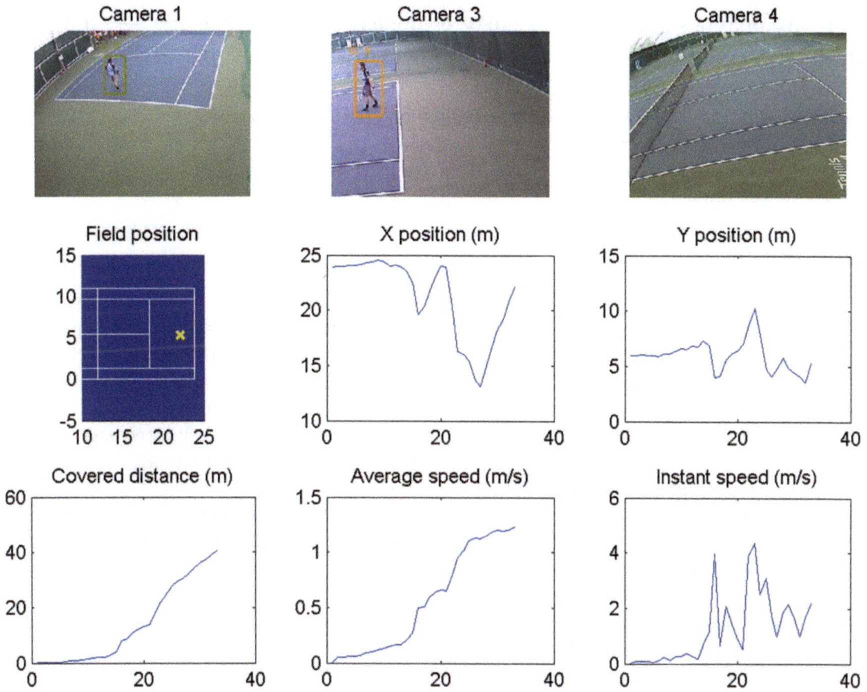

Fig. 9.19 Sample frame of the analytics video

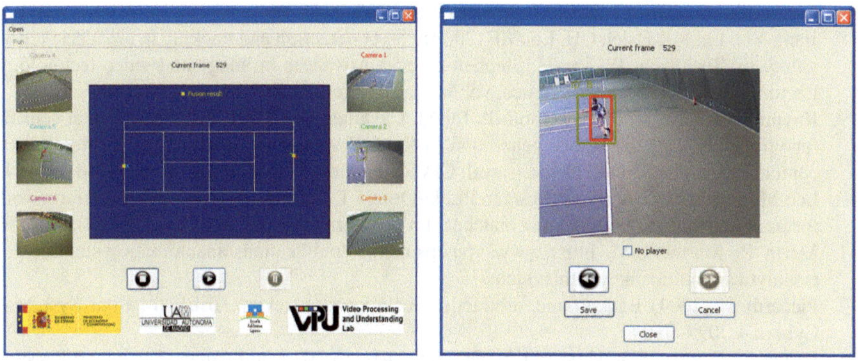

Fig. 9.20 GUI: main window (*left*) and position edit window (*right*)

differences, minimizing the final position error. Parallelizing the processing of each one of the cameras would greatly improve the speed of the system. Also new fusion techniques can be developed trying to improve the simple fusion used, for example, adding weights to the contribution of each camera (this weight may depend on the distance from each camera to the player in that frame). Finally, additional and more complex analytics of each player can be estimated: areas of the field where the player stays longer, acceleration of the players, interactions between players, etc.

Acknowledgments This work has been partially supported by the Spanish Government (TEC2011-25995).

References

1. Cavallaro A, Steiger O, Ebrahimi T (2005) Semantic video analysis for adaptive content delivery and automatic description. IEEE Trans Circuits Syst Video Technol 15(10):1200–1209
2. Connaghan D, Conaire CO, Kelly P, O'Connor NE (2010) Recognition of tennis strokes using key postures. In: IET irish signals and systems conference, June 2010, pp 245–248
3. Cucchiara R, Grana C, Piccardi M, Prati A (2001) Detecting objects, shadows and ghosts in video streams by exploiting color and motion information. In: International conference on image analysis and processing, Sept 2001, pp 360–365
4. Conaire CÓ, Connaghan D, Kelly P, O'Connor NE, Gaffney M, Buckley J (2010) Combining inertial and visual sensing for human action recognition in tennis. In: First ACM international workshop on analysis and retrieval of tracked events and motion in imagery streams, New York. ACM, pp 51–56
5. Hartley R, Zisserman A (2004) Multiple view geometry in computer vision, 2nd edn. Cambridge University, Cambridge, ISBN: 0521540518
6. Huang Y, Llach J, Bhagavathy S (2007) Players and ball detection in soccer videos based on color segmentation and shape analysis. Multimedia content analysis and mining. Lecture Notes in Computer Science, vol 4577. Springer, Heidelberg, pp 416–425
7. Inamoto N, Saito H (2007) Virtual viewpoint replay for a soccer match by view interpolation from multiple cameras. Trans Multimedia 9(6):1155–1166
8. Jiang YC, Lai KT, Hsieh CH, Lai MF (2009) Player detection and tracking in broadcast tennis video. In: Toshikazu W, Fay H, Stephen L (eds) Advances in image and video technology. Lecture Notes in Computer Science, vol 5414. Springer, Heidelberg, pp 759–770
9. Kayumbi G, Mazzeo PL, Spagnolo P, Taj M, Cavallaro A (2008) Distributed visual sensing for virtual top-view trajectory generation in football videos. In: International conference on content-based image and video retrieval, CIVR '08, New York, July 2008. ACM, pp 535–542
10. Leo M, Mosca N, Spagnolo P, Mazzeo PL, D'Orazio T, Distante A (2010) A visual framework for interaction detection in soccer matches. Int J Pattern Recognit Artif Intell 24(04):499–530
11. Martn R, Martnez JM. http://www-vpu.eps.uam.es/publications/anautomaticsystemforsportsanalyticsinmulticameratennisvideos/
12. Piccardi M (2004) Background subtraction techniques: a review. IEEE Int Conf Syst Man Cybern 4:3099–3104
13. Poppe C, Bruyne SD, Verstockt S, de Walle RV (2010) Multi-camera analysis of soccer sequences. In: International conference on advanced video and signal based surveillance, Aug 2010, pp 26–31
14. Salembier P, Ruiz J (2002) On filters by reconstruction for size and motion simplification. In: International symposium in mathematical, morphology, pp 425–434
15. SanMiguel JC, Martnez JM (2012) A semantic-based probabilistic approach for real-time video event recognition. Comput Vis Image Underst 116(9):937–952
16. Shan Y, Yang F, Wang R (2007) Color space selection for moving shadow elimination. In: International conference on image and graphics, IEEE computer society, Washington, DC, pp 496–501
17. Tsai PS, Meijome T, Austin PG (2007) Scout: a game speed analysis and tracking system. Mach Vis Appl 18(5):289–299

18. Tennis dataset. http://www.cdvp.dcu.ie/tennisireland/tennisvideos/acm_mm_3dlife_grand_challenge/
19. Xinguo Y, Farin D (2005) Current and emerging topics in sports video processing. In: International conference on multimedia and expo, July 2005, pp 526–529
20. Xu M, Orwell J, Jones G (2004) Tracking football players with multiple cameras. Int Conf Image Process 5:2909–2912
21. Yan F, Christmas WJ, Kittler J (2005) A tennis ball tracking algorithm for automatic annotation of tennis match. In: British machine vision conference. British machine vision association, Sept 2005
22. Yu X, Sim CH, Wang JR, Cheong LF (2004) A trajectory-based ball detection and tracking algorithm in broadcast tennis video. Int Conf Image Process 2:1049–1052

Chapter 10
Data Fusion with a Dense Sensor Network for Anomaly Detection in Smart Homes

Kevin Bing-Yung Wong, Tongda Zhang and Hamid Aghajan

Abstract Research into assistive technologies for the elderly has been increasingly driven by the rapidly expanding population of older adults in many developed countries. One area of particular interest is technologies that enable aging-in-place, which allows older adults to remain in their own homes and live an independent life. Our work in this space is based on using a network of motion detectors in a smart home to extract patterns of behavior and classify them as either typical or atypical. Knowledge of these patterns can help caregivers and medical professionals in the study of any behavioral changes and enable better planning of care for their patients. Once we define and extract these patterns, we can construct behavioral feature vectors that will be the basis of our behavioral change detection system. These feature vectors can be further refined through traditional machine learning approaches such as K-means to extract any structure and reduce the dimensionality of the data. We can then use these behavioral features to identify significant variations across time, which could indicate atypical behavior. We validated our approach against features generated from human labeled activity annotations, and found that patterns derived from raw motion sensor data can be used as proxies for these higher level annotations. We observed that our machine learning-based feature vectors show a high correlation with the feature vectors derived from the higher level activity annotations and show a high classification accuracy in detecting potentially atypical behavior.

K.B.-Y. Wong (✉) · T. Zhang · H. Aghajan
Department of Electrical Engineering, Stanford University, Stanford, CA, USA
e-mail: kbw5@stanford.edu

T. Zhang
e-mail: tdzhang@stanford.edu

H. Aghajan
e-mail: hamid@icdsc.org

P. Spagnolo et al. (eds.), *Human Behavior Understanding in Networked Sensing*,
DOI 10.1007/978-3-319-10807-0_10

10.1 Introduction

The World Health Organization (WHO) and the US Department of Health have both predicted a rapid rise in the proportion of older adults that make up the populations of developed countries. Globally, it is predicted that the number of people older than 60 will triple between 2000 and 2050 from 600 million to 2 billion, while considering just the United States alone, the number of citizens older than 65 is expected to grow from 40.3 to 72.1 million in 20 years [1, 2]. This rapidly growing and aging population segment is of great concern in terms of their healthcare and management, since eldercare is traditionally very labor intensive and costly.

In response to the concern of how to care for an increasing elderly population, many assistive and monitoring technologies are being examined to reduce the need for caretakers and to enable the aging population to retain a measure of independence [3–7]. These efforts are mostly intended to enable aging-in-place, which is defined by the Center for Disease Control as "The ability to live in one's own home and community safely, independently, and comfortably, regardless of age, income, or ability level" [8]. This would reduce the infrastructure costs of eldercare, and would align better with the wishes of older adults. A survey conducted by AARP, an American advocacy group that addresses issues concerning older adults, indicated that 84 % of people over the age of 50 wish to remain in their current homes, with the percentage increasing to 95 % for respondents over the age of 75 [9].

The use of long-term health and wellbeing indicators is also beneficial for self-reflection as a motivational tool to change possibly unhealthy trends in lifestyle. These systems could be used by healthcare professionals and caregivers to augment existing doctor visits to provide doctors with a more continuous view of a patient's heath and wellbeing, as well as alert them if any sudden changes occur. The "Quantified Self" movement is an example of this recent trend for self reflection and health monitoring. Using environmental sensors would allow a monitoring system to unobtrusively monitor a patient continuously while they are in the home with no active compliance from the patient [10].

10.2 Related Work

There has been a great deal of work in developing assistive technologies for the elderly, with the goal of enabling so-called "aging in place." A common type of assistive technologies are those that monitor for anomalous activities or events, one such system developed by Shin et al., used a network of 5 PIR(Passive InfraRed) sensors to track the mobility of 9 elderly occupants of government sponsored housing [11]. This system first derived indicators of mobility, such as the percentage of time the motion sensors were triggered and how often the user would move between motion sensors, to look for changes in these indicators over time. The authors detected these changes by using 24 different SVDD (Support Vector Data Descriptors) based classifiers, one for each hour of the day, to classify normal activities [12]. Since the SVDD classifiers would generate warnings for any abnormal activity, their system would often generate false warnings due to the irregular behavior patterns of the users, such as waking up late and performing cleaning activities during different times of day. Other work by O'Brien et al. also used PIR sensors in the home as a primary input, but their work was focused on visualization techniques to potentially identify movement disorders for the older adults [13]. Cuddihy et al. used the same PIR-based motion sensors with the goal of identifying periods of unusually long inactivity of occupants in their homes to generate alerts to caregivers [14]. More general work by Fine et al. used location-based information to build feature vectors to determine classes of normal or abnormal activities using a clustering-based approach [15].

The CASAS project, led by Diane Cook at Washington State University, has been studying a related field of identifying Activities of Daily Life or ADL, which are defined as common activities that a person performs to care for themselves, using data mining and machine learning to automatically identify important activities through finding the most common pattern in motion sensor data [16–19]. ADL's could be useful to describe the behavior of a smart environment's occupant and identify abnormalities if certain ADL's are not completed. Some of the recent work by Jakkula et al., focuses on using one class SVM's to classify anomalous behavior using an annotated dataset based on motion and door sensors in a home setting [20]. Anomaly detection by monitoring drifts and outliers of detected parameters were also studied by Jain et al., however that research focused less on ambient sensors and more on wearable health monitors [21]. More theoretical approaches to activity detection, such as work by Kalra et al. have focused on machine learning and statistical models for ADL detection [22].

There have been many other proposed approaches toward detecting, representing, and analyzing activity and behavioral patterns in a home setting. One such approach by Lymberopoulos et al. uses a home sensor network to track a user's motion and presence throughout the home [23]. Using region occupancy and the associated occupancy time, they create a set of symbols that encode the location, duration of the user's presence, and the time of day the user was present in a specific area in the home. From these symbols, they discover frequent sequences of symbols and their likelihoods to extract the users activity patterns form their 30 day dataset. Vision centric approaches by Gómez-Conde el al. [24], focus on detecting abnormal behavior using cameras and computer vision techniques such as motion detection and object segmentation to develop tele-assistance applications for the elderly. Their system mainly focuses on the sensing and classification of events, not recognizing longer term patterns or behaviors. Other research projects such as [25, 26] also focus more on shorter term monitoring and on techniques for person tracking and fall detection. Due to the general lack of long-term monitoring data and privacy issues with data collection, there has not been a significant body of work dedicated to long-term behavioral and health monitoring based on cameras.

10.3 Methodology

We examine the task of detecting atypical behaviors using two different approaches, using region-based occupancy patterns, derived from measuring how an occupant spends time in specific regions in their home, and concurrency-based models, which find important areas of a home automatically based on how an occupant moves through their home. For both approaches to atypical behavior detection, we use long-term datasets from WSU's CASAS project [16]. CASAS was intended as a smart home testbed, to evaluate algorithms for activity recognition and home automation. Common to the three datasets that we used, are a fairly dense deployment of 20+ PIR motion sensors, configured to have a small field of view. Judging from the documentation, we estimated that the motion sensors had a detection area of 8 m [27]. These motion sensor deployments do not offer the rich data available from cameras, but they sidestep several privacy issues inherent with placing cameras in people's homes. Since motion sensors can only detect the presence of motion in their fields of view, they will be better tolerated, even if data is recorded and stored for later processing or evaluation. Archiving video data for later processing would have significant privacy concerns for occupants, not to mention the logistics of storing months or years of video from multiple cameras.

Our initial experiments centered on a CASAS dataset featuring a single occupant for a 220 day experiment, codenamed "Aruba" by CASAS. The apartment layout and sensor placements can be seen in Fig. 10.1. We wanted to start with a single occupant, since motion sensors cannot differentiate between multiple people. For our region occupancy-based atypical behavior detector, we later extended our work to include a

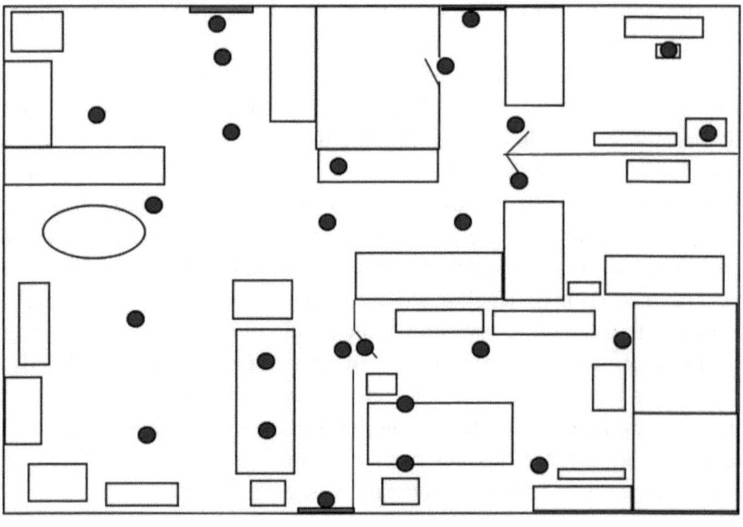

Fig. 10.1 "Aruba" apartment sensor layout

shorter 30 day dataset that contained an occupant with a pet, codenamed "Milan," and finally a 180 day dataset that contained a couple living together, codenamed "Tulim." All of the datasets that we evaluated had activities that were human annotated, and we used this as a baseline input to our atypical behavior system to compare against features derived directly from the motion sensors.

The following sections describes how we used the CASAS motion sensor-based data for both region occupancy and concurrent activation-based atypical behavior detection.

10.3.1 Region Occupancy-Based Atypical Behavior Detection

In order to identify atypical behaviors of a smart home's occupant, we need to have a representation for the occupant's behaviors. One clear choice is to use occupant activities to form a behavioral model, however, identifying activities using PIR's is a complicated task, since some important activities, such as sleeping, is marked by an absence of motion. We then hypothesized that activities in a home are closely tied to specific regions of a home, for example, cooking mostly takes place in the kitchen, and sleeping takes place mostly in the bedroom. Using that observation, we decided to use region occupancy as a proxy for occupant activities to generate daily patterns of behavior, which we can then compare across days to identify outliers, which we treat as atypical. These observations are illustrated in Fig. 10.2, in which we show both region occupancy and annotated activity patterns for each 30 minute window across 220 days of data collection, with each horizontal line in the image representing the occupant's occupied regions or activities for one day. The coloring for the patterns is different, since there is a different number of regions and activities, but there is still a clear visual similarity between the two. The following sections describe our steps to derive these region occupancies and atypical detections from the raw sensor data.

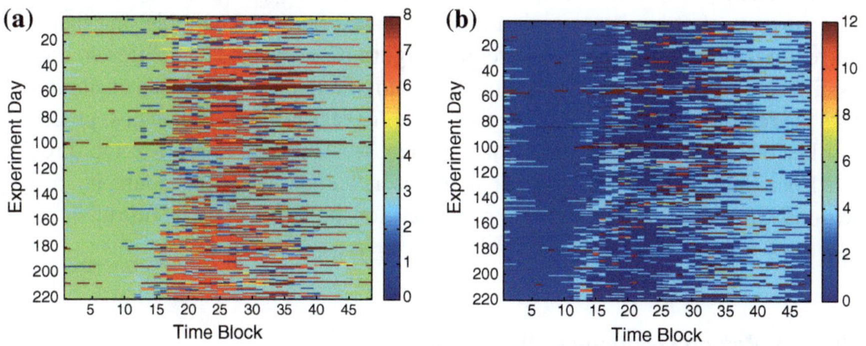

Fig. 10.2 Comparisons of region occupancy patterns to annotated activity patterns, based on most frequent region/activity in each 30 min time window. **a** Region occupancy patterns. **b** Annotated activity patterns

10.3.1.1 Initial Processing

The CASAS data consists of a series of PIR motion sensor activation events, which represent times in which an occupant or a guest moved within the detection area of one of the PIR's used in the deployment. These PIR's are located in Fig. 10.1 as the dark circles, and were mainly concentrated in the kitchen, living, and bedroom areas of the testbeds.

We first took these activation events, and examined them manually to look for sensor malfunctions. For example, for one day in the "Aruba" dataset, all of the motion sensors were triggered simultaneously for several hours. After we identified these days, we removed them from the dataset so they would not skew our results.

Next, we estimated the position of the occupant within the apartment based on PIR activation events. Since the user can activate many PIR's at any one moment, using the locations of the activated PIR's as the user's position would be quite noisy and subject to rapid changes. Thus, we decided to use a relatively simple approach to estimate the occupant's position by averaging the locations of the activated motion sensors within a small time window. Most of the PIR sensors used in the instrumented apartment were ceiling mounted units with a relatively small detection radius of 8 ft. With these pieces of information, we are able to determine the position and time of all motion detection events. This result was then temporally smoothed and used to assign a region label to every point in the occupant's estimated trajectory, as described in the next section.

10.3.1.2 Region Labeling

As a first step in forming the region occupancy patterns that we will later use for atypical behavior detection, we assign each point in the occupant's trajectory with a region label that corresponds to the room or semantic region where the occupant is currently located. For the "Aruba" dataset, the region labels include: *Kitchen*, *Dining Area*, *Living Room*, *Bedroom*, *Guest Bedroom*, *Office*, *Hallway* and *Outside*. The current scheme to map region labels is based on a lookup table that maps the current position of the user to one region. Figure 10.3 describes the different regions as different colored boxes overlaid on the deployment map for the dataset. Table 10.1 lists the region identifiers used. The time series of region labels is then post processed to filter out region changes that last less than 3 s. This acts to remove rapid region label oscillations that would occur if the user walked along the boundary of two regions. Similar region maps were generated for the "Milan" and "Tulim" datasets, as shown in Fig. 10.4a, b, respectively.

10.3.1.3 Region Occupancy Histograms

We decided to represent the time series of region occupancies, described in the previous section, as a set of region occupancy histograms for consecutive

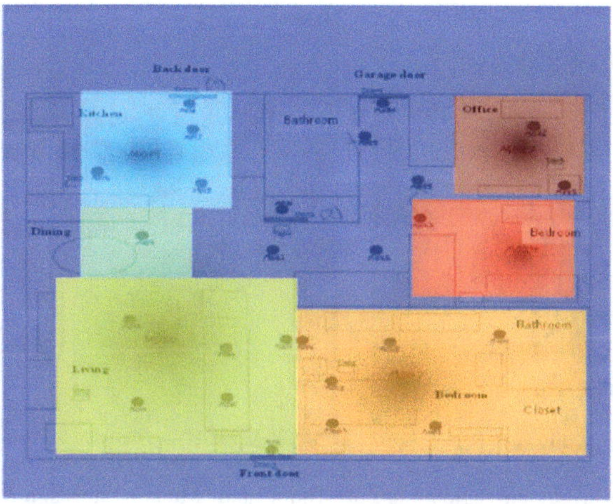

Fig. 10.3 Region map

Table 10.1 List of region labels used for processing

Identifier	Region description
0	Hallway
1	Kitchen
2	Dining area
3	Living room
4	Main bedroom
5	Guest bedroom
6	Office
7	Outside apartment
8	Inside with visitors

non-overlapping regions in time. These region occupancy histograms are more compact than the region time series, and can be interpreted more quickly than a long sequences of region occupancies. To form the actual region occupancy histograms that we used as a proxy for the occupant's behaviors, we first subdivided each day's data into smaller 30 minute chunks, and calculated the region occupancy histogram for each chunk. The size for the time chunk was chosen so that it would still be a reasonably compact size, to limit processing time for our experiments.

The result was 48 region histograms that represented the daily region occupancy patterns for the occupant of the apartment. We initially used several methods to summarize these 48 histograms to form even more compact representations, including using just the region with the highest occupancy for every time chunk. Other alternatives included using a Bag of Words representation along with a PCA to reduce the dimensionality of the data. We ultimately settled on simply concatenating these 48 histograms into a single feature vector to represent the occupant's region

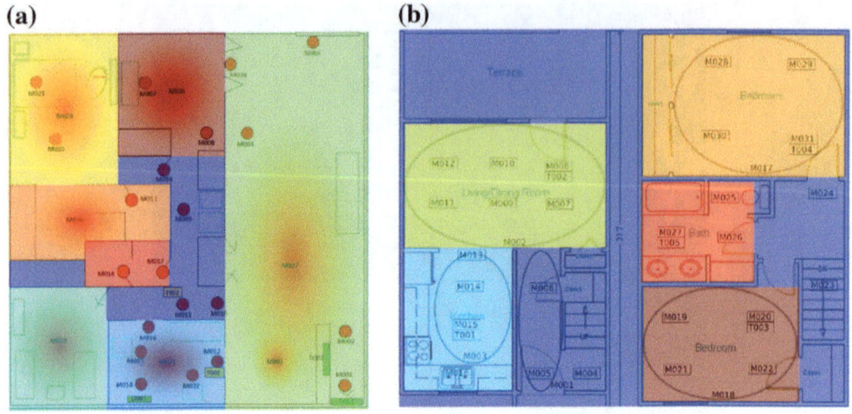

Fig. 10.4 Sensor layout and region maps of “Tulim” and “Milan” testbeds. **a** Milan testbed with region overlay. **b** Tulim testbed with region overlay

occupancy for each day, which we refer to as “Complete Region Histograms,” since the compact representations did not perform significantly better, and were difficult to interpret. We later augmented these concatenated region histograms with region-specificmotion detection histograms, which represented the number of motion events in each region during the same time chunk, which formed “Complete Region and Motion Histograms” features.

For the sake of completeness, we experimented with using only the motion histograms, formed by histograms of the region a motion sensor was activated per time period, and an even finer histogram of which motion sensor was activated per time period. However, our results for these last sets of histograms showed poor correlation with our ground truth-based activity classifier. Table 10.2 briefly describes some of the different features that we evaluated.

10.3.1.4 Identifying Atypical Daily Patterns

After mapping the occupant’s position to regions, and forming histogram-based patterns using region occupancy, we sought to identify region occupancy patterns that were atypical. We started by calculating how dissimilar each day’s pattern was to every other day in our dataset. For our “Complete Region and Motion Histograms,” we used the Euclidian distance between each pattern of concatenated histograms as our dissimilarity metric.

We can compactly represent the dissimilarity between all of the days of a dataset in the form of a distance matrix, where every entry (i, j) represents the dissimilarity between day i and day j, which is shown in Fig. 10.5 for both region occupancy and annotated activity-based patterns. We note that days that were very dissimilar to every other day, the red bands in the distance matrix, appear to be identical for both

Table 10.2 Different region/occupancy features considered for anomaly detection

Region occupancy feature	Associated distance metric	Description of descriptor
Most occupied region	Edit distance	The most frequently occupied region is used to represent each time period
"Bag of words feature"	Edit distance	The region occupancy histogram for a time period is mapped to the closest K-means based cluster for each time period
"Complete Region Histograms"	Euclidian distance	A concatenated vector of region occupancy histograms is used to represent each time period
"Complete Region and Motion Histograms"	Euclidian distance	The concatenated region occupancy histograms are appended with a histogram of region-based motion detection events
"Motion Only"	Euclidian distance	A histogram of region-based motion detection events for each time period

region occupancy and annotated activity-based patterns. Initially, we summed these dissimilarity of a single day i to every other day together to form a global dissimilarity metric for day i. Since lower values indicate a lower dissimilarity of a day's patterns to every other day in the dataset, we can use this global dissimilarity metric to classify days as atypical. To do this, we set a threshold on the global dissimilarity of each day to classify days with a high dissimilarity as atypical. A histogram of these global dissimilarity for every day can be seen in Fig. 10.6, we note that the histogram seems normally distributed, except that the distribution has a very long tail. We decided to find the average and standard deviation of these global dissimilarity values, and classify values that deviated from more than one standard deviation from the mean as atypical.

Our first approach used data from every day in the dataset in order to form global dissimilarity metrics to classify days as atypical, however, this is not a practical solution, since it assumes that we have access to data in the future. We wanted to also evaluate a sliding window approach to classification, where we would step through one day at a time and only classify the days based on the current and past data only. This approach may not identify the current day or past days as atypical if there is not enough historical data, for example, if the system just stared to collect data. So as each day is added to the sliding window, we reclassify all days using dissimilarity for all of the data up to the current day. We also experimented with different finite sliding window sizes, but we felt that the size of our daily region occupancy patterns was quite small, on the order of 10 KB, so we could reasonable store a lifetime's worth of occupancy data in less than 1 GB of memory.

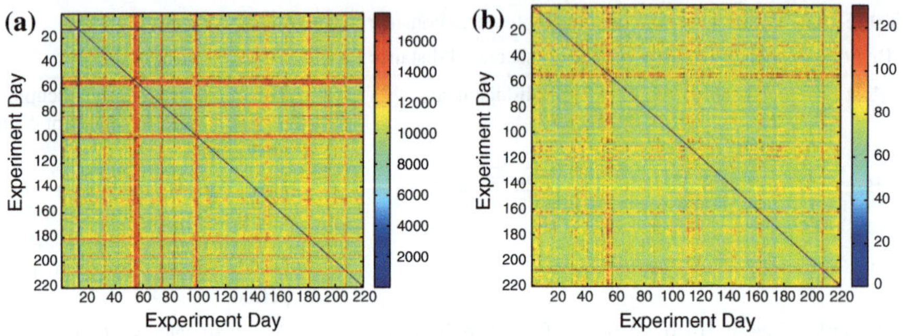

Fig. 10.5 Comparisons of distance matrices of the "Complete Region and Motion Histograms" patterns and CASAS annotated activities. **a** Region occupancy. **b** Annotated activity

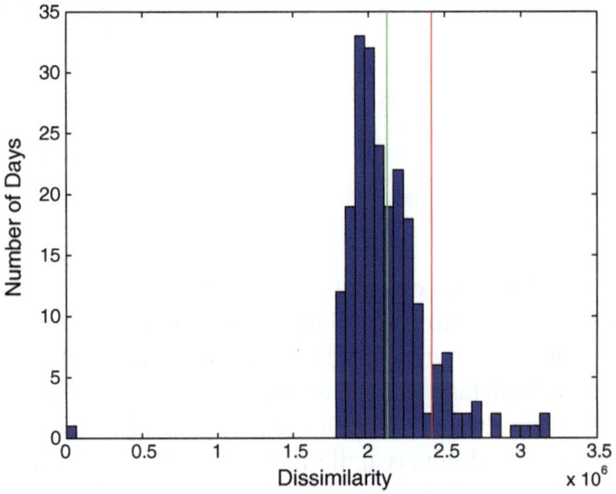

Fig. 10.6 Histogram of global dissimilarity values for the "Aruba" dataset

Lastly, we evaluated an alternative method of calculating dissimilarity other than our global dissimilarity metric. We decided to use the Local Outlier Factor or LOF, original proposed by Breunig et al. as a method to identify outliers in a dataset by comparing the local density around each point in the dataset [28]. The LOF algorithm also works on distance matrices, so we used our existing matrices calculated using our region occupancy patterns as an input and calculated the LOF for every day of our "Aruba" dataset. LOF has one parameter k, which is used to determine the size of the local neighborhood used to calculate the local density, we choose to use a value of 30, determined empirically. The LOF algorithm returns a value that represents the degree that a particular point is an outlier, but with no fixed threshold, we used the same method of choosing a threshold as with our global dissimilarly approach, after plotting a histogram of the LOF values as seeking a similar distribution as with dissimilarity.

10.3.1.5 Evaluating Region-Based Atypical Behavior Detector

To evaluate the performance of using region occupancy-based behavior patterns to identify atypical behaviors, we leveraged the activity annotations included with the CASAS dataset, the activities included in the "Aruba" dataset are shown in Table 10.3. Using the same procedure as with the region occupancy patterns, we instead used activity patterns segmented into the same 30 minute time chunks. These activity patterns were histograms of the amount of time the occupant performed one of the annotated activities in each time chunk. With these activity histograms we used the same methods as with the region occupancy histograms to form daily descriptors and compared each day to every other day.

After using these annotated activity patterns to classify days as atypical we treated these classifications as a ground truth and compared them against the classification results from our region occupancy-based classifier and presented the resulting comparison as a confusion matrix. We also compared how the region-based dissimilarity compared to the activity-based dissimilarity for each day in the dataset. When both the region-based and activity-based dissimilarities are plotted against each other, we can evaluate how well the two relate to each other visually as well as calculate a correlation coefficient. A high degree of correlation can be used to determine if the region occupancy can be used as an effective proxy for annotated activities.

For the original "Aruba" dataset, we noticed that the "Complete Region and Motion Histograms," as described in Table 10.2 had the highest correlation coefficient at 0.916115, which indicates that region occupancy is a very good proxy for annotated activities for the purposes of atypical behavior detection. Figure 10.7a, shows the correlation plot and Fig. 10.7b shows a confusion matrix of the region occupancy-based classifier output when compared to the output of an annotated activity-based classifier. This approach yielded an accuracy of over 95 % and a precision of over 90 % for identifying atypical days.

Table 10.3 List of annotated activities in CASAS dataset

Identifier	Activity
1	Sleeping
2	Bed to toilet
3	Meal preparation
4	Relax
5	Housekeeping
6	Eating
7	Wash dishes
8	Leave home
9	Enter home
10	Work
11	Resperate

(a)

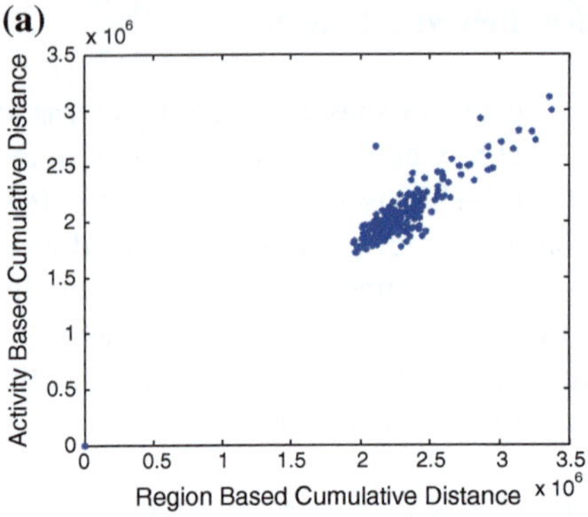

(b)

		Activity Based	
		Normal	Abnormal
Region	Normal	191	8
	Abnormal	2	19

Fig. 10.7 Correlation between region-and activity-based daily dissimilarity and a classification confusion matrix for the "Aruba" dataset. **a** Plot of daily total dissimilarity of the "Complete Region and Motion Histogram" patterns versus the CASAS annotated activities, correlation coefficient: 0.916115. **b** Confusion matrix of region-based abnormality detector of the "Complete Region and Motion Histograms" based classifier

We further wanted to verify that our approach was suitable for other homes and living situations, which is why we evaluated out approach for the "Milan" and "Tulim" datasets, which featured different apartment layouts and more than one occupant. Figure 10.4a, b show the layouts and regions, which are highlighted in different colors, for the "Milan" and "Tulim" testbeds, respectively. For these two datasets, we found that adding in the raw motion data to form the "Complete Region and Motion Histograms" yielded slightly worse performance compared to using just region occupancy. This can be attributed to the continued presence of multiple occupants, who would have generated many more motion events compared to the"Aruba" testbed, which just had a single occupant. From the correlation plots and confusion matrices of the "Milan" testbed, shown in Fig. 10.8a, b, we note that the correlation was quite lower than "Aruba" at 0.638051, this is probably due to the short duration of the "Milan" test set, which was considerable shorter at only 30 days. The "Tulim" testbeds correlation and confusion matrices, shown in Fig. 10.9a, b, show a better correlation of 0.801184, which is promising, considering "Tulim" had two occupants, which could imply that the occupants were frequently in the same region and performed the same activities, which for a coupling living together, seems highly likely.

We also wanted to study what effect using a sliding window approach rather than a global approach for atypical behavior detection would have on our classification accuracy. We found that using a sliding window, in which daily region occupancies patterns were added one at a time, did increase the number of false positives, which can be seen in Fig. 10.10a when compared to the global approach, which is reproduced in Fig. 10.10b. Most of these false positives occurred early in the dataset, when there was not enough region occupancy histogram to adequately separate out atypical from normal behavior.

(a)

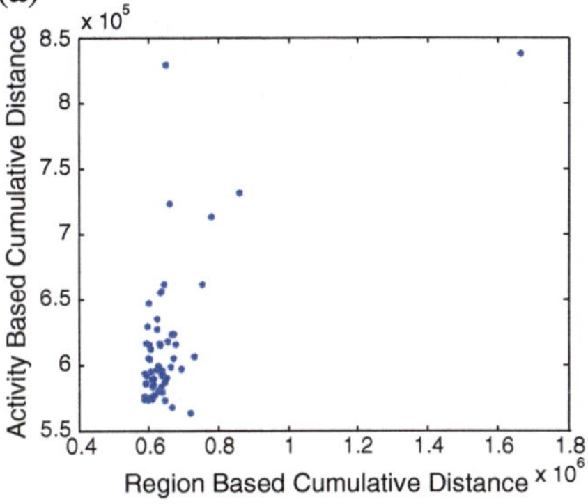

(b)

		Activity Based	
		Normal	Abnormal
Region	Normal	80	1
	Abnormal	0	2

Fig. 10.8 Correlation between region and activity-based daily dissimilarity and a classification confusion matrix for the "Milan" dataset. **a** Plot of daily total dissimilarity of the "Complete Region Histograms" patterns versus the CASAS annotated activities for the "Milan" dataset, correlation coefficient: 0.638051. **b** Confusion matrix of region-based abnormality detector of the "Complete Region Histograms" based classifier for the "Milan" dataset

(a)

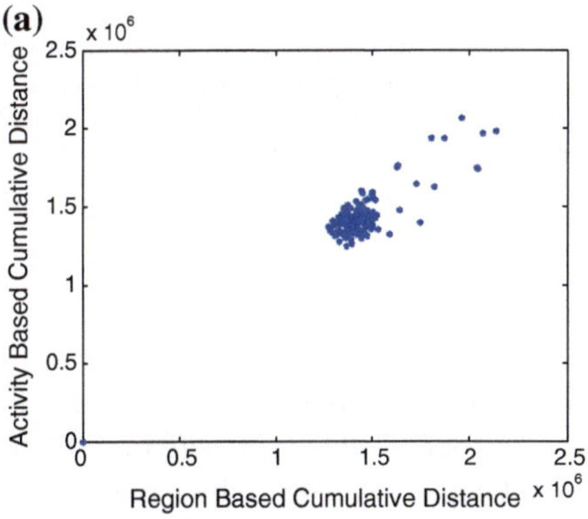

(b)

		Activity Based	
		Normal	Abnormal
Region	Normal	174	2
	Abnormal	2	7

Fig. 10.9 Correlation between region-and activity-based daily dissimilarity and a classification confusion matrix for the "Tulim" dataset. **a** Plot of daily total dissimilarity of the "Complete Region Histograms" patterns versus the CASAS annotated activities for the "Tulim" dataset, correlation coefficient: 0.801184. **b** Confusion matrix of region-based abnormality detector of the "Complete Region Histograms" based classifier for the "Tulim" dataset

Lastly, we compared the performance of a LOF-based classify compared to a classify based on global dissimilarities of annotated activities, to evaluate other methods of identifying outliers. We found good correlation between the two, 0.86167, as shown in Fig. 10.11a. The confusion matrix of classification results, as shown in Fig. 10.11b , were not as good as with the global or sliding window approaches, with more false positive and negative classifications. This increase in false classifications could be due to an overly conservative threshold that we applied to the LOF value to determine if a day was an outlier.

(a)

		Activity Based: Normal	Activity Based: Abnormal
Region Based	Normal	184	6
	Abnormal	7	23

(b)

		Activity Based: Normal	Activity Based: Abnormal
Region Based	Normal	187	6
	Abnormal	4	23

Fig. 10.10 Comparing a sliding window approach to a global approach for atypical behavior detection. **a** Sliding window approach, 220 day maximum size. **b** Global approach

(a)

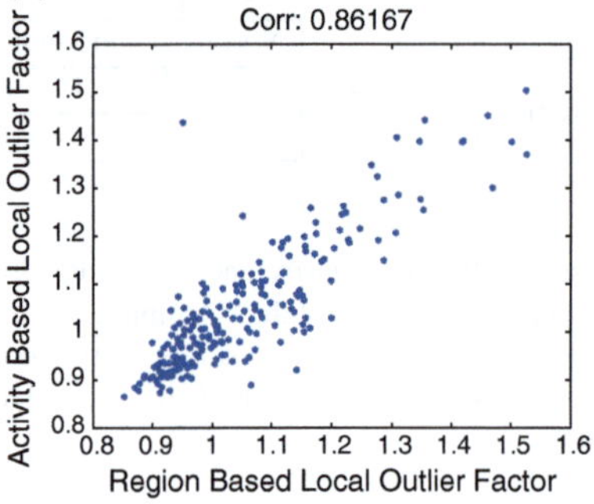

(b)

		Activity Based: Normal	Activity Based: Abnormal
LOF Region Based	Normal	182	8
	Abnormal	9	21

Fig. 10.11 Correlation between region-and activity-based LoF scores and a classification confusion matrix for the "Aruba" dataset. **a** Plot of daily LoF of the "Complete Region and Motion Histograms" patterns versus the CASAS annotated activities for the "Aruba" dataset, correlation coefficient: 0.86167. **b** Confusion matrix of region-based abnormality detector using a LoF- based classifier for the "Aruba" dataset

10.3.1.6 Interpreting Atypical Patterns

The previous section primarily evaluated how well region-based atypical behavior compared to a similar classification process using human annotated activities. In this section, we examine the results of the atypical behavioral detector by looking at the region occupancy patterns of the days classified as normal or atypical.

Figure 10.12 shows features that correspond to normal days, with each horizontal line corresponding to a day's region occupancy patterns. Each one is stacked on top of each other, so looking at vertical columns would represent the region occupancy at the same time across days. These histogram patterns have been resorted, so that the components of the histograms that represent the same region are adjacent to each other, with highlighted boxes separating the different region's occupancy. The labels above each block represent the semantic region that the block represents. Each region block is broken up into 48 columns, representing the 48 time chunks in which the histograms were originally calculated, so each day's occupancy of that region is encoded left to right, with the far left side representing midnight. We can then examine each block to determine how the occupancy of a specific region varies within a day, and throughout the dataset by looking horizontally and vertically respectively. When examining the occupancy patterns for the bedroom, we see a high occupancy for the

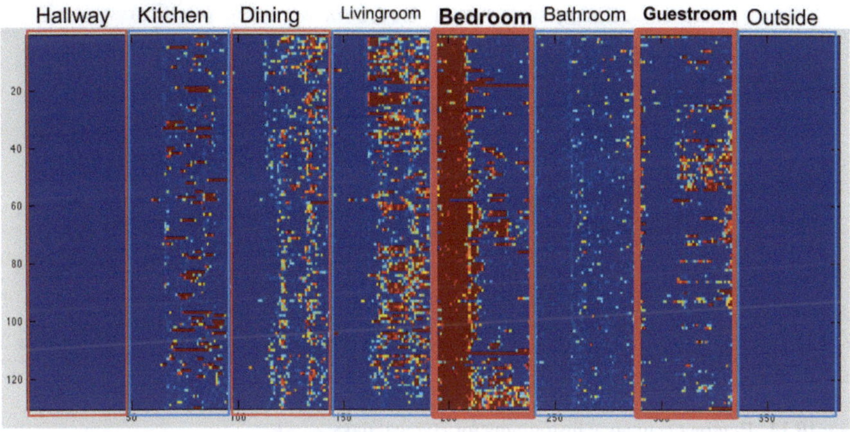

Fig. 10.12 Region occupancy histograms for normal days

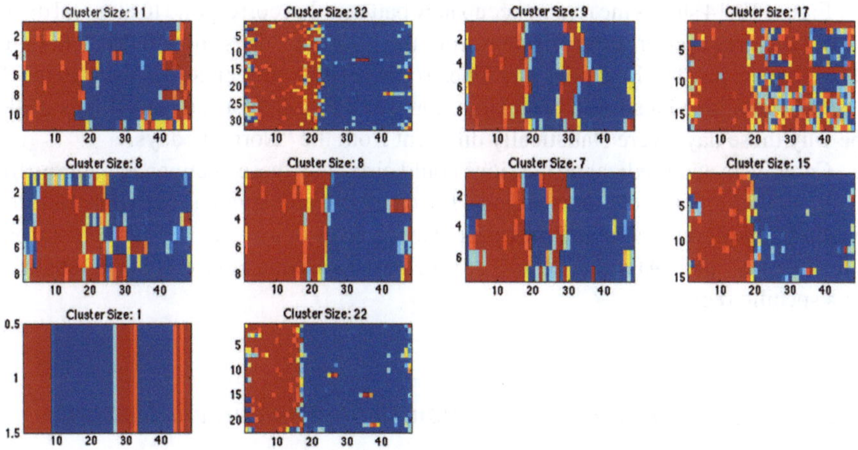

Fig. 10.13 Cluster analysis of bedroom occupancy patterns for normal days

early hours, most likely representing sleep. Also note that the normal days do not have significant Guest room occupancy during the same early hours time period.

Using the bedroom as an example, we sought to understand the variations of the bedroom region occupancy for our "Normal" days. We performed a clustering analysis of the bedroom occupancies using k-means, which yielded 10 unique activity patterns for normally classified behavior. These bedroom occupancy clusters can be seen in Fig. 10.13. We note that these cluster represent different sleep and wake times, and that these clusters of bedroom occupancy could be used to monitor sleep habits be used to specifically monitor for atypical sleep patterns by comparing the bedroom occupancy patterns with these common "Normal" bedroom occupancy clusters.

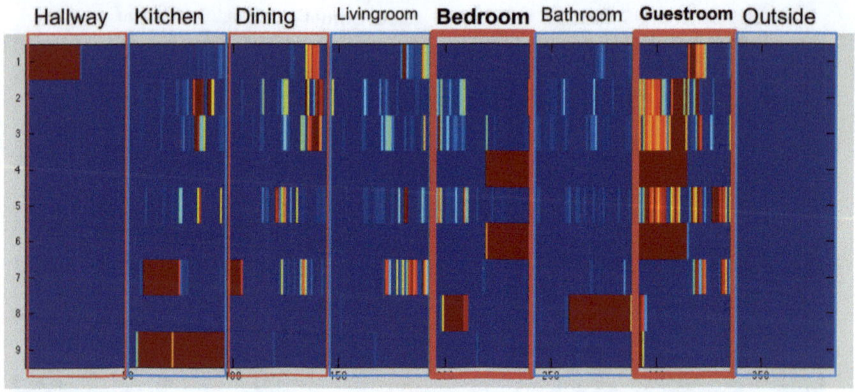

Fig. 10.14 Region occupancy histograms for atypical days

Figure 10.14 shows the region occupancy patterns that correspond to atypical days. These patterns appear quite different from the "Normal" days show in Fig. 10.12. If we compare just the Bedroom and Guestroom regions, it seems like there is much higher overnight Guestroom occupancy compared to the "Normal" days. This could be why these days were statistically different from the "Normal" days.

Caregivers and medical professions could also view these occupancy patterns for both normal an atypical days to look for causes of the atypical classification, for example, they could compare the occupancy patterns of specific regions across both the "Normal" and "Atypical" classes to see of the classification was due to changes in a specific region.

10.3.2 Atypical Behavior Detection Using Concurrent Hotspot

In a motion sensor network, a concurrent activation event is when a moving object enters an area that overlaps with multiple sensors' detecting region and generates one or more motion detection events. In this section, we will develop and use a concurrent activation model to find concurrent hotspots (the location where occupants move frequently). Then, an occupant's daily behavior at these hotspots will be used to estimate how likely that occupant is displaying anomalous behavior.

The basic intuition behind this analysis is that people tend to maintain regular daily routines and the behavior at the concurrent hotspots are able to summarize the occupant's daily activity. So any deviation of a occupant's behavior at these concurrent hotspots might indicate atypical behavior.

10.3.2.1 Finding Concurrent Hotspots

Since a concurrent hotspot is the location where occupants move frequently, we need to first define a concurrent event and the location of such events.

Assuming that a motion sensor network consists of N binary motion sensors, defined as sensors only have two possible states $\{0, 1\}$. In the cause of motion sensors, a 0 state means that no motion is detected, and 1 indicates the sensor is being triggered by motion at this time.

The model of a single sensor's activation can be demonstrated with Fig. 10.15. To simplify the activation model, the detection region of a motion sensor is considered a circular area. If an object is moving inside the detection region, the sensor will be activated; conversely, if the moving object is outside the detection boundary, the sensor will not be triggered. However, some exceptions could generate false detections, PIR-based motion sensors can be triggered by sudden local changes in temperature, such has air moving through a heating or cooling vent. We define the probability that a sensor is activated with no moving object present as false positive rate β. Our previous work shows that this model fits the CASAS Aruba data set quit well, with an estimated false positive rate of $\widetilde{\beta} = 0.0406$, was calculated by a Genetic Optimization algorithm.

With this single sensor's activation model, we can now turn to the concurrent activation case. Suppose a moving object is at the location with coordinates (x_u, y_u) with k sensors being activated at the same time. Intuitively, that object is somewhere in the overlapping detection areas of those k sensors. Assuming that all of sensors have the same detection area size and have detection centers located at $\{(x_{\lambda 1}, y_{\lambda 1}), (x_{\lambda 2}, y_{\lambda 2}), \ldots, (x_{\lambda k}, y_{\lambda k})\}$, the most likely estimation of user's location $(\hat{x}_u, \hat{y}_u)$ is given by the following equation:

$$\hat{x}_u = \frac{1}{k}\sum_{i=1}^{k} x_{\lambda i} \qquad (10.1)$$

$$\hat{y}_u = \frac{1}{k}\sum_{i=1}^{k} y_{\lambda i}$$

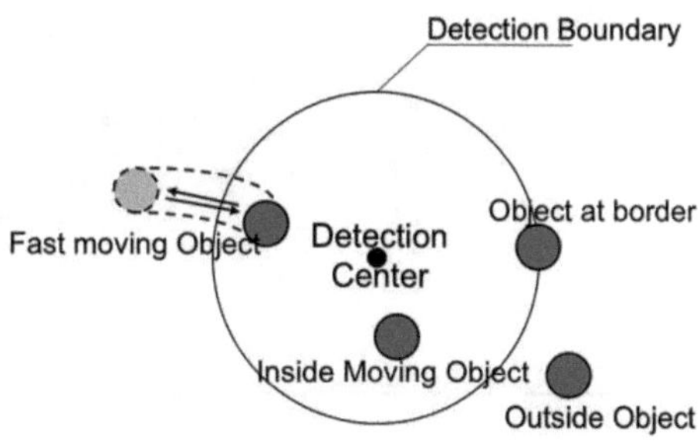

Fig. 10.15 Model of a single sensor's activation

Equation 10.1 is simply averages of locations of all the activated sensors. This approach is easy to implement but it ignores the fact that some of the sensors are activated by false positive events as we mentioned earlier. For example, if some of the active sensors amount those k activated sensors are activated by environmental temperature changes or some other accidental factors (false positive), the above approach described by Eq. 10.1 might give a result far away from the occupant's actual location.

In order to limit of the influence caused by false positive motion detection events, we leverage a Concurrency Graph that contains prior knowledge of overlapping areas of sensors' detection regions. The Concurrency Graph is defined as a weighted graph $G = (V, E)$, which consists of a set of motion sensors V as nodes and a set of edges E. A concurrent activation event will increase the weight of edges between any pair of activated sensors by one. Therefore, the higher the weight of a edge, more likely those two involved sensors will be activated at the same time.

After filtering out the edges with weight less than a certain threshold $T = \lambda \cdot \widetilde{\beta}^2$, where λ is the total number of concurrent events, and $\widetilde{\beta}$ is the false positive rate, most of the edges created by false positive activation can be removed.

Figure 10.16 shows the concurrency graph built on the "Aruba" dataset from 2010-11-01 to 2010-12-01. The red circles in the figure are the sensor nodes; the links are the edges between nodes; and numbers on the edges are the weights of corresponding edges. Figure 10.17 shows the concurrency graph after filtering out edges using the threshold mentioned above.

With the Concurrency Graph, if we have k activated sensor, instead of calculating the average location directly, we mark the corresponding k nodes in the concurrency graph Fig. 10.17. This will generate one or more sub graphs, where we choose the subgraph, G_u, with largest number of nodes to estimate the occupant's location with Eq. 10.2.

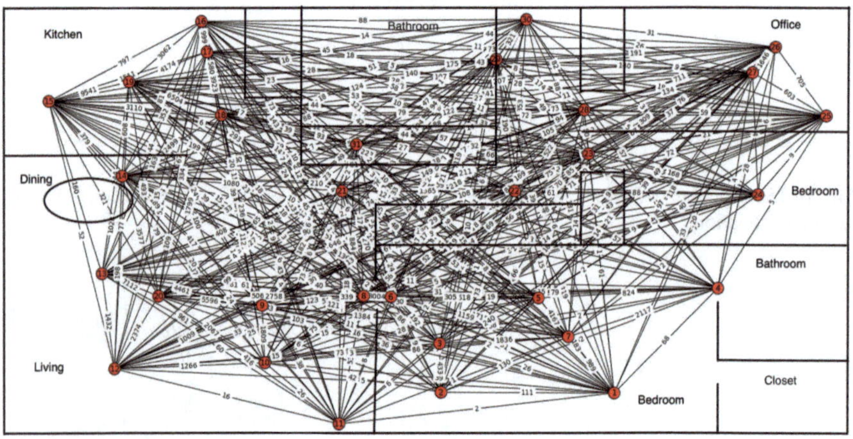

Fig. 10.16 Concurrency graph for 2010–11

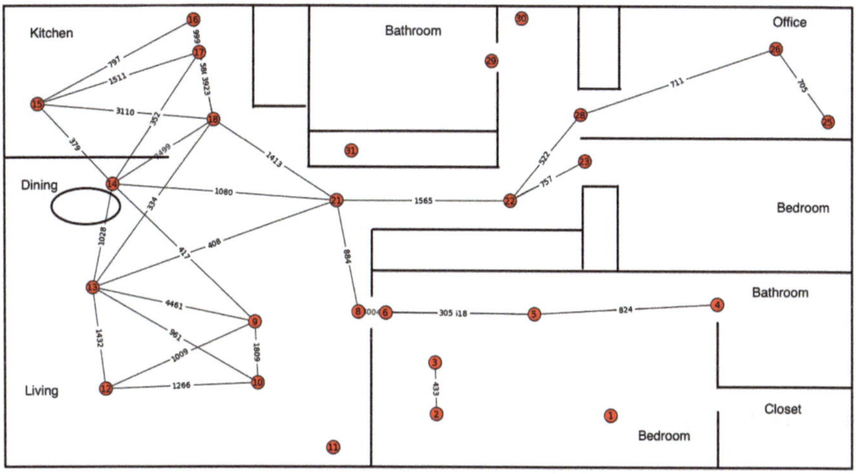

Fig. 10.17 Concurrency graph for 2010–11 with thresholding and area sensor deleted

$$
\begin{aligned}
\hat{x_u} &= \frac{1}{|G_u|} \sum_{i:s_i \in G_u} x_i, \\
\hat{y_u} &= \frac{1}{|G_u|} \sum_{i:s_i \in G_u} y_i
\end{aligned}
\tag{10.2}
$$

We define the concurrent hotspots as center of areas where an occupant frequently moves. Every time the activation state of any sensor changes, an estimation of the user's location can be calculated by Eq. 10.2. To find the concurrent hotspots we just defined, we go through the whole "Aruba" dataset and get a sequence of estimated user's active locations $\{(\hat{x}_{u1}, \hat{y}_{u1}), \ldots, (\hat{x}_{un}, \hat{y}_{un})\}$. If we can cluster the sequence into several groups, then the centroids of these clusters will be the hotspots that we are looking for.

We choose to use K-Means as our clustering algorithm, to decide how many clusters, k to use, we plotted the clustering error or cost, defined as the distance of every point to their assigned cluster, versus the number of clusters, as shown in Fig. 10.18. As can be seen from the figure, a value $k = 10$ is a good choice since it is the turning point of the cost curve. While K-means has a component of randomness, as initial cluster centroids are randomly selected, which may yield a different result, multiple experiments resulted in very similar centroid sets. We picked one of these sets shown in Fig. 10.19, where the red circles are the hotspots found, and the size of the circle indicates the size of the cluster, which represents how many concurrency events it encompasses.

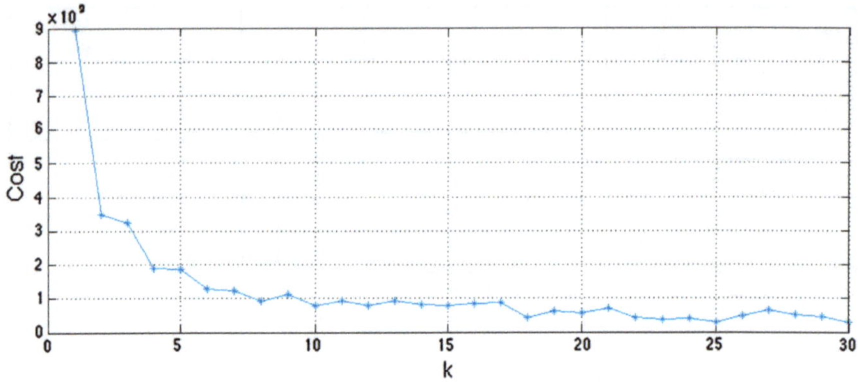

Fig. 10.18 Kmeans: cost versus cluster number

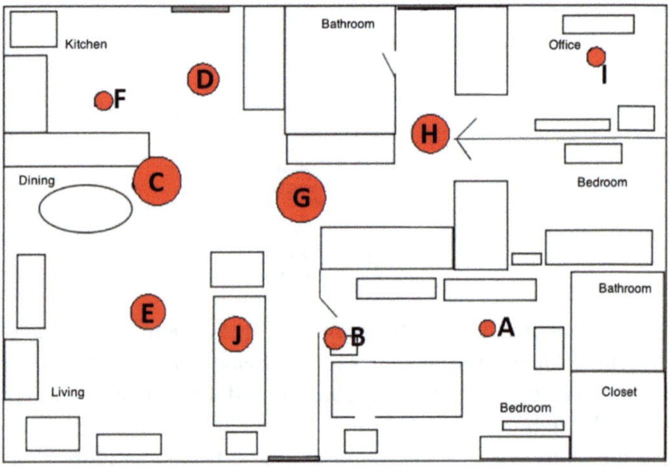

Fig. 10.19 Hotspot distribution

10.3.2.2 Hotspot-Based Occupant's Behavior Modeling Selection

The hotspots we found in the previous section are calculated by clustering locations where the occupant frequently moves. As a result, different clusters represents the centers of the occupant's activities to some extent. For examples, clusters *A* and *B* in Fig. 10.19 are related to the occupant's activities in the bedroom (sleeping, walking, and so on); clusters *D*, *G*, and *H* represent walking through hallway; cluster *E* reflects occupant's movements inside the living room; cluster *J* is for the sofa related activity; cluster *F* acts as the indicator of the occupant's cooking activity; and cluster *I* is the occupant's behavior in the office.

With the help of concurrent hotspots, a occupant's daily activities can be divided into different clusters according to their relative locations to the hotspots. To summarize the occupant's daily active level at each concurrent hotspot, we use Algorithm 1 that can summarize the occupant's active level of one day into a 1×10 vector $V = [v_1, v_2, \ldots, v_{10}]$. The algorithm is described as follows:

Algorithm 1: Active Level Summary with Hotspots

Data: $H = \{h_1, h_2, \ldots, h_{10}\}$
$E = \{(\hat{x}_{u1}, \hat{y}_{u1}), (\hat{x}_{u2}, \hat{y}_{u2}), \ldots, (\hat{x}_{un}, \hat{y}_{un})\}$
Result: $V = [v_1, v_2, \ldots, v_{10}]$
initialize V to a zero vector ;
foreach $(\hat{x}_u, \hat{y}_u) \in E$ **do**
  $\hat{i} = \arg\min_{i:h_i \in H} \left(distance(h, (\hat{x}_u, \hat{y}_u))\right)$;
  $wcore = ScoreMapping(t)$;
  $v_{\hat{i}} = v_{\hat{i}} + wcore$;
end

In Algorithm 1, H is the Hotspots Set, where that h_i is the location of the ith concurrent hotspot; E is a sequence of user's active locations estimated by Eq. 10.2 for a day; $ScoreMapping(t)$ is a function that map time duration t into a active level score. Therefore, the algorithm calculates the active level score of the occupant and accumulates the score for each concurrent hotspot.

The $ScoreMapping(t)$ function in the above algorithm defines how we evaluate a occupant's active level from the amount of time they are moving at one location. For example, if the $ScoreMapping()$ is linear, the algorithm just accumulates the time an occupant spends in a certain hotspot. In this chapter, a super linear function is chosen as $ScoreMapping()$ which indicates that a long-time continuous activity has more impact than several short-time activities together.

For the whole CASAS "Aruba" dataset, we apply Algorithm 1 for each day and get a $N \times 10$ result matrix, where N is the total number of days, and each row is the output result of the algorithm 1 for the corresponding day. Therefore, a column $C_j = [v_j^{(1)}, v_j^{(2)}, \ldots, v_j^{(N)}]^T$ $(j = 1, 2, \ldots, 10)$ of the result matrix is the occupant's active level scores at the jth hotspot for N days.

Now we can use this resulting model derived from time spend in each hotspot to detect abnormal activity of the occupant. Our assumption is that the occupant's activity level at each concurrent hotspot satisfies is a specific distribution.

Therefore, we set up a distribution library which contains Normal, Rayleigh, Rician, t location-scale, Weibull, and Generalized extreme value distributions. For each concurrent hotspot, we fit the occupant's active level scores to every distributions in our distribution library. And we choose the distribution with the highest log likelihood as the behavior model for the occupant at that hotspot. Table 10.4 shows the result for each concurrent hotspot.

The histogram of occupant's active level scores at hotspots A and B, and the result curves of corresponding fitted distribution are showed in Fig. 10.20a, b. It can be seen that some of the curves fit the active level scores well. The Table 10.5 summaries the best probabilistic models and parameters for all the concurrent hotspots.

For at location-scale distribution with parameter μ, σ, ν, the probabilistic density function is

Table 10.4 Concurrent hotspot model fitting

HotSpot	Normal	Rayleigh	Rician	t location-scale	Weibull	Generalized extreme value
A	−1232.68	−1256.35	−1230.19	−1199.89	−1236.12	−1205.71
B	−1500.01	−1585.86	−1500.38	−1499.56	−1500.57	−1498.22
C	−1316	−1287.56	−1287.56	−1300.66	−1286.7	−1260.19
D	−1299.57	−1279.22	−1279.22	−1275.59	−1278.62	−1243.49
E	−1326.36	−1308.94	−1308.94	−1314	−1307.84	−1283.66
F	−1287.33	−1259.48	−1259.48	−1268.75	−1258.69	−1235.75
G	−1139.27	−1117.72	−1117.7	−1129.07	−1117.58	−1094.88
H	−1534.13	−1534.16	−1534.16	−1533.94	−1531.83	−1530.7
I	−1339.2	NA	NA	−1214.28	NA	−1112.02
J	−1577.44	−1608.62	−1576.43	−1572.18	−1579.38	−1574.47

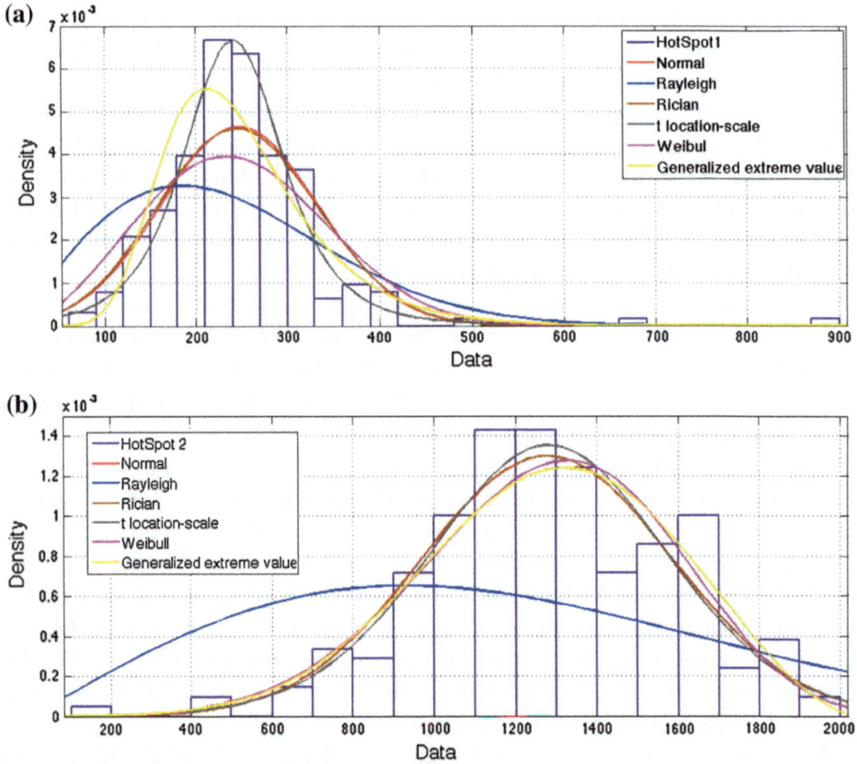

Fig. 10.20 Histogram and model fitting for hotspot A and B. **a** Hotspot A. **b** Hotspot B

Table 10.5 Hotspot model fitting

Hotspot	Probabilistic model	Parameters
A	t location-scale	$\mu = 240.839$ $\sigma = 56.1281$ $\nu = 3.93679$
B	Generalized extreme value	$k = -0.371485$ $\sigma = 321.032$ $\nu = 1183.27$
C	Generalized extreme value	$k = 0.294019$ $\sigma = 70.3057$ $\nu = 154.99$
D	Generalized extreme value	$k = 0.222946$ $\sigma = 67.6701$ $\nu = 178.837$
E	Generalized extreme value	$k = 0.175264$ $\sigma = 84.0357$ $\nu = 205.644$
F	Generalized extreme value	$k = 0.245482$ $\sigma = 64.3452$ $\nu = 137.352$
G	Generalized extreme value	$k = 0.201744$ $\sigma = 33.6826$ $\nu = 78.0005$
H	Generalized extreme value	$k = -0.152369$ $\sigma = 330.334$ $\nu = 509.017$
I	Generalized extreme value	$k = 1.35126$ $\sigma = 20.4538$ $\nu = 12.7242$
J	t location-scale	$\mu = 1297.43$ $\sigma = 368.005$ $\nu = 6.48294$

$$p(x;\mu,\sigma,\nu) = \frac{\Gamma(\frac{\nu+1}{2})}{\sqrt{\nu\pi}\,\Gamma(\frac{\nu}{2})}\left(1 + \frac{(\frac{x-\mu}{\sigma})^2}{\nu}\right)^{-\frac{\nu+1}{2}}$$

For a generalized extreme value distribution with parameter k, σ, ν, the probabilistic density function is

$$p(x;k,\sigma,\nu) = \frac{1}{\sigma}\left[1 + \nu(\frac{x-k}{\sigma})\right]^{-\frac{1}{\nu}-1} \exp\left(-\left[1 + \nu(\frac{x-k}{\sigma})\right]^{-\frac{1}{\nu}}\right)$$

With fitted probabilistic model of each concurrent hotspot, we propose a multi-variable distribution model PM that models the occupant's daily active level score vector (the 1 by 10 vector that contains active score for each hotspot):

$$V = [v_1, v_2, \ldots, v_{10}] \sim \mathrm{PM}(p_1, p_2, \ldots, p_{10}) \tag{10.3}$$

where p_i $(i = 1, 2, \ldots, 10)$ is the probabilistic distribution model for hotspot i showed in Table 10.5. The model (Eq. 10.3) is the representation random distribution model for user's daily active level at each concurrent hotspot.

10.3.2.3 Abnormal and Typical Active Level Detection

We define the normalness of a day as log likelihood the occupant's active level score vector which is calculated by our proposed PM model (Eq. 10.3).

Given the active score vector $V = [v_1, v_2, \ldots, v_{10}]$ and the distribution model is $\mathrm{PM}(p_1, p_2, \ldots, p_{10})$, the likelihood of the active level scores can be calculated by the following equation:

$$L = \prod_{i=1}^{10} p_i(v_i) \tag{10.4}$$

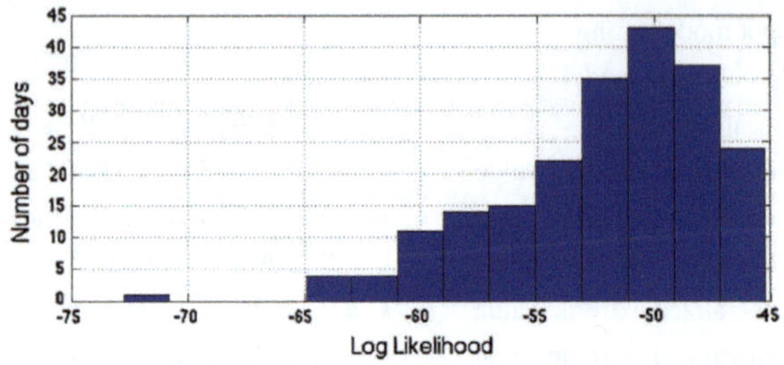

Fig. 10.21 The histogram of log probability score

Then, the log likelihood's calculation becomes straightforward:

$$\text{Log}(L) = \sum_{i=1}^{10} \log(p_i(v_i)) \tag{10.5}$$

Using Eq. 10.5, the higher the value of Log(L) indicates that a specific day is more likely to be a normal day. Similarly, the lower the value, the more likely that day is a atypical day. The histogram of the log likelihood of all the days is shown in Fig. 10.21.

Setting the lower threshold $T_{\text{low}} = -57$ and the higher threshold $T_{\text{high}} = -47$, days with log likelihood greater than T_{high} are marked as typical, days with log likelihood less than T_{low} are considered as abnormal days. Using this rule, we have the result that {1, 2, 6, 32, 54, 56, 57, 73, 74, 76, 83, 90, 99, 100, 103, 107, 108, 109, 111, 132, 142, 143, 155, 167, 170, 181, 200, 201, 207} are classified as be atypical, and days {7, 20, 23, 28, 30, 31, 35, 38, 42, 43, 53, 58, 65, 69, 71, 72, 78, 85, 88, 89, 91, 94, 05, 06, 13, 17, 22, 24, 26, 38, 48, 64, 68, 76, 77, 78, 89, 93, 94, 96, 103, 105, 210} are marked as typical, all the other days are normal.

In summary, the whole process of detecting the occupant's abnormal behavior is very straightforward. It starts from location estimation based on concurrency graph, representing user's daily active level using a score vector, to calculating the log likelihood of the score vector. Therefore, The proposed method offered us a simple method to interpret the information from binary motion sensors directly into a user daily behavior summary.

10.4 Future Work

The two approaches that we have used so far, region occupancy-based and concurrency-based show promise in identifying whole days as"Normal" or "Atypical," however, it is not clear why a specific day was classified as "Atypical." Our future work seeks to address this issue by incorporating features that more closely

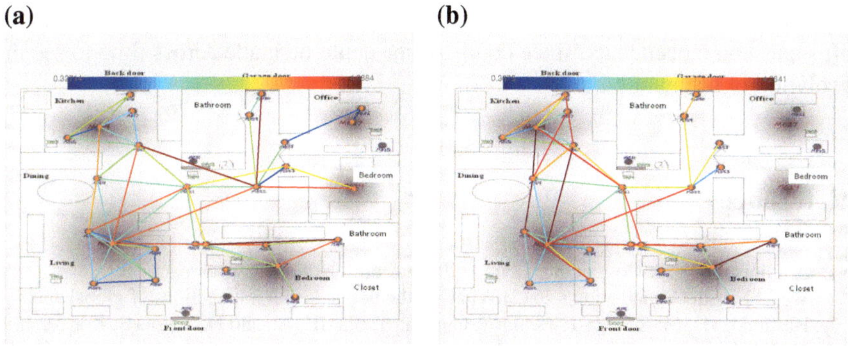

Fig. 10.22 Variation of occupant mobility between two months. **a** Occupant apartment transversals, month 2. **b** Occupant apartment transversals, month 5

correlates with an occupants health and wellbeing. For example, Fig. 10.22 shows an occupant's motion between PIR sensors for the "Aruba" dataset between two one moth periods. Most of the upper left and lower portions are similar between the two months, but on the left graph, the occupant shows more movement into and out of the office and guest bedrooms and less movement in and around the kitchen. If we used these compact representations of how an occupant moves around a home in our classification system, the atypically classified day's mobility patterns could directly aid caretakers/healthcare professionals in diagnosing mobility difficulties if movement around the apartment decrease or significantly changes.

One other extensions that we are evaluating is to determine if the motion activity in any one region or hotspot is atypical, which would future give healthcare professionals an indication as to where these atypical events are occurring. Similar work is also being planned to look for long-term shifts or changes in an occupants mobility and behavior, in order to look for more subtle changes in mobility over time.

10.5 Conclusion

Longitudinal data collection and interpretation is now becoming more practical with ambient and wearable sensors technologies. With this reality, our approach of using region occupancy patterns can be used to model behavior and to identify common patterns and atypical daily patterns of smart home occupants. We show that both region occupancy-and concurrency-based hotspots derived from simple motion sensors can be used to identify "Atypical" days and that patterns from these days can be further analyzed to look for specific causes of the "Atypical" classification. This has the potential of reducing the work load of caretakers and healthcare professionals if the occupants are elderly or otherwise need monitoring, since they only would have to evaluate the atypical days closely. Additionally, common behavioral patterns and atypical patterns could be useful as diagnostic tools to indicate lifestyle changes for all smart home occupants, since comparisons could be made across time to see the evolution of behavior patterns.

References

1. Administration for Community Living (2012) A profile of older Americans
2. World Health Organization (2012) What are the public health implications of global ageing?
3. Hashimoto H, Matsunaga T, Tsuboi T, Ohyama Y, She JH, Amano N, Yokota S, Kobayashi H (2007) Comfortable life space for elderly—using supporting systems based on technology. In: SICE, 2007 annual conference, Sept 2007, pp 3037–3042
4. O'Brien A, Ruairi RM (2009) Survey of assistive technology devices and applications for aging in place. In: Second international conference on advances in human-oriented and personalized mechanisms, technologies, and services, CENTRIC'09, pp 7–12, Sept 2009
5. Pollack ME (2005) Intelligent technology for an aging population: the use of ai to assist elders with cognitive impairment. AI Mag 26(2):9–24
6. Tran BQ (2002) Home care technologies for promoting successful aging in elderly populations. In: Engineering in medicine and biology, 2002, 24th annual conference and the annual fall meeting of the biomedical engineering society EMBS/BMES conference, 2002, proceedings of the second joint, vol 3, Oct 2002, pp 1898–1899
7. Wang L, Wang Z, He Z, Gao X (2010) Research of physical condition monitoring system for the elderly based on zigbee wireless network technology. In: 2010 international conference on E-Health networking, digital ecosystems and technologies (EDT), vol 1, pp 32–35, Apr 2010
8. Cdc—healthy places—healthy places terminology, Mar 2014
9. Kochera A, Straight AK, Guterbock TM, AARP (Organization) (2005) Beyond 50.05: a report to the nation on livable communities: creating environments for successful aging, AARP, 2005
10. Quantified self: self knowledge through numbers, Mar 2012
11. Shi JH, Lee B, Park KS (2011) Detection of abnormal living patterns for elderly living alone using support vector data description. IEEE Trans Inf Technol Biomed 15(3):438–448
12. Tax DMJ, Duin RPW (2004) Support vector data description. Mach Learn 54(1):45–66
13. O'Brien A, McDaid K, Loane J, Doyle J, O'Mullane B (2012) Visualisation of movement of older adults within their homes based on pir sensor data. In: 2012 6th international conference on pervasive computing technologies for healthcare (PervasiveHealth), May 2012, pp 252–259
14. Cuddihy P, Weisenberg J, Graichen C, Ganesh M (2007) Algorithm to automatically detect abnormally long periods of inactivity in a home. In: Proceedings of the 1st ACM SIGMOBILE international workshop on systems and networking support for healthcare and assisted living environments, HealthNet'07, ACM, New York, pp 89–94
15. Fine BT (2009) Unsupervised anomaly detection with minimal sensing. In: Proceedings of the 47th annual southeast regional conference, ACM-SE 47, ACM, New York, pp 60:1–60:5
16. Cook DJ (2012) Learning setting-generalized activity models for smart spaces. Intell Syst IEEE 27(1):32–38
17. Rashidi P, Cook DJ (2010) Mining and monitoring patterns of daily routines for assisted living in real world settings. In: Proceedings of the 1st ACM international health informatics symposium, IHI'10, ACM, New York, pp 336–345
18. Rashidi P, Cook DJ, Holder LB, Schmitter-Edgecombe M (2011) Discovering activities to recognize and track in a smart environment. IEEE Trans Knowl Data Eng 23(4):527–539
19. Roley SS, DeLany JV, Barrows CJ, Brownrigg S, Honaker D, Sava DI, Talley V, Voelkerding K, Amini DA, Smith E, Toto P, King S, Lieberman D, Baum MC, Cohen ES, Cleveland PA, Youngstrom MJ (2008) Occupational therapy practice framework: domain & practice, 2nd edn. Am J Occup Ther 62(6):625–683

20. Jakkula VR, Cook DJ (2011) Detecting anomalous sensor events in smart home data for enhancing the living experience. In: Artificial intelligence and smarter living, volume WS-11-07 of AAAI workshops, AAAI
21. Jain G, Cook D, Jakkula V (2006) Monitoring health by detecting drifts and outliers for a smart environment inhabitant. In: Proceedings of the international conference on smart homes and health telematics
22. Kalra L, Zhao X, Soto AJ, Milios AE (2012) A two-stage corrective markov model for activities of daily living detection. In: ISAmI'12, pp 171–179
23. Lymberopoulos D, Bamis A, Savvides A (2008) Extracting spatiotemporal human activity patterns in assisted living using a home sensor network. In: Proceedings of the 1st international conference on PErvasive technologies related to assistive environments, PETRA'08, ACM, New York, pp 29:1–29:8
24. Gómez-Conde I, Olivieri DN, Vila XA, Rodriguez-Liñares L (2010) Smart telecare video monitoring for anomalous event detection. In: 2010 5th Iberian conference on information systems and technologies (CISTI), June 2010, pp 1–6
25. Cardile F, Iannizzotto G, La Rosa F (2010) A vision-based system for elderly patients monitoring. In: 2010 3rd conference on human system interactions (HSI), May 2010, pp 195–202
26. Rougier C, Meunier J, St-Arnaud A, Rousseau J (2011) Robust video surveillance for fall detection based on human shape deformation. IEEE Trans Circuits Syst Video Technol 21(5):611–622
27. Sahaf Y (2011) Comparing sensor modalities for activity recognition. PhD thesis, Washington State University
28. Breunig MM, Kriegel H-P, Ng RT, Sander J (2000) Lof: Identifying density-based local outliers. Sigmod Rec 29(2):93–104

20. Jakkula, V., Cook, D.J. (2011) Detecting anomalous sensor events in smart home data for enhancing the living experience. Artificial intelligence and smarter living, volume WS-11-07 of AAAI Workshops, AAAI.

21. [illegible]

22. [illegible]

23. [illegible]

24. [illegible]

25. [illegible]

Chapter 11
People Counting Across Non-overlapping Camera Views by Flow Estimation Among Foreground Regions

Naoko Nitta, Ryota Akai and Noboru Babaguchi

Abstract Counting the number of people traveling across nonoverlapping camera views generally requires every person who has exited a camera view to be reidentified when he/she reenters another camera view. A typical solution is to detect an individual person exiting or entering each camera view and establish their correspondence based on their visual appearances and the knowledge of the camera topology, transition time between cameras, etc. One of the main challenges is that the appearances of different people can be similar, while the appearance of the same person can vary in different camera views. On the other hand, a recent approach for counting people within a single camera view is "crowd-centric", which is to extract foreground regions and estimate the crowd density of the regions. Considering that people often walk together with their acquaintances but not with strangers, the reidentification solution can be applied to the foreground regions to reidentify the groups of people. In this case, another problem arises, that is, people sometimes meet or part outside the field of views of the cameras. Thus, a foreground region can have correspondence with multiple foreground regions. Our proposed method handles both of these problems by estimating the flows from the foreground regions exiting the camera views to those entering other camera views based on the confidence levels of their correspondence and the constraints defined by the relationships among their areas. The estimated flows are then summed up to count the people traveling across each pair of cameras.

N. Nitta (✉) · R. Akai · N. Babaguchi
Graduate School of Engineering, Osaka University, 2-1 Yamada-oka,
Suita, Osaka 565-0871, Japan
e-mail: naoko@comm.eng.osaka-u.ac.jp

R. Akai
e-mail: akai@nanase.comm.eng.osaka-u.ac.jp

N. Babaguchi
e-mail: babaguchi@comm.eng.osaka-u.ac.jp

P. Spagnolo et al. (eds.), *Human Behavior Understanding in Networked Sensing*,
DOI 10.1007/978-3-319-10807-0_11

11.1 Introduction

Information concerning the number and direction of people traveling in a real environment such as streets, stations, shopping malls, airports, stadiums, and amusement park can be useful for various purposes including marketing, navigation, and crowd management [9, 25]. Manually counting the number of people is a very tedious and time-consuming work; therefore, automated counters by using various technologies such as computer vision and infrared beams have been developed. In particular, since cameras are installed at various locations for security purposes recently, automated counters based on computer vision are considered as one of the most practical solutions.

Many methods have been proposed for counting the number of people who travel within a camera's field of view (FOV) [14]. Traditional "individual-centric" approaches detect every individual person in a camera view [5] and count the number of people moving in the same direction [3]. However, since people can often get occluded in crowded scenes and an approximate number of people generally suffices for the marketing and navigation purposes, recent approaches try to solve the problem without explicit detection/tracking of individual persons. These "crowd-centric" approaches generally extract foreground regions corresponding to a group of people moving in the same directions and estimate the crowd density of the extracted regions [2, 11, 12, 17, 18].

Meanwhile, many cameras are required for monitoring an area, which is larger than the FOV of a camera. However, due to the limitations of the resources, these cameras are often installed so that their FOVs do not overlap. In this case, every person who has exited a camera view needs to be reidentified when he/she reenters its spatially adjacent camera view [10]. Many methods have been proposed for tracking persons across cameras with nonoverlapping FOVs [22] or for reidentifying individual persons [1, 21]. Given the images of an individual person when he/she exits or enters each camera view, these methods generally rely on the appearance based similarity between the images to establish their correspondence. In addition, since the appearance of the same person can change largely in different camera views and the appearance of different persons can be similar, the contextual information such as the topology of the camera network and the transition time between cameras are often used. Such techniques can be considered as "individual-centric" approaches in that they firstly need to detect every individual person.

Since people often form groups with their acquaintances and keep their social distances from other groups of strangers while walking in public, we consider that people counting across multiple cameras with nonoverlapping FOVs can also be realized in a "crowd-centric" way, by reidentifying groups of people each of which is detected as a foreground region when they exit or enter camera views [16]. However, since people in a group detected in a camera view can split and merge in the "blind area" outside the FOVs of cameras, a group of people detected as a foreground region in one camera view can be detected as several foreground regions in other camera views, which complicates their reidentification. In order to handle the split-merge problem and to simultaneously decrease the errors in people counting caused by the false reidentification due to the appearance variations of the same person in different camera views or the appearance similarity among different persons, we propose to estimate the flows from multiple foreground regions, which have exited camera views to multiple foreground regions, which have entered different camera views based on the confidence levels of their correspondence and the constraints defined by the relationships among their areas. In other words, while the "individual-centric" approach yields a one-to-one correspondence among the foreground regions containing an individual person, the proposed method yields a weighted many-to-many correspondence among the foreground regions, which can contain a group of people. Then, the number of people traversing between the FOVs of a pair of cameras can be estimated by summing up the flows between the foreground regions, which have exited one camera view and entered the other camera view.

11.2 Related Work

Many methods have been proposed for counting the people traveling within a single camera's FOV. As stated above, the most intuitive and direct approach is "individual-centric", which is to detect each individual person in the camera view and count them. The main component of this approach is the detection of individual persons. A diversity of features including histogram of oriented gradient (HOG) [4], edgelet [24], shapelet [19], and local binary patterns (LBP) [23] and classifiers including AdaBoost and support vector machine (SVM) have been used. However, it is still difficult to robustly detect individual persons especially in low resolution images and under partial occlusion [5].

As an approach to avoid the detection of individual persons, the "crowd-centric" approach, which extracts the foreground region and estimates its crowd density by using a regression model to establish a direct mapping between the holistic features, such as the area, the total edge count, and the texture in the foreground region, and the actual number of people has been proposed [2, 11, 12, 17, 18]. Since the area occupied by the same number of people can differ according to their distance from the camera due to the perspective distortion, the geometric correction, or perspective normalization is generally performed, for example, to scale each pixel by a weight before extracting the holistic features. When monitoring a wide area, which should provide far-view low resolution images, these "crowd-centric" approach is considered to be more appropriate.

When monitoring an area wider than the FOV of a single camera, multiple cameras need to be used. They are either spatially adjacent or far away and their FOVs are either overlapped or nonoverlapped. Although little work has been done for people counting across multiple cameras [10], mainly three types of relevant technologies have been developed: camera network topology identification, person reidentification, and multi-camera tracking [22]. The camera network topology identification is to identify overlapping or spatially adjacent nonoverlapping camera views. Each camera view has entry/exit locations where objects enter or exit the camera view. The paths connecting the entry/exit locations among different cameras can be identified based on the distribution of people's transition time without establishing the correspondence among the individual persons entering or exiting the camera views. The basic assumption is that, if two camera views are overlapped or spatially adjacent, a distribution of the transition time of all pairs of the individual persons entering and exiting the camera views within a certain time interval should have peaks [15, 20]. People counting across multiple cameras with spatially adjacent nonoverlapping views can be considered as the estimation of the temporally changing strength among all pairs of the camera views. In this case, since the persons exiting a camera view can enter any other camera view, the correspondence among the individual persons captured by different cameras needs to be established.

The problems of the person reidentification and multi-camera tracking are similar in that their target is to establish the correspondence among the images of an individual person observed in different camera views. Their typical approach is to use appearance cues of individual persons such as color, shape, and texture. The appearance relationships between camera views can be learned from the training data of the images of the individual persons in different camera views whose correspondences are manually labeled or can be incrementally learned without any supervised input [6]. The potential true match can be ranked in the order of the correspondence likelihood or the match and no-match can be distinguished by binary classification models. For the person reidentification, since the images of an individual person can be captured by spatially distant cameras on different days, the appearance of the same person can change especially largely and the appearance of different persons can be similar. Therefore, recent efforts have focused on designing the features which capture the most distinguishing aspects of an individual person or learning distance models for robust matching [1]. For the multi-camera tracking, the correspondence should be established between the images of an individual person captured by spatially adjacent cameras within a short time interval. Although the appearance change of the same person can be relatively smaller, the appearance of the same person can still change largely due to the differences in lighting, resolution, pose, etc., and the appearance of different persons can be similar, which makes it hard to identify the same persons based only on the appearance cues. Thus, other contextual information such as the topology of the camera network and the transition time between cameras, which are either manually given or learned from the training data, are often used. Further, in order to handle the changes in the appearance between two camera views, the brightness transfer function (BTF) between each pair of cameras is also learned from the training data [8]. Considering the possibility of detecting a group of people exiting a camera view as a foreground region, an optimal graph matching algorithm was proposed to split the group into individuals to find the corresponding individuals in another camera view [13].

As done in [10], detecting an individual person entering or exiting the camera views and establishing their correspondence can be considered as the "individual-centric" approach for people counting across multiple nonoverlapping camera views. Such approach can be realized by the reidentification or multi-camera tracking techniques. On the other hand, the target of our work is to propose a "crowd-centric" approach by establishing the correspondence among the foreground regions, which can contain a group of people. Traditional one-to-one correspondence among the foreground regions established by the "individual-centric" approach can not handle the case where a group of people split after exiting a camera view and its subgroups of people enter different camera views or multiple groups of people merge after exiting camera views and enter another camera view together. Instead, our "crowd-centric" approach estimates the flows among the foreground regions to establish weighted many-to-many correspondence. This should also decrease the maximum errors in the estimated number of people caused by the false correspondence due to the appearance variations of the same person or the appearance similarity among different persons.

11.3 People Counting Across Nonoverlapping Camera Views

Assuming that an area is monitored by J cameras with *spatially adjacent nonoverlapping* views as shown in Fig. 11.1, the target of our work is to count the number of people traversing across each pair of cameras' fields of views (FOVs) C_i and C_j. More concretely, given $D = \{d^i_m \mid i = 1, \ldots, J;\ m = 1, \ldots, M_i\}$, a set of M_i foreground regions d^i_m, which have exited the entry/exit location in the view of the

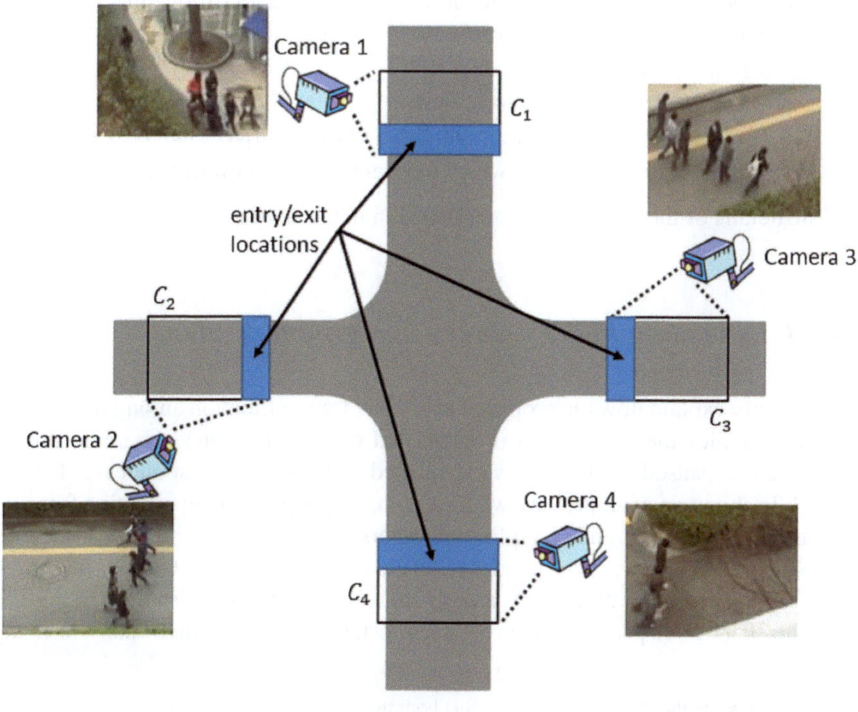

Fig. 11.1 Example of multiple cameras with nonoverlapping views

camera i within a time interval of T, and $A = \{a_n^j \mid j = 1, \ldots, J;\ n = 1, \ldots, N_j\}$, a set of N_j foreground regions a_n^j, which have entered the entry/exit location in the view of the camera j within the same time interval,[1] the proposed method counts the number of people $V_{i,j}$ traversing from C_i to C_j.

When a group of people who have exited a camera view always enter one of other camera views as the same group after a while, $V_{i,j}$ can be counted by reidentifying the groups of people across the cameras i and j, which is to check if d_m^i corresponds to a_n^j, and by summing up the number of the reidentified groups of people. However, a group of people in a foreground region can split and merge outside the FOVs of the cameras. Therefore, instead of reidentifying them, the proposed method estimates the flows between the foreground regions, allowing the flows between multiple d_m^is and a_n^js according to the confidence level of each pair of foreground regions to contain the same persons. This approach is also considered to handle the problems that the appearance variance of the same person in different camera views and the appearance similarity among different persons can lead to false reidentification, and as a result, can increase the errors in people counting.

Figure 11.2 shows the overview of the proposed method, which is composed of the following two steps:

(1) Flow Estimation among Foreground Regions
The confidence level of every pair of d_m^i in D and a_n^j in A to contain the same persons is determined based on their appearance cues and transition time. According to the determined confidence levels and their areas, the flows among all pairs of d_m^i in D and a_n^j in A are estimated.

(2) Count Estimation across Camera Views
$V_{i,j}$ is estimated by summing up the flows between d_m^is, which have exited the view of the camera i and a_n^js which have entered the view of the camera j.

The details of the two steps are described in the following subsections.

11.3.1 Estimating Flows Between Foreground Regions

Let us firstly explain how the proposed approach, flow estimation among foreground regions, handles the split-merge problem and can decrease the maximum errors, which can be caused by the falsely established one-to-one correspondence. Firstly, Fig. 11.3a shows an example case where a group of people split after exiting from C_2 and separately enter C_1 and C_3 (split) with a person who has exited from C_4 (merge). Establishing one-to-one correspondence would yield at least the total error of 2 when identifying a_1^1 as d_1^4 and a_1^3 as d_1^2, and fail to estimate the flows from C_2 to C_1. On the other hand, our proposed approach can establish the weighted many-to-many

[1] Here, we assume that T is determined so that both the entry and exit of each person are captured in the time interval.

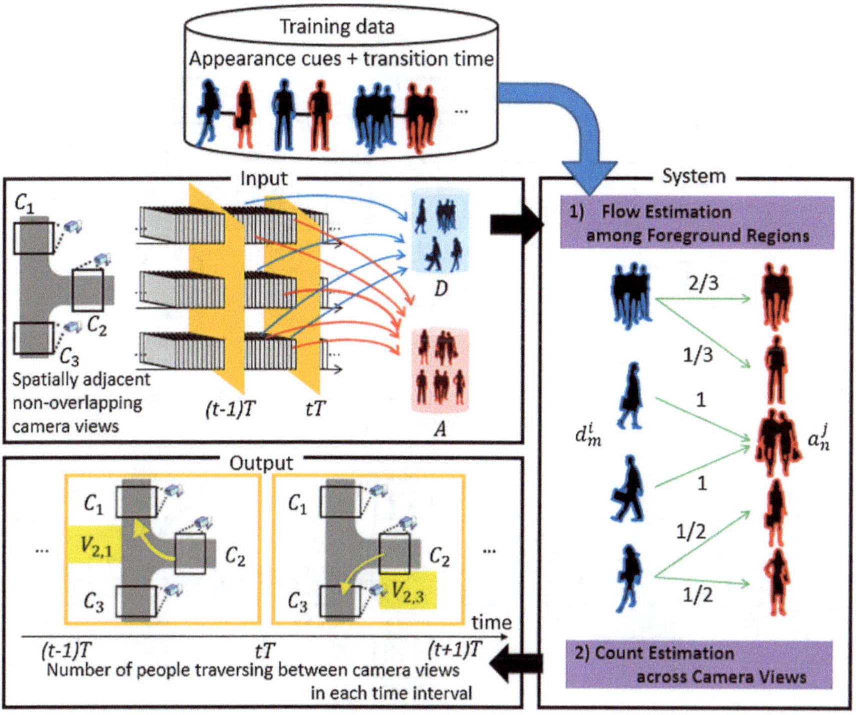

Fig. 11.2 Overview of proposed method

correspondence among d_1^2, d_1^4 and a_1^1, a_1^3 according to the confidence level for each pair of foreground regions to contain the same persons; and therefore, can estimate the flows from C_2 and C_4 to both C_1 and C_3 without an error in the best-case scenario. Secondly, Fig. 11.3b shows an example case where two persons simultaneously exit C_1 and C_2 and enter C_3 and C_4. In this case, the error for the one-to-one correspondence can be as good as 0 when a_1^3 and a_1^4 are correctly identified as d_1^2 and d_1^1. However, when the appearance of each person changes a lot in different camera views or the appearances of the two persons are similar, a_1^3 and a_1^4 can be falsely identified as d_1^1 and d_1^2 and the error in people counting can be as bad as 4 . On the other hand, by estimating the flows from both d_1^1 and d_1^2 to both a_1^3 and a_1^4 according to the confidence level of their correspondence, the proposed method can estimate the flows across all pairs of cameras. This can increase the error compared to when they are correctly identified; however, can decrease the error compared to when they are falsely identified. Considering that the reidentification performance of the state-of-the-art approaches is still about 20 % [1] for the images of an individual person under different viewpoints or illumination variations as in the ViPER dataset [7], the proposed approach would be effective in decreasing the errors in people counting.

Generally, the person reidentification or multi-camera tracking techniques establish the correspondence among the individual persons based on their appearance

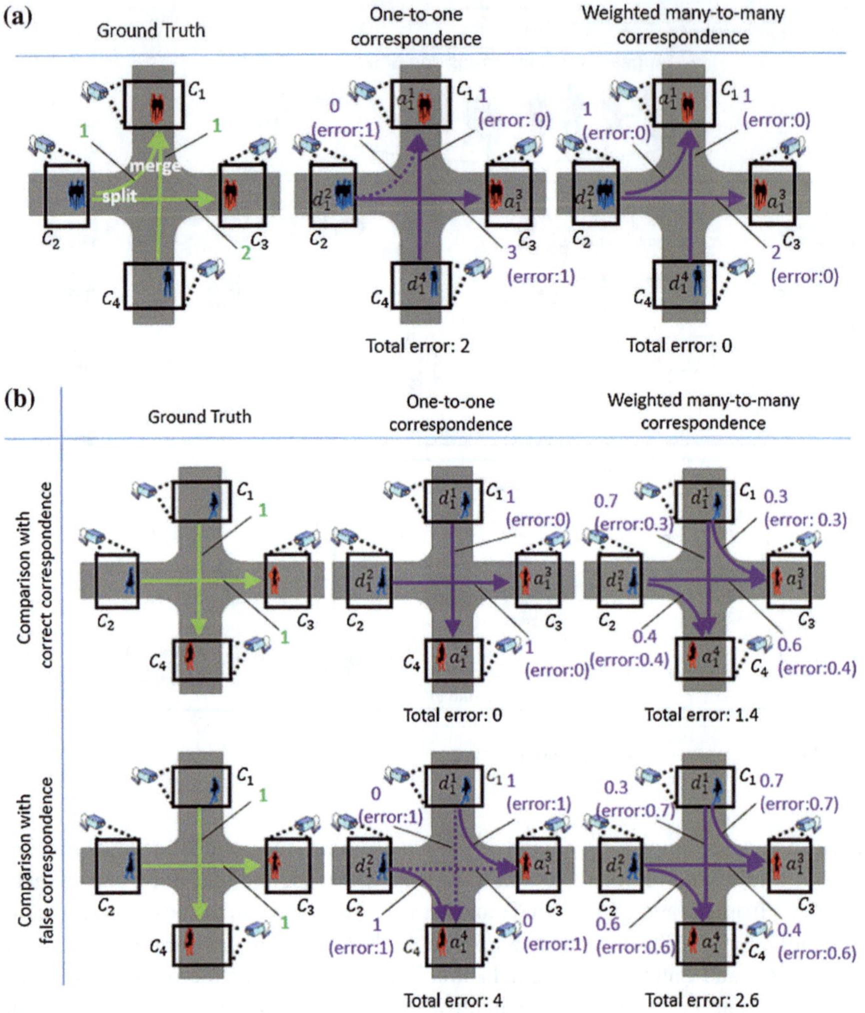

Fig. 11.3 Ideas of proposed method. **a** Split-merge problem. **b** False one-to-one correspondence problem

similarity. For multi-camera tracking, the transition time among the camera views can also be used as the contextual information. Such appearance similarity and transition time between each pair of cameras can be learned from the training data of the pairs of the foreground regions whose correspondence is manually labeled. Here, 2-class support vector machine (SVM) is used to predict if any pair of d_m^i and a_n^j contains the same persons. As the features for the SVM, the Bhattacharryya distance of the HSV color histograms and the absolute difference of the areas are used as the appearance cues and the difference of the times (frame numbers) of the exit and entry of the foreground regions d_m^i and a_n^j is used as the transition time.

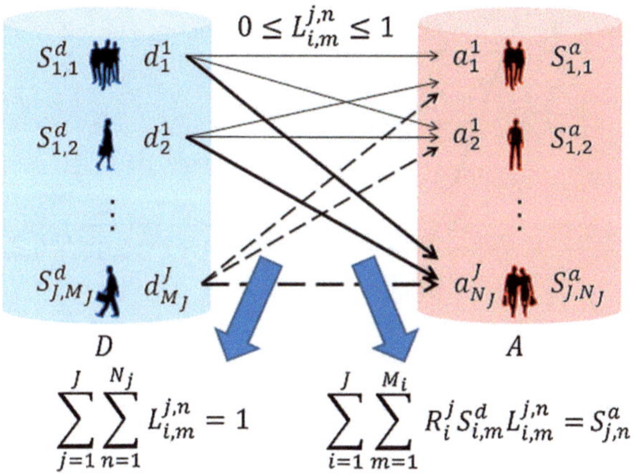

Fig. 11.4 Flows across foreground regions in D and A

Figure 11.4 shows the flows across multiple foreground regions in D and A. Intuitively, $L_{i,m}^{j,n}$ represents the ratio of the people in d_m^i who have traveled to a_n^j. Thus, for each d_m^i, $L_{i,m}^{j,n}$ should satisfy the conditions:

$$0 \le L_{i,m}^{j,n} \le 1, \tag{11.1}$$

$$\sum_{j=1}^{J}\sum_{n=1}^{N_j} L_{i,m}^{j,n} = 1. \tag{11.2}$$

In addition, when defining the areas of d_m^i and a_n^j as $S_{i,m}^d$ and $S_{j,n}^a$, respectively, the flow from d_m^i to a_n^j can be represented by $S_{i,m}^d L_{i,m}^{j,n}$. Considering that an object in the view of the camera i appears R_i^j times larger in the view of the camera j, $L_{i,m}^{j,n}$ should also satisfy the condition:

$$\sum_{i=1}^{J}\sum_{m=1}^{M_i} R_i^j S_{i,m}^d L_{i,m}^{j,n} = S_{j,n}^a. \tag{11.3}$$

For each d_m^i, when there is only one a_n^j, which contains the same persons as d_m^i with a high level of confidence, $L_{i,m}^{j,n}$ should be close to 1 for only one a_n^j and 0 for all other a_n^js. On the other hand, when there are several a_n^js, which appear to have traveled from d_m^i, $L_{i,m}^{j,n}$ should be proportional to the possibility that a_n^j have traveled from d_m^i. Thus, $c_{i,m}^{j,n}$, the confidence level of the prediction of the SVM, is determined by $l_{i,m}^{j,n}$, the distance of the pair of d_m^i and a_n^j to the decision boundary, by using a

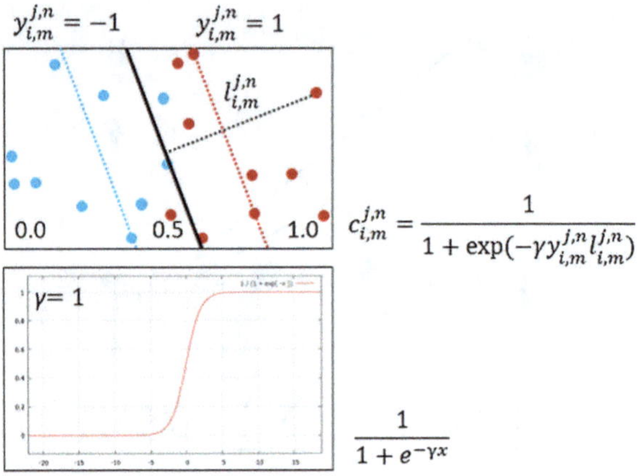

Fig. 11.5 Confidence level of the prediction of SVM

sigmoid function ς_γ as follows:

$$c_{i,m}^{j,n} = \varsigma_\gamma(y_{i,m}^{j,n}, l_{i,m}^{j,n}) = \frac{1}{1 + \exp(-\gamma \times y_{i,m}^{j,n} \times l_{i,m}^{j,n})}, \tag{11.4}$$

where γ is the gain and $y_{i,m}^{j,n}$ represents if d_m^i and a_n^j are predicted to contain the same persons ($y_{i,m}^{j,n} = 1$) or not ($y_{i,m}^{j,n} = -1$). Figure 11.5 graphically illustrates how the confidence level is determined. Then, $L_{i,m}^{j,n}$ is initialized by normalizing $c_{i,m}^{j,n}$ so that $L_{i,m}^{j,n}$ satisfies Eq. (11.2).

$$L_{i,m}^{j,n} = \frac{c_{i,m}^{j,n}}{\sum_{j=1}^{J} \sum_{n=1}^{N_j} c_{i,m}^{j,n}}. \tag{11.5}$$

Now, $L_{i,m}^{j,n} = 0$ represents that d_m^i and a_n^j are highly unlikely to contain the same persons based on their appearance cues and transition time. By keeping them intact, $L_{i,m}^{j,n}$ should also satisfy Eq. (11.3). Thus, $L_{i,m}^{j,n}$ is updated to $\hat{L}_{i,m}^{j,n}$ as follows:

$$\hat{L}_{i,m}^{j,n} = L_{i,m}^{j,n} \times \frac{S_{j,n}^{a}}{\sum_{i=1}^{J} \sum_{m=1}^{M_i} R_i^j S_{i,m}^{d} L_{i,m}^{j,n}}. \tag{11.6}$$

By substituting $\hat{L}_{i,m}^{j,n}$ as $c_{i,m}^{j,n}$, $L_{i,m}^{j,n}$ is iteratively updated by Eqs. (11.5) and (11.6) until the total changes in $L_{i,m}^{j,n}$ after an iteration represented by ε converges after Eq. (11.5), so that $L_{i,m}^{j,n}$ approximately satisfies both Eqs. (11.2) and (11.3).

Finally, in order to avoid the tiny amount of noisy flows among the foreground regions, $L_{i,m}^{j,n}$ is set to 0 when $L_{i,m}^{j,n} < \lambda$ and then is normalized again by Eq. (11.5).

11.3.2 Count Estimation

Since $S_{i,m}^{d}$ represents the area of persons in a camera view, it is converted to the number of persons $N_{i,m}^{d}$ by the linear function:

$$N_{i,m}^{d} = \alpha_i \times S_{i,m}^{d} + \beta_i. \tag{11.7}$$

The parameters α_i and β_i are determined by the linear regression using a set of the training data consisting of the foreground regions extracted from the view of the camera i with manually labeled number of persons in the regions. Since d_m^i and a_n^j are extracted from the same entry/exit locations in the camera views, their areas would depend only on the number of people and the geometric correction within each camera view is not applied. Then, the number of people $V_{i,j}$ traversing from C_i to C_j is calculated as follows.

$$V_{i,j} = \sum_{d_m^i \in D} \sum_{a_n^j \in A} N_{i,m}^{d} L_{i,m}^{j,n}. \tag{11.8}$$

Further, R_i^j in Eq. (11.3) in the previous section is determined as

$$R_i^j = \frac{\alpha_i}{\alpha_j}. \tag{11.9}$$

11.4 Experiments

An intersection in a university campus is monitored by two cameras as shown in Fig. 11.6. The top left and bottom right images are the views of the two cameras. The resolution and the frame rate of the videos are 640×360 and 30 fps, respectively. From each camera view, two rectangular regions are extracted as shown in Fig. 11.6 to simulate the situation where four cameras, namely CAM 1, 2, 3, and 4, are monitoring the intersection. In the experiments, the numbers of people traversing between the FOVs of each pair of these four cameras are estimated. Although the FOVs of CAM1 and CAM2 seem to be overlapped in the figure, the overlapped region is only handled as the FOV of CAM2 so that their FOVs can be considered as nonoverlapped. Thus, no group of people simultaneously appears in more than two camera views.

A 120-min video captured on February 3, 2014 and another 120-min video captured on February 25, 2013 are used to obtain the training and test samples, respec-

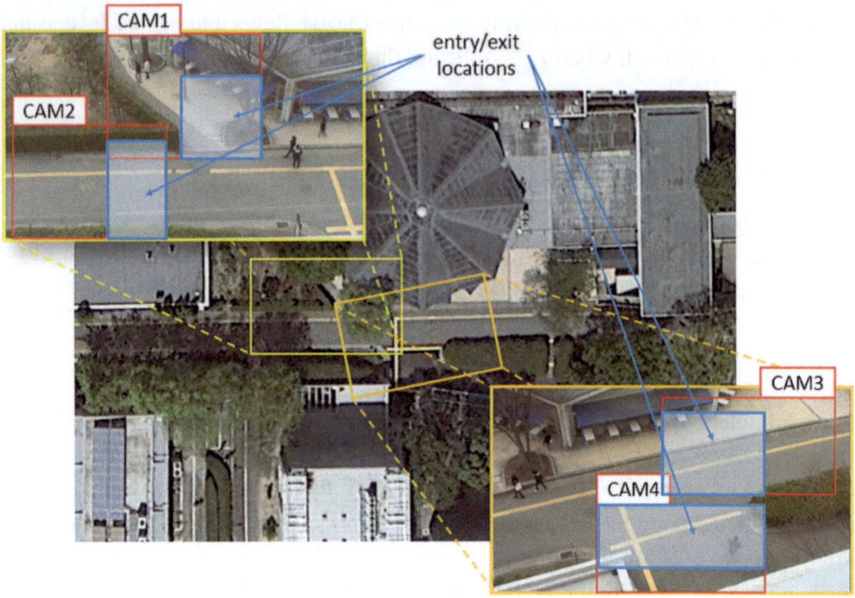

Fig. 11.6 Intersection monitored by cameras

tively, which are pairs of d^i_m and a^j_n. d^i_m and a^j_n were manually selected from the foreground regions, which were extracted from the entry/exit locations in the camera views by the background subtraction. For each pair of cameras i and j, the pairs of d^i_m and a^j_n containing the same persons and the same number of pairs of d^i_m and a^j_n containing only different persons were manually prepared as the positive and negative training samples for the SVM, respectively. Table 11.1 shows the number of the positive/negative samples for each pair of cameras.[2] Further, the number of people in the training samples were specified manually and used to obtain the parameters α_i and β_i in Eq. (11.7) for each camera by the linear regression.

Given all the foreground regions D and A extracted from the 120-min test video, we firstly evaluated the accuracy of the SVM by examining if the correct a^j_n is ranked in the top P when ranking all a^j_n in the order of the initial $c^{j,n}_{i,m}$. $c^{j,n}_{i,m}$ is obtained by Eq. (11.4) for each d^i_m and indicates the likelihood of a^j_n to contain the same persons in d^i_m according to their appearance cues and transition time. As can be seen

Table 11.1 Number of training samples for each pair of cameras

Camera pair	1–2	1–3	1–4	2–3	2–4	3–4
♯ of positive/negative samples	79	179	104	81	70	56

[2] Since no one entered the camera view he/she had exited in the videos used in the experiments, we did not consider such camera pairs, e.g., 1–1.

Table 11.2 Accuracy of SVM

P	1	2	3
Acc@ P	26.9 % (316/1,175)	48.5 % (570/1,175)	66 % (775/1,175)

in Table 11.2, for only 26.9 % of d^i_m, the corresponding a^j_n ranked first. This result indicates that, due to the appearance variance of the same group of people in different camera views and the appearance similarity among different groups of people, the false correspondence is likely to be established by relying only on the SVM. However, for 66 % of d^i_m, the corresponding a^j_n ranked within the top 3, which indicates that estimating some flows to a^j_n in the top ranks can be effective in decreasing the errors caused by the false correspondence.

Given the test samples, which have entered or exited the camera views within every $T = 5$ min, the number of people traversing each pair of the four cameras is estimated. The results were evaluated with the absolute errors between the estimated and the actual number of people. Table 11.3 shows the total number of people who have exited the four camera views in each time interval with the number of people who merged and split outside the FOVs of the cameras. The numbers in the brackets represent the numbers of the foreground regions. Figure 11.7 shows the actual number of people traversing between each pair of cameras in each time interval.

The effectiveness of the proposed approach was evaluated by comparing with when establishing one-to-one correspondence for the foreground regions. In order to establish one-to-one correspondence, when d^i_m has only one a^j_n, which is predicted to contain the same persons by the SVM, they are considered as a match. Then, the correspondence among other d^i_m and a^j_n is established in a greedy manner in the order

Table 11.3 Actual number of people in each time interval (Numbers in brackets are the number of the foreground regions)

Time interval (min)	All	Split	Merge	Time interval (min)	All	Split	Merge
0–5	58(40)	8(2)	0(0)	60–65	74(52)	5(1)	3(3)
5–10	64(57)	0(0)	0(0)	65–70	73(50)	3(1)	0(0)
10–15	72(50)	4(1)	2(2)	70–75	87(66)	2(1)	9(4)
15–20	87(59)	0(0)	19(8)	75–80	60(49)	0(0)	0(0)
20–25	89(62)	7(2)	0(0)	80–85	67(47)	0(0)	0(0)
25–30	86(45)	8(1)	0(0)	85–90	70(51)	11(1)	9(6)
30–35	79(54)	0(0)	0(0)	90–95	51(41)	4(1)	0(0)
35–40	74(53)	3(1)	0(0)	95–100	76(51)	4(1)	0(0)
40–45	89(64)	2(1)	0(0)	100–105	53(38)	0(0)	5(2)
45–50	60(45)	3(1)	0(0)	105–110	59(41)	0(0)	0(0)
50–55	82(59)	4(1)	0(0)	110–115	65(35)	25(4)	3(2)
55–60	61(39)	0(0)	0(0)	115–120	38(27)	4(1)	5(2)

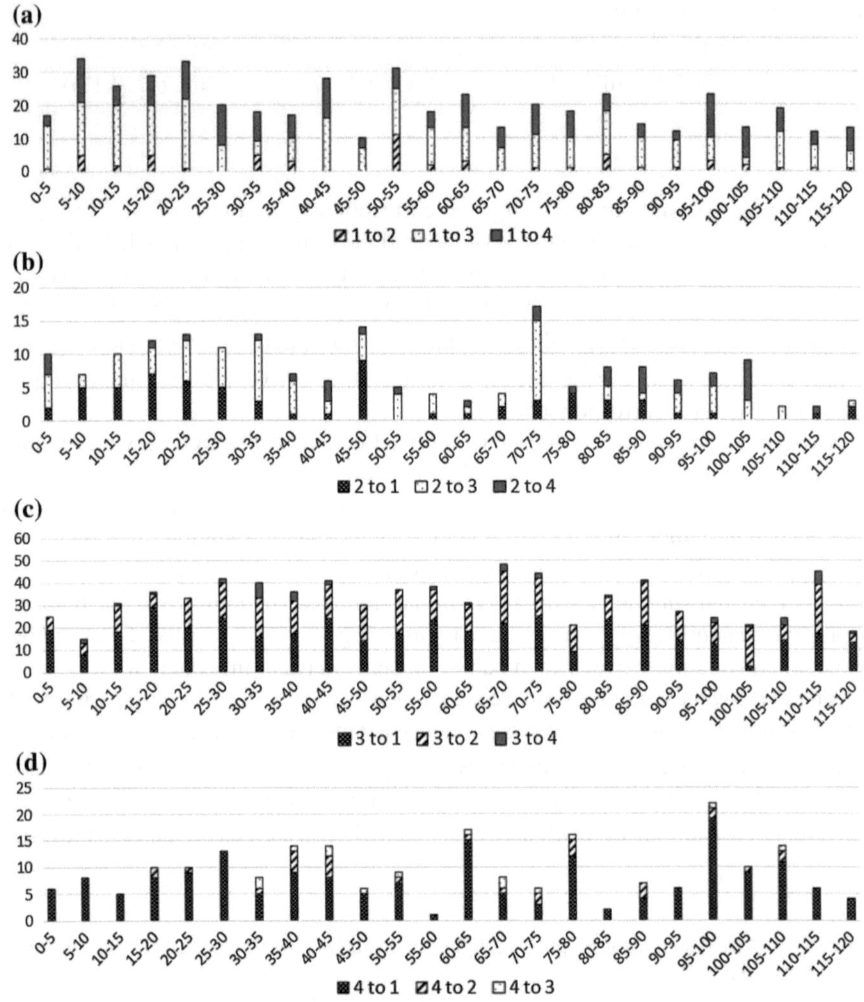

Fig. 11.7 Actual number of people traveling across camera views. **a** From CAM1 to CAM2, 3, and 4. **b** From CAM2 to CAM1, 3, and 4. **c** From CAM3 to CAM1, 2, and 4. **d** From CAM4 to CAM1, 2, and 3

of the prediction confidence of the SVM $c_{i,m}^{j,n}$. This corresponds to the "one-to-one correspondence" approach indicated in Fig. 11.3, where each d_m^i is associated with at most one a_n^j in a way that the sum of the matching confidence of all matched pairs would approximately be maximized. Such approximate solution of the combinational optimization problem was able to increase the number of the correct matches and the accuracy improved from 26.9 to 37.0 % as shown in Table 11.4. By using the obtained correspondence, the number of people traversing each pair of cameras is estimated also as described in Sect. 11.3.2 for the comparative approach. For the proposed

Table 11.4 Accuracy after greedy approach

Match	False	Miss	Accuracy of foreground correspondence	Accuracy of camera correspondence
435	731	9	37.0 % (435/1175)	61.7 % (725/1175)

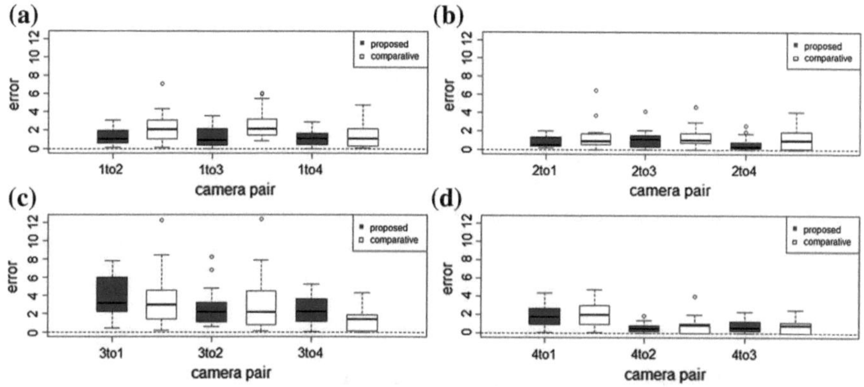

Fig. 11.8 Absolute errors between estimated and actual number of people. **a** Errors in flows from CAM1. **b** Errors in flows from CAM2. **c** Errors in flows from CAM3. **d** Errors in flows from CAM4

approach, the gain of the sigmoid function was set as $\gamma = 1.0$, the iterations were repeated until $\varepsilon < 0.001$, and λ was set as $\lambda = 0.1$.

Figure 11.8 is the box plot of the absolute errors between the actual numbers of people traversing between each pair of cameras and the numbers estimated by the comparative and proposed approaches. The false correspondence of the foreground regions does not affect the results of people counting if the falsely matched a_n^j appears in the same camera view as the correct a_n^j. When evaluating if the correct camera correspondence is established for each d_m^i for the comparative approach, the accuracy improved largely to 61.7 % as shown in Table 11.4, which explains the relatively small errors in the estimation by the comparative approach considering that the accuracy of the foreground region correspondence was only 37.0 %. Nevertheless, for most pairs of cameras, the proposed approach was able to further decrease the errors compared to the comparative approach. Figure 11.9 shows an example of the correspondence established by each approach. By the comparative approach, when groups of people split or merge outside the FOV of the cameras, they can only be matched with at most one of their subgroups as d_1 and a_1 in the example. Further, as the result of the split/merge, D and A can have different numbers of the foreground regions. Then, no correspondence can be established for some foreground regions such as d_{12} in this example. On the other hand, the proposed approach can estimate the flows from multiple foreground regions in D to multiple foreground regions in A. Thus, a group of people can be matched with its multiple subgroups such as a_1, which is matched

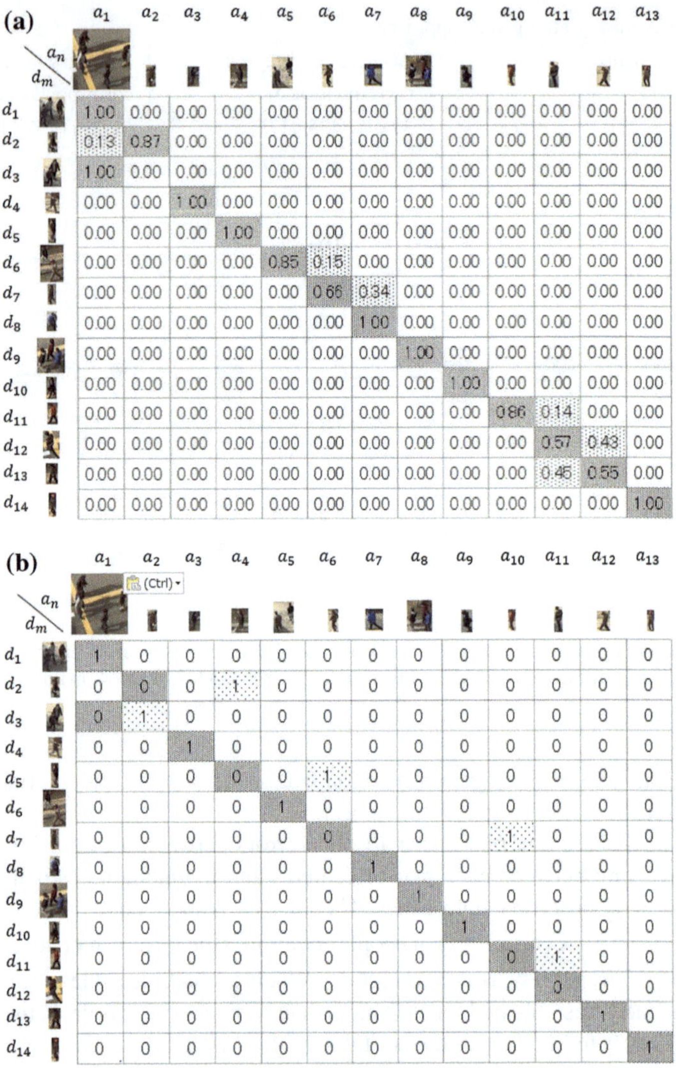

(a)

d_m \ a_n	a_1	a_2	a_3	a_4	a_5	a_6	a_7	a_8	a_9	a_{10}	a_{11}	a_{12}	a_{13}
d_1	1.00	0.00	0.00	0.00	0.00	0.00	0.00	0.00	0.00	0.00	0.00	0.00	0.00
d_2	0.13	0.87	0.00	0.00	0.00	0.00	0.00	0.00	0.00	0.00	0.00	0.00	0.00
d_3	1.00	0.00	0.00	0.00	0.00	0.00	0.00	0.00	0.00	0.00	0.00	0.00	0.00
d_4	0.00	0.00	1.00	0.00	0.00	0.00	0.00	0.00	0.00	0.00	0.00	0.00	0.00
d_5	0.00	0.00	0.00	1.00	0.00	0.00	0.00	0.00	0.00	0.00	0.00	0.00	0.00
d_6	0.00	0.00	0.00	0.00	0.85	0.15	0.00	0.00	0.00	0.00	0.00	0.00	0.00
d_7	0.00	0.00	0.00	0.00	0.00	0.66	0.34	0.00	0.00	0.00	0.00	0.00	0.00
d_8	0.00	0.00	0.00	0.00	0.00	0.00	1.00	0.00	0.00	0.00	0.00	0.00	0.00
d_9	0.00	0.00	0.00	0.00	0.00	0.00	0.00	1.00	0.00	0.00	0.00	0.00	0.00
d_{10}	0.00	0.00	0.00	0.00	0.00	0.00	0.00	0.00	1.00	0.00	0.00	0.00	0.00
d_{11}	0.00	0.00	0.00	0.00	0.00	0.00	0.00	0.00	0.00	0.86	0.14	0.00	0.00
d_{12}	0.00	0.00	0.00	0.00	0.00	0.00	0.00	0.00	0.00	0.00	0.57	0.43	0.00
d_{13}	0.00	0.00	0.00	0.00	0.00	0.00	0.00	0.00	0.00	0.00	0.45	0.55	0.00
d_{14}	0.00	0.00	0.00	0.00	0.00	0.00	0.00	0.00	0.00	0.00	0.00	0.00	1.00

(b)

d_m \ a_n	a_1	a_2	a_3	a_4	a_5	a_6	a_7	a_8	a_9	a_{10}	a_{11}	a_{12}	a_{13}
d_1	1	0	0	0	0	0	0	0	0	0	0	0	0
d_2	0	0	0	1	0	0	0	0	0	0	0	0	0
d_3	0	1	0	0	0	0	0	0	0	0	0	0	0
d_4	0	0	1	0	0	0	0	0	0	0	0	0	0
d_5	0	0	0	0	0	1	0	0	0	0	0	0	0
d_6	0	0	0	0	1	0	0	0	0	0	0	0	0
d_7	0	0	0	0	0	0	0	0	0	1	0	0	0
d_8	0	0	0	0	0	0	1	0	0	0	0	0	0
d_9	0	0	0	0	0	0	0	1	0	0	0	0	0
d_{10}	0	0	0	0	0	0	0	0	1	0	0	0	0
d_{11}	0	0	0	0	0	0	0	0	0	0	1	0	0
d_{12}	0	0	0	0	0	0	0	0	0	0	0	0	0
d_{13}	0	0	0	0	0	0	0	0	0	0	0	1	0
d_{14}	0	0	0	0	0	0	0	0	0	0	0	0	1

Fig. 11.9 Example of established correspondence with group merge. The *dark shaded cells* represent the actual correspondence. The *light shaded cells* represent the falsely established correspondence. **a** Weighted many-to-many correspondence (Proposed approach). **b** One-to-one correspondence (Comparative approach)

with d_1 and d_3. The flows across different numbers of foreground regions can also be estimated. In the example, estimating the flows from d_{12} to a_{11} led to the estimation of the flows from d_{11} to a_{10}, then from d_7 to a_6, d_5 to a_4, and d_2 to a_2 in a chain reaction, which can reduce the errors caused by the false correspondence. Figure 11.10 shows another example when there is no group split/merge. Estimating the flows among multiple d_m to a_n can estimate some flows between the correct pairs of the foreground

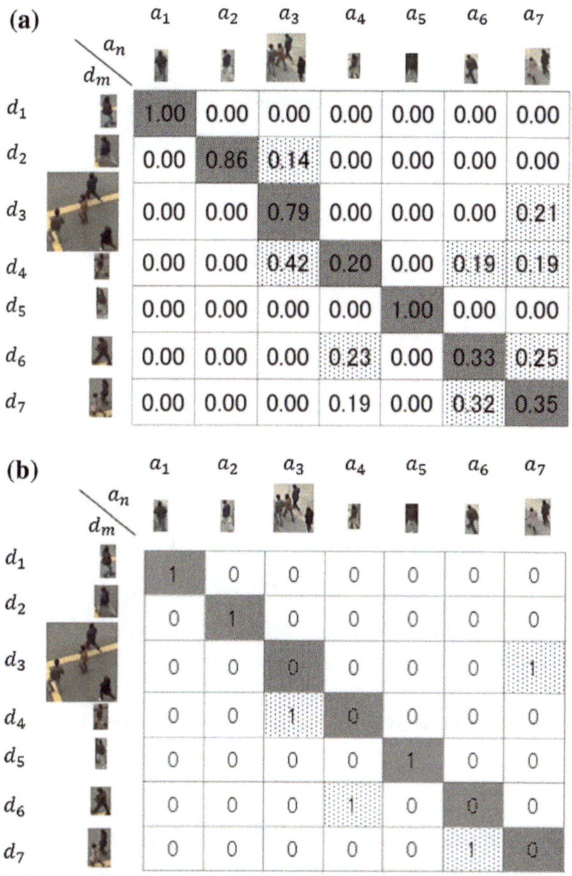

Fig. 11.10 Example of established correspondence without group split/merge. The *dark shaded cells* represent the actual correspondence. The *light shaded cells* represent the falsely established correspondence. **a** Weighted many-to-many correspondence (Proposed approach). **b** One-to-one correspondence (Comparative approach)

regions which were not established by one-to-one correspondence. While the errors were increased for some pairs such as d_2 and a_2, the errors were decreased for other pairs such as d_3 and a_3, d_4 and a_4, d_6 and a_6, and d_7 and a_7. Figure 11.11a shows an example where the proposed approach successfully estimated the number of people traversing between the pairs of cameras by comparing the results with the ground truth and the results estimated by the comparative approach.

By contrast, the proposed approach obtained larger errors for the number of people traveling from CAM3 as shown in Fig. 11.8c, especially from CAM3 to CAM4. As can be seen in Fig. 11.11b, noisy flows were often estimated between the incorrect pairs of the FOVs of the cameras. In addition to the appearance variations/similarity of the persons, the area difference of the same group of people in different camera

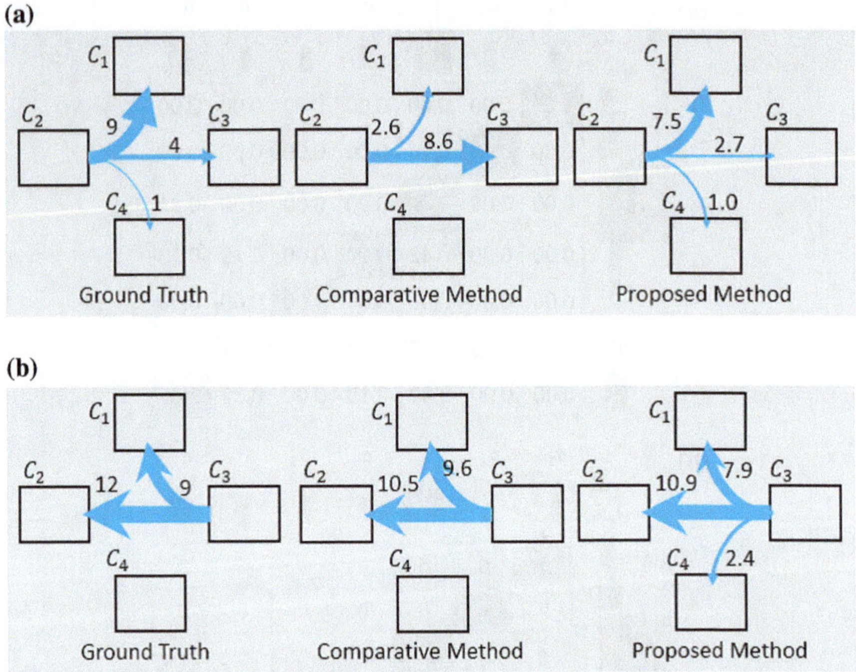

Fig. 11.11 Examples of results **a GOOD** Time interval: 45–50 min **b BAD** Time interval: 75–80 min

views can largely affect the flows obtained by Eq. (11.6). For example, in Fig. 11.9, a_5 contains the same persons in d_6, but is smaller than d_6. As a result, the flows from d_6 to a_5 are restricted to 0.85, giving the remaining flows to other foreground regions such as a_6. a_7 also contains the same person in d_8, but is larger than d_8. Then, a_7 requires more flows from other foreground regions such as d_7. Both of these decreased the flows between the correct pairs of the foreground regions d_7 and a_6 and increased the flows between the incorrect pairs of the foreground regions such as from d_6 to a_6 and from d_7 to a_7. Such small amount of incorrect flows can accumulate as the numbers of the foreground regions in D and A increase especially between the pairs of cameras where no people traverses. Since the number of people exiting the view of CAM3 are much larger compared to those exiting the views of other cameras and it was often the case that no people traveled to CAM4 as shown in Fig. 11.7, the errors accumulated between CAM3 and CAM4. Thus, a way to handle such difference in the areas of the foreground regions of the same group of people in the normalization by Eq. (11.6) needs to be devised.

Finally, we discuss the efficiency of the proposed method. The experiments were conducted on a PC with a Intel(R) Core(TM) i7-2600 (3.40 GHz) CPU and 3.49 GB memory. After extracting the features from the foreground regions, the comparative

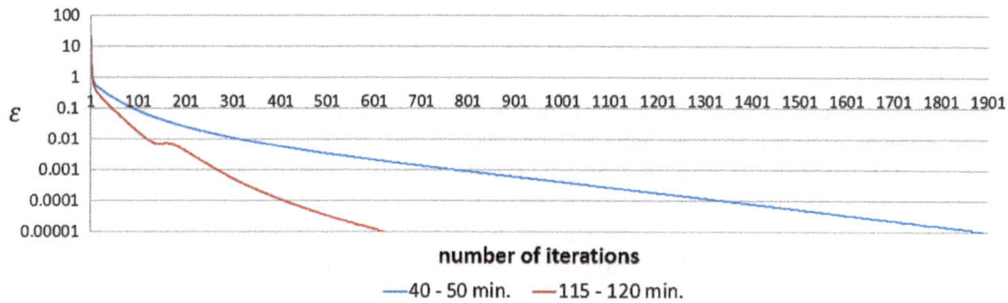

Fig. 11.12 Relationships between number of iterations and changes in estimated flows $L_{i,m}^{j,n}$

approach took only about 1 millisecond per a time interval of $T = 5$ min on average, while the proposed approach took from 0.96 to 23.2 s depending on the number of the combinations of the foreground regions d_m^i and a_n^j and the number of iterations. Figure 11.12 shows the changes of the estimated flows $L_{i,m}^{j,n}$ represented by ε after iterations for the time interval of 40–45 min which took 0.96 s and of 115–120 min which took 23.2 s. Although the iterations were stopped when $\varepsilon < 0.001$ in the experiments and the processing time can be considered still acceptable compared to the duration of the processed video, changing the threshold can largely influence the computation time and the errors. As λ and γ would also affect the errors, such parameters should be changed adaptively considering their effects both on the computation time and the errors.

11.5 Conclusions

We proposed a method for counting the number of people over an area monitored by multiple cameras with spatially adjacent nonoverlapping views by estimating the flows among the foreground regions which have exited and entered the camera views. For 120-min videos capturing an area in a university campus by four virtual cameras, the proposed approach was able to estimate the number of people traveling in the monitored area every 5 min with the average errors of 1.52 persons per pair of cameras with the standard deviation of 1.54.

As future work, more experiments are necessary to evaluate the effects of changing the parameters. The number of the cameras needs to be increased to more accurately examine how the errors caused by the false correspondence of the foreground regions can be alleviated. Further, the estimated number of people traversing between each pair of cameras' FOVs can be used as the transition probability between the FOVs, which can additionally be used to improve the confidence level of the foreground correspondence. How to handle the error accumulations across cameras with no traffic especially due to the area difference of the foreground regions of the same group of people in different camera views needs to be devised.

References

1. Bedagkar-Gala A, Shah SK (2014) A survey of approaches and trends in person re-identification. Image Vis Comput 32(4):270–286
2. Chan AB, Vasconcelos N (2012) Counting people with low-level features and bayesian regression. IEEE Trans Image Process 21(4):2160–2177
3. Chen T-H, Hsu C-W (2003) An automatic bi-directional passing-people counting method based on color image processing. In: IEEE international carnahan conference on security technology, pp 200–207
4. Dalal N, Triggs B (2005) Histograms of oriented gradients for human detection. In: IEEE conference on computer vision and pattern recognition, vol 1, pp 886–893
5. Dollar P, Wojek C, Schiele B, Perona P (2012) Pedestrian detection: an evaluation of the state of the art. IEEE Trans Pattern Anal Mach Intell 34(4):743–761
6. Gilbert A, Bowden R (2008) Incremental, scalable tracking of objects inter camera. Comput Vis Image Underst 111(1):43–58
7. Gray D, Brennan S, Tao H (2007) Evaluating appearance models for recognition, reacquisition, and tracking. In: IEEE international workshop on performance evaluation of tracking and surveillance
8. Javed O, Shafique K, Rasheed Z, Shah M (2008) Modeling inter-camera space-time and appearance relationships for tracking across non-overlapping views. Comput Vis Image Underst 109(2):146–162
9. Jacques S Jr, Musse SR, Jung CR (2010) Crowd analysis using computer vision techniques. IEEE Signal Process Mag 27(5):66–77
10. Kettnaker V, Zabih R (1999) Counting people from multiple cameras. In: IEEE international conference on multimedia computing and systems, vol 2, pp 267–271
11. Kilambi P, Ribnick E, Joshi AJ, Masoud O, Papanikolopoulos N (2008) Estimating pedestrian counts in groups. Comput Vis Image Underst 110(1):43–59
12. Kong D, Gray D, Tao H (2005) Counting pedestrians in crowds using viewpoint invariant training. In: British machine vision conference
13. Lian G, Lai J, Zheng W-S (2011) Spatial-temporal consistent labeling of tracked pedestrians across non-overlapping camera views. Pattern Recognit 44(5):1121–1136
14. Loy CC, Chen K, Gong S, Xiang T (2013) Crowd counting and profiling: methodology and evaluation. In: Modeling, simulation and visual analysis of crowds, Springer, New York, pp 347–382
15. Makris D, Ellis T, Black J (2004) Bridging the gaps between cameras. In: IEEE conference on computer vision and pattern recognition, vol 2, pp II-205–II-210
16. Nitta N, Nakazaki T, Nakamura K, Akai R, Babaguchi N (2013) People counting across spatially disjoint cameras by flow estimation between foreground regions. In: IEEE workshop on activity monitoring by multiple distributed sensing, pp 414–419
17. Paragios N, Ramesh V (2001) A mrf-based approach for real-time subway monitoring. In: IEEE conference on computer vision and pattern recognition, vol 1, pp I-1034–I-1040
18. Ryan D, Denman S, Fookes C, Sridharan S (2009) Crowd counting using multiple local features. In: Digital image computing: techniques and applications, pp 81–88
19. Sabzmeydani P, Mori G (2007) Detecting pedestrians by learning shapelet features. In: IEEE conference on computer vision and pattern recognition, pp 1–8
20. Tieu K, Dalley G, Grimson WEL (2005) Inference of non-overlapping camera network topology by measuring statistical dependence. In: IEEE international conference on computer vision, vol 2, pp 1842–1849
21. Vezzani R, Baltieri D, Cucchiara R (2013) People re-identification in surveillance and forensics: a survey. ACM Comput Surv 46(2):29:1–29:3
22. Wang X (2013) Intelligent multi-camera video surveillance: a review. Pattern Recogn Lett 34(1):3–19
23. Wang X, Han TX, Yan S (2009) An hog-lbp human detector with partial occlusion handling. In: IEEE international conference on computer vision, pp 32–39

24. Wu B, Nevatia R (2005) Detection of multiple, partially occluded humans in a single image by bayesian combination of edgelet part detectors. In: IEEE international conference on computer vision, vol 1, pp 90–97
25. Zhan B, Monekosso DN, Remagnino P, Velastin SA, Xu L-Q (2008) Crowd analysis: a survey. Mach Vis Appl 19(5–6):345–357

Chapter 12
2D Human Pose Estimation and Tracking in Non-overlapping Cameras

Murtaza Taj, Ali Hassan and Abdul Rafay Khalid

Abstract This chapter will discuss approaches to 2D human pose estimation and tracking in a non-overlapping camera network. It will demonstrate the limitations of current approaches and suggest strategies to overcome them. In particular, computational intractability due to high dimensional limb space, violation of articulation constraints, and view-point dependence. The chapter is divided into three major components; namely, search space reduction, pose validation, and view-invariant pose tracking in a non-overlapping camera network. Firstly, we present approaches for search space reduction, such as Kinematic Tree based sub-region selection for each limb, Mean-Shift based maxima search on the likelihood surface, and temporal based reduction of search in parameter space. Secondly, we devise a PCA based Pose Validation strategy to prune out anatomically incorrect hypotheses. Thirdly, we propose to incorporate articulation constraints while keeping the problem tractable. Finally, we enable view-invariance through the fusion of only two pose detectors and an articulated skeleton tracker.

12.1 Introduction

Human pose estimation from a single image or an image sequence such as the case of a monocular camera or multiple non-overlapping cameras has gained significant attention in recent years. It has multiple applications in human computer interaction, behaviour monitoring, surveillance and entertainment. There are many approaches

M. Taj (✉) · A. Hassan · A.R. Khalid
Department of Computer Science,
LUMS School of Science and Engineering,
Lahore, Pakistan
e-mail: murtaza.taj@lums.edu.pk

A. Hassan
e-mail: ali.hassan1287@gmail.com

A.R. Khalid
e-mail: arkhalid1@gmail.com

P. Spagnolo et al. (eds.), *Human Behavior Understanding in Networked Sensing*,
DOI 10.1007/978-3-319-10807-0_12

that estimate a 3D human pose using multiple overlapping sensors particularly cameras [20, 23]. In the case of a network of non-overlapping cameras, the problem is similar to that of pose estimation from a monocular camera.

The problem of human pose estimation and tracking in monocular images is to automatically extract and track the position and orientation of limbs and their joint angles over time. This problem is inherently challenging as muscles, body tissue and clothing obscure the skeleton structure. Moreover, the human skeleton has high degrees of freedom and complex kinematics. It is composed of articulated joints[1] between pairs of limbs which implies that position, orientation and scale of each limb is constrained by its adjacent limbs. Incorporating articulation into pose estimation is thus the correct way of formulating the problem. Since the search in this combined space makes the problem intractable, this fundamental constraint is usually violated by introducing independence assumption between limbs [1, 2, 5, 7, 8, 16, 17]. This leads to an anatomically invalid pose solution which violates biomechanical limitations over part motion. Several attempts have been made to overcome these limitations by imposing a joint prior between pairs of limbs [17]. This limitation can also be overcome by considering the limbs are planes articulated at a point for which a linear least square solution can be formulated [4].

When applying pose estimation techniques to non-overlapping cameras, one of the challenges is the continuously changing view of a person. To enable continuous pose estimation and tracking over a wide range of views, either a bank of viewpoint-specific detectors can be trained [2] or a fusion methodology can be designed that just fuses output from a frontal and a profile pose detector with a tracker to achieve viewpoints invariance. In contrast to fusion of homogeneous classifiers, fusion of heterogeneous set of detectors and trackers is a significantly more challenging problem. To overcome this limitation, decoding strategies can be used that allows for fusion of complementary information from heterogeneous algorithms.

Existing 2D pose estimation approaches cannot be applied directly to a camera network due to their speed and viewpoint limitations. In this chapter we discuss several improvements on these approaches that can make 2D Pose estimation algorithms suitable for multi-camera setups. These include search space reduction using both spatial as well as temporal cues and view-invariance using *Fusion* of a frontal and a profile pose detector. Other improvements include replacing spring-like connection model with *articulated skeleton tracking* [4] and reducing false detections by imposing kinematic constraints while detecting each limb instead of post detection. A Principal Component Analysis (PCA) based validation criterion is also discussed to further enforces the correctness of the obtained 2D pose.

[1] In this work, by articulated skeleton we refer to a skeleton in which each pair of adjacent limbs shares a common point (a joint) called articulation point. This common point introduces a joint constraint on the movement of these limbs called articulation constraint.

12.2 Background

One of the initial approaches in 2D pose estimation was Pictorial Structures (PS) [8], which models the object as a collection of distinctive parts with geometric relationships between them. This model characterizes local visual properties of object parts and proposes spring-like connections between pairs of parts. Seminal work on 2D pose estimation was conducted by Ramanan et al. [16] in which an edge template for each limb of a person is learned. Template matching is then performed on test images at various positions, orientations and scales to find the best location for each limb. Although the method produced promising results, search in a 4 dimensional space is its major computational bottleneck. Eichner et al. [5] proposed a search space reduction methodology based on foreground highlighting and the Grabcut algorithm to segment background pixels. However, this method relies on segmentation, which may remove edges belonging to the body parts. Even after segmentation, the search for each limb is carried over the entire foreground region. On the other hand, this chapter suggest a strategy that does not require segmentation and searches only in the expected limb region. In addition, these methods rely on loose articulation constraints they may generate anatomically incorrect poses. In order to counter this, a PCA based pose validation criteria that ensures the pruning of invalid hypotheses has shown improvements [9].

Most work on pose estimation [5, 16, 22, 25] is viewpoint specific, focusing either on profile or on frontal pose. However, viewpoint independence can be introduced by training a bank of viewpoint specific Support Vector Machine (SVM) classifiers [1]. The output of these classifiers can then be fed into another bank of SVMs that establish which classifier output should be considered correct. Due to limited training data, it is not possible to train a classifier for every viewpoint, limiting the scalability of such approaches. In contrast, we devise a novel method that achieves similar view-invariance utilizing only two view-specific pose detectors while achieving computational tractability [9].

In many real scenarios, it is often challenging to identify every limb in a 2D pose due to occlusions and lack of visible features. Discriminative-part based model addresses this problem by representing each limb as multiple parts with spring-like connections [7, 24]. Only a rough stick man like figure can be estimated through these models in which limbs in a pair of parts could be loosely connected. This results in many incorrect poses and lack of accuracy in parts localization. The connection between parts can be better represented by *articulation constraints* between each part-pair. Articulation constraint restricts the part estimation from being significantly off from the estimated location of other parts which results in better accuracy. Introducing articulation constraint requires augmenting the spatial relational model with model relative orientation, position and foreshortening [17] which restricts the number of possible solutions, and hence improves robustness in cluttered scenes. Furthermore, it inherently estimates the articulation point between part-pairs. The augmented spatial relational model requires parameter search in higher dimensional space and needs more computations as compared to modelling each limb independently.

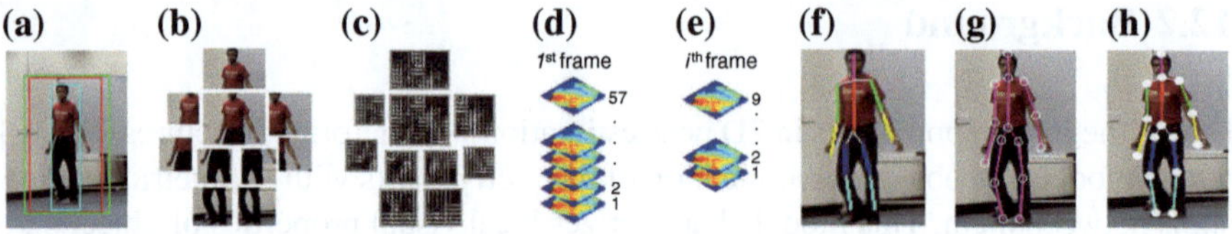

Fig. 12.1 Sample intermediate steps of the algorithm. **a** Input image with Person detection and TLD tracker (*red*: Person detector, *cyan*: tracker, *green*: fused bounding box). **b** Cropped portions showing search space reduction through kinematic tree. **c** Histogram of oriented gradients. **d** Heat maps from SVM scores for 3 sizes and 19 orientations on 1st frame only. **e** Heat maps from SVM scores for 3 sizes and 3 orientations for each subsequent frame showing further reduction in search space through tracking. **f** Pose estimated by detector. **g** Pose estimated by articulated skeleton tracker. **h** Final pose after fusion

One efficient method to impose articulation constraints has been proposed by Yasser et al. [4], which models the articulated joints as a system of 2D planes. The motion of these joints can be estimated using the relative transformation between the 2D planes. The major advantage of this method is a linear least squares solution for affine cameras which is tractable and unlike [22], it does not require 2D to 3D estimation. This method works well for textured planes, however, it is sensitive to occlusion, suffers from frequent drifts in tracking, and requires manual initialization. To overcome these problems, we propose to initialize the articulated tracker using input from a pose detector. To avoid drifts and achieve consistent tracking, we fused two view-specific pose detectors with this tracker. It is interesting to note that when the frontal pose detector fails, a profile detector usually provides the desired estimation and vice versa. Similarly, when both these detectors fail, tracking under articulation constraints can continue to estimate the 2D pose while drift in tracking is kept in check by the detectors [9]. Thus these approaches provide complementary information about the 2D human pose and their *fusion* should achieve better performance. One can fuse different algorithms; a person detector [14], an Open Tracking-Learning Detection (TLD) bounding box tracker [12], frontal and profile pose detectors and an articulated skeleton tracker to obtain consistent tracking of person bounding box and its pose (10 limb articulated skeleton) over a video sequence from multiple non-overlapping cameras. Figure 12.1 shows the overview of such approach.

12.3 Pose Detection

12.3.1 Problem Formulations

In Pictorial Structures [1, 8, 17] (PS), a body is defined as a configuration of body parts $L = \{\mathbf{l}_1, \mathbf{l}_2, \ldots, \mathbf{l}_N\}$ where each part $\mathbf{l}_i$ is defined as $\mathbf{l}_i = \{x_i, y_i, s_i, \theta_i\}$, representing its position (x_i, y_i), scale s_i and orientation θ_i.

Given image observation $\mathbf{z}$, the goal is to estimate the posterior of part configuration L as $p(L|\mathbf{z}) \propto p(\mathbf{z}|L)p(L)$, where $p(\mathbf{z}|L)$ is the likelihood of the image observation $\mathbf{z}$ given a particular part configuration L and a prior $p(L)$. The likelihood term is decomposed into the product of single part likelihoods $p(\mathbf{z}|L) = \prod_{i=1}^{N} p(\mathbf{z}|\mathbf{l}_i)$. The desired part configuration L is then obtained using a maximum a posteriori (MAP) approach as:

$$\underset{L}{\operatorname{argmax}}\ p(L|\mathbf{z}) = \underset{L}{\operatorname{argmax}}\ p(\mathbf{z}|L)p(L). \tag{12.1}$$

These parts are detected by searching the entire parameter space for each part and then a kinematic tree is used to filter false hypotheses.

12.3.2 Detector

In order to determine the part likelihood $p(\mathbf{z}|L)$, we need to train detectors for each limb. This is achieved by first cropping limb regions for each part from the input images. Histogram of Oriented Gradients (HoG) features are then computed on the patches after scale and orientation normalization. These features can then be used to train an SVM for each part, either with a linear kernel or an intersection kernel. However, the intersection kernel is preferred due to its superior performance [14]. At the classification stage, a candidate region is again transformed into the same HoG space and a likelihood (classification confidence) is obtained for each limb from its trained SVM.

To reduce the number of false limb detections due to background clutter, a kinematic tree prior $p(L)$ that describes dependencies between part pairs $(\mathbf{l}_i|\mathbf{l}_j)$ is imposed [17]. The tree prior $p(L)$ can be modelled by a Gaussian distribution in the transformed space of part joints, $\hat{\mathbf{l}}$.

The posterior $p(L|\mathbf{z})$ is obtained by applying each part prior on the likelihood obtained from respective SVMs for all limbs. Exceptions include the torso and head, as the torso is defined as a root node. Instead of performing a full search in the space for each limb, a reduced search can be performed. For example, in the spatial domain, the search space can be reduced by filtering the pixels that do not belong to the body part by using image segmentation approaches or by applying kinematic tree constraints (see Sect. 12.4). Kinematic structure also imposes restrictions on movement of individual limbs over any given time. Temporal constraint can further be exploited to reduce the search space in all four dimensions which is discussed in Sect. 12.4.

Furthermore, the MAP estimate from the set of all possible pose hypotheses L will be the same as the MAP estimate from a subset of hypotheses corresponding to highly likely limb hypotheses only. Instead of full search, these highly likely limb hypotheses can be obtained by just estimating the peaks of the density such as by using Mean Shift (see Sect. 12.4.4).

A kinematic tree not only reduces the spatial search space, but also helps in restricting the generation of false hypotheses. False hypotheses can also be filtered by projecting such hypotheses in a low-dimensional sub-space of valid poses. Pose validation is discussed in Sect. 12.5.

12.4 Search Space Reduction

12.4.1 Foreground Highlighting

Foreground highlighting has been proposed to reduce the search space in spatial parameter space (x, y) [5] (Fig. 12.1b). This approach is based on segmenting the given image into foreground and background regions to limit the search in foreground regions only. This segmentation can be performed by applying any semi-supervised segmentation approaches such as K-Nearest Neighbour or Graph based partitioning (Grab cut).

These approaches require a manual initialization of foreground and background regions. Such initialization can also be done automatically by using face detectors. Assumptions such as the person being upright can also be used to obtain an estimate of a possible torso region. Regions of the image, away from the face and torso can then be used for initialization of background region. However, this method searches the entire highlighted region for each limb as it does not provide information about possible location of the limbs. Incorrect foreground highlighting and full feature space search (all sizes, orientations and highlighted pixel positions) increases the chances of incorrect limb estimation. Moreover, once the background regions are removed from the image, the low-level image features such as edge features along the limbs are degraded resulting in low limb likelihood.

12.4.2 Kinematic SSR

Most of the pose estimation literature assumes that fully cropped images of a person are available, having the subject in the center and minimal background pixels [16, 25]. In order to perform pose estimation in real scenarios, methods such as person [14] and face detectors [5] are needed to localize the bounding box (BBox) enclosing the person. Many of these person detectors such as HoG based person detector [3] result in a very loose/enlarged BBox around a person.

Searching the entire BBox for each limb location could result in significant amount of computations, particularly in case of enlarged BBoxes. Unlike [1, 17], it is not necessary to search the entire region inside a BBox, instead a small sub-region containing head and torso can be obtained from the output of face detection. Using these estimates, kinematic constraints can be applied to reduce the spatial search space for each limb. To apply these constraints, a kinematic tree chain can be traversed

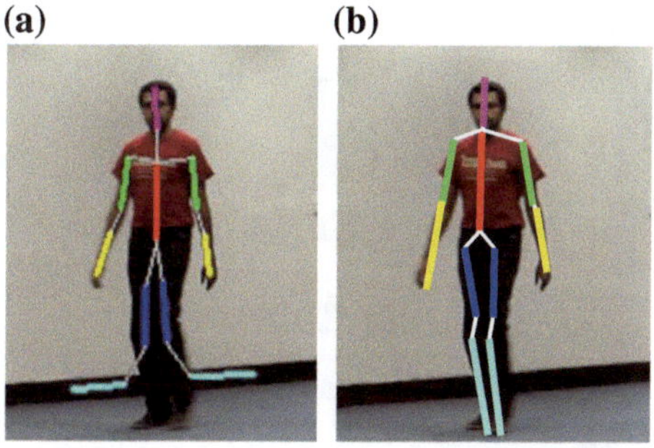

Fig. 12.2 Sample result showing effect of pose estimation on search space reduction. **a** Search space reduction through foreground highlighting [5]. **b** Proposed KTSSR and PCA

and possible sub-regions for each limb can be identified (Fig. 12.1c). This can reduce the search in the spatial dimensions to <35 % of the full search for each limb.

12.4.3 Temporal SSR

A biomechanical skeleton can only perform a highly constrained motion during a time step δt. Furthermore, assuming δt to be very small, say <1 second, this motion will also be very smooth and can be modelled with a smooth curve. This leads to the idea that given the pose estimation in a previous frame, the pose search in current frame can be highly reduced. To this extent, it is enough just to perform the full parameter space search in the first frame only. The search space of all the consecutive frames can be reduced to only a few possibilities which reduces the computations as well as chances of incorrect estimation as shown in Fig. 12.2.

To fully exploit the temporal redundancy in pose estimation it is desired to consistently track the person across the image sequence. For consistent tracking, it is desirable to track a compact BBox of a person that excludes protruding limbs (as in the person detector output) to protect the tracker from drifting into the background. One can fuse the output from the upper body detector[2] to obtain a such compact BBox. Tracking of these detected BBoxes can help in reducing the search in size as well as orientation dimensions.

At the time of initialization several orientations and scales (say 19 and 3 respectively) can be tried, however in each subsequent frames only very few corresponding orientations (say 3) need to be tested. This not only results in a significant boost in performance, but it also reduces the detection of false limbs due to background clutter. This kinematic temporal search space reduction (KTSSR) may limit the chances of recovering in case of incorrect estimation from PS. To cater for this, a pose validation step can be performed before applying temporal SSR. This is discussed in Sect. 12.5.

[2] http://groups.inf.ed.ac.uk/calvin/calvin_upperbody_detector/.

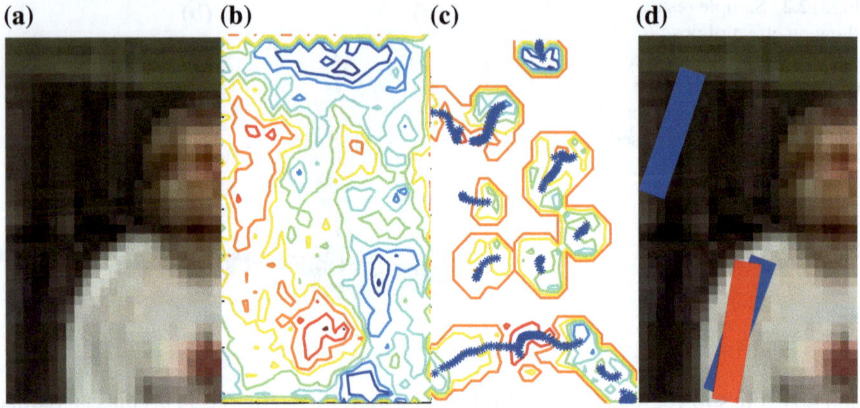

Fig. 12.3 **a** Cropped image patch for upper arm. **b** Exhaustive search over spatial space. **c** Proposed Mean-shift estimate showing that peaks can be recovered without traversing the entire space resulting in saving computations. **d** Recovered limb hypotheses

12.4.4 Mean-Shift

The MAP formulation of Eq. (12.1) requires a part likelihood and a prior. If the size and orientation of the limb is fixed, the resulting likelihood surface can be approximated as a mixture of densities (Fig. 12.3). Furthermore, the set of hypotheses that maximizes the full posterior includes either one of the peaks or nearby hypotheses. The problem is thus reduced to that of finding the modes or peaks of the distribution, without computing the entire surface. This can be reformulated as a problem of kernel density estimation (KDE) using Mean-shift (MS) [10, 13].

MS is a nonparametric mode seeking technique that does not require prior knowledge of the number of peaks. Moreover, MS climbs the gradient of a probability distribution to find the nearest dominant mode or peak and does not impose constraints on the shape of the data. Furthermore, as the algorithm climbs the gradient, the hypotheses near the peaks are automatically estimated as a part of the process. Given n samples $(\mathbf{l}_1, \mathbf{l}_2, \ldots, \mathbf{l}_n)$ on a 2D space $\mathbb{R}^2$ using $\mathbf{l}_i = (x_i, y_i)$ only, the multivariate KDE obtained with kernel $\mathbf{K}(\mathbf{l})$ and bandwidth h is:

$$f(\mathbf{l}) = \frac{1}{nh^2} \sum_{i=1}^{n} \mathbf{K}\left(\frac{\mathbf{l} - \mathbf{l}_i}{h}\right). \tag{12.2}$$

The MS algorithm maximizes the density whose modes are located at the zeros of the gradient, $\triangledown f(l) = 0$. Due to similarity in limbs and background clutter, the response surface is usually multi-modal resulting in multiple peaks. In order to ensure all such peaks are estimated, stratified sampling over the spatial dimension can be used. Figure 12.3 shows that the peaks of the surface can be estimated without

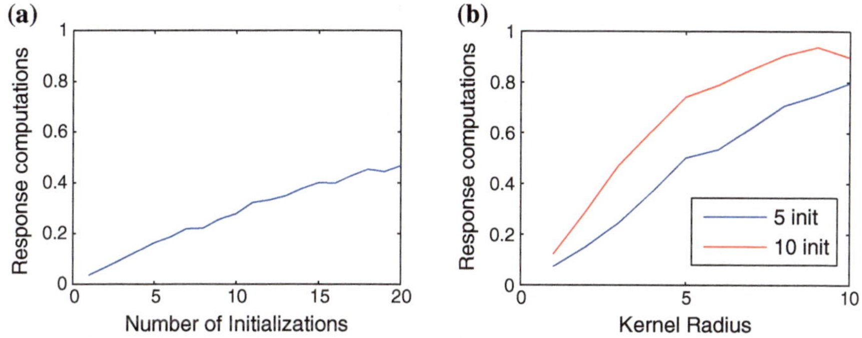

Fig. 12.4 Effect of kernel size and initializations on computation cost. **a** Increase in number of initializations. **b** Increase in bandwidth

traversing the entire surface, provided that there are sufficient number of initialization and there are non-flat regions in the space.

Flat regions in the space can be dealt with by choosing an appropriate kernel and by increasing its bandwidth. Given the nature of the response map and due to its convenient mathematical properties, an isotropic uniform density function is a popular choice for the kernel **K**. Thus, only two parameters need to be tuned for estimating all the peaks, i.e. the number of initialization and the kernel bandwidth. The implications of changing these parameters on the amount of computations can be seen in Fig. 12.4. It can be observed that increase in kernel bandwidth is much more costly than having more initializations.

The bandwidth h of the kernel is a free parameter that exhibits a strong influence on the resulting estimate. Intuitively, one wants to chose h as small as the data allows and for the Gaussian Kernel it is directly proportional to the variance of the data. The response surface to be estimated is generally computed using a sliding window operation with high overlap between the two consecutive windows resulting in a smooth surface with low variance. Hence, for each estimate it is enough to compute 9 samples that fall within the 3×3 window centered over the previous estimate.

This approach can also be extended to higher dimensions such as 3D ($\{x_i, y_i, \theta_i\}$) and full 4D limb space ($\{x_i, y_i, \theta_i, s_i\}$) . The limitation of using 3D and 4D variants of MS is that they require dense sampling over the size and orientation space as well. The search in angular dimension can be dense, if the range of angles to be tested is narrow and is finely sampled, which is generally the case in 2D pose estimation and tracking. In case of detection only, using many values for limb scale and full angular range of $-pi$ to pi with small step sizes is computationally very expensive. Two variants of Mean-Shift algorithm can be used, MS2D for pose detection only and MS3D for pose tracking. MS2D works for the spatial dimension only. A partial response surface containing the peaks is estimated for each size s_i and orientation θ_i, which are then combined to obtain the final pose of a limb. MS3D is more applicable in case of pose tracking where the angular dimension can be densely sampled, while the size estimates have been provided by the tracker.

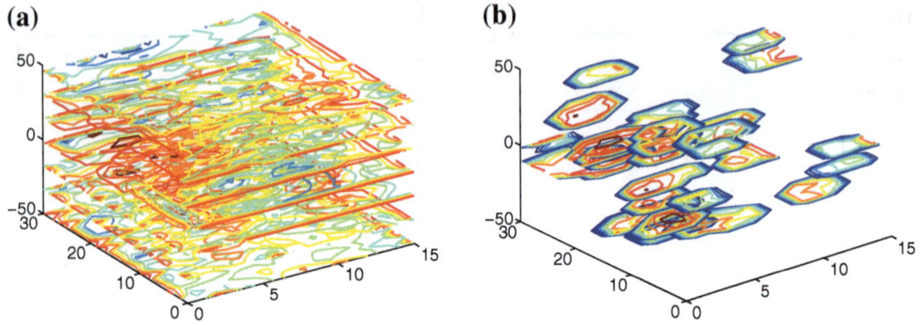

Fig. 12.5 **a** Exhaustive search in 3D space of position and orientation. **b** Reduced space sampled by 3D-Mean shift

It can be shown that similar results can be achieved without performing exhaustive search in 3D space (see Fig. 12.5), thus resulting in significant savings in computations.

12.5 Pose Validation

Many real world objects can have limb like appearances, such as portion of furniture, door frames, poles, pillars, and road marks. Due to perspective distortion, these objects may appear very close to an articulated body in an image and can even have similar sizes and can be identified as possible limb candidates. In most cases,a skeleton estimated by incorporating these false limbs does not adhere to the anatomical constraints.

A simple method for pose validation has been proposed which is similar to Eigen Faces based facial recognition. For each 20 point skeleton (PS), a pairwise distance between points is computed resulting in a 190 (C_2^{20}) dimensional feature vector. These features are then normalized by the largest distance within the vector and are used as a signature for this skeleton. For N skeletons, this results in a $N \times 190$ dimensional feature matrix. PCA can be performed on this feature space and the top few (e.g. 20) principal components can be selected for skeleton reconstruction. At the validation stage, all the candidate skeletons can be projected into the same 190 dimensional space. The one having highest similarity with the components is selected as being valid. Similarity criteria such as reciprocal of $L2$-norm in the PCA space $\frac{1}{1+\| \cdot \|}$ can be used for valid hypothesis selection. This approach is not only simple and fast, but also requires less data. This approach can be further improved by introducing online update of PCA. Figure 12.6 shows a comparison of the top 4 candidates from MAP with top 4 selected based on validation criterion.

The limitation of this approach is that we require different PCA pose validation detectors, for frontal and profile poses. We reconstruct each pose at each time using both these spaces and select the one with best reconstruction. We also use this

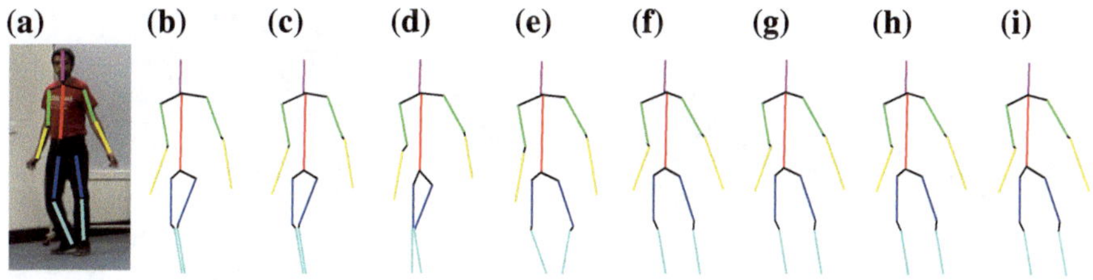

Fig. 12.6 **a** Correct pose from ground truth. **b–e** Top 4 poses selected using MAP. **f–i** Top 4 poses selected using PCA

Table 12.1 Comparison between ours and other state-of-the-art algorithms

Method	T	UA	LA	H	Total
Eichner et al. [5]	98.7	82.8	59.8	97.9	80.1
Sapp et al. [19]	100	95.3	63.0	96.2	85.5
Yang et al. [24]	100	96.6	**70.9**	99.6	89.1
Black et al. [25]	99.6	94.7	62.8	99.2	85.6
Ours	**100**	**98.1**	57.8	**100**	85.3

Key T Torso, *UA* Upper arms, *LA* Lower arms

reconstruction as a switching mechanism between the pose detectors. The consistency of the detector and the tracker is imposed through fusion of pose detection with the Articulated Skeleton (AS) tracking, which is discussed next in Sect. 12.6.

12.5.1 Example—Search Space Reduction and Pose Validation

In this example, the frontal pose detector was trained on standard 2D Pose estimation datasets such as Leeds Sport Pose [11], TUD Multiview Pedestrian [1] and Human Eval [21], using 171, 74 and 155 images respectively. The profile detector was trained on 344 images from TUD-Multiview dataset only. We also included flipped version of all the images resulting in total 1488 training images. Joint priors and PCA basis were also trained on the same data.

Two of the improvements on the PS model discussed in this chapter are search space reduction and PCA validation. This extended model is compared with four recent 2D pose extraction algorithms [5, 19, 24, 25] on the Buffy testset[3] (consisting of 276 images) using the values reported in [25] (see Table 12.1). Unlike [5, 19, 24, 25] no retraining is performed on this dataset and the initial training also does not contain any images from Buffy series. Despite this, the extended method performed consistently better when compared to other approaches.

[3] http://www.robots.ox.ac.uk/~vgg/data/stickmen/buffy_stickmen_v3.01.tgz.

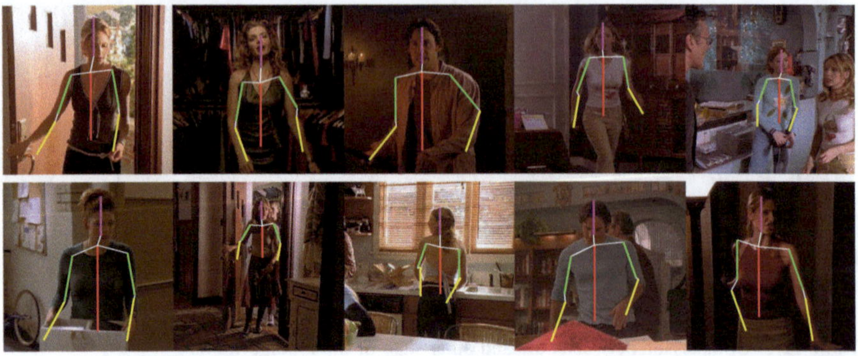

Fig. 12.7 Qualitative evaluation on the Buffy testset showing good performance, particularly on failure scenarios of [25]

The only exception is in case of lower arm where Eichner et al. [5] has produced better results. For consistency, we have used the same parameters for each limb, however the lower arm in particular has the flexibility of being anywhere in a comparatively larger area. Perhaps, slightly increased number of initializations for lower arm could have produced better results at the cost of increasing the number of computations.

Quantitative evaluation was performed using the standard Percentage of Correctly estimated body Parts (PCP) performance criterion (v3.01).[4] PCP scores for [24] are comparatively better for lower arm only because this criterion evaluates individual parts without considering overall pose validity. This means that an invalid pose can have higher PCP score when compared to a valid pose, which is the reason in this case. Discriminantly trained part-based model [24] allows very loose spring like connections, which may result in invalid poses. This is inconsistent with the hypotheses of having articulated joints that share a common point between limbs. This filters out inconsistent poses and increases robustness against track drifting. Figure 12.7 shows the qualitative evaluation on the Buffy dataset, particularly where [25] performed poorly.

12.6 Articulated Skeleton Tracking

Tracking of Articulated Skeletons (AS) [4] can be thought of as motion estimation with articulation constraints. The major difference between PS and AS is in the explicit formulation of the articulation constraint. In AS, as proposed by [4], if two limbs $\mathbf{l}_i$ and $\mathbf{l}_j$ share a common point $\mathbf{p}_a$, and they undergo an affine transformation A_i and A_j respectively, then:

[4] PCP computes the distance between the estimated skeleton and the ground truth, skeletons found closer than a set threshold (commonly set to 0.5) are considered correct.

$$A_i \mathbf{p}_a = A_j \mathbf{p}_a, \quad (12.3)$$

$$\Longrightarrow (A_i - A_j)\mathbf{p}_a = 0. \quad (12.4)$$

This extends the parameter space of each limb with parameters of joining limbs. PS ignores this relative parameter space and estimate parameters of each limb independently, thus gaining computational efficiency at the cost of accuracy. It has been shown that if we consider two moving limbs $\mathbf{l}_i$ and $\mathbf{l}_j$ articulated at point $\mathbf{p}_a = (x_a, y_a)$ as planes π_i and π_j, then for affine cameras, a linear least square solution can be formulated [4]. This reduces the problem to that of finding corresponding pixels in two consecutive frames for which the brightness constancy assumption is proposed. Under this assumption, motion estimation can be solved as a sum of squared distance minimization problem, which leads to solving a linear system of the form $\Gamma\mathcal{A} = B$ subjected to the articulation constraint.

This method has shown promising results in estimating upper body posture of vehicle drivers, i.e. estimating the 5 limbs and 6 points skeleton after manual initialization. In this work, we extend this model for the full human skeleton having 10 limbs and 15 point skeleton, and also eliminate the need for manual initialization.

Each limb is approximated by a plane and their joints can be defined as articulation points. For a frontal pose skeleton of 15 points and 10 limbs (see Fig. 12.8a), there exist 13 articulation planes, 12 articulations lines and 24 constraints (see Fig. 12.8b). There are 6 affine parameters to be estimated per plane totalling 78 parameters for 13 planes resulting in a 24×78 dimensional constraint matrix D. Thus the constraint equation for the system could be written in matrix form as $D\mathcal{A} = 0$, where $\mathcal{A}$ is the 78×1 dimensional matrix of unknowns. The additional constraints are obtained using affine flow for each plane. Similarly, parameters for profile pose can be deduced from Fig. 12.8.

Since this approach is sensitive to initialization errors and occlusions, we introduce the automatic initialization of the algorithm through frontal and/or profile pose estimation. Unlike a vehicle driver, many of the articulated points on a freely moving 2D

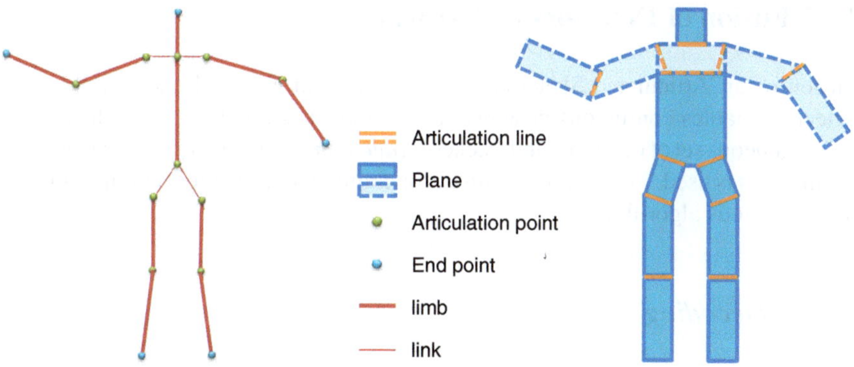

Fig. 12.8 (*Right*) 2D human pose with 13 planes and 12 articulation lines. (*Left*) 10 limbs, 15 points human skeleton with 10 articulation points and 5 end points

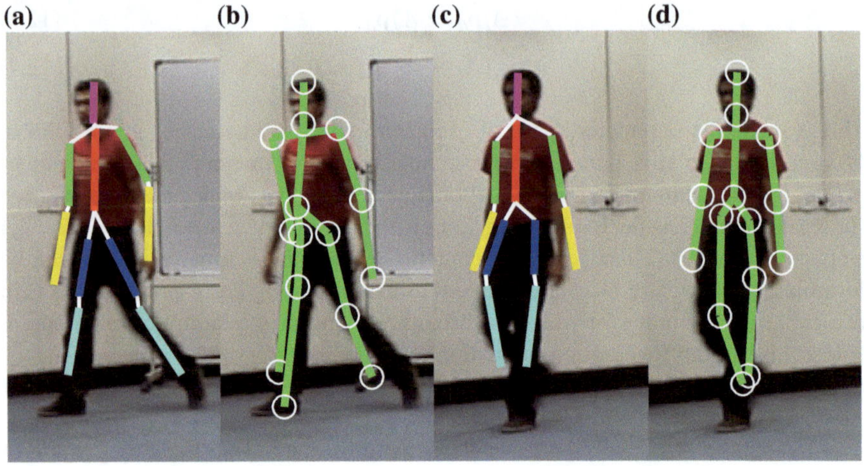

Fig. 12.9 Comparison between frontal pose estimation and AS tracker elaborating the need for fusion. **a** 2D pose estimated from the frontal pose detector. **b** AS tracking showing a drifting issue. **c** 2D pose from the same frontal pose detector with incorrect right lower arm detection. **d** AS tracking showing better estimation of articulation point on left knee joint as compared to estimated 2D pose

skeleton undergo self occlusions. In fact, since human walking patterns are periodic, these occlusions occur at a very regular interval. This restricts the tracking of AS to hardly one walk cycle of a person after which the tracker starts to drift (see Fig. 12.9). To enable extended tracking of a person with repetitive self occlusions and occlusions due to continuously changing viewpoints, we introduce fusion of outputs from Frontal and Profile pose detectors, person detector and tracker and Articulated Skeleton (AS) tracker. Next, we briefly discuss frontal and profile pose detectors followed by our fusion strategy.

12.7 Fusion of Detectors and Trackers

Fusion of an Articulated Skeleton (AS) tracker with a frontal and a profile pose detector, enables continuous pose estimation and tracking. To perform fusion of a heterogeneous set of detectors and trackers, a *decoding* strategy to filter out inaccurate estimations is used. This allows for *fusion* of complementary information from these heterogeneous algorithms.

12.7.1 Decoding

In order to obtain the best pose tracking at each frame the problem is to decide which set of detector and tracker outputs should be combined. Considering that the output of each detector and tracker will be either 0 or 1 i.e. $y \in \{0, 1\}$ representing success or failure respectively, a decoding strategy [18] can be used. Considering there are n detectors and trackers, there are 2^n possible combinations. These set of combinations C can be defined as:

$$C = \begin{pmatrix} 0\,0 \cdots 0\,0 \\ 0\,0 \cdots 0\,1 \\ \vdots\ \vdots\ \ddots\ \vdots \\ 1\,1 \cdots 1\,1 \end{pmatrix}. \tag{12.5}$$

Out of these 2^n combinations, the score for each option can be obtained as $C \times \Omega$, where $\Omega = \{\omega_1, \ldots, \omega_n\}$ are the set of weights.

Unlike multiple classifiers of the same type learned on different classes [1], fusing output from multiple heterogeneous algorithms is a much more difficult and challenging problem. Fusion of output from multiple heterogeneous algorithms requires normalization of their confidence on a uniform scale. These confidence scores can be based on a variety of different measures such as classification error, probability score, maximum likelihood value, correlation score, entropy, uncertainty estimate or residual error and differ in their ranges as well as sensitivity to noise. Thus a per-score normalization function is desired to project these scores on a uniform scale. This problem can be solved by learning a per algorithm normalization factor $\mathbf{b} = \{b_1, \ldots, b_n\}$. Thus, the decoding can be formulated as:

$$\hat{c} = \arg\max_i C_i \omega_i b_i, \tag{12.6}$$

where b_i can be a regression coefficient. To obtain b_i, one can evaluate the performance of each algorithm against the ground truth. This can be achieved by comparing the obtained outputs such as bounding boxes and articulated poses with the ground truth. This allows comparing the performance of any set of heterogeneous algorithms on a uniform scale.

12.7.2 Fusion

No single detector or tracker can ensure a perfect bounding box (BBox) over the entire sequence. Multiple detectors and trackers can be fused to increase the chances of obtaining the correct BBox. By using Eq. (12.6), a decision can be obtained to select the set of algorithms that performed reliably on the current frame. A BBox enclosing the estimated pose can then be obtained from the selected pose detectors and trackers. The bounding boxes can then be fused with those obtained from the person detector and tracker. Let us assume the $\mathbf{X}_b = \{x_b^{tld}, x_b^{pd}, x_b^{f}, x_b^{p}, x_b^{a}\}$ is the set of 5 bounding boxes from the TLD tracker, person detector, frontal pose detector, profile pose detector and the articulated pose tracker respectively. The updated BBox can be obtained as:

$$\hat{x}_j^b = \frac{\sum_{i \in P} x_b{}^i c^i \omega^i b^i}{\sum_{i \in P} c^i}_{i=\{tld,pd,p\}}, \tag{12.7a}$$

$$\hat{y}_j^b = \frac{\sum_{i \in P} y_b{}^i c^i \omega^i b^i}{\sum_{i \in P} c^i}_{i=\{tld,pd,f,p,a\}}, \tag{12.7b}$$

where $j = \{1, 2\}$. Equation (12.7a, 12.7b) will result in a BBox that will contain the person's head, torso and legs. It will exclude the arms of the person from the BBox. This can be achieved by excluding the x-components of bounding boxes from the articulated pose detector and tracker. This compact BBox will help the tracker in learning the visual appearance of the object only, as a minimum portion of background is included in the BBox. In case all of the decision components are zero for any component of BBox, the values from previous frames can be used.

Similarly, the poses obtained from multiple pose detectors and trackers can be fused. Let us assume the $\mathbf{X}_{\text{pose}} = \{\mathbf{X}^i_{\text{pose}}\}_{i \in P}$ is the set of 2D poses. To obtain the final pose, these poses can be linearly combined as:

$$\hat{\mathbf{X}}_{\text{pose}} = \frac{\sum_{i \in P} \mathbf{X}^i_{\text{pose}} c^i \omega^i b^i}{\sum_{i \in P} c^i}, \tag{12.8}$$

where $P = \{f, p, a\}$ refers to the frontal and profile detectors and the articulation point tracker respectively. This formulation allows giving higher weight to better performing algorithms and vice versa in the final 2D pose (see Fig. 12.10).

The final fused bounding box $\hat{\mathbf{X}}_b$ and pose $\hat{\mathbf{X}}_{\text{pose}}$ is then fed back to all the detectors and tracker. The updated bounded box ensures that the person tracker does not drift over time. It also reduces the search space. Similarly, the fused pose reduces the search space of detectors to a small subset of the entire space. It is also used to reinitialize the articulated pose tracker. In case of complete failure of all the pose detectors and tracker, the pose from the previous frame is propagated to the next frame.

12.7.3 Example—Fusion

In this example we compared the performance of the algorithm with [1, 5] on 3 standard datasets (HumanEvalI, TUD-Stadtmitte and ETH Moving camera [6]), and a Smart Lab dataset consisting of 887 frames and 255 frames respectively.

The fundamental hypothesis behind introducing articulation constraints on bone joints is: "introducing articulation constraint improves the consistent estimation and tracking of 2D human pose estimation in video". Validating this hypothesis involves multiple advancements including: a tractable solution for articulated pose estimation, a fusion of multiple heterogeneous trackers and detectors, PCA based pose validation and KTSSR. We have analyzed each of these modules of the algorithm on a video

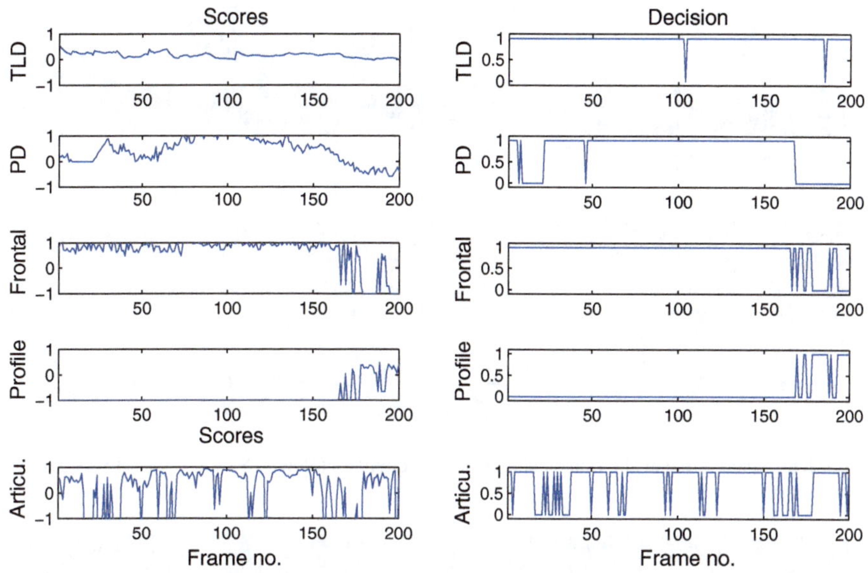

Fig. 12.10 *Left* Confidence scores from detectors and trackers. *Right* Decision showing selected combination of detectors and trackers. It can be seen as frontal pose detector fails during turning, profile pose detector attempt to perform pose estimation and manage to perform successful detection

Table 12.2 Comparison between modules of proposed approach, final proposed solution and state-of-the-art

Desc.	Det.	T	UL	LL	UA	LA	H	Total
[5]	75.3	75.3	64.7	34.1	75.3	73.1	75.3	64.5
D	96.5	96.5	86.5	67.4	96.1	**83.2**	96.5	86.0
DP	96.1	96.1	85.9	67.3	95.7	82.0	96.1	85.4
DPS	96.5	96.5	85.9	71.2	96.1	76.9	96.5	85.3
DPSA	**100**	**98.4**	**93.9**	**81.4**	**98.8**	80.2	**100**	**90.7**

Key D PS Detector, *DP* PD with PCA, *DPS* DP with search space reduction, *DPSA* DPS with AS and fusion, *T* torso, *UL* upper legs, *LL* lower legs, *UA* upper arms, *LA* lower arms, *H* head

sequence and compared its performance with [5], using PCP after applying detection rate (see Table 12.2).

The first two rows of Table 1 compares performance of our pose detectors with [3]. The preceding three rows show gradual improvements made by each contribution of our approach. There are two key observations from Table. 12.2, (i) 2D pose detection rate has increased to 100 % with consistent improvements at each module, and (ii) the total 2D pose estimation score has increased to 90.7 %. Both these scores are superior when compared to [5] which shows the efficacy of the proposed methodology.

Qualitative comparison of the proposed approach on a single and multiple target scenarios is shown in Figs. 12.11 and 12.12 respectively. We used sequences S2/C1 and S2/C2 from HumanEvaII dataset [21]. In this dataset, the person view is

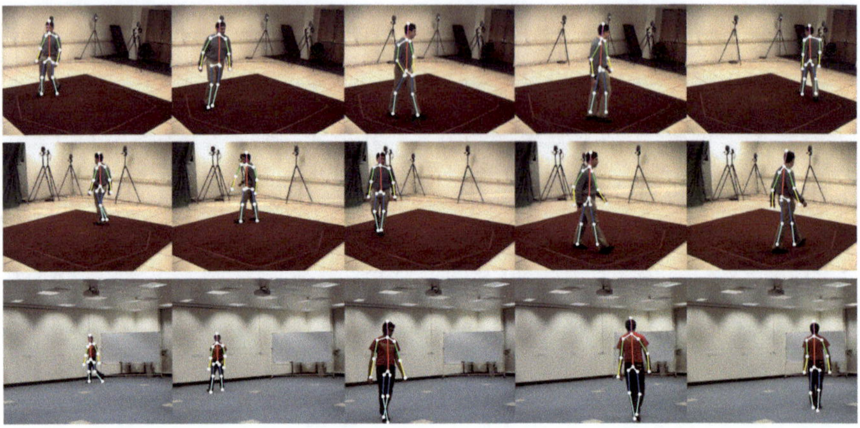

Fig. 12.11 Qualitative evaluation on single target sequences. (*Row 1*) S2/C1. (*Row 2*) S2/C2. (*Row 3*) Smart lab

Fig. 12.12 Qualitative evaluation on challenging multi-target real-life scenarios. (*Left*) Static camera (*Right*) Moving Camera

continuously changing with respect to the camera making it appropriate for evaluating view-invariance. To test the robustness on varying sizes, a Smart Lab sequence (Fig. 12.11 (Row 3)) is used. These results validate another key contribution that fusion of only 2 view-specific pose detectors with articulated tracker eliminates the need for having 8 view-specific PS detectors as suggested in [1]. Furthermore, unlike [15], it eliminates the need for large amount of viewpoint specific training data. Moreover, the use of few pose detectors requires far less computation and there is no need to try all viewpoint specific pose detectors each time, provided that there is a fusion and detector switching mechanism.

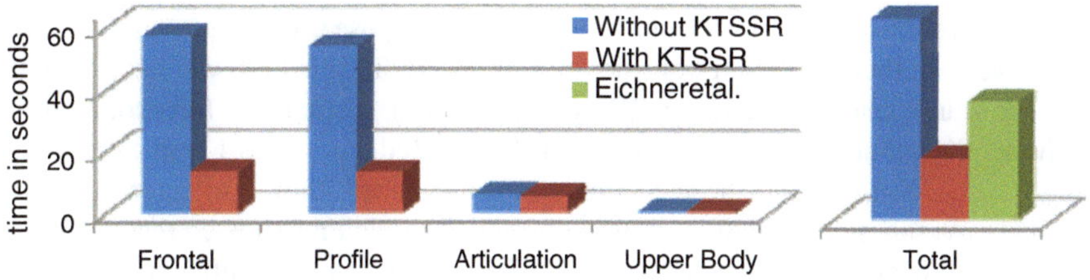

Fig. 12.13 Comparison of execution time in with and without KTSSR and their comparison with Eichner et al. [5]

The trade-off of only using two detectors is a slight increase in error (10 pixels on HumanEvaII dataset) as compared to [1] due to ambiguities related to symmetry in PS. These can be partially overcome by introducing face detection and additional temporal smoothness constraints. 3D tracking is also used to remove flip ambiguities, which is very challenging with only two detectors.

The method was also tested on real world outdoor scenarios (TUD-Stadtmitte and ETH Moving Camera datasets), having multiple people performing unconstrained motion. Promising results were obtained on both these datasets as shown in Fig. 12.12.

12.7.4 Example—Computational Cost

Figure 12.13 shows the reduction in computational cost achieved through KTSSR. Overall the execution time is reduced by a factor of 3. It also shows that the total execution time for 10 limb articulated pose estimation is much <10 limb PS. This further establishes that articulated tracker make the problem tractable. The average computation time for a 960×544 image on a PC with a Core $i7$ processor and 8 GB RAM, using a MATLAB based implementation, is around 55 s for the 1st frame and 13 s for each subsequent frame.

If we carefully analyze the algorithm for limb detection, it involves computation of a response from a classifier at large number of locations for each limb. Except in case of Mean-shift, all these computations are independent of each other and can be performed in parallel on a Graphic Processing Unit (GPU). Similarly, computations of some of the limbs are independent of other. For e.g. once the torso is identified, the computations for arms and legs can be performed in parallel. This parallel nature of 2D pose estimation suggest that further significant computation gains can be obtained by using a GPU.

12.8 Summary

This chapter discusses various improvements in 2D Pose estimation to make it feasible for multi-camera networks. The major challenges in deploying 2D Pose estimation algorithms in multi-camera networks were identified and solutions were explored. The algorithm must be robust against varying viewpoints. For this, the fusion of frontal and profile detectors with person and pose trackers proves to be quite effective. Another important consideration is speed. To this end, we discuss methods for search space reduction in 2D pose estimation, particularly foreground highlighting, Kinematic and Temporal Search Space Reduction and Mean-Shift based approaches. Not only do these methods improve speed, they also filter out many unlikely hypotheses and thus increase accuracy. Experiments showed that even after eliminating over 80 % of the computation, there is no significant effect on accuracy. Finally, we discuss the need for a self-evaluation criterion such as PCA as an essential aid for pruning out invalid hypotheses and determining the failure cases of the algorithm.

References

1. Andriluka M, Roth S, Schiele B (2010) Monocular 3d pose estimation and tracking by detection. In: CVPR, San Francisco, pp 623–630
2. Andriluka M, Roth S, Schiele B (2012) Discriminative appearance models for pictorial structures. Int J Comp Vis 99(3):259–280
3. Dalal N, Triggs B (2005) Histograms of oriented gradients for human detection. In: Proceedings of IEEE international conference on computer vision and pattern recognition, vol 1, pp 886–893
4. Datta A, Sheikh YA, Kanade T (2008) Linear motion estimation for systems of articulated planes. In: IEEE CVPR, June 2008
5. Eichner M, Marin-Jimenez M, Zisserman A, Ferrari V (2012) 2D articulated human pose estimation and retrieval in (almost) unconstrained still images. Int J Comp Vis 99:190–214
6. Ess A, Leibe B, Van Gool L (2007) Depth and appearance for mobile scene analysis. In: IEEE ICCV, Oct 2007
7. Felzenszwalb PF, Girshick RB, McAllester D, Ramanan D (2010) Object detection with discriminatively trained part-based models. IEEE Trans PAMI 32:1627–1645
8. Fischler MA, Elschlager RA (1973) The representation and matching of PS. IEEE Trans Comput 22(1):67–92
9. Hassan A, Taj M (2014) 2D articulated pose tracking: a hybrid approach. In: Proceedings of IEEE international conference on image processing, Paris, Oct 2014
10. Lucey S, Saragih J, Cohn J (2011) Deformable model fitting by regularized landmark mean-shifts. Int J Comp Vis 91(2):200–215
11. Johnson S, Everingham M (2010) Clustered pose and nonlinear appearance models for human pose estimation. In: Proceedings of British machine vision conference, pp 1–11
12. Kalal Z, Mikolajczyk K, Matas J (2012) Tracking-learning-detection. IEEE Trans PAMI 34:1409–1422
13. Khalid AR, Hassan A, Taj M (2014) Efficient 2D pose estimation using mean-shift. In: Proceedings of IEEE international conference on image processing, Paris, Oct 2014
14. Maji S, Berg AC, Malik J (2008) Classification using intersection kernel support vector machines is efficient. In: IEEE CVPR, Anchorage, Alaska
15. Pishchulin L, Jain A, Andriluka M, Thormaehlen T, Schiele B (2012) Articulated people detection and pose estimation: reshaping the future. In: CVPR, Providence
16. Ramanan D (2006) Learning to parse images of articulated objects. In: NIPS, Vancouver
17. Ramanan D (2011) Visual analysis of humans, Chapter 11: part-based models for finding people and estimating their pose, Springer, pp 199–224
18. Sadeghi MA, Farhadi A (2011) Recognition using visual phrases. In: IEEE CVPR, Colorado Springs, USA, June 2011

19. Sapp B, Toshev A, Taskar B (2010) Cascaded models for articulated pose estimation. In: Proceedings of the European conference on computer vision, Berlin, Heidelberg, pp 406–420
20. Shotton J, Fitzgibbon A, Cook M, Sharp T, Finocchio M, Moore R, Kipman A, Blake A (2011) Real-time human pose recognition in parts from single depth images. In: Proceedings of IEEE international conference on computer vision and pattern recognition, pp 1297–1304
21. Sigal L, Balan AO, Black MJ (2006) Humaneva: synchronized video and motion capture dataset for evaluation of articulated human motion. Int J Comp Vis 87(1):4–27
22. Simo-Serra E, Quattoni A, Torras C, Moreno-Noguer F (2013) A joint model for 2D and 3D pose estimation from a single image. In: Proceedings of the conference on computer vision and pattern recognition (CVPR)
23. Wu C, Aghajan H (2008) Human pose estimation in vision networks via distributed local processing and nonparametric belief propagation. In: Proceedings of the 10th international conference on advanced concepts for intelligent vision systems, ACIVS'08, Springer, Berlin, pp 1006–1017
24. Yang Y, Ramanan D (2011) Articulated pose estimation with flexible mixtures-of-parts. In: IEEE CVPR, Washington
25. Zuffi S, Freifeld O, Black MJ (2012) From pictorial structures to deformable structures. In: IEEE CVPR, Washington

Chapter 13
Exploiting Crowd Synthesis for Multi-camera Human Tracking

Zhixing Jin and Bir Bhanu

Abstract There are many challenges to achieve a robust performance for tracking in a video network. In this chapter, we propose a method that integrates both detection and crowd synthesis approaches to achieve robust tracking performance. The experiments are conducted on PETS 2009 data set, and the performance is evaluated by multiple object tracking precision and accuracy criteria based on the position of each pedestrian on the ground plane. It is demonstrated that the information from crowd synthesis can provide significant advantage for tracking multiple pedestrians through multiple cameras.

13.1 Introduction

Tracking pedestrians, especially tracking them in crowds, has been an attractive topic for computer vision researchers for many years. Many pedestrian tracking approaches have been proposed till today, for the applications in various scenarios such as surveillance, security, and monitoring. To improve tracking performance, especially in extremely complicated situations, approaches are developed to be more and more sophisticated. On one head, more advanced features, models, and learning strategies have been proposed and extended, such as histogram of oriented gradient (HOG) [6] and Haar-like features [16], Ada-Boosting-based online learning [9], and multiple instance learning [2]. On the other hand, we may also increase the number of cameras in the system and fuse information from multiple cameras. By setting up a video network with multiple cameras, the area under surveillance can be greatly expanded if these cameras have nonoverlapping field-of-views (FOVs). If the cameras in a video network have overlapping FOVs, then tracking accuracy can be improved,

Z. Jin (✉) · B. Bhanu
The Center for Research in Intelligent Systems, University of California,
Riverside, CA 92521, USA
e-mail: jinz@cs.ucr.edu

B. Bhanu
e-mail: bhanu@cris.ucr.edu

P. Spagnolo et al. (eds.), *Human Behavior Understanding in Networked Sensing*,
DOI 10.1007/978-3-319-10807-0_13

particularly for crowded scenes, since the possibility that a pedestrian is occluded in all camera views is significantly smaller than that using a single camera [8, 22].

In the proposed approach, we are focused on the situation where pedestrians are crowded with many occlusions. Therefore, a multi-camera tracking system is used to relieve the severe occlusion problem. In such a system, it is necessary to correspond information from different views; therefore, estimating pedestrian locations in the real-world is required and it is usually achieved by adopting homography-related methods. However, currently in almost all the systems, the estimated real-world locations is only utilized in data correspondence, but the relationship between them has been rarely explored.

Pedestrian locations are actually spatially and temporally highly relevant. For example, in most cases, instead of walking alone, pedestrians are actually self-organized into groups and walk together [17]. In addition, pedestrians are able to avoid collisions, even in an extremely crowded scene. In the area of computer graphics, there is such a category of approaches that models and simulates the pedestrian behaviors, known as crowd simulation. It has crucial importance for the applications such as designing emergency evacuation routes and resource management. Basically, the purpose of crowd simulation is to mimic the realistic behavior for every virtual individuals in a crowd under the given constraints (e.g., collision avoidance). Currently, most of the crowd simulators are aimed at simulating and predicting pedestrian walking, and some of them have really impressive results [11, 18, 21]. A typical crowd simulator requires the information of direction and velocity, as well as the starting and ending locations for each pedestrian. Since these types of information can be acquired in a multiple camera tracking system, it is natural to integrate crowd simulation algorithms into a vision system for tracking to predict pedestrian behaviors, and therefore, to improve tracking performance.

In this chapter, we propose a novel way to combine a multiple camera tracking system and a crowd simulator. In our integrated system, each camera has its own independent tracker based on the tracking-by-detection approach [4], which uses pure vision-based features. The simulator used is the RVO2 library [21], which works separately from the tracking system. At each time step, a distribution of possible positions for each pedestrian in the scene is generated by the simulator based on his/her historical location and velocity information. This distribution is then fused together with the information from trackers to estimate the new location for each pedestrian. Finally, trackers are updated according to the new patches, which are calculated based on these new locations. The system diagram is illustrated in Fig. 13.1.

The rest of the chapter is organized as follows. Section 13.2 presents related work, including tracking approaches and crowd simulation methods. Section 13.3 describes the details of our proposed approach. Section 13.4 demonstrates the experimental results and finally Sect. 13.5 concludes the chapter.

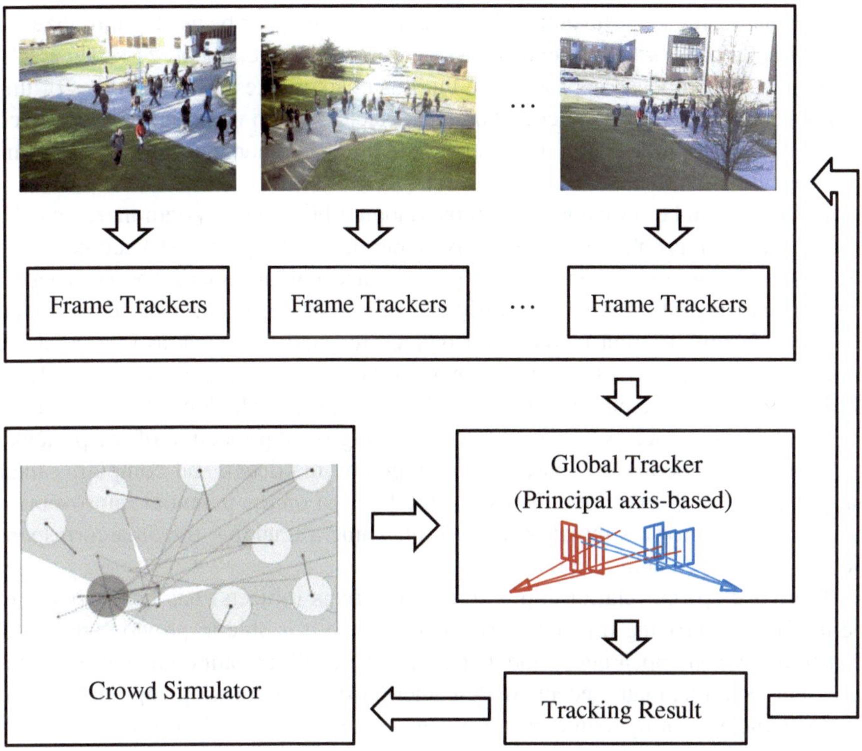

Fig. 13.1 The system diagram. At each time step, the global tracker obtains information from all the camera views and the crowd simulator, and then computes the tracking results on the ground plane. The tracking results are then used to update the frame trackers and the crowd simulator

13.2 Related Work

Most of the *state-of-the-art* tracking approaches have the components of classification and/or detection, and are based on online learning strategies, including: Online Ada-Boosting [9], Semi-Boosting [10] and Online Multiple Instance Learning [2] trackers. A general processing approach for this kind of tracker is to train a classifier for the object's appearance model from the first one or several frames, and then update the classifier as the tracking continues. At each time step, a likelihood map can be computed within a certain searching window based on the object's previous location, and its new location is defined as the location where the likelihood reaches the maximal. The update for the classifier also depends on the new location for an object. This process may cause the drifting problem, because as the classifier keeps updating itself during tracking, it may eventually represent a different appearance model than the model was learned at the very beginning. Therefore, in addition to classification, detection approaches, especially human detectors are also integrated into the tracking system [1, 4], since human detector is generally more confident than the online tracker. The output from human detectors can be used to initialize the online tracker, and/or to correct the classifier during the tracking process. The tracking part in the proposed approach used in this chapter takes the advantages of this combination of online classifier and human detector, which was originally proposed in [4]. It contains three components: a particle filter, a human detector and an online boosting classifier.

When the number of cameras with overlapping FOVs in a system increases, the severe occlusion problem may be resolved, but the tracking process becomes more complicated. For example, the data correspondence among cameras becomes necessary when fusing information from different views. This has not been perfectly solved till today. Many different methods for data correspondence, such as region-based, point-based, and principal axis-based, have been reported in recent years [7, 22]. In this chapter, the principal axis-based method is adopted, which calculates the real-world location of each pedestrian by finding the ground projection of the principal axis for each camera view (based on homography matrices), and computing their intersections [8]. Furthermore, since we are focused on the potential improvement brought by the crowd simulation to multiple camera tracking, the data correspondences between cameras are fixed.

The basic spatial relationship among pedestrians (objects) has been proven to be useful in improving tracking performance since it is able to provide additional constraints when appearance models change due to illumination change or occlusion. For example, many recent single-camera pedestrian tracking approaches have explored the possibility to integrate grouping strategy in the tracking process [5, 19], and general object tracking approaches can also benefit when structure information is utilized [23]. For multi-camera applications, group information has also been studied [15, 24].

Additionally, in the research area of crowd simulation, more complicated spatial and temporal constraints between pedestrians have been explored. There are many sophisticated crowd simulation models proposed in the recent years. Examples include: the social force model, which is derived from physics and social-psychology [11]; the Reciprocal Velocity Obstacles (RVO2) library, which finds the optimal collision avoidance strategy [21]; the combination of rule-based approaches and local collision avoidance [18]; and the continuum dynamics model, which is able to simulate extremely large and dense crowds [20]. These crowd simulation models have a wide range of applications, even in industry such as movie making. Except the macroscopic techniques, most of the crowd simulation approaches simulate each pedestrian separately. For instance, the social force model uses a particle to represent each individual and defines several types of forces on each particle (individual), and the crowd simulation can be computed as the existing simulation for a particle system. In the proposed approach, the crowd simulator adopted is the RVO2 library [21], because it only requires the information of the current location and desired velocity of each pedestrian, which is quite easy to obtain in a multi-camera tracking system. In addition, the library is computationally efficient, allowing us to repeat the calculation for many times at each time step to get the distribution of possible locations.

An example of integrating crowd simulation in a single-camera pedestrian tracking system has been proposed in our previous work [12].

13.3 Technical Approach

The system has two major components. As shown in Fig. 13.1, the first component uses the *state-of-the-art* tracking-by-detection algorithm (frame tracker), which is able to track pedestrians based on information from camera. The second component calculates the pedestrian positions in the real world (global tracker). It integrates the information from the crowd simulator as well as the projection from each frame tracker, and estimates the real position for each pedestrian on the ground plane.

13.3.1 Frame Tracker

The frame tracker adopted in this approach is a sophisticated tracking-by-detection method combining a particle filter, a boosting classifier, and a human detector [4]. Since our main purpose is to investigate the benefit of crowd simulation, the original technique is modified to eliminate possible errors brought by various steps, as well as to speed up the single camera tracking process. The framework for the modified frame tracker in this approach is shown as Fig. 13.2. For readers who are interested in the complete approach, please refer to the paper [4].

The tracking is accomplished mainly based on a *bootstrap filter*. The state for each pedestrian $\mathbf{x} = \{x, y, u, v\}$, consists of the information of position (x, y) and velocity (u, v) of each particle (on image frames). Since importance resampling is used at every time step and $w^i_{t-1} = 1/N$, the weight of each particle at every time step w^i_t only depends on the likelihood of the current observation, $p(o_t|\mathbf{x}^i_t)$, which will be described as the observation model at the end of this section.

The particle filter uses a simple constant velocity motion model

$$(x, y)_t = (x, y)_{t-1} + (u, v)_{t-1} + \varepsilon_{(x,y)} \tag{13.1}$$

$$(u, v)_t = (u, v)_{t-1} + \varepsilon_{(u,v)} \tag{13.2}$$

where $\varepsilon_{(x,y)}$ and $\varepsilon_{(u,v)}$ are two independent zero-mean normal distributions. The variances $\sigma^2_{(x,y)}$ and $\sigma^2_{(u,v)}$ are set proportional to the initial patch size, and then decrease as the number of successfully tracked frames increases. For simplicity, we skip the *Iterative Likelihood Weighting* procedure used in the original tracker to deal with abrupt and fast camera motion. Furthermore, we initialize each tracker by manual annotations to ensure that each pedestrian has a corresponding tracker. The termination strategy of a tracker is the same as in the original work: the tracker stops if there are no associated detection results for a while.

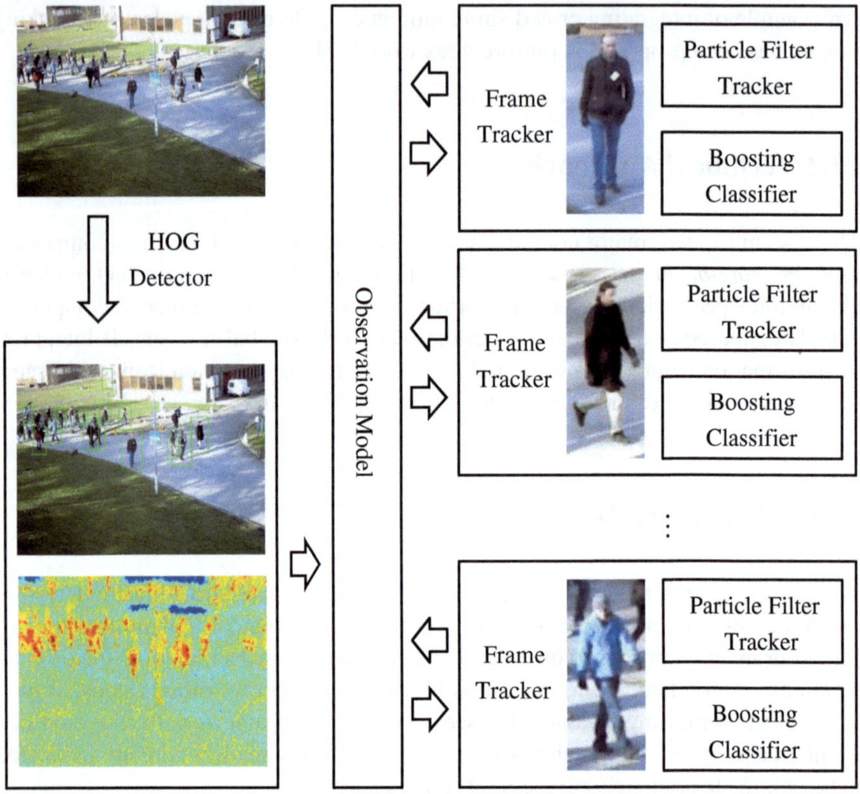

Fig. 13.2 The framework for the frame trackers in this approach. A particle filter and a boosting classifier are maintained for each single pedestrian. At each time step, after particle transition, the outputs from the HOG detector and the boosting classifier are combined based on the observation model, and is then used to update the tracker

The information provided by the human detector includes two parts, the detection results and the confidence map. At each time step, the detection results are associated to trackers. A function [4] calculates the matching scores between each detected patch and tracked patch

$$S(\mathrm{tr}, d) = g(\mathrm{tr}, d) \cdot \left(c_{\mathrm{tr}}(d) + \alpha \cdot \sum_{p \in \mathrm{tr}}^{N} p_{\mathcal{N}}(d - p) \right) \tag{13.3}$$

where tr and d are the positions of the tracker and the detected patch, respectively. N denotes the number of particles for each tracker. $p_{\mathcal{N}}(d - p)$ is the normal distribution based on the Euclidean distance between the detection and particle, $c_{\mathrm{tr}}(d)$ is the evaluation from the classifier for the detected patch, and $g(\mathrm{tr}, d)$ is the gating function

$$g(\mathrm{tr}, d) = p(\mathrm{size}_d|\mathrm{tr})p(\mathrm{pos}_d|\mathrm{tr})$$
$$= \begin{cases} p_{\mathcal{N}}\left(\frac{\mathrm{size}_{\mathrm{tr}}-\mathrm{size}_d}{\mathrm{size}_{\mathrm{tr}}}\right) \cdot p_{\mathcal{N}}(|d-\mathrm{tr}|), & \text{if } |\mathbf{v}_{\mathrm{tr}}| < \tau_v \\ p_{\mathcal{N}}\left(\frac{\mathrm{size}_{\mathrm{tr}}-\mathrm{size}_d}{\mathrm{size}_{\mathrm{tr}}}\right) \cdot p_{\mathcal{N}}(\mathrm{dist}(d, \mathbf{v}_{\mathrm{tr}})), & \text{otherwise} \end{cases} \tag{13.4}$$

where $\mathbf{v}_{\mathrm{tr}}$ is the velocity estimated for current tracker and $\mathrm{dist}(d, \mathbf{v}_{\mathrm{tr}})$ is the distance from the detected position to the line where the vector of velocity lies (distance between point and line). The distribution $p_{\mathcal{N}}(\mathrm{dist}(d, \mathbf{v}_{\mathrm{tr}}))$ has a shape similar to a 2D cone, where the possible positions of the tracker are constrained to in the next frame when the current velocity exceeds certain threshold τ_v.

After the matching scores have been computed for every pair between trackers and detected patches, we use a greedy strategy to determine their final associations. At every iteration, the algorithm finds the largest matching score $s^*(\mathrm{tr}^*, d^*)$ in the current remaining pairs of trackers and detected patches. If s^* is greater than a predefined threshold τ, then this pair of tracker and detected patch (tr^*, d^*) is marked as associated. One constraint is that one tracker (detected patch) can be associated to at most one detected patch (tracker). The procedure continues until there is no pair that has a matching score greater than the threshold τ. By using this greedy strategy, it is not guaranteed that we can get the global optimal solution (e.g., the maximum summation of matching scores). However, the result obtained using greedy method is usually acceptable with a much lower computational cost.

Another important component combined in this tracker is the boosting classifier from [9]. For each tracker, there is a corresponding classifier. This classifier uses a boosting mode, which consists of a series of weak classifiers. When the tracker is initialized, the classifier is also initialized based on the information from the first frame. The positive sample is the patch at the current tracker location and the negative samples come from the nearby patches (including background and/or other pedestrians). At each frame, after the patch location is updated, this classifier also updates using the most recent information.

The outputs from the detector and the classifier are integrated based on the observation model, which calculates the weight for each particle in the particle filter.

$$w_{\mathrm{tr},p} = \beta \cdot \mathcal{I}(\mathrm{tr}) \cdot p_{\mathcal{N}}(p - d^*) + \gamma \cdot d_c(p) \cdot p_O(\mathrm{tr}) + \eta \cdot c_{\mathrm{tr}}(p) \tag{13.5}$$

The first two terms in Eq. (13.5) are based on the output of the detector, and the third term is obtained from the classifier. $\mathcal{I}(\mathrm{tr})$ is the indicator function. It equals to 1 if there is an associated detected patch d^* for this tracker tr and equals to 0 otherwise. In the second term, $d_c(p)$ is the confidence computed by the detector at position p (scaled to [0, 1]). $p_O(\mathrm{tr})$ is called *interobject occlusion reasoning*, which is designed for the situation when the detection is failed because of the occlusion. It is defined as

$$p_O(\mathrm{tr}) = \begin{cases} 1, & \text{if } \mathcal{I}(\mathrm{tr}) = 1 \\ \max\limits_{\mathrm{tr}':\mathcal{I}(\mathrm{tr}')=1} p_{\mathcal{N}}(\mathrm{tr} - \mathrm{tr}'), & \text{else if } \exists \mathcal{I}(\mathrm{tr}') = 1 \\ 0, & \text{otherwise} \end{cases} \tag{13.6}$$

In [4], authors apply two different human detectors: Implicit Shape Model (ISM) [14] and Histogram of Oriented Gradient (HOG) [6]. But in our tracker, we only use the HOG detector, because it is more generalized and has a more widely usage.

13.3.2 Crowd Simulator

The crowd simulation algorithm in the proposed approach is based on the RVO2 library [21]. This model solves an optimization problem using a strategy named Optimal Reciprocal Collision Avoidance (ORCA). The library is very computationally efficient and only requires the information for the current position and desired velocity of each pedestrian. For more details, the reader can refer to the original paper.

RVO2 introduces a concept called velocity obstacles, with the definition as

$$VO^T_{A|B} = \{v | \exists t \in [0, T] : v \cdot t \in D(p_B - p_A, r_A + r_B)\} \tag{13.7}$$

where p_A and p_B are the positions for two pedestrians A and B, and r_A, r_B are their radii. $D(p, r)$ indicates a circle centered at p with radius r. From the definition, $VO^T_{A|B}$ is the set of relative velocities of A with respect to B, which will cause a collision in the future within the time period $[0, T]$. Therefore, the best velocity solution to avoid collisions is the set of velocities that is (1) most adjacent to the desired velocity, (2) not fell into the velocity obstacle set (that is why it is called "obstacle"). The global optimal solution can be efficiently computed using linear programming. The efficiency of the library enables us to run the simulator multiple times at each time step to get a distribution rather than a single solution.

In the current multiple camera tracking system, the position of each pedestrian in the real ground plane is easy to acquire using homography. However, the desired velocity is not explicitly given as we have no idea about where a pedestrian will finally move to and how long will this movement be. That is, neither the direction nor the speed of the desired velocity can be directly obtained based on the current information. An alternative way is to use the historical information. We use a Monte Carlo simulation process to estimate the desired velocity based on its derivatives (accelerations) from the last m frames. Let the acceleration set of a pedestrian k be $A^t_k = \{a^{t-m}_k, a^{t-m+1}_k, \ldots, a^{t-1}_k\}$, and the corresponding weight for each acceleration be

$$w^{t-i}_k = \frac{m - i + 1}{\sum_{j=1}^m j}, \qquad i = 1, \ldots, m \tag{13.8}$$

According to Eq. (13.8), the weight assigned to more recent acceleration will be larger. Then, a set of n accelerations $A'_k = \{a'_{k,1}, a'_{k,2}, \ldots, a'_{k,n}\}$ $(n > m)$ can be generated for estimating a distribution of desired velocity

$$v'_{k,i} = v_k + a'_{k,i} + \varepsilon_{a,k} \tag{13.9}$$

where v'_{k_i} is the estimated velocity corresponding to $a'_{k,i}$, and v_k is the current velocity. $\varepsilon_{a,k}$ is a zero-mean normal distribution with variance $\sigma_{a,k} \propto \max_{i,j} ||a_k^{t-i} - a_k^{t-j}||$. In addition, to handle the sudden stopping situation (i.e., the velocity suddenly changes to 0), one fifth of the elements in the estimated velocity set are 0's.

To reduce the computation, not all possible combinations of different velocities are calculated. Instead, for each pedestrian, we pick up the velocity with the same index (i.e., i) and form $n = |A'_k|$ sets $C_i = \{v_{1,i}, v_{2,i}, \ldots\}$. So the total number of possible locations calculated for each pedestrian is n in this case.

13.3.3 Global Tracker

The global tracker is used to integrate the information from the frame trackers and the output of the crowd simulator, and to provide a final decision of the current position of each pedestrian in the real ground plane.

The first step we need to do is to recover the homography matrix for each view. The homography matrix is defined as a 3×3 matrix

$$H_v = \begin{bmatrix} h^v_{11} & h^v_{12} & h^v_{13} \\ h^v_{21} & h^v_{22} & h^v_{23} \\ h^v_{31} & h^v_{32} & 1 \end{bmatrix} \tag{13.10}$$

Given two points (x, y) (ground point) and (x_v, y_v) (frame point), the projection from the ground point to the frame point can be express as

$$\begin{bmatrix} x_v \\ y_v \\ 1 \end{bmatrix} = H_v \begin{bmatrix} x \\ y \\ 1 \end{bmatrix} \tag{13.11}$$

Note that normally H_v is invertible, which means that we can also project the frame point back onto the ground using its inversion. The homography matrices are computed by manually selecting four corresponding points from different views.

The principal-axis based integration is then adopted for calculating the final ground position. A principal axis of a pedestrian is the line connecting the pedestrian's head to the feet. In our approach, the principal axis is defined as the vertical line in the middle of the patch for simplicity. If the result obtained from the frame tracker of each view is accurate, then the projection of the principal axis in the ground plane will intersect at a single point, which is the position of the pedestrian on the ground plane. It is proven that the principal axis-based integration is very robust in fusing the information from different cameras [7, 22].

The principal axis-based integration in the proposed approach is modified to use particle information from different views. For each particle in a frame tracker, we compute the principal axis of the patch associated to this particle and then project the principal axis back on to the ground plane. Then, the intersection points between principal axes from different views are calculated. We also assign a weight for each intersection point

$$w^0_{\text{tr1},p1,\text{tr2},p2} = w_{\text{tr1},p1} \cdot w_{\text{tr2},p2} \tag{13.12}$$

where $w_{\text{tr1},p1}$ and $w_{\text{tr2},p2}$ are the weights of the particles $p1$ in tracker tr1 and $p2$ in tracker tr2, calculated by Eq. (13.5). In this case, the intersection of higher weighted particles gets a higher weight. To speed up the computation of intersection, not all the possible combinations are tried, instead we experimentally choose $2 * N$ (N is the number of particles in frame tracker) pairs of particles between each two different views.

The integration of the output from the crowd simulator is based on radial basis function. For a particular point g, its "simulation term" is defined as

$$\text{sim}(g) = \sum_{q \in Q_k} p_{\mathcal{N}}(g - Q_k) \tag{13.13}$$

where Q_k is the set of possible locations of pedestrian k (its size $|Q_k| = 2N$) and $p_{\mathcal{N}}(g - Q_k)$ is a zero-mean normal distribution. For each intersection point g_i, the final weight

$$w'_{g_i} = w^0_{g_i} + \delta \text{sim}(g_i) \tag{13.14}$$

And the final location of each pedestrian on the ground plane is calculated by a weighted sum

$$G = \frac{1}{Z} \sum_i w'_{g_i} g_i \tag{13.15}$$

where Z is the normalization factor. After the location for each pedestrian on the ground plane is decided, we use the homography matrices H_v's to project this position back to different views. And the weights for each particle is reevaluated using a Gaussian filter.

13.4 Experimental Results

In this section, we describe the details for our experimental setting, as well as the results and related discussion. The programming of this algorithm is done in C++ with the widely distributed library OpenCV.

13.4.1 Experimental Setting

Our experiments are conducted on the PETS 2009 dataset with medium density crowd (i.e., S2.L2). The dataset originally has four views. However, according to the provider, View 4 suffers from frame rate instability, so we avoid using this view in our experiment. In addition, View 3 has a large tree on the right part of the field of view, which causes severe occlusions especially with medium density of crowd, even during annotation. As a result, the frame tracking is performed only based on View 1 and View 2 in our experiments, and we use View 1, 2, and 3 for testing. The image of the ground plane is obtained using Google Maps (satellite view). The homography matrix for each view is calculated using the function provided in OpenCV, based on four manually annotated points.

The ground-truth is obtained by annotation. Each pedestrian is annotated for its bounding box every five frames, and the bounding boxes for the frames in between are calculated based on linear interpolation. With the annotation of bounding box, the principal axis is determined as the vertical line in the middle of the bounding box. The ground-truth of the position of each pedestrian on the ground plane is computed by intersecting the principal axes projected from View 1 and View 2 (since we cannot guarantee that all the annotations of View 3 are correct because of the occlusion from the big tree).

The HOG detector used in our experiment also comes from OpenCV, with the smallest detection size as 48×96. In order to keep the detection result acceptable, we resize the original image frame to 1920×1440, which makes the smallest pedestrian in a frame have a similar size to 48×96.

The parameter setting used in the frame tracker follows the original work [4]. For example, we set $\beta : \gamma : \eta$ in the observation model Eq. (13.5) to 20:2:1. The δ in Eq. (13.14) is experimentally decided as 2η ($\delta = 0$ is used as the situation without integrating crowd simulator).

For the crowd simulator, RVO2 library, it has 10 parameters for each pedestrian. Among those 10 parameters, three of them keep changing during the tracking (current position, current velocity, and desired velocity) and they vary from individual to individual. The rest seven of them are: the time step of the simulation, the maximal number of neighbors each pedestrian can observe, the maximal speed of a pedestrian, the maximal observation distance of a pedestrian, the radius of a pedestrian, the minimal amount of time a pedestrian is safe with respect to other pedestrians, and the minimal amount of time a pedestrian is safe with respect to static obstacles. Except for the time step of the simulation, the rest of the parameters can actually differ across individuals, but in our experiment we simply set them the same to all individuals. These seven parameters are optimized based on the UCSD crowd dataset [13]. We set the pedestrians in the UCSD and PETS datasets to have the same radius when projected to the ground plane so that the parameters trained on UCSD crowd dataset can be directly applied in the current experiment. However, the UCSD dataset itself is not used in the current experiment since it is for single camera tracking.

13.4.2 Results

Figures 13.3 and 13.4 are qualitative illustrations of tracking results for View 1 and View 2, comparing the results from the multiple camera tracker with/without crowd simulation. For View 3, because the size of target patch is unknown, we only quantitatively calculated the accuracy of tracking. Only the pedestrians appear in both views are evaluated.

For each view, we define the tracking as accurate if the projected point of the position for a pedestrian from the ground plane to the frame falls into a rectangle around its feet area. This rectangle has its height equals to a quarter of the annotation height, its width equals to half of the annotation width, with its location vertically at the bottom and horizontally in the middle of the bounding box. The accuracy of tracking one pedestrian for each view is then calculated as

$$\text{acc}_v = \frac{\#\,\text{accurately tracked frames}}{\#\,\text{tracked frames}} \tag{13.16}$$

On the ground plane, we use multi-object tracking precision (MOTP) and multi-object tracking accuracy (MOTA) [3] to measure the performance of the proposed approach, using a point-based distance

$$s(\text{tr}, \text{gt}) = \max\left(0, \frac{||p_{\text{tr}} - p_{\text{gt}}||_2}{r_p} - 1\right) \tag{13.17}$$

where r_p denote the radius of a pedestrian on the ground plane (which is the same as the radius parameter used in our crowd simulator). p_{tr} and p_{gt} are the position from the multi-camera tracker and the ground-truth respectively.

Table 13.1 shows the tracking accuracy with/without crowd simulator for three views. Table 13.2 shows the MOTP and MOTA results with/without crowd simulator on the ground plane.

The result of MOTP and MOTA with crowd simulator are 57.1 and 31.9 %, respectively. When no information from crowd simulator is integrated [set δ in Eq. (13.14) to 0], the MOTP and MOTA are 59.2 and 9.79 %. The MOTP only evaluates the precision for *matched* objects, and fewer matches between observations and ground-truths will possible increase its value, so the integration of crowd simulation does not necessarily improve the performance on this metric. On the other hand, since the scene is so crowded with many pedestrians in it, the MOTA performance is not extremely impressive. However, according to these results as well as the tracking accuracies in each view, we can easily observe that the performance is significantly improved by integrating the crowd simulator.

To further investigate the performance improvement brought by the crowd simulator, we conduct experiments using a modified tracking system as well. Instead of projecting particles from different camera views onto the ground plane and adjusting their weights according to the estimated locations from crowd simulator, we project the simulated locations back to each camera view and adjust the particle weights

Fig. 13.3 Some sample images for view 1. The *left* column are the results from the tracker with simulation. The *middle* column are the results without simulation. The *right* column are the corresponding ground-truth by annotation. Pedestrians who only appear in one view are not shown

there. This requires modification for the observation model (Eq. 13.14), and makes the sampling step for the particle intersections on the ground plane unnecessary. Therefore, with the similar computational efficiency, the skipping of the sampling

Fig. 13.4 Some sample images for view 2. The *left* column are the results from the tracker with simulation. The *middle* column are the results without simulation. The *right* column are the corresponding ground-truth by annotation. Pedestrians who only appear in one view are not shown

step can lead to a better performance since more information is preserved. The MOTP and MOTA for View 1 and View 2 are reported in Table 13.3 (The tracked patch is considered as accurate if its overlapping ratio with ground-truth patch is over 0.5).

Table 13.1 The tracking accuracy with/without crowd simulator for three views

View	With simulator (%)	Without simulator (%)
1	86.9	76.4
2	87.1	77.7
3	82.3	72.5

The statistics is based on active trackers

Table 13.2 The MOTP and MOTA evaluation for the tracking results generated by the system with/without crowd simulator

	With simulator (%)	Without simulator (%)
MOTP	57.1	59.2
MOTA	31.9	9.79

Table 13.3 The MOTP and MOTA with/without crowd simulator for View 1 and View 2

View	Evaluation	With simulator (%)	Without simulator (%)
1	MOTP	71.2	67.8
	MOTA	62.4	41.8
2	MOTP	70.4	68.7
	MOTA	59.8	49.3

The statistics is based on active trackers

13.5 Conclusions

In this chapter, we proposed a multi-camera tracking approach that combines *state-of-the-art* single camera tracking-by-detection method and a crowd simulation approach (RVO2 library). The purpose of this approach is to investigate the influence on the tracking performance when the crowd simulation output is additionally integrated into a vision-based tracking approach. The experiments are conducted on PETS 2009 dataset with medium density crowd and the performance is evaluated on different views as well as on the ground plane. The experimental results demonstrate that the multi-camera pedestrian tracking with a crowd simulator significantly outperforms the one without a crowd simulator. This means that the utilization of the spatial and temporal relationship between pedestrians can be really important and helpful for pedestrian tracking.

References

1. Andriluka M, Roth S, Schiele B (2008) People-tracking-by-detection and people-detection-by-tracking. Comput Vis Pattern Recogn 2008:1–8
2. Babenko B, Yang M-H, Belongie S (2011) Robust object tracking with online multiple instance learning. IEEE Trans Pattern Anal Mach Intell 33(8):1619–1632

3. Bernardin K, Stiefelhagen R (2008) Evaluating multiple object tracking performance: the clear mot metrics. J Image Video Process 2008:1:1–1:10
4. Breitenstein MD, Reichlin F, Leibe B, Koller-Meier E, Van Gool L (2011) Online multiperson tracking-by-detection from a single, uncalibrated camera. IEEE Trans Pattern Anal Mach Intell 33(9):1820–1833
5. Chen X, Qin Z, An L, Bhanu B (2014) An online learned elementary grouping model for multi-target tracking. IEEE conference on computer vision and pattern recognition (CPVR), pp 1242–1249
6. Dalal N, Triggs B (2005) Histograms of oriented gradients for human detection. In: Proceedings of the 2005 IEEE computer society conference on computer vision and pattern recognition (CVPR'05), vol 01. IEEE Computer Society, Washington, DC, pp 886–893
7. Du W, Piater Justus (2007) Multi-camera people tracking by collaborative particle filters and principal axis-based integration. In: Proceedings of the 8th Asian conference on computer vision—volume part I, ACCV'07. Springer, Berlin, pp 365–374
8. Eshel R, Moses Y (2010) Tracking in a dense crowd using multiple cameras. Int J Comput Vis 88(1):129–143
9. Grabner H, Bischof H (2006) On-line boosting and vision. In: Proceedings of the 2006 IEEE computer society conference on computer vision and pattern recognition, CVPR '06, IEEE computer society, vol 1, Washington, DC, pp 260–267
10. Grabner H, Leistner C, Bischof H (2008) Semi-supervised on-line boosting for robust tracking. In: Proceedings of the 10th European conference on computer vision: part I, ECCV '08. Springer, Berlin, pp 234–247
11. Helbing D, Farkas I, Vicsek T (2000) Simulating dynamical features of escape panic. Nature 407:487
12. Jin Z, Bhanu B (2012) Single camera multi-person tracking based on crowd simulation. In: IEEE international conference on pattern recognition (ICPR), Nov 2012, pp 3660–3663
13. Jin Z, Bhanu B (2013) Optimizing crowd simulation based on real video data. In: IEEE international conference on image processing (ICIP), Sept 2013, pp 3186–3190
14. Leibe B, Leonardis A, Schiele B (2008) Robust object detection with interleaved categorization and segmentation. Int J Comput Vis 77(1–3):259–289
15. Lian G, Lai J, Zheng W (2011) Spatial-temporal consistent labeling of tracked pedestrians across non-overlapping camera views. Pattern Recogn 44(5):1121–1136
16. Lienhart R, Maydt J (2002) An extended set of haar-like features for rapid object detection. In: IEEE international conference on image processing (ICIP) vol 1, pp I-900–I-903
17. Moussaïd M, Perozo N, Garnier S, Helbing D, Theraulaz G (2010) The walking behaviour of pedestrian social groups and its impact on crowd dynamics. PLoS ONE 5:e10047
18. Ondřej J, Pettré J, Olivier A, Donikian S (2010) A synthetic-vision based steering approach for crowd simulation. In: ACM SIGGRAPH 2010 papers, SIGGRAPH '10, ACM, New York, pp 123:1–123:9
19. Qin Z (2012) Improving multi-target tracking via social grouping. Comput Vis Pattern Recognit 2012:1972–1978
20. Treuille A, Cooper S, Popović Z (2006) Continuum crowds. In: ACM SIGGRAPH, pp 1160–1168
21. van den Berg J, Guy SJ, Lin MC, Manocha D (2009) Reciprocal n-body collision avoidance. In: 14th international symposium on robotics research, Sept 2009
22. Weiming H, Min H (2006) Principal axis-based correspondence between multiple cameras for people tracking. IEEE Trans Pattern Anal Mach Intell 28(4):663–671
23. Zhang L, van der Maaten L (2014) Preserving structure in model-free tracking. IEEE Trans Pattern Anal Mach Intell 36(4):756–769
24. Zheng W, Gong S, Xiang T (2009) Associating groups of people. In: Proceedings of BMVC, pp 23.1–23.11. doi:10.5244/C.23.23

Part III
Multi-robot Systems

Multi-robot systems (MRS) is an innovative robotic research field, due to both the challenging nature of the involved research and the multiple potential applications to different topologies of areas: autonomous sensor networks, building surveillance, transportation of large objects, air and underwater pollution monitoring, forest fire detection, transportation systems, or search and rescue after large-scale disasters. Problems that can be handled by a single multi-skilled robot may benefit from the usage of a robot team, since robustness and reliability can often be increased by combining several robots that are individually less robust and reliable. On the other hand, new problems like communication, synchronization, and cooperation come to light and require the attention of the community.

In this context, the term robot has to be intended as generic autonomous agent, so including UAVs (Unmanned Aerial Vehicles) and UUVs (Unmanned Underwater Vehicles).

Chapter 14
Distributed Probabilistic Search and Tracking of Agile Mobile Ground Targets Using a Network of Unmanned Aerial Vehicles

Liang Sun, Stanley Baek and Daniel Pack

Abstract As technologies in digital computation, sensing, wireless and wired communications, embedded systems, and micro-electro-mechanical systems continue to advance in the coming years, it is certain that we will see a variety of distributed sensor networks (DSNs) being deployed in an increasing number of systems such as power distribution systems, engineering structures and buildings, smart homes, environmental monitoring systems, biomedical systems, military systems, and others. In addition, unlike the traditional networks of sensors, the mobility afforded by autonomous systems, embedded systems, and humans who carry smart sensing devices will contribute in creating new and exciting future sensor networks. These future networks of sensors that take advantage of man-machine interactions will also introduce new applications yet unknown to us. In this paper, we present the origin and time line of DSN development, analyze the benefits and challenges of DSNs, and present a mobile sensor network in the form of an unmanned aerial vehicle (UAV) team using distributed mission area probability maps to search and track mobile ground targets. We propose a novel update strategy for the probability map used by UAVs to store probability information of dynamic target locations in the search area. Two update laws are developed to accommodate maps with different scales. Simulation results are used to demonstrate the validity of the proposed probability-map update strategy.

L. Sun (✉) · D. Pack
Department of Electrical and Computer Engineering,
The University of Texas at San Antonio, San Antonia, TX, USA
e-mail: liang.sun@utsa.edu

D. Pack
e-mail: daniel.pack@utsa.edu

S. Baek
Department of Electrical and Computer Engineering, The University of Michigan, Dearborn, MI, USA
e-mail: stanbaek@umich.edu

P. Spagnolo et al. (eds.), *Human Behavior Understanding in Networked Sensing*,
DOI 10.1007/978-3-319-10807-0_14

14.1 Introduction

Sensors perceive real-world by capturing physical phenomena and converting them into electric signals. Combining these sensors, integrating them into a network of sensors, and applying its capability to applications, which benefit from synergistic sensor information, are the key functions of sensor networks. Today, a network of sensors, mostly static, detects catastrophic infrastructure failures, conserves precious natural resources, increases economic productivity, enhances security, and enables new applications such as context-aware systems and smart home technologies [1]. New sensor network technologies are also beginning to emerge with mobile sensor platforms, allowing smart and dynamic sensor placement in response to changing environment [2].

14.1.1 History of Distributed Sensor Networks

The origin of sensor networks can be traced back to defense applications developed during the Cold War. The Sound Surveillance System (SOSUS), a system of acoustic sensors at the bottom of the ocean, was deployed by the United States to detect and track submarines [3]. This system was later used by the National Oceanographic and Atmospheric Administration (NOAA) to monitor the migration patterns of whales and seismic signals indicating pending earthquakes [4, 5]. Sensor networks of air defense radars were also deployed during the Cold War era to defend England, the continental United States and Canada. Although research was focused on satisfying particular mission needs—in the case of SOSUS, acoustic signal processing and interpretation, tracking and fusion—these research produced some key technologies for modern sensor networks [6].

The research on distributed sensor networks was catalyzed around 1980 with the Distributed Sensor Network (DSN) project sponsored by the Defense Advanced Research Projects Agency (DARPA). By this time, the ARPAnet (the predecessor of the Internet) had been operational for a number of years, with about 200 hosts at universities and research institutions [6]. Focused on distributed computing, signal processing, and tracking, the DSNs postulated the possibility of spatially distributed sensing nodes designed to operate in a collaborative manner [3]. To support the distributed systems, in the late 1980s, researchers at Carnegie-Mellon University developed a communication oriented operating system kernel, Accent, to support transparent access and fault-tolerant behavior of a DSN [7, 8].

Recent advances in inexpensive low-power microprocessors, wireless networking, and micro-electro-mechanical systems (MEMS) technologies have accelerated the development of wireless sensor networks. The DARPA's Sensor Information Technology (SensIT) program focused on the development of a new class of software for networks of distributed microsensors. The program pursued two key thrusts: (a) development of novel networking techniques for rapidly deployable ad hoc microsensors in the battlefield, and (b) leveraging the distributed computing resources to extract right and timely information from a sensor field, including detection, classification, and tracking of targets [9].

In 1993, the University of California, Los Angeles initiated development of Wireless Integrated Network Sensors (WINS). Combining sensing, signal processing, decision making, and wireless networking capabilities in a compact, low power system, WINS was developed for monitoring and control capabilities of transportation, manufacturing, health care, environmental, and safety and security systems [11]. The advances in integrated circuit technology at the same time enabled mass production of powerful compact sensors, radios, and processors at low cost. One of the achievements of WINS is the demonstration of the feasibility of algorithms for operation of multihop wireless sensor nodes and networks at micropower level [12, 13].

In the late 1990s, the Smart Dust research project at Berkeley pursued fabrication of sensor nodes incorporating a power supply and sensing, communication, and computing hardware in a volume less than a few cubic millimeters [14, 15]. Thanks to ongoing breakthroughs in nanofabrication techniques, these sensor nodes (or motes) are expected to be the size of a grain of sand in the near future. After completion of the Smart Dust research project in 2001, as shown in Fig. 14.1, the project led to multiple follow-on research projects such as Network Embedded Systems Technology (NEST) [16], Wireless Embedded Systems (WEBS) [17], and Center for Embedded Networked Sensing (CENS) [18].

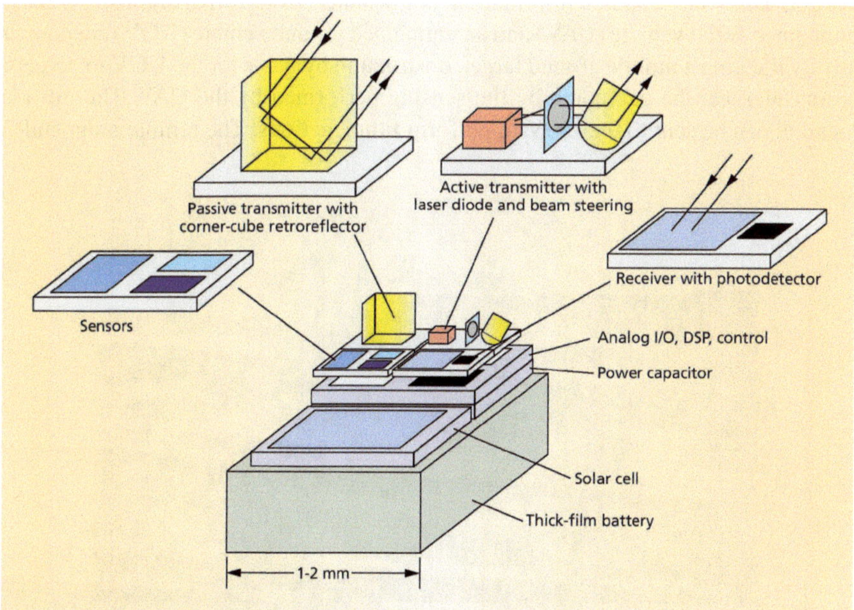

Fig. 14.1 Conceptual diagram showing a Smart Dust mote's major components: a power system, sensors, an optical transceiver, and an integrated circuit (Courtesy of [10])

14.1.2 Benefits and Challenges of Distributed Sensor Networks

In the family of DSNs, mobile DSNs have been widely used in applications for environment monitoring [19], target tracking [20, 21], and search and rescue missions [22]. Mobile sensor nodes offer advantages over static sensor networks since mobile agents can control the coverage and connectivity of the network. A typical mobile DSN consists of sensor nodes that can autonomously relocate and continuously sense, compute, and communicate. Nodes in a mobile DSN are typically scattered in space to collect information using dynamic topologies. Due to the limited communication range of sensors, however, collected information can be communicated only when each two nodes are within a communication range. Another characteristic of mobile DSNs is data distribution. In a static DSN, data can be distributed using fixed routing or flooding, while dynamic routing is used in a mobile DSN [23].

Mobile DSNs offer capabilities of distributed wireless remote sensing and processing, which translate to an improved survivability and adaptation in any environment. It is extremely difficult, for example, to conduct precise manual deployment of sensor networks for damage assessment in disaster areas or for intelligence, surveillance and reconnaissance (ISR) missions over a remote, dangerous battlefield. Nevertheless, mobile sensor nodes can proceed to areas of interest after initial deployment to complete required missions. In a surveillance and tracking mission, mobile autonomous sensor nodes can collaborate and make decisions, distributed or central, based on the shared information. For instance, as shown in Fig. 14.2, when an unmanned aerial vehicle (UAV) and an unmanned ground vehicle (UGV) are cooperatively tracking a mobile ground target, obstruction by walls for the UGV to perceive an intruder, can be overcome by the sensing performed by the UAV. The intruder location can be sent to the UGV to perform future actions. The remote independent

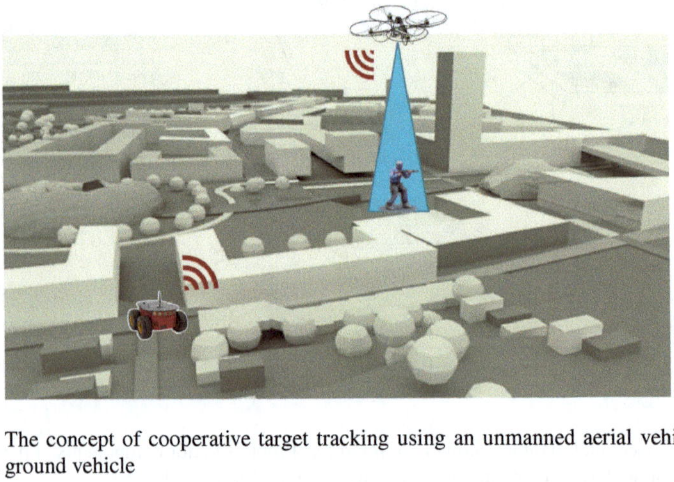

Fig. 14.2 The concept of cooperative target tracking using an unmanned aerial vehicle and an unmanned ground vehicle

processing capability of DSNs also increases the mission robustness. The advance of cooperative data fusion techniques, such as consensus and auction algorithms, enables a DSN to quickly combine information collected by distributed sensors.

Distributed mobile sensor networks, with their advantages, come with challenges and constraints. Challenges include deployment of resources, localization of platforms, self-organization for missions, navigation and control, allocation of tasks, energy consumption, maintenance of capabilities, and distributed data processes.

14.1.3 Cooperative Search and Tracking for Mobile Targets

Searching of mobile targets in an area using a mobile sensor network with unknown a priori target information is a challenging task. A typical formulation of confidence indicating target locations within a search area requires a grid map and an assignment of each cell in the grid with a probability value between 0 and 1. The resulting map is referred to as a probability map, which has been widely used in the past for target search and tracking. In this paper, we present a technique for cooperative search and tracking of mobile targets by a team of UAVs using probability maps. In particular, a novel strategy for updating a probability map by each agent of the sensor network is presented and validated using MATLAB simulations.

In the past, probability maps have been adopted by researchers working in the area of target search and tracking. Bertuccelli and How [24] presented a statistical framework to calculate a minimum observation time required for an agent to achieve a desired confidence level for the existence of a stationary target. They extended their work in [25] by working with slow moving targets (top speed 2 m/s). A binary value (0 or 1) was assigned to each cell based on detection results. Since agents of the network must work with independent maps, a consistent map among agents was required to store the information. Bourgault et al. [26] proposed a decentralized search strategy for a team of sensor platforms to locate a lost target based on the Bayesian rule. An optimal path planning algorithm was presented to maximize the cumulative probability of target detection. The work was extended for multiple target search [22] and tracking missions [27]. Detailed vehicle, process and observation models were adopted in [28] to validate the proposed strategy. In these scenarios, the prediction and update of a probability map were performed by a recursive Bayesian filter. However, a priori information of a lost target, such as the target's top speed and a last reported location, was assumed known. Millet et al. [29] developed a decentralized search algorithm for stationary targets. Each agent updates its individual probability map based on its observation using the Bayesian rule and performs the map fusion when other neighbors enter a space within its communication range. Mirzaei et al. [30] proposed a decentralized cooperative search and coverage algorithm for stationary targets, in which a probability map was updated using a Bayesian filter. To solve the coverage problem, the entire search region was partitioned into a Vironoi diagram and a dynamic programming method was used to obtain optimal paths for mission vehicles. Chung et al. [31] presented a framework for search and identification of multiple heterogeneous moving targets. The detection and identification formulation and update are conducted separately using the Bayesian rule. A centralized map was required to perform the optimization of the path planning and target identification. The study exposed the scalability issue for a large search area. Hu et al. [32] developed a decentralized search algorithm for stationary targets. A nonlinear transformation of a probability map was performed to reduce the communication bandwidth and a consensus-based fusion algorithm was proposed. A coverage control strategy, similar to the one used in [30], was adopted for the path planning. Finally, the asynchronous issue of the data fusion was studied.

Among the previous work for target search and tracking, the research for stationary targets has been well documented [24, 29, 30, 32], while for the ones working with moving targets, some a priori information was usually assumed known [27, 31]. A search task involving multiple moving targets using multiple sensor platforms without a priori information of targets, however, has not been well studied. The current work aims to contribute toward this unexplored area of research.

Suppose there is an unknown number of mobile ground targets to be searched and tracked by a team of unmanned aerial vehicles with gimbaled video sensors. We assume that the number of UAVs is insufficient with respect to the size of the mission area to perform a sweep search. The objective of the mission is to search for, locate, and track as many targets as possible in a mission area. To formulate the problem, we provide each UAV with a probability map of the mission area divided into cells and assign values between 0 and 1 to represent the target existence in each cell. A novel decentralized uncertainty propagation law is developed to globally update the individual probability map of each UAV by spreading the location uncertainty of mobile targets in a cell onto its neighbors using a conservative heuristic method. A measurement update step is then conducted to regionally update the probability values of cells in regions exposed by collective sensors of the UAV team. The effectiveness of the proposed strategy is validated in simulations when it was incorporated in a path planning strategy [33, 34] for search mission.

In this chapter, the shared information among UAVs is assumed to be UAV states and video sensor measurements. Sensors are assumed to have the same accuracy, and communications among UAVs are assumed to be robust, allowing UAVs to have identical probability maps throughout the search mission.

The rest of the paper is structured as follows. Section 14.2 introduces the notations used to formulate the search problem. A novel update law using a probability map in a multi-mobile-target search and tracking problem is developed in Sect. 14.3. In Sect. 14.4, algorithms for cooperative search and tracking along with the strategy for sensor placement are briefly presented. Section 14.5 presents the simulation results to validate the proposed update law for the probability map. The conclusion of our work is given in Sect. 14.6.

14.2 Problem Statement

The search area, $\mathbb{A}$, is assumed to be a plane ground and is mapped onto a set of M grid cells, $\{(x, y) \in \mathbb{A} | 0 \leq x \leq B_x, 0 \leq y \leq B_y\}$, each of which is an $\ell \times \ell$ square, where x and y are the Cartesian coordinates of the center of each cell, respectively, B_x and B_y are the boundaries of the region in the x and y directions, and ℓ is the length of the cell.

We first define the following events.

- $E_{x,y,k}$: A target is actually in cell (x, y) at time step k.
- $D_{x,y,k,i}$: A target is detected in cell (x, y) at time step k by agent i.

Each cell in $\mathbb{A}$ is associated with a probability of target existence at time step k, modeled as a Bernoulli distribution

$$\mathscr{P}\left(E_{x,y,k}\right) = q = 1 - \mathscr{P}\left(\overline{E}_{x,y,k}\right),$$

where a bar above an event denotes its complement. Then target existence can be modeled as

$$\text{Target existence} = \begin{cases} \text{A target is present} & q > 0.5, \\ \text{Unknown} & q = 0.5, \\ \text{No target is present} & q < 0.5. \end{cases} \tag{14.1}$$

Suppose that n UAVs with unique IDs, U_i, $i = 1, 2, \ldots, n$, fly above a search area with constant velocities and constant altitudes, which are assumed to be different among UAVs to avoid collisions. The position of UAV i at time step k is denoted as $\mathbf{p}^u_{i,k} \triangleq \left(p^u_{i,k,x}, p^u_{i,k,y}, p^u_{i,k,z}\right)^T \in \mathbb{R}^{3\times 1}$. UAV i also maintains an individual probability map, with an initial probability value of each cell set to 0.5, indicating we are not sure of target existence. At each time step the camera sensor of agent i captures an image of the area, $\Omega_{i,k}$. UAV i is equipped with a pan-tilt camera sensor with a limited field of view (FOV), μ_i, and a limited sensing radius, R_i. The footprint of the sensor on the ground is obtained by first projecting the camera field of view (μ_i) onto the ground and then confining it by the sensing range (R_i), as shown in Fig. 14.3. At time step k, each agent i independently takes a measurement over the sensor exposure area, $\Omega_{i,k}$, denoted as the shaded region in Fig. 14.3.

The number of targets and a priori information, such as locations and movement patterns, are assumed unknown, while the target's top speed, $V^{\max}_{\text{target}}$, is assumed to be known. The target size is assumed large enough to be identified by sensors with a predefined detection probability when it enters on exposure area of the sensor.

Given the above definitions and assumptions, the problem we seek to solve is a distributed update law for the probability map on each agent based on sensor measurements. We present, in the next section, a heuristic strategy for each cell in the probability map to propagate its probability values based on the uncertainty values

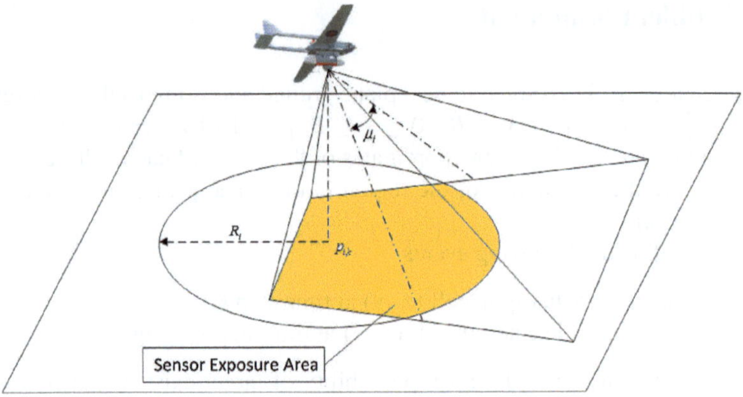

Fig. 14.3 Sensor exposure area (*shaded area*) of a UAV at $\mathbf{p}_{i,k}$ equipped with a pan-tilt video sensor with a field of view of μ_i and a limited sensing range R_i

of its neighboring cells in the previous time step. The probability values of cells in the sensor exposure area is then updated according to the measurement outcomes, such as detection or absence of targets.

14.3 Probability Map Update

For static target search, the target presence probability in a cell depends on the number of "looks" committed over the cell by a UAV team. However, when searching mobile targets in an area without a priori information, such as the number of targets and potential target locations, update rules for static search are not valid any more. In this section, we present a heuristic strategy of updating the probability map for mobile target search and tracking.

At each time step, every UAV first applies an uncertainty propagation step to update the probability value of each cell of its probability map. Depending on sensor detection results, "No target detected" or "Target detected", a measurement update step is then applied to update the probability values for cells that fall in the sensor exposure region.

14.3.1 Uncertainty Propagation Step

Since we have no a priori information, each cell with probability 0.5 may contain a target. We can designate the maximum speed of a target, $V_{\text{target}}^{\max}$, but the orientation of the target movement is unknown. Assuming that the step size of updating the probability map is T_s, the target existence probability of cell (x, y), at time k, will

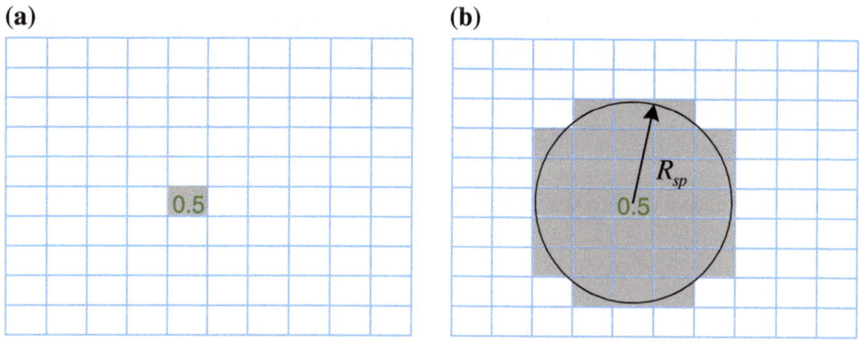

Fig. 14.4 Probability map update for a cell with the probability value of 0.5. **a** Time step k: before the update. **b** Time step $k+1$: after the update

spread, at time $k+1$, to its neighbors. This event can be described by a circle, whose center is at (x, y) and whose radius is $R_{\text{sp}} = V_{\text{target}}^{\max} T_s$, as shown in Fig. 14.4. The first update step of the probability in each cell is expressed as

$$\mathscr{P}_{i,k+1}(x, y) = 0.5, \quad \forall (x, y) \in \mathbb{C}, \tag{14.2}$$

$$\mathbb{C} \triangleq \left\{(x, y) \mid \left\|(x, y) - \left(x', y'\right)\right\| \le R_{\text{sp}}\right\},$$

where $\left(x', y'\right)$ is the coordinate of the center of a cell that satisfies

$$\mathscr{P}_{i,k}\left(x', y'\right) = 0.5. \tag{14.3}$$

The uncertainty propagation step can be explained as follows: at time step k, if a cell has a probability value of 0.5 (unknown target existence), the probability will spread to its neighboring cells at time $k+1$. The maximum traveling distance of a potential target equals to R_{sp}, and the area in which the potential target may stay can be expressed by a circle, defined by $\mathbb{C}$ in Eq. (14.2). Thus, at time step $k+1$, each cell in the region defined by the circle with radius R_{sp} would have an equal probability of holding that potential target. Therefore, this uncertainty should be spread out using the conservative manner in Eq. (14.2).

An issue would arise if the size of the cell (ℓ) is greater than the spreading pace (R_{sp}), which implies that one time step is not long enough to spread the probability neighboring cells. In this case, the probability value of the neighboring cells can be gradually changed to reflect the uncertainty spread. The following strategy can be used to update the probability map for such a case. The time to spread the uncertainty from a cell with probability value of 0.5 over the cells next to it can be calculated by

$$T_{\text{sp}} = \frac{\ell}{R_{\text{sp}}} T_s = \frac{\ell}{V_{\text{target}}^{\max}},$$

where ℓ is the side length defining the cell size. The probability change of neighboring cells at each step toward 0.5 can be calculated by

$$\mathscr{P}_{\text{unit}} = \frac{0.5}{T_{\text{sp}}} = \frac{0.5V_{\text{target}}^{\max}}{\ell}. \tag{14.4}$$

Then an alternative update law is given by

$$\begin{aligned} \mathscr{P}_{i,k+1}(x,y) &= \mathscr{P}_{i,k}(x,y) + \mathscr{P}_{\text{unit}} \cdot \text{sgn}\left(0.5 - \mathscr{P}_{i,k}(x,y)\right), \ \forall (x,y) \in \mathbb{C}, \\ \mathbb{C} &\triangleq \left\{(x,y) \mid \left\|(x,y) - \left(x',y'\right)\right\| \leq \ell\right\}, \\ \mathscr{P}_{i,k}\left(x',y'\right) &= 0.5, \end{aligned} \tag{14.5}$$

where

$$\text{sgn}(z) = \begin{cases} 1 & z > 0, \\ 0 & z = 0, \\ -1 & z < 0. \end{cases}$$

14.3.2 Measurement Update

After the uncertainty propagation step, the post process of updating the probability map will be conducted separately in two different scenarios: no detection or detection of targets. The next subsections present the detailed procedures.

14.3.2.1 No Target Detected

When no target is found at time step $k+1$ in region $\Omega_{i,k+1}$, the probability of the cells therein is updated using the following Bayesian rule [30]

$$\mathscr{P}\left(E_{x,y,k+1} | \overline{D}_{x,y,k+1,i}\right) = \frac{\mathscr{P}\left(E_{x,y,k+1}\right)\mathscr{P}\left(\overline{D}_{x,y,k+1,i} | E_{x,y,k+1}\right)}{\mathscr{P}\left(\overline{D}_{x,y,k+1,i}\right)}, \ (x,y) \in \Omega_{i,k+1}.$$

The probability values of the cells outside $\Omega_{i,k+1}$ remain the same. Define the probability of true positive and false positive sensor measurements as two constants, $\alpha \triangleq \mathscr{P}\left(D_{x,y,k+1,i} | E_{x,y,k+1}\right)$ and $\beta \triangleq \mathscr{P}\left(D_{x,y,k+1,i} | \overline{E}_{x,y,k+1}\right)$, respectively. The probability that a target is not detected in the cell (x,y), $\mathscr{P}\left(\overline{D}_{x,y,k+1,i}\right)$, can be calculated by [30]

$$\begin{aligned}\mathscr{P}\left(\overline{D}_{x,y,k+1,i}\right) &= \mathscr{P}\left(\overline{D}_{x,y,k+1,i}|E_{x,y,k+1}\right)\mathscr{P}\left(E_{x,y,k+1}\right)\\ &\quad+\mathscr{P}\left(\overline{D}_{x,y,k+1,i}|\overline{E}_{x,y,k+1}\right)\mathscr{P}\left(\overline{E}_{x,y,k+1}\right)\\ &= (1-\alpha)\,\mathscr{P}\left(E_{x,y,k+1}\right)+(1-\beta)\left(1-\mathscr{P}\left(E_{x,y,k+1}\right)\right).\end{aligned}$$

14.3.2.2 Target Detected

When targets are detected in region $\Omega_{i,k}$, each target will be associated with a dynamic model whose motion is predicted and updated using a Kalman filter. Target detection algorithms are assumed to be capable of distinguishing two targets that are next to each other.

Let the location and the velocity of a target at time k be $\mathbf{p}_k^t \triangleq \left(p_{k,x}^t, p_{k,y}^t\right)^T \in \mathbb{R}^{2\times 1}$ and $\mathbf{v}_k^t \triangleq \left(v_{k,x}^t, v_{k,y}^t\right)^T \in \mathbb{R}^{2\times 1}$, respectively. Selecting the system state as $\chi_k = \left(\left(\mathbf{p}_k^t\right)^T, \left(\mathbf{v}_k^t\right)^T\right)^T$ and system output at time step k as $\phi_k = \chi_k$, and assuming that the unknown system input is zero, the target dynamics is given by

$$\begin{aligned}\chi_{k+1} &= A\chi_k + \xi_k\\ \phi_k &= C\chi_k + \eta_k,\end{aligned}$$

$$A = \begin{pmatrix} 1 & 0 & T_s & 0\\ 0 & 1 & 0 & T_s\\ 0 & 0 & 1 & 0\\ 0 & 0 & 0 & 1\end{pmatrix},\quad C = \begin{pmatrix} 1 & 0 & 0 & 0\\ 0 & 1 & 0 & 0\end{pmatrix},$$

where ξ_k is the process noise at time step k, representing modeling error and disturbances on the system, and η_k is the measurement noise at time step k, representing the sensor noise [35]. The random variables ξ_k and η_k are zero-mean Gaussian random processes with covariances Q and R, respectively.

Defining the estimated state of χ as $\hat{\chi}$ and the estimation covariance at time k as P_k, the prediction step of the Kalman filter is given by [36]

$$\begin{aligned}\hat{\chi}_k^- &= A\hat{\chi}_{k-1}^+\\ P_k^- &= AP_{k-1}^+A^T + Q,\end{aligned}$$

where the superscripts $-$ and $+$ represent the variable values obtained before and after the update step, respectively. Defining the Kalman gain at time step k as L_k, when a measurement is available, the update step of the Kalman filter is given by

$$L_k = P_k^- C^T \left(C P_k^- C^T + R \right)^{-1}$$
$$P_k^+ = (I - L_k C) P_k^-$$
$$\hat{\chi}_k^+ = \hat{\chi}_k^- + L_k \left(\phi_k - C \hat{\chi}_k^- \right),$$

where I is an identity matrix.

Let the standard deviations of state estimates in the x and y directions be σ_x and σ_y, respectively, which are assumed $\sigma_x = \sigma_y$. For a Gaussian distribution, 99.73 % of the realization lies within three standard deviations of the mean [37]. Select a circular region

$$\mathbb{F} \triangleq \left\{ (x, y) \mid \left(x - \hat{p}_{k,x}^t \right)^2 + \left(y - \hat{p}_{k,y}^t \right)^2 \leq (3\sigma_x)^2 \right\},$$

whose center is at the estimated position of the target and whose radius is three times of standard deviation of the position estimation, $3\sigma_x$ (or $3\sigma_y$). Select the values for a Gaussian distribution in region $\mathbb{F}$ and rescale these values to the range [0.5, 1]. The highest value of the resulting cell in the region represents the highest confidence of target existence, while the cells with probability close to 0.5 reveal a relative low possibility of target existence. Probability values of the cells in region $\mathbb{F}$ are then updated using the scaled values accordingly.

14.4 Sensor Management and Path Planning for Search and Tracking

The objective of search is to maximize the possibility of detecting targets in the region of interest, while the objective of tracking is to minimize the overall uncertainty of target locations, i.e., the trace of the estimation covariance matrix [35] of the targets, which have been found. For UAVs equipped with pan-tilt video sensors, two tasks need to be solved: the sensor management, i.e., which orientation the sensor should point towards, and the path planning.

14.4.1 Search Mode

Until a target is found, UAVs operate in the search mode. Due to the projection distortion effect of video sensors, the gimbal is commanded to consistently point downward to obtain the best resolution of the image. For the path planning algorithm, we use the guidance law for multiple UAVs searching multiple mobile targets, reported in [33, 34]. The desired heading angle of UAV i, ψ_i, can be calculated by the following equation.

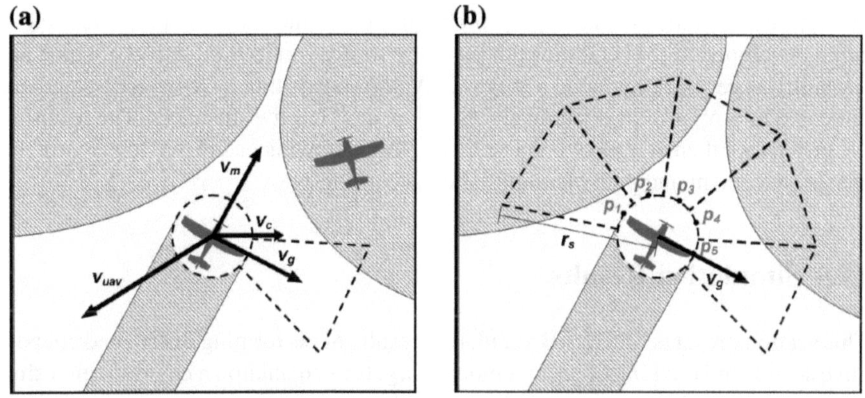

Fig. 14.5 An optimal path planning algorithm for cooperative target search. **a** The four vectors involved in the determination of the desired heading of a UAV. **b** The unitary vector v_g points in the direction of the *trapezoid-shaped* segment (one out of five in this case) with the highest probability of target detection (*white area*) [33]

$$\psi_i = \omega_g v_g + \omega_{\mathrm{UAV}} v_{\mathrm{UAV}} + \omega_c v_c + \omega_m v_m, \tag{14.6}$$

where v_g is the goal vector that points in the direction of the area around the UAV that has the largest probability of finding a target, as depicted in Fig. 14.5; v_{UAV} is a vector responsible for UAV to UAV collision avoidance; v_c is a vector used to maintain the UAV within a predetermined search area by operating as an obstacle avoidance vector that concerns itself only with search boundaries within a radial comfort range around the UAV; v_m is a momentum vector that incorporates in ψ_i to maintain the previous heading; and ω_g, ω_{UAV}, ω_c, and ω_m are corresponding weights for aforementioned vectors, respectively.

A set of optimized weights is given in [33] as $\omega_g = 0.63$, $\omega_{\mathrm{UAV}} = 0.26$, $\omega_c = 0.27$, and $\omega_m = 0.03$. It can be seen that the largest weight ω_g makes v_g play the most significant role among vectors in Eq. (14.6) of determining the desired heading angle for UAV i. Therefore, a proper dynamic probability map is essential for a UAV team to maximize the probability of detecting targets in a search area.

14.4.2 Tracking Mode

When a target is found, UAVs switch to the tracking mode. It is noted that there are other operating modes, such as validating target, re-acquiring target, and approaching target, which are beyond the scope of this work. For a UAV tracking multiple targets, sensor management plays a significant part in decreasing the uncertainty of target states. The path planning algorithm for UAVs to cooperatively track multiple mobile targets is also a challenging problem. To use the sensor management algorithm developed in [38] and the path planning strategy in [39] effectively, which are for multi-target tracking using a single UAV, the targets that have been detected are allocated into N_u groups dynamically based on their relative distances. The resulting N_u groups are then assigned to the nearest UAVs' allowing each UAV to perform the sensor placement and path planning tasks, accordingly.

14.5 Simulation Results

This section presents MATLAB simulation results of performing distributed cooperative search and tracking of ground mobile targets in an unknown environment using a team of two UAVs. As shown in Fig. 14.6, the mission area of search and tracking targets and allowed flying zone are enclosed by two large (black and red, respectively) rectangles. Two search areas, a circular region on the left and a rectangular region on the right (blue lines), are specified by a user. Two UAVs are commanded out from the home position (the origin) toward the search areas for a search and track mission. Each UAV is depicted as a small colored circle. The gray thin tail attached to each UAV represents the historical UAV trajectory. The gray rectangle around the head of each UAV represents the sensor exposure area. In Fig. 14.6, the UAVs are in the "Fly to Search Area" mode, so the gimbal is regulated pointing downward, resulting in square sensor exposure areas. In this simulation, a total of three targets, shown as small colored rectangles, are making random walk movements in the mission area. The two subfigures arranged vertically on the right side are probability maps for the two UAVs, respectively. The probability values are displayed using a "gray" colormap defined in MATLAB, which maps value 0 to color black, value 1 to color white, and value 0.5 to color gray. The title line of each probability map shows the unique UAV ID and its current mode.

Key parameters used in the simulation are presented in Table 14.1. The simulation step size T_S was selected as 0.3 s. The actual top speed of the targets in the simulation

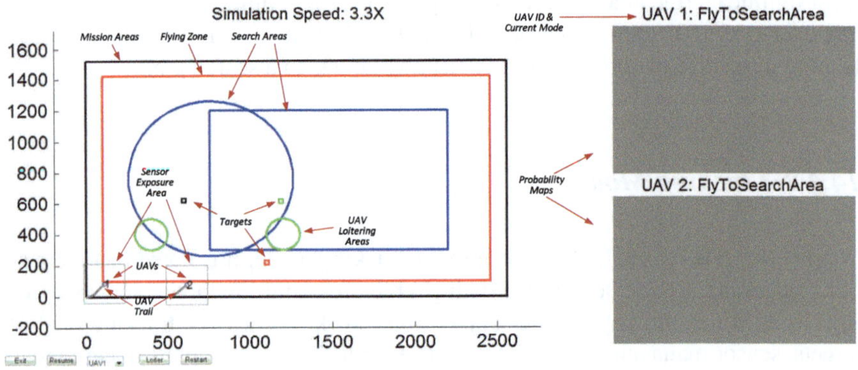

Fig. 14.6 Simulation snapshot: initialization

Table 14.1 Simulation parameters

Map size		UAVs	
Mission area (m^2)	2,560 × 1,520	Speed (m/s)	20
Flying zone (m^2)	2,360 × 1,320	Minimum turning radius (m)	100
Cell size (m^2)	20 × 20	Sensor range radius (m)	300
Search area 1 (m^2)	$\pi \cdot 500^2$	Sensor FOV (deg)	56
Search area 2 (m^2)	1,440 × 900	Sensor slew rate (deg/s)	150

was 10 m/s. R_{sp} is then calculated as 3 m, which is smaller than the side length of the cell, ℓ (20 m). Therefore, the update law (14.5) should be used. The spread pace $\mathscr{P}_{unit}$ is then calculated by using Eq. (14.4) as $\mathscr{P}_{unit} = 0.075$. The probability map is recursively updated at each time step by using the strategy proposed in Sect. 14.3. To simplify the calculation, we select $\alpha = 1$ and $\beta = 0$ in the simulation.

Figures 14.7 and 14.8 present a series of snapshots of the simulation run in which two UAVs searched and tracked three targets in an unknown area. To simplify the problem, UAVs are assumed to communicate all of their knowledge regarding targets

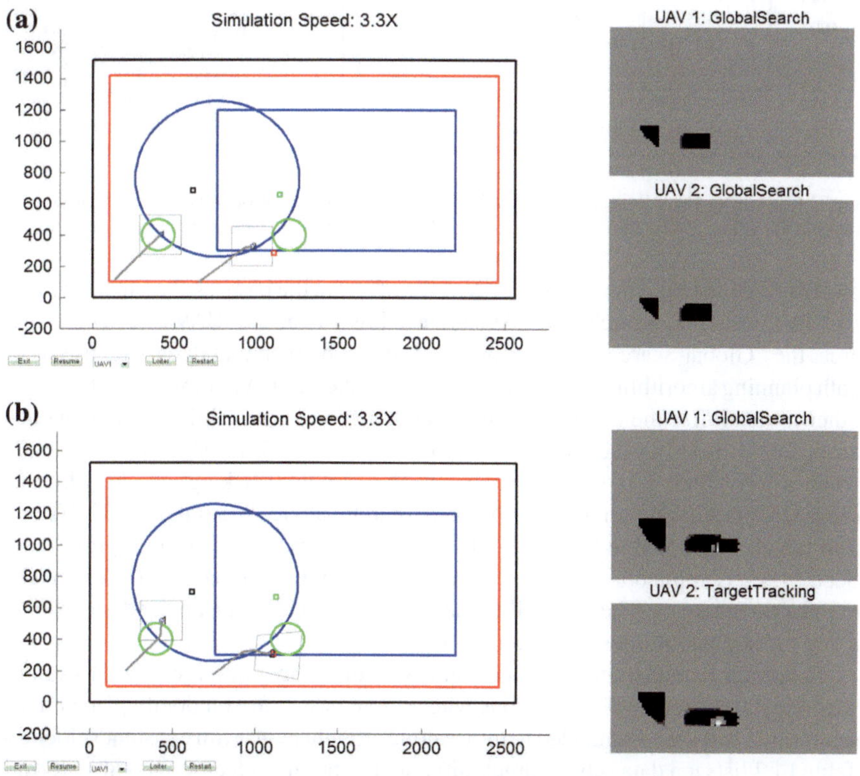

Fig. 14.7 Group one of simulation snapshots: search and tracking of three mobile targets using two UAVs. **a** UAVs enter search areas ($t = 10$ s). **b** One UAV finds a target ($t = 11$ s)

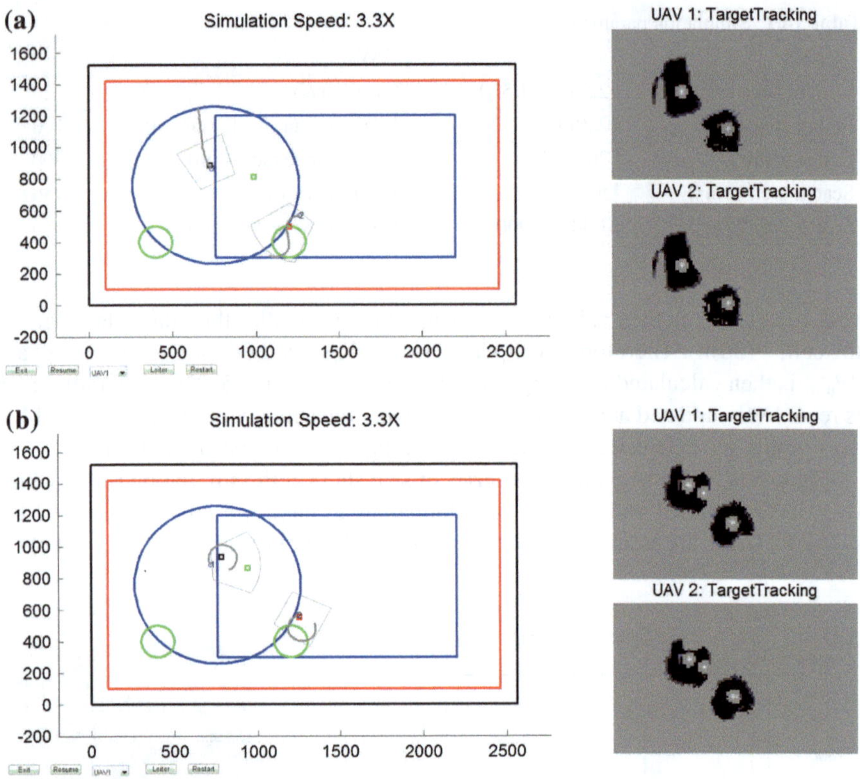

Fig. 14.8 Group two of simulation snapshots: search and tracking of three mobile targets using two UAVs. **a** Two UAVs find two targets. ($t = 30$ s). **b** Two UAVs track three targets. ($t = 66$ s)

and the UAV status. After the two UAVs take off from the base, as shown in Fig. 14.6, they fly toward their search areas. As shown in Fig. 14.7a, after UAVs reach the search area, the "Global Search" mode is initiated. It can be seen that due to the use of the path planning algorithm proposed in Sect. 14.4.1, the two UAVs move apart from each other to maximize the coverage of the search area. The probability map is updated accordingly by using the strategy described in Sect. 14.3. As shown in Fig. 14.7b, when a UAV finds a target, it switches to the "Target Tracking" mode, while the other UAV is still operating in the "Global Search" mode. When the two UAVs both find targets, as shown in Fig. 14.8a, the cooperative tracking algorithm proposed in Sect. 14.4.2 is applied accordingly. Figures 14.8b shows that the two UAVs are able to track three targets. The probability maps of the two UAVs are updated accordingly using the strategy proposed in Sect. 14.3.

To further demonstrate the effectiveness of the proposed target search strategy, we conducted a series of simulations where three targets are randomly placed in the search area and are commanded to move along straight paths with constant velocities. Table 14.2 lists ten data sets of target initial locations and velocities and time periods that the UAV team took to locate the targets. However, when a UAV detects a target,

Table 14.2 Simulation configuration for two UAVs to perform search and track missions

Target initial locations (m)	Target velocities (m/s)	Time (s)
(2300, 1300), (2300, 1300), (2300, 1300)	(−2, 0), (−4, −2), (0, −5)	106
(600, 600), (1100, 200), (1200, 600)	(0, 4), (−0.5, 5), (−3, −3)	29
(200, 200), (800, 200), (600, 300)	(2, 1), (0.5, 3), (1, 5)	135
(1500, 800), (1500, 800), (1500, 800)	(−2, 1), (3, 3), (5, −5)	128
(100, 100), (200, 1300), (2300, 200)	(5, 4), (5, −2), (−4, 2)	21
(350, 100), (200, 900), (1000, 500)	(5, 0), (4, −1), (3, 2)	90
(500, 800), (500, 800), (500, 800)	(5, 0), (4, −1), (3, 2)	83
(1300, 1300), (1300, 1300), (1300, 1300)	(0, −5), (2, −5), (−3, −4)	77
(2300, 800), (2300, 800), (2300, 800)	(−5, 0), (−4, −1), (−3, 1)	100
(1300, 1300), (2300, 800), (200, 800)	(0, −4), (−6, 0), (5, 0)	47

it switches to the tracking mode in which the UAV keeps tracking detected target(s) using the strategy introduced in Sect. 14.4.2. So the "Time" column in Table 14.2 lists the time periods starting from the beginning of the simulation until all three targets are found or until two UAVs both switch to the tracking modes. It can be seen from Table 14.2 that both UAVs are able to detect targets in all cases and the maximal time used is 135 s in a mission area with dimension of $2{,}5604 \times 1{,}520\,\mathrm{m}^2$.

14.6 Conclusion

This paper presents the use of mobile sensor network to search and track multiple mobile targets in an unknown area. The network is made of a team of UAVs equipped with pan-tilt video sensors. We introduced a novel update strategy for the probability map used by UAVs to store probability information of target locations in the search area. Two update laws are proposed to accommodate maps with different scales. The simulation results show the rationality of the proposed probability-map update strategy. The future work will focus on the comparison study and cooperative tracking guidance law for multiple UAVs.

References

1. Dargie W, Poellabauer C (2011) Fundamentals of wireless sensor networks: theory and practice. Wiley, New York
2. Estrin D, Girod L, Pottie G, Srivastava M (2001) Instrumenting the world with wireless sensor networks. In IEEE international conference on acoustics, speech, and signal processing (ICASSP), vol 4, pp 2033–2036
3. Sohraby K, Minoli D, Znati T (2007) Wireless sensor networks: technology, protocols, and applications. Wiley, Hoboken
4. Bryan C, Nishimura C (1995) Monitoring oceanic earthquakes with SOSUS: an example from the caribbean. Oceanography 8(1):4–10

5. Nishimura C, Conlon D (1994) IUSS dual use: monitoring whales and earthquakes using SOSUS. Mar Technol Soc J 27(4):13–21
6. Chong C, Kumar S (2003) Sensor networks: evolution, opportunities, and challenges. Proc IEEE 91(8):1247–1256
7. Rashid R, Julin D, Orr D, Sanzi R, Baron R, Forin A, Golub D, Jones M (1989) Mach: a system software kernel. In: IEEE computer society international conference: intellectual leverage, digest of papers, Feb 1989, pp 176–178
8. Rashid RF, Robertson GG (1981) Accent: a communication oriented network operating system kernel, vol 15, New York, pp 64–75
9. Kumar S, Shepherd D (1993) SensIT: sensor information technology for the warfighter. In: Proceedings of 4th international conference on information fusion, pp TuC1-2–TuC1-9
10. Warneke B, Last M, Liebowitz B, Pister KSJ (2001) Smart Dust: communicating with a cubic-millimeter computer. Computer 34(1):44–51
11. Asada G, Dong M, Lin TS, Newberg F, Pottie G, Kaiser WJ, Marcy HO (1998) Wireless integrated network sensors: low power systems on a chip. In: Proceedings of the 24th European solid-state circuits conference, Sept 1998, pp 9–16
12. Agre JR, Clare LP, Pottie GJ, Romanov NP (1999) Development platform for self-organizing wireless sensor networks. In: Aerosense 1999, Orlando, April 1999
13. Pottie GJ, Kaiser WJ (2000) Wireless integrated network sensors. Commun ACM 43(5):51–58
14. Kahn JM, Katz RH, Pister KSJ (1999) Next century challenges: mobile networking for smart dust. In: International conference on mobile computing and networking, pp 271–278
15. Kahn JM, Katz RH, Pister KSJ (2000) Emerging challenges: mobile networking for smart dust. J Commun Netw 2(3):188–196
16. http://webs.cs.berkeley.edu/nest-index.html. Accessed on 20-May-2014
17. http://smote.cs.berkeley.edu:8000/tracenv/wiki. Accessed on 20-May-2014
18. http://research.cens.ucla.edu/research/. Accessed on 20-May-2014
19. Corke P, Wark T, Jurdak R, Hu W, Valencia P, Moore D (2010) Environmental wireless sensor networks. Proc IEEE 98(11):1903–1917
20. Atia GK, Veeravalli VV, Fuemmeler JA (2011) Sensor scheduling for energy-efficient target tracking in sensor networks. IEEE Trans Signal Process 59(10):4923–4937
21. Hongju C, Su G, Jiannan H (2012) A distributed cross-layer framework for target tracking in three-dimensional wireless sensor networks. Future wireless networks and information systems, Lecture Notes in Electrical Engineering, vol 143, Springer, Berlin, pp 653–661
22. Wong EM, Bourgault F, Furukawa T (2005) Multi-vehicle bayesian search for multiple lost targets. In: IEEE international conference on robotics and automation, Apr 2005, pp 3169–3174
23. Yick J, Mukherjee B, Ghosal D (2008) Wireless sensor network survey. Comput Netw 52(12):2292–2330
24. Bertuccelli LF, How JP (2005) Robust UAV search for environments with imprecise probability maps. In: 44th IEEE conference on decision and control and 2005 European control conference, Dec 2005, pp 5680–5685
25. Bertuccelli LF, How JP (2006) Search for dynamic targets with uncertain probability maps. In: American control conference, June 2006
26. Bourgault F, Furukawa T, Durrant-Whyte HF (2003) Coordinated decentralized search for a lost target in a Bayesian world. In: IEEE/RSJ international conference on intelligent robots and systems, vol 1, Oct 2003, pp 48–53
27. Furukawa T, Bourgault F, Lavis B, Durrant-Whyte HF (2006) Recursive Bayesian search-and-tracking using coordinated UAVs for lost targets. In: IEEE international conference on robotics and automation, May 2006, pp 2521–2526
28. Bourgault F, Furukawa T, Durrant-Whyte HF (2006) Optimal search for a lost target in a Bayesian world. Field and service robotics, Springer tracts in advanced robotics, vol 24. Springer, Berlin, pp 209–222
29. Millet PT, Casbeer DW, Mercker T, Bishop JL (2010) Multi-agent decentralized search of a probability map with communication constraints. In: AIAA guidance, navigation and control conference

30. Mirzaei M, Sharifi F, Gordon BW, Rabbath CA, Zhang YM (2011) Cooperative multi-vehicle search and coverage problem in uncertain environments. In: IEEE conference on decision and control and European control conference, Dec 2011, pp 4140–4145
31. Chung TH, Kress M, Royset JO (2009) Probabilistic search optimization and mission assignment for heterogeneous autonomous agents. In: IEEE international conference on robotics and automation, May 2009, pp 939–945
32. Hu J, Lihua X, Kai-Yew L, Xu J (2013) Multiagent information fusion and cooperative control in target search. IEEE Trans Control Syst Technol 21(4):1223–1235
33. DeLima P, Pack D (2008) Toward developing an optimal cooperative search algorithm for multiple unmanned aerial vehicles. In: International symposium on collaborative technologies and systems, May 2008, pp 506–512
34. DeLima P, Pack D, Jr Sciortino JC (2007) Optimizing a search strategy for multiple mobile agents. In: Society of photo-optical instrumentation engineers (SPIE) conference series, vol 6563
35. Beard RW, McLain TW (2012) Small unmanned aircraft: theory and practice. Princeton University Press, Princeton
36. Maybeck PS (1979) Stochastic models, estimation, and control, Mathematics in Science and Engineering. Academic press, Boston
37. Pukelsheim Friedrich (1994) The three sigma rule. Am Stat 48(2):88–91
38. Farmani N, Sun L, Pack D (2014) An optimal sensor management technique for unmanned aerial vehicles tracking multiple mobile ground targets. In: International conference on unmanned aircraft systems, Orlando, May 2014
39. Farmani N, Sun L, Pack D (2014) Optimal UAV sensor management and path planning for tracking multiple mobile targets. In: ASME 2014 dynamic system and control conferences, San Antonio, October 2014

Chapter 15
A Heterogeneous Robotic Network for Distributed Ambient Assisted Living

Antonio Petitti, Donato Di Paola, Annalisa Milella, Pier Luigi Mazzeo, Paolo Spagnolo, Grazia Cicirelli and Giovanni Attolico

Abstract Networks of robots and sensors have been recognized to be a powerful tool for developing fully automated systems that monitor environments and daily life activities in Ambient Assisted Living applications. Nevertheless, issues related to active control of heterogeneous sensors for high-level scene interpretation and mission execution are still open. This work presents the authors' ongoing research about the design and implementation of a heterogeneous robotic network that includes static cameras and multi-sensor mobile robots for distributed target tracking. The system is intended to provide robot-assisted monitoring and surveillance of large environments. The proposed solution exploits a distributed control architecture to enable the network to autonomously accomplish general-purpose and complex monitoring tasks. The nodes can both act with some degree of autonomy and cooperate with each other. The chapter describes the concepts underlying the designed system architecture and presents the results of simulations performed in a realistic scenario to validate the distributed target tracking algorithm. Preliminary experimental results obtained in a real context are also presented showing the feasibility of the proposed system.

A. Petitti (✉) · D. Di Paola · A. Milella · G. Cicirelli · G. Attolico
Institute of Intelligent Systems for Automation (ISSIA)—National Research Council (CNR), Bari, Italy
e-mail: petitti@ba.issia.cnr.it

D. Di Paola
e-mail: dipaola@ba.issia.cnr.it

A. Milella
e-mail: milella@ba.issia.cnr.it

G. Cicirelli
e-mail: grace@ba.issia.cnr.it

G. Attolico
e-mail: attolico@ba.issia.cnr.it

P.L. Mazzeo · P. Spagnolo
National Institute of Optics (INO)—National Research Council (CNR), Lecce, Italy
e-mail: pierluigi.mazzeo@ino.it

P. Spagnolo
e-mail: paolo.spagnolo@ino.it

P. Spagnolo et al. (eds.), *Human Behavior Understanding in Networked Sensing*,
DOI 10.1007/978-3-319-10807-0_15

15.1 Introduction

The development of environment and activity monitoring systems, based on heterogeneous networks of sensors, constitutes an active investigation field, with many potential applications, including safety, security, ambient intelligence and health-care assistance. In real scenarios, such as buildings, airports, road and rail networks, or sport grounds, a single sensor is not able to monitor the whole environment or to track a moving object or a person for a long period of time, due to field of view limitations. Furthermore, integrating information from multiple sensors is a basic requirement for achieving an adequate level of robustness and scalability. Typical solutions include the use of fixed camera networks that are able to cooperate to monitor wide areas and track objects beyond the capabilities of each single sensor [21]. However, fixed cameras may pose some critical limitations in large environments and wherever infrastructure preparation is expensive or unfeasible. As an alternative, mobile and multi-functional robots have been proposed as means to reduce the environment structuring and the number of devices needed to cover a given area [8]. The use of robots significantly expands the potential of monitoring systems, which can evolve from the traditional passive role, in which the system can only detect events and trigger alarms, to an active one, in which a robot can be used to interact with the environment, with humans or with other robots for more complex cooperative actions [17].

In this chapter, a Distributed Ambient Assisted Living (DAAL) system is proposed. It is based on a distributed architecture exploiting fixed and mobile heterogeneous sensors to intelligently monitor large environments and track human activities. The proposed cooperative monitoring system integrates fixed calibrated cameras with a team of autonomous mobile robots equipped with different sensors. A conceptual representation of the system is shown in Fig. 15.1. The system is being developed as part of the project BAITAH (Italian National Research Program PON-BAITAH—"Methodology and Instruments of Building Automation and Information Technology for pervasive models of treatment and Aids for domestic Healthcare"), aimed at identifying and developing ICT-based Ambient Intelligence technologies to support the independent living of fragile people in their domestic environments. In this project, mobile sensors are intended to provide two main contributions: they can supply information about the observed human target in areas that are out of the field of view of fixed cameras (thus reducing complexity and costs of the required infrastructure), and they can move close to the target to increase precision and reliability of scene analysis whenever fixed sensors are unable to provide robust estimates. In designing such a system, a major challenge is the integration of high-level decision-making issues with primitive simple behaviors for different operative scenarios. This aim requires a modular and reconfigurable system, capable of simultaneously addressing low-level reactive control, general purpose and monitoring tasks and high-level control algorithms in a distributed fashion. This chapter presents an overview of both the system architecture and the implemented algorithms.

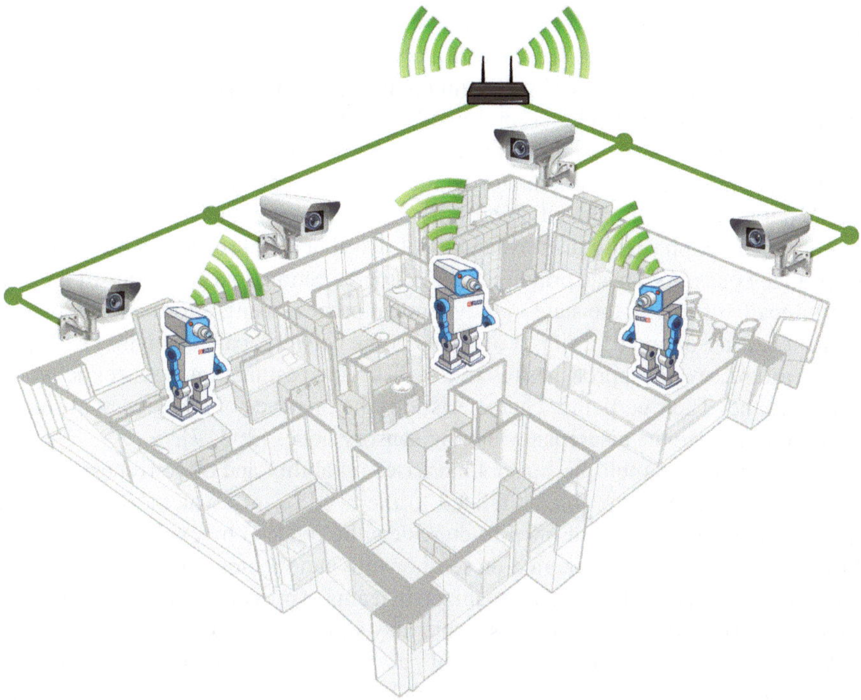

Fig. 15.1 Conceptual representation of the proposed ambient assisted living system

The remainder of the chapter is structured as follows. Section 15.2 presents related work. In Sect. 15.3 the distributed algorithmic framework for the ambient assisted living system is presented. In Sect. 15.4 details about the implementation of the system in a real-world scenario are provided. Results of simulation tests are shown in Sect. 15.5, while preliminary real-world experiments using the proposed system are described in Sect. 15.6. Finally, conclusions are drawn in Sect. 15.7.

15.2 Related Work

In the last few years, many researchers have focused their attention on Ambient Assisted Living (AAL) technologies [10, 17]. Among the several research challenges in the AAL domain, one of the main issue regards the monitoring of people activities [9]. It is easy to note that this scenario is based on an accurate and robust tracking of people in the environment. This can be achieved exploiting the most recent techniques in multi-target tracking using distributed architectures. Several papers have addressed the problem of multi-target tracking by means of distributed camera networks. In [20], for example, the Kalman–Consensus filter [14] is used in order to fuse the information coming from each camera of the network in a decentralized way. The presence of a consensus step significantly increases the system performance as shown by experimental results. In [19] an extension of [20] to wide-area scene understanding is presented. To optimize the dynamic scene analysis, a control framework for a PTZ camera network is introduced. In [21], a survey of distributed multi-camera systems for target tracking on planar surfaces is provided. In [22], a review of distributed algorithms for several computer vision applications is presented, emphasizing the advantages of distributed approaches with respect to centralized ones. As a basic principle, in distributed estimation, each node of the network locally estimates the state of a dynamical process using information provided by its local sensor and by a subset of nodes of the network, called neighbors [24]. In the literature, several approaches relative to distributed estimation in sensor networks can be found. Their particular characteristic is the presence of an agreement step in order to minimize the discrepancy among sensory nodes [2, 3, 7].

While the use of multiple sensors increases reliability and effectiveness in large environments, it poses problems related to the need of infrastructures that can be heavy and expensive. These infrastructures can be reduced by exploiting the flexibility of moving sensors mounted on semi or fully autonomous vehicles that can be employed as individual agents or organized in teams to provide intelligent distributed monitoring of broad areas. Mobile sensors may significantly expand the potential of AAL technologies beyond the traditional passive role of event detection and alarm triggering from a static point of view. Mobile robots can actively interact with the environment, with humans or with other robots to accomplish more complex cooperative actions [1, 23]. Nevertheless, mobile surveillance devices based on autonomous vehicles are still in their initial stage of development and many issues are currently under investigation [5, 6, 12].

15.3 Distributed Ambient Assisted Living

In this chapter a Distributed Ambient Assisted Living (DAAL) framework is introduced. The proposed DAAL system is a multi-agent[1] heterogeneous network for distributed monitoring of people in an indoor environment. It is composed by a network of *fixed cameras*, to execute surveillance tasks in areas of relevant interest, and *mobile robots*, that are able to perform local and specific monitoring tasks to completely cover the environment. Integration among the various agents, fixed and mobile, is performed via a distributed control architecture which uses a wireless network as a communication channel. In this section, first, the target detection algorithms, used by either the fixed or the mobile agents, are described. Then, the distributed target tracking algorithm is presented.

[1] Hereinafter, the nodes of the network will be also named as *agents* in order to emphasize their detection, communication and computation capabilities.

15.3.1 Target Detection Using Fixed Cameras

Fixed cameras of the DAAL system are distributed in different locations of the environment to optimize the target detection task. Each fixed node is equipped with the following functionalities [9].

Motion Detection. The binary shape of moving objects (e.g., people) is extracted. Specifically, a statistical background model is generated by evaluating mean value and standard deviation for each point. Then, foreground moving regions are detected by estimating, for each pixel, the similarity between the current frame and the background model.

Shadow Removal. This task is necessary because foreground pixels may correspond not only to real moving objects, but also to their shadows. The shadow pixels need to be removed, as they alter the real shape of objects and decrease the precision of their localization. A connectivity analysis is, finally, performed to aggregate pixels belonging to the same moving object.

Object Tracking. The detected moving objects, after shadow removal, are tracked over time. Statistical (tracked object life time) and spatial information are extracted for each of them. This task enables the association of each moving region to the corresponding target object, based on its appearance. Furthermore, it reduces false detections due to noise or light reflections.

3D Moving Object Localization. The intersection of the central axis of the rectangular bounding box containing the moving region with its lower side provides the estimate of object position on the ground plane. The corresponding 3D position is evaluated using a pre-calibrated homographic matrix between the image plane and the 3D ground plane.

15.3.2 Target Detection Using the Mobile Robots

Robots used in the DAAL system are equipped with an RGB-D sensor, namely the Microsoft Kinect camera, to detect people in the environment [15]. The Kinect sensor, through the 3D data representation, allows to robustly track the positions of a group of people in the environment and to detect their movements [18]. Furthermore, in the case the Kinect is mounted on a robot, the presence of a relative motion between the camera and the global reference system should be taken into account in order to obtain better results.

In the DAAL system people are identified in the scene captured by the Kinect camera onboard the robot and then a single person of interest is selected. Once the robot is focused on a person, a tracking algorithm keeps track of the position of that person and a control algorithm allows the robot to move toward the person in order to improve the tracking performance. Thus, each mobile robot is equipped with the following functionalities.

Person Tracking. Through an algorithm for segmentation and recognition of the human skeleton, that takes advantage of both the RGB color information and the depth information of the image [13], the robot detects all the people in the scene. Then a person of interest is selected, for instance the person nearest to the robot or the one who made a given gesture. To improve the estimation of the position of each single person of interest and to improve the performance in realistic situations affected by noise, the tracking algorithm uses a Kalman filter that improves the estimation of the position. Finally, the correct position, obtained from the output of the Kalman filter, can be used as the input for the motion controller.

Person Following. The person follower controller is basically a motion control algorithm which requires two different inputs: the updated position of the person of interest, given by the person tracker algorithm, and the information about static and dynamic obstacles. In particular, the algorithm sets a trajectory planner with the position of the person as the point of arrival and at the same time the robot is aware of the obstacles in the environment obtained by the use of predefined map. In this way, the person follower controls the motion of the robot, exploiting the robust performance of a map-based navigation system, following the position of a person of interest.

15.3.3 Distributed Target Tracking Algorithm

At the final stage of the DAAL system all the information coming for the various sensors are fused using a distributed framework. To this end, the DAAL system exploits the *fully distributed* Consensus-based Distributed Target Tracking (CDTT) algorithm [16], to enhance the performance of the people tracking in a heterogeneous sensor network. The CDTT consists of a two-phase iterative procedure: an estimation step and a consensus step. In the estimation phase, each node of the network gives an estimate of the position of the target. If the node can directly take a measurement, then it will estimate the target position by means of a Kalman filter. Otherwise, the node will take a prediction of the target motion according to the embedded linear motion model of the Kalman filter. In the consensus phase, all the estimates in the network converge to a common value via a *max-consensus* protocol, performed on a measurement accuracy metrics called *perception confidence value*. This approach was proved to provide good performance in heterogeneous sensor networks composed by nodes with limited sensing capabilities [7]. The CDTT approach is totally distributed, as it does not involve any form of centralization. Moreover, it guarantees the agreement of the network nodes on the target position. The reader is referred to [16] for further information.

15.4 System Implementation

The DAAL system was implemented in the Robotics Laboratory of CNR ISSIA, Bari, Italy. In this section, details about the implementation of the system are provided.

In the DAAL network, each agent corresponds to an independent software component that is executed on the robots embedded PC for the mobile agents and on a workstation for the fixed cameras. This architectural solution provides several advantages. First, the system is totally plug-&-play, i.e., to increase the number of sensors it is sufficient to add a new camera (with its IP address) to the network, so that no further effort to program new cameras is required. Software maintenance is easy and immediate, avoiding the broadcast updating of each camera software. Moreover, algorithms for motion detection and shadow removal, as the ones explained in the previous section, are based on the evaluation of pixel correlation that requires a very fast processing unit to run in real time and that cannot be done efficiently with embedded cameras. The team of agents forms a peer-to-peer network. The network nodes differ only for their own sensor capabilities. In particular, every agent is able to detect an event (e.g., to perceive moving people or objects) and to localize an event (e.g., tracking the position of a person) in the environment using one or more sensor devices, whereas, in addition, mobile agents are able to execute tasks, through their actuators. The detailed description of fixed and mobile nodes are given in the following.

15.4.1 Setup of Fixed Nodes

The fixed agent software runs on a workstation linked to each camera by the network infrastructure. The schematic representation of interconnections among nodes composing the Fixed Node module is shown in Fig. 15.2. For each connected camera

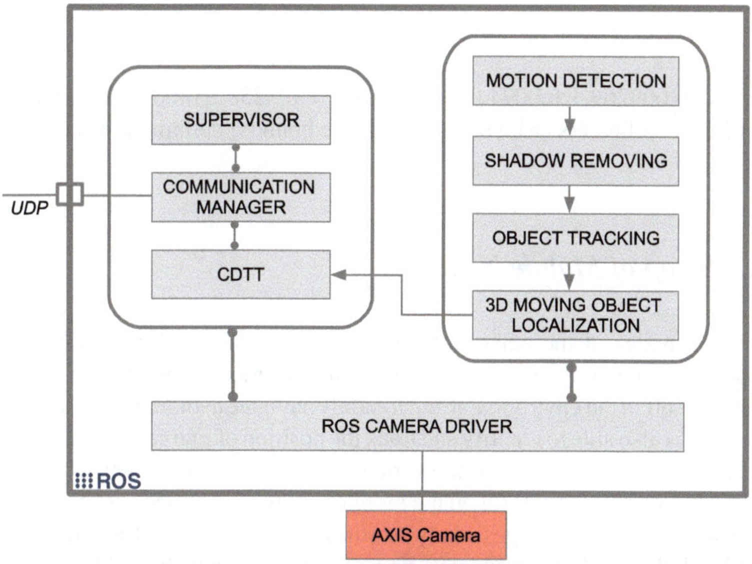

Fig. 15.2 Schematic representation of interconnections among nodes composing the Fixed Node module

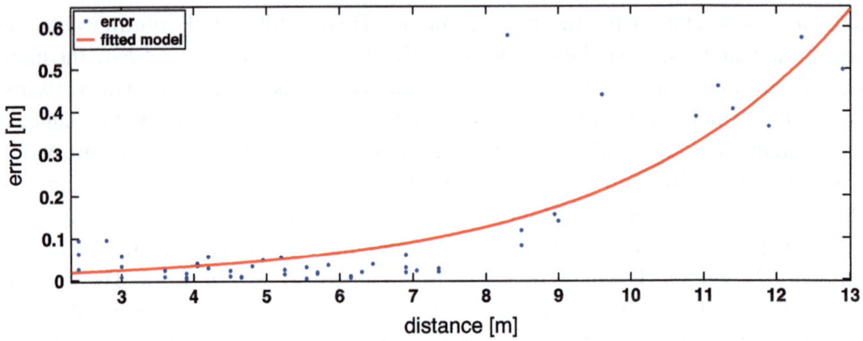

Fig. 15.3 The measurement error model for one of the cameras: $f(x) = a\,e^{bx}$. The error is limited when the sensor-target distance is under 7–8 m, and, above that, the error increases. This suggests that the camera should be deployed ensuring a maximum distance to the object under 7–8 m

an autonomous thread integrated in the Robot Operating System (ROS)[2] framework is implemented, to execute some well-defined ordered tasks as explained in Sect. 15.3.

Moreover in a real-world implementation, the measurement error of cameras should be taken into account. The measurement error of the cameras depends on the distance of the target relative to the sensor. In order to characterize the measurement error, an error model is fitted from a series of measurement errors obtained by the comparison of the position measured by the camera and the real position of the target (the real position of the target is retrieved by means of a theodolite). Figure 15.3 shows the model fitted as an exponential function for one of the cameras:

$$f(x) = a\,e^{bx}, \tag{15.1}$$

where $a = 0.009269 \pm 0.0074$ [meters] and $b = 0.3258 \pm 0.0696$ 1/[meters] are the value of the coefficients (with 95 % confidence bounds) defining the actual function $f(x)$.

15.4.2 Setup of Mobile Nodes

The mobile nodes of the network consist of mobile robots. Each mobile agent is equipped with sensory devices to interact with the environment. Every node is able to localize itself in the environment and to safely navigate avoiding static and dynamic obstacles. It is also able to identify and track the position of a target in the environment. ROS has been adopted as a framework for communication management, sensor acquisition and actuator control on the mobile robots. It is an open source framework that presents several packages ready to run in order to control all the devices of a robotic platform. ROS provides a *Navigation Stack*, which enables the robot to

[2] http://www.ros.org.

navigate in a known environment avoiding obstacles, as well as sensor management packages [11]. The most important characteristic of ROS is its modular structure that makes it possible to modify or substitute some modules. In order to develop a customized monitoring architecture, new functionalities have been developed and added to the native ROS framework. Specifically, the structure of the navigation stack of ROS has been modified in order to add surveillance capabilities to the mobile nodes. A coordinate transformation from local to global coordinates was also introduced for the people tracking task.

In Fig. 15.4 a schematic representation of the mobile node module is reported. All ROS nodes run on the on-board laptop, except for *sicktoolbox_wrapper* and *p2os_driver*, which runs on the embedded pc of the robot. As can be seen, the Navigation Stack of ROS produces robot position estimates, as well as information about obstacles on the basis of laser measurements. The ROS node *motion_control*, implemented by our research team, sends velocity references to *p2os_driver* ROS node, responsible of the robot guidance. The *people_tracker* node estimates the relative position of people with respect to the robot, on the basis of the skeleton information received from *openni_tracker*. The relative coordinates of detected people, transformed in the world reference frame, provide input data to the distributed target tracking algorithm.

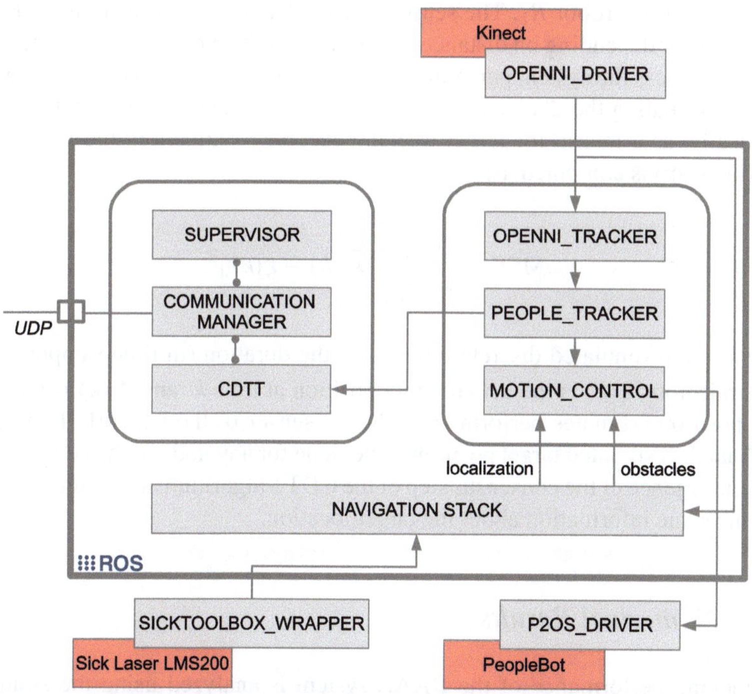

Fig. 15.4 Schematic representation of interconnections among nodes composing the Mobile Node module

15.5 Simulation Results

This section deals with the evaluation of the DAAL system through a numerical simulations' campaign. The evaluation is focused on the tracking task performance. The setup and results of such simulations are described below.

15.5.1 Simulation Setup

The DAAL system performance is tested in a realistic scenario with a setup similar to the real one. A target moving inside a given environment, according to various random trajectories, is simulated for the target tracking task. The analysis is focused on the evaluation of the presence of mobile nodes in the network, specifically, the simulations investigate if the presence of mobile nodes increases the tracking performance according to a given evaluation index. A network composed by three cameras, named as C_1, C_2, C_3, and one robot, R_1, is assumed (as in the real DAAL system). Heterogeneity in the sensor network is due to the different sensing ranges of sensors, set on the basis of real devices' characteristics. Specifically, the sensing area is defined as a circular sector area placed at the front of the sensor with radius of $r_{C_1} = 10\,\mathrm{m}$ for camera C_1, $r_{C_2} = 8.5\,\mathrm{m}$ for camera C_2, $r_{C_3} = 7\,\mathrm{m}$ for camera C_3, and $r_{R_1} = 5\,\mathrm{m}$ for robot R_1. The sensors are modeled as range-bearing, with measurement error depending on distance and bearing of the target relative to the sensor. In order to assess the system performance, attention is focused on the *tracking accuracy,* by evaluating the discrepancy between estimated and actual target trajectory. Specifically, as a metric for target tracking accuracy estimation, the mean square error (in norm) is computed as:

$$\mathrm{MSE} = \frac{1}{k_f} \sum_{k=1}^{k_f} \|\overline{\boldsymbol{\xi}}_i(k) - \boldsymbol{\xi}(k)\|^2 \tag{15.2}$$

where k is the simulated discrete time, k_f is the duration (in time samples) of the target trajectory, $\boldsymbol{\xi}(k)$ is the actual target position at time k, and $\overline{\boldsymbol{\xi}}_i(k)$ is the global target position estimates performed by the ith sensor of the network. It should be noted that the estimated target position is the same for any node of the network, since after convergence of the consensus step of the CDTT algorithm all the network nodes share the same information about the target location.

15.5.2 Numerical Results

The tracking performance of the DAAL system is analyzed using the simulation setup described in Sect. 15.5.1. A campaign of Monte Carlo simulations is run in two different cases. In the first case, the mobile robot is kept at a fixed position, thus

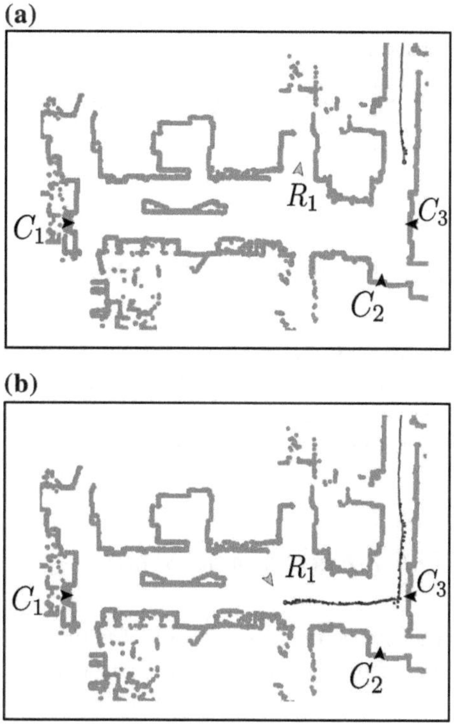

Fig. 15.5 DAAL system evaluation: simulation of a random generated target trajectory for a network of 3 fixed nodes (in *black*) and 1 mobile node (in *green*). The *red line* indicates the actual trajectory of the target, while the *blue dots* are the estimated positions of the target returned by the CDTT algorithm. **a** The mobile robot surveys an assigned area of interest of the environment. **b** As soon as the target enters this area, the mobile node approaches it to perform a more accurate measure

acting as a fourth static node. In the second case, the mobile robot can move in the surroundings of its initial location.

A set of 250 random target trajectories is run both for the case of static nodes only and for the scenario including the mobile node. The tracking simulation for one of the trajectories is shown in Fig. 15.5. It refers to the simulation performed using a mobile node (green arrow) in addition to the static ones (black arrows). A solid red line denotes the actual target trajectory, while the estimated positions at each time step k are marked by blue circles. Initially (Fig. 15.5a), the target is sensed by the static node C_2, while the other nodes are aware of the target position thanks to the consensus convergence. As soon as the target enters the area surveyed by the mobile node (Fig. 15.5b), the latter approaches the target to perform a more accurate measure.

The numerical results of the simulation campaign are reported in Table 15.1, showing a mean square error of 0.2339 m and 0.1523 m, for the static network and for the network including the mobile node, respectively. As can be noted, the presence of a mobile node increases the tracking accuracy. This is mainly due to two reasons: first, the mobile node can approach the target, so that it can measure the position of the target with higher accuracy according to the adopted range-bearing sensor model. In addition, the mobile node can track the target also in areas hidden to the fixed nodes, thus increasing the overall coverage of the network.

Table 15.1 Average MSE and variance in the tracking of 250 repeated random target trajectories: comparison between results with and without the presence of a mobile node

Method	Average MSE (m)	Variance (m^2)
w/ Mobile Agent	0.15	0.06
w/o Mobile Agent	0.23	0.02

15.6 Experimental Results

In this section, the DAAL system is validated through experimental tests conducted in a real-world scenario. The evaluation is focused on the distributed target tracking task. First, we describe the environment setup, then the system and the results of the experimental tests are presented.

15.6.1 Environment Setup

The environment setup used for the experimentation of the system is shown in Fig. 15.6. The picture shows the map of a corridor of the ISSIA-CNR building, as it is built by the *gmapping* node available in ROS using the laser data acquired by a mobile robot during a complete exploration of the environment. In this experimentation, three fixed cameras and one mobile robot have been employed. The positions of the fixed cameras (C_1, C_2, C_3) and of the mobile robot (R_1) are overlaid on the map. The mobile agent is able to localize itself in the environment and, using its on-board sensors, it is able to carry out surveillance tasks, such as people detection and tracking. Cameras are calibrated, therefore events detected in the image plane can be located in the real world and their positions can be communicated to the mobile agent. The mobile robot can explore areas that are unobservable by the fixed cameras and improve the accuracy in detecting events by reaching proper positions in

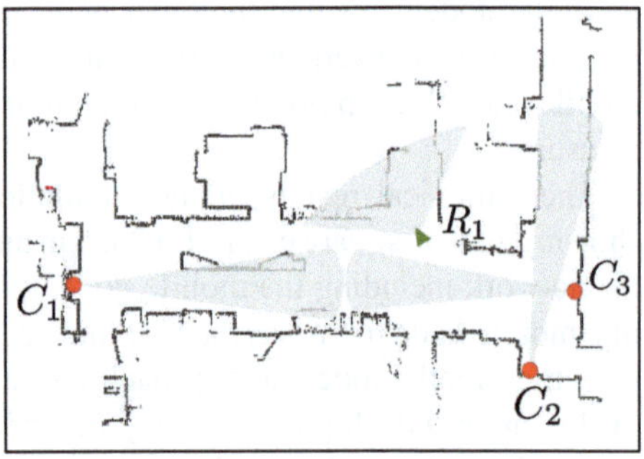

Fig. 15.6 Map of one corridor of the office with overlaid the position of three static cameras (*red circles*) and one mobile agent (*green triangle*)

the environment. Hence, the proposed system could be useful to reduce the number of fixed sensors or to monitor areas (e.g., cluttered environments) in which the field of view of fixed cameras can be temporarily and dynamically reduced.

15.6.2 System Setup

The fixed nodes are three wireless IP cameras (C_1, C_2, C_3) with different spatial resolution, located in different points of the environment (see map in Fig. 15.6). C_2 and C_3 are Axis IP color cameras with a 640×480 pixel resolution and an acquisition frame rate of 10 frames/s. C_1 is a Mpixel Axis IP color camera with $1{,}280 \times 1{,}024$ pixel resolution and full frame acquisition rate of 8 frames/s (see Fig.15.7, on the right). A calibration step to estimate intrinsic and extrinsic parameters was

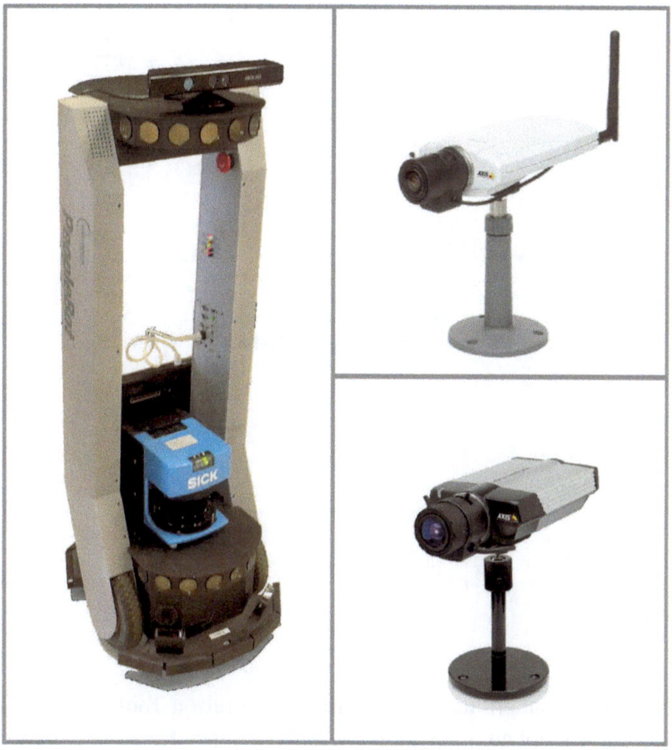

Fig. 15.7 The nodes of the network. On the *left*, the mobile agent PeopleBot. The robot is equipped with a laser range-finder SICK LMS200 and a Kinect. On the *right*, two different AXIS cameras: on the *top*, a Mpixel Axis IP color camera with 1,280 × 1,024. On the *bottom*, an Axis IP color cameras with a 640 × 480 pixel camera

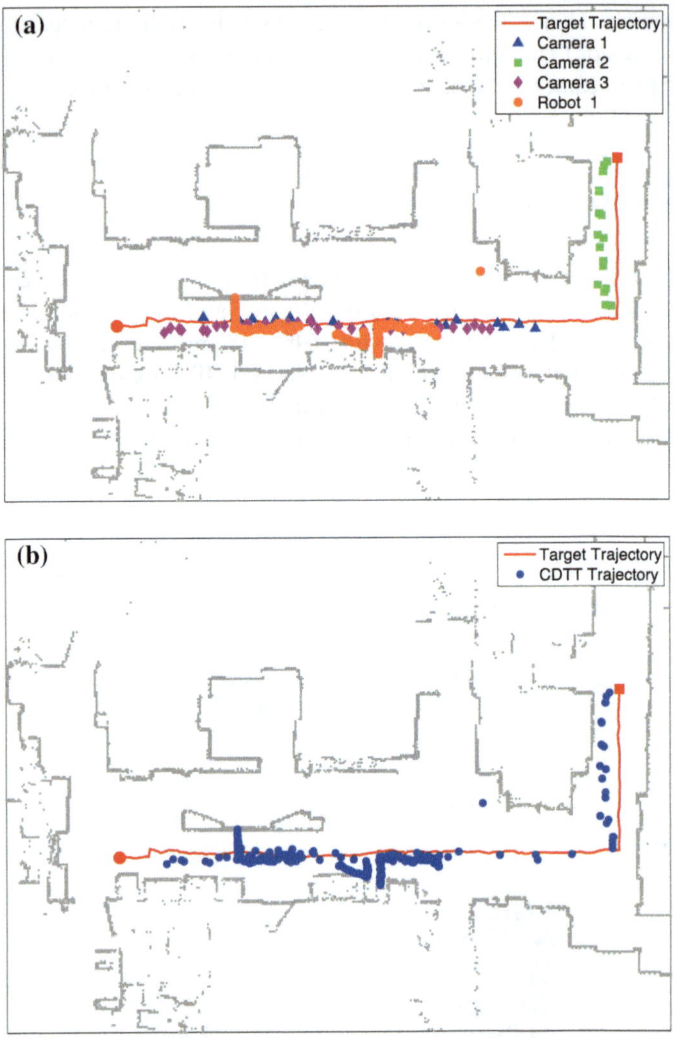

Fig. 15.8 Trajectory 1. The measurement of the position of the target carried out by each of the sensor of the network (**a**) and the CDTT trajectory recovered on line and in distributed fashion by the network (**b**)

performed for each camera using the Matlab Calibration Toolbox,[3] so that camera coordinates can be mapped to the global world reference frame provided by the map built by the mobile robots.

The mobile agent (denoted as R_1 in Fig. 15.6) consists of a PeopleBot mobile robot platform equipped with a laser range-finder, a Kinect, and an on-board laptop

[3] The toolbox is available on http://www.vision.caltech.edu/bouguetj/calib_doc/index.html.

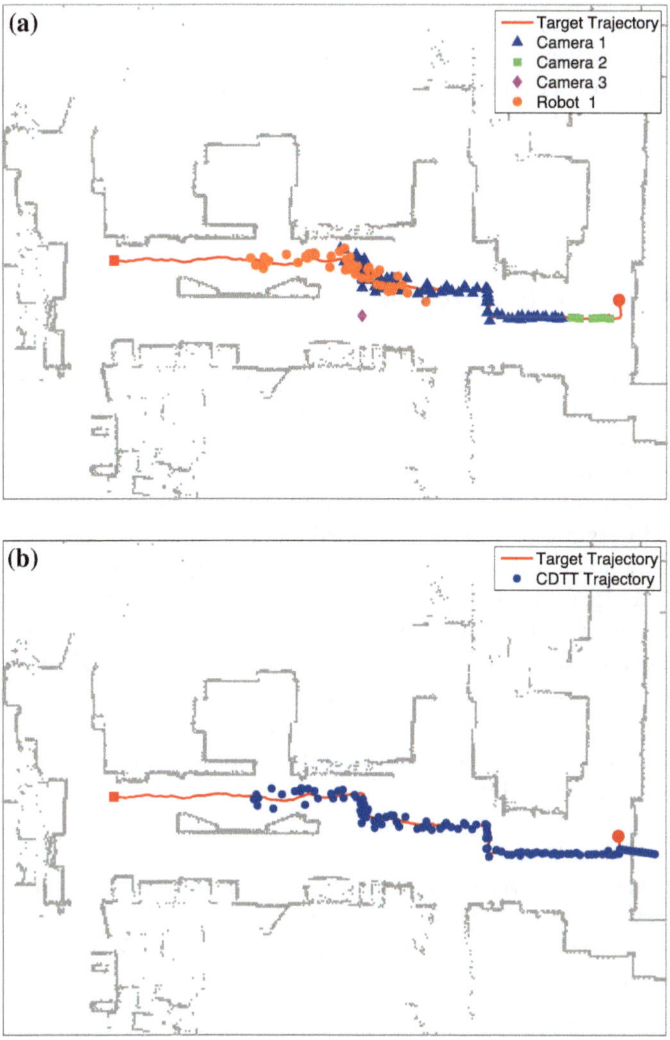

Fig. 15.9 Trajectory 2. The measurement of the position of the target carried out by each of the sensor of the network (**a**) and the CDTT trajectory recovered on line and in distributed fashion by the network (**b**)

(see Fig.15.7, on the left). The SICK laser is connected with the embedded robot control unit. The Kinect camera and the PeopleBot control unit are connected with the laptop, via a USB cable and a crossover cable, respectively. The laser range-finder is used to build a map of the environment and to localize the vehicle. The Kinect is used for both navigation (e.g., obstacle avoidance) and high-level tasks such as people detection and tracking.

The DAAL system performance is tested in a real time application in which a network of three cameras and a robot is used to monitor a large environment and track the position occupied by a given target. The target to be tracked is a person moving in the environment following two given trajectories. The robot is equipped with an on board Kinect camera whose field of view is 58° horizontal, 45° vertical, 70° diagonal, and the operational range is between 0.8 m (2.6 ft) and 3.5 m (11 ft) [4].

15.6.3 Results of Experiments

In the experimentation, the target follows two different trajectories in the environment, as shown in Figs. 15.8 and 15.9. Specifically, in Figs. 15.8a and 15.9a, the target trajectory is denoted by a red line, while the target positions as estimated by the three cameras and the robot are denoted by different markers. In Figs. 15.8b and 15.9b the target trajectory (red line) is compared with the trajectory (blue dots) as estimated by the CDTT algorithm. It should be noted that the estimated target position is the same for any node of the network, since after convergence of the consensus step of the CDTT algorithm all the network nodes share the same information about the target location. In order to quantify the tracking performance, we suppose that the target is moving with a constant velocity and we calculate the MSE, as done for the simulated case. Results are collected in Table 15.2, showing a mean square error of 1.15 and 0.75 m, for Trajectory 1 and Trajectory 2, respectively. Figure 15.10 shows two frames, acquired from the Kinect camera on the robot during the tracking of the Trajectory 1 depicted in Fig. 15.8.

Table 15.2 Average MSE and variance in the tracking of a person moving in the laboratory by means of a network of 4 nodes, 3 fixed and 1 mobile

Case	Average MSE (m)	Variance (m^2)
Trajectory 1 (Fig. 15.8)	1.15	0.86
Trajectory 2 (Fig. 15.9)	0.75	0.16

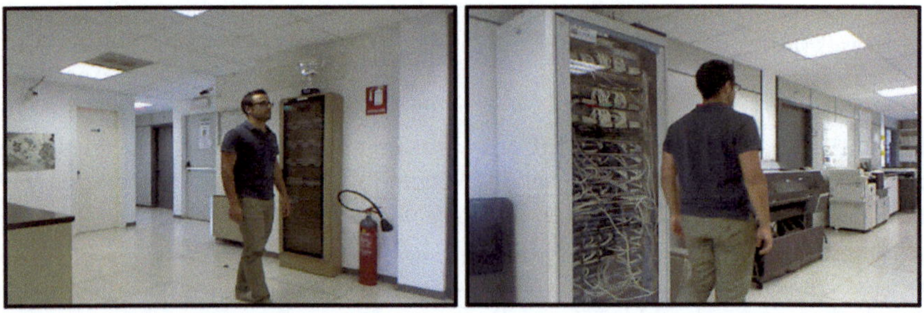

Fig. 15.10 Two different instants of the tracking of Trajectory 1, acquired from the Kinect sensor

15.7 Conclusions

In this chapter, a novel activity monitoring architecture for Ambient Assisted Living applications has been introduced. The main contribution is the combination of fixed and mobile nodes in the monitoring network: mobile sensors enable the complete coverage of large environments with fewer fixed sensors and increase the accuracy of measurements by reaching the most favorable position to observe the current target. The global logical architecture used by the system has been presented. The software agents developed to work on fixed and mobile nodes have been described. Simulations of the behavior of the system in a realistic environment (with sensor parameters closely corresponding to the characteristics of the real fixed and mobile sensors) have been carried out and the results have been shown. They have been obtained using a distributed target tracking algorithm developed by some of the authors. Furthermore, preliminary experimental results obtained by the real sensors in our lab environment are presented, showing the feasibility and effectiveness of the proposed system.

Acknowledgments This research is supported by the National Research Program PON-BAITAH - "Methodology and Instruments of Building Automation and Information Technology for pervasive models of treatment and Aids for domestic Healthcare". The authors thank Arturo Argentieri for technical support in the setup of the system presented in this work.

References

1. Burgard W, Moors M, Fox D, Simmons R, Thrun S (2000) Collaborative multi-robot exploration. In: Proceedings of IEEE international conference on robotics and automation, ICRA'00, vol 1, pp 476–481
2. Carli R, Chiuso A, Schenato L, Zampieri S (2008) Distributed kalman filtering based on consensus strategies. IEEE J Sel Areas Commun 26(4):622–633
3. Cattivelli FS, Sayed AH (2010) Diffusion strategies for distributed kalman filtering and smoothing. IEEE Trans Autom Control 55(9):2069–2084
4. Cruz L, Lucio D, Velho L (2012) Kinect and rgbd images: challenges and applications. In: 25th SIBGRAPI conference on graphics, patterns and images tutorials (SIBGRAPI-T), pp 36–49
5. Di Paola D, Milella A, Cicirelli G, Distante A (2010) An autonomous mobile robotic system for surveillance of indoor environments. Int J Adv Rob Syst 7(1):19–26
6. Di Paola D, Naso D, Cicirelli G, Milella A, Distante A (2008) Multi-sensor surveillance of indoor environments by an autonomous mobile robot. In: IEEE 15th international conference on mechatronics and machine vision in practice, pp 23–28
7. Di Paola D, Petitti A, Rizzo A (2014) Distributed kalman filtering via node selection in heterogeneous sensor networks. Int J Syst Sci pp 1–12
8. Giannini S, Di Paola D, Rizzo A (2012) Coverage-aware distributed target tracking for mobile sensor networks. In: IEEE 51st annual conference on decision and control (CDC), pp 1386–1391
9. Leo M, Spagnolo P, D'Orazio T, Mazzeo PL, Distante A (2010) Real-time smart surveillance using motion analysis. Expert Syst 27(5):314–337
10. Magherini T, Fantechi A, Nugent CD, Vicario E (2013) Using temporal logic and model checking in automated recognition of human activities for ambient-assisted living. IEEE Trans Human-Machine Syst 43(6):509–521

11. Marder-Eppstein E, Berger E, Foote T, Gerkey B, Konolige K (2010) The office marathon: robust navigation in an indoor office environment. In: International conference on robotics and automation
12. Milella A, Di Paola D, Mazzeo PL, Spagnolo P, Leo M, Cicirelli G, D'Orazio T (2010) Active surveillance of dynamic environments using a multi-agent system. In: 7th IFAC symposium on intelligent autonomous vehicles, IAV 2010, vol 7, pp 13–18
13. Mitchell R (2010) Primesense releases open source drivers, middleware for kinect. www.joystiq.com
14. Olfati-Saber R (2007) Distributed kalman filtering for sensor networks. In: 46th IEEE conference on decision and control, pp 5492–5498
15. Park J-H, Shin Y-D, Bae J-H, Baeg M-H (2012) Spatial uncertainty model for visual features using a kinect sensor. Sensors 12(7):8640–8662
16. Petitti A, Di Paola D, Rizzo A, Cicirelli G (2011) Consensus-based distributed estimation for target tracking in heterogeneous sensor networks. In: 50th IEEE conference on decision and control and european control conference (CDC-ECC), pp 6648–6653
17. Rashidi P, Mihailidis A (2013) A survey on ambient-assisted living tools for older adults. IEEE J Biomed Health Inf 17(3):579–590
18. Shotton J, Fitzgibbon A, Cook M, Sharp T, Finocchio M, Moore R, Kipman A, Blake A (2011) Real-time human pose recognition in parts from single depth images. In: IEEE conference on computer vision and pattern recognition (CVPR), pp 1297–1304
19. Song B, Ding C, Kamal A, Farrell J, Roy-Chowdhury A (2011) Distributed camera networks: Integrated sensing and analysis for wide area scene understanding. IEEE Signal Process Mag
20. Song B, Kamal A, Soto C, Ding C, Farrell J, Roy-Chowdhury A (2010) Tracking and activity recognition through consensus in distributed camera networks. IEEE Trans Image Process 19(10):2564–2579
21. Taj M, Cavallaro A (2011) Distributed and decentralized multicamera tracking. IEEE Signal Process Mag 28(3):46–58
22. Tron R, Vidal R (2011) Distributed computer vision algorithms. IEEE Signal Process Mag 28(3):32–45
23. Vig L, Adams JA (2007) Coalition formation: from software agents to robots. J Intell Rob Syst 1:85–118
24. Xu Y, Gupta V, Fischione C (2013) In: Chellappa R, Theodoridis S (eds) Distributed estimation. E-reference signal processing. Elsevier (to appear)

Chapter 16
Cooperative Multi-robot Patrol in an Indoor Infrastructure

David Portugal and Rui P. Rocha

Abstract Multi-robot patrol (MRP) is essentially a collective decision-making problem, where mobile robotic units must coordinate their actions effectively in order to schedule visits to every critical point of the environment. The problem is commonly addressed using centralized planners with global knowledge and/or calculating a priori routes for all robots before the beginning of the mission. However, distributed strategies for MRP have very interesting advantages, such as allowing the team to adapt to changes in the system, the possibility to add or remove patrol units during the mission, and leading to trajectories that are much harder to predict by an external observer. In this work, we present a distributed strategy to solve the patrolling problem in a real world indoor environment, where each autonomous agent decides its actions locally and adapts to the system's needs using distributed communication. Experimental results show the ability of the team to coordinate so as to visit every important point of the environment. Furthermore, the approach is able to scale to an arbitrary number of robots as well as overcome communication failures and robot faults.

16.1 Introduction

This work addresses multi-robot systems (MRS) for cooperative patrolling missions in realistic scenarios. To patrol is herein defined as "the activity of going around or through an area at regular intervals for security purposes" [1]. It requires every position in the environment, or at least the ones that need surveillance, to be regularly visited to verify the absence of anomalies. Additionally, it aims at monitoring

D. Portugal (✉) · R.P. Rocha
Institute of Systems and Robotics (ISR), University of Coimbra (UC),
3030-290 Coimbra, Portugal
e-mail: davidbsp@isr.uc.pt

R.P. Rocha
e-mail: rprocha@isr.uc.pt

P. Spagnolo et al. (eds.), *Human Behavior Understanding in Networked Sensing*,
DOI 10.1007/978-3-319-10807-0_16

environments, obtaining information, searching for objects, and clearing areas in order to guard the grounds from intrusion. Consequently, performing a patrolling mission with a team of any given number of autonomous and cooperative robots distributed in space represents a complex challenge. Being monotonous and repetitive, patrolling missions may also be dangerous (e.g., patrolling in hazardous environments). Therefore, using MRS in this context enables to safeguard human lives in applications like mine clearing, search and rescue operations, or surveillance, reducing the risk to human operators, which can be occupied in nobler tasks like monitoring the system from a safer location [2, 3].

In Multi-robot patrol (MRP), it is common to abstract the environment through a topological, graph-like map and robots are expected to have improved sensing abilities, meaning that they need to visit regularly all important places in the environment without necessarily going everywhere. Thus, agents should coordinate their actions in a shared environment while continuously deciding which place to move next after clearing their locations, having the ultimate goal of achieving optimal group performance.

The problem is commonly addressed using centralized planners with global knowledge and/or calculating a priori routes for all robots before the beginning of the mission. However, the deterministic nature of such methods do not capture the repetitive, and hence dynamic aspect of the problem, nor the synchronization issues that arise when a timing among the visits of certain zones is required. On the other hand, distributed strategies for MRP have very interesting advantages, such as allowing the team to adapt to changes in the system, the possibility to add or remove patrol units during the mission, and leading to trajectories that are much harder to predict by an external observer.

In this work, a distributed algorithm is proposed to solve the problem. The patrolling route of each robot is progressively built online and according to the state of the system. Furthermore, all robots are endowed with autonomous decision-making capabilities, being able to decide their moves by resorting to Bayesian decision, instead of following routes computed by a centralized entity.

In the next section, a literature review is conducted and the contributions of the chapter are described. Afterward, the MRP Problem is defined and the performance metric is presented in Sect. 16.3. The following section describes the distributed multi-robot patrolling strategy adopted in this chapter. Section 16.5 presents the experimental setup and the results obtained in real world indoor patrolling missions, as well as a discussion of the facets of the problem. Finally, the chapter ends with conclusions and open issues for future research.

16.2 Related Work

An overview of multi-robot strategies for area patrol missions is presented in this section. The MRP problem is also known in the literature as repetitive sweeping, multi-robot monitoring, and graph coverage, and the interest in this field stems from the variety of possible approaches, the potential applications of such algorithms in several distinct areas, and the key social function of these systems.

Important theoretical contributions to the MRP have been presented by [4–6]. Considering the *idleness* criterion (cf. Sect. 16.3), it was shown that the problem is NP-Hard, i.e., no polynomial time algorithm is known to compute an optimal solution to the problem. Also, it was shown that in theory, it can be optimally solved with a single robot by finding a Traveling Salesman Problem (TSP) tour in the graph that describes the environment. However, such computation is also NP-Hard. For the multi-robot case the problem remains open with several different algorithms in terms of motion rules, communication paradigm, cooperation scheme, etc. being proposed by several research groups in the last decade.

Numerous works employ graph theory tools like spanning trees [7] or graph partitioning [8] to compute minimal-cost cycles that assign efficient routes for each robot in the patrolling mission. Auctions and market-based coordination are also popular among MRP literature as in the case of [9], where agents bid to exchange vertices of the patrol graph to increase overall patrol performance. Diverse other concepts have also been explored, such as simple reactive architectures [10], task allocation [11], artificial forces [12], Gaussian process theory [13], evolutionary algorithms [14], swarm intelligence [15], Markov decision process [16], linear programming modeling [17], and others. A survey of methods in the literature for MRP can be found in [18].

Research on adversarial patrolling, a variant of the classical multi-robot area patrol, has addressed important issues such as applying unpredictable actions in the patrolling method so that intruders will not have access to the patrolling trajectory information to avoid being detected by agents [19], and studying strategies to detect intruders with high probability [20]. In identical surveillance application scenarios, where the threat of having adversarial agents is a central issue, the problem can also be addressed using game-theoretic approaches [21, 22].

Most contributions to the literature propose patrolling methods and overlook other relevant problems that should be addressed in MRP missions, e.g., robustness to failures and scalability. Furthermore, the vast majority of related work verifies their results only in simulations with different types of assumptions; some exceptions being the works described in [9, 23] and a few others. Clearly, there is a lack of implementation using physical MRS in noncentralized architectures. This serves as a motivation for the need to continuously coordinate teams of robots in patrolling missions in a distributed way, to validate these systems in the real-world and the possibility to add or remove patrolling agents (e.g., due to failures).

As will be seen, the main advantages of the patrolling framework presented in this chapter are the adaptability to the system's needs, which results from providing the robots with autonomous decision-making capability; the straightforwardness of implementation; and the quality of the technique leading to a scalable and fault-tolerant solution, which represents the main contribution of this work to the state of the art.

16.3 Problem Definition

In this work, the problem of efficiently patrolling a given environment with an arbitrary number of robots is studied. Agents are assumed to have an a priori map of the environment and through a graph extraction algorithm [24], they obtain an undirected, connected and metric navigation graph $\mathcal{G} = (\mathcal{V}, \mathcal{E})$ with $v_i \in \mathcal{V}$ vertices and $e_{ij} \in \mathcal{E}$ edges. Each vertex represents a specific location that must be visited regularly and each edge represents the connectivity between these locations, having a weight $|e_{i,j}|$ defined by the metric distance between v_i and v_j. $|\mathcal{V}|$ represents the cardinality of the set $\mathcal{V}$ and $|\mathcal{E}|$ represents the cardinality of the set $\mathcal{E}$. Seeing as undirected graphs are assumed, then: $|\mathcal{E}| \leq \frac{|\mathcal{V}| \cdot (|\mathcal{V}|-1)}{2}$.

Informally, a good strategy is one that minimizes the time lag between two passages to the same place and for all places [4]. Thus, the MRP problem can be reduced to coordinate robots in order to frequently visit all vertices of the graph, ensuring the absence of atypical situations with respect to a predefined optimization criterion.

In order to address and compare the performance of different patrolling algorithms, it is important to establish an evaluation metric. Diverse criteria have been previously proposed to access the effectiveness of multi-robot patrolling strategies. Typically, these are based on the idleness of the vertices, the frequency of visits or the distance traveled by agents [23]. In this work, the first one has been considered [25, 26], given that it measures the elapsed time since the last visit from any agent in the team to a specific location. Idleness is intuitive to analyze and brought into confrontation with the possibility of attacks to the system, seen as it uses time units. Thus, in the following equations, we define important variables used in the upcoming sections of the chapter.

The instantaneous idleness of a vertex $v_i \in \mathcal{V}$ in time step t is defined as:

$$\mathcal{I}_{v_i}(t) = t - t_l, \tag{16.1}$$

wherein t_l corresponds to the last time instant when the vertex v_i was visited by any robot of the team.

Consequently, the average idleness of a vertex $v_i \in \mathcal{V}$ in time step t is defined as:

$$\overline{\mathcal{I}_{v_i}}(t) = \frac{\overline{\mathcal{I}_{v_i}}(t_l) \cdot C_i + \mathcal{I}_{v_i}(t)}{C_i + 1}, \tag{16.2}$$

where C_i represents the number of visits to v_i. Considering now $\overline{\mathcal{I}_{\mathcal{V}}}$ as the set of the average idlenesses of all $v_i \in \mathcal{V}$, given by:

$$\overline{\mathcal{I}_{\mathcal{V}}} = \{\overline{\mathcal{I}_{v1}}, ..., \overline{\mathcal{I}_{v_i}}, ..., \overline{\mathcal{I}_{v|\mathcal{V}|}}\}, \tag{16.3}$$

the maximum average idleness of all vertices $\max(\overline{\mathcal{I}_{\mathcal{V}}})$ in time step t is defined as:

$$\max(\overline{\mathcal{I}_{\mathcal{V}}})(t) = \max\{\overline{\mathcal{I}_{v_1}}(t), ..., \overline{\mathcal{I}_{v_i}}(t), ..., \overline{\mathcal{I}_{v_{|\mathcal{V}|}}}(t)\}. \tag{16.4}$$

For the sake of simplicity, the argument (t) is omitted whenever timing is not relevant. Finally, in order to obtain a generalized measure, the average idleness of the graph $\mathcal{G}$ ($\overline{\mathcal{I}_{\mathcal{G}}}$) is defined as:

$$\overline{\mathcal{I}_{\mathcal{G}}} = \frac{1}{|\mathcal{V}|} \sum_{i=1}^{|\mathcal{V}|} \overline{\mathcal{I}_{v_i}}. \tag{16.5}$$

A similar assumption to other works in the literature [4, 10] is taken in the beginning of the experiments, where for all $v_i \in \mathcal{V}$, $\mathcal{I}_{v_i}(0) = 0$, as if every vertex had just been visited, when the mission started. As a consequence, there is a transitory phase in which the $\overline{\mathcal{I}_{\mathcal{G}}}$ values tend to be low, not corresponding to the reality in a steady-state phase, as will be seen in the results section. For this reason, the final $\overline{\mathcal{I}_{\mathcal{G}}}$ value is measured only after convergence in the stable phase.

Considering a patrol path as an array of vertices of $\mathcal{G}$, the multi-robot patrolling problem can be described as the problem of finding a set of R robot trajectories $\mathbf{x}$ that visit all vertices $v_i \in \mathcal{V}$ of the graph $\mathcal{G}$, using an arbitrary team of R robots, with the overall team goal of minimizing $\overline{\mathcal{I}_{\mathcal{G}}}$:

$$f = \underset{\mathbf{x}}{\operatorname{argmin}}(\overline{\mathcal{I}_{\mathcal{G}}}), \tag{16.6}$$

by finding:

$$\mathbf{x} = \{x_1, ..., x_r, ..., x_R\}, \tag{16.7}$$

such that:

$$x_r = \{v_a, v_b, ...\}, \tag{16.8}$$

$$v_a, v_b, ... \in \mathcal{V},$$

$$1 \leq r \leq R,\ R \in \mathbb{N},$$

subject to:

$$\forall v_i \in \mathcal{V}, \exists x_r \in \mathbf{x} : v_i \in x_r. \tag{16.9}$$

Note that x_r represents the patrolling path of robot r, which has an arbitrary dimension that depends on each robot's decisions and $v_a, v_b, ...$ are generic vertices in $\mathcal{V}$, which do not imply any specific order.

In this work, instead of relying in precomputed routes, which is common in classical approaches, the patrolling route x_r of each robot is built online according to the state of the system. Furthermore, all robots are able to decide their own moves instead of following routes that are computed by a centralized coordinator.

16.4 A Distributed Strategy for MRP

In [27], it was shown that methods based on Bayesian principles can effectively solve the MRP problem in different environment topologies. These methods can cope with uncertainty and robots' actions are selected according to the state of the system, leading to adaptive and distributed cooperative patrolling. More specifically, in the State-Exchange Bayesian Strategy (SEBS) each robot takes other teammates' actions into account while, at the same time, aiming to maximize a local gain function, which guarantees that every vertex of the navigation graph is visited regularly by all agents.

In order to compare the performance of diverse state of the art MRP techniques, we have used Stage [28], a recognized multi-robot simulator designed to support research into multi-agent autonomous systems. Stage simulates not only a population of mobile robots, but also sensors and objects in a two-dimensional environment. Moreover, it is realistic for many purposes, having a well-known status of being a robust simulation platform. In order to program the robots, the robot operating system (ROS) [29] was adopted. It was also verified that the nodes developed using Stage would work with little or no modification with real robots.

In the comparative analysis conducted, SEBS outperformed the remaining methods [27]. As a consequence, in this work it is chosen as the preferred strategy for coordination of a team of mobile robots, in a patrolling mission in a real world indoor infrastructure.

In the following subsections, we review the SEBS strategy. Using this strategy, agents decide asynchronously which place to move next when they reach their location, according to prior information about the team and the environment. Having this in mind, a fundamental random variable, which represents the act of moving (or not) to a neighbor vertex v_A is defined as:

$$\text{move}(v_A) = \{\text{true}, \text{false}\}, \tag{16.10}$$

The variables, which influence each robot's decision to move to a specific vertex, are presented in the next subsections with special focus on the selection of proper statistical distributions to model the data, so as to ensure the quality of the results. Afterward, it is shown how the local decision-making process is automated, applying Bayes Rule.

16.4.1 Gain

After reaching a given location of the environment, which needs to be visited, each robot is faced with a decision, where it must decide the next move within the shared environment. Therefore, the Gain G_A of moving from the current vertex (v_0) to a neighbor vertex (v_A), assuming constant speed (c) is defined as:

$$G_A(t) = c \cdot \left(\frac{\mathcal{I}_{v_A}(t) - \mathcal{I}_{v_A}(t + \Delta t)}{|e_{\text{val}}|} \right), \tag{16.11}$$

where in $t + \Delta t$ is the arrival time in v_A, and $\Delta t = {}^{|e_{0A}|}/_{c}$. $G_A(t)$ is proportional to a difference in the idleness values, representing a gain that the robot expects to obtain in moving to a given vertex. Note however that $G_A(t) \geq 0$ because $\mathcal{I}_{v_A}(t + \Delta t) = 0$ when the robot reaches v_A. For simplicity of notation, let us omit (t) in G_A, since every computation is done instantaneously.

In most cases, $|e_{\text{val}}|$ is equal to $|e_{0A}|$, which represents the distance between v_0 and v_A, given by the weight of the edge that connects them. However, the constraint (16.12) is imposed in order to control the impact of $|e_{\text{val}}|$, avoiding seldom situations where robots may get trapped in local optima (i.e., repeatedly visiting vertices that are very close to each other):

$$|e_{\text{val}}| = \begin{cases} |e_{\min}|, \text{ if } \max\{e_{0A}, ..., e_{0\beta}\} > 2\min\{e_{0A}, ..., e_{0\beta}\} \quad \wedge \quad |e_{0A}| < |e_{\min}|; \\ |e_{0A}|, \text{ otherwise.} \end{cases} \tag{16.12}$$

Naturally, greater values of gain rapidly have more influence in the robot's decision. Hence, the distribution function $F(g)$ of G_i is defined as a monotonically increasing function with the exponential model, as illustrated in Fig. 16.1a:

$$F(g) = ae^{bg}; \quad a > 0, \tag{16.13}$$

where:

$$F(0) = L \Leftrightarrow a = L, \tag{16.14}$$

and:

$$1 = Le^{bM} \Leftrightarrow b = \frac{\ln\left({}^{1}/_{L}\right)}{M}. \tag{16.15}$$

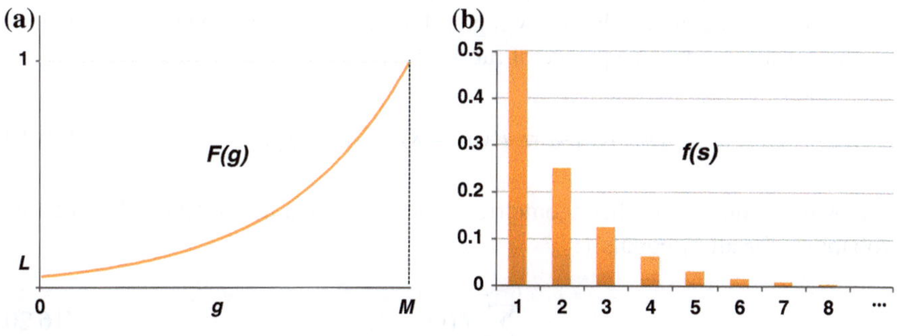

Fig. 16.1 Distribution Functions. **a** Gain, $F(g)$, **b** State, $f(s)$

This results in:

$$F(g) = L \cdot \exp\left(\frac{\ln\left(1/L\right)}{M} g\right), \tag{16.16}$$

with:

$$L, M > 0 \quad \text{and} \quad g < M. \tag{16.17}$$

L and M are constants that control the distribution function. Particularly, L is the y-intercept, which controls the probability values for lower gains and M is the gain saturation, beyond which the probability values are maximum; $F(g \geq M) = 1$. These constants are simply defined as $L = 0.1$ in the experiments conducted; and M is calculated through (16.11) using an upper bound of $\mathcal{I}_{v_A}$.

16.4.2 State

If the robots only depended on the Gain variable, they would aim to obtain the best reward for themselves, neglecting the global objective of the patrolling team and acting independently of their teammates, i.e., they would follow a greedy approach. However, in collective operations with a common goal, coordination between agents is fundamental for the success of the mission. Particularly in the MRP context, it is highly undesirable that agents move to the same positions. Instead, they should communicate their goals to ensure the distribution in the shared environment. As a result, a random variable, the vertex state S_i, is defined to model the number of robots that intend to visit a given vertex v_i involved in the decision process of robot r, which is currently located in vertex v_0:

$$S_i \in \mathbb{N}_0 \cap [0, R-1]; \quad R > 1. \tag{16.18}$$

As previously, it is necessary to define a statistical distribution $f(s)$ to model the vertex state. The greater the number of teammates in a given region in the vicinity of a robot, it becomes increasingly unlikely for the robot to move in that direction. To describe this behavior, the following probability mass function has been defined, which uses a geometric sequence of ratio 1/2:

$$f(s)_{R\to\infty} = P(S_i = s)_{R\to\infty} = \frac{1}{2^{s+1}}, \tag{16.19}$$

as shown in Fig. 16.1b. This geometric sequence is used to guarantee that the total probability for all S_i equals 1:

$$\sum_{s=0}^{R-1} f(s) = 1, \tag{16.20}$$

Equation (16.19) assumes that the number of robots R is unknown and can be arbitrarily high. Nevertheless, given that the robots communicate among themselves in order to coordinate, it is more realistic to consider R as known and with finite values. Thus, the following approximation to (16.19) is assumed:

$$f(s) = P(S_i = s) = \frac{2^{R-(s+1)}}{2^R - 1}; \quad R > 1. \tag{16.21}$$

16.4.3 Robot Decision

Each decision to move from a vertex v_0 to a neighbor v_A is independent and agents have the ability to choose the action, which has the greatest expectation of utility, weighted by the effects of all possible actions.

Having this in mind, robots locally update the idleness values online, by communicating to other robots when they reach any vertex of the navigation graph, in a distributed way. This enables the calculation of the Gain of moving from the current vertex to any of its neighbors. Similarly, by receiving other robots' intentions, agents can calculate the vertex state.

Having the likelihood distribution models $P(G_i|\text{move})$ and $P(S_i|\text{move})$ defined respectively by $F(g)$ and $f(s)$; and considering the prior knowledge as uniform, $P(\text{move})$, where all decisions are equiprobable; agents calculate the probability of moving to a specific vertex i, given its gain G_i and the vertex state S_i, by applying

Algorithm 1: State Exchange Bayesian Strategy (SEBS).

while *true* **do**
  `add` $(v_n \text{ to } x_r)$; //current vertex
  forall $v_i \in N_{\mathcal{G}}(v_n)$ **do**
    $G_i \leftarrow c \cdot \left(\frac{\mathcal{I}_{v_i}(t) - \mathcal{I}_{v_i}(t+\Delta t)}{|e_{val}|}\right)$;
    $P(G_i|move(v_i)) \leftarrow L \cdot \exp\left(\frac{\ln(1/L)}{M} G_i\right)$;
    $S_i \leftarrow$ `count_intentions_to` (v_i);
    $P(S_i|move(v_i)) \leftarrow \frac{2^{R-(S_i+1)}}{2^R-1}$;
    $P(move(v_i)|G_i, S_i) \propto P(move(v_i))P(G_i|move(v_i))P(S_i|move(v_i))$;
  //Next vertex is the neighbor of the current vertex with highest posterior probability.
  $v_{n+1} \leftarrow \underset{i \in N_{\mathcal{G}}(v_n)}{\text{argmax}} \; P(move(v_i)|G_i, S_i)$
  `write_msg_arrival_to` (v_n);
  `write_msg_intention_to` (v_{n+1});
  while *move_robot to* v_{n+1} **do**
    `read_msg_arrival_and_intentions_to` $(\mathcal{V})$;
    `update` $(\mathcal{I}_{\mathcal{V}}(t))$;
  $v_n \leftarrow v_{n+1}$;

Bayes rule:

$$P(\text{move}(v_i)|G_i, S_i) = \frac{P(\text{move}(v_i))P(G_i|\text{move}(v_i))P(S_i|\text{move}(v_i))}{P(G_i)P(S_i)}. \quad (16.22)$$

The denominator term is a normalization factor [30], being omitted for simplification purposes. Finally, the decision-making process of the agent consists of choosing the move from v_0 to the vertex v_j with the maximum probability among all vertices of the neighborhood $N_{\mathcal{G}}(v_0)$ of v_0:

$$\text{move}_j = \mathsf{true} : \; j = \underset{i \in N_{\mathcal{G}}(v_0)}{\mathtt{argmax}} \, P(\text{move}(v_i)|G_i, S_i) \quad (16.23)$$

Algorithm 1 presents a high-level pseudo-code of the SEBS approach, which runs locally on each mobile robot.

16.5 Results and Discussion

In this section, the implementation of a system for multi-robot patrol in a real-world environment is presented to demonstrate the potential of employing mobile robots as a potential solution in surveillance missions. Aiming to fill a gap in the state of the art, the SEBS distributed approach is validated in a large indoor scenario, where fully autonomous agents decide locally and sequentially their patrol routes according to the state of the system, as previously described. Beyond the coordination, which arises from the distributed communication of agents, it is also shown that the approach is robust to robot faults and communication failures.

Experiments were conducted in the floor 0 of the Institute of System and Robotics (ISR), in the University of Coimbra (UC), Portugal. Figure 16.2 shows the floor plan and the extracted topological map on top of the 67.85×26.15 m environment. The resulting topology is a noncomplete, connected and sparse graph, like most real world environments. In these tests, robots must overcome noisy sensor readings, localization issues, and even robot failures, which are usually ignored or not precisely modeled in simulation experiments. Therefore, a team of three Pioneer-3DX robots equipped with an Hokuyo URG-04LX-UG01 laser was used, as seen in Fig. 16.3.

The Pioneer 3-DX is a lightweight two-wheel differential drive robot for indoor use, equipped with two high-speed, high-torque, reversible-DC motors. Each motor has a high resolution optical quadrature shaft encoder for precise position, speed sensing, and advanced dead-reckoning. These robots are highly popular due to their versatility, reliability, and durability. They can operate continuously for 8–10 h, with a maximum load of 23 kg on top of the platform. In terms of dimensions, the robot has a diameter of 45.5 and 23.7 cms of height, as shown in Fig. 16.4. The robot easily handles small gaps and minor bumping, and its middle-size lends itself very well to navigation in tight quarters and cluttered spaces, such as classrooms,

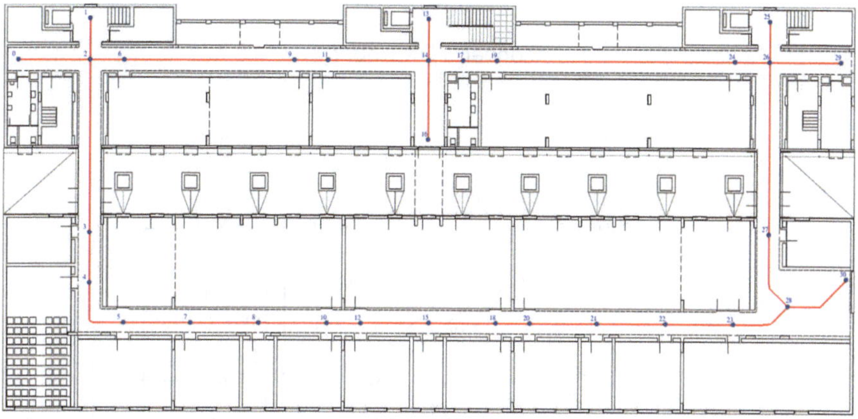

Fig. 16.2 Topological map of the "ISR-Floor0" Environment

Fig. 16.3 A team of Pioneer 3-DX robots

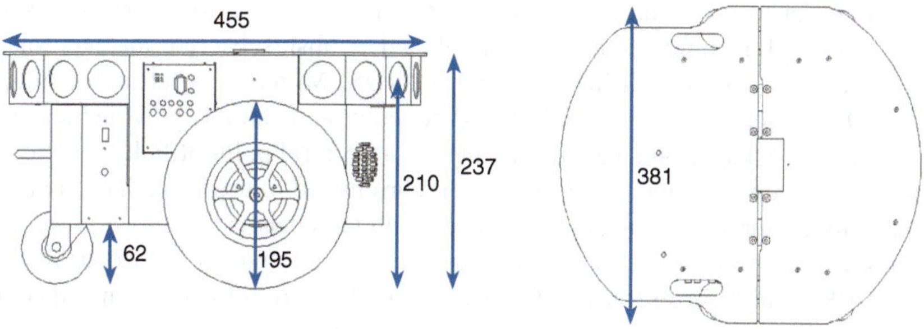

Fig. 16.4 Robot's dimensions (in mm)

laboratories, and small offices. A laptop on top of each robot was used to extend its processing capability. Each laptop runs the ROS navigation stack with the Adaptive Monte Carlo (AMCL) algorithm for localization purposes, being responsible for controlling the robot's motion. The ROS architecture running inside each robot is depicted in Fig. 16.5. A *patrolling* node, i.e., a ROS application, was added to the

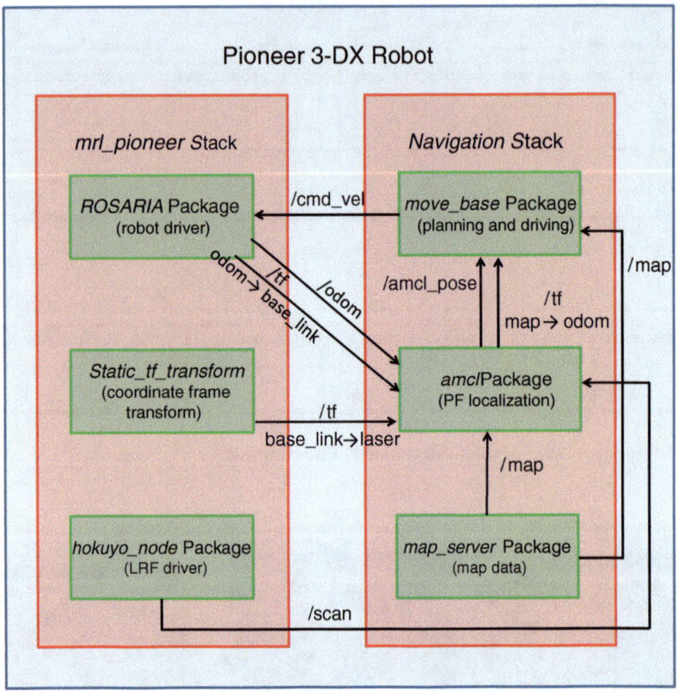

Fig. 16.5 ROS system running on each robot

architecture, having the responsibility to decide the robot's moves and send goals to the *move_base* node, which translates them into velocity commands for the robot base, in order to reach the given goal. All robots are limited to a maximum speed of 1 m/s. As for communication, a distributed publish/subscribe mechanism has been used, due to its built-in integration in ROS. Moreover, each robot runs its own ROS master node (*roscore*). Multimaster communication is provided using the *wifi_comm*[1] package. This means that there is no central point of failure in the system. Also, given that robots only share their current and future immediate goals, the bandwidth requirements are negligible even with large teams.

In the beginning of each test, the graph of the environment is loaded by every robot. A ROS node is responsible for advertising the start of the mission and collect results during the experiments. Not only is the average graph idleness along time $\overline{\mathcal{I}_{\mathcal{G}}}$ examined, but also the median $\widetilde{\mathcal{I}_{\mathcal{G}}}$, the standard deviation σ, and the maximum average idleness of a vertex along time, $\max(\overline{\mathcal{I}_{\mathcal{V}}})$.

Firstly, experiments with one, two, and three robots were conducted. Each experiment was repeated three times. Afterward, in order to further demonstrate the scalability of the approach, virtual robots were added to the team, and 3 trials with 6 agents (3 + 3) and 9 agents (3 + 6) were also conducted. It is noteworthy that

[1] Available at http://www.ros.org/wiki/wifi_comm.

adding virtual simulated agents to the physical teams of robots was only made possible by the hardware abstraction layer of ROS and its modular structure. Finally, to prove its robustness, experiments which included failures in the robots at different time instants are analyzed, as well as the impact of communication failures in the performance of the team. In all experiments, $|e_{\min}| = 7.5\,\text{m}$ has been used.

Aiming at comparing the total time of the mission (τ) in various conditions, each experiment finishes after four complete patrolling cycles. This stopping condition is adequate, as the $\overline{\mathcal{I}_\mathcal{G}}$ converges in all experiments. During the course of the experiments reported, the total estimated distance traveled by the robots was 23 km.

16.5.1 Scalability Experiments

Initially, experiments with one to three robots in the "ISR-Floor0" Environment were conducted. An overview of these results is shown in the top rows of Table 16.1. It can be seen that the $\overline{\mathcal{I}_\mathcal{G}}$ values, as well as the total mission time τ, decrease with team size, as expected. Additionally, the median is fairly close to the average idleness value, meaning that most data is spread around the mean.

An interesting result is the maximum average idleness, $\max(\overline{\mathcal{I}_\mathcal{V}})$, which is low for the case of one robot. This can be explained due to the existence of a main loop in the environment, which leads to fairly uniform visits to all vertices of the graph. In the cases of 2 and 3 robots, the value is higher compared to $\overline{\mathcal{I}_\mathcal{G}}$, because robots occasionally meet in the environment and need to coordinate by changing their heading direction. Consequently, no cycles are followed in such situations, and

Table 16.1 Overview of the scalability experiments

Team size	$\overline{\mathcal{I}_\mathcal{G}}$	$\max(\overline{\mathcal{I}_\mathcal{V}})$	$\overline{\mathcal{I}_\mathcal{G}}$	σ	τ
1	336.676	412.207	370.994	78.769	1648.828
	332.745	407.897	366.677	77.892	1631.590
	331.615	406.387	365.345	77.626	1625.550
2	168.921	309.455	137.267	64.210	1237.821
	180.761	296.085	180.293	56.064	1184.341
	170.267	328.300	146.890	62.603	1313.201
3	128.875	273.670	116.269	54.893	1094.682
	116.248	216.020	95.150	44.356	864.081
	112.954	200.030	101.923	36.066	800.121
6(3+3)	71.097	152.625	65.483	27.130	610.500
	72.165	140.725	67.043	24.418	562.900
	77.332	150.145	72.938	27.350	600.580
9(3+6)	48.623	102.305	47.395	16.499	409.220
	50.239	90.580	54.157	16.083	362.320
	51.687	105.12	52.271	19.622	420.480

All values in seconds

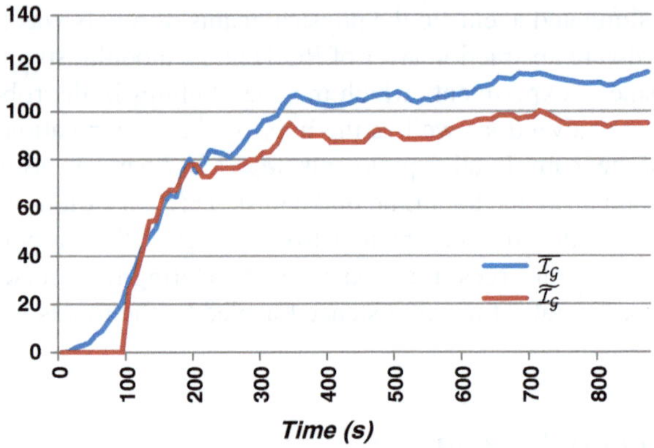

Fig. 16.6 Evolution of the idleness in a trial with 3 robots

the frequency of visits becomes less balanced. This can be confirmed by the standard deviation, which is around 23 % using 1 robot, and 35 and 37 % for a team size of 2 and 3 robots, respectively.

Figure 16.6 shows the evolution of the idleness in an experiment with 3 robots. After four patrolling cycles, $\overline{\mathcal{I}_\mathcal{G}}$ converges, meaning that it is no longer affected by the initial conditions, seeing as all vertices start with a null value of idleness.

The distributed patrolling method used supports an arbitrary high team size. However, we were limited by the physically available robots, which were $R = 3$. In order to test the approach with greater team size and further assess its scalability, virtual agents running in the Stage simulator were added to the team, resulting in a mixed team of real and simulated robots, which interact seamlessly via ROS. Three trials were conducted with a total of 6 agents comprising 3 physical robots and 3 simulated ones, and three additional trials were performed with a team size of 9, comprising 3 physical robots and 6 simulated ones. Similarly to the work in [23], the software layer is used unchanged both on real robots and in simulation.

Results in the bottom rows of Table 16.1 show that the overall values of $\overline{\mathcal{I}_\mathcal{G}}$, $\max(\overline{\mathcal{I}_\mathcal{V}})$, $\widetilde{\mathcal{I}_\mathcal{G}}$, σ and τ are within the expected, following the trend shown in the cases of two and three robots. In order to analyze how well the MRP strategy scales, Balch's speedup measure [31], a classical scalability metric, was calculated:

$$v(R) = \frac{\Psi(1)/R}{\Psi(R)}, \tag{16.24}$$

where $\Psi(R)$ is the performance for R robots, given by $\overline{\mathcal{I}_\mathcal{G}}$. Figure 16.7 presents a speedup chart using different team sizes. It can be seen that speedup and interference are negatively correlated, since the system enters progressively in sublinear performance ($v < 1$) with team size, due to the more frequent existence of spatial limitations, which in turn, increases the interference between robots, causing the performance to decrease. The interference between robots is measured as the overall

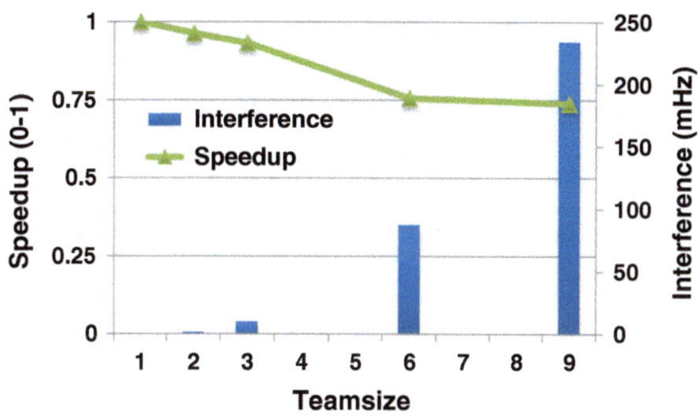

Fig. 16.7 Interference and Speedup against team size

frequency (in Hz) that different agents share nearby areas, having to avoid each other, in every experiment. These results show that the SEBS algorithm is able to scale to high number of robots, working independently of the team size. In addition, it is also illustrated that as the team size increases, the individual contribution of each robot decreases progressively as expected. This is in fact common to every MRP method tested in the literature.

16.5.2 Fault-Tolerance

One of the advantages of using autonomous robots with decision-making abilities is the absence of a centralized coordinator, which would represent a critical point of failure. A distributed robotic system, such as the one described enables redundancy, remaining functional if any of the agents fails.

In order to demonstrate the robustness of the patrolling method, three additional experiments using the Pioneer 3-DX robots were planned. In these experiments, a robot is shutdown during the course of the mission so as to understand the effect of the faults in the overall performance, as well as how the system evolves.

In the first experiment, a robot is shutdown after 200 s from the start of the mission. Similarly, in the second and third experiments, a robot is shutdown after 400 and 600 s, respectively. Teammates assume that the robot has failed when no message has been received from it for a period larger than 2 min.

Generally, Table 16.2 shows that the results obtained in the first experiment resembles those obtained with two robots, as most of the experiment is spent with only two agents due to the failure occurring near the beginning. On the other hand, the results of the second and third experiment are closer to those obtained with three robots, even though the performance is inferior, as expected.

Analyzing now the influence of the faults in the evolution of the results, one can verify that in all three cases when the shutdown occurs the values of $\overline{\mathcal{I}_{\mathcal{G}}}$ and $\widetilde{\mathcal{I}_{\mathcal{G}}}$ increase after a while, which is particularly visible in Fig. 16.8a, b.

Table 16.2 Experiments with 3 robots with failure of a robot in different instants of time (all values in secs)

Failure time (s)	$\overline{\mathcal{I}_{\mathcal{G}}}$	$\max(\overline{\mathcal{I}_{\mathcal{V}}})$	$\overline{\mathcal{I}_{\mathcal{G}}}$	σ	$\mathcal{T}$
200	160.975	330.225	144.846	62.825	1320.901
400	140.128	232.290	134.177	45.934	929.161
600	135.209	235.700	139.797	41.262	942.801

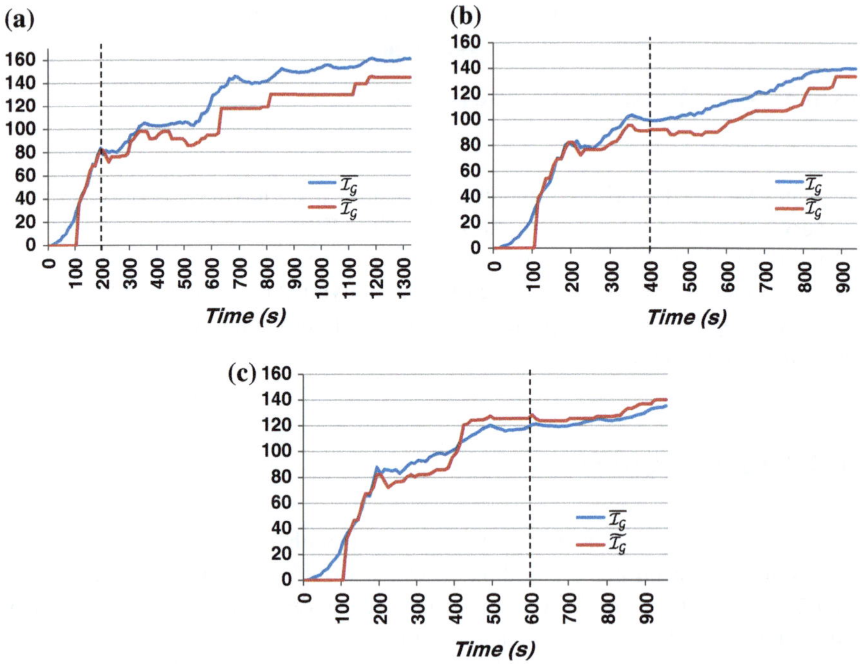

Fig. 16.8 Evolution of the idleness along time in experiments with robot failures **a** Failure at 200 s, **b** Failure at 400 s, **c** Failure at 600 s

Therefore, the MRP system using the proposed distributed strategy is resilient against robots' individual failures, presenting a graceful degradation of performance as long as at least one robot remains operational.

16.5.3 Influence of Communication Errors

The model proposed to solve the MRP problem assumes that agents are able to communicate seamlessly with other teammates during the course of the mission. However, this is not always the case, especially if a mobile *ad-hoc* network should be maintained and robots are occasionally far apart. In this section, multi-robot simulations in Stage were run in the "ISR-Floor0" map in order to test the robustness of the SEBS approach with different rates of communication failures.

When a message is not received by a robot, it does not update the instantaneous idleness time values and, consequently, it keeps incomplete information about the state of the system. This information becomes more incomplete with the increasing number of undelivered messages. Additionally, when robots are close to each other, if messages are not received, they may decide to move to the same places and interfere with their teammates' plans. The success of resolving such situations hugely depends on each robot's local planner and the ability to avoid dynamic obstacles. In these simulations, this is taken care by the ROS navigation stack.

In order to simulate different rates ξ of communication failures, a robot will ignore messages with a probability equivalent to ξ. In the reported experiments, the rates considered were: $\xi = \{0\,\%, 25\,\%, 50\,\%, 75\,\%, 100\,\%\}$. Furthermore, the system has also been tested allowing only local communication, restricted to robots within two edges of distance in the graph $\mathcal{G}$. This is a particular situation where it is ensured that robots are able to receive all the other nearby robots' intentions, and are thus able to coordinate themselves. Nevertheless, they are expected to make poor decisions as they are maintaining incomplete information about the system.

The chart in Fig. 16.9 presents an overview of the simulation results with different rates of communication failures, using team sizes of 2, 4, and 6 robots. Team performance is once again measured in terms of $\overline{\mathcal{I}_\mathcal{G}}$. The graph shows that performance gracefully degrades as ξ increases. The decrease of performance is approximately constant for the 25 %, 50 % and 75 % cases. However, when no communication is allowed, i.e., $\xi = 100\,\%$, the performance of the algorithm drops strongly, especially for larger teams, which are much more influenced by the lack of coordination in the multi-robot system, as robots constantly interfere with one another. This reduction of performance, especially for greater team sizes, is evident in the bars for $\xi = 100\,\%$; with 36.54 % for 2 robots, 51.30 % for 4 robots, and 66.84 % for 6 robots.

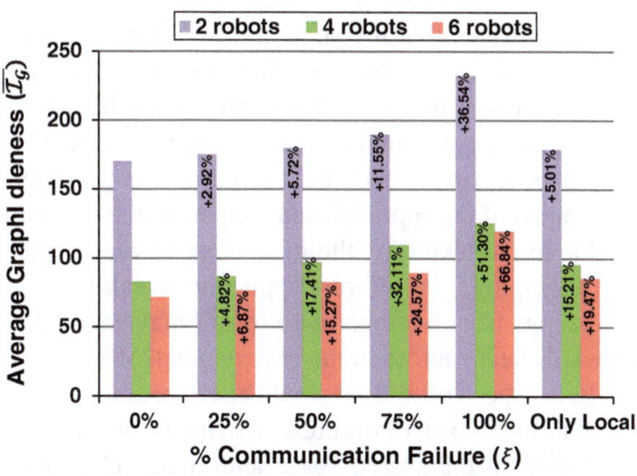

Fig. 16.9 Influence of communication failures in team performance

Also illustrated in the rightmost side of the chart is how performance is affected when communication is restricted to local interactions within 2 hops in $\mathcal{G}$. In this situation, robots are able to coordinate themselves by not competing to the same goals and not interfering with teammates. Despite that, they do not have contact with agents that are further away and, as a consequence, they will make uninformed decisions quite often. It can be seen that the system is able to perform well assuming such restrictions, especially for smaller team sizes. The performance obtained using only local communication closely resembles to that obtained when dropping 50 % of the messages for all team sizes.

In short, these results show that the approach is robust to communication failures and only slightly degrades its performance when communication error rate is moderate (e.g., 25 %). Evidently, the higher the rate of failures, the more affected performance is. Moreover, communication failures have more impact in the performance of systems with larger number of robots.

16.6 Conclusions and Future Work

The implementation of a distributed MRS for patrolling of an indoor infrastructure has been described. Breaking away from conventional techniques, our work goes beyond classical centralized approaches that rely on precomputed cyclic routes or partition schemes for MRP, giving the robots the autonomy to deal with uncertainty and select actions according to the state of the system at the time.

Previous results had shown the superior performance of the approach when compared with other state of the art MRP strategies in simulated environments [27]. This work confirms the potential and flexibility of employing Bayesian-based formalism to solve the MRP. The proposed approach accounts for the future immediate state of the system, preventing robots from competing to reach the same goals, consequently reducing interference and enhancing scalability.

Results have demonstrated that the approach is robust to robot faults and communication failures, and has the ability to adapt to constraints, e.g., different agent velocities, since the decision-making is done online with the information that each agent has collected about the system. Experiments were conducted using real robots and mixed teams of both virtual and real agents in a large indoor infrastructure proving the effectiveness of the approach and the potential to use it in the real world.

In the future, due to its flexibility, the model can be easily extended with more variables in order to employ it in different applications and/or use others sensors in the robots; e.g., readings from a temperature sensor may be included in the model, guiding robots towards heat sources in the environment. Moreover, even though the method allows different speed profiles, it would be interesting to study its influence in the mission, as well as the impact of unforeseen dynamic obstacles in the real world, such as people walking in the shared space and affecting the robot's navigation. Finally, we intend to devise an analytical method to compute the most adequate team size for a patrolling mission according to the environment topology and temporal constraints.

Acknowledgments This work has been supported by a Ph.D. grant (SFRH/BD/64426/2009), the CHOPIN research project (PTDC/EEA-CRO/119000/2010), and the Institute of Systems and Robotics (project Est-C/EEI/UI0048/2011), all of them funded by the Portuguese science agency "Fundação para a Ciência e a Tecnologia".

References

1. Webster's Online Dictionary (2014). Available at: http://www.webster-dictionary.org
2. Murphy R (2004) Human-robot interaction in rescue robotics. IEEE Trans Syst Man Cybern Part C Appl Rev 34(2):138–153
3. Rocha R P, Portugal D, Couceiro M, Araújo F, Menezes P and Lobo J (2013) The CHOPIN project: Cooperation between Human and robotic teams in catastrophic incident. In: Proceedings of the 2013 international symposium on safety, security and rescue robotics (SSRR 2013), Sweden, Linköping
4. Chevaleyre Y (2004) Theoretical analysis of the multi-agent patrolling problem. In : Proceedings of the 2004 international conference on agent intelligent technologies (IAT'04), China, Beijing, pp 30–308
5. Smith S, Rus D (2010) Multi-robot monitoring in dynamic environments with guaranteed currency of observations. In: Proceedings of the 49th IEEE conference on decision and control, USA, Atlanta, Georgia, pp 514–521
6. Pasqualetti F, Franchi A, Bullo F (2012) On cooperative patrolling: optimal trajectories, complexity analysis, and approximation algorithms. IEEE Trans Rob 28(3):592–606
7. Fazli P, Davoodi A and Mackworth AK (2013) Multi-robot repeated area coverage. In: Autonomous robots, 34(4), Springer Science, May 2013, pp 251–276
8. Portugal D, Rocha R (2010) MSP Algorithm: multi-robot patrolling based on territory allocation using balanced graph partitioning. In: Proceedings of 25th ACM symposium on applied computing (SAC 2010), Special track on intelligent robotic systems, Switzerland, Sierre, pp 1271–1276
9. Pippin C, Christensen H and Weiss L (2013) Performance based task assignment in multi-robot patrolling. In Proceedings of the 2013 ACM symposium on applied computing (SAC'13), Portugal, Coimbra, pp 70–76
10. Machado A, Ramalho G, Zucker J and Drogoul A (2003) Multi-agent patrolling: an empirical analysis of alternative architectures. In: Multi-agent-based simulation II, Lecture notes in computer science, vol 2581. Springer, pp 155–170
11. Sempé F and Drogoul A (2003) Adaptive patrol for a group of robots. In: Proceedings of the 2003 IEEE/RSJ international conference on intelligent robots and systems (IROS'2003), Las Vegas, Nevada, USA
12. Sampaio P, Ramalho G and Tedesco P (2010) The gravitational strategy for the timed patrolling. In: Proceedings of the IEEE international conference on tools with artificial intelligence (ICTAI'10), Arras, France, pp 113–120
13. Marino A, Parker L, Antonelli G, Caccavale F (2009) Behavioral control for multi-robot perimeter patrol: a finite state automata approach. In: Proceedings of the IEEE international conference on robotics and automation (ICRA'09), Kobe, Japan, pp 831–836
14. Aguirre O, Taboada H (2012) An evolutionary game theory approach for intelligent patrolling. In: Procedia computer science, vol 12, part II, Elsevier, pp 140–145
15. Yanovski V, Wagner IA, Bruckstein AM (2003) A distributed ant algorithm for efficiently patrolling a network. Algorithmica 37:165–186

16. Marier J, Besse C and Chaib-draa B (2010) Solving the continuous time multiagent patrol problem. In: Proceedings of the 2010 IEEE international conference on robotics and automation (ICRA'10), Anchorage, Alaska, USA
17. Keskin BB, Li S, Steil D, Spiller S (2012) Analysis of an integrated maximum covering and patrol routing problem. In: Transportation research Part E: Logistics and transportation, vol 48, Elsevier, pp 215–232
18. Portugal D, Rocha R (2011) A survey on Multi-robot patrolling algorithms. Technological innovation for sustainability, IFIP advances in information and communication technology series, vol 349. Springer, Berlin, pp 139–146
19. Sak T, Wainer J and Goldenstein S (2008) Probabilistic multiagent patrolling. In: Advances in artificial intelligence, proceedings of the 19th Brazilian symposium on artificial intelligence (SBIA 2008), Lecture Notes in Computer Science, vol 5249, Springer, pp 124–133
20. Agmon N, Kaminka G, Kraus S (2011) Multi-robot adversarial patrolling: facing a full-knowledge opponent. J Artif Intell Res (JAIR) 42:887–916
21. Basilico N, Gatti N, Rossi T, Ceppi S and Amigoni F (2009) Extending algorithms for mobile robot patrolling in the presence of adversaries to more realistic settings. In: Proceedings of the 2009 IEEE/WIC/ACM international conference on intelligent agent technology (IAT'09), Milan, Italy, pp 557–564
22. Pita J, Tambe M, Kiekintveld C, Cullen S, Steigerwald E (2011) GUARDS-innovative application of game theory for national airport security. In: Proceedings of the 22nd international joint conference on artificial intelligence (IJCAI'11), vol 3. Spain, Barcelona, pp 2710–2715
23. Iocchi L, Marchetti L and Nardi D (2011) Multi-robot patrolling with coordinated behaviours in realistic environments. In: Proceedings of the international conference on intelligent robots and systems (IROS'2011), San Francisco, CA, USA, pp 2796–2801
24. Portugal D and Rocha RP (2013) Retrieving topological information for mobile robots provided with grid map. In: Agents and artificial intelligence, communications in computer and information science (CCIS) series, vol 358. Springer, Berlin, pp 204–217
25. Portugal D, Rocha RP (2011) On the performance and scalability of multi-robot patrolling algorithms. In: Proceedings of the 2011 IEEE international symposium on safety, security, and rescue robotics (SSRR 2011), Japan, Kyoto, pp 50–55
26. Portugal D and Rocha RP (2013) Multi-robot patrolling algorithms: examining performance and scalability. In: Advanced robotics journal, special issue on safety, security, and rescue robotics, 27(5), pp 325–336
27. Portugal D and Rocha RP (2012) Decision methods for distributed multi-robot patrol. In: Proceedings of the 10th international symposium on safety, security and rescue robotics (SSRR'2012), College Station, Texas, USA
28. Vaughan R (2008) Massively multi-robot simulation in stage. J Swarm Intell 2(2–4):189–208
29. Quigley M, Gerkey B, Conley K, Faust J, Foote T, Leibs J, Berger E, Wheeler R, Ng A (2009) ROS: an open-source robot operating system. In: Proceedings of the IEEE international conference on robotics and automation (ICRA'2009), workshop on open source software, Japan, Kobe
30. Jansen F and Nielsen T (2007) Bayesian networks and decision graphs, 2nd edition, Springer
31. Balch T, Arkin R (1994) Communication in reactive multiagent robotic systems. Auton Robots 1(1):27–52

Chapter 17
Distributed Thermal Identification and Exploitation for Multiple Soaring UAVs

José Antonio Cobano, David Alejo, Santiago Vera, Guillermo Heredia, Salah Sukkarieh and Aníbal Ollero

Abstract This chapter discusses the problem of cooperatively sensing the wind map of an area in order to efficiently harvest the wind energy with fixed-wing gliding UAVs, known as soaring. Moreover, a cooperative system with multiple gliding fixed-wing UAVs is presented for long endurance missions. This system is composed by three main blocks that include thermal detector, path planning, and collision avoidance. The main advantage is its low computational load, making it suitable for real-time applications. Extensive simulation results in several scenarios are given to test the complete system. In addition, real experiments have been carried out with real gliding aircrafts of the Robotics Vision and Control Group (GRVC) of the University of Sevilla in the Airfield of La Cartuja (Sevilla). The results of these experiments show the convenience of the proposed method.

17.1 Introduction

The interest in using multiple Unmanned Aerial Vehicles (UAVs) has been increasing in recent years taking into account potential applications in different missions such as exploration, data collection, mapping, surveillance, coast control, fire detection,

J.A. Cobano · D. Alejo (✉) · S. Vera · G. Heredia · A. Ollero
University of Seville, Camino de Los Descubrimientos s/n, Seville, Spain
e-mail: dalejo@us.es

J.A. Cobano
e-mail: jcobano@us.es

S. Vera
e-mail: svera@us.es

G. Heredia
e-mail: guiller@us.es

A. Ollero
e-mail: aollero@us.es

S. Sukkarieh
The University of Sydney, Sydney, NSW 2006, Australia
e-mail: salah@acfr.usyd.edu.au

P. Spagnolo et al. (eds.), *Human Behavior Understanding in Networked Sensing*,
DOI 10.1007/978-3-319-10807-0_17

monitoring, and many more. In all these cooperative missions, the UAVs should visit different places during their flight in order to explore the area. The common problem in this kind of missions is the short endurance of many vehicles. They have to land in order to refuel or recharge batteries. Extending the flight duration of multiple UAVs cooperating for long endurance missions arises as a critical issue in many applications.

New ideas such as the so-called autonomous soaring have been proposed to extend the flight endurance of a single glider aerial vehicle [5]. Soaring could be defined as flight in which a propulsion system is not used and favorable wind conditions are exploited to extend flight duration. This phenomenon was noticed in some birds by observing how they are able to fly without flapping their wings [25]. The clearest example is the Wandering Albatross that covers large areas with minimal energy consumption [27]. In 1885, Lancaster [18] published a work on soaring of birds. Thus, soaring flight became an important research area. There are two types of soaring, static and dynamic soaring. The first one uses rising air to gain energy and the second one uses wind gradients or distributions.

Aerial vehicles should be capable of extracting energy from the atmosphere to gain altitude in order to stay aloft [23]. This energy can be extracted from different sources such as wind gusts over surfaces (such as the ocean), shear generated by flow around geographic obstacles, and meteorological shear from temperature inversions. This work will consider vertical movements of the atmosphere, also so-called thermals. Thermals are caused by convection in the lower atmosphere and could be exploited to increase the altitude of multiple UAVs. This process is also known as static soaring where UAV flies through air which is rising relative to the surrounding air. On the other hand, dynamic soaring obtains kinetic energy by using trajectories through distributions of wind speed.

This chapter addresses long endurance cooperative missions with multiple glider aerial vehicles. The mission is given by a set of places defined by point of interest (PoIs) which should be visited. Existence of thermals in the environment is considered. Thus, the aerial vehicles should cooperatively visit the PoIs and each aerial vehicle should detect and identify the thermals present in the environment during the mission in order to exploit their energy and gain altitude, and so extend the flight duration. Cooperative missions with multiple vehicles allow faster detection and more efficient exploitation of the thermals, since each vehicle transmits to the rest of the teams the location of the thermals it has identified. The guidance and control of an autonomous soaring UAV is not addressed in this work, but we use the approach in [4]. A path planner is also needed to efficiently carry out the cooperative mission. The planner has to consider constraints such as energy available of the UAV at the current instant and locations of the thermals which will influence the computation of collision-free trajectories. Moreover, collision avoidance is a critically important aspect in applications with multiple UAVs to successfully perform the mission. Therefore, a collision avoidance block should be implemented to ensure the fulfillment of the mission. In summary, the objectives of the chapter are:

1. Explore all the PoIs without landing and decrease the total time of the mission.
2. Identify the presence of thermals in the environment in order to exploit them and extend the flight duration.
3. Compute safe trajectories to perform the mission.

A new system made up different blocks is developed in order to meet the objectives. The path planner block considers a method to assign each PoI or thermal point (TP) to a vehicle. A thermal detector block is added to detect and identify thermals during the mission. The conflict detection and resolution block is based on the RRT* (optimal rapidly exploring random trees) planning algorithm. Studies with many simulations show the performance and advantages of the developed system. Experiments have been carried out in the airfield of La Cartuja (Seville, Spain) with the gliding fixed-wing UAV shown in Fig. 17.1 in order to show the reliability of the system.

The chapter is organized into nine sections. The state of the art is presented in Sect. 17.2. The developed system is described in Sect. 17.3. Section 17.4 presents the thermal model, the features of the environment considered and the algorithm to detect and identify the thermals. The path planner is explained in Sect. 17.6, and the conflict detection and resolution algorithm is described in Sect. 17.6. The simulations and experiments performed are shown in Sects. 5.2.1 and 17.8, respectively. Finally, the conclusions are detailed in Sect. 17.9.

Fig. 17.1 Gliding fixed-wing UAV used in the experiments

17.2 State of the Art

First studies on soaring were based on the flight patterns of birds [25]. Soaring UAVs capable of extracting energy from the atmosphere to gain altitude in order to stay aloft have been presented in [23].

The works presented in [5, 13, 28] show the first analysis on autonomous thermal soaring. Other results with an autonomous soaring controller are reported in [12].

The static soaring problem is applied to the vehicle routing problem with time windows (VRPTW) in [15]. It develops an exact solution method including pre-processing, route optimization, and route validation . The total flight time minimization is achieved, and a considerable increase in the level of autonomy of a soaring UAV is attained.

Detection and identification of thermals have also been addressed in the literature [3, 21]. Models of thermals should be considered in the studies and several of them are presented in [4, 17].

Energy-constrained motion planning is done by considering the problem of a gliding UAV searching for a ground target while simultaneously collecting energy from known thermal energy sources [22]. Path planning is also addressed in other studies. A graph-based method for planning energy-efficient trajectories over a set of waypoints is presented in [8]. A method to generate a spatio-temporal map of the wind and a path planning to generate energy-gain paths based only on local observations of the wind is presented in [19]. The trajectory generation for autonomous soaring is also addressed in [9, 14].

The coordination of multiple UAVs in order to perform a long endurance mission considering the detection of thermals and the computation of collision-free trajectories has been studied in [17]. UAVs communicate to each other the location of potential thermals in the area but the simulation shown only considers one UAV.

Reference [7] describes a new algorithm for maximizing the flight duration of a group of UAVs using thermals located in the area. A simultaneous perturbation stochastic approximation method (SPSA) is used to detect the center of the thermal and the method treats the thermal center drift effectively. It is assumed that there exists a path planning algorithm that keeps the vehicles from colliding with each other. This work considers small unmanned powered glider, so the propulsion system or soaring can be used.

Reference [11] presents a method for distributed mapping of the wind field. The map is discretized and a Kalman filter is used to estimate the vertical wind speed and associated covariance in each cell. Flocks of small UAVs are considered to maximize the endurance. Reference [6] investigates the possible benefits of using a cooperating team of small UAVs to increase the probability of finding thermal lift. A collision-free trajectory planning algorithm is not implemented to optimize the search of thermals in [6, 11]. These works and [15] consider lifetime and drift of the thermals. Moreover, the proposed system allows applications in real time because of its low computational needs.

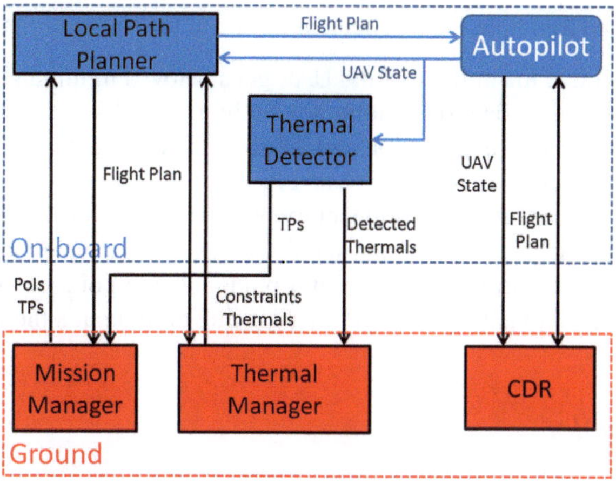

Fig. 17.2 Block diagram of the system

17.3 Overview of the System

This section describes the proposed system for long endurance missions with multiple gliding fixed-wing UAVs. It assigns the PoI to the UAVs and computes the collision-free trajectory for each UAV if a collision is detected. During the flight, each UAV should detect and identify unknown thermals. Figure 17.2 shows the block diagram.

17.3.1 Local Path Planner

The local path planner block (PP) is responsible for generating the flight plan of the UAV taking into account the knowledge of the wind map, i.e., detected thermals so far, and the PoIs to be visited. In order to do this, it should communicate with the thermal manager block and the mission manager block.

This block uses a path planning algorithm called Bounded Recursive Heuristic Search method (BRHS) [10], which is based on a depth-first search algorithm (DFS).

The basic behavior of this block is the following: it periodically generates a new flight plan taking into account the current location of the UAV (from the Autopilot), position of the remaining PoIs and thermal points (TPs), and minimum flying altitude of the UAV related to the available energy.

The flight plan is computed every second in order to adapt to unexpected events and the execution time is below one millisecond. When a new flight plan is generated and is significantly different of the current flight plan, PP transmits the new flight plan to the Autopilot.

The generated flight plan can be defined by one of the following four alternatives:

1. One waypoint: If the altitude of the UAV goes below a minimum flying altitude, the UAV is commanded to go Home for landing.
2. Two waypoints: Current location and a PoI or TP. UAV does not need a thermal to gain altitude and can reach a PoI or TP.
3. Three waypoints: Current location, entry point and exit point of the thermal. The UAV cannot reach a PoI or TP and should access to a thermal first to gain energy.
4. Four waypoints: Current location, entry point and exit point of the thermal, and a PoI. UAV could visit a PoI or TP after gaining altitude in a thermal.

17.3.2 Autopilot

Each UAV should be equipped with an Autopilot to be capable of following 3D flight plans. It is also responsible for estimating the state of the UAV (3D position) and providing other blocks with this information.

In the experimental platforms currently developed in the Robotics, Vision and Control Group of the University of Seville, we have installed an Ardupilot Mega 2.5 of the company 3DRobotics [1]. This is an open-source autopilot that is easily configured and gives good performance. The experimental setup is shown in Fig. 17.3.

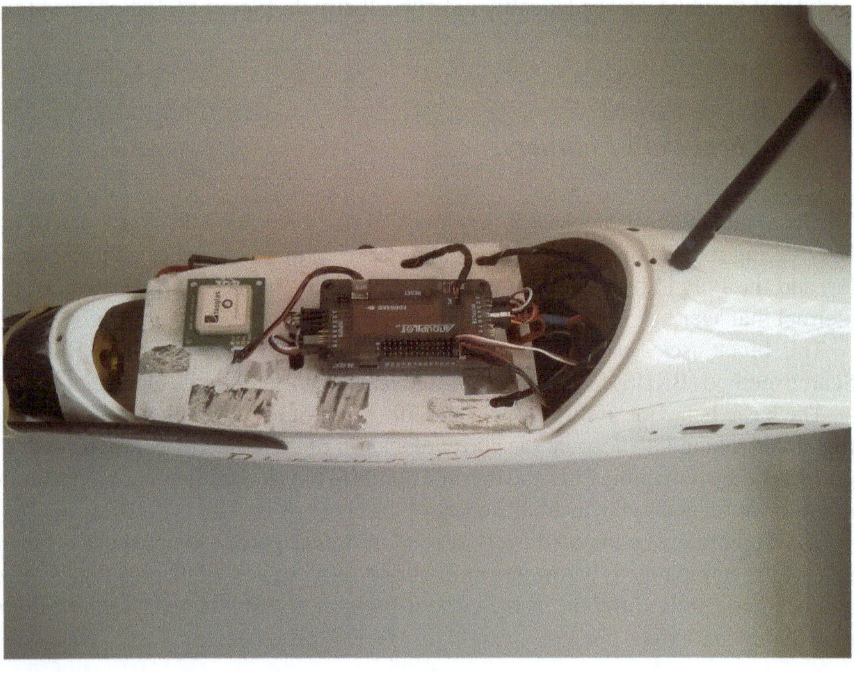

Fig. 17.3 Experimental setup of one of the gliding fixed-wing aircraft UAV

17.3.3 Thermal Detector

The thermal detector (TD) is responsible for detecting new thermals in the environment from changes of energy of the UAV, that is altitude of the UAV. It is constantly monitoring the UAV state in order to check for unexpected ascensions. Each UAV has onboard its own TD.

Whenever an unexpected ascension occurs and it meets some requirements, a new thermal is added to the system and new points are added and sent to the Mission Manager in order to actively sense the characteristics of the thermal. The details of these procedures are given in Sect. 17.4. The characteristics of the new thermal are also sent to the thermal manager block.

17.3.4 Mission Manager

The mission manager (MM) block stores the list of remaining PoI and TPs to be visited by the UAVs. It is also responsible for assigning and reassigning these waypoints to the UAVs as requested by the PP modules.

In the proposed system, two types of points to visit are distinguished: PoIs and TPs. Both could be considered as an exploration process: PoI to explore some places, and TPs to explore potential thermals. PoIs are set by the operator and TPs are generated when the location of a potential thermal is received from TD block. The TPs are computed to provide a better estimation of the center of a detected thermal.

Initially, the list shows all the PoI defined in the environment. The list is updated every time one PoI is visited or a thermal is detected. The PP of each UAV proposes visiting a PoI or TP when generating its flight plan. *MM* should assign to a UAV a PoI or TP if its estimated time of arrival (ETA) to it is the lowest one so far. In order to prevent oscillatory behaviors, whenever an UAV_i proposes visiting a PoI_k or TP_k that has been already assigned to a UAV_j, the ETA of UAV_i not only should to be lower than the ETA of UAV_j but also should decrease this time with a given margin, t_{visit}. Otherwise, PoI_k or TP_k continues being assigned to UAV_j.

17.3.5 Thermal Manager

The thermal manager (TM) block stores the information on the thermals and manages the access to them. It communicates to each PP the existing thermals in the space and the temporal constraints to access a thermal.

Whenever an UAV needs to gain energy, it should request access to any thermal to the TM block. This block checks whether the flight plan proposed by each UAV to gain altitude is safe or not. A flight plan to access to a thermal is safe when the vertical separation between two UAVs within the thermal is larger than a safety margin, d_{safety}. The outputs are temporal constraints to access to the thermal. If a flight plan is not safe, TM sends the temporal constraints to meet the vertical separation to the corresponding UAV.

17.3.6 Collision Detection and Resolution Block

The collision detection and resolution block (CDR) is responsible for ensuring collision-free trajectories between UAVs in the system outside the thermals. Note that the thermal manager block arbitres the access of UAVs to the thermals, so the collisions inside thermals should not occur.

This module can be divided into two different blocks: the detection and the resolution blocks. The first block takes as inputs the state of the UAVs in the systems and their current flight plans in order to detect conflicts between their trajectories. The second block is activated whenever a conflict is detected and will modify the flight plans of involved UAVs in order to prevent potential collisions.

17.4 Thermal Detector

This section describes how the wind map of the environment is generated and the potential thermals are detected. The parameters that define a thermal are: center of the thermal (C), vertical wind velocity (w), radius (R), maximum altitude (A), and drift of the thermal, (V_{drift}) .

The environment is divided into uniform two-dimensional cells. A value of the vertical wind velocity is assigned in each cell. Each UAV will estimate the vertical wind velocity of the center of the thermal from the changes of energy. The UAV speed is constant, so only changes of altitude are taken into account.

17.4.1 Thermal Model

The model of the thermal used is based on the model presented in [3]. Some modifications are performed to compute a more realistic initial wind map:

- A spatially uncorrelated zero-mean Gaussian noise is added to the wind field.
- The lifetime of the thermal is considered. Thus, the vertical wind velocity distribution that defines the thermal decreases with respect to time.
- The drift of the thermal is considered. Thus, center of the thermal is in relative movement to the ground.

In this work, a test set has been generated to validate the proposed system. An algorithm to randomly generate the wind maps has been implemented. The inputs are: number of thermals at the start, lifetime of each thermal, drift of each thermal, zero-mean Gaussian noise considered, size of the environment and the cells, probability to generate new thermals during the mission and separation between the thermals. Thus, different wind maps can be generated.

17.4.2 Thermal Detection Algorithm

The thermal detection algorithm is implemented in the TD block. Algorithm 1 presents the thermal detection algorithm which output will be the position of the detected thermal, $thermal_{\text{origin}}$. Changes of altitude, Δh, are considered to detect a potential thermal from the current altitude, h_i and the previous one h_{i-1}. Whenever $\Delta h > 0$ (see line 4), the origin of a potential thermal is stored when the first increasing of the altitude is obtained (see line 5) or the continuation of the climb is considered (see line 7) when the altitude continues increasing. On the other hand, whenever $\Delta h < 0$, two cases are possible: the descent takes place after a climb (see line 11) or the UAV was already descending (see line 18). In the first case, algorithm decides if a thermal is detected. A thermal is detected if the altitude gained during the climb, h_{gain}, is greater than $H_{\text{threshold}}$. Otherwise, a thermal is not detected and values of the thermals are initialized, $thermal_{\text{origin}}$, h_{gain} and h_{final}.

Once a thermal is detected, the parameters of the thermal are estimated. Center of the thermal, vertical wind velocity, and radius are estimated as those used by Allen [3]. Drift of the thermal and more precise parameters are estimated when a UAV passes through the thermal again. Figure 17.4 shows how a thermal is detected when

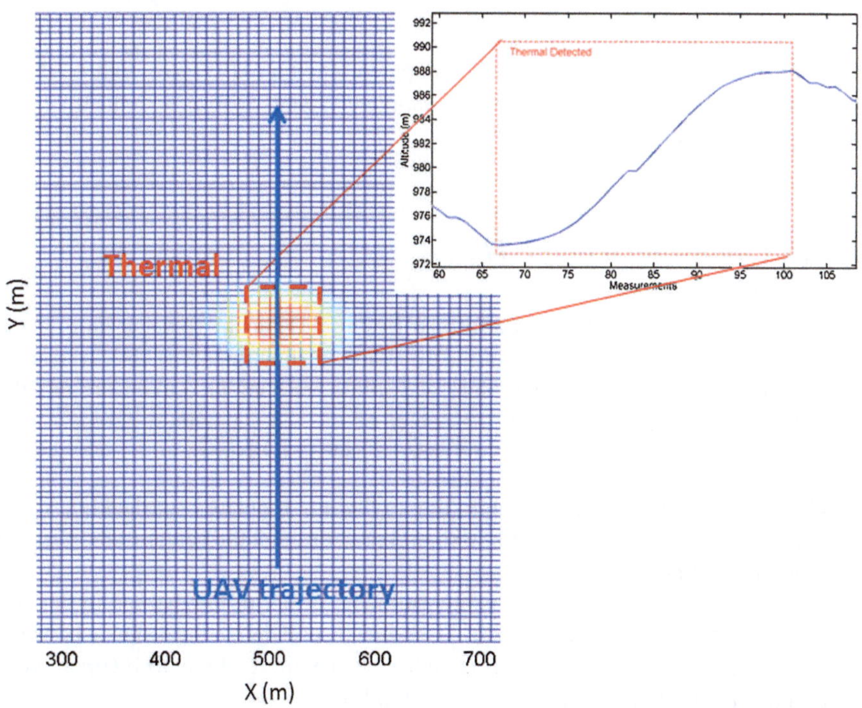

Fig. 17.4 Detection of a thermal when a UAV passes through it by using Algorithm 1

Algorithm 1: Thermal detection algorithm

$h_{\text{gain}} \leftarrow 0, h_0 \leftarrow 0$
$thermal_{\text{origin}} \leftarrow (0, 0, 0)$
for Each aircraft position, $\boldsymbol{p_i} = (x_i, y_i, h_i)$ **do**
  $\Delta h = h_i - h_{i-1}$
  if $\Delta h > 0$ **then**
    $h_{\text{final}} \leftarrow h_i$
    if $thermal_{\text{origin}} = (0, 0, 0)$ **then**
      $thermal_{\text{origin}} \leftarrow \boldsymbol{p_i}$
      $h_0 \leftarrow h_i$
    end if
  else
    if $h_i > h_{\text{final}}$ **then**
      if $h_{\text{gain}} > H_{\text{threshold}}$ **then**
        Thermal Detected. Estimate the center:
        $thermal_{center} \leftarrow \frac{thermal_{\text{origin}} + \boldsymbol{p_i}}{2}$
      end if
      $h_{\text{gain}} \leftarrow 0, h_0 \leftarrow 0$
      $thermal_{\text{origin}} \leftarrow (0, 0, 0)$
    end if
  end if
end for

a UAV passes through it. The drift is computed when an UAV passes through the thermal again by considering the how the estimated center evolves with the time, and making a minimum squares adjustment.

17.4.3 Computation of the TPs

The computation of the TPs is performed by the TD block from the data of the detected thermal: estimated center of the thermal and direction of the UAV trajectory passing through the thermal. Two more waypoints are computed to ensure that the UAV trajectory will pass through the center of the thermal with a perpendicular direction to the first one (see Fig. 17.5). The steps followed are:

1. Compute the perpendicular straight line to the first trajectory (dashed black line in Fig. 17.5). This new straight line should pass through the center of the thermal (solid black line in Fig. 17.5).
2. Consider a circle whose center is the estimated center of the thermal in the first pass (dashed red circle in Fig. 17.5). Its radius, r, will define the distance between the TPs and the center of the thermal, it has been empirically set to 100 m in order to make the flight plan flyable by our autopilot.
3. Compute the cross points between the new straight line and the circle. The two points computed, TP_1 and TP_2, along with the center of the thermal, TP_c, will be the set of TPs to explore the thermal.

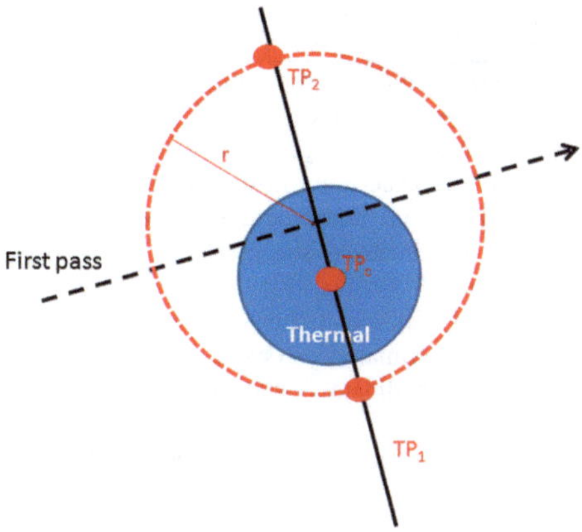

Fig. 17.5 Computation of the TPs to pass through a thermal again. TP_1, TP_c, and TP_2 are computed from the first pass (estimated center of the thermal and UAV trajectory)

The TPs computed, the tuple (TP_1, TP_c, TP_2), are sent to the MM block and each UAV can apply for passing through PoI or TPs to improve the computation of the parameters of a thermal.

17.5 Path Planner

The proposed path planning algorithm is called BRHS method and is based on a DFS algorithm [24, 26]. A drawback of the DFS is that it may not finish in certain situations. For example, if it is used in a graph with cycles, it will expand all nodes in a cycled branch that may not contain the goal node, so it will keep exploring that branch infinitely. For this reason, a bounded method is chosen in order to make the execution time finite in all cases. On the other hand, the DFS does not consider any cost to compute the solution. In our case, the traveled distance is the cost and it is considered to compute the best successor in each branch and the execution is recursive.

Bounding the exploration also presents some drawbacks. In particular, the method is not complete because the exploration may end before a goal is reached. In these cases, a heuristic has to be considered. The proposed heuristic considers the distance to the closest goal.

The inputs of the algorithm are: current location of the UAV, time, position of the remaining PoI and TPs, thermals in the space, minimum altitude of the UAV to fly, and maximum depth that BRHS can reach. The output is a flight plan given by a set of waypoints. Each waypoint is defined by: 2D position of the waypoint, estimated altitude of the UAV will have when reaching the waypoint (considering the descending angle as a constant that depends on the characteristics of the UAV), ETA to the waypoint (cost), and the distance that should be traveled to reach the waypoint from the current location.

Algorithm 2 shows the behavior of the BRHS algorithm. This algorithm starts from the initial node defined by the current localization, altitude and time of the UAV. It will calculate the reachable nodes from the current node by invoking Algorithm 3. If the

Algorithm 2: BRHS Algorithm

```
Require: initial_node, depth
  best ← initial_node
  successor_list ← get_successors(initial_node)
  for Each successor in successor_list do
    if is_final_node(successor) then
      candidate ← successor
    else
      if depth == 1 then
        estimate_cost(successor)
        candidate ← successor
      else
        candidate ← BRHS(successor, depth - 1)
      end if
    end if
    if candidate.cost < best.cost + t_visit then
      best ← successor
    end if
  end for
  return best
```

current node is a goal it will get it if the cost , or the maximum depth has been reached it stops and estimates the cost of the node if necessary. Else, it will recursively call the algorithm starting with the current node. Accordingly, Algorithm 3 calculates the successors that are reachable in an action range (A_r) from a node. The action range

Algorithm 3: Get_successors

```
Require: parent_node
  successor_list = Ø
  Calculate A_r (Eq. 17.1)
  for Each PoI in PoI_list do
    near_thermal = get_nearest_thermal(PoI)
    if parent_node.distance(PoI) + PoI.distance(near_thermal.location)< A_r α then
      new_state ← get_estimated_state(PoI)
      if PoIA.is_available(new_state) then
        successor_list.append(new_state)
      end if
    end if
  end for
  for Each T in thermal_list do
    if parent_node.disaccording tance(T.location) < γ_s then
      new_state ← get_estimated_state(T.location)
      if TM.is_safe(new_state) then
        successor_list.append(new_state)
      end if
    end if
  end for
  return best
```

of the UAV is calculated with Eq. 17.1.

$$A_r = \frac{h - h_{\min}}{tg\gamma}. \tag{17.1}$$

Where current altitude h, minimum altitude $h_{\min}$, and the gliding angle ψ (see Sect. 17.6). α is a safety coefficient that is usually set to 1.2. Finally, γ_s is used to not consider very distant thermals, reducing the execution time of the algorithm.

A flight plan could not be computed if all the PoI have already been visited or the rest of PoIs to visit are not reachable. The goal is to keep flying all the UAVs if a new PoI is added or a new thermal is detected in the environment and allows visiting some PoI which have not been visited yet. When an UAV cannot reach any detected thermal, it is automatically commanded to go to Home in order to land.

17.6 Conflict Detection and Resolution

UAVs should maintain as much as possible a minimum separation among them for safety purposes. The proposed system should not let a UAV enter in a thermal if a vertical separation is violated and should also ensure that the horizontal and vertical separation are satisfied outside the thermals. Therefore, a collision detection and avoidance system is necessary when the UAVs fly outside the thermals.

Periodically, the trajectories of the UAVs are estimated by considering their flight plans, current state and integrating the model described in Eq. (17.2) in a determinate time horizon. A potential collision is detected if there exists a time when two cylinders of radius r_{xy} and altitude r_z, centered in each UAV overlap.

Whenever a potential collision between two or more UAVs is detected in the system, a collision-free trajectory planning algorithm is executed. It is based on a RRT* planning algorithm. RRT* makes two main modifications to the original RRT planning algorithm [16].

An UAV model should be considered to compute the trajectories. The controlled UAV model proposed in [20] has been used in order to generate feasible trajectories. The main modifications to the original model are the constant descent rate, assumption of constant airspeed, and the addition of the vertical wind velocity that is retrieved from the wind map. The configuration space of this model is composed by three spatial coordinates (x, y, z) and the heading θ. However, new samples are generated randomly in this space, but coordinates z and θ are calculated in the interpolation phase in order to ensure that the final trajectories are flyable. Therefore, the equations that model the behavior of the UAV are:

$$\begin{aligned} \dot{x} &= v_i \cos(\theta) \\ \dot{y} &= v_i \sin(\theta) \\ \dot{\theta} &= \alpha_\theta \left(\theta^c - \theta\right) \\ \dot{h} &= -v \tan\psi + w_z \end{aligned} \tag{17.2}$$

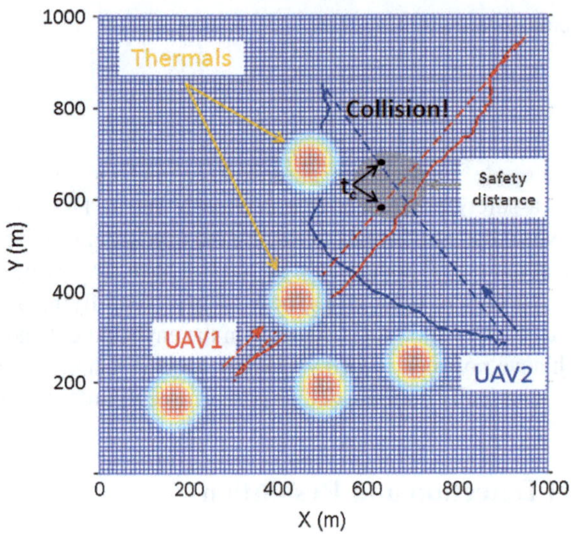

Fig. 17.6 UAV trajectories computed from the RRT* planning algorithm to solve a collision (instant t_c): *solid line* is the solution trajectory and *dashed line* is the initial trajectory

where ψ is the gliding angle of the aircraft. This angle relates the horizontal traveled distance with the descent of the UAV in the absence of wind and without propulsion.

It is known that the RRT* algorithm is only capable of minimizing the length of the trajectories [16]. As long as this algorithm is applied only outside the thermals, this is a very fair approximation of energy-efficient trajectories.

Figure 17.6 shows two collision-free trajectories computed to solve a collision detected between two UAVs. Both change their initial trajectory to avoid the collision. The trajectories generated by RRT* should be then smoothed before being sent to the autopilot. The algorithm has been implemented in C++ using the Open Motion Planning Library using the contrib package where an implementation of the RRT* algorithm is available. More than a hundred test cases have been used as bench-test and the average run time was of 2.53 s with a standard deviation of 1.5 s. This allows the algorithm to be used in the system for real-time applications.

17.7 Simulation Results

Many simulations with several UAVs have been performed to show the behavior of the system and how thermals are identified with cooperative gliding fixed-wing UAV. The configuration parameters are listed below.

- **Wind Map**. Cellsize = 10 m, drift = 0.5 m/s, lifetime = 25 min, noise σ = 0.3 m/s, windspeed = 3 m/s.

- **CDR.** $r_{xy} = 50\,\text{m}$, $r_z = 25\,\text{m}$
- **Planner.** $t_{\text{visit}} = 5\,\text{s}$, $\text{depth}_{\text{max}} = 4$
- **UAV Model.** $\phi = 0.08\,\text{rad}$, $v = 13.89\,\text{m/s}$, $h_{\text{min}} = 80\,\text{m}$.

Next a study to analyze the behavior of the system with several cooperative UAVs is presented. A wind map generated randomly is considered. Initially, twelve thermals are created (thermals 1–12). Five thermals more are created during the mission in different times (thermals N1–N5) (see Fig. 17.7). Each UAV does not have any information about their location or strength, so the thermals are unknown to the system. Ten simulations are performed in each case by changing the initial position of each UAV. Table 17.1 shows the results obtained by considering different number of UAVs. The time of the mission and the number of thermals detected is shown. Figure 17.7 presents one of the simulations to show how the exploration is carried out with three UAVs.

It is important to highlight the main advantages of the proposed system. It ensures the safety of the system. Each UAV takes into account the drift estimated to exploit

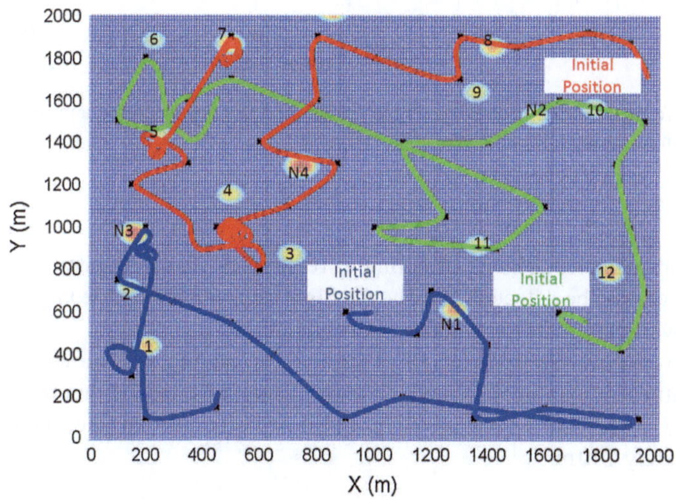

Fig. 17.7 Mission with three UAVs: UAV trajectories to pass through fifty PoI (*black points*). Wind map considered corresponding with $t = 450\,\text{s}$

Table 17.1 Detection and identification of thermals considering ten simulations

UAVs	Elapsed time (s)	Thermals detected
1	1345.31 ± 57.20	4.63 ± 1.51
2	759.92 ± 42.02	4.81 ± 1.68
3	498.844 ± 36.01	5.75 ± 1.92
4	466.24 ± 44.03	6.89 ± 0.84
5	344.25 ± 31.63	5.73 ± 1.34

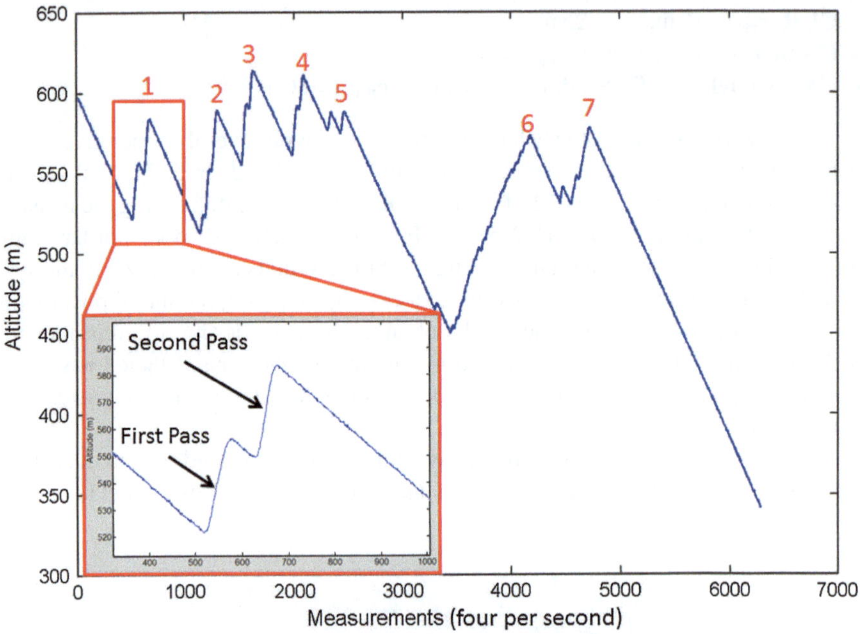

Fig. 17.8 Vertical profile of the UAV flight. Seven thermals are identified and the UAV passes through each thermal twice to estimate its parameters

the thermals detected. The mission time is reduced by using cooperative UAVs and more thermal can be detected. Finally, the flight duration is extended to carry out the mission, while thermals exist in the environment.

In order to show how the detection of thermal is done, Fig. 17.8 shows the evolution of the altitude in a simulation with an UAV. It identifies seven thermals (thermals 4, 1, N3, 7, 5, 10, and 12 of Fig. 17.7), and it exploits the sixth thermal by gaining approximately 140 m.

17.8 Experimental Results

Experiments have been performed with two gliding fixed-wing UAVs in the airfield of La Cartuja (Seville) in order to test the behavior of the whole system in real time. One of them is a real gliding fixed-wing UAV and the other is simulated. The thermals are emulated; that is, when the real UAV accesses a simulated thermal, it simulates the gaining of energy by using the propulsion system to gain altitude. The rest of the flight is carried out without propulsion. The following variables of the UAV were set: gliding angle (0.11 rad), airspeed (13.89 m/s).

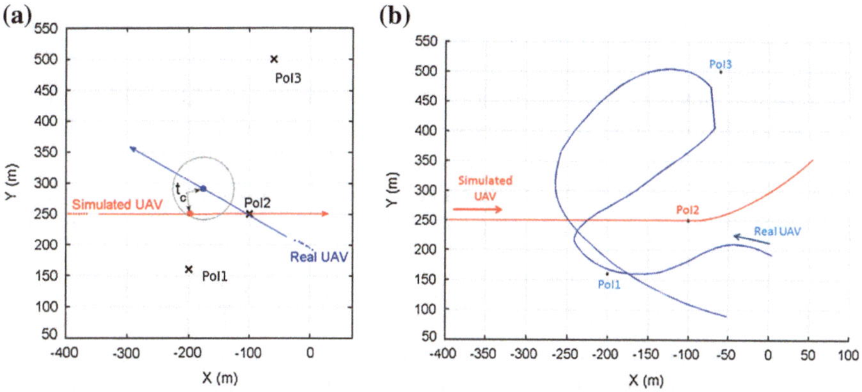

Fig. 17.9 Real and simulated flight in 2D to explore the environment in the airfield of La Cartuja (Seville). A potential collision is detected (**a**) and real UAV avoids it (**b**). Therefore, the real UAV passes through PoI1 and PoI3, and the simulated UAV passes through PoI2

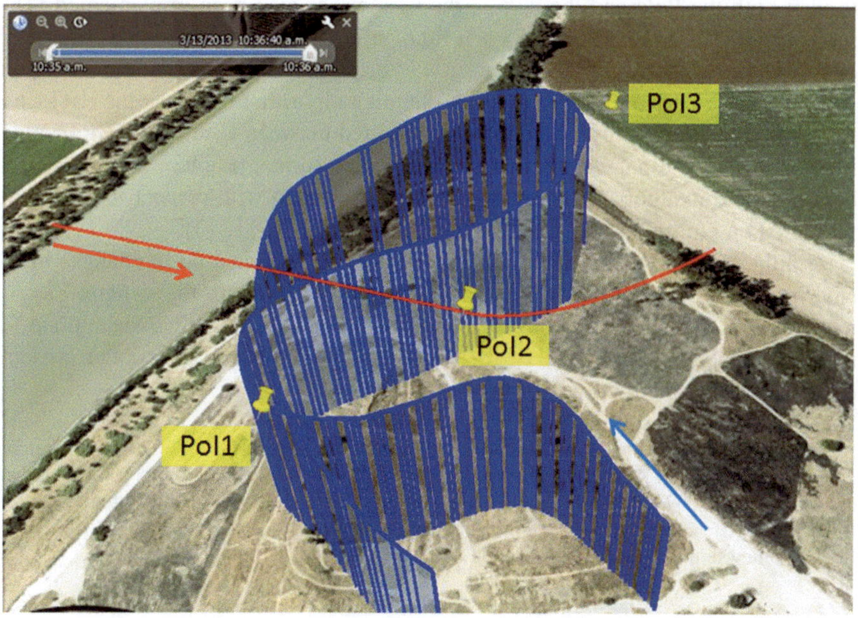

Fig. 17.10 UAV Trajectories and location of thermal represented in the airfield of La Cartuja (Seville): real gliding fixed-wing UAV (*blue*), simulated gliding fixed-wing UAV (*red*)

Figure 17.9 shows a potential collision and the solution trajectory of the real gliding fixed-wing UAV in 2D. Both UAVs fly to the PoI2 but real UAV changes its trajectory to avoid the collision, so it passes through PoI1. Finally, Fig. 17.10 presents the trajectories in the airfield of La Cartuja (Seville).

17.9 Conclusions

The chapter considers long endurance cooperative missions with multiple gliding fixed-wing UAVs. The goal is to explore an environment as much as possible without landing. Multiple UAVs can be used in order to decrease the time to perform the mission and increasing the probability of detecting unknown thermals. A new system has been proposed to extend the flight duration by harvesting energy that comes from thermals.

A thermal detection algorithm is implemented to identify unknown thermals and exploit them. First, a potential thermal is detected from the changes of altitude of a UAV. Then an algorithm computes two extra waypoints to ensure that a UAV will pass through the center of the thermal with a perpendicular direction to the first one. The thermal parameters are estimated after the second pass and these parameters are sent to the TM block.

These thermals are considered as a shared resource of the system. A distributed path planning algorithm (BFRS) that automatically guides the UAVs in the system to visit both the PoIs and the TPs in the system has also been implemented. This algorithm will ask the TM block each time an UAV needs to enter in a thermal in order to gain energy.

Moreover, a collision-free trajectory planning algorithm based on the RRT* has been implemented to solve the collisions detected between UAVs. The RRT* planning algorithm presented in [2] has been adapted to this problem by considering the energy. This algorithm is an important contribution with respect to the works presented on multiple UAV in autonomous soaring [6, 7, 11, 17].

Simulations demonstrate the utility of the system by adapting to changes in the environment while maximizing the endurance of the UAVs in the system. Experiments that have been carried out on a real platform shows that it can be applied for real-time applications because of its low computational needs. This latter presents an important contribution with respect to [6, 11].

Acknowledgments This work was supported by the European Commission FP7 ICT Programme under the International Research Exchange Network "Multi-UAV Cooperation for long endurance applications" (SI-0971/2012) and the CLEAR Project (DPI2011-28937-C02-01) funded by the Ministerio de Ciencia e Innovacion of the Spanish Government. David Alejo is granted with a FPU Spanish fellowship from the Ministerio de Educación, Cultura y Deporte.

References

1. 3DRobotics (2014) Apm multiplatform autopilot
2. Akgun B, Stilman M (2011) Sampling heuristics for optimal motion planning in high dimensions. In: International conference on intelligent robots and systems (IROS2011), San Francisco, California (USA), 25–30 Sept 2011, pp 2640–2645
3. Allen MJ (2005) Autonomous soaring for improved endurance of a small uninhabited air vehicle. In: Proceedings of the 43rd aerospace sciences meeting, AIAA

4. Allen MJ (2006) Updraft model for development of autonomous soaring uninhabited air vehicles. In: 44th AIAA aerospace sciences meeting and exhibit, AIAA 2006–1510, pp 9–12
5. Allen MJ (2007) Guidance and control of an autonomous soaring uav. NASA TM-214611, February 2007
6. Andersson K, Kaminer I, Jones KD, Dobrokhodov V, Lee DJ (2009) Cooperating uavs using thermal lift to extend endurance. In: AIAA unmanned unlimited conference, Seatle, Washington, USA, April 6–9, 2009
7. Granichin O, Antal C, Levi S (2010) Adaptive autonomous soaring of multiple uavs using simultaneous perturbation stochastic approximation. In: Proceedings of the 49th IEEE conference on decision and control, Atlanta, GA, USA
8. Chakrabarty A, Langelaan JW (2011) Energy-based long-range path planning for soaring-capable unmanned aerial vehicles. J Guid Control Dyn 34(4):1002–1015
9. Clarke JHA, Chen WH (2012) Trajectory generation for autonomous soaring uas. Int J Automation Comput 9(3):248–256
10. Cobano JA, Alejo D, Vera S, Heredia G, Ollero A (2013) Multiple gliding uav coordination for static soaring in real time applications. In: IEEE international conference on robotics and automation (ICRA2013), Karlsruhe, Germany, pp 782–787, 6–10 May, 2013
11. Depenbusch NT, Langelaan JW (2011) Coordinated mapping and exploration for autonomous soaring. In: AIAA Infotech@Aerospace Conference, St. Louis, Missouri, USA, March 29–31, 2011
12. Edwards DJ (2008) Implementation details and flight test results of an autonomous soaring controller. In: AIAA guidance, navigation, and control conference, AIAA, paper 2008–7244, Reston, VA, Aug 2008
13. Hazard M (2009) Unscented kalman filter for thermal parameter identification. In: AIAA region II student conference, AIAA, Washington, DC, USA
14. Kagabo WB, Kolodziej JR (2011) Trajectory determination for energy efficient autonomous soaring. In: 2011 American control conference, San Francisco, CA, USA, pp 4655–4660, June 29 - July 01
15. Kahveci N, Ioannou P, Mirmirani D (2007) Optimal static soaring of uavs using vehicle routing with time windows. In: AIAA aerospace sciences meeting and exhibit, AIAA-2007-158, AIAA, Washington, DC, USA
16. Karaman S, Frazzoli E (2011) Sampling-based algorithms for optimal motion planning. Int J Robot Res 30(7):846–894
17. Klesh A, Kabamba P, Girard A (2009) Optimal cooperative thermalling of unmanned aerial vehicles. Optim Coop Control Strateg 381:355–369
18. Lancaster I (1885) The problem of the soaring bird. University of Chicago Press, Chicago
19. Lawrance NRJ, Sukkarieh S (2011) Path planning for autonomous soaring flight in dynamic wind fields. In: Proceedings of the IEEE international conference on robotics and automation, ICRA2011, Shanghai, China
20. McLain TW, Beard RW, Beard A (2003) Coordination variables, coordination functions, and cooperative timing missions
21. Metzger DE, Hedrick JK (1974) Optimal flight paths for soaring flight. In: Proceedings of the 2nd international symposium on the technology and science of low speed and motorless flight
22. Nguyen J, Lawrance N, Fitch R, Sukkarieh S (2013) Energy-constrained motion planning for information gathering with autonomous aerial soaring. In: IEEE international conference on robotics and automation (ICRA2013), Karlsruhe, Germany, pp 3825–3831, 6–10 May, 2013
23. Patel CK, Kroo IM (2008) Theorical and experimental investigation of energy extraction from atmospheric turbulence. In: Proceedings on 26th congress of international council of the aeronautical sciences, Anchorage, Alaska, USA, 14–19 Sept, 2008
24. Rasmussen SJ, Shima T, Mitchel JW, Sparks AG, Chandler P (2004) State-space search for improved autonomous uavs assignment algorithm. In: Proceeding on 43rd IEEE conference on decision and control, Atlantis, Paradise Island, Bahamas, pp 2911–2916
25. Rayleigh L (1883) The soaring of birds. Nature 27:534–535

26. Russell S, Norvig P (2003) Artificial intelligence: a modern approach, 2nd edn. Prentice-Hall, New Jersey
27. Guionnet T, Martin J, Shaffer SA, Weimerskirch H, Costa DP (2000) Fast and fuel efficient optimal use of wind by flying albatrosses. Proc R Soc Lond Biol Sci 267:1869–1874
28. Wharington J (1998) Autonomous control of soaring aircraft by reinforcement learning. PhD thesis, Royal Melbourne Institute of Technology, Melbourne, Australia

Chapter 18
Distributed Coordination of Networked Robots for Perimeter Surveillance Tasks

José J. Acevedo, Begoña C. Arrue, Iván Maza and Aníbal Ollero

Abstract Perimeter surveillance is a relevant task which can be performed in a more efficient manner using multiple robots than a single robot. This chapter addresses the perimeter surveillance tasks using a team of heterogeneous robots and assuming limited communications conditions and zones with different priorities. A partitioning strategy, where the whole perimeter is divided in segments and these segments are assigned to the different robots, is proposed. The robots patrol their assigned segments, while keeps at least periodic connectivity between them. The refresh time is used as criterion to optimize each zone surveillance, while an urgency criterion is proposed to allocate dynamically the robots among the zones based on their priorities. Different algorithms and protocols based on the coordination variables and the one-to-one coordination are proposed to coordinate the robots to converge to the desired partitioning strategy in a distributed manner. The presented system is fully decentralized and distributed, robots converge to a cooperative behavior from local decisions. A set of experimental and simulated results are provided to test, analyze and compare the convergence, efficiency, scalability and robustness of the proposed solutions.

18.1 Introduction

Perimeter surveillance missions has been widely studied in the scientific literature about robotics and automation. For instance, a robot for surveillance tasks is designed in [1], while a whole system using ground stations is presented in [2] to protect a

J.J. Acevedo (✉) · B.C. Arrue · I. Maza · A. Ollero
Grupo de Robótica, Visión y Control, Escuela Superior de Ingenieros, Universidad de Sevilla, Camino de Los Descubrimientos S/n, 41092 Sevilla, Spain
e-mail: jacevedo@us.es

B.C. Arrue
e-mail: barrue@us.es

I. Maza
e-mail: imaza@us

A. Ollero
e-mail: aollero@us.es

P. Spagnolo et al. (eds.), *Human Behavior Understanding in Networked Sensing*,
DOI 10.1007/978-3-319-10807-0_18

border against intruders. Other authors, as in [3, 4], address the cooperation between ground stations and UAVs in border defense missions. Reference [5] proposes a robust solution to the perimeter surveillance problem using behavioral control. Anyway, the use of multiple robots offers higher efficiency, coverage and robustness than a single robots, as is stated in [6, 7]. In this chapter, the cooperation between mobile and fixed agents for perimeter surveillance missions is studied.

Assuming null information about where and when the intruders to detect (or event to monitor) can appear in the perimeter, it can be assumed that the probability of intruder appearing is equal along the whole perimeter. So, any position into the perimeter should be monitored with the same frequency. It is a frequency-based approach, where the criterion to optimize is the frequency in which any position in the path is visited (or monitored) by a robot, [8]. It is equivalent to optimize the refresh time or elapsed time between each pair of consecutive visits, [9].

In [10], different patrolling strategies are proposed for surveillance mission (defined as the min-idleness problem) from a frequency-based approach. In [11] the cyclic patrolling strategy is explained assuming identical robots, a closed path and communications constraints. Authors of [9] describe the partitioning strategy to coordinate a set of video cameras in surveillance missions and assuming asynchronous communications. Both, the cyclic and the partitioning strategies, are analyzed and compared in [12] from a refresh time criterion. The partitioning strategy is proposed in this chapter because it useful for non-closed paths, exploits the heterogeneous capabilities of the robots and keeps unless periodic connectivity (as was defined in [13]) even under communications constraints.

However, if there are some information about the probability of intruders appearing along the perimeter, the refresh time approach can not be the more suitable. For instance, considering intelligent intruders, a deterministic solution as the above mentioned patrolling strategies would not be useful. Authors of [14] address the problem assuming potential intelligent intruders and maximize the probability to detect them. In [15], a monitoring problem with multiple identical robots assuming positions with different priorities is posed and solve using a metric called urgency. The priority represents how often the position should be visited. In this chapter, the priorities are also defined along the perimeter and the urgency is used as optimizing criterion.

The coordination of multiple robots is a challenging topic in distributed multi-robot systems, more assuming communications constraints. Different coordination techniques have been proposed for cooperative surveillance missions. A peer-to-peer method is proposed in [9, 16] to solve perimeter surveillance missions in a cooperative manner following a partitioning strategy and assuming asynchronous communications. It is based on sharing the actually assigned segments between each pair of contacting robots and dividing the union between both according to their capabilities. A similar method is named one-to-one coordination and introduced in [17, 18] to solve area monitoring missions with multiple aerial robots. This method is used also [19] to patrol a path with multiple robots following a path partitioning strategy.

Other methods based on coordination variables are proposed in [20–22] to solve perimeter surveillance missions, but assuming no different priorities.

The coordination variables can be defined as the minimum amount of variables that all the robots should share to solve the problem in an independent but coherent manner. Authors of [23] analyze how the consensus can be reached in few iterations using the coordination variables. The challenge here is how to share the same coordination variables considering only asynchronous communications between neighbors robots. It can be difficult to define which information to interchange between the robots to accomplish correctly the mission in a distributed manner.

A totally distributed and decentralized solution is posed in this chapter to address a cooperative perimeter surveillance mission assuming priorities. An urgency criterion helps to normalize the refresh time along the whole perimeter, regardless the different priorities. The surveillance mission is redefined as a two levels problem. The first one is a dynamic allocation problem to assign the robots between the paths in order to minimize the maximum urgency along the whole perimeter. It is solved using a one-to-one coordination method. The second one is a cooperative patrolling strategy to optimize the refresh time of each path. A robust coordination variables based algorithm allows the robots to converge in few iterations to a partitioning strategy in a distributed manner ensuring periodic connectivity even under communications constraints.

The rest of the chapter is organized as follows. Section 18.2 states the perimeter surveillance problem with multiple robots assuming priorities and defines the different optimizing criteria. It is redefined as a dynamic allocation problem in Sect. 18.3, where the issue is to assign the robots among the paths to minimize the maximum urgency along the whole perimeter. In Sect. 18.4 the partitioning strategy is chosen to patrol a non closed path assuming communications constraints in a cooperative manner using a team of heterogeneous robots. An algorithm based on the coordination variables is presented in Sect. 18.5 to allow the robots to converge to the partitioning strategy from a distributed manner, showing validation results. A one-to-one coordination method is proposed in Sect. 18.6 to allow the fixed nodes manage the dynamic allocation of robots between their adjacent paths. Section 18.7 shows the conclusions.

18.2 Perimeter Surveillance Missions with a Team of Mobile Robots

Figure 18.1 illustrates the problem addressed in this chapter.

Let us consider a perimeter B as the union of a set of adjacent and non overlapped paths $\{B_1, B_2, \dots, B_M\}$. Given a curve b which defines the whole perimeter B, each zone B_i can be defined as follows:

$$B_i := \left\{ b(x) \in \mathbb{R}^2 : x \in [l_{i-1}, l_i] \right\}, \tag{18.1}$$

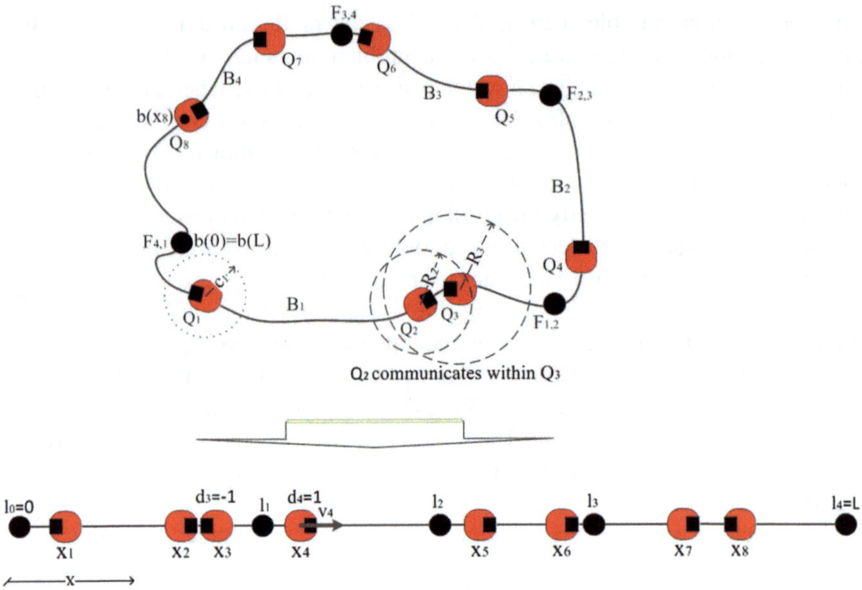

Fig. 18.1 A perimeter B defined as the union of 4 paths with different priorities has to be monitored by a team of 8 mobile robots with different speed capabilities and 4 fixed nodes

where x define the distance to the initial perimeter position $b(0)$ along the curve b, $l_0 = 0$, $l_i - l_{i-1} = L(B_i)$ and $L : H \rightarrow L(H)$ is a function which computes the length of the input path H. Therefore, the length of the whole border B can be computed as the sum of the length of all the adjacent paths.

$$L = L(B) = \sum_{i=1}^{M} L(B_i) = l_M \tag{18.2}$$

On other hand, a priority P_i can be defined for each zone B_i. The priority of a path defines the probability of appearing an intruder or event of interest in this zone with respect to others. A higher priority indicates a higher probability.

Finally, let us assume that there is a fixed node (or ground station) $F_{i,i+1}$ located between each pair of adjacent paths B_i and B_{i+1}. These nodes should receive information from both adjacent zones and estimates coherently their priorities. It means, the priority of a zone B_i should be equally estimated by its two adjacent fixed nodes (or ground stations) $F_{i,i+1}$ and $F_{i-1,i}$.

Given the this scenario, a perimeter surveillance missions is addressed using a team of mobile robots $Q := \{Q_1, Q_2, \ldots, Q_N\}$. The robots of the team Q should cooperate to perform the surveillance mission along the perimeter B, accounting their own capabilities and the different zones priorities and lengths.

For sake of simplicity, it is assumed that the robots just can move along the curve b (it means, the above described perimeter) while run a collision avoidance system. Then, each robot Q_i state at time t can be defined by three values:

- The actual position of the robot Q_i in the perimeter curve b, $x_i(t) \in [0, L]$. It defines the actual position of Q_i in the plane, $b(x_i) \in \mathbb{R}^2$.
- The actual motion speed of the robot Q_i to travel the curve b, $v_i(t)$. It is assumed a maximum motion speed $v_i^{\max}$ for any robot.
- The actual sense in which Q_i travel the curve b, $d_i(t)$. A value $d_i = 1$ indicates that robot moves following a clockwise sense, while $d_i = -1$ indicates a counterclockwise sense.

On the other hand, the control inputs variables would be v_i and d_i, and the dynamic control model can be defined as follows:

$$\frac{dx_i(t)}{dt} = d_i(t)v_i(t), \forall i = 1, 2, \ldots, N, \tag{18.3}$$

where $d_i(t) = \{-1, 1\}$ and $v_i(t) \leq v_i^{\max}$, $\forall i, t$.

The team of mobile robots can be considered heterogeneous since each robot can have different capabilities. Let us define three different capabilities:

- The maximum motion speed $v_i^{\max}$ as is defined above.
- The communications range R_i, which defines the maximum distance between a pair of robots Q_i and Q_j to interchange information between them. Therefore, two robots will be able to communicate between them, if they are close enough.
- The coverage range c_i, which defines the segment $C_i(t) \in B$ which is being monitored by Q_i at time t.

However, the effects of the coverage and communications ranges in the perimeter surveillance problem are just limited to reduce the total length to patrol. Therefore, these parameters will be considered equal for all the robots later throughout this chapter. It means, $c_i = c \approx 0$ and $R_i = R \approx 0$, respectively, because they are considered too small with respect to the total perimeter length. Then, the robots will be assumed heterogeneous because of their different maximum motion speeds.

18.2.1 Refresh Time Criterion

Assuming no information about the potential location in the perimeter of the intruders or events of interest, a frequency criterion seems to be the more efficient option to optimize the surveillance problem. The frequency-based approach assumes that the probability of appearing an event in a position x without being detected is increasing while the frequency of visit for this position x is decreasing. The actual frequency of visit of a position x at time t is inversely related to the refresh time $RT(x, t)$ or elapsed time since the last visit to that position (as was defined in [12]). It is also defined as idleness in [10], but applied along a perimeter.

Given an updating time dT, the refresh time can be periodically recomputed as follows:

$$RT(x,t) := \begin{cases} RT(x, t-dT) + dT, \text{if } b(x) \notin \bigcup_{i=1}^{N} C_i(t) \\ 0, \text{ in other case} \end{cases}, \tag{18.4}$$

where $RT(x,0) = 0, \forall x \in B$ and $t = kdT$ with $k \in \mathbb{N}$.

Let us define two different refresh time based criteria to optimize the perimeter surveillance task:

- The maximum refresh time computed along the whole perimeter B, $RT^{\max}(t)$.

$$RT^{\max}(t) := \max_{0 \le x \le L} (RT(x,t)) \tag{18.5}$$

- The average refresh time computed along the whole perimeter B, $\overline{RT}(t)$.

$$\overline{RT}(t) := \frac{1}{L} \int_{0}^{L} RT(x,t)\mathrm{d}x \tag{18.6}$$

Then, assuming a perimeter formed by a single zone ($M = 1$), the objective will be minimizing the maximum value of a refresh time criterion computed along a mission. In this chapter the criterion to minimize is the maximum refresh time.

$$J := \max_{t}(RT^{\max}(t)) \tag{18.7}$$

Theorem 18.1 *The minimum maximum refresh time computed along a perimeter B which length is L while is patrolled by a team of N mobile robots* $Q := \{Q_1, Q_2, \ldots, Q_N\}$ *is computed when they move at their maximum motion speeds* $v := \{v_1^{\max}, v_2^{\max}, \ldots, v_N^{\max}\}$ *and is lower bounded by* $\frac{L}{\sum_{i=1}^{N} v_i^{\max}}$.

Proof Assuming that all the robots move at their maximum motion speed, during a time of T' s, Q_j would cover a length of $T'v_j^{\max}$. During the same time, another robot Q_k would cover a length of $T'v_k^{\max}$. Then, considering that the segments covered by the robots are not overlapped, during that time, the whole team of robot would cover a total length of $T' \sum_{i=1}^{N} v_i^{\max}$.

From here, it can be deduced the time T that the whole team would take to cover the total length L.

$$L = T \sum_{i=1}^{N} v_i^{\max} \tag{18.8}$$

$$T = \frac{L}{\sum_{i=1}^{N} v_i^{\max}} \tag{18.9}$$

In the best case scenario, each robot could travel the same segment again and again. Therefore, each position into the segment would be without being visited T seconds. It means, $RT^{\max}(t) = T, \forall t$.

If any of the robots move with a motion speed less than its maximum speed, $v_i < v_i^{\max}$, it is easy to deduce from expression (18.9) that T would be increased and, therefore, the maximum refresh time $RT^{\max}$ too.

18.2.2 Urgency Criterion

Nevertheless, in this chapter, some information about the perimeter is known. The perimeter is divided in M adjacent paths with different priorities (it means different "a priori" probabilities of intruder appearing). Then, a frequency-based criterion could not be suitable because zones with the highest priorities should be the most frequently visited ones.

Therefore, the priorities can be related to the refresh times. Given a path B_i which priority is P_i, RT_i defines the maximum refresh time computed along a mission. So, another path B_j which priority is P_j should be patrolled with a maximum refresh time $RT_j = \frac{P_i}{P_j} RT_i$.

The urgency is defined to normalize the refresh time along the whole perimeter, even assuming zones with different priorities. The urgency $U(x,t)$ in a position x at time t can be computed periodically using an updating time dT as follows.

$$U(x,t) := \begin{cases} U(x,t-dT) + P(x)dT, \text{if } b(x) \notin \bigcup_{i=1}^{N} C_i(t) \\ 0, \text{ in other case} \end{cases}, \tag{18.10}$$

where $U(x,0) = 0, \forall x \in B$ and $P : x \to P(x)$ is a function which returns the priority of the position $b(x)$.

Based on the urgency, two different criteria can be defined to optimize the perimeter surveillance task:

- The maximum urgency computed along the whole perimeter B, $U^{\max}(t)$.

$$U^{\max}(t) := \max_{0 \le x \le L} (U(x,t)) \tag{18.11}$$

- The average urgency computed along the whole perimeter B, $\overline{U}(t)$.

$$\overline{U}(t) := \frac{1}{L} \int_{0}^{L} U(x,t) \mathrm{d}x \tag{18.12}$$

So, the cost function to minimize can be redefined as follows.

$$J := \max_t(U^{\max}(t)) \tag{18.13}$$

Theorem 18.2 *The minimum maximum urgency computed along a perimeter B divided into non overlapped paths* $\{B_1, B_2, \ldots, B_M\}$ *which lengths are* $\{L(B_1), L(B_2), \ldots, L(B_M)\}$ *and priorities are* $\{P_1, P_2, \ldots, P_M\}$ *and patrolled by a team of N mobile robots* $Q := \{Q_1, Q_2, \ldots, Q_N\}$ *which maximum motion speeds are* $v := \{v_1^{\max}, v_2^{\max}, \ldots, v_N^{\max}\}$ *is lower bounded by* $\frac{\sum_{j=1}^{M} P_j L(B_j)}{\sum_{k=1}^{N} v_k^{\max}}$.

Proof From expression (18.10), the urgency of a position x at time t can be defined based on its refresh time as $U(x,t) = P_i RT(x,t)$, where P_i is the priority of the path where the position x is located. From here, it can be deduced that the maximum urgency computed along a path B_i is $P_i RT_i^{\max}$, where $RT_i^{\max}$ is maximum refresh time computed along the path B_i, $RT_i^{\max} = \max_t \max_{l_{i-1} \le x \le l_i} (RT(x,t))$.

The maximum urgency $U_i^{\max}$ along a path B_i can be defined as follows.

$$U_i^{\max} := P_i RT_i^{\max} \tag{18.14}$$

From Theorem 18.1, it can be deduced its lower bound as $U_i \ge P_i \frac{L(B_i)}{v_B i}$, where $v_B i$ is the sum of the maximum motion speeds of the robots which are patrolling the path B_i. So, the maximum urgency of a path B_i can be redefined as refresh time of a path which length is $P_i L(B_i)$.

Therefore, the maximum urgency of the perimeter B can be computed as the maximum refresh time of a perimeter which length is $\sum_{i=1}^{M} P_i L(B_i)$. So, according to previous results, the maximum urgency along a perimeter B is lower bounded as follows.

$$U^{\max}(t) \ge \frac{\sum_{j=1}^{M} P_j L(B_j)}{\sum_{k=1}^{N} v_k^{\max}}, \forall t \tag{18.15}$$

Theorem 18.3 *The minimum maximum urgency along a perimeter B can be obtained if and only if all the paths* $\{B_1, B_2, \ldots, B_M\}$ *obtains the same maximum urgency.*

Proof Assuming that all the paths obtains the same urgency, and according to Theorem 18.2 and expression (18.14), the following equation for each path B_i can be posed.

$$\frac{P_i L(B_i)}{v_{Bi}} = \frac{\sum_{j=1}^{M} P_j L(B_j)}{\sum_{k=1}^{N} v_k^{\max}} \tag{18.16}$$

From here, it is easy to calculate the sum of speeds of the robots that should patrol each path B_i.

$$v_{Bi} = \frac{P_i L(B_i) \sum_{k=1}^{N} v_k^{\max}}{\sum_{j=1}^{M} P_j L(B_j)} \quad (18.17)$$

Now, the sum of it value for all the segments should be equal to the sum of maximum motion speeds of all the robots. It is accomplished as follows.

$$\sum_{i=1}^{M} v_{Bi} = \sum_{i=1}^{M} (\frac{P_i L(B_i) \sum_{k=1}^{N} v_k^{\max}}{\sum_{j=1}^{M} P_j L(B_j)}) = \sum_{i=1}^{M} (P_i L(B_i)) \frac{\sum_{k=1}^{N} v_k^{\max}}{\sum_{j=1}^{M} P_j L(B_j)} = \sum_{k=1}^{N} v_k^{\max} \quad (18.18)$$

So, if a path B_i is patrolled by a team of robots which sum of maximum motions speed is greater than v_{Bi} as is calculated in (18.17), there should be another path B_j patrolled by a team of robots which sum of maximum motions speed is less than v_{Bj} as is calculated in (18.17). It is easy to deduce that the maximum urgency of the path B_j defined as $\frac{P_j L(B_j)}{v_{Bj}}$ would be increased and, then, the maximum urgency of the whole perimeter B too.

18.3 Allocating the Robots Among the Paths

As it will be shown in the following sections, the lower bounds for the maximum refresh time and urgency (defined by Theorems 18.1 and 18.2) can not be reached in real perimeter surveillance missions, assuming non-closed perimeters, communications constraints, heterogeneous robots or paths with different priorities. Anyway, the objective posed in this chapter is to obtain the minimum maximum urgency along the whole perimeter as close as possible from the optimal one.

Assigning a sub-team of robots $Q^{(i)} = \{Q_j, Q_{j+1}, \ldots, Q_{k-1}, Q_k\}$ for each path B_i, the theoretical maximum refresh time for this path would be as follows.

$$RT^{\max}(Q^{(i)}) := \frac{L(B_i)}{\sum_{n=j}^{k} v_n^{\max}} \quad (18.19)$$

And the theoretical maximum urgency would be as follows.

$$U^{\max}(Q^{(i)}) := P_i \frac{L(B_i)}{\sum_{n=j}^{k} v_n^{\max}} \quad (18.20)$$

Therefore, the problem can be divided in two problems. The first one implies to obtain in a distributed manner the best cooperative strategy to patrol each path B_i using its assigned sub-team of robots $Q^{(i)}$. The second one can be addressed as a distributed dynamic allocation problem, where the robots have to be assigned among the paths to get the theoretical minimum maximum urgency along the whole perimeter.

$$J := \max_{i=1..M} U^{\max}(Q^{(i)}) \tag{18.21}$$

18.4 Cooperative Path Patrolling Strategies

Given a path B_i which length is $L(B_i)$ and a sub-team of robots $Q^{(i)}$ as are defined in the previous section, a cooperative patrolling strategy should be defined to minimize the maximum refresh time along the path.

18.4.1 Cyclic Strategy

According to the cyclic strategy, all of them move along the path at the same speed v, in the same direction and equally spaced. Then, the positions of a pair of robots Q_n and Q_{n-1} with $j < n \leq k$ into the path B_i will be related as follows.

$$x_n - x_{n-1} = \frac{L(B_i)}{k-j} \tag{18.22}$$

Assuming that the path B_i is closed, $b(l_{i-1}) = b(l_i)$, in a steady state, the refresh time along the whole path is as Fig. 18.2 shows and the maximum refresh time can be computed as follows.

$$RT^{\max} = \frac{L(B_i)}{(k-j)v} \tag{18.23}$$

It will be equal to the theoretically optimal one defined in expression (18.9) if and only if all the robots have the same maximum motion speed $v_n^{\max} = v, \forall n = k, \ldots, j$, as is stated in [18]. In this case, the average refresh time can also be calculated easily from the Fig. 18.2.

$$\overline{RT} = \frac{L(B_i)}{2(k-j)v} \tag{18.24}$$

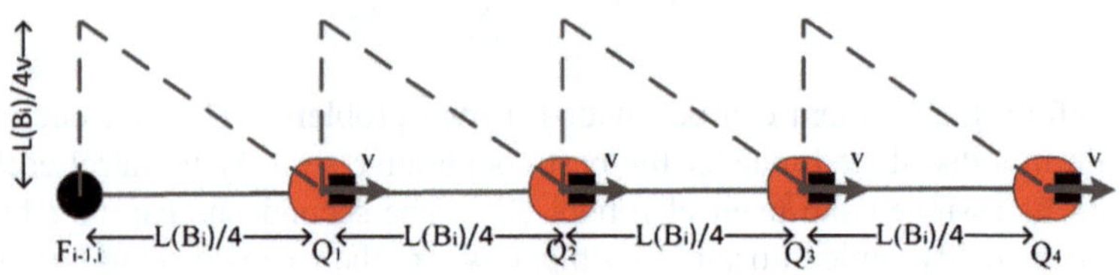

Fig. 18.2 This figure shows as the refresh time along a closed path changes while a team of 4 robot executes a cyclic strategy

However, assuming robots with different motion speeds or non closed paths this strategy can not be applied. Also, assuming communications constraints with a communications range smaller with respect to the total path length, the robots could not be communicate between them to coordinate their motions.

18.4.1.1 Heterogeneous Team of Robots in a Cyclic Strategy

When the team of robots is not homogeneous (there are robots with different maximum motion speeds), but the path is closed, the cyclic strategy can be applied by defining a same motion speed v for all the robots. The Slowest robots will not take part of the solution, while fastest robots should reduce its motion speed to v. Assuming $v_j^{max} \leq v_{j+1}^{max} \leq \cdots \leq v_k^{max}$, the theoretical maximum and average refresh time can be computed as follows.

$$RT^{max} = \frac{L(B_i)}{(k-m+1)v} \tag{18.25}$$

$$\overline{RT} = \frac{L(B_i)}{2(k-m+1)v} \tag{18.26}$$

with $m = \min(k, \ldots, j) | v_m^{max} \geq v$.

Obviously, assuming different maximum motion speeds, the optimal values for refresh time are not reached.

18.4.1.2 Dealing with the Communications Constraints in the Cyclic Strategy

In [11], authors apply the cyclic strategy to solve a perimeter surveillance problem and considering a closed route. The communications constraints are addressed by the authors and solved by stopping a robot to interchange informations with the other robots. This solutions is not robust since a failure in this stopped robot would lead the system to a totally in-communicated conditions.

So, considering a fixed node into a closed path B_i which length is $L(B_i)$ and a team of $k-j$ homogeneous mobile robots which can move with the same maximum motion speed v, it is possible to compute the latency (or time since a event is detected until it is shared with the rest of the team). Applying the cyclic strategy, each pair of nearby robots is separated a distance of $\frac{L(B_i)}{k-j}$ along the path. So, each $\frac{L(B_i)}{v(k-j)}$ seconds a different robots communicate with the fixed node. In the worst case scenario, a robot detects an event just after communicates with the fixed node. Then, this robot takes $\frac{L(B_i)}{v}$ seconds to inform the fixed node. Now, the fixed node has to inform the rest of the robots. Therefore, theoretically the latency, as was defined in [12], can be upper-bounded as follows.

$$LT \leq \frac{L(B_i)}{v} + (k - j - 1)\frac{L(B_i)}{(k-j)v} \approx 2\frac{L(B_i)}{v} \quad (18.27)$$

These values for the refresh times and the latency are not near to optimal ones. Also, in the presented problem, assuming more tha one path ($M > 1$), these paths can not be closed. Therefore, the cyclic strategy is not useful for the perimeter surveillance problem proposed in the previous section.

18.4.2 Partitioning Strategy

These drawbacks can be tackled using a partitioning strategy, obtaining near optimal solution from a refresh time criterion. Considering a path B_i which length is L_i and a sub-team of $k - j$ robots Q_i as is defined in the previous sections, a partitioning strategy implies that the whole path B_i is divided in $k - j$ non-overlapping segments $\{S_j, S_{j+1}, \ldots, S_k\}$.

$$\begin{aligned} S_j \cup S_{j+1} \cup \cdots \cup S_k &= B_i \\ S_j \cap S_{j+1} \cap \cdots \cap S_k &= \emptyset \end{aligned} \quad (18.28)$$

Now, each robot Q_n is in charge to patrol a different segment. To minimize the refresh time along the whole path, each robot Q_n moves along its segments with a back and forth motion (from one endpoint to the other one again and again) at its maximum motion speed $v_n^{\max}$, as is shown in Fig. 18.3. Also, the length of each segment $L(S_n)$ has to be related to the robot maximum speed.

$$L(S_n) = v_n^{\max} \frac{L(B_i)}{\sum_{m=j}^{k} v_m^{\max}}, \quad \forall n = j, \ldots, k, \quad (18.29)$$

From here, it is easy to deduce that all the robots in the sub-team would take the same time T' to cover their assigned segments. Then the neighbor robots can be coordinated to meet periodically in their common endpoint.

$$T' = \frac{L(S_n)}{v_n^{\max}} = \frac{L(B_i)}{\sum_{m=j}^{k} v_m^{\max}} \quad (18.30)$$

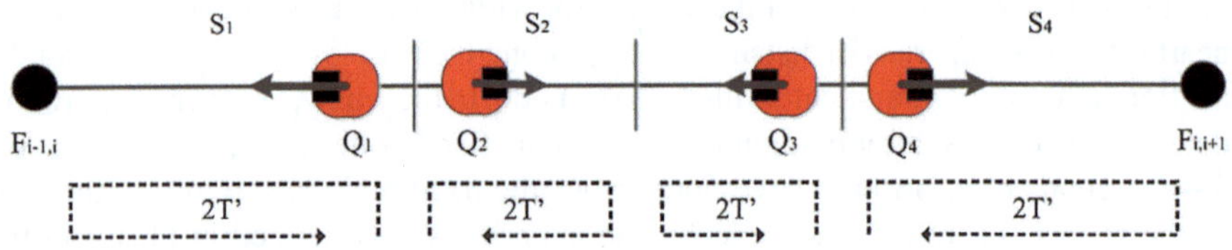

Fig. 18.3 A team of 4 heterogeneous mobile robots performs a partitioning strategy to patrol cooperatively a path

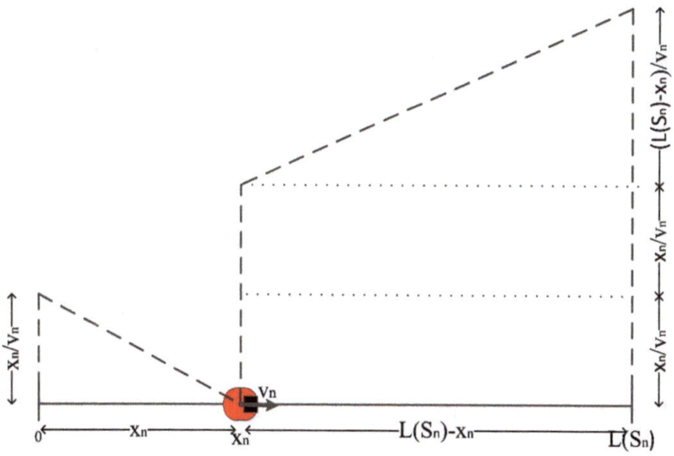

Fig. 18.4 This figure shows the refresh time computed along a segment S_n in a steady state while a team of robots performs partitioning strategy along the path B_i

Figure 18.4 illustrates the refresh time computed along a segment S_n in a steady state and depending on the position of the robot Q_n, while it is performing a partitioning strategy.

The theoretical maximum refresh time can be computed as the time that a robot takes to cover its assigned segment twice.

$$RT^{\max} = 2T' = 2\frac{L(B_i)}{\sum_{m=j}^{k} v_m^{\max}} \tag{18.31}$$

The average refresh time computed for a segment S_n can be extrapolated to the whole path B_i, because all the robots take the same time T' to patrol their assigned segments. So, as the Fig. 18.4 shows, the average refresh time computed along a segment S_n depends on the robot position x_n.

$$\overline{RT}(t) = \frac{\frac{x_n^2(t)}{2v_n^{\max}} + \frac{(L(S_n)-x_n(t))^2}{2v_n^{\max}} + \frac{(L(S_n)-x_n(t))2x_n(t)}{v_n^{\max}}}{L(S_n)} \tag{18.32}$$

Now, simplifying and deriving it with respect a $x_n(t)$ and equating to zero, it is possible compute for which $x_n(t)$ the average refresh time is maximum.

$$\frac{d\overline{RT}(t)}{dx_n(t)} = \frac{\frac{L(S_n)}{v_n^{\max}} - \frac{2x_n(t)}{v_n^{\max}}}{L(S_n)} = 0$$

$$x_n(t) = \frac{L(S_n)}{2} \tag{18.33}$$

Replacing the obtained value for $x_n(t)$ in the expression (18.32) and accounting the expression (18.30), the average refresh time can be upper-bounded as follows.

$$\overline{RT} = \frac{3}{4} \frac{L(B_i)}{\sum_{m=j}^{k} v_m^{\max}} \qquad (18.34)$$

In general, the partitioning strategy gets better results than the cyclic one when the robots are heterogeneous, according to a refresh time criterion. It is because the partitioning strategy allows the robots to exploit their different capabilities (maximum motion speeds) to patrol the whole path in a cooperative manner.

18.4.2.1 Periodic Connectivity

Considering a communications range R short with respect to the whole path length, it is not possible the continuous connectivity between all the robots. However, without communications between robots, they can not interchange informations about detected events or intruders or coordinate to converge to the cooperative patrolling strategy.

In the next section, an algorithm for the robots to converge to the partitioning strategy in a distributed manner and assuming asynchronous communications will be presented.

On the other hand, according to the partitioning strategy, all the robots take the same time T' to cover their assigned path. Therefore, each pair of neighbors can be coordinated to meet periodically. So, the robot motions allow them to be within their communications range and non continuous, but periodic connectivity can be ensured.

The periodic connectivity between neighbor robots ensures the information propagation between all the robots in a finite time. The latency time is upper-bounded as follows approximately a half of the upper-bounds of the latency for the cyclic strategy.

$$LT \leq 2T' + T' + (k - j - 3)T' = (k - j)T' = (k - j)\frac{L(B_i)}{\sum_{m=j}^{k} v_m^{\max}} \qquad (18.35)$$

18.5 Distributed Coordination to Converge to the Partitioning Strategy

A distributed algorithm based on the concept of *coordination variables* is designed to patrol the path B_i according to the partitioning strategy and assuming asynchronous and limited communications The coordination variables considered are: the path length L and the sum of the motion speeds of all the robots which are patrolling the path speed^{sum}. The problem will be solved coherently for all the robots in a distributed manner, when all of them have the same values for their coordination variables. It is described in Algorithm 1 and executed in an independent manner for each robot. There are not robots which rule the rest.

In addition to the coordination variables (L and speed^{sum}), each robot Q_n should store its own maximum motion speed ($v_n^{\max}$), the segment which it is patrolling (defined as $[a, b]$) and a set of local variables to execute the presented algorithm. These local variables are: the sum of speeds of the robots that each one has on each side of the path (speed$_n^{\text{left}}$ and speed$_n^{\text{right}}$) and the total length of path that each one has left on each side (L_n^{left} and L_n^{right}).

Algorithm 1 Algorithm based on coordination variables to patrol a path using a partitioning strategy from a distributed manner.

```
Initialization
while !ABORT do
  if Meet a neighbor then
    Interchange information
    Update local variables
    Update coordination variables
    Compute segment to patrol
    Go to common segment endpoint
    Continue patrolling its segment
  end if
  if Reach path endpoint then
    Initialize local variables
    Reverse to patrol its segment
  end if
  Monitor path
  Update local variables
  Move along the path
end while
```

At first, each robot Q_n initializes their local variables depending on its initial position in the path. Then, the robots start to move along the path at their maximum motion speed and according to their actual direction while monitor the environment looking for new unexpected events or intruders. Meanwhile, each robot updates its own local variables, specifically L_n^{right} and L_n^{left} according to its actual position x_n and its actual direction d_i.

Even when a robot Q_n reaches its segments endpoints $[a, b]$, it keeps moving along the path, unless it meet another robot or arrive to a path endpoint. If a robot Q_n reaches a path endpoint ($x_n = l_{n-1}$ or $x_n = l_n$), it initializes its local variables depending on its actual direction d_n and reverse direction $d_n \leftarrow -d_n$ to continue patrolling its segment.

On the other hand, if a pair of robots Q_n and Q_m meet, they trust information that each other gives about its own side. It means, if Q_m is on the right of Q_n, Q_m sends information to Q_n about the right side (L_m^{right} and speed$_m^{\text{right}}$) and Q_n to Q_m about its left side (L_n^{left} and $\text{speed}_n^{\text{left}}$). Then each robot can update its own local information using the received information.

$$
\begin{aligned}
L_m^{\text{left}} &\leftarrow L_n^{\text{left}} \\
\text{speed}_m^{\text{left}} &\leftarrow \text{speed}_n^{\text{left}} + v_n^{\max} \\
L_n^{\text{right}} &\leftarrow L_m^{\text{right}} \\
\text{speed}_n^{\text{right}} &\leftarrow \text{speed}_m^{\text{right}} + v_m^{\max}
\end{aligned}
\tag{18.36}
$$

Using these local variables each robot Q_n can update its coordination variables.

$$
\begin{aligned}
L &\leftarrow L_n^{\text{left}} + L_n^{\text{right}} \\
\text{speed}^{\text{sum}} &\leftarrow \text{speed}_n^{\text{left}} + \text{speed}_n^{\text{right}} + v_n^{\max}
\end{aligned}
\tag{18.37}
$$

Now, each robot Q_n uses all its information to compute the segment that must patrol.

$$
\begin{aligned}
a &\leftarrow l_{i-1} + \text{speed}_n^{\text{left}} \frac{L}{\text{speed}^{\text{sum}}} \\
b &\leftarrow a + v_n^{\max} \frac{L}{\text{speed}^{\text{sum}}}
\end{aligned}
\tag{18.38}
$$

Finally, both robots move together to their common segment endpoint and then they continue patrolling their segments. Therefore, this algorithm minimizes the required information to share between robots because each one just communicates with their neighbors.

18.5.1 Dynamic Solution

This algorithm provides a dynamic solution since robots updates their coordination variables and decides its new assigned segments periodically. A dynamic solution allows the system to adapt to variations in the initial problem parameters, such as amount of robots, motions speeds or total path length. Therefore, a dynamic solution provide flexibility and tolerance to faults as a communications lost. On the other hand, a decentralized system provide also fault-tolerance because there is not an indispensable robot or central unit to complete the mission. Therefore, a dynamic, distributed and decentralized system such as is proposed in this section increases the robustness of the solution.

For instance, a system of $k - j$ robots is performing the Algorithm 1 to patrol a path B_i in a distributed manner. Assuming a fully steady state, a robot Q_n meets its neighbors Q_{n-1} and Q_{n+1} periodically.

Q_n meets Q_{n-1} on its left and receives information about its left side. So, Q_n, according to expression (18.36), updates its sum of speeds of its left.

$$\text{speed}_n^{\text{left}} = v_{n-1}^{\max} + \text{speed}_{n-1}^{\text{left}} \tag{18.39}$$

After, Q_n meets Q_{n+1} and send it information about its left side. Then Q_{n+1}, can updates its sum of speeds of its left.

$$\text{speed}_{n+1}^{\text{left}} = v_n^{\max} + \text{speed}_n^{\text{left}} = v_n^{\max} + v_{n-1}^{\max} + \text{speed}_{n-1}^{\text{left}} \tag{18.40}$$

If Q_n goes out from the problem, Q_{n-1} and Q_{n+1} will meet. Then, Q_{n-1} will send information about its left side and Q_{n+1} will be able to compute its new local variable $\text{speed}_{n+1}^{\text{left}}$ correctly without the lost robot Q_n.

$$\text{speed}_{n+1}^{\text{left}} = v_{n-1}^{\max} + \text{speed}_{n-1}^{\text{left}} \tag{18.41}$$

This process is repeated until the last robots and all of them can update correctly in a finite time the new coordination variables and calculate correctly a new segment to patrol, adapting to the lost of a robot. This logic would be similar for the rest of local variables.

18.5.1.1 Validating the Dynamic Feature with Experimental Results

Two different experiments have been performed to illustrate how the proposed system is able to adapt to changes in the initial conditions.

The experiments have been carried out using a team of Pioneer-3AT which have to patrol path defined by the walls of a room. The robots uses a laser to follow the wall. The robots can move at a maximum motion speed of 1 m/s, but some of them (red and green in Fig. 18.5) have been limited by software to 0.6 m to validate system with non homogeneous robots. During the experiments a sensing range of 2 m and a communications range (simulated via software) of 4 m are considered. An application which executes the Algorithm 1 for each robot talks to a Player Server [24] running in each Pionner.

In the first experiment, four robots are patrolling the path and, at time $t = 250$ s, the fifth (green) robot goes into the path and joins to the team in the mission. Finally, at time $t = 420$ s, a robot (the red one) goes out from the path. Figure 18.6 the robots positions into the path along the time of the mission. It shows as the robots adapt and the system converges such as each robot patrol a segment which length is related to its own maximum speed.

In Fig. 18.7, the maximum and average refresh times computed (based on robots positions and external timers for a set of way-points in the path) along the time during the experiments are shown. It shows how close to the theoretical maximum (defined for the partitioning strategy by (18.31) and (18.34)) are the results obtained

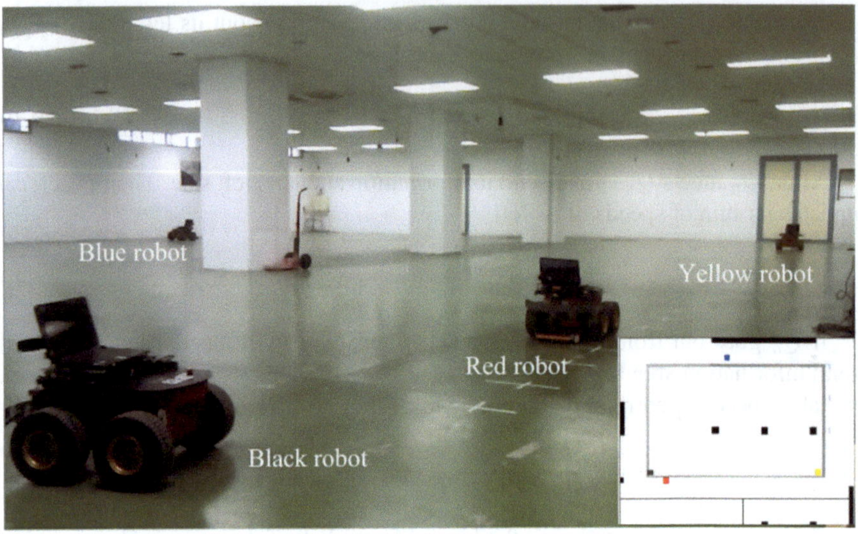

Fig. 18.5 Snapshot from experiments. The initial and end path position is next to the farthest column in the coordinates (9, 0) m

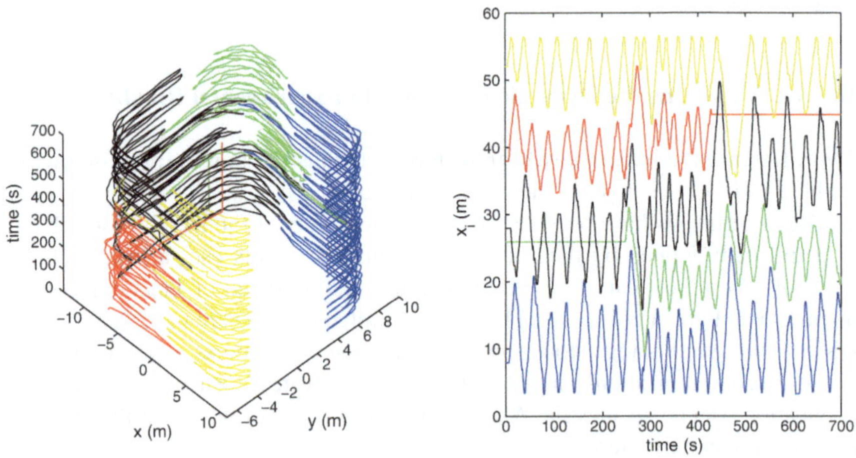

Fig. 18.6 This figures shows the results obtained in the experiment with 5 robots. On the *left* the actual position of the robots along the time. On the *right* its position into the path (x_i) along the time. Each robot is represented by a different color. In http://www.youtube.com/watch?v=WqRKXqcuWKg, a video from this experiment can be viewed

using the proposed algorithm. This experiment probes that the proposed algorithm allows the robots to adapt dynamically to lost of robots, even under communications constraints. As it is obvious, refresh times are decreasing while the number of robots is increasing.

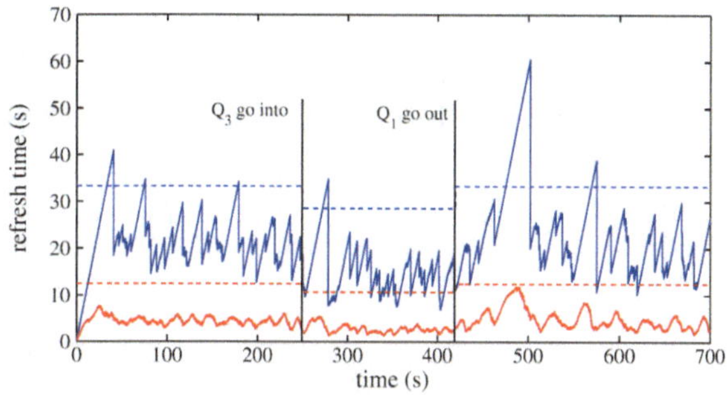

Fig. 18.7 This figure shows the maximum (*solid blue line*) and average (*solid red line*) refresh time computed along the path during the experiment with 5 robots. *Dashed lines* defines the theoretical maximum values using the partitioning strategy such as is stated in expressions (18.31) and (18.34)

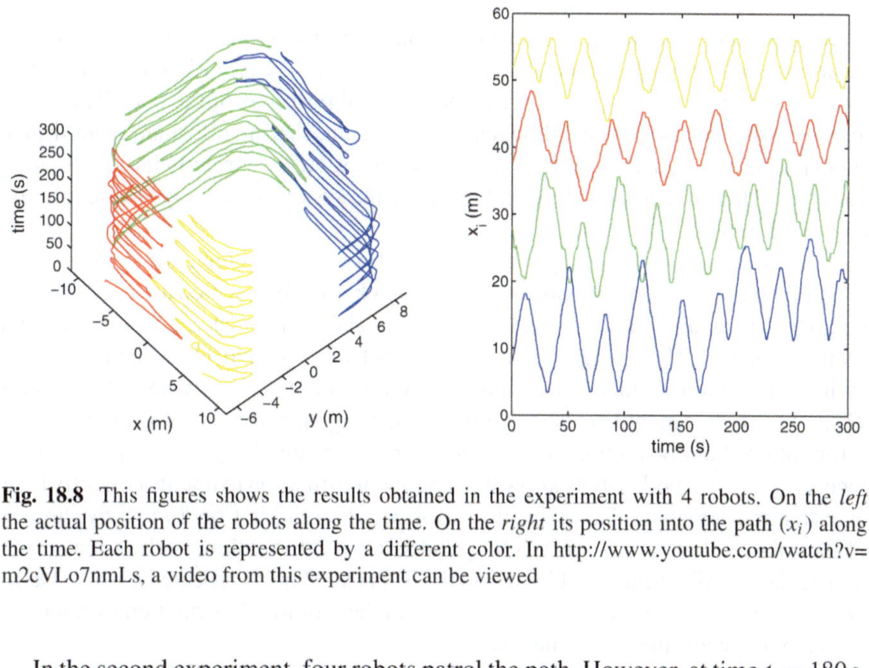

Fig. 18.8 This figures shows the results obtained in the experiment with 4 robots. On the *left* the actual position of the robots along the time. On the *right* its position into the path (x_i) along the time. Each robot is represented by a different color. In http://www.youtube.com/watch?v=m2cVLo7nmLs, a video from this experiment can be viewed

In the second experiment, four robots patrol the path. However, at time $t = 180$ s, the path length is decreased. The multi-robot system is able to adapt to this variation dynamically, as is shown in Figs. 18.8 and 18.9.

18.5.2 Convergent Solution

When all the robots have the correct values for the coordination variables, all of them can compute correctly the segment to patrol and the whole multi-robot system

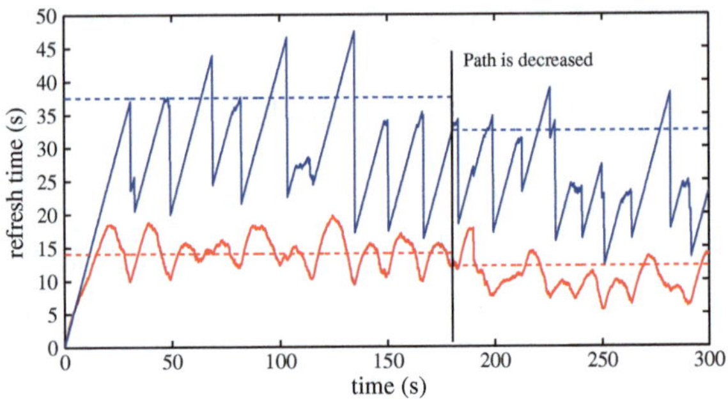

Fig. 18.9 This figure shows the maximum (*solid blue line*) and average (*solid red line*) refresh time computed along the path during the experiment with 4 robots. *Dashed lines* defines the theoretical maximum values using the partitioning strategy such as is stated in expressions (18.31) and (18.34)

converges. According to the problem description, the robots just move along the path in two possible opposite directions. Also, the Algorithm 1 explicitly forces the robots to reverse direction when they get the end or initial positions of the path. Therefore, all the robots will meet its neighbors again and again, sharing information until each robot has information about all the robots and can calculate correctly its coordination variables. Then, the proposed algorithm allows the system to converge to the solution described in Sect. 18.4.

The question is: how many meeting the robots need to converge to the desired solution? It is a time-complexity analysis. Given $k-j$ robots which are patrolling the path B_i, it is assumed that robots know nothing about the other robots (amount and motions speeds). Then, after the first meeting between Q_j and Q_{j+1}, both calculate their coordination variables accounting only two robots. Then, when Q_{j+1} meets Q_{j+2}, they both can update their variables assuming three robots but Q_j only knows information about two robots. This process can be repeated $k-j-1$ times until Q_{k-1} meets Q_k and, so, both robots know the required information to update correctly their coordination variables. However, this information could not be known by the rest of the robots. Now, Q_{k-1} meets Q_{k-2} and sends it information, such as it also can update the coordination variables correctly. This reasoning is repeated $k-j-2$ until Q_{j+1} meets Q_j and then the $k-j$ robots can the required information to calculate correctly the coordination variables.

From this reasoning, it can be concluded that, using the proposed algorithm based on the coordination variables, the robots need less than $2(k-j)$ meeting to converge to the partitioning strategy. It means, the convergence time-complexity is increasing linearly with the amount of robots in the system.

On the other hand, peer-to-peer (or one-to-one) based algorithms has been proposed in the literature [16, 19] to solve the path surveillance problem with multiple robots converging to a path partitioning strategy. Authors of [16] probe that the convergence time-complexity of its peer-to-peer coordination technique increases quadratically with the amount of robots.

Table 18.1 Relation between the convergence times using the algorithm based on the one-to-one coordination and the algorithm described in this chapter

Number of robots	1	2	3	4	5	6	7	8
Average value	1.00	0.98	1.67	2.41	2.54	3.39	3.81	4.10
Standard deviation	0.00	0.08	0.87	1.75	1.57	2.16	2.95	2.54

18.5.2.1 Results to Validate the Convergence Advantages

The proposed distributed algorithm based on the coordination variables and the one described in [19] based on a peer-to-peer (one-to-one) approach have been developed in MATLAB to compare their convergence times. A large amount of scenarios has been simulated with different number of robots and different perimeter lengths. The simulated robots implement a quad-rotor dynamical model which maximum motion speed have been limited. The initial positions and maximum motion speeds have been defined randomly using an standard uniform distribution from 0.2 to 0.5 m/s. The communications range have been limited to 4 m. Each scenario has been executed using both the algorithm based on the coordination variables and the one based on the one-to-one coordination. The convergence time has been calculated for both algorithms, assuming that a system has converged if the maximum difference between the segment actually assigned to each and the theoretically optimal one (defined by expression (18.29)) is less than 5 %.

The results are summarized in Table 18.1. This table shows the average relation between the convergences times computed using the one-to-one coordination and the coordination variables algorithms, depending on the number of robots. It shows that increasing the number of robots, the algorithm based on the coordination variables converges much faster than the one-to-one coordination algorithm.

18.6 One-to-one Coordination for Dynamic Allocation

Each path B_i is patrolled by a sub-team of robots $Q^{(i)}$ that patrols it using the coordination variables based Algorithm 1 to implement a partitioning strategy from a refresh time criterion. It is a dynamic algorithm able to adapt to variations in the number of robots from a distributed manner, converging to the best possible partitioning strategy in few iterations and under communications constraints. On the other hand, between each pair of adjacent paths B_i and B_j, there are a fixed node $F_{i,j}$.

However, the actual distribution of the robots among the different paths could not be the best from an urgency criterion, such as is shown in Sect. 18.3. As communications are considered limited and as the initial priorities conditions are assumed variables, a centralized allocation is not useful. So, a distributed and dynamic allocation method based on the one-to-one coordination is proposed.

Section 18.5 shows that the proposed algorithm assures all the robots in a path B_i to share the correct coordination variables about their problem (it means, the path length $L(B_i)$ and the total sum of speeds $\text{speed}_i^{\text{sum}}$) in a finite time. So, according to expression (18.31), each robot can compute the theoretical maximum refresh time along the path using the partitioning strategy.

The fixed nodes are used as path allocation manager. When a robot Q_n in a path B_i meets a fixed node $F_{i,j}$, it sends information to the node about its own path length $L(B_i)$, the path priority P_i and sum of speeds of the robots $\text{speed}_i^{\text{sum}}$ in the path. On the other hand, the fixed node sends information to the robot about the length $L(B_j)$, priority P_j and sum of speeds $\text{speed}_j^{\text{sum}}$ from its other adjacent path B_j. As the robots from both paths reaches periodically the ends of the paths, the fixed node can update periodically the information about both paths.

Therefore, the robot Q_n in a path B_i which has met a fixed node $F_{i,j}$ has information about both paths and can compute the maximum urgency of both paths, according to expression (18.20). Also, it can estimate the maximum urgency of both path if it moves to the other path B_j. The fixed node $F_{i,j}$ can also calculate the same values.

$$\begin{aligned} U_i &\leftarrow U^{\max}(Q^{(i)}) \\ U_j &\leftarrow U^{\max}(Q^{(j)}) \\ U_i' &\leftarrow U^{\max}(Q^{(i)} - \{Q_n\}) \\ U_j' &\leftarrow U^{\max}(Q^{(j)} + \{Q_n\}) \end{aligned} \tag{18.42}$$

Now, the robot Q_n decides in an independent manner to move to the other path B_j if the change is profitable. It means, according to the urgency criterion defined in Sect. 18.3, if the estimated maximum urgency between both paths is less than the actual maximum urgency between them.

$$\max(U_i, U_j) > \max(U_i', U_j') \longrightarrow \quad Q_n \ \texttt{moves from}\ B_i\ \texttt{to}\ B_j \tag{18.43}$$

In case than actual and estimated maximum urgency are equal, the robot Q_n will move if and only if the sum of the actual urgencies are greater than the sum of the estimated urgencies.

On the other hand, as the fixed node has the same information, it can deduce the decision of the robot and update correctly the information about its both adjacent paths.

Therefore, each robot uses a one-to-one method to choose the path to patrol based only in the information about the actual and estimated urgencies of both paths. From local decisions, the whole system converges to global solution close to the optimal one.

18.6.1 Protocols for Changing Paths

The proposed method is based on the idea that fixed nodes has a totally updated information about its two adjacent paths. However, fixed nodes can not know if another robot is going out or into its adjacent paths by the other paths endpoints while it is enabling that a robots move by its adjacent paths endpoints, because this information would take a minimum time to be propagated from one to the other endpoint (as described in Sect. 18.4). So, this method enables any robot in the end segments of any path to move to the other adjacent path if it is profitable from an maximum urgency criterion and based to possible non updated information. Some protocols to be used together or separately are proposed to mitigate this effects.

- One direction policy. Assuming a closed perimeter, robots can move between paths following an only direction.
- Token-based method. Only one robot in the system carries a token and only it can move between adjacent paths. In case, this change is not profitable from an urgency-based criterion, it does not move and leaves the token in the fixed node. So, if another robot reaches this fixed node, it takes the token and decides, according to the urgency criterion, if it should move between paths. On the other, when a robot owns the token, it can move from one to the other fixed node of its own present path (see Sect. 18.6.2).
- Probabilistic protocol. When a robot reaches a fixed node, both the node and the robot share a common random value rnd. So, the robot uses this value to decide if it should move between paths.
- Timer-based protocol. A different threshold based on the its unique identifies is defined for each fixed node. The fixed nodes set up a time to its threshold and this timer is continuously decreasing. A robot can move between paths if this change is profitable and if the timer of common fixed node is less than zero. In any case, the timer is again set to its own threshold when a robot reaches a fixed node which timer is less than zero.

18.6.1.1 Comparing Path Change Protocols

The presented system has been implemented in a distributed and decentralized manner, using different MATLAB objects and simulating the constrained communications, to test its performance using different path changes protocols.

Ten different scenarios assuming four paths with different priority distributions over a 15×15 m perimeter and nine homogeneous quad-rotors moving at a maximum motion speed of 0.5 m/s have been executed. The priority distributions has been chosen randomly using an standard distributions for each scenario. Also, each scenario has been executed during 1,000 s once for each different protocol: no control methods (not-2d), one-direction (not-1d), token method (tok-2d), token and one-direction (tok-1d), probabilistic method (prob-2d), probabilistic and one-direction (prob-1d), timer (timer-2d) and timer and one-direction (timer-1d).

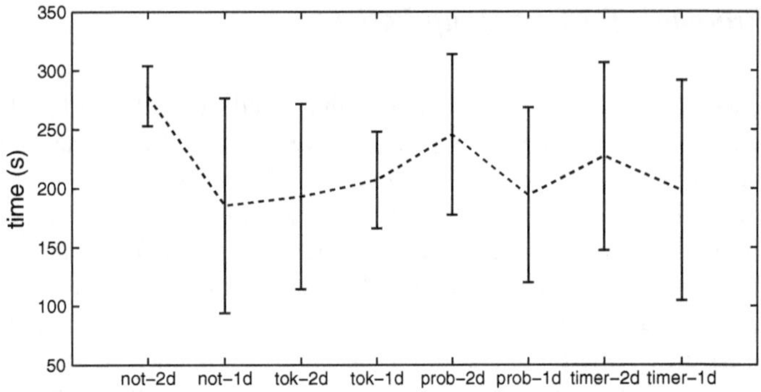

Fig. 18.10 This figure shows the average convergence times (± its standard deviation) computed during the simulations depending on the different changing path protocols: no control methods (not-2d), one-direction (not-1d), token method (tok-2d), token and one-direction (tok-1d), probabilistic method (prob-2d), probabilistic and one-direction (prob-1d), timer (timer-2d) and timer and one-direction (timer-1d)

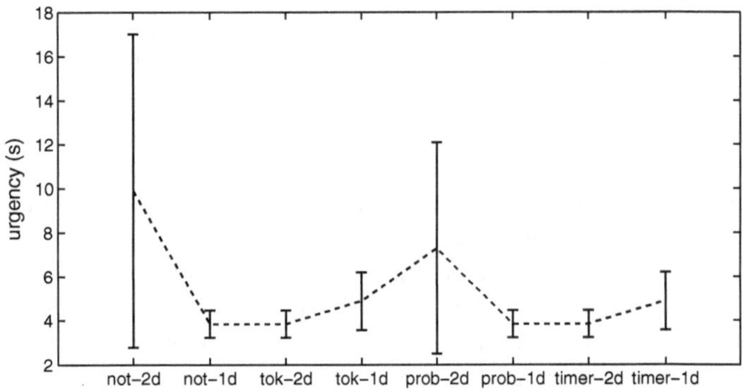

Fig. 18.11 This figure shows the average maximum urgency (± its standard deviation) computed during the simulations depending on the different changing path protocols: no control methods (not-2d), one-direction (not-1d), token method (tok-2d), token and one-direction (tok-1d), probabilistic method (prob-2d), probabilistic and one-direction (prob-1d), timer (timer-2d) and timer and one-direction (timer-1d)

Simulations results about the method convergence time depending on the different protocols are summarized in Fig. 18.10.

These results shows a faster convergence using the one-directions protocols. The average maximum urgency computed during the simulation for the different protocols are shown in Fig. 18.11.

According to obtained results, no more than the one-direction protocol seems to be necessary to obtains a quick and close to optimal performance.

18.6.2 Segment Swapping Policies

The proposed approach, such as is described above, converges to a solution very dependent of initial conditions (initial robots positions) when the robots have different maximum motion speeds and then, the maximum urgency would be lower limited by these initial robots positions. It is because, according to the described method, only the robots in the end segments can move between paths. However, it could be more profitable if a robot in one of the middle segments of a path moves to another path.

Therefore, the Algorithm 1 is slightly modified to allow the neighbors robots to swap their segments when they meet, such that any robot in the path can reach the fixed nodes and move to another path. It implies, not only to swap their segments to patrol, but also interchange their local and coordination variables. Then, different policies to decide if a pair of neighbor robots must or not swap their segments are proposed.

- Token-based policy. The robot which owns the token swaps directly the segments with its neighbors in order to go from one fixed node to the other as soon as possible. It is related to the token-based protocol to move between paths described in Sect. 18.6.1.
- Speed-based policy. This policy assumes that slower robots should be nearer to the fixed nodes because it ensures a finer change between paths.
- Probabilistic-based policy. When two robots meet, they share a common random value and use it to decide if they must or not to swap their segments.
- Mixed criterion. This criterion mixes the probabilistic and speed criterion to decide the swapping.

18.6.2.1 Analyzing the Swapping Policies

Ten different scenarios over a triangular closed perimeter are executed for the different swapping policies to analyze their performance. The team of robots is considered heterogeneous, such as their maximum motion speeds are randomly chosen using a standard distribution between 0.3 and 0.5 m/s. The perimeter is formed by three straight paths between three vertexes (0, 0), (20, 0) and (10, 15). So, different priority distribution are randomly chosen for each scenario. The one-direction protocol is used to enable the change between paths.

Each scenario is run during 1,000 s once for each swapping policy: no control method (not), token-based (tok), speed-based (speed), probabilistic criterion (prob) and mixed criterion (mix).

Figures 18.12 and 18.13 summarizes the convergence time and the average maximum urgency computed during the simulations depending on the swapping policy used.

Notice that the speed-based criterion converges faster and obtains the better performance from a maximum urgency criterion.

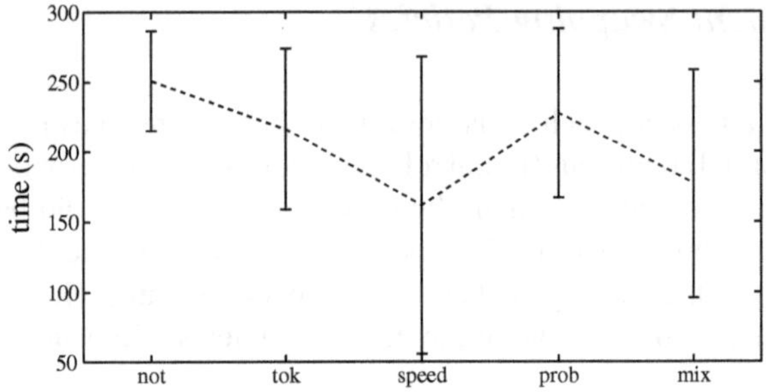

Fig. 18.12 This figure shows the average convergence time (± its standard deviation) computed during the simulations and depending on the different segment swapping policies: no control method (not), token-based (tok), speed-based (speed), probabilistic criterion (prob) and mixed criterion (mix)

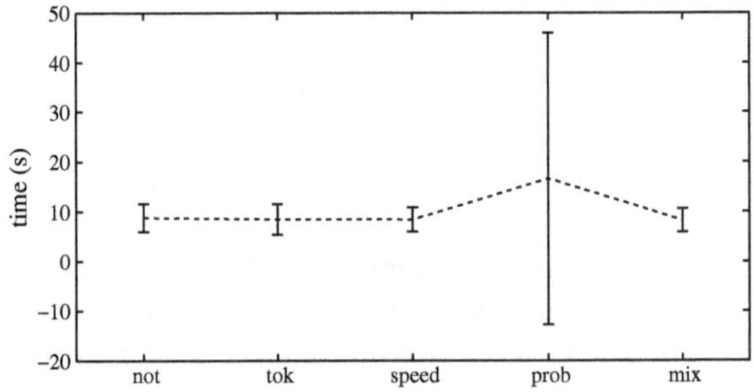

Fig. 18.13 This figure shows the average maximum urgency (± its standard deviation) computed during the simulations depending on the different segment swapping policies: no control method (not), token-based (tok), speed-based (speed), probabilistic criterion (prob) and mixed criterion (mix)

18.7 Conclusions

This chapter addresses a perimeter surveillance mission with multiple robots, where the perimeter can be divided in a set of adjacent paths with different priorities. Each priority represents the probability of event appearing in this path relative to the other paths. The refresh time criterion is not useful to optimize the problem. So, the urgency criterion is defined to normalize the refresh time along the whole perimeter.

The lower bounds of the maximum urgency for a path is defined depending on the set of robots. Then, the problem can be solved in two levels: a patrolling strategy to monitor cooperative each path to minimize its maximum refresh time and a dynamic allocation of the robots between the different paths to minimize the maximum urgency.

The partitioning strategy is proposed, such as each sub-team of robots can cooperate to monitor its assigned path, exploiting the robots different maximum motion speeds and keeping periodic connectivity among them even under communications constraints. An algorithm based on the coordination variables allows the robots to converge to the partitioning strategy from a distributed and decentralized manner. Analysis and validation results show than the proposed algorithm converges in fewer iterations than other peer-to-peer methods and than the robustness of the distributed system.

The fixed nodes manage the dynamic allocation of the robots between their adjacent paths when they meet them. The fixed nodes receive from and send information to the contacted robots, such as they can decide in an independent manner if moving from one to the other paths would improve the performance from a maximum urgency criterion. Also, it is proposed that robots can swap their segments into each path in order to allow any robot to reach the fixed node to move between paths. A set of different protocols for moving between paths or segment swapping are defined and tested to analyze which obtains the best performance. These results show that allowing that robots move between paths following an only direction and a speed-based protocol for segment swapping are sufficient to obtain very high performance and a low convergence time.

References

1. Beainy F, Commuri S (2009) Development of an autonomous atv for real-life surveillance operations. In: 17th mediterranean conference on control and automation, 2009. MED '09, June 2009, pp 904–909
2. Darbha S, Krishnamoorthy K, Pachter M, Chandler P (2010) State aggregation based linear programming approach to approximate dynamic programming. In: 49th IEEE conference on decision and control (CDC), 2010, December 2010, pp 935–941
3. Frew EW (2009) Combining area patrol, perimeter surveillance, and target tracking using ordered upwind methods. In: IEEE international conference on robotics and automation, 2009. ICRA '09, May 2009, pp 3123–3128
4. Girard AR, Howell AS, Hedrick JK (2004) Border patrol and surveillance missions using multiple unmanned air vehicles. In: 43rd IEEE conference on decision and control, 2004. cdc, 1:620–625, December 2004
5. Marino A, Parker L, Antonelli G, Caccavale F (2009) Behavioral control for multi-robot perimeter patrol: A finite state automata approach. In: IEEE international conference on robotics and automation, 2009. ICRA '09, May 2009, pp 831–836
6. Maza I, Caballero F, Capitan J, Martinez de Dios JR, Ollero A (2011) A distributed architecture for a robotic platform with aerial sensor transportation and self-deployment capabilities. J Field Robot 28(3):303–328
7. Viguria A, Maza I, Ollero A (2010) Distributed service-based cooperation in aerial/ground robot teams applied to fire detection and extinguishing missions. Adv Robot 24(1–2):1–23
8. Elmaliach Y, Shiloni A, Kaminka GA (2008) A realistic model of frequency-based multi-robot polyline patrolling. In: Proceedings of the 7th international joint conference on autonomous agents and multiagent systems—Vol 1, AAMAS '08, Richland SC, international foundation for autonomous agents and multiagent systems, pp 63–70
9. Baseggio M, Cenedese A, Merlo P, Pozzi M, Schenato L (2010) Distributed perimeter patrolling and tracking for camera networks. In: 49th IEEE conference on decision and control (CDC), 2010, December 2010, pp 2093–2098

10. Chevaleyre Y (2004) Theoretical analysis of the multi-agent patrolling problem. In: Proceedings of the IEEE/WIC/ACM international conference on intelligent agent technology, 2004. (IAT 2004), September 2004, pp 302–308
11. Pasqualetti F, Durham JW, Bullo F (2012) Cooperative patrolling via weighted tours: performance analysis and distributed algorithms. Robot IEEE Trans 28(5):1181–1188
12. Pasqualetti F, Franchi A, Bullo F (2012) On cooperative patrolling: optimal trajectories, complexity analysis, and approximation algorithms. Robot IEEE Trans 28(3):592–606
13. Hollinger G, Singh S (2010) Multi-robot coordination with periodic connectivity. In: IEEE international conference on robotics and automation (ICRA), 2010, May 2010, pp 4457–4462
14. Agmon N, Kaminka GA, Kraus S (2011) Multi-robot adversarial patrolling: facing a full-knowledge opponent. J Artif Int Res 42(1):887–916
15. Smith SL, Rus D (2010) Multi-robot monitoring in dynamic environments with guaranteed currency of observations. In: 49th IEEE conference on decision and control (CDC), 2010, December 2010, pp 514–521
16. Carli R, Cenedese A, Schenato L (2011) Distributed partitioning strategies for perimeter patrolling. Am Control Conf (ACC) 15:4026–4031
17. Acevedo JJ, Arrue BC, Diaz-Baez JM, Ventura I, Maza I, Ollero A (2013) One-to-one coordination algorithm for decentralized area partition in surveillance missions with a team of aerial robots. J Intell Robot Syst 70:1–17
18. Acevedo JJ, Arrue BC, Maza I, Ollero A (2013) Cooperative large area surveillance with a team of aerial mobile robots for long endurance missions. J Intell Robot Syst 70:329–345
19. Acevedo JJ, Arrue BC, Maza I, Ollero A (2013) Distributed approach for coverage and patrolling missions with a team of heterogeneous aerial robots under communication constraints. Int J Adv Robot Syst 10(28):1–13
20. Acevedo JJ, Arrue BC, Maza I, Ollero A (2013) Cooperative perimeter surveillance with a team of mobile robots under communication constraints. In: International conference on intelligent robots and systems, November 2013
21. Beard RW, McLain TW, Nelson DB, Kingston D, Johanson D (2006) Decentralized cooperative aerial surveillance using fixed-wing miniature UAVs. Proc IEEE 94(7):1306–1324
22. Kingston D, Beard RW, Holt RS (2008) Decentralized perimeter surveillance using a team of UAVs. Robot IEEE Trans 24(6):1394–1404
23. Geng X (2009) Consensus-reaching of multiple robots with fewer interactions. In: WRI world congress on computer science and information engineering, 2009, 5:249–253, April 2009
24. Richard T (2003) Vaughan Brian Gerkey and Andrew Howard. The player/stage project: Tools for multi-robot and distributed sensor systems. In: Proceedings of the 11th international conference on advanced robotics (ICAR 2003), Coimbra, Portugal, June 2003, pp 317–323

Chapter 19
Social-Aware Coordination of Multi-robot Systems Based on Institutions

José N. Pereira, Porfírio Silva, Pedro U. Lima and Alcherio Martinoli

Abstract Institutional robotics (IR) is an approach to the coordination of multi-robot systems that draws inspiration from social sciences, namely from institutional economics. Using the concept of institution, it aims to provide a comprehensive strategy for specifying social interactions (e.g., norms, roles, hierarchies) among robots. In previous work, we have introduced a control methodology for multi-robot systems that takes into account institutions in order to create an Institutional Agent Controller (IAC) that captures such social interactions. In this chapter, the IAC design methodology is validated in a case study concerned with a swarm of 40 real, resource-constrained robots which has to maintain wireless connectivity. We then investigate a second case study dealing with more complex social interactions, showing that institutional roles can effectively help a multi-robot system to coordinate and improve performance in a given task of social nature. Given the fact that institutions are one of the tools in use within human societies to shape social interactions, our

---

This work was partially supported by Fundação para a Ciência e a Tecnologia (FCT) through grants SFRH/BD/33671/2009 (first author, as part of the Joint Doctoral Program IST-EPFL) and SFRH/BPD/35862/2007 (second author), as well as by FCT ISR/IST Pluriannual funding through the PIDDAC program funds, and by EU under FP7/2007-2013—Challenge 2—Cognitive Systems, Interaction, Robotics—grant agreement 601033—MOnarCH.

J.N. Pereira (✉) · A. Martinoli
Distributed Intelligent Systems and Algorithms Laboratory—EPFL,
EPFL ENAC IIE DISAL, Station 2, 1015 Lausanne, Switzerland
e-mail: jose.pereira@epfl.ch

A. Martinoli
e-mail: alcherio.martinoli@epfl.ch

P. Silva · P.U. Lima
Institute for Systems and Robotics—Instituto Superior Técnico,
Universidade de Lisboa, Av. Rovisco Pais 1, 1049 Lisboa, Portugal
e-mail: porfiriosilva@isr.ist.utl.pt

P.U. Lima
e-mail: pal@isr.ist.utl.pt

P. Spagnolo et al. (eds.), *Human Behavior Understanding in Networked Sensing*,
DOI 10.1007/978-3-319-10807-0_19

intuition is that IR can also facilitate coordination with humans in scenarios involving many-to-many human–robot interactions. We discuss how the IR concepts and the IAC design methodology can be implemented in real-world scenarios where multiple robots must interact with multiple humans in a socially aware manner.

19.1 Introduction

In robotics, the transition from constrained laboratory environments to real-world environments is not a trivial step. For human actors carrying out any task in real-world environments, even without any robotic systems present, the need for coordination with other actors is ubiquitous. Consider that simply traveling from point *A* to point *B* requires coordinating with others, be it on foot (using common sense rules to avoid colliding with others), by car (using a more elaborate set of rules, i.e., the "road code"), or any other mode of transport. More importantly, most tasks in our daily lives involve the trade of services or goods for money. This requires not only coordinating with others in order to physically carry out such a trade but also the underlying acceptance that the money being received can then be accepted by some other actors. The collective acceptance of such an idea is in itself a form of society-wide coordination.

For multi-robot systems to be truly immersed in real-world environments, this type of coordination must be considered. Robots need to consider complex social interactions with multiple anonymous robots and multiple anonymous human actors. This anonymity reflects not only the fact that interacting agents might never have met before but also that such agents might not have to coexist at the same time or place for the interaction to occur.

Our goal is to formalize rules specifying social interactions for specific tasks in a way that resembles the organizational aspects of human society. Our intuition is that by doing so we will be able to consider complex social interactions within multi-robot systems, ease the effort of their transition to real-world environments populated with human actors, and facilitate coordination with such actors in scenarios involving many-to-many human–robot interactions.

To do so, we follow the *Institutional Robotics* (IR) approach [23] to the coordination of multi-robot systems (described in Sect. 19.2). This approach takes inspiration from social sciences, namely from *institutional economics* [10], and aims to provide a comprehensive strategy for specifying complex social interactions among a team of robots and possibly between a team of robots and human actors. In [20], we formalized institutions—the central concept in IR—using an abstract representation (executable Petri Nets), allowing their design and execution for multi-robot systems, so as to obtain behaviors capturing the social interactions of interest. Our methodology (described in Sect. 19.3) composes a set of institutions in order to create an institutional agent controller able to execute a desired task and observe the specified social interactions.

An initial validation study was performed in [20], by comparing our methodology with other approaches. To do so, we considered a swarm robotics case study concerned with a robot swarm which has to maintain wireless connectivity and a certain degree of spatial compactness, taking into account only simple social interactions. However, the validation presented in [20] was carried out only in simulation. In Sect. 19.4, we advance our validation effort by considering a real-world implementation of the case study with a swarm of up to 40 real, resource-constrained robots, further increasing our confidence in the approach's robustness and scalability. This real-world implementation was reported in [19].

Considering a case study concerned only with simple interactions allows us to perform a more grounded validation effort. However, we are interested in tackling more complex social interactions with the IR approach. In Sect. 19.5, we present a second case study (briefly described in [18]) where a team of robots must coordinate while navigating through the environment in order to accomplish a transportation task. In this case study, we increase the complexity of the social interactions by focusing on a specific form of institution: the institutional role. We compare the IR approach with a self-organized approach in order to identify situations in which it might prove advantageous.

The IR approach will also be considered in social robotics scenarios implemented in real-world human-populated environments. In Sect. 19.6, we discuss how the IR approach can enforce social-aware coordination in such a scenario, and how we will be able to verify our intuition about the impact of IR in many-to-many human–robot interactions.

19.2 Institutional Robotics and Related Work

Institutional robotics [23] is an approach to the coordination of multi-robot systems that draws inspiration from the social sciences, namely from institutional economics' concepts [10]. It combines the notions of institution [11, 21], coordination artifact [25], and environment [28], aiming to provide a comprehensive strategy for specifying social interactions (e.g., norms, roles, hierarchies) among robots. Under IR, robots are situated not only in a physical but also in an institutional environment, where their interactions are guided by institutions. Cooperation is achieved by this regulation of social interactions since the robots know not only how to behave in a given scenario but also what to expect from other robots and the environment.

In IR, the coordination system is a network of institutions. Institutions are coordination artifacts of different types (organizations, norms, hierarchies, social roles, etc.). They are generic, meaning that they are not designed for any specific set of robots. Robots are able to modify, at some extent, not only the physical environment but also the institutional environment. From an institutional perspective, institutions are taken as the main tool of any sophisticated society, and individuals are both constructive within and constructed through institutional environments.

Market-based multi-robot coordination [7, 31] is a previous example of importing some economic views into robotics. Inspired by market mechanisms, researchers have proposed systems like MURDOCH [9] and TraderBots [8] to achieve flexible allocation of subtasks using auctions between robots. In these systems, robots act as agents trying to maximize their individual profits, calculated based on rewards from tasks and resources expended. The underlying assumption is that with every robot trying to maximize its individual profit, team coordination, and efficiency will be improved. A limitation of the market-based approach is that, despite some application to the allocation of roles [26], the great majority of the work available only deals with task allocation, leaving other mechanisms (e.g., cooperative decision-making) out of the picture.

Self-organization is another possible, scalable mechanism that has been proposed for the coordination of, often large, distributed robotic systems [1, 2, 6]. Self-organizing systems are characterized as being fully reactive and relying on local interactions (and possibly local, broadcast communication), both between robots and between robots and the environment, in order to achieve coordination. However, the design of truly social distributed robotic systems should take into account the objective social interactions arising from the combination (and dependencies) of goals of heterogenous agents [5]. The simple, local interactions considered by self-organizing systems might not capture well this aspect.

19.3 Institutional Agent Controllers

We model institutions using a formal representation, leading to a standard design and execution platform (in real robots, submicroscopic realistic simulations, and microscopic multi-agent systems). Institutions encapsulate relevant behavioral rules for robots, specifying social interactions of different types among actors in a given scenario. They represent the basic building blocks for creating shared coordinated working environments. Moreover, concurrent execution of institutions has to be regulated since not all behaviors can be executed simultaneously. We use *Petri Nets* (PNs) as the formal framework and follow their usual definition as described in [3].

Formalizing institutions for modeling and execution of robot controllers means that we need to take into account robot's actions and sensor readings. *Executable Petri Nets* (EPNs) are PNs that have actions and boolean conditions (verifiable by sensor readings) associated with places and transitions, respectively. The basic intuition behind this definition is that by associating actions with places we are able to define which actions are to be executed at each time step. This is done simply by checking if the corresponding place is marked. By associating transitions with conditions verified by sensor readings, we trigger state changes in the EPN due to changes in the robot's environment.

We represent each institution by an EPN that can be executed independently or together with other institutions. We also represent robot's *individual behaviors* by EPNs. While the institutions specify behaviors that have a *social nature*, i.e., they relate the robot to other robots in some way, the individual behaviors specify a set of basic behaviors that have exclusively an *individual nature*, i.e., they relate the robot with the surrounding environment and its own goals. The composition of the individual behavior with a set of institutions generates a robot controller.

Definition An *Institution I* is a four-tuple $(Inst, initial_I, final_I, d_I)$ where:

- *Inst* is an EPN;
- $initial_I, final_I \in Cdt$ are initial and final conditions for the execution of *Inst*;
- $d_I \in D = \{AllowAll, StopInd, StopInst, StopAll\}$ is the associated deontic operator.

The EPN *Inst* specifies the desired behavior that should be performed by the robot. This behavior is not always being executed, its start and end are dictated by conditions $initial_I$ and $final_I$, which the robot verifies at each time step. Thus, we say that an institution I at each time step can be *active* or *idle*. Each institution also includes a deontic operator d_I which is used when combining it with the robot's individual behavior and further institutions, allowing or stopping the concurrent execution of institutions and/or individual behavior. *Inst* must be designed, but institutions can be kept simple and further behavioral complexity is the result of composition, in a modular fashion.

EPNs can be represented by macro places in a hierarchical fashion, using two distinct layers. We consider that each institution I is part of a lower layer and is represented by one macro place m_I in the higher layer. By adding bidirectional arcs between each transition in I and m_I, we guarantee that if m_I is marked, I is active, otherwise it is idle. This allows us to compose our institutions at the higher layer where relationships among the institutions and the individual behavior should be specified while keeping relationships between actions and conditions separated in the lower layer.

The composition of individual behaviors and institutions is performed algorithmically by adding, in the higher layer, places and transitions that restrict their concurrent execution, according to the specification provided by the deontic operators. Both layers can be then merged algorithmically to obtain a full EPN that can be used as controller. This EPN is designated as the *Institutional Agent Controller* (IAC). Each robot runs its IAC in a social collective setting mediated by institutions. An example of a specific IAC for the wireless connected swarm case study is displayed in Fig. 19.2 and will be discussed in detail in the next section.

19.4 Validation of IAC Methodology

In order to validate the IAC methodology for design and execution of robotic controllers using institutions, we follow a two-phase approach. The first phase is to compare the IAC methodology with other methods, and assess its capability to replicate results obtained with such methods. In [20], we considered the wireless connected swarm case study, previously investigated in [16, 29, 30], and applied to it our IAC methodology. We performed submicroscopic simulations, characterized by a low degree of abstraction and where intra-robot details such as individual sensors and actuators are captured, both with the IAC designed and with a Finite State Automata (FSA) approach originally proposed in [16]. We concluded that the IAC methodology was able to replicate results obtained with the more traditional FSA approach.

The second phase is to validate the IAC methodology in real-world environments. In this section, we focus on this phase. To do so, we perform real-world experiments of the case study and compare results obtained in reality with those obtained in submicroscopic simulations.

In [30], the authors report an implementation using a small number of real robots (4–8 robots) where local communication was achieved with a combination of a global wireless network and an overhead camera delimiting the communication range. A first goal of this work is to move one step further the realism of the physical implementation by using real local communication channels and a large number of robots (tests were performed with sets of 20 and 40 robots). We chose to use 40 robots in order to maintain as much as possible a parallel with the original case study experiments, where 40 simulated agents were used [29]. A second goal of such implementation is to show that the IR approach is able to handle such real scenarios, and in particular maintain the wireless connectivity of a swarm of 40 real, resource-constrained robots, further increasing our confidence in the approach's robustness and scalability.

19.4.1 Materials and Methods

Our platform is the *e-puck* robot [15], a differential drive robot of 7 cm in diameter. In order to endow the robots with scalable wireless communication capabilities, we use a radio communication module developed at DISAL [4]. This module is ZigBee compliant and uses TinyOS [12]. A bounded communication range is obtained using software-controllable power emission and a dedicated hardware attenuator.

For implementing our submicroscopic simulations, we used *Webots* [14], a flexible, 3D realistic simulator, and considered kinematic models of the *e-puck* robot. The original case study considered a perfect circular bounded communication radius and perfect package reception inside that radius (radial disk model). In this work, communication between *e-pucks* is also simulated realistically using the network simulation engine OMNeT++ [27] as a plugin for *Webots*. The OMNet++ engine handles channel coding, noise, fading signal propagation, as well as a non-circular communication footprint. Figure 19.1a offers a visualization of the *Webots* submicroscopic simulations. Figure 19.1b displays an image of the arena during execution taken with the overhead camera.

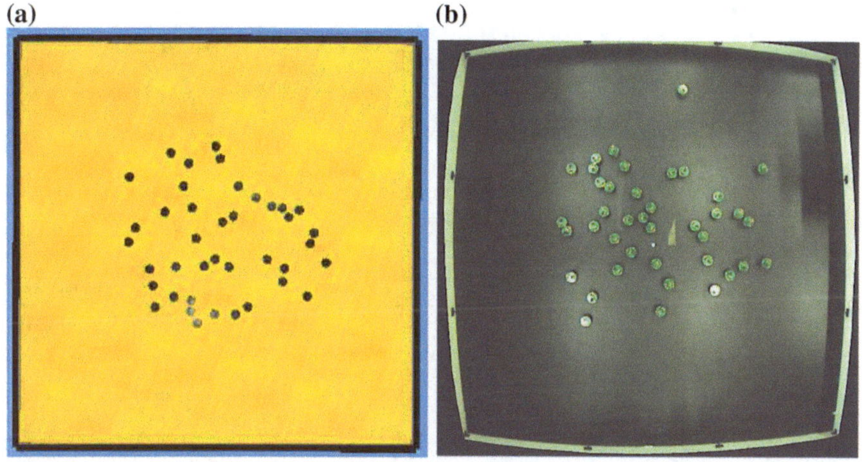

Fig. 19.1 **a** *Webots* simulation screenshot, 40 *e-puck* robots simulated. **b** Real-world experiment screenshot, 40 *e-puck* robots

19.4.2 Task Description and Decentralized Control Algorithm

In the wireless connected swarm case study, a decentralized control algorithm is implemented to maintain wireless connectivity and a certain degree of spatial compactness of a robotic swarm (with N robots) in an unbounded arena using exclusively, as information at the robot level, the current number of wireless connections to the neighbors. The communication is local and its bounded range is a parameter of the robotic system. Let X be the number of connections perceived by a robot. In the default state (defined as *forward*), the robot simply moves forward. If at any time the robot senses the loss of a connection and X falls below a threshold α (where $\alpha \in \{0, \ldots, N-1\}$), the robot assumes it is going in the wrong direction and switches to state *coherence*. In this state, the robot performs a 180° turn in order to recover the lost connection. Upon recovering the lost connection, the robot performs a random turn and moves back to the default state. If the connection is not recovered, the robot simply moves to the default state. If an obstacle is detected the robot immediately switches to state *avoid*, where it performs obstacle avoidance for a given number of time steps, after which it returns to its previous state.

While this simple algorithm has limited robustness, it allows the swarm to maintain its connectivity to a certain extent, with its spatial compactness being controlled by the communication range and by the threshold α. It is implemented in [29] using a FSA controller with states defined as above.

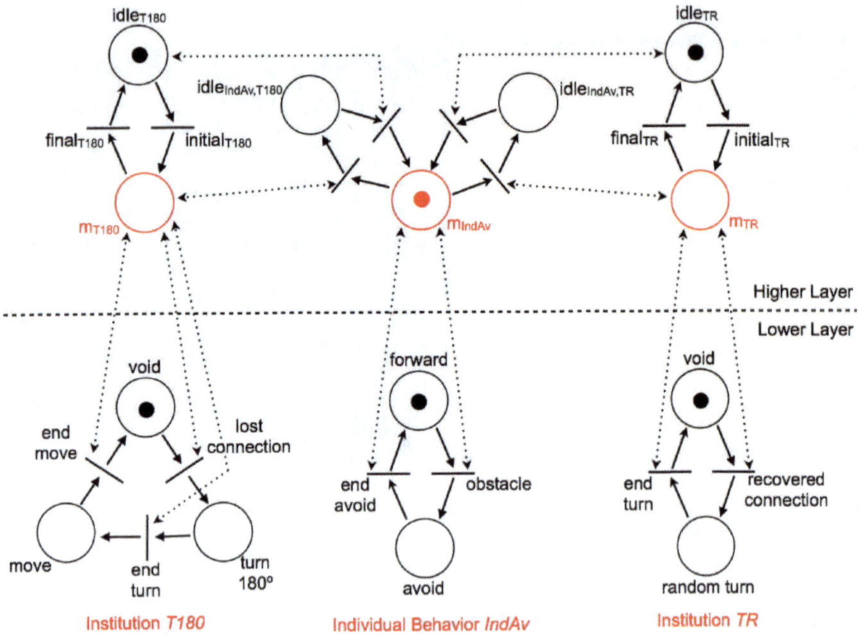

Fig. 19.2 IAC for the wireless connected swarm. *Dotted* arcs represent bidirectional arcs. Lower layer: EPNs for individual behavior *IndAv* and institutions $T180$ and *TR*. Higher layer: composition of individual behavior and institutions

19.4.3 Institutional Agent Controller

In our IAC implementation, robots execute an individual behavior *IndAv* (*Individual Avoidance*) and two institutions T 180 (*Turn* 180°) and TR (*Turn Random*), all specified by EPNs shown in the lower layer of Fig. 19.2. Individual behavior *IndAv* specifies a behavior relating the robot to its environment, consisting on simple obstacle avoidance. Institutions $T180$ and *TR* implement the social rules, dealing with loss and recovery of connections. $T180$ specifies that upon losing a connection the robot performs a 180° turn followed by moving forward for a small number of steps. Institution *TR* specifies that if a connection is recovered the robot performs a random degree turn.

To consider institutions as defined in Sect. 19.3, we need initial and final conditions and deontic operators. For institution $T180$, we say that initial condition $initial_{T180}$ is "loss of connection detected and number of connections is less than α" and the final condition $final_{T180}$ is "move forward procedure has ended." For institution *TR*, we say that initial condition $initial_{TR}$ is "recovery of connection detected and previous number of connections is less than α" and the final condition $final_{TR}$ is "random turn procedure has ended." The deontic operator associated with both institutions is *StopInd*, specifying that institutions and individual behavior cannot be executed concurrently.

We now have all the elements needed to obtain the IAC that specifies our desired behavior. The composition of the individual behavior *IndAv* and institutions $T180$ and *TR* (specified separately by EPNs shown in the lower layer of Fig. 19.2) is shown in the higher layer of Fig. 19.2. The final controller is the full EPN of Fig. 19.2, obtained after merging the two layers.

19.4.4 Experimental Setup

We replicated, to the best possible extent, the conditions of the original case study presented in [29]. Therein, the authors considered 40 robots in an unbounded arena performing the task over 10,000 s. In this work, we carry out experiments (both real robot experiments and *Webots* simulations) with sets of $N = 20$ and $N = 40$ robots in a 3 by 3 meters bounded arena performing the task over 1,800 s. The connection threshold is dependent on the size of N and is set to $\alpha = 8$ for $N = 20$ and $\alpha = 16$ for $N = 40$. The communication radius of the *e-puck* is intended to be 0.7 m, instead of the original 2.0 m, in order to keep the ratio between communication and physical radius presented in the original paper. We set the transmission power of the *e-puck* communication module to an appropriate value that allows us to roughly achieve the desired communication radius.

To compare the performance of our submicroscopic simulations and real-world experiments we performed 100 runs of the simulation for each $N = 20$ and $N = 40$, and 10 runs of real-world experiments for $N = 20$ and 5 runs for $N = 40$. During runs, we stored the number of time steps robots spent with each number of connections (between 0 and $N - 1$). We also recorded videos of the arena during the real-world experiments using an overhead camera and the *SwisTrack* software [13]. We processed the videos offline, using *SwisTrack* to perform background subtractions and blob detection, in order to extract and store the position of each robot in each frame. We also stored information about the position of robots at each time step of our simulations.

19.4.5 Results and Discussion

In this work, we are interested in two main metrics that represent and allow us to analyze different aspects of the swarm behavior: connectivity and displacement.

Connectivity tells us, on average, how many robots have a particular number of wireless connections during the time needed to perform a run of the experiment. To measure connectivity we use data gathered by the robots about the number of time steps spent with each number of connections. Robots with α or more connections are not concerned with recovering lost connections and are likely to be moving away from the swarm. On the other hand, robots with less than α connections are actively trying to regain connections and are likely to be moving toward the swarm. Thus, we can expect the swarm connectivity to peak at α, i.e., at each time step we will have more robots with α connections than with any other number of connections. *Displacement* measures the distance between the swarm center of mass and the center of the arena. Given the stochastic nature of the movement of the robots, displacement will start close to zero (runs start with robots gathered closely in the center of the arena) and will increase throughout the run. The motion of the swarm as a whole resembles a random walk through the arena. Comparing the values for displacement in tests made with simulated and real robots will give us additional insights into how well the simulator is capturing reality. This metric would be somewhat different if considered in the original case study, given that an unbounded arena was considered.

In Fig. 19.3a, b, we present the connectivity metric results for $N = 20$ and $N = 40$. In green, we display results obtained with submicroscopic simulations, while in red and blue we display results with real robots. The blue line was obtained with data about number of connections as perceived and recorded by the robots. On the other hand, the red line was obtained in offline processing using *SwisTrack* by counting, for each robot, how many other robots were present in a 0.7 m range, somehow emulating a perfectly radial communication disk. The differences in these two lines can be

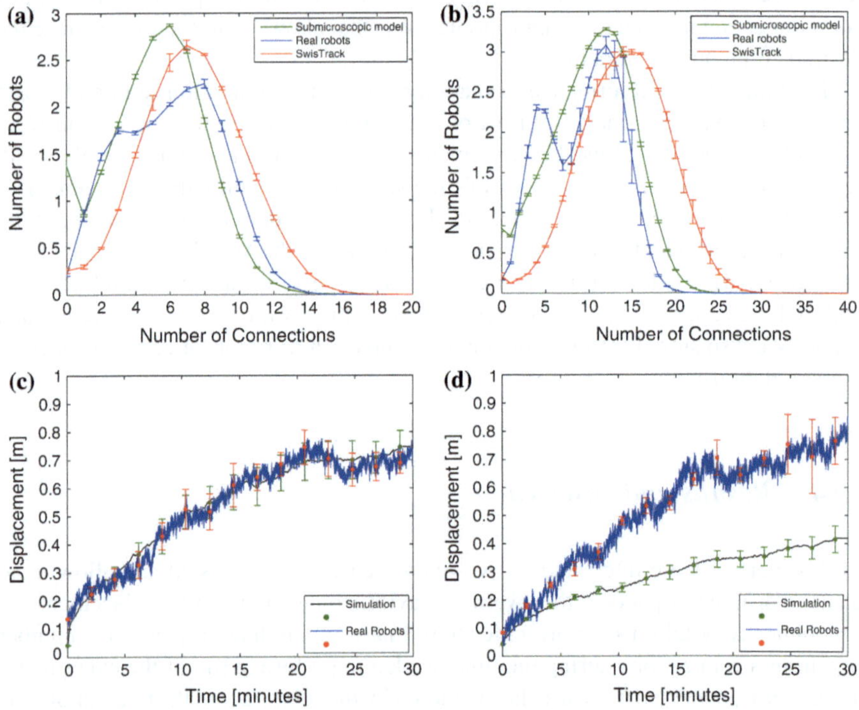

Fig. 19.3 *Top* Connectivity metric: average number of robots with a particular number of connections during a run. *Bottom* Displacement metric: average distance of swarm center of mass to arena center throughout a run. *Left* Results for 20 robots and $\alpha = 8$. *Right* Results for 40 robots and $\alpha = 16$. Variance shown for different runs

explained by the spatially irregular coverage of the wireless radio communications. The blue line reflects more accurately this noisy nature by spreading the number of robots more evenly between 3 and 9 connections in Fig. 19.3a and producing a second local maximum for 4 connections in Fig. 19.3b. This maximum can be explained by the increase in N and α. The increase in α forces robots to try to keep more neighbors in their communication radius, leading to robots aggregating in a smaller space. This effect is magnified by the increase of robots in the swarm. Thus, when robots lose or gain connections they lose 1 or 2 connections with $N = 20$ but they lose 4 or 5 connections with $N = 40$. The video data processed with *SwisTrack* always gives the correct number of neighbors since all robot positions are known, thus the red line better reflects the overall swarm behavior. We can see that connectivity measured with *SwisTrack* has a very good agreement with the connectivity measurements obtained in our submicroscopic simulations. The slight shift of the curve of the simulations in relation to the curve of *SwisTrack*, representing that robots have on average slightly less connections, is most likely a product of the inclusion of wireless communication realism (noisy fading and ellipsoidal communication area) in the simulations through the OmNET++ plugin. These results show that, despite the high influence of noise in real-world wireless communication, the overall swarm behavior implemented using an IR distributed control approach is able to maintain the expected connectivity. The results also show a very good agreement with the results presented in the original case study work [29].

In Figs. 19.3c, d, we present the displacement metric results for $N = 20$ and $N = 40$. Real robots results are obtained only using the video data processed with *SwisTrack*, since robots do not have localization capabilities and are unaware of their own location as well as the location of others. As expected, displacement distance is close to zero at the beginning and increases throughout the run. For $N = 20$, submicroscopic simulations and real robot experiments show perfect agreement. However, for $N = 40$, despite distance increasing in both simulation and real robots, we observe that the rate of increase is doubled from simulation to real robots. A possible explanation for this effect is the difference in the obstacle avoidance behavior. While in submicroscopic simulations *e-pucks* are considered as perfect cylindrical blocks, in reality *e-pucks*' bodies are translucent. This leads to some collisions between robots, being this effect greatly increased when the number of robots is doubled and they are forced to aggregate in a smaller space (because α is also doubled). Robots motion becomes less predictable and more stochastic and as a result the displacement of the whole swarm is increased, much in the same manner as a random walk with increased turning probability.

19.5 Coordination Through Institutional Roles

As discussed previously, institutions can take several forms: organizations, norms, hierarchies, roles, etc. In the wireless connected swarm case study, we experimented with institutional norms in a low complexity task, used for IAC validation only.

We now focus on another important institutional form, the institutional role. Our objective is to observe if coordination of a multi-robot system can be improved by using institutional roles, possibly in combination with other types of institutions. Also, the task to be accomplished by the robots in this case study is of higher complexity (w.r.t. the wireless connected swarm case study), with complexity of social interactions among robots depending on the approach taken.

We consider the following scenario and task. Robots are situated in an arena consisting of two rooms connected by a narrow corridor (see Fig. 19.4a). The width of the corridor allows only for one robot. In the left room, robots can pick up "virtual payloads" (in infinite supply) that can be deployed in the right room. Both picking up and deploying virtual payloads happen after a fixed amount of time has elapsed since the robots enter the respective rooms. In order for the robots to recognize their topological location, the walls have different colors, yellow in the left room, green in the right room, and blue in the corridor.

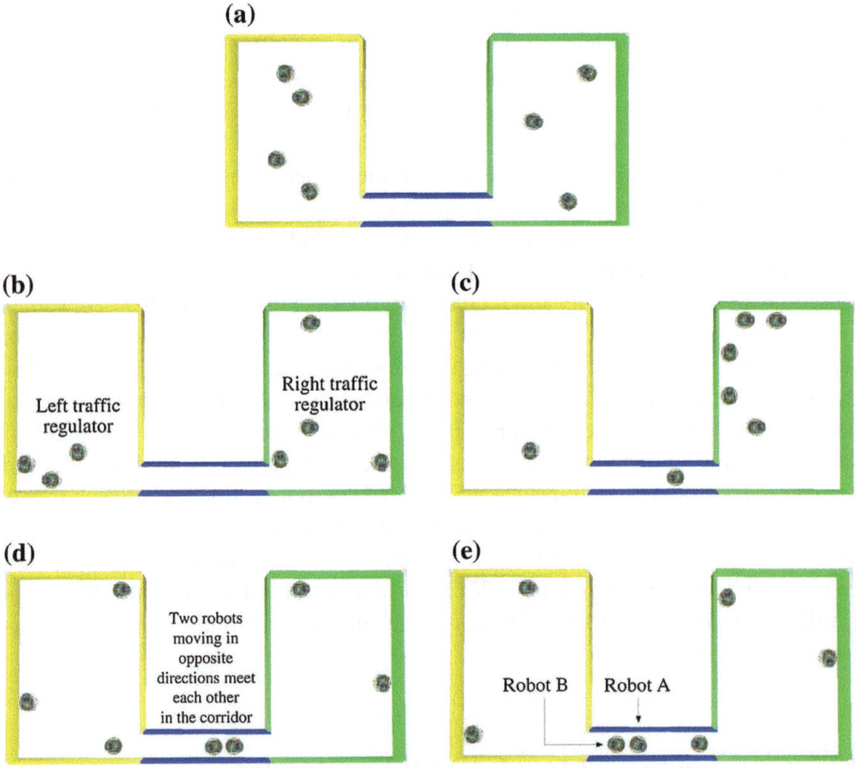

Fig. 19.4 Screenshots from submicroscopic simulations: **a** initial deployment of robots in the rooms; **b** regulators in their final positions at each entrance of the corridor; **c** queue formed behind right traffic regulator, while robot moves in the corridor. **d** two robots encounter each other in the corridor; **e** after adopting the role, robot A switches the role with robot B

The team goal is to maximize the number of deployed virtual payloads. Robots pick up the virtual payload in the left room. They must then navigate through the corridor and deploy the payload in the right room. The corridor connecting the rooms is too narrow for two robots moving in opposite directions to pass one another. In order to avoid congestion in the corridor, the traffic between the two rooms must to be coordinated so that robots only attempt to traverse the corridor in one direction at a time.

We show how such coordination can be achieved when the constituent robots are given the capacity to assume an institutional role, that of traffic regulator. We compare this institutional approach to a self-organized approach to the same task and try to identify in which situations one is preferable to the other.

19.5.1 Institutional Approach

We designate by *transporting* robots all robots that are transporting virtual payloads, and thus, actively accomplishing the task. Robots performing an institutional role are designated as *regulators* (we use also *traffic regulators* interchangeably).

19.5.1.1 Transporting Robots

Initially, all robots are transporting robots. They are placed randomly in the two rooms (see Fig. 19.4a) where they attempt to locate a wall and perform a wall-following behavior by keeping a wall on their right hand side, using readings from their proximity sensors. This wall-following behavior is complemented with some use of the camera in order to avoid conflicts with other transporting robots and help localization in the arena. Robots use their camera when, based on the readings from their proximity sensors, there is the possibility that they might be entering or leaving the corridor, or when an obstacle is detected. Based on the colors detected in the captured images, the robot can distinguish between other robots and walls of different colors. By navigating in this manner through the arena, robots are able to pick up virtual payloads and deploy them.

19.5.1.2 Traffic Regulation

If the need for traffic regulation arises due to a conflict between two transporting robots in the corridor, two robots assume the institutional role of traffic regulators. The two traffic regulators place themselves at the opposite ends of the corridor so that each regulator can control the flow of transporting robots entering the corridor from one of the rooms (see Fig. 19.4b). The goal of the regulators is to ensure that robots only move through the corridor in one direction at a time. The regulating robots are synchronized so that only one of them will let transporting robots enter the corridor from their respective rooms at any one time. The synchronization between the regulators is facilitated by an external program running on a *Webots* supervisor node, although it could also have been designed in a decentralized manner.

The regulators use their short-range communication capabilities to emit messages to guide the transporting robots trying to enter the corridor. A traffic regulator periodically emits messages when it has to prevent transporting robots from entering the corridor from the room in which it is placed. Transporting robots have to be inside the short-range communication radius of the regulators (set to 15 cm) to receive messages. If a transporting robot receives a message to stop, it will stop and begin to relay the stop message so other transporting robots behind it will stop too. As a result, the transporting robots will form a queue (see Fig. 19.4c). When the first robot in the queue receives a message to proceed, it forward the message to any robots that may be behind it, and the queued up robots will start to move.

19.5.1.3 Allocation of the Traffic Regulator Role

When two robots moving in opposite directions encounter one another in the corridor (see Fig. 19.4d), they send a message to the supervisor to determine if they should adopt the role as traffic regulators. Each of the robots specifies from which room it came. If no other robot has yet assumed the role in the room specified by the robot, the supervisor instructs the robot to assume the traffic regulator role in that room. The robot, now that it has adopted the role, has to retreat to the room from which it came and place itself next to the entrance of the corridor. However, after two robots moving in opposite directions have assumed the role as regulators, other robots may already have entered the corridor and prevent them from navigating to the entrance of the corridor (see Fig. 19.4e). In order to speed up conflict resolution in this case, the role is propagated to the last robot that entered the corridor from a given direction. Role propagation takes place in the following way: a traffic regulator (robot A) has been assigned the role, but has not yet navigated to the right location. During its retreat, robot A encounters another robot (robot B) in the corridor, both robots detect one another. Robot A stops, while robot B immediately sends a message to the supervisor in order to discover if it should assume the role as a traffic regulator. Despite the fact that a traffic regulator has already been assigned to the room from which robot B came (namely robot A), the regulator it is still located inside the corridor and not yet coordinating traffic. Thus, the supervisor sends a message to robot A to cancel the role assignment and instructs robot B to adopt the role instead. Robot A abandons the role, turns around and assumes the behavior of a regular transport robot.

After exiting the corridor, the regulator sends a message to the supervisor stating that it has made it outside of the corridor, preventing the supervisor from propagating the role further. The regulator navigates to a specific position at the entrance of corridor and sends another message to the supervisor stating that it is ready to regulate traffic. This specific position (see Fig. 19.4b) is chosen to allow transporting robots to enter the corridor while at the same time being close enough to the regulator to receive the messages that it emits.

When the regulators in both rooms are ready, the regulation process begins. The supervisor sends messages to both regulators and instructs one of them to let transporting robots enter the corridor, while the other regulator is instructed to prevent robots from entering the corridor from its side. After a certain amount of time, the supervisor sends messages to both regulators to stop robots trying to enter from either side. This allows the corridor to clear before robots from the opposite direction are let through. After another fixed period of time, the supervisor sends a message to the regulators instructing them to allow traffic in the opposite direction of that from the last cycle. After a given number of these switches, both regulators abandon the role and the system goes back to the initial state. This is done so that all robots have a chance to accomplish the task and no robot has the role for the entire duration of the experiment.

19.5.2 Institutional Agent Controller

As before, when using the IAC methodology to design robotic controllers that implement our institutional approach, our aim is to specify behaviors that have a social nature as institutions and behaviors that have an individual nature as the robots' individual behavior.

The individual behavior of the robots specifies how the task at hand is accomplished. Picking up virtual payloads and deploying them is a behavior that has an individual nature, since it relates the robot only to the environment in which it is located. A single robot could accomplish the deployment task, although performance would be critically reduced. Thus, we specify the individual behavior *Ind* as an EPN that accomplishes exactly that behavior.

The main social behavior of the corridor case study is the traffic regulator institutional role. This is clearly a behavior that has a social nature. We consider that this behavior is specified as an institution I_R that manages the role of traffic regulator. Its initial condition initial_R is the detection of a conflict in the corridor and its final condition final_R is the end of regulation (time limit). Since we do not want this behavior to be executed concurrently with any other behavior, the deontic operator of institution I_R will be *StopAll*. The EPN Inst_R to be executed by the robots follows the sequence of actions described in Sect. 19.5.1.

However, the institutional role is not the only social behavior present. Institutional roles depend on other robots' behaviors, in the sense that other must recognize and/or permit such role playing by particular robots. A second social behavior present in the institutional approach to this task is the recognition and compliance with the traffic regulator. The behavior corresponds to an institution I_M that manages the reception of messages from the traffic regulators and their relay, which is implemented with the EPN Inst_M. Its initial condition $\mathit{initial}_M$ is the reception of a stop message and its final condition final_M is the reception of a go message. We do not want this behavior to be executed concurrently with the individual behavior, so its deontic operator will be *StopInd*.

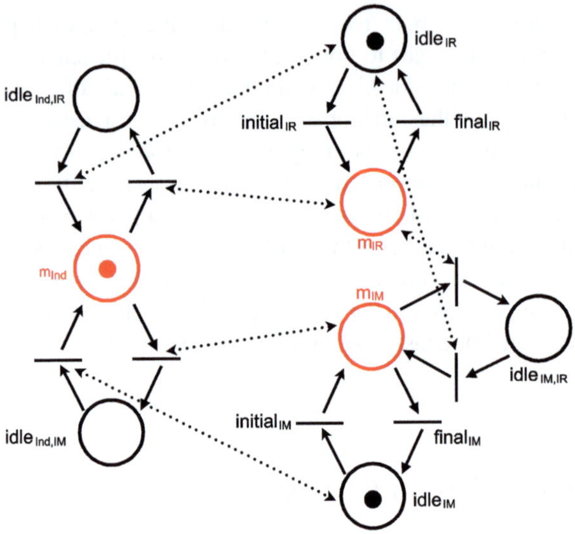

Fig. 19.5 Higher layer composition net of IAC for corridor case study. As before, *dotted arcs* represent bidirectional arcs. Places in *red* are macro places for behaviors in the lower layer. Place m_{Ind} represents the individual behavior Ind. Place m_{IR} represents institution I_R. Place m_{IM} represents institution I_M

In Fig. 19.5, we show the higher layer composition of our two institutions and individual behavior. The IAC for this case study is the result of merging this net with the lower layer EPNs. More details, including the lower layer EPNs can be found in [17].

19.5.3 Self-organized Approach

We implemented a different solution to our task which does not use institutional roles to regulate traffic. This solution is based on the principles of swarm robotics and the robots rely exclusively on self-organization to solve the task. Conflicts between robots moving in opposite directions in the corridor are solved in the following way: whenever a robot moving in one direction encounters a robot moving in the opposite direction in the corridor, it waits for a period of time proportional to the time that it has been in the corridor. If, during this period, a waiting robot detects that the other robot gives up, turns around and moves back to the room it came from, the waiting robot continues to traverse the corridor. Otherwise, if the time proportional to the time the waiting robot has been in the corridor expires, the waiting robot turns around and heads back to the side of the arena from where it came. No further optimization of the self-organized approach was carried out. For instance, solutions using basic local communication could lead to better performances.

19.5.4 Experimental Setup

As with the previous case study, we use the *e-puck* robots as our robotic platform. We consider that each robot is endowed with two different forms of communication: short-range and long-range. Long-range communication can be achieved using Bluetooth, while short-range communication can be achieved using the *e-puck* proximity sensors as an infrared communication device.

We prepared different setups in order to evaluate how parameters such as the size of the robotic team and the length of the corridor affect the performance. Three different corridor lengths L (50, 100, and 200 cm) were considered. For each corridor length, we ran experiments with different numbers of robots N (7 and 20 robots). For each of the six resulting setups, we performed 30 runs for both the institutional approach and for the self-organized approach. Each run had a duration of $T = 900$ s. Other parameters, such as the area of the rooms or the time intervals during with the regulators allow or stop robots entering the corridor, are directly dependent on N and L and are described in detail in [17].

19.5.5 Results and Discussion

Our metric of interest is the *number of transportations*, described as the total number of successful virtual payload deployments (a pickup in the left room followed by deployment of the virtual payload in the right room) achieved by the team during a run of the experiment.

In Fig. 19.6, we display the distributions of the number of transportations for all six experimental setups. The results for the institutional approach are presented in

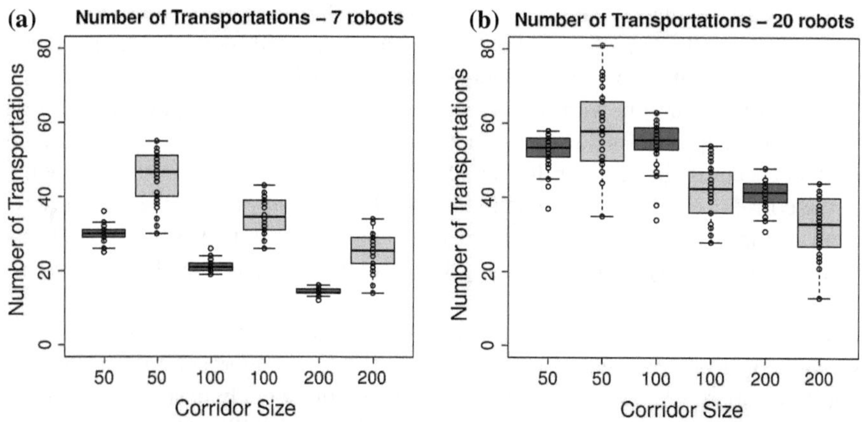

Fig. 19.6 Distribution of number of transportations for teams with **a** $N = 7$ robots and **b** $N = 20$ (institutional in *dark gray*, self-organized in *light gray*)

dark gray, while results for the self-organized approach are presented in light gray. The number of transportations decreases as the length of the corridor increases. This is naturally explained by the fact that the robots spend more time traversing the longer corridors.

When $N = 7$ (Fig. 19.6a), we observe that the robots following the self-organized approach always manage to perform more transportations than the robots following the institutional approach. This is due to the fact that not all robots in the institutional approach are performing transportations. While in the self-organized approach all the robots are devoted to transporting virtual payload, in the institutional approach two of the robots instead assume the institutional role of traffic regulators. This means that some of the team's resources are spent on coordination. In small teams, a proportionally larger share of robots are dedicated to coordination (28.5 % in the case of $N = 7$ robots with 2 traffic regulators). Moreover, in the self-organized approach, conflicts are easily solved the first time a (proportionally) large group of robots meets in the corridor, resulting in the robots forming a line and thus making future conflicts rare. This emergent coordination allows the self-organized approach to perform more transportations when the team is small.

When $N = 20$ (Fig. 19.6b), we observe an increase in the number of transportations for both approaches, although the increase for the institutional approach is considerably larger than for the self-organized approach. For $L = 50$ cm, there is not a significant difference between both approaches, except that the variance is much larger in the self-organized approach. However, for the longer corridors, the robots following the institutional approach perform more transportations. For teams with $N = 20$ robots, a smaller share of resources are dedicated to coordination (10 % in this case).

Larger teams have a greater need for regulation than smaller ones, as they are more prone to conflicts occurring often, simply due to their larger number of robots. Since only two robots are devoted to the regulation at any time, larger teams spend less of their resources in coordination than smaller ones. Thus, larger teams have their need for regulation satisfied while allowing a larger share of robots to perform the transport task. The coordination of the team provided by the traffic regulators gives some advantage over the self-organized approach.

The larger variation, with respect to experiments with $N = 7$, in results for the institutional approach is due to the fact that, with a higher number of robots more conflicts occur in the corridor. It is less likely that the first two robots that encounter in the corridor eventually become regulators. Robots may switch the role between them multiple times, leading to a difference in the time that it takes before the traffic regulators effectively start coordinating the rest of the team (and therefore a difference in number of transportations).

For different sizes of the team and different corridor lengths, we observe that the variance of results is always smaller in the institutional approach than in the self-organized approach. This suggests that the regulation not only positively affects the performance of the system, but also its performance reliability. Other metrics such as the number of conflicts in the corridor and the time duration of transports were also studied. These results are described in [17].

19.6 Discussion on Social-Aware Coordination of Multi-robot Systems in Human-Populated Environments

The corridor case study addresses three crucial issues for institutional roles: role allocation (how some robots start playing a role), role recognition (how robots recognize that some others are playing a role), and role permission (how robots permit other robots to play a role and behave accordingly). These three issues specify one of three elements involved in the ontology of institutional reality (according to [21, 22]): the assignment of status functions. Assigning status functions, that attribute some deontic powers, to objects or persons is one of the means human societies have to coordinate. In human societies, institutions exist because of the collective agreement of its members on the assignment of status functions. For instance, money, as a function, does not depend on the material chosen for banknotes or coins, but depends on the collective agreement to use such physical support to represent wealth and aid trade.

In the previous section, we addressed the allocation, recognition, and permission, of the traffic regulator role. We saw that the allocation is made when a conflict occurs inside the corridor, and depends on whether other robots are already executing the role. The recognition of this role by transporting robots is made through a second institution, that associates the reception of a "stop" message with the knowledge that a regulator is in place and is coordinating the team. Role permission is also implied in this second institution, since it specifies how to behave accordingly. Every robot *can* play the role, so in fact every robot *has permission* to do so, meaning that transporting robots will accept the order of the regulator and conform to it. One can view this permission as the existence of a collective agreement by the robots to assign a status function to one particular robot playing the role. Institutional roles are one possible example of the type of coordination we discussed earlier: society-wide coordination.

Another relevant aspect of the corridor case study concerns the distinction between "role" and "individual." No robot is specifically designed to play the traffic regulator role. In the IR approach, playing a role is justified if there is a collective need for coordination, not as a right or an inherent feature of any individual. Particularly, if we consider scenarios taking place in human-populated environments, institutional roles might also be played by humans, much in the same manner as they do when robots are not present. It is our intuition that, in certain scenarios, considering an IR approach will not only improve the coordination of the multi-robot system but will also facilitate the social interaction between robots and humans. Such intuition comes as a consequence of our goal to specify complex social interactions for multi-robot systems in a way that resembles the organizational aspects of human society.

The next main objective in the implementation and validation of the IR approach is to consider experiments in real-world scenarios populated with human actors. Robots will interact with these actors and such interaction should be based on coordination through common social rules, described as institutions. Such experiments will validate our intuition.

Let us consider a service robotics example scenario, focused on social robotics, using networked heterogeneous robots and sensors to interact with children, staff, and visitors, engaging in edutainment activities in the pediatric infirmary of a hospital. The infirmary environment includes not only bedrooms but also playing areas and also a school room. Besides being a realistic scenario, the ethical regulations enforced by hospitals for pediatric wards introduce important constraints, not only of a technical nature but also on what type of human–robot interactions are socially acceptable and how they are implemented. In order to deal with these constraints, we can consider institutional norms and institutional roles.

Institutional norms will allow the robots to comply with the social norms specified by both the ethics regulations and the staff of the pediatric infirmary. This will enforce that any coordination mechanism adopted by the robots is socially aware. For a simple example of how such norms will be taken into account, consider a task where two robots must fetch a child from her bedroom and guide her to a playing area. This action will require coordination not only between the two robots but also between the robots and the child. Suppose, however, that another child in the same room is being observed by a staff member. In this case, an institutional norm can specify that the robots should not go into room (to avoid disturbing the medical examination) and should instead produce a visual sign to call the child to join them. Such norms can constrain the normal coordination procedure between robots and children to enforce social-awareness.

Institutional roles are also of great importance in this scenario. The robots must recognize that some individuals are playing a role that gives them some deontic powers not available to other individuals. However, there must also be recognition that these individuals might change but the role remains the same, for instance, different nurses have the same powers as long as they are on duty. In terms of human–robot interaction, recognizing that certain human actors have some deontic powers that others do not, not only makes the robots aware of the social structure of the interaction but also allows better coordination of the robots. For instance, a command to "go away" might originate different responses depending on who gives it. If issued by a doctor, a coordinated effort between all robots to move to a safe area might be in order, if issued by a child the robot should just leave the area nearby.

Due to the complexity of both the environment where they are set and the mission to be accomplished, social robotics scenarios in real-world environments populated with human actors can consider not only distributed control and coordination of a robotic system but also centralized behavioral planning. Social-aware coordination based on institutions can be present at both these levels. At the centralized level, institutions can be used to enforce the social-awareness of the plans developed. At the individual robot (distributed) level, institutions ensure that social norms are always taken into account in the execution of plans, even in the event of an unplanned change in the environment or a loss of communication with the centralized planner.

In the IAC methodology proposed for distributed control and coordination, the nature of behaviors (individual vs. social) and their implementation are extremely important. The implementations of behaviors as EPNs allows the combination of multiple institutions and individual behaviors into a single controller that executes a desired task while taking into account the institutional environment. The focus of centralized planning is on how to produce a sequence of behaviors for multiple robots that, when executed at appropriate times and locations, achieve a desired goal. From the perspective of the planner, the way in which behaviors are implemented (at the individual robot level) is not of importance but rather where, when, and by whom those behaviors are executed. Thus, the EPN specification of institutions is not very relevant at the centralized planner level and the definition of institutions must be reformulated.

Given the different needs of the planner, we consider the following definition for institutions (in the context of centralized planning) as a tuple (following previous work described in [24] that considered a similar definition):

$$\langle \text{activity, place, physical artifacts, roles, norms} \rangle \tag{19.1}$$

The determining factor in guiding the behavior of the robot is the *activity* in which humans want it to be involved. There must be a comprehensive and closed list of possible activities. In the case of the pediatric infirmary scenario, some examples are "good-morning room tour," school-time, play-time.

Each activity can only be initiated at an appropriate *place*. A preparatory action may be necessary since the robot must be in a suitable place. For instance, was the robot at the corridor when accepting the command "it's time for school," it must first go to the school room. Certain activities can only take place at a specific location, while other activities can take place at different locations. Each activity must take place at a location which is appropriate from the humans' point of view, so as not to be intrusive.

Then, a set of *physical artifacts* and a set of *roles* are used to confirm that the robot is at a suitable location for the intended activity, and that it has the human partners needed for that activity. For example, there is a whiteboard at school and nowhere else; there must be a teacher at school, although we can also find a teacher outside the school; certain activities can only take place in the presence of at least one child. *Norms* express the desired relations between robots and humans, using the institution as a coordination artifact.

Our research will proceed concurrently on three fronts: improving the IAC distributed methodology; introducing the IR approach in the context of centralized planning; and ensuring that both distributed and centralized approaches to IR are coherent in the design, representation and execution of institutions.

19.7 Conclusion

In this work, we describe and discuss several aspects of the IR approach to the coordination of multi-robot systems. Previously, we introduced a methodology based on the formalization of the central concept of IR—institutions—using EPNs, that allows us to design and execute robotic controllers (IAC) that produce behaviors capturing complex social interactions. Herein, we advance the IR approach in three fronts: we move forward in the validation of the IAC methodology by considering a real-world case study; we tackle a case study dealing with more complex social interactions and compare the IR approach with a self-organized approach; and we discuss how the IR approach might be applied in a particular real-world human-populated scenario.

First, we describe a real-world implementation of the wireless connected swarm case study, following an IR approach. We observed that such approach was able to maintain the wireless connectivity of a swarm of 40 real, resource-constrained robots. Results on connectivity show that, despite the high influence of noise in real-world wireless communication, the overall swarm behavior implemented using an IR distributed control approach is able to maintain the expected connectivity.

With the corridor case study, we have demonstrated how concepts from institutional robotics can be applied in a robotics task, focusing on one specific form of institution, namely the institutional role. We have shown that coordination artifacts set up as institutional roles can effectively help a robotic team organize and improve performance in a given task. Nevertheless, this is not true in all cases. For instance, we showed that for smaller teams, emergent coordination from a set of simple control rules is sufficient for the team to achieve a good performance. With the increase of the size of the robotic team, and the consequent decrease in proportion of robots devoted to institutional roles, we see benefits of using institutional roles, not only in the overall performance of the task but also in its reliability.

The next main objective in the implementation and validation of the IR approach is to consider experiments in real-world scenarios populated with human actors. This will be achieved in the scope of the MOnarCH[1] project. This project focuses on social robotics, dealing with the use of networked robots in an hospital setting, much the in same way as the example presented in Sect. 19.6. The development of the MOnarCH project will provide us with an ideal testbed to test our intuition that the IR approach will ease the effort of the transition to real-world environments populated with human actors and facilitate coordination with such actors in scenarios involving many-to-many human–robot interactions.

References

1. Beni G (2005) Swarm robotics. In: Sahin E, Spears WM (eds) Swarm intelligence to swarm robotics. Springer, Berlin, pp 1–9
2. Bonabeau E, Dorigo M, Theraulaz G (1999) Swarm intelligence: from natural to artificial systems. Oxford University Press, New York
3. Cassandras CG, Lafortune S (2008) Introduction to discrete event systems, 2nd edn. Springer, New York

[1] MOnarCH—Multi-Robot Cognitive Systems Operating in Hospitals, FP7-ICT European project. More info at http://monarch-fp7.eu/.

4. Cianci C, Raemy X, Pugh J, Martinoli A (2006) Communication in a swarm of miniature robots: the e-puck as an educational tool for swarm robotics. Simulation of adaptive behaviour (SAB-2006), swarm robotics workshop, Rome, pp 103–115
5. Conte R, Castelfranchi C (1995) Cognitive and social action. London University College of London Press, London
6. Correll N, Martinoli A (2011) Modeling and designing self-organized aggregation in a swarm of miniature robots. Int J Robot Res 30(5):615–626
7. Dias M, Zlot R, Kalra N, Stentz A (2006) Market-based multirobot coordination: a survey and analysis. In: Proceedings of the IEEE (Special issue on multirobot coordination), vol 94, pp 1257–1270 July 2006
8. Dias MB, Zlot R, Zinck M, Gonzalez JP, Stentz AT (2004) A Versatile implementation of the traderbots approach for multirobot coordination. In: Groen FCA, Bonarini A, Amato N (eds) Intelligent Autonomous Systems 8 (Proceedings of the international conference on intelligent autonomous systems IAS 2004), IOS Press, pp 325–334
9. Gerkey BP, Mataric MJ (2002) Sold !: auction methods for multirobot coordination. IEEE Trans Rob 18(5):758–768
10. Hodgson GM (2000) What is the essence of institutional economics? J Econ Issues 34(2):317–329
11. Hodgson GM (2006) What are institutions? J Econ Issues XL(1):1–25
12. Levis P, Madden S, Polastre J, Szewczyk R, Woo A, Gay D, Hill J, Welsh M, Brewer E, Culler D (2004) Tinyos: an operating system for sensor networks. Ambient intelligence. Springer, New York
13. Lochmatter T, Roduit P, Cianci C, Correll N, Jacot J, Martinoli A (2008) SwisTrack—a flexible open source tracking software for multi-agent systems. In: 2008 IEEE/RSJ international conference on intelligent robots and systems, IEEE, pp 4004–4010
14. Michel O (2004) Webots TM: professional mobile robot simulation. Adv Rob 1(1):39–42
15. Mondada F, Bonani M, Raemy X, Pugh J, Cianci C, Klaptocz A, Magnenat S, Zufferey J, Floreano D, Martinoli A (2009) The e-puck, a robot designed for education in engineering. In: Proceedings of the 9th conference on autonomous robot systems and competitions, vol 1, pp 59–65
16. Nembrini J, Winfield AFT, Melhuish C (2002) Minimalist coherent swarming of wireless networked autonomous mobile robots. from animals to animats. In: Proceedings of the seventh international conference on simulation of adaptive behavior, pp 273–282
17. Pereira JN (2014) Advancing social interactions among robots: an institutional economics-based approach to distributed robotics systems. PhD thesis, IST-EPFL joint doctoral initiative - instituto superior Técnico (IST), École Polytechnique Fédérale de Lausanne (EPFL)
18. Pereira JN, Christensen AL, Silva P, Lima PU (2010) Coordination through institutional roles in robot collectives (extended abstract). In: van Der Hoek Se, Kaminka, Lespérance, Luck (eds) Proceedings of 9th international conference on autonomous agents and multiagent systems, Toronto, pp 1507–1508
19. Pereira JN, Silva P, Lima PU, Martinoli A (2013) An experimental study in wireless connectivity maintenance using up to 40 robots coordinated by an institutional robotics approach. In: Proceedings of the IEEE/RSJ international conference on intelligent robots and systems (IROS), pp 5073–5079
20. Pereira JN, Silva P, Lima PU, Martinoli A (2014) Formalization, implementation, and modeling of institutional controllers for distributed robotic systems. Artif Life 20(1):127–141
21. Searle JR (2005) What is an institution? J Instit Econ 1(1):1–22
22. Searle JR (2006) Social ontology: some basic principles. Anthropol Theory 6(March):12–29
23. Silva P, Lima PU (2007) Institutional robotics. In: Proceedings of ECAL 2007—9th European conference on artificial life, Lisboa, Portugal, pp 157–164
24. Silva P, Ventura R, Lima PU (2008) Institutional environments. In: Proceedings of workshop AT2AI-6: from agent theory to agent implementation, AAMAS 2008—7th international conference on autonomous agents and multiagent systems, Estoril, Portugal, pp 157–164

25. Tummolini L, Castelfranchi C (2006) The cognitive and behavioral mediation of institutions: towards an account of institutional actions. Cogn Syst Res 7(2–3):307–323
26. Vail D, Veloso M (2003) Dynamic multi-robot coordination. In: Schultz AC, Parker LE, Schneider FE (eds) Multi-robot systems: from swarms to intelligent automata, Volume II (Proceedings from the 2003 international workshop on multi-robot systems), Springer, pp 87–100
27. Varga A (2002) Software tools for networking: OMNeT++. IEEE Netw Interact 16(4):683–689
28. Weyns D, Schumacher M, Ricci A, Viroli M, Holvoet T (2005) Environment, a first-order abstraction in multiagent systems. Knowl Eng Rev 20(2):127–141
29. Winfield AFT, Liu W, Nembrini J, Martinoli A (2008) Modelling a wireless connected swarm of mobile robots. Swarm Intell 2(2–4):241–266
30. Winfield AFT, Nembrini J (2006) Safety in numbers: fault-tolerance in robot swarms. Int J Model Ident Control 1(1):30–37
31. Xu L, Stentz AT (2011) Market-based coordination of coupled robot systems. In: IEEE/RSJ international conference on intelligent robots and systems (IROS), pp 2784–2789

Chapter 20
Design of Safety Map with Collectives of Smartphone Sensors

Dang Viet Chau, Masao Kubo, Hiroshi Sato and Akira Namatame

Abstract Recently, there have been strong demand and interest for developing methods to analyze driving data for extracting traffic safety information. In this chapter, we study a method to extract incident factors that interfere with smooth driving for making safety map by using smartphone as a terminal data logger. In automobile research field, several methods for detecting sudden braking have been proposed; however, the detection of the factors those disturb the driving process, which drivers should pay attention, has not been fully discussed. Our method is based on smartphone with GPS information, therefore sophisticated equipments such as speed cameras are not required. We highly expect to utilize data from community in which each member shares smartphone data for generating incident map collectively. In our method, we apply the IMAC method (a dynamic map generating method) [1] for generating safety map. We carry out computer simulations and take real-world experiments in order to validate a part of safety map which generated by the proposed method. The result shows that based on the proposed method, safety map are correctly archived.

20.1 Introduction

In recent years, there is an opportunity to share traffic information to create a safer society. One of them is the construction of online safety traffic map. Safety map provides information relating to daily traffic safety information and traffic system alert [2, 3]. All of safety map products as examples shown above are all made by hand.

D.V. Chau · M. Kubo · H. Sato · A. Namatame (✉)
National Defense Academy, Yokosuka, Japan
e-mail: nama@nda.ac.jp

M. Kubo
e-mail: masaok@nda.ac.jp

H. Sato
e-mail: hsato@nda.ac.jp

D.V. Chau
e-mail: ed13003@nda.ac.jp

P. Spagnolo et al. (eds.), *Human Behavior Understanding in Networked Sensing*,
DOI 10.1007/978-3-319-10807-0_20

There is an opportunity to automatically analyze large amount of data and use them to create traffic safety map. By analyzing a large amount of data, it is potential to quickly provide information about traffic environment. Example of using probe car's log data for analyzing near-miss accidents [4]. The Honda company [5] does a pioneer work for building safety map using sudden braking data which collected from vehicle's braking sensors. In this work, we expect to benefit of smartphone's GPS data to discover incident factors from smartphone log data [6–9].

It is necessary to acquire position information and discover relating incident hotspots to automatically create traffic safety map from smartphone log data. In traffic road environment, there are obstacles that effect smooth driving, for example, traffic signal, zebra crossing line, slowdown area, and so on. We refer them as *incident factor*.

Automatically generating safety map is a new challenge in ITS field. As shown in Table 20.1, it is common to get incident information by questionnaire method. There are some challenges of detecting incident factors on road by using probe car acceleration data; however, these methods are high cost approach. It is common to detect road incidents by using roadside sensors and cameras; however, this method also requires setup large scale equipments. From above reasons, the current approaches have their own scalability limitations. Nowadays, many people have their own smartphone with high capacity and computing power; to record vehicle data it is not required to spend additional cost on external equipments. For general application, people can put smartphone on any places on their vehicle. Thus, smartphone should not be fixed installed on vehicle to record vehicle's behavior data. Smartphone GPS signal is not available in some areas, thus data accuracy at these areas is low accuracy and it becomes a big challenge. Therefore, we propose a novel method to utilize GPS information.

To detect incident spots, we apply the IMAC model which is a method to create the occupancy grid map [1]. Occupancy grid map evenly divides the space into grid; each grid state is updated by using neighbor-related information. IMAC is often used by robot car to make robot map [10]. Occupancy grid map method also can be used

Table 20.1 Literature related to automatic safety map generation: The labels g, p, s stand for government data, probe car, and smartphone, respectively

Information for safety map	Related works
Accident spots	Reports released by public agencies
Congestion detection	Herrera et al. [7, 8] (s), Fagan et al. [12]
Road condition classification	Li et al. [13] (p), Mohan et al. [14] (s), Fazeen et al. [15] (s)
Road width estimation	Zhang et al. [16] (p)
Intersection detection	Fathi et al. [17] (p)
Dangerous intersection detection	Higuchi et al. [18] (p), Yamazaki et al. [19] (p)
Anomaly braking point detection	Mohan et al. [14] (s), Honda project [5] (p)
Traffic signal, stop line detection	Dang et al. [20] (s)
Map making	Cao et al. [21] (s), Hilton et al. [22] (g), [5] (p, s)
Automatic accident report	White et al. [23] (s), Thompson et al. [24] (s)

to automatically create map by using LRF (Laser Range Finder) or sonar [11]. The problem is that occupancy grid map only deal with static map such as presenting if things are available or not at a location, so that it cannot be used with a dynamic environment such as traffic road.

The IMAC model is an extend version of occupancy grid map model, in which assume each grid is a two-state Markov chain [1]. Therefore, it can be used for representing a dynamic environment such as traffic road. We propose a method for automatically creating map from smartphone log data.

In order to create an occupancy grid map, it is necessary to observe states of corresponding locations to each grid. To observe such information, it is usually to use a laser range finder or sonar. In case of using a smartphone, it is impossible to directly observe the state of a given location. Therefore, to estimate the state of grids, we estimate the state of the vehicle by using information observed by smartphone. The computer simulation result shows that we can create a reasonable incident map by the proposed method.

This chapter is organized as follows. Related works are discussed in Sect. 20.2. Driving models are discussed, and rules of how to learn vehicle states based on driving model is discussed in Sect. 20.3. Section 20.4 shows the experiment results. Section 20.5 gives a conclusion and future work.

20.2 Challenges for Automatic Safety Map Generation

20.2.1 What Is Safety Map?

Some examples of safety map are provided by public agencies. For instance, Kanagawa prefecture in Japan provides safety map including accident locations, near-miss locations, and school zones [2]. Kitashitara county of Aichi prefecture [3] provides a map of road conditions [25–27], where includes accident locations, near-miss locations, and details analysis of near-miss information. The important information for creating safety map are accident locations, near-miss locations, road width, no traffic signal intersections, zebra crossing, traffic volumes, road with school zone, road condition, and so on. We call such above information is information support safety.

20.2.2 Automatic Safety Map Generation and Related Research

Making map from information support safety by hand is a very hard work. In recent years, there are some automatic methods to archive such kinds of map. Beside traditional method such as installing inductive loop in roadside, probe car, SNS, and smartphone are getting popular. Table 20.1 shows the main related works with publishing year.

Li et al. use GPS and sensor data to evaluate road condition [13]. Mohan et al. and Fazeen et al. use accelerometer and GPS data to detect road bump, manhole and create map by using five smartphones on a vehicle at the same time [14, 15]. Accident and congestion is likely to occur in places where road width changes regularly. Zhang et al. use probe car to collect GPS data and proposed method to detect road lance and width information [16]. Accident is also likely to occur at road intersection. Fathi et al. use probe car to collect GPS data and proposed method to detect intersections without prior knowledge about road database [17]. Higuchi and Nakajima et al. use probe car driver recorder data to detect sudden braking, sudden wheeling, near-miss locations [4, 18]. They also create near-miss map based on probe car's data for Shizuoka prefecture. Yamazaki et al. use JSAE database and probe car data to analyze time series of accelerometer data to detect near-miss locations, and predict dangerous locations on road [19]. Hilton et al. use kernel density method to analyze the USA government accident database and public the result over the internet for public use (http://saferroadmap.org) [22].

Since traffic safety map under as hardcopy version is created for each region generally, obtaining safety support information for global is quite difficult. However, it is possible to acquire safety information at national level by using above web site. Honda company [5] public their database of sudden braking over the internet (http://safetymap.jp). Based on the web site with sudden braking locations, they ask community for contributing experiences to confirm the fidelity of data. This method can utilize power of community to grow up the database; however, it is need to double check the accuracy of these pieces of data before use.

20.2.3 Driving Models

There have been significant contributions on driving models in ITS and automobile fields. Prior to developing driver models, it is important to establish what elements should be contained, Macadam [28] provides a comprehensive list of these essential aspects as well as some secondary ones that may be used to enhance the model. In his work, Macadam quotes Rashevsky who is of the opinion that the model must consider the vehicle and the driver as one entity that may not be separated. He also characterizes human drivers based on physical limitations and physical attributes. Physical limitations refer to input channels that humans have such as visual, vestibular, kinesthetic, auditory, and tactile channels.

Some of the earliest driver models made use of control theory by Levesque [29]. This approach has been used by a number of researchers. Control theory methods can be considered appropriate for modeling given that a driver is a very complex controller whose task is to maintain the course of the vehicle and arrive at the desired destination. One of the early control theory models was developed by Tustin; the model focused on the linear part of driver behavior while the nonlinear portions were regarded as a remnant Jurgensohn [30]. Attempts were made to describe the

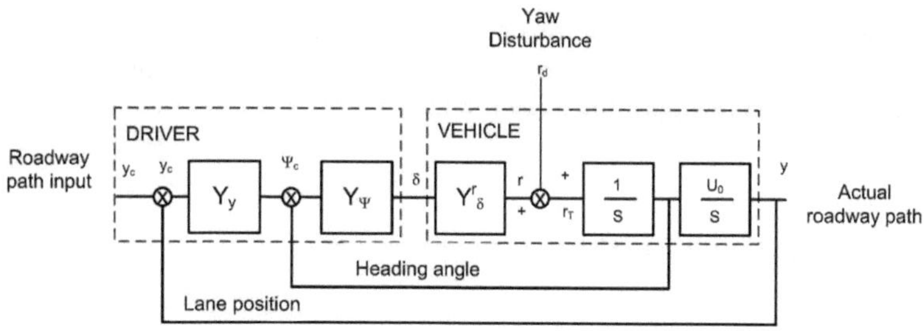

Fig. 20.1 Lateral control model by Weir and Chao [31]

remnant; however, they were relatively unsuccessful as they can generally only be regarded as an error which is quite difficult to model mathematically.

An observation with regard to the remnant is that it is relatively small and that most of the behavior is described by the linear portion; however, employing this method is not very well regarded as there are inaccuracies that are known to exist in the model. Ultimately, the research by Tustin revealed that modeling human behavior through the use of mathematical equations is extremely difficult given the amount of variation that exists in human behavior, especially from person to person. Common practice in the development of driver models that use control theory principles is to divide the model in two separate parts where one portion is responsible for longitudinal control and the other portion is responsible for lateral control [31]. A model of this nature is presented by Weir and Chao (Fig. 20.1).

The lateral portion of the model contains two feedback loops, one that considers the heading angle of the vehicle and the other that considers the lateral lane position. In addition to the feedback loops, the model also considers a random yaw rate disturbance. While the model is presented showing consideration for the lane position in the outer loop, it is possible to consider other parameters like path angle, sideslip, and lateral acceleration; however, the latter two are less desirable since they are more difficult to perceive by the driver. A dynamic model of the vehicle is required which is not difficult to obtain as it may already be known or can be measured if necessary. For the driver model, there are two describing functions that are used which relate to variables chosen for the feedback loops. When constructing this driver model, a combination of different approaches is used which consists of the crossover model, control principles, and experimental data acquired from either a driving simulator or an instrumented vehicle. The other portion of the model is for longitudinal control. This model is less complex than the one used to describe the lateral position as there is only one feedback loop with one describing function because only the throttle pedal position is considered and braking is neglected. To increase the accuracy of the longitudinal model, a speed disturbance is added which may simulate environmental factors such as wind and changes in terrain.

In the scenario of our incident map generation (using smartphone log data), there is not any driving model suitable for our objective. Our objective of desired driving model is that it can model the vehicle behaviors by using smartphone as a data logger installed on it and ignore the driver behavior difference. In the next section, we propose a basic driving model for modeling a vehicle behavior and generating incident map by using smartphone data log.

20.3 The Proposed Method

When encounter obstacles, to avoid accident, driver usually make deceleration or acceleration. Therefore, to detect incident locations, we analyze behavior of vehicle for deceleration and acceleration (Figs. 20.2 and 20.3). We do not mount smartphone for a fixed location, then we calculate acceleration from speed change. Moreover, since position accuracy of smartphone GPS is low, we propose a method to create a map that takes into account GPS noise.

We use the IMAC model [1] for generating incident map. This kind of map and occupancy grid map [11, 32] are the same type which can be used to record the presence or absence of objects in each grid. Basic occupancy grid map is suitable for recording an object is present steadily on a location corresponding to each grid. However, incidents with dynamic properties such as traffic signals that temporarily prevents passing over, to address them in occupancy grid map is very difficult. IMAC model is a two-state Markov chain in which each grid is composed of *free* or *occupied* state, and is suitable for recording semi-static objects [20]. To create incident map as discussed above, it is necessary to detect states for each grid is being *occupied* or *free*. This chapter, we propose a method to infer states of grid from GPS data.

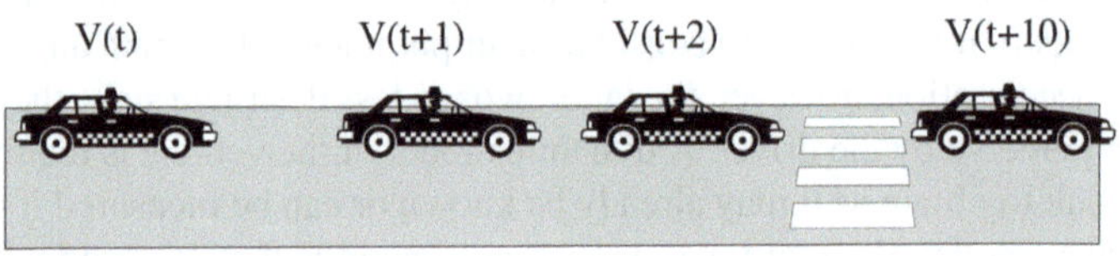

Fig. 20.2 Incident at zebra crossing *line*

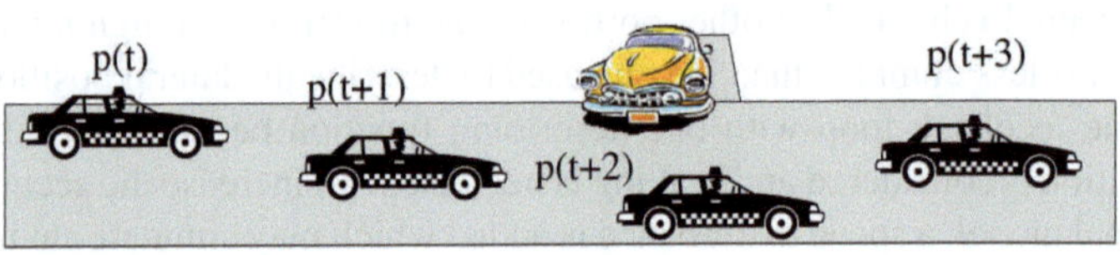

Fig. 20.3 Incident by obstacles

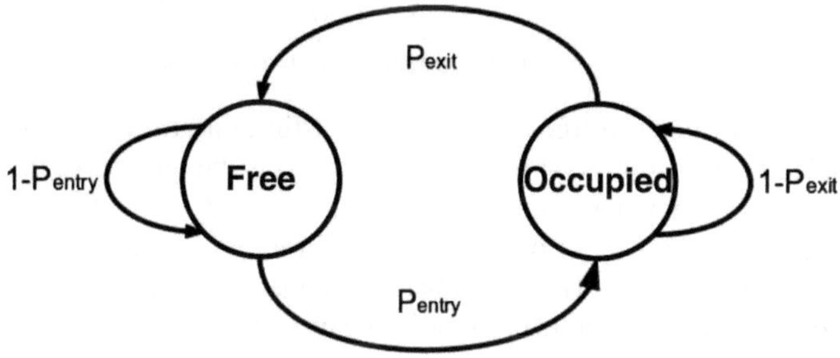

Fig. 20.4 State transition of a grid of IMAC

20.3.1 Independent Markov Chain Occupancy Grid Map

The IMAC (Independent Markov Chain Occupancy Grid Map) [1] is an occupancy grid map based on the proposed model of Luber [33]. Each grid has two states, which being in *occupied* state or *free* state. Assuming that observations of a moving object are independent events, thus the observations can be modeled as a Poisson process. A Poisson process describes probability to observe a number of events within a given time as in Fig. 20.4. Here,

$$P = \begin{pmatrix} 1 - P_{\text{entry}} & P_{\text{entry}} \\ P_{\text{exit}} & 1 - P_{\text{exit}} \end{pmatrix} = \begin{pmatrix} 1 - \lambda_{\text{entry}} & \lambda_{\text{entry}} \\ \lambda_{\text{exit}} & 1 - \lambda_{\text{exit}} \end{pmatrix} \tag{20.1}$$

The stationary transition state $w = \left(w_{\text{free}}, w_{\text{occupied}}\right)$ is

$$w \begin{pmatrix} 1 - \lambda_{\text{entry}} & \lambda_{\text{entry}} \\ \lambda_{\text{exit}} & 1 - \lambda_{\text{exit}} \end{pmatrix} = w \tag{20.2}$$

then

$$\left(w_{\text{free}}, w_{\text{occupied}}\right) = \left(\frac{\lambda_{\text{exit}}}{\lambda_{\text{exit}} + \lambda_{\text{entry}}}, \frac{\lambda_{\text{entry}}}{\lambda_{\text{exit}} + \lambda_{\text{entry}}}\right) \tag{20.3}$$

The state transition probability is estimated as follows. The estimated state transition probability of grid m is $\hat{\lambda}_{m,\text{exit}}, \hat{\lambda}_{m,\text{entry}}$

$$\hat{\lambda}_{m,\text{exit}} \sim P_{m,\text{exit}} = p(m = \text{free}|m = \text{occupied}) \tag{20.4}$$

$$\hat{\lambda}_{m,\text{entry}} \sim P_{m,\text{entry}} = p(m = \text{occupied}|m = \text{free}) \tag{20.5}$$

After we got the observations for grid m, we calculate $\hat{\lambda}_{m,\text{exit}}, \hat{\lambda}_{m,\text{entry}}$ as follows:

$$\hat{\lambda}_{m,\text{exit}} = \frac{\#\text{events : occupied to free} + 1}{\#\text{observations when occupied} + 1} \tag{20.6}$$

$$\hat{\lambda}_{m,\text{entry}} = \frac{\text{\#events : free to occupied} + 1}{\text{\#observations when free} + 1} \tag{20.7}$$

where #events: occupied to free is the number of times a grid is observed turning from occupied to free, #observations when occupied is the number of observations done in *occupied* state and #*events*: *free to occupied* and #observations when free are the respective quantities for observing a grid turning from *free* to *occupied* and observing a grid in *free* state. The additional +1 in Eqs. (20.6) and (20.7) follow from the initialization of all the parameters to one. The interpretation of $\hat{\lambda}_{m,\text{exit}}$ as a Poisson rate parameter is the expected number of state change events per observation, given that we are in *occupied* state.

20.3.2 Road State Estimation

Algorithm 1 Grid property update algorithm

```
if vehicleIsStop_i(t) == true then
  for all grid q in map do
    for all grid m : | m in neighbor(x_i,span_min) do
      Increase number of observations in occupied by w(x_i(t), q)
      if vehicleIsStop_i(t − 1) == false then
        Increase number of entry event by w(x_i(t), m)
      end if
    end for
  end for
else
  for all grid q in map do
    for all grid m : | m in neighbor(x_i, k_s v_i(t)) do
      Increase number of observations in free by w(x_i(t), q)
    end for
    if vehicleIsStop_i(t − 1) == true then
      for all grid m : | m in neighbor(x_i,span_min) do
        Increase number of exit event by w(x_i(t), q)
      end for
    end if
  end for
end if
```

20.3.2.1 The Proposed Algorithm Description

If grid state (*free* and *occupied*) observations are large enough, we can infer $(\lambda_{\text{exit}}, \lambda_{\text{entry}})$ by using Eqs. (20.6) and (20.7), therefore we can utilize this result to create incident map for traffic road. Below we explain a method to infer states of grid which locates near the vehicle from GPS log data.

We propose a method to use GPS data only for creating incident map even if smartphone posture is unknown. The method is used to classify *free* state and *incident* state on road by using GPS log data recorded from a smartphone installed on a vehicle. There are some methods for inferring road states from GPS changes, however, we use a very basic method for this objective. We will extract road state information of a vehicle when it stop by using GPS change. When a vehicle stops, area ahead is in *occupied* state. Another challenge when using smartphone GPS signal is that GPS data contains noise. Smartphone GPS accuracy is lower in compared to accuracy of military and construction GPS receiver. A large differences between vehicle's true position and GPS location can be predicted. Algorithm updates the map by considering the likelihood that the location is the true position of the vehicle. We also shows the proposed algorithm that takes into account GPS noise as in Algorithm 1. In this section, we explain principle of how to infer grid states from noiseless GPS data. In next section, we explain driving model which apply in the algorithm. Then, we also explain the method to infer neighboring states when using the driving model with deceleration.

Algorithm 2 Linear Deceleration and Constant Acceleration Driving Model (LD and CA)

1: **if** $incident(x_{obs}) = true \wedge isInsight_i(x_{obs}) = true \wedge caution_i(x_{obs}) = true \wedge v_i \leq kdis_i(t, x_{obs})$ **then**
2: $speed\ down : \frac{dx_i}{dt} = k\ dis_i(t, x_{obs})^n$
3: $where\ k = \dot{x}_i(0)/dis_i(0, x_{obs})$ and n=1
4: **else if** $v_i(t) <$ *MAX_SPEED* **then**
5: *Constant Acceleration*
6: **end if**

20.3.2.2 LD Deceleration Driving Model

Algorithm 2 shows the vehicle deceleration and acceleration behavior. In the second line, driver decreases speed according to the distance to the obstacle that the vehicle may collide. When the incident is resolved, driver accelerates constantly up to *MAX_SPEED*.

In Algorithm 2, i is the vehicle number, $x_i(t)$, $v_i(t)$ is the position and speed of the vehicle i at time t.

$incident(x)$ returns true if there is an incident at location x, otherwise $incident(x)$ returns false.

$isInsight_i(x)$ returns true if the driver if vehicle i watches incident at location x, otherwise $isInsight_i(x)$ returns false.

$caution_i(x)$ returns true if the driver of vehicle i predicts it is going to collide with incident at location x, otherwise $caution_i(x)$ returns false.

$dis_i(t, x_{\text{obs}})$ is the distance between vehicle i at time t and the obstacle x_{obs}, *MAX_SPEED* is vehicle maximum speed.

In this driving model, when the driver detects an obstacle (x_{obs}), a collision with obstacle can be avoided because the driver decreases the speed according to the distance to obstacle $dis_i(x_{\text{obs}})$. The vehicle behavior progress before incident is as follow. The incident position x_{obs}, the speed down equation is:

$$\frac{dx_i}{dt} = k\, \text{dis}_i(t, x_{obs})^n \tag{20.8}$$

In this study, we consider the problem of $n = 1$ in Eq. (20.8).

$$k = v_i(0)/\text{dis}_i(0, x_{obs}) \tag{20.9}$$

$$x_i(t) = (1 - e^{kt})\text{dis}_i(0, x_{obs}) \tag{20.10}$$

$$\dot{x}_i(t) = ke^{-kt}\text{dis}_i(0, x_{obs}) \tag{20.11}$$

assuming v_{min} is the minimum speed, the time until vehicle stops is

$$\frac{\log \frac{\text{dis}_i(0, x_{obs})}{v_{min}}}{k} \tag{20.12}$$

Figure 20.5 shows the speed change versus vehicle's location on a straight line road. There is a traffic signal at location 200 m on the road. The vehicle repeats to run from left to right when it reaches at the end. During trip on the left of traffic signal, if vehicle detects the signal turned red, its speed decreasing follow Eq. (20.8); when the signal turns green, it increases its speed until *MAX_SPEED*. The vehicle visual range

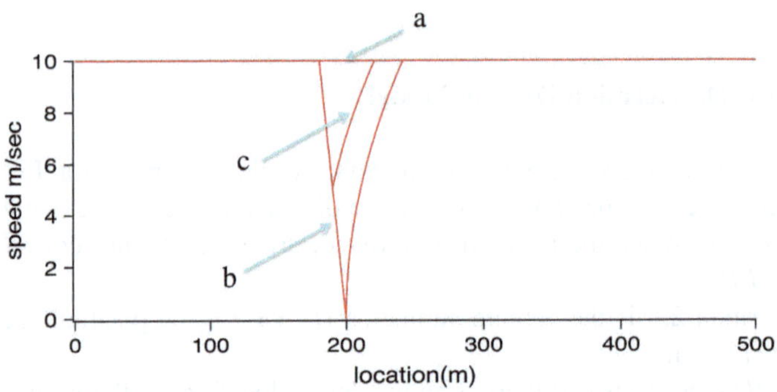

Fig. 20.5 Linear deceleration driving model and constant acceleration driving model

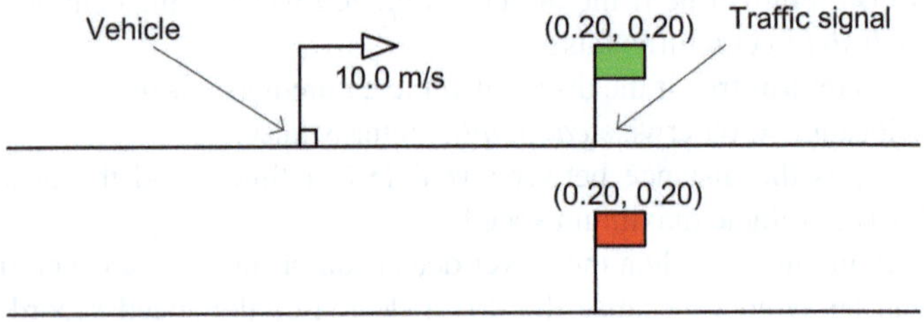

Fig. 20.6 A case of slow down on straight road with a single traffic signal

is set to 20 m, the acceleration =1.2 m/s, *MAX_SPEED* = 10 m/s, $v_{\min} = 0.1$ m/s. Figure 20.5 shows three cases of the relation between vehicle speed and its locations before the traffic signal. If the vehicle is in location before the signal 100 m, then its speed is keeps at 10 m/s. If the signal is green (a), then the vehicle keeps remain its speed and pass through the traffic signal. In case (b), the vehicle decreases speed and stop before the red signal; case (c), the signal turns green before the vehicle stops. The example of case (b) is shown in Fig. 20.6. Both case (b) and case (c), if the signal turns red, then from location 180–200 m, the vehicle starts to decrease its speed. We can confirm that the vehicle speed and distance to the signal is in direct proportion. In case (b), if the vehicle speed decreases less than $v_{\min} = 0.1$ m/s, it is considered to be stop and it waits for green signal. When the signal turns green, the vehicle starts to increase constantly its speed until reach *MAX_SPEED* = 10 m/s. In case (c), right after traffic signal turns green, the vehicle also starts to increase constantly its speed until reach *MAX_SPEED* = 10 m/s.

20.3.2.3 Stop Detection Rule

We describe a simple method how to infer vehicle states by using its location data $x_i(t)$. The vehicle is determined in stop state if its speed $v_i(t)$ is slower than a threshold value Th_s.

$$\text{vehicleIsStop}_i(t) = \begin{cases} \text{true} & v_i(t) < Th_s \\ \text{false} & \text{(otherwise)} \end{cases} \tag{20.13}$$

where $\text{vehicleIsStop}_i(t)$ is the speed state of the vehicle i at time t which hold an boolean value.

20.3.3 Road State Update Algorithm

In this section, we estimate road states by using vehicle estimated states. When a vehicle stops, there may be an obstacle appeared which infers with smooth driving. On the contrary, there is not any incident in front of the vehicle if it moves smoothly. In particular, if the vehicle follows the LD model, the distance to the incident, in Eq. (20.8) is

$$\text{dis}_i(t, x_{\text{obs}}) = v_i(t)/k \tag{20.14}$$

We can estimate locations of safety area is equal to or less than the distance right before the vehicle and the incident. Therefore, by choosing appropriate parameters k, we can set the safety area to be directly proportion to $\text{dis}_i(t, x_{\text{obs}})$. Utilizing this property, the grid map of road (IMAC grid) is updated using Algorithm 3. When the vehicle stops, IMAC's *occupied* of the grid just before the vehicle location increases

1, otherwise, if the vehicle moves, IMAC's *free* of the grid that inside safety area are increased to 1.

Algorithm 3 Grid property update algorithm without noise

if *vehicleIsStop*$_i(t)$ = *true* **then**
  for all *grid m* : | *m in neighbor*(x_i,*span*$_{min}$) ***do***
    Increase number of observations in occupancy by 1
    if *vehicleIsStop*$_i(t-1)$ = *false* **then**
      Increase number of entry event by 1
    end if
  end for
else
  for all *grid m* : | *m in neighbor*(x_i, $k_s v_i(t)$) ***do***
    Increase number of observations in free by 1
  end for
  if *vehicleIsStop*$_i(t-1)$ = *true* **then**
    for all *grid m* : | *m in neighbor*(x_i,*span*$_{min}$) ***do***
      Increase number of exit event by 1
    end for
  end if
end if

In Algorithm 3, neighbor(x_i, d) is the rectangle area with starting point is the vehicle i location and d length. k_s is safety parameter with a constant value.

20.3.4 Simulation Proof of Road State Update Algorithm

This section focuses on noiseless GPS data. We use Algorithm 3 to create the incident map.

At the beginning, we describe the IMAC-based proposed algorithm for creating an incident map. Figure 20.7 shows the simulation result of transition observations for a one-way road with a traffic signal at location 200 m, the vehicle repeats to run from the begin to the end of the road, using Algorithm 3. Assuming that we correctly

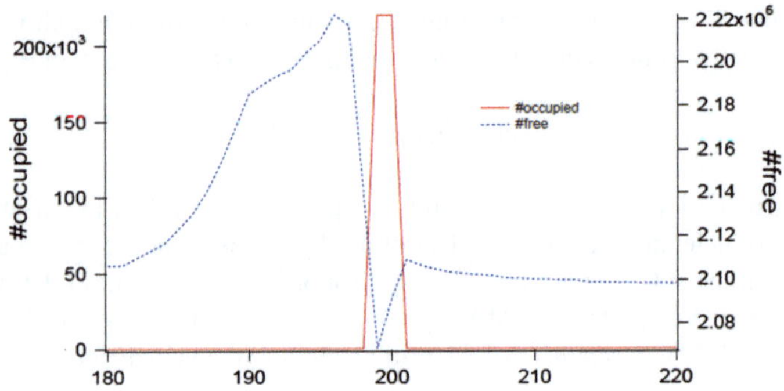

Fig. 20.7 Example of IMAC result based on state estimation: transition observations

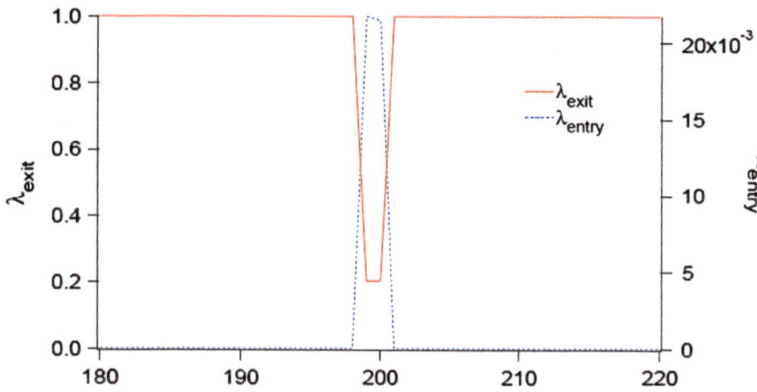

Fig. 20.8 Example of IMAC result based on state estimation: probability

estimate k, then set $k_s = 1/k$. The traffic signal changes between green and red based on a probability value. We set the probability that traffic signal turns from green to red by 0.02 and red to green by 0.2. The vehicle virtual range is 20 m. If the signal turns red, the vehicle starts to decrease its speed from location 180 m. During speed down, *#free* observation is increased.

At the signal location, *#occupied* observation is increased. The straight road simulation result of grid map of IMAC is shown in Fig. 20.8. The red solid line is λ_{exit}, the blue dotted line is λ_{entry}. From preset probability value of traffic signal, the results should be $\lambda_{exit} = 0.2$, $\lambda_{entry} = 0.02$ at the traffic signal. Otherwise, at the location without signal, $\lambda_{exit} = 1.0$, $\lambda_{entry} = 0.0$. The estimated results of signal location 200 m is approximately the probability of traffic signal, $\lambda_{exit} = 0.2$, $\lambda_{entry} = 0.0217$. From the simulation result, we can estimate the incident map based on the IMAC model by using Algorithm 3 with a suitable chosen of k_s.

From the simulation result, it is confirmed that we can estimate λ_{exit} exactly and λ_{exit} value does not depend on k_s (Fig. 20.9).

20.3.5 Verification of Impact on the Estimated Map of the Driving Model

In this section, we make clear the impact of the driving model parameters on incident map creation process. The parameter includes max speed (m/s) (*MAX_SPEED*), acceleration (m/s^2), visual range (m). We test the driving model impact by changing the input values in the simulation setting.

Figure 20.10 shows the relation between the estimated λ_{exit} and λ_{entry} value at the traffic signal location and the visual range of the vehicle. In this simulation, $k_s = 1$, we got the value of $\lambda_{exit} \approx 0.2$ and it does not depend on the visual range. And, when the visual range is getting larger the λ_{entry} value getting better (closer to the true value). We archived this result because the vehicle has more chances to observe the traffic signal state when it has long visual range (Fig. 20.10).

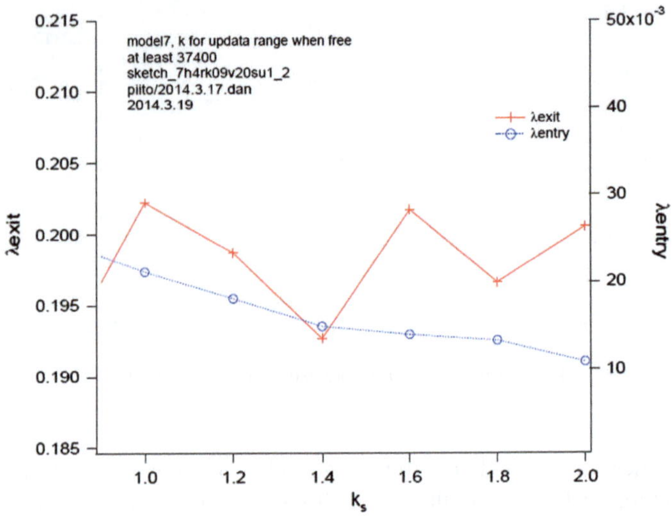

Fig. 20.9 Example of IMAC result based on state estimation

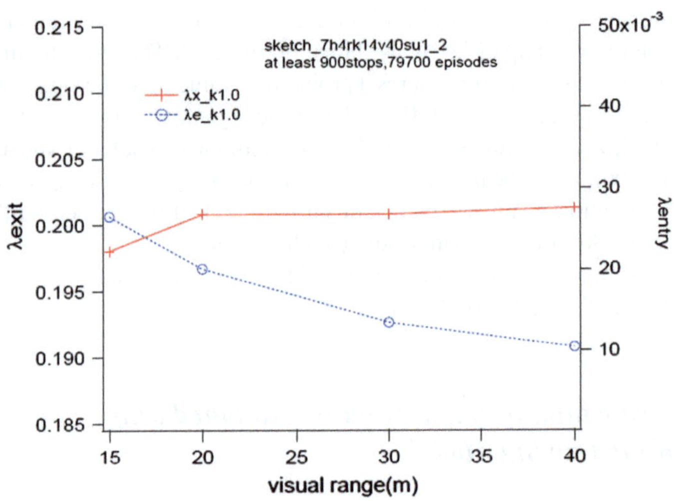

Fig. 20.10 Difference visual range simulation

Figures 20.11 and 20.12 shows the impact of acceleration on the estimated λ_{exit} and λ_{entry} value. In this simulation, the max speed changes from 0.5 to 3.0 m/s^2, and $k_s = 1$. As can be seen from the experimental results, it was found that the speed does not affect substantially the estimation result in this range. From the simulation result, we confirmed that the driving model parameters does not make an big impact on the estimated grid map λ_{exit} and λ_{entry}. Moreover, the impact on λ_{exit} is less than the impact on λ_{entry} in most cases.

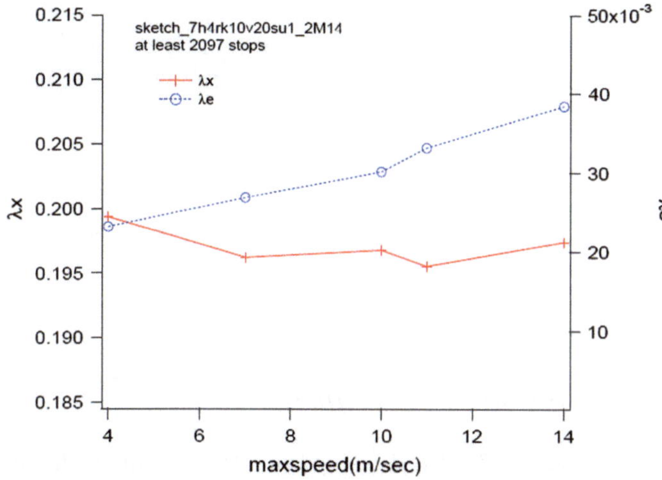

Fig. 20.11 The estimated map with different speed

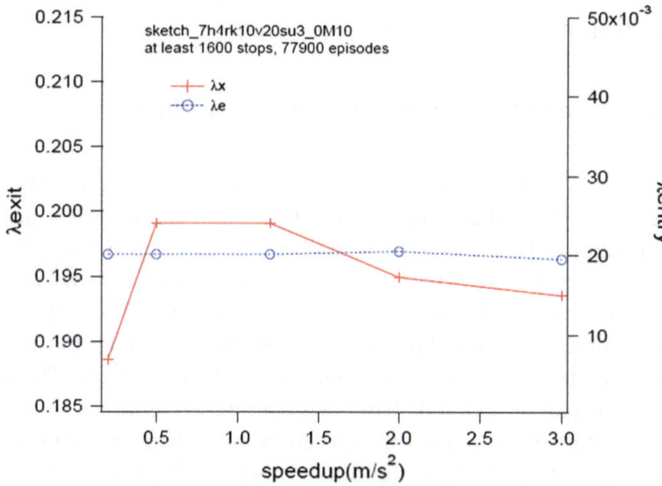

Fig. 20.12 The estimated map with different acceleration

20.3.6 GPS Noise Solution

Until now, we only deal with noiseless GPS data. Since GPS has noise, there is possibility that Algorithm 3 would update the different location on road far from the true position. We assume that the GPS location follows the probability distribution of $N(0, \sigma)$, in Algorithm 3, and instead of increment by 1, we use a weight parameter w for that increment. Now, the update rule for the grid m with the value $w(x_i(t), g)$ is

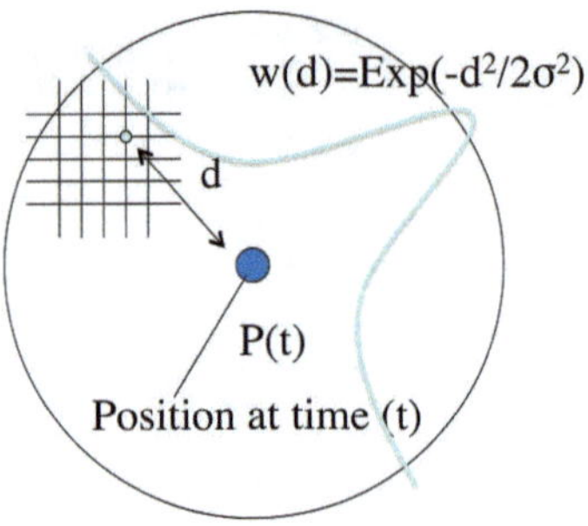

Fig. 20.13 GPS noise solution (*circle* update)

$$w(x_i(t), g) = f(dis_i(t, g))/f(0) = e^{-dis_i(t,g)^2/2\sigma^2} \tag{20.15}$$

where $f(x) = \frac{1}{\sqrt{2\pi\sigma^2}} e^{-x^2/2\sigma^2}$. The detail update rule is shown in Algorithm 1. The algorithm updates IMAC grids from 1 to w (Fig. 20.13).

20.4 Experiments

20.4.1 Experiment 1: Around a Campus Building

We use an apple IPhone 4 s for recording GPS information at 100 Hz sampling. We carry out an experiment around a campus building which does not include much real traffic situations. The vehicle is an 2005 version Mazda 6, the smartphone is put on vehicle's door pocket. The test track for experiment is shown in Fig. 20.14. The white line plots with red dot are the vehicle's test track. The test track follows clockwise direction. There are three stop lines A, B, C at which the vehicle stops for 10, 6, 4 s. The test track includes about 60 rounds about 5 km. The dataset for experiment is overlaid on a Google Satellite map (Fig. 20.15).

The first half part of dataset 1 will be used as input data for the proposed algorithm to generate map. As shown in Fig. 20.15, most of GPS paths are out of test track because of GPS noise. From the dataset, the position information can be acquired by GPS of a smartphone installed in vehicle, but it was found that the accuracy is very poor.

The grid map of λ_{exit} is shown in Fig. 20.16. As shown in Fig. 20.16, for the λ_{exit}, at three stop lines A, B, C; the grid map has low value of λ_{exit}. At stop line A, vehicle stops for 10 s, the sampling by smartphone is 100 Hz, therefore the idea value of $\lambda_{exit} = (1/10\,s)/100\,Hz = 0.001$. Nearby locations of stop line A, there are many gray star grids, and together with λ_{exit} value, it is confirmed that the grid map of λ_{exit} can be correctly estimated. For the stop line B, the vehicle stops for 6 seconds, therefore the idea value of $\lambda_{exit} = (1/6\,s)/100\,Hz = 0.00167$. Nearby locations of stop line B, there are many gray dot grids, and together with λ_{exit} value,

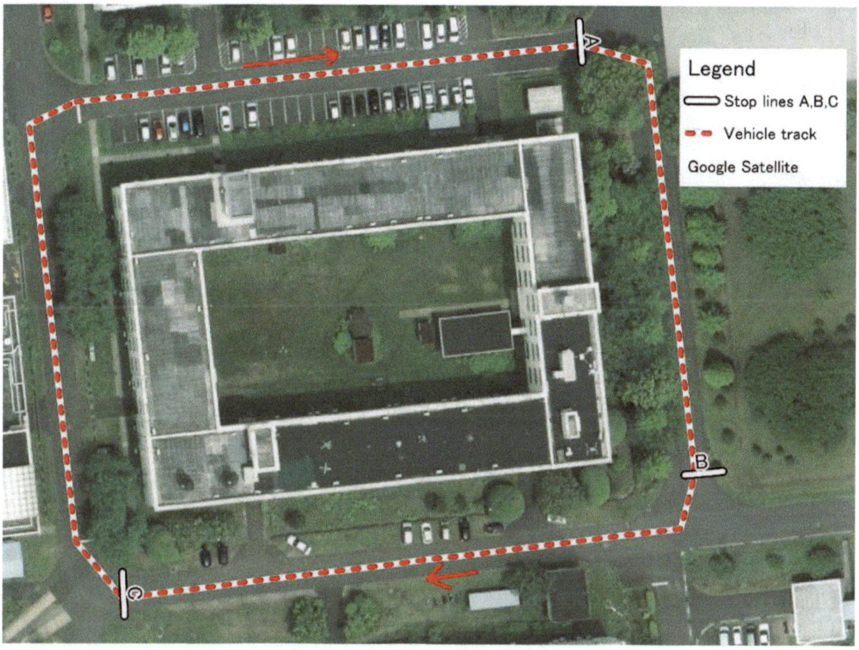

Fig. 20.14 Test track

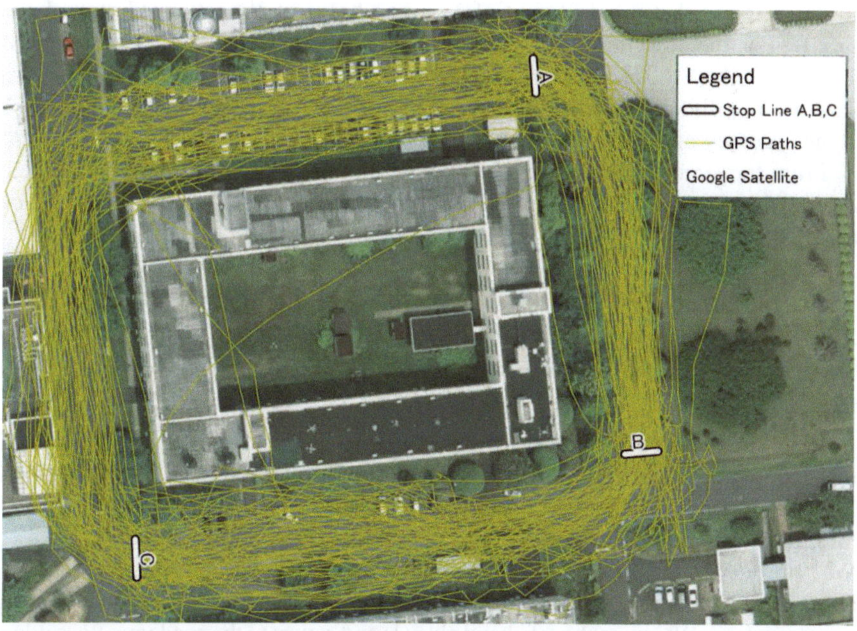

Fig. 20.15 Dataset for incident map generation. GPS paths: log data collecting from IPhone; stop line A, B, C; google satellite: ground truth map (dataset 1)

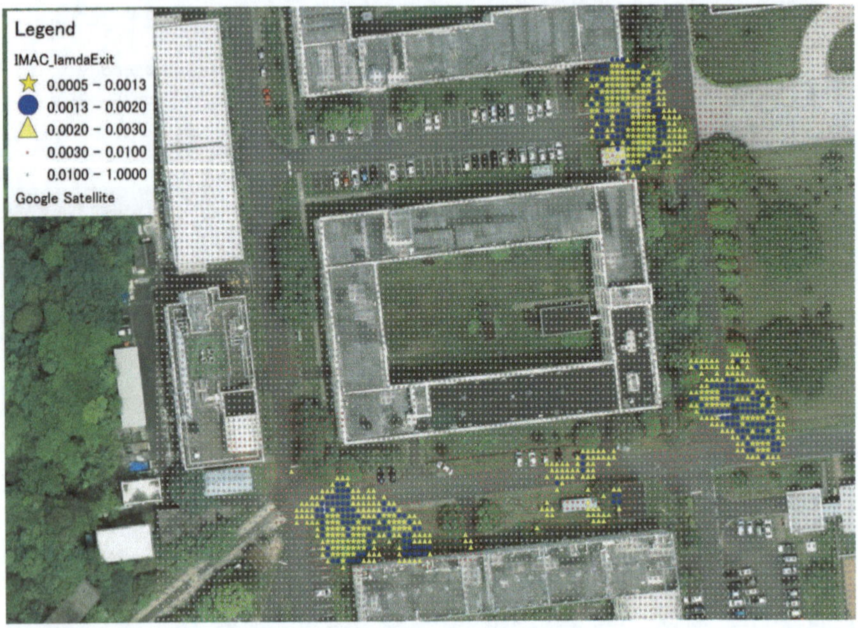

Fig. 20.16 The estimated map by dataset 1 (λ_{exit})

it is confirmed that the grid map of λ_{exit} can be correctly estimated around stop line B. For the stop line C, the vehicle stops for 4 s, therefore the idea value of $\lambda_{\text{exit}} = (1/4\,\text{s})/100\,\text{Hz} = 0.0025$. Nearby locations of stop line C, the grid map value of λ_{exit} should contain gray triangle; however, in comparing with stop lines A, B the accuracy of the λ_{exit} is low.

From the simulation results, it was found that the estimated grid map correctly detects three stop lines by using the proposed method in the case of one vehicle are used.

20.4.2 Experiment 2: Traffic Road Environment

We evaluate the proposed method for generating incident map by a real traffic environment. In the last experiment, there is only one test vehicle on the experiment. In this experiment, there are other vehicles as obstacles on traffic road. We drove about 20 times in July 2013 around our academy (mabori, yokosuka, kanagawa prefecture, Japan). Figure 20.17 shows the path we drove. The driving route is as follows. We start our academy (A) at about 83 m height above sea level and go down to E at about 1 m height above sea level passing through B, C, and D. Then we turn right at E and run to G. We run to the left-hand side (J) and return to the academy. We seldom meet a traffic congestion while we stop at the red light of traffic signals. There is a

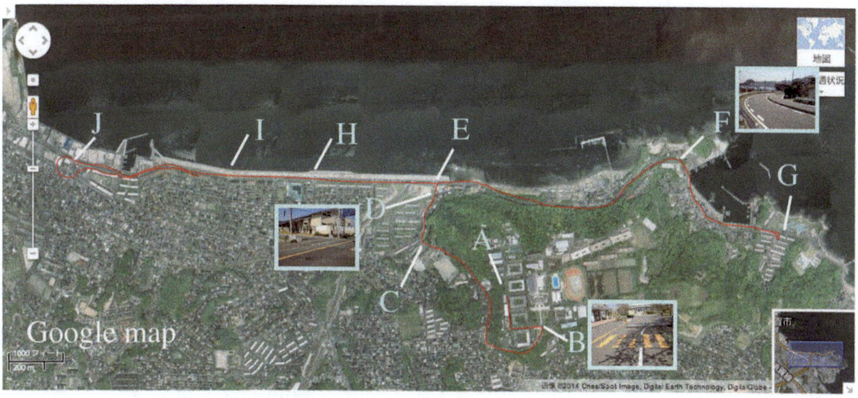

Fig. 20.17 Cartography in general traffic environment: course

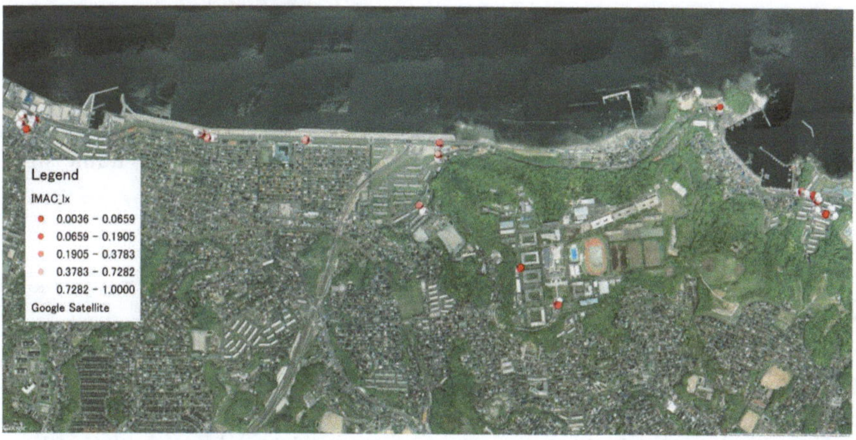

Fig. 20.18 The grid map of λ_{exit} in traffic road

stop line at B. There are traffic signals at C, E, H, and I. Location F is an entrance gate before a building.

Figure 20.18 shows the λ_{exit} of the estimated incident map. At the location B, C, D, the value of λ_{exit} is small. We confirm in the ground true map (google map) that there is a stop signal at location B, and there is a traffic signal at each location C, E, I, and H. The vehicle gradually decreases its speed at location F. From the result, the proposed algorithm can be used to generate correctly incident map in real-world environment.

Figure 20.19 shows the incident map at the location from A to C which generated by using only the speed down state. Using only the speed down state not the stop state, the proposed method also can be used to generate incident factors. The green

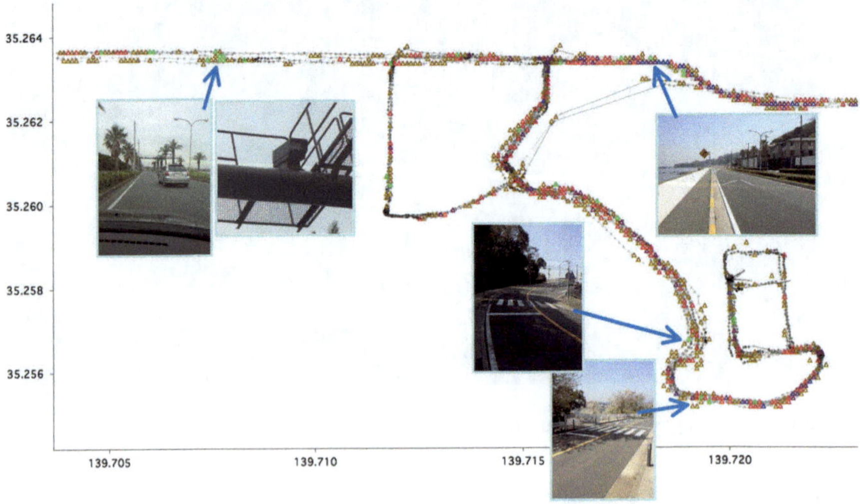

Fig. 20.19 The incident map by vehicle deceleration

marks are the locations with high value of λ_{exit}, at which include no traffic signal zebra crossing lines.

20.5 Conclusion

In recent years, there is an opportunity to automatically analyze large amount of data, and use them to create a traffic safety map. There are many proposals to detect and share the sudden braking data; however, none of them is successful to detect and generate map of incident factors that interfere with smooth driving such as zebra crossing, traffic signals, and so on. In this chapter, we proposed a method to generate map of incident factors which interfere with smooth driving by using smartphone log data.

The proposed method estimates road states from the change of GPS data over time. For this purpose, we proposed the LDCA driving model which ensures a short safety area before the vehicle according to its current speed. The LDCA driving model is validated by a computer simulation using noiseless data. Two experiments including a GPS noise reducing algorithm were also carried out in order to test the proposed method in real-world environment. The experiment results show that the proposed method can be used to generate a incident map by using smartphone GPS data.

References

1. Saarinen J, Andreasson H, Achim JL (2012) Independent Markov chain occupancy grid maps for representation of dynamic environment, 2012 IEEE/RSJ international conference on intelligent robots and systems (IROS), pp 3489–3495
2. Kanagawa police safety map http://www.police.pref.kanagawa.jp/mes/mesf0152.htm
3. Aichi Kirashitara county safety map http://www.pref.aichi.jp/cmsfiles/contents/0000041/41119/sitara-jikomap.pdf
4. Nakajima Y, Makimura K, Mashiko T (2005) Near-miss data for urban transport administration. IBS annual report 2005, pp 81–86
5. Honda safety map project http://safetymap.jp/
6. http://g-book.com/pc/smart_G-BOOK/
7. Herrera JC, Work DB, Herring R, Ban XJ, Jacobson Q, Bayen AM (2010) Evaluation of traffic data obtained via GPS-enabled mobile phones: the mobile century field experiment. Transp Res C: Emerg Technol 18(4):568–583
8. Herrera JC, Bayen AM (2010) Incorporation of Lagrangian measurements in freeway traffic state estimation. Transp Res B: Methodol 44(4):460–481
9. Demonstration promotion of probe technology export, H23 Trade and Investment business facilitation support program, Hitachi Co., Ltd, Nippon Koei Co. Ltd and Center for Information Cooperation CICC
10. http://www.meti.go.jp/committee/kenkyukai/seisan/juntenchoueisei/003_02_2.pdf
11. Thrun S, Burgard W, Fox D (2005) Probabilistic robotics. MIT press, Cambridge
12. Fagan D, Meier R (2010) Highly-dynamic, pervasive monitoring of traffic congestion levels. Proceedings of ITRN2010, pp 1–8
13. K Li, Misener JA, Hedrick K (2007) On-board road condition monitoring system using slip-based tyre road friction estimation and wheel speed signal analysis. Proc Inst Mech Eng K: J Multi-body Dyn 221(1):129–146
14. Mohan P, Venkata N, Ramjee R (2008) Nericell rich monitoring of road and traffic conditions using mobile smartphones. In: Proceedings of the 6th ACM conference on embedded network sensor systems, pp 323–336
15. Fazeen M, Gozick B, Dantu R, Bhukhiya M, Gonzalez MC (2012) Safe driving using mobile phones. IEEE Trans Intell Transp Syst 13(3):1462–1468
16. Zhang L, Thiemann F, Sester M (2010) Integration of GPS traces with road map. In: Proceeding of IWCTS'10 Proceedings of the second international workshop on computational transportation science, pp 17–22
17. Fathi A, Krumm J (2010) Detecting road intersections from GPS traces. Geogr Inf Sci 6292:56–69
18. Study of outcome measures with potential accident data. IBS annual report 205, pp 85–86
19. Yamazaki S, Funakubo A, Tanizawa Y (2011) Estimation of dangerous routes using the near-miss incident data of probe-car
20. Dang CV, Sato H, Shirakawa T, Namatame A (2014) Occupancy grid map of semi-static objects by mobile observer. In: Proceedings of the international symposium on artificial life and robotics 19th 2014
21. Cao L, Krumm J (2009) From GPS traces to a routable road map, Proceeding of GIS'09 proceedings of the 17th ACM SIGSPATIAL international conference on advances in geographic information systems, pp 3–12
22. Hilton BN, Horan TA, Burkhard R, Schooley B, SafeRoadMaps: communication of location and density of traffic fatalities through spatial visualization and heat map analysis information visualization http://saferoadmaps.org
23. White J, Thompson C, Turner H, Dougherty B, Schmidt DC (2011) Wreckwatch: automatic traffic accident detection and notification with smartphones. J Mob Netw Appl 16(3):285–303
24. Thompson C (2010) Using smartphones to detect car accidents and provide situational awareness to first responders. Third international ICST conference on mobile wireless middleware, operating systems, and applications, Lecture Notes of the Institute for Computer Sciences, Social Informatics and Telecommunications Engineering vol 48, pp 29–42

25. Nagai M, Yohei M, Kamata M, Motokiso K, Study on near-miss analysis using the drive recorder, Research report part 1
26. Fujita M, Yohei M, Kotake M, Kamata M, Nagai M, Study on near-miss analysis using the drive recorder, Originally research report part 2
27. Fujita M, Kotake M, Kamata M, Nagai M, Yohei M (2007) Study on near-miss analysis using the drive recorder, rear-end collision near-miss analysis using the database. In: The Society of Automotive Engineers Society of Automotive Engineers Proceedings, vol 38(4), pp 151–156
28. Macadam CC (2003) Understanding and modeling the human driver. Veh Syst Dyn 40(1–3):101–134
29. Levesque A, Johrendt J (2011) The state of the art of driver model development. SAE Technical Paper 2011-01-0432. doi:10.4271/2011-01-0432
30. Jurgensohn T (2007) Control theory models of the driver. Modelling driver behaviour in automotive environments. Springer, London
31. Weir HD, Chao KC (2007) Review of control theory models for directional and speed control. Modelling driver behaviour in automotive environments. Springer, London, pp 293–311
32. Fox D, Burgard W, Thrun S (1999) Markov localization for mobile robots in dynamic environments. J Artif Intell Res (JAIR) 11:391–427
33. Luber M, Tipaldi GD, Arras KO (2011) Place-dependent people tracking. Int J Robot Res 30(3):280

Glossary

Antenna An electrical device which converts electric power into radio waves, and vice versa; it is usually used with a radio transmitter or radio receiver.

Artificial Neural Networks Computational models inspired by an animal's central nervous systems (in particular the brain) which is capable of machine learning as well as pattern recognition. Artificial neural networks are generally presented as systems of interconnected "neurons" which can compute values from inputs.

Background Subtraction An algorithm for Motion Detection, based on a comparison between current image and a reference (background) model.

Bhattacharrya distance A measurement of the similarity of two discrete or continuous probability distributions.

Bayesian Networks A probabilistic graphical model (a type of statistical model) that represents a set of random variables and their conditional dependencies via a directed acyclic graph (DAG).

Data Fusion Integration of data coming from different sources/devices/algorithms.

Directional Antenna An antenna which radiates greater power in one or more directions allowing for increased performance on transmit and receive and reduced interference from unwanted sources.

Embedded system A computer system with a dedicated function within a larger mechanical or electrical system.

Expectation Maximization (EM) An iterative method for finding maximum likelihood or maximum a posteriori (MAP) estimates of parameters in statistical models, where the model depends on unobserved latent variables.

Euclidean distance The *ordinary* distance between two points that one would measure with a ruler, and is given by the *Pythagorean formula*.

Flight Plan A predefined sequence of aerial paths for a UAV.

Foreground Region An area with specific issues that make it different form the surrounding scene (i.e., a moving object).

Graph A representation of a set of objects where some pairs of objects are connected by links; the interconnected objects are represented by mathematical abstractions called *vertices*, and the links that connect some pairs of vertices are called *edges*.

Hole An uncovered area in a Wireless Sensor Network; it can be due to the failures of sensors, or miscalculations in the planning phase.

Homography A geometric transformation for mapping a plane onto another one.

P. Spagnolo et al. (eds.), *Human Behavior Understanding in Networked Sensing*,
DOI 10.1007/978-3-319-10807-0

Homotopy A transformation that allows to "continuously pass" from a generic function/curve/distribution set to another one.

K-Nearest Neighbor A nonparametric method used for classification and regression; in both cases, the input consists of the k closest training examples in the feature space.

Kalman Filter An algorithm that uses a series of measurements observed over time, containing noise (random variations) and other inaccuracies, and produces estimates of unknown variables that tend to be more precise than those based on a single measurement alone. It is used for object tracking (to predict the next position by starting from the previous ones).

Kernel methods A class of algorithms for pattern analysis based on the use of Kernel functions, which enable them to operate in a high-dimensional, implicit feature space without ever computing the coordinates of the data in that space, but rather by simply computing the inner products between the images of all pairs of data in the feature space.

Local Binary Patterns A type of feature used for classification in computer vision.

Machine Learning A branch of artificial intelligence, concerns the construction and study of systems that can learn from data.

Mean-shift A nonparametric feature-space analysis technique for locating the maxima of a density function given discrete data sampled from that function.

Mission A single task that a robot must do.

Motion Detection An approach to detect moving object in a video sequence.

Multi-camera system A system that integrates information coming from several cameras. They can be connected in different ways (1-to-1, star configuration, ...)

Omnidirectional Antenna A class of antenna which radiates radiowave power uniformly in all directions in one plane, with the radiated power decreasing with elevation angle above or below the plane, dropping to zero on the antenna's axis.

Optical Flow The pattern of apparent motion of objects, surfaces, and edges in a visual scene caused by the relative motion between an observer and the scene.

Path Planner A task devoted to decide the best path for an agent.

Perimeter The union of a set of adjacent and nonoverlapped paths.

Perimeter surveillance The act of monitoring the perimeter of an area.

Petri Nets One of the several mathematical modeling languages for the description of distributed systems.

Principal Component Analysis A statistical procedure that uses an orthogonal transformation to convert a set of observations of possibly correlated variables into a set of values of linearly uncorrelated variables called Principal Components.

Protocol A set of rules in a specific issue.

Robot An autonomous agent programmed with a sequence of *missions*.

ROS-Robot Operating System An open-source operating system preinstalled on several coomercial/academic robots.

Shadow Removal An algorithm for the suppression of shadows, erroneously extracted by a foreground segmentation algorithm.

Skeleton A thin version of a shape that is equidistant to its boundaries.

Smart camera A vision system which, in addition to image capture circuitry, is capable of extracting application-specific information from the captured images, along with generating event descriptions or making decisions that are used in an intelligent and automated system.

Support Vector Machines Supervised learning models with associated learning algorithms that analyze data and recognize patterns, used for classification and regression analysis.

Thermal Detector A task devoted to detect and identify thermals during the mission of an agent.

Token A criteria for task scheduling (a token allows an agent, and only it, to act a task).

Tracking The process of locating a (moving) object (or multiple objects) over time in a frame sequence; the objective of tracking is to associate target objects in consecutive video frames.

Webots A professional robot simulator widely used for educational purposes.

Index

P. Spagnolo et al. (eds.), *Human Behavior Understanding in Networked Sensing*,
DOI 10.1007/978-3-319-10807-0

MIX
Papier aus verantwortungsvollen Quellen
Paper from responsible sources
FSC® C105338

If you have any concerns about our products,
you can contact us on
ProductSafety@springernature.com

In case Publisher is established outside the EU,
the EU authorized representative is:
Springer Nature Customer Service Center GmbH
Europaplatz 3, 69115 Heidelberg, Germany

Printed by Libri Plureos GmbH
in Hamburg, Germany